THE
ARMED CONFLICT SURVEY
2019

The worldwide review of
political, military and humanitarian
trends in current conflicts

published by

 Routledge
Taylor & Francis Group

for

The International Institute for Strategic Studies

The International Institute for Strategic Studies
Arundel House | 6 Temple Place | London | WC2R 2PG | UK

THE ARMED CONFLICT SURVEY 2019

First published May 2019 by **Routledge**
4 Park Square, Milton Park, Abingdon, Oxon, OX14 4RN

for **The International Institute for Strategic Studies**
Arundel House, 6 Temple Place, London, WC2R 2PG, UK

Simultaneously published in the USA and Canada by **Routledge**
52 Vanderbilt Avenue, New York, NY 10017

Routledge is an imprint of Taylor & Francis, an Informa business

DIRECTOR-GENERAL AND CHIEF EXECUTIVE Dr John Chipman
EDITOR Dr Francesca Grandi
DIRECTOR OF EDITORIAL Dr Nicholas Redman
ASSOCIATE EDITOR Alex Goodwin
EDITORIAL Clea Gibson, Sara Hussain, Jessica Watson, Carolyn West
DESIGN AND PRODUCTION John Buck, Kelly Verity

CONFLICTS Adam Wunische (Afghanistan), Dr Karena Avedissian (Armenia–Azerbaijan (Nagorno-Karabakh)), Antônio Sampaio (Brazil (Rio de Janeiro)), Professor Yonatan Morse (Cameroon), Thierry Vircoulon (Central African Republic), Gonzalo Croci (Colombia (BACRIMs)), Janosch Kullenberg (Democratic Republic of Congo), Douglas Farah & Caitlyn Yates (El Salvador & Honduras), Christopher Shay (India (CPI–Maoist)), Dr Alex Waterman (India (Northeast)), Mohd Tahir Ganie (India–Pakistan (Kashmir)), Benedict Robin (Iraq), Elisabeth Marteu (Israel–Palestine), Folahanmi Aina (Lake Chad Basin (Boko Haram)), Dr Umberto Profazio (Libya), Allison Chandler (Mali (Sahel)), Professor Laura Atuesta (Mexico (Cartels)), Elliot Brennan & Elliot Dolan-Evans (Myanmar (EAOs)), Dr Adam Higazi (Nigeria (Farmer–Pastoralist)), Dr Zoha Waseem (Pakistan), Michael Hart (Philippines), Dr Eleanor Beevor (Somalia), Dr Andrew Tchie (South Sudan), Jeremy Walden-Schertz (Southern Thailand), Chedine Tazi (Sudan (Darfur, Blue Nile & South Kordofan)), Katy Walsh Glinert (Syria), Katrina Marina (Ukraine)

KEY TRENDS Shifaa Alsairafi & Elisabeth Marteu (Humanitarian Aid as a Weapon of War), Professor Alex Braithwaite (Armed Conflict and Forced Displacement), Shiloh Fetzek (The Security Implications of Climate Change), Antônio Sampaio (Conflict Expansion to Cities)

THE CHART OF ARMED CONFLICT Nicholas Crawford
COVER IMAGES Getty

British Library Cataloguing in Publication Data
A catalogue record for this book is available from the British Library

Library of Congress Cataloguing in Publication Data

ISBN 978-0-367-27358-3
ISSN 2374-0973

Tanzanian soldiers from the UN
peacekeeping mission in Central
African Republic (MINUSCA)

Contents

Editor's Introduction

It is somewhat artificial to analyse conflicts by year. Political, military and humanitarian trends rarely stop at the calendar mark. The logic of armed violence unfolds according to the incentives and the constraints of the actors organising it. Conflict drivers are deeply interwoven in a country's political and socio-economic challenges, often rooted in historical pitfalls.

An in-depth analysis of the conflicts active in the past year, however, allows us to reflect on what we learned from recent events and hone our understanding of the drivers and dynamics shaping today's wars. The 33 conflict reports in *The Armed Conflict Survey 2019* aim to do exactly that – to explain why armed conflicts occur, what drives and what sustains them. The introductions at the beginning of the regional sections identify what features set each conflict apart, and what dynamics recur across different theatres. The four essays opening the book delve into those key trends, tracing how they unfold and drive conflict developments in the short to long term.

Our annual review is thus necessarily a balancing exercise between understanding the continuity of conflict drivers and dynamics, and spotting the new trajectories that they are likely to both generate and follow. This combination offers the reader the analytical tools necessary to see through the complexity of modern armed conflicts and the insights needed to draw informed conclusions from them.

Dynamics of armed conflict in 2018

The growing challenge of criminal networks, the merging of transnational and local dynamics, and the targeting of civilians characterised armed conflicts in 2018.

War has been an instrument of statecraft for centuries. What 'statecraft' looked like in 2018, however, differed profoundly not only from the inter-state wars of the past centuries, but also from the intra-state wars that became prevalent following the Second World War. Ideology-driven insurgencies that aim to oust or shape a state, or separate from it, are by no means disappearing. Yet armed actors pursuing narrow economic interests are today more prominent and the challenge they pose to governments is ever increasing. The conflict in the Central African Republic (CAR) is a good example of these developments, where the two factions that started the current conflict in 2013 had splintered into at least 17 local militias by the end of 2018. Scattered throughout the country, and collectively controlling about 70% of its territory, few of these groups pursue a political agenda. Some still seek their 'fair' share of political offices and rents, but many just wish to maintain control over 'their' areas, to exploit natural resources, profit from smuggling routes and the cattle business, and tax the communities that they ostensibly protect from local banditry or ethnic violence.

Similarly, in several conflicts, the drugs trade is an integral part of the war ecosystem. At the frontiers of Afghanistan and Myanmar, for example, armed groups engage in the full supply chain of narcotics – from protecting crops, to controlling smuggling routes, to directing trafficking. In Central America, the trafficking of illicit goods and other criminal activities has given rise to gangs, which now dictate the behaviour of the citizens living in their areas of control, enforce social norms and even provide basic livelihoods. In El Salvador, Guatemala and Honduras, the *maras* exploit, infiltrate and bend the political system to their criminal purposes, undermining state institutions but not dislodging them. The crucial role of illicit drugs in sustaining criminal networks, especially in Latin America, is set to continue. The United Nations Office on Drugs and Crime (UNODC) foresees 'a potential supply-driven expansion of drug markets' in 2019, with opium and cocaine production 'at the highest levels ever recorded'.

Regardless of their origin and stated intents, armed groups that engage in criminal activities have posed an increasingly fundamental challenge to the state in 2018. Controlling territory is in itself a political act, even when the objective of such control is to pursue self-interest. The natural outcome of armed criminal activity is the creation, in that territory, of a parallel political economy, be it local or national, and the widespread use of armed violence to sustain it. This dynamic plays out in a variety of ways in different conflicts, and the relation between criminal armed groups and the state varies accordingly. Armed groups can substitute the state. With a much more established presence in isolated and peripheral communities, they are often the sole actors providing a semblance of public services (mostly in the form of protection). Armed groups may also coexist with the state, operating in lawless pockets of territory that provide safe haven to their criminal activities. Finally, armed groups corrupt the state. Their power and wealth are such that they can keep security forces out of their territories, fashion themselves as the alternative to the state and manipulate institutions to serve their goals.

An accurate understanding of armed conflict must rely on explanations drawing on multiple factors – many of which are often local in nature. The conflicts active in 2018 exposed a close link between global and local dynamics and their mutually reinforcing effects on generating and sustaining violence. Transnational networks, such as groups pursuing global jihad, as well as geostrategic competition or global climatic change, all shape and intertwine with micro-level and communal sources of conflict. Jihadism made inroads in West Africa and Southeast Asia thanks to its ability to adopt local narratives and incorporate local grievances into its agenda. Internationalised radical Islamist networks have begun to connect militants in East Africa as well, transmitting funds and expertise across different countries (such as Mozambique, Somalia, Sudan, Tanzania and Uganda). When looking for new grounds, their recruitment strategies mixed financial opportunities with ideological messages. For example, in northern Mozambique, radical groups have achieved considerable success in attracting recruits angered at the political class, whose practices of resource extraction have long excluded the local population and failed to redistribute the country's natural wealth. Their innovative recruitment approaches have included start-up loans. In the Middle East and the Horn of Africa, external influences manifested instead in the more traditional form of foreign-power interventions. Geopolitical and geo-economic competition played out on the battlefields of Syria and Yemen as well as through bilateral security and commercial deals along the Red Sea and the Gulf of Aden, with China, Russia and Gulf states all pursuing their geostrategic interests in Somalia and Sudan.

This year's *Armed Conflict Survey* adds important pieces to our understanding of the complex causes of armed conflict. The essay 'The Security Implications of Climate Change' offers an insightful perspective on how climate change may exacerbate conflict – for example, by affecting the socio-economic dynamics that fuelled the anti-Assad mobilisation in 2011. The regime's impending military victory in Syria, made possible by Russian support, has not eliminated those underlying grievances. If plans for reconstruction begin but do not include a strategy to manage resources (such as water and land) more equitably and effectively, the potential for economic disruption and its harmful social consequences will persist unchanged. Understanding the effect of climate change on conflict dynamics reminds us that the developing world is bearing its most severe effects and it is where most active conflicts concentrate. Climate change also draws our attention to the urban–rural link. Rural societies are the first to suffer the effects of changing climatic patterns, which reduce the prospects for agriculture-based economies and add pressure on the most vulnerable populations. The effects of poor harvest also transmit quickly to urban centres in countries with weak governance capacity, where social safety nets and alternative livelihoods are unavailable. Conflict also travels to and from cities and most active armed conflicts have a significant urban component. This year's essay, 'Conflict Expansion to Cities' explores how conflict becomes entrenched in local socio-economic dynamics and how it morphs into something new, generating new grievances.

Consequences of armed conflict in 2018

It is no novelty that civilians bear the brunt of armed violence and its consequences in contemporary wars. Widespread violence against civilians remained a central characteristic of many active conflicts in 2018, but in some cases, it was also a strategic choice. Syria and Yemen were both examples of this. In the former, chemical attacks were an integral part of the government's strategy to debilitate civilian support of rebel groups. In Yemen, the parties' control and competition over vital distribution hubs deliberately cut basic services and humanitarian aid to civilians. Furthermore, warring parties often pursued ways to manipulate the tools meant to moderate the consequences of violence on civilians. The essay 'Humanitarian Aid as a Weapon of War' details the various ways in which that occurred – including the use (or restriction) of assistance to deliver a political message, as a tool of repression or as a source to fund the war. These strategies expose a worrying trend. Multilateral humanitarian mechanisms are increasingly used to serve state interests, systematically corroding normative constraints against targeting civilians.

Although civilian suffering is by no means abating, there is little consensus on how to measure it. How are the indirect consequences of a conflict to be factored in? Should only direct targeting of civilians be counted? The incidence of epidemics in war settings suggests that this is hardly satisfactory. The spread of Ebola in the Democratic Republic of the Congo (DRC) and cholera in Yemen, and the expansion of human trafficking from Syrian refugee camps, show that the plight of civilian populations during an armed conflict goes well beyond the immediate threat of violence.

Notwithstanding the complexity of defining civilian suffering in war and including all its different elements, even the basic metrics remain notoriously hard to measure in environments that by definition offer limited access and are predicated on the breakdown of state capacity (to collect data among other things). The challenges of gathering and counting fatalities should not prevent us from acknowledging one of the most evident, destabilising and disrupting consequences of conflict – displacement. This year's essay on 'Armed Conflict and Forced Displacement' delves into this complex relationship and shows how the two phenomena are deeply interwoven and mutually reinforcing. Crucially, armed groups often manipulate the movement of people and may use displacement as a strategic tool, in turn prolonging and exacerbating conflict and facilitating its spillover.

Conflict resolution in 2018

Be they criminal or political, the motives of armed groups do not fundamentally change fighting or recruitment patterns in armed conflict. In Colombia, the Marxist-Leninist National Liberation Army (ELN) competes with drug-trafficking organisations for areas in the jungle with access to gold mines or coca laboratories, as well as for youth in the slums hoping for lucrative tasks. Different motives do present different dilemmas to peacemakers, however. The conflicts active in 2018 show how the political and socio-economic dynamics of an area or a country change with conflict. Armed violence creates, sustains and enforces new political economies that have particularly pernicious effects on conflict resolution. The traditional tools of peacemaking, peacekeeping and peacebuilding face growing stress from armed groups that operate with the backing of transnational illicit traffics or are able to capture state institutions and reshape local economies. Criminal organisations pursue interests that are more difficult to accommodate within the framework of the rule of law; and the vast wealth from illicit activities gives them independence from political patronage and thus leverage.

The increasingly complex nature of conflict drivers also poses questions on how to design new counter-insurgency and counter-terrorism strategies. Mexico provides an example of some of these dilemmas. The militarised response to drug cartels that began in 2006 fuelled rivalries between, as well as within, armed criminal groups by decapitating their leadership. Decades-long efforts to defeat criminal organisations in Latin America have shown that a highly militarised response cannot eradicate the problem if states do not simultaneously address complex socio-economic and politico-institutional challenges. Do any of these lessons apply in different contexts, for example, in sub-Saharan Africa, where Islamist militias are devising innovative strategies to expand across borders, capitalising on ever-increasing youth unemployment rates, governance vacuums and local violence?

The end of the Syrian and the Afghan conflicts seemed to be in sight by December 2018. With donors already thinking of the post-conflict reconstruction phase, the creation and implementation of this process will have major repercussions on the prospects as well as the sustainability of peace. Without a mutually recognised political agreement supporting the reconstruction efforts, however, both countries will remain vulnerable to recurring and widespread violence if not fully fledged war. The United States-trained Afghan troops will face major challenges once the coalition leaves, including incomplete training and a limited capacity to attract new recruits as well as little legitimacy among the population. Although the Assad regime has defeated its adversaries, it is easy to see how a government so fundamentally lacking in legitimacy across the majority of the country will face difficulties in holding the country together. Globally, multilateral organisations face growing operational challenges and diminishing political support, leaving more space for regional mechanisms. Bilateral initiatives are growing in prominence. Their effectiveness might be a simple by-product of the external focus of interveners on narrow state interests, however, and an eventual shift away from multilateral solutions will hardly ensure improved civilian protection.

The Chart of Armed Conflict

This year's 'Chart of Armed Conflict' shows, with more detail than in previous years, the geography of the violence occurring in the conflicts covered in *The Armed Conflict Survey*. The Chart draws on the geolocated armed clashes and violent incidents recorded in the Armed Conflict Database, the online data-repository companion to *The Armed Conflict Survey*.

The map shows the deployment of multilateral missions to conflict-affected and post-conflict countries. Since last year, two multilateral missions have been terminated. In March 2018, the UN Mission in Liberia (UNMIL) closed down after completing its mandate, and in January 2019, the Israeli government refused to renew the mandate of the Temporary International Presence in Hebron (TIPH) in the Occupied Palestinian Territories, claiming that the civilian observer mission was operating against Israel. A new multilateral mission also began in early 2019, with the deployment of the UN Mission to Support the Hudaydah Agreement (UNMHA) – a group of observers tasked with monitoring the redeployment of armed forces out of the Yemeni port city.

The amount of aid money spent on civilian peacebuilding, conflict prevention and resolution continues to increase, as the line chart 'Breakdown of conflict-related aid spend by type' shows. Spending on the removal of landmines and explosive remnants of war has also increased. Iraq is a major recipient of this money as it demines the

territory recaptured from the Islamic State, also known as ISIS or ISIL.

There is interesting variation in how donors allocate their conflict, peace and security aid. Germany is by far the largest contributor to civilian peacebuilding, conflict prevention and resolution, whereas the United States spends far more than Germany on security-sector reform, and the United Kingdom is the largest contributor of programmatic funds to international peacekeeping operations. The UK's spend through multilateral programmes and institutions is also reflected in the 'Top 20 contributors to multilateral ODA' chart: the UK is the largest contributor of core funds to multilaterals and the second-largest contributor overall after the US. The European Union is in the top four largest sources of funds for both emergency relief and conflict, peace and security aid.

Aside from the EU, a number of multilateral institutions are among the top 20 donors for both kinds of aid. The Central Emergency Response Fund (CERF), the UN High Commissioner for Refugees (UNHCR) and the World Food Programme (WFP) are among the top 20 sources of emergency aid. Alongside EU institutions, four multilaterals are among the top 20 sources of conflict, peace and security aid: the Inter-American Development Bank (IDB), the International Development Association (IDA), the UN Peacebuilding Fund and the Organization for Security and Co-operation in Europe (OSCE). As two of these organisations are regional, the geographic distribution of contributions is slightly skewed, but Germany remains the largest contributor, ahead of the US. In general, European countries are the main users of the multilateral system for discretionary aid spend.

Syria attracts the highest per capita aid flows of all the countries affected by conflict. A large proportion of the funds, however, is likely spent on refugees in neighbouring countries. Turkey is the largest donor of emergency relief aid worldwide, but of that amount, 99% is allocated to Syria; in turn, Turkey is responsible for 77% of the total emergency relief aid allocated to Syria. Turkey does not provide a breakdown of this spending, but the vast majority is spent within Turkey to address the challenge of hosting some 3.5 million refugees in 2017 – the year for which the aid data is available.

Notes on Methodology

The Armed Conflict Survey reviews and analyses the armed conflicts that are active worldwide every year. We define an armed conflict as a sustained military contest between two or more organised actors making purposive use of armed force. The inclusion of a conflict in the book is based on this definition and the methodology detailed below, which are the same as for the Armed Conflict Database.

Armed conflicts in 2018

This year's *Armed Conflict Survey* includes 33 armed conflicts that were ongoing during the 2018 calendar year (from 1 January to 31 December) in six world regions (Americas, Asia-Pacific, Europe and Eurasia, Middle East and North Africa, South Asia and sub-Saharan Africa). The list of conflicts in the 2019 edition differs slightly from the 2018 edition. Firstly, the armed conflict in Cameroon was added this year. Regular fighting ensued after separatist groups took up arms against government forces in the country's Southwest Region, with the aim to create an independent Anglophone nation-state (Ambazonia). Secondly, certain conflicts have been grouped together based on common key characteristics, such as drivers or meaningful links between armed groups. This year's northeast India report includes all conflicts fought in Assam, Manipur and Nagaland by ethnic nationalist groups against the central government. The conflicts in Myanmar have also been merged, pitting ethnic armed organisations (EAOs) at the country's periphery against Naypyidaw. Similarly, this year's edition features only one conflict report for Colombia – the criminal bands (BACRIMs) controlling the drug trade in the country's rural areas. The same report includes also the National Liberation Army (ELN), which has adopted tactics virtually indistinguishable from those of the criminal bands.

Despite these groupings, the unit of analysis in *The Armed Conflict Survey* remains the armed conflict itself – the military confrontation between armed actors – rather than the country where it occurs.

Most armed conflicts take place within the boundaries of a state and are therefore listed under those country names, although many do not affect the national territory as a whole. In Sudan, for example, the central state fights various armed groups in the Blue Nile and South Kordofan provinces and in the Darfur region, but Khartoum has never become a theatre in these long-standing wars. Other conflicts, such as the Boko Haram insurgency, unfold across state boundaries, in this case involving territories in Cameroon, Chad, Niger and Nigeria. The opposite and extreme case in this category is Rio de Janeiro, the only armed conflict in *The Armed Conflict Survey 2019* that is limited to an urban centre.

Classification of armed conflicts

Conflict parties may be state or non-state actors. According to the types of actors involved and the interactions between them, armed conflicts fall into one of three categories: international (or inter-state), internal or internationalised. An *international* armed conflict takes place between two or more states (or a group of states) on the territory of one or several states, as well as the global commons. An *internal* armed conflict is fought by a government (and possibly allied armed groups) against one or more non-state actors or between two or more non-state armed groups. An *internationalised* armed conflict is an internal conflict, in which the kernel of the dispute remains domestic, but one or more external states intervenes militarily. Such involvement may include training, equipping or providing military intelligence to a conflict party or participating in the hostilities, either directly or through local proxies and sponsored actors.

Criteria for inclusion

The Armed Conflict Survey's definition of armed conflict requires combat between opposing actors. In order to be included, an armed confrontation must possess two characteristics: *duration* and *intensity*. We require an armed conflict to run for at least three months and feature violent incidents on a weekly or fortnightly basis. For wars between states – which feature substantial levels of military mobilisation, simultaneous and numerous armed clashes or significant fatalities – the duration threshold may be relaxed.

The third test for inclusion is the *organisation* of the conflict parties, namely their ability to plan and execute military operations. The scale of the attacks is not a factor in this determination – for the purpose of inclusion in *The Armed Conflict Survey*, for example, planting improvised explosive devices (IEDs) is equivalent to battlefield clashes. For armed conflicts that involve state parties, the deployment of armed forces or militarised (not regular) police is required. In the case of non-state conflict parties, the logistical and operational capacity of the group is key. This indicator includes access to weapons and other military equipment, as well as the ability to devise strategies and carry out operations, coordinate activities, establish communication between members (often based on existing social networks), and recruit and train personnel. The organisation of an armed actor does not require territorial control or a permanent base in an area. *The Armed Conflict Survey* also remains agnostic with regard to the type of organisational structure that armed groups adopt. Not all non-state groups engaged in armed conflicts have a distinct and effective chain of command, such as many of those operating in sub-Saharan Africa. Armed groups can be highly decentralised, maintain an amorphous structure, rely on a transnational network or have a global reach – a hierarchical military structure is therefore not an inclusion criterion.

The Armed Conflict Survey applies also two criteria for removal. Over time, certain armed conflicts lose the characteristics required for inclusion and are removed after two years. An armed conflict terminated through a peace agreement also ceases following the military demobilisation of all conflict parties, as in the case of the Revolutionary Armed Forces of Colombia (FARC) conflict, which was dropped for this year's edition.

Methodological differences

Defining armed conflict simply as a military phenomenon rather than a legal one, *The Armed Conflict Survey* does not aim to determine the applicability of international humanitarian law to different conflict situations (as in the Geneva Conventions or the Rome Statute). Contrary to other datasets (notably the Uppsala Conflict Data Program (UCDP) and the Peace Research Institute Oslo's Correlates of War Project (PRIO)), *The Armed Conflict Survey*'s definition of armed conflict does not involve a numerical threshold of battle-related deaths.

The Armed Conflict Survey's methodology does not make distinctions based on the motivations driving an armed conflict, which may be political, ideological, religious or criminal. The book thus includes cases of internal conflicts where only criminal organisations, rather than revolutionaries or separatists, fight each other and the state (such as in El Salvador, Honduras, Mexico and Rio de Janeiro).

Finally, *The Armed Conflict Survey* excludes cases involving the one-sided application of lethal force, terrorist attacks and public protests. Government repression, as well as ethnic cleansing or genocide, regardless of the scale, are not included if they occur outside a conflict situation, until the population displays a capacity to fight back through an armed, organised resistance, or another state wages war – as in the case of the Khmer Rouge regime in Cambodia when Vietnam invaded in 1979. Terrorist attacks may lead to the domestic deployment of armed forces, but these events are too rare to pass the intensity test. Situations with widespread but unorganised criminal activity are also excluded.

Key statistics

For each conflict, *The Armed Conflict Survey 2019* reports key statistics relevant to the context under analysis. The information in the tables at the beginning of each conflict report indicates the type of conflict and the figures on displacement (refugees and internally displaced persons (IDPs)) and the number of people in need of humanitarian aid (people in need).

Refugees

The Armed Conflict Survey adopts the definition in Article 1A(2) of the 1951 UN Convention Relating to the Status of Refugees (also known as the Refugee Convention), according to which a refugee is a person who 'owing to a well-founded fear of being persecuted for reasons of race, religion, nationality, membership of a particular social group or political opinion, is outside the country of his nationality and is unable, or owing to such fear, is unwilling to avail himself of the protection of that country; or who, not having a nationality and being outside the country of his former habitual residence as a result of such events, is unable or, owing to such fear, is unwilling to return to it'.

'Refugees total' refers to the total number of refugees since the beginning of the conflict, as of the latest available date (December 2017 or December 2018). 'Refugees new' refers to the number of refugees displaced in 2018, as of the latest available date.

Internally displaced persons (IDPs)
The Armed Conflict Survey adopts the definition in the 1998 UN Guiding Principles on Internal Displacement, according to which IDPs are 'persons or groups of persons who have been forced or obliged to flee or to leave their homes or places of habitual residence, in particular as a result of or in order to avoid the effects of armed conflict, situations of generalized violence, violations of human rights or natural or human-made disasters, and who have not crossed an internationally recognized state border'.

'IDPs total' refers to the total number of IDPs since the beginning of the conflict, as of the latest available date (December 2017 or December 2018). 'IDPs new' refers to the number of IDPs displaced in 2018, as of the latest available date.

People in need
The Armed Conflict Survey refers to people in need of humanitarian aid following the criteria set out by the UN Office for the Coordination of Humanitarian Affairs (OCHA), which refer to basic services such as food, shelter, water and sanitation, healthcare and non-food items (such as clothing, hygiene kits). The figures refer to the latest date available and are rounded according to the methodology shown in **Table 1**.

Sources
All figures for refugees, IDPs and people in need are drawn from the same standardised open sources, compiled by the relevant specialised international agencies (exceptions in parentheses):

Refugees
- UN High Commissioner for Refugees (UNHCR), Mid-Year Trends, 2018 (Annex 2)
- United Nations Relief and Works Agency for Palestine Refugees (UNRWA), Palestinian refugees (Israel–Palestine)
- UN Office for the Coordination of Humanitarian Assistance (OCHA), 'Humanitarian Response Plans' (Iraq, Syria)

Internally displaced persons (IDPs)
- Internal Displacement Monitoring Centre (IDMC), 'Global Report on Internal Displacement', 2018
- OCHA, 'Cameroon: Insecurity and underfunding severely hamper scale-up of humanitarian response', November 2018 (Cameroon)
- OCHA, 'Humanitarian Response Plan 2019', February 2019 (Central African Republic)
- International Organization for Migration (IOM), 'Displacement Tracking Matrix' (Iraq, Libya)
- OCHA, 'Lake Chad Basin Crisis Overview', January 2019 (Lake Chad)
- OCHA, 'Humanitarian Needs Overview', 2019 (Myanmar)
- OCHA, 'UN Coordinated Support to People Affected by Disaster and Conflict, Global Humanitarian Overview (GHO)', 2019 (Somalia)
- UNHCR, 'Mid-Year Trends', 2018 (Syria)
- UNHCR Ukraine, 'Registration of Internal Displacement', 2018 (Ukraine)
- IISS, Armed Conflict Database (The Philippines)

People in need
- OCHA, 'GHO', 2019
- OCHA, 'Humanitarian Bulletin, October 2018', 20 November 2018 (Iraq)
- Humanitarian Country Team, Humanitarian Needs Overview, 2019 (Israel–Palestine)
- UNHCR, 'Mid-Year Trends', 2018 (Syria)

Military data
Through the book, unless otherwise indicated, all figures related to military strength and capability, defence economics and arms equipment are from *The Military Balance*. The figures on violent incidents are from the Armed Conflict Database, unless otherwise indicated.

Table 1: Rounding methodology

Range	Rounding	Test for Maximum Variance			
		Actual	Rounded to	Difference	Variance
501 to 1000	50	525	550	−25	−0.047619048
1,001 to 5,000	100	1,050	1,100	−50	−0.047619048
5,001 to 10,000	500	5,250	5,500	−250	−0.047619048
10,001 to 50,000	1,000	10,500	11,000	−500	−0.047619048
50,001 to 100,000	5,000	52,500	55,000	−2,500	−0.047619048
100,001 to 500,000	10,000	105,000	110,000	−5,000	−0.047619048

GLOBAL TRENDS

Migrants stranded in the Strait of Gibraltar
in September 2018, before they were
rescued by the Spanish Civil Guard and
the Salvamento Marítimo agency

Humanitarian Aid as a Weapon of War

Between 2017 and 2018, more people were at risk of starvation than at any other time since the Second World War, with 20 million people facing the threat of famine in South Sudan, Yemen, Somalia and Nigeria. These famines are consequences of political decisions and a direct result of ongoing armed conflicts. In these conditions, international humanitarian agencies have been facing major obstacles to intervene, and have been subject to blockades, deadly attacks and political instrumentalisation.

In the course of 2018, conflict dynamics in Yemen, Syria, South Sudan and Palestine illustrated some of the ways in which humanitarian aid can be used as a weapon of war, such as the use of political famine and the blockade of emergency relief; the manipulation of international humanitarian actors to finance state repression; the diversion of aid as a source of funding and enrichment; and politicised aid conditionalities. These dynamics have fuelled violence and prolonged conflict, resulting in the need for further funding and further aid operations, as well as endangering humanitarian workers. This vicious circle becomes all the more difficult to halt when donors are also those who manipulate humanitarian aid to serve political interests.

Using aid strategically

Since the Second World War, international aid has become an increasingly important dimension of foreign policy and diplomatic competition. The Marshall Plan was the first and most critical element of the United States' strategy of 'containing' the Soviet Union by exporting democracy and capitalism to Western Europe through massive injections of financial aid. Using aid as an instrument of power in contexts of conflict and fragility is therefore not a new phenomenon.

Yet the nature of humanitarian emergencies, and the humanitarian responses to them, has dramatically changed over the past 15 years. Humanitarian emergencies have increased in number and in duration. Between 2005 and 2017, the number of crises receiving an internationally led response almost doubled from 16 to 30, and the average length of a crisis rose from four to seven years.[1] The human cost of conflict has also continued to increase, with a total population of concern of 70.4 million people (including refugees, asylum seekers, returnees, stateless persons and internally displaced people) reported in June 2018.[2] After years of decline, the number of undernourished people rose in 2017 (to 821m people), primarily due to armed conflicts and the consequences of climate change. In 2018, the total number of people in need of aid reached a record 141m, representing an 11% increase compared to 2016. In parallel, requirements for consolidated aid appeals increased by 20% to US$23.9 billion. Syria, Yemen, Iraq, Palestine and South Sudan were the five top recipients of humanitarian assistance (combining international and inter-agency funding) in 2018.[3]

Most crises have become complex humanitarian emergencies combining multiple risks and vulnerabilities, and facing 'internationalisation' through increasing external assistance and civil/military interventions. In 2017, international humanitarian funding amounted to US$27.3bn, with OECD–DAC donors giving US$19.6bn.[4] If the US (US$6.68m) and the European institutions (nearly US$2.25bn through the European Commission, in addition to member states' bilateral aid such as Germany with US$2.99bn and the UK with US$2.52bn) remain the world's leading providers of humanitarian aid, new countries have emerged, such as Saudi Arabia (US$385m) and the United Arab Emirates (US$281m), who were ranked among the top 20 humanitarian aid contributors in 2017.[5]

The policies of these new actors, however, demonstrates that humanitarian aid has entered the strategic toolkit of states seeking to project more influence and power. The UAE and Saudi Arabia donate aid mostly to countries within their spheres of influence, aiming to build a sense of Arab or Muslim solidarity in the Middle East and Africa. Their contribution has also been increasingly driven by anti-Iranian objectives in the aftermath of the upheavals of the Arab Spring in 2011. This has been particularly the case in Iraq and Yemen, where Riyadh and Abu Dhabi have been donating billions in aid (cash transfer, humanitarian and development aid, reconstruction programmes, etc.) to counter Iran's influence. Interestingly, Iran has never been recorded as a significant humanitarian donor, as it has directed its aid policy exclusively to Middle Eastern and Central Asia's Shia communities through informal solidarity networks.

China has also entered the humanitarian field. Even though Beijing does not release official data on its humanitarian expenditures, it has been developing a robust bilateral aid policy and has become a significant player in many fragile states, including in Africa.[6] China's humanitarian assistance is considered to be related to three kinds of national interest: diplomatic interests, international reputation and indirect economic and commercial interests.[7]

The combination of protracted conflict with the instrumentalisation of humanitarian-aid policy has had a pernicious effect on the ground, resulting in the selection of aid recipients by donors, according to ideological motivations; redundancy and competition between donors; larger-scale blockage of food deliveries and mass starvation; diversion of funds and goods by governments or armed groups to fuel repression or insurgency; and a rise in the targeting, abduction and killing of humanitarian-aid workers. Humanitarian aid can be used as a weapon of war in different ways and can result in provoking, prolonging or intensifying conflict. In Somalia, for instance, aid agencies have been suspected of paying and therefore enriching al-Shabaab terrorists to access areas under the group's control during the 2011 famine.[8] In Myanmar, the government has been pursuing a policy of starvation in Rakhine State since 2017 to force out the remaining Rohingya population. In Central African Republic, Russia is competing for influence with France and delivering arms to the central government, sometimes under false humanitarian motives and operations.[9] All these strategies are not only devastating for people in need; they are also strongly detrimental to humanitarian agencies' efficiency and credibility.

The dynamics of aid and violence in Yemen, Syria, South Sudan and Palestine in 2018 exemplify different aspects of this process of 'weaponisation of aid', but the contamination of humanitarian-aid operations will have long-term geostrategic consequences for all four conflicts.

Yemen: restricted access

The war between the Houthi rebel movement and forces loyal to President Abd Rabbo Mansour Hadi that began in 2014 has provoked what United Nations Secretary-General António Guterres described in December 2017 as the world's worst humanitarian crisis. This situation is largely due to the interference of regional powers in the war to advance their financial, military and ideological goals.

The crisis has drawn international attention and triggered generous financial support, especially from Saudi Arabia and the UAE, two major parties to the conflict. According to the UN Office for the Coordination of Humanitarian Affairs (OCHA), the 2018 response plan for Yemen required US$2.96bn to be effective, of which 80% has been funded and mobilised – a remarkable success compared to other humanitarian appeals. In total, 133 aid organisations operate in 332 out of Yemen's 333 districts, with 57 working in the nutrition and food-security sectors.[10] Despite these positive achievements, as of December 2018, 20m people, representing two-thirds of the population, were facing severe food insecurity. As of mid-December 2018, 36% of the population (10.8m people) were in IPC Phase 3 (Crisis); 17% of the Yemeni population (5m people) were in IPC Phase 4 (Emergency); and 63,500 were categorised as IPC Phase 5, meaning that they were at risk of starvation, death or destitution.[11]

Saudi Arabia's King Salman Humanitarian Aid and Relief Centre (KSRelief) claims that the Arab coalition backing the Hadi government has donated as much as US$18bn in aid since 2015. In 2018 alone, Saudi Arabia and the UAE were reported to have given US$534m and US$467m respectively in support of the UN response plan for Yemen.[12] However, Riyadh and Abu Dhabi have also been waging airstrike campaigns on Yemen against the Houthi rebels since 2015, thereby increasing the need for humanitarian aid. As leaders of the coalition against the Houthis, they are also controlling the access of humanitarian organisations to Yemen, which results in regional disparities in aid distribution. Between the end of 2017 and February 2018, the Saudi-led coalition blockaded for weeks the Hudaydah port, Yemen's only aid and goods pipeline, cutting the total amount of aid entering the country by almost half. To compensate for this loss, the Saudi-led coalition delivered a new aid plan, the Yemen Comprehensive Humanitarian Operations (YCHO), which further reduced the aid flow through Hudaydah while significantly increasing the capacity of the ports of Aden, Jizan, Mukallah and Mokha, all ports under the control of the Saudi-led coalition and the Hadi government.[13] This effectively choked the supply of aid to populations in the Houthi-controlled areas, in particular in the Hajjah, Hudaydah, Sa'ada and Ta'izz governorates, which today host the people facing the greatest threat of starvation.[14] In this way, the actions of the Saudi-led coalition had the effect of using 'the threat of starvation as an instrument of war', as stated by the UN Panel of Experts on Yemen.[15]

The Saudi-led coalition also imposed severe restrictions and extensive search mechanisms on vessels carrying humanitarian and commercial goods in the Red Sea, despite the existence of the UN Inspection and Verification Mechanism for YEMEN (UNVIM). While verification by UNVIM only takes 28 days, the Saudi-led coalition's mechanism may last for many weeks and often results in the denial of entry to vessels for arbitrary reasons, despite warnings on the impact that the delay of goods' delivery could have on civilian populations.[16] The coalition also refuses to cooperate with UN officials in supplying a list of prohibited items.

The Houthi forces are also exacerbating the humanitarian crisis in areas under their control in the hope that public condemnation of Saudi Arabia will offset any liability for their actions. Throughout the war, they have obstructed the delivery of humanitarian assistance in various ways. The Houthis controlled the two main entry points in Ta'izz from March 2015 to March 2016, during which time they stopped United Nations International Children's Emergency Fund (UNICEF), Norwegian Refugee Council (NRC) and Deem for Development trucks carrying humanitarian supplies, forcing them to take longer and more dangerous routes in order to deliver essential supplies. They have also detained and tortured humanitarian-aid workers,[17] confiscated their equipment and interfered in the selection of beneficiaries and areas of operation. As of late December 2018, World Food Programme director David Beasly stated that aid was only reaching 40% of eligible beneficiaries in the rebel-held capital, Sana'a, while only a third were receiving aid in the

rebels' northern stronghold of Sa'ada, partly due to the corruption of executives who were using their influence over humanitarian access to generate profit despite warnings from the UN Food Agency.[18]

Aid donations to Yemen have also been leveraged in the Gulf Cooperation Council (GCC) by Qatar to gain international backing in its ongoing diplomatic row with Saudi Arabia, the UAE, Egypt and Bahrain. Qatar initially sent air pilots and 1,000 ground troops and 200 army vehicles to support the Hadi government, but withdrew them after it became embroiled in the embargo in June 2017. Qatar has since donated nearly US$100m in humanitarian aid to Yemen; used public announcements of its donations to criticise the war and its consequences on the civilian population; and provided relief through several charity and development organisations as a way to increase its standing in the region.[19]

Syria: aid as repression tool

Since the beginning of the Syria conflict in 2011, the regime of President Bashar al-Assad has manipulated the international humanitarian system and blocked organisations from delivering aid to people in need as a way to weaken local oppositions. As a consequence, starvation and deprivation continued to increase in 2018, not only due to the violence of the fighting but also because international aid has been used as a tool for repression.

In early 2019, 400,000 civilians were still reported as besieged throughout Syria, and 6.8m internally displaced people needed humanitarian assistance.[20] In 2017, Syrian authorities granted only 27% of requests to deliver aid to civilians.[21] As the Syrian regime intensified food blockades and healthcare attacks as a strategy to sustain its massive military campaign to regain full control of the country, the humanitarian crisis deepened in 2018. In the first half of 2018, almost 400,000 civilians were trapped in the Damascus suburb of Eastern Ghouta as the regime restricted all humanitarian supplies, including food delivery and medical aid. In Idlib and the surrounding areas, by the end of 2018, nearly 3m people were caught up in the fighting between the regime, supported by Russian airplanes, and the rebels, who included several jihadi groups trying to preserve their last stronghold.

At the root of these events is the agreement between OCHA and the Syrian government in 2012 to centralise all operations in Damascus and put humanitarian assistance under the government's control in coordination with the Syrian Arab Red Crescent. The Red Crescent has been suspected of delivering aid according to partisan criteria, while the regime has provided the UN with the list of national organisations it ought to partner with, including many controlled by Assad and his relatives.[22] The regime has also been suspected of intervening in the UN's needs assessments, even redacting UN documents prepared for donor fundraising.[23] Finally, large portions of aid money were captured by the regime through a tax on relief staff's salaries, thus generating at least US$1bn in revenue.[24] In September 2016, 73 aid groups accused the UN system of complicity with the regime, suspended their cooperation with the UN and demanded a transparent investigation into its operations in the country.[25] By diverting aid, the Assad regime managed not only to compromise humanitarian principles, but also to breach international sanctions imposed in 2011 by the EU and the US on Syrian individuals and entities connected to the regime.[26]

Either because they were not granted access, or because they wanted to avoid the regime control, many humanitarian agencies chose to operate across the border from Turkey and Jordan and work with local partners to access civilians in areas held by the opposition. The escalation of violence in the southern governorates of Daraa, Quneitra and Sweida in June 2018, however, forced the suspension of cross-border operations from Jordan, which resumed only at much lower pace in September. As the regime retook most of the opposition strongholds the same month, cross-border activities were then renamed 'operations to newly accessible areas' by the regime as well as UN agencies. Even though humanitarian agencies have been obliged and constrained to coordinate their operations with Damascus, not least because it was the only way to reach certain areas, their pragmatism has been extremely detrimental to their efficiency and reputation.

South Sudan: aid as funding source

Since hostilities erupted in South Sudan between the government and opposition forces in December 2013, the humanitarian situation has deteriorated, with aid regularly looted, destroyed or blocked, as well as being used as a source of funding by warring parties.[27]

In September 2018, around 60% of the population (nearly 6m people) faced IPC Phase 3 (Crisis) or worse, acute food insecurity. At the peak of the lean season (July–August), 1.7m were in IPC Phase 4 (Emergency) while 47,000 people were categorised as IPC Phase 5 (Catastrophe). As warring parties suspected that aid agencies were providing assistance to the opposite side's fighting forces, both government and opposition groups established bureaucratic impediments to control the activities of the agencies. In South Sudan, humanitarian organisations have been able to negotiate access directly with armed groups – a rare occurrence – but these channels of negotiation and mitigation did not impede warring parties from restricting access to conflict-affected areas.[28]

Between 2017 and 2018, persistent and systematic denial of life-saving assistance to people in need was documented in the greater Baggari area of Wau county, where nearly 25,000 people were reported to be at risk of famine in September 2017.[29] Government forces have been accused of disrupting aid delivery by restricting movement, threatening and intimidating humanitarian workers, and interfering with field operations. During the offensive conducted in June–July 2018 to regain control of rebel-held areas in Wad Alel and areas south and southwest of the city of Wau, the security forces disrupted humanitarian access, prevented human-rights investigators from reaching sites and attacked civilian property.[30]

Since 2011, humanitarian funding for South Sudan has surpassed US$9.5bn (most of which was part of the coordinated South Sudan Humanitarian Response Plan).[31] Humanitarian actors have become South Sudan's 'new oil fields', with 173 organisations registered to operate in emergency programmes.[32] The government has reportedly diverted international funding to consolidate power, imposing illegal taxes at checkpoints, confiscating aid assets and increasing annual work-permit fees for international staff. At the end of 2017, the Ministry of Labour increased work permit fees from US$100 to up to US$4,000, diverting at least US$7m from the provision of life-saving assistance that year.[33] One international non-governmental organisation with an in-country staff of fewer than 200

> Using humanitarian aid as a weapon of war can result in provoking, prolonging or intensifying conflict

people estimated in 2018 that it spent approximately US$350,000 per year on administrative taxes and fees paid to official or quasi-official entities. NGOs also reported that they have to negotiate humanitarian access (with different fees and conditions of access) with at least 70 distinct armed groups across the country. In view of evidence of diversion of aid and massive corruption, the US initiated a comprehensive review of its aid programmes in South Sudan in May 2018 to ensure that international assistance 'does not contribute to or prolong the conflict, or facilitate predatory or corrupt behavior'.[34]

Palestine: aid cut as political message

Since it erupted in 1948, the Israel–Palestine conflict has mobilised massive international assistance and support, but it has also polarised the international community following the opposite Israeli and Palestinian interests, as demonstrated by the United States' decision in 2018 to cut aid to the United Nations Relief and Works Agency for Palestine Refugees (UNRWA).

Established in 1950, UNRWA is the official structure in charge of Palestine refugees, whose numbers have risen from 750,000 in 1950 to nearly 5m today (810,000 are officially registered in the West Bank and East Jerusalem, 1.3m in the Gaza Strip, 2.2m in Jordan, 450,000 in Lebanon and 527,000 in Syria). The agency is responsible for their official registration as 'Palestine refugees' and provides them with humanitarian and development assistance. For the current US administration, however, the very existence of UNRWA perpetuates the problem of the Palestinian refugees. Accordingly, in January 2018, the US State Department released US$60m for the agency but withheld US$65m for 'future consideration'. In August, it declared that the US would no longer fund 'this irredeemably flawed operation', and criticised other countries for not sharing the funding burden.[35]

The decision is only partly motivated by economic concerns. Until 2018, the US was the main funder of UNRWA with an average annual donation of approximately US$355m. The Trump administration has repeatedly expressed discontent over America's 'disproportionate' contribution to multilateral bodies and initiatives, such as NATO and UN peacekeeping operations, but there is a broader geostrategic dimension in its decision. By cutting its support for UNRWA and undermining the refugee

status of millions of Palestinians, the US intends to hasten the resolution of the Israel–Palestine conflict. It hopes that such a move will oblige Arab countries to 'share the burden' by granting refugees full citizenship and therefore erasing the issue in future negotiations. As with the US decision to recognise Jerusalem as the capital of Israel, the main objective of cutting aid to UNRWA is to reshape the course of the conflict by unilaterally overcoming one of its most difficult and contentious issues.[36]

The weakening of UNRWA, however, is likely to negatively affect the lives of millions of Palestinians. Thanks to additional contributions from other states, the agency announced in November 2018 a cash deficit of 'only' US$21m and began implementing several drastic cost-saving measures, including the non-renewal of staff members' contracts; the reduction of the emergency-cash assistance to Palestinian refugees in Yarmouk in Syria; and the interruption of a mental-health programme implemented in the Bedouin community in the West Bank.[37] Only the core services (education, health and relief) and emergency programmes have been maintained.

Even though the US decision recalled the necessity to reform UNRWA as well as to solve the 70-year-old Israel–Palestine conflict, it has been too biased to effectively foster peace or improve the lives of millions of Palestine refugees. Beyond the clear pro-Israel stance of the US decision, the situation of UNRWA is also symptomatic of the intrinsic financial dependence of humanitarian interventions on voluntary donations, and therefore of their extreme vulnerability to geopolitical and ideological fluctuations.

The consequences of using aid for strategic purposes

As the number of protracted conflicts increases, at times fuelled by warring parties diverting aid to finance their war efforts, the long-term consequences for the humanitarian system become increasingly severe.

Firstly, in the past two decades, armed groups have increasingly targeted aid workers, considering them as parties to the conflict and thus legitimate targets (as in East Timor in 1999 and Iraq in 2003, among others). Extortion, intimidation and the kidnapping of humanitarian workers have become increasingly common, eroding the 'humanitarian space' and the principle that relief supplies and relief workers are neutral. The London-based group Humanitarian Outcomes documented that 139 humanitarian-aid workers were killed in 22 countries in 2017, with another 102 wounded and 72 kidnapped, especially in conflict-affected areas such as South Sudan, Syria, Afghanistan and Central African Republic.

In South Sudan, for instance, at least 12 aid workers were killed in 2018, bringing the toll to more than 100 since December 2013. In February, rebel forces detained 29 aid workers in greater Baggari area and released them after one day. In April, ten aid workers were abducted for five days in Yei in the former Central Equatoria State. Even though humanitarian organisations have tightened their security measures and created specific training and doctrine (including a new approach to identify which armed-group leaders to work with), the number of victims among humanitarian workers is likely to continue to increase.[38]

Secondly, aid has for years been accused of all evils. Some have referred to it as a standardised, decontextualised instrument and 'a machine turning out ready-made solutions'.[39] Others have seen in international assistance a primary form of political and ideological action serving 'political humanitarianism'.[40] Already facing a plethora of criticisms and challenges, aid operations are likely to be further contested and put into question. The international community will have to identify the best and safest way to supply aid while preventing all parties (such as governments, armed groups and donors) from using it to fuel violence and advance their interests. This requirement is, however, biased by a major constraint: among those who create norms and humanitarian rules are sometimes the same actors who compete through humanitarian proxy wars. The challenges the United Nations faces to ensure the respect of international humanitarian law and aid operations is partly due to the geopolitical competition between the UN Security Council's five permanent members. This is evident today in Syria, where the post-conflict reconstruction phase has already become hostage of opposite interests between Russia and China on one side and the US, France and the United Kingdom on the other. As the Assad regime regains control over Syria, Russia is intending to shame the anti-Assad coalition for the imposition of sanctions against the regime and its

allies, and for their lack of appetite to support the post-war stabilisation and restoration process. On their part, the US and the EU have been refusing to finance the reconstruction of Syria in the absence of a conflict-resolution agreement, claiming that such efforts only benefit those loyal to the regime, further exacerbating the tensions that are at the very heart of the civil war. As international donors are also warring parties in charge of arming and ultimately mediating and negotiating post-conflict agreements, they are often not equipped to create a just and sustainable peace or sustain a viable humanitarian–development nexus.

Finally, after decades of decline, famines are on the rise again. In 2017, three of the four reported cases of famines (northeastern Nigeria, South Sudan, Yemen and Somalia) were caused by an armed conflict. In Nigeria, villages in the path of the war between Boko Haram and the army have been stripped of assets, income and food. In 2018, the government and several opposition groups in South Sudan signed a new peace agreement, but the prospects for a lasting peace remained uncertain. Yemen has become the biggest impending humanitarian crisis in the world. In 2017, Stephen O'Brien, then head of OCHA, declared that 'the scale of the various crises today is greater than at any time since the United Nations was founded. Not in living memory have so many people needed our support and solidarity to survive and live in safety and dignity.'

The use of starvation as a method of warfare is already prohibited by the Geneva Conventions, the Rome Statute of the International Criminal Court and UN Security Council Resolution 2417 on armed conflict and hunger (unanimously adopted in May 2018). However, to date, no international court has prosecuted a case of starvation crimes, leading observers to doubt that the perpetrators of the current political famines or their supporters (including China, France, Russia, the UK and the US) will ever be prosecuted. Listing political starvation as a crime against humanity could be an important political and judicial step to ensure respect for international humanitarian law.[41]

> Warring parties diverting aid leads to severe long-term consequences

Notes

1   United Nations Office for the Coordination of Humanitarian Affairs (OCHA), 'World Humanitarian Data and Trends 2018', 2018, p. 3.
2   UN High Commissioner for Human Rights (UNHCR), 'Mid-Year Trends 2018', 21 February 2019, p. 3.
3   Development Initiatives, 'Global Humanitarian Assistance 2018 Report', 2018, p. 21.
4   Requirements for inter-agency consolidated appeals amounted to US$23.9bn; total funding for consolidated appeals amounted to US$14.2bn. OCHA, 'World Humanitarian Data and Trends 2018', p. 7.
5   Development Initiatives, 'Global Humanitarian Assistance 2018 Report', p. 38.
6   The top five recipients of Chinese aid from 2000 to 2014 were Cuba, Côte d'Ivoire, Ethiopia, Zimbabwe and Cameroon. Axel Dreher, Andreas Fuchs, Bradley Parks, Austin M. Strange and Michael J. Tierney, 'Aid, China, and Growth: Evidence from a New Global Development Finance Dataset', AidData Working Paper no. 46, AidData at William and Mary, 2017.
7   Miwa Hirono, 'Exploring the links between Chinese foreign policy and humanitarian action: Multiple interests, processes and actors', HPG Working Paper, Humanitarian Policy Group, Overseas Development Institute (ODI), January 2018, p. iii.
8   Ashley Jackson and Abdi Aynte, 'Talking to the other side: Humanitarian negotiations with Al-Shabaab in Somalia', HPG Working Paper, Humanitarian Policy Group, ODI, December 2013.
9   Laurent Larcher, 'Centrafrique, main basse de Moscou', La Croix, 3 October 2018.
10 OCHA, 'Yemen: Organizations 3W Operational Presence: November 2018', 9 January 2019.
11 Integrated Phase Classification (IPC) reflects the phase classification of food security and the humanitarian assistance protocol attached to it. OCHA, 'Yemen Humanitarian Update: 13 December 2018–15 January 2019', January 2019.
12 OCHA, 'Yemen Humanitarian Update, 1–13 December 2018', December 2018.
13 Embassy of Saudi Arabia in Washington DC, 'Yemen Comprehensive Humanitarian Operations: Unprecedented Relief to the People of Yemen', 22 January 2018. The Aden expansion allows the port to receive 58,000 tonnes of food per month, 66,000 tonnes of bulk food shipments, 58,000 tonnes of shelter and non-food humanitarian goods, and 405,000 tonnes of fuel.
14 OCHA, 'Yemen Humanitarian Update, 1–13 December 2018'.
15 UN Panel of Experts, 'Final Report on Yemen', S/2018/594, UN Security Council, 26 January 2018, p. 3.
16 UNHCR, 'Situation of human rights in Yemen, including violations and abuse since September 2014', A/HRC/39/43, 17 August 2018.
17 Human Rights Watch, 'Yemen: Houthi Hostage Taking: Arbitrary Detention, Torture, Enforced Disappearance Go Unpunished', 25 September 2018.
18 UN Panel of Experts, 'Final Report on Yemen': 'Executives such as Motlaq Amer al-Marrani, the deputy head of the Sana'a-based National Security Bureau, was using his influence over humanitarian access in order to generate profit. As a consequence, the UN Food Agency threatened to suspend some aid shipments to Yemen if the Houthi rebels did not stop theft and fraud in food distribution', p. 49.
19 Hassan Hassan, 'Qatar Won the Saudi Blockade', Foreign Policy, 4 June 2018.
20 UN, 'Global Humanitarian Overview 2019: Trends in Humanitarian Needs and Assistance', 30 November 2018.
33 '2018 worst year in Syria's humanitarian crisis: U.N. official', Reuters, 18 May 2018.
35 Emma Beals and Nick Hopkins, 'Aid groups suspend cooperation with UN in Syria because of Assad "influence"', Guardian, 8 September 2016.
36 Reinoud Leenders, 'UN's $4bn aid effort in Syria is morally bankrupt', Guardian, 29 August 2016.
37 Annie Sparrow, 'How UN Humanitarian Aid Has Propped Up Assad', Foreign Affairs, 20 September 2018.
38 Rick Gladstone, '73 Syrian Aid Groups Suspend Cooperation with U.N.', New York Times, 8 September 2016.
39 Sanctions were imposed for Syria's repression and violation of human rights and have been updated several times since 2011.
40 Erol Yayboke, 'Accessing South Sudan: Humanitarian Aid in a Time of Crisis', CSIS Briefs, Center for Strategic and International Studies, 27 November 2018.
41 'Instruments of Pain (II): Conflict and Famine in South Sudan', Briefing no. 124, International Crisis Group, 26 April 2017.
42 UN Panel of Experts, 'Final Report on South Sudan, S/2018/292', UN, 11 April 2018, p. 17–19.
44 'South Sudan: Soldiers Attack Civilians in Western Region Abuses by Both Sides Underline Need for Justice', Human Rights Watch, 24 October 2018.
45 OCHA, 'Republic of South Sudan 2018 (Humanitarian Response Plan)', Financial Tracking Service.
46 OCHA, 'South Sudan: Operational Presence (3W: Who does What, Where): September 2018', September 2018.
48 UN Panel of Experts, 'Final Report on South Sudan'.
50 White House, 'Statement from the Press Secretary on the Civil War in South Sudan', United States Government, 8 May 2018.
51 US Department of State, 'On U.S. Assistance to UNRWA', 31 August 2018.
52 On 6 December 2017, US President Donald Trump announced the US recognition of Jerusalem as the capital of Israel. The US Embassy in Israel relocated from Tel Aviv to Jerusalem in May 2018.
53 United Nations Reliefs and Works Agency (UNRWA), 'Statement of UNRWA Commissioner-General, To The Advisory Commission', 21 November 2018.
56 International Committee of the Red Cross, 'Protracted Conflict and Humanitarian Action: some recent ICRC experiences', 6 September 2016.
57 Ben Ramalingam, Aid on the Edge of Chaos: Rethinking International Cooperation in a Complex World (Oxford: Oxford University Press, 2013).
58 Joanna Macrae and Nicholas Leader, 'Apples, Pears and Porridge: The origins and impact of the search for "coherence" between humanitarian and political responses to chronic political emergencies', Disasters, vol. 25, no. 4, December 2001, pp. 290–307.
60 Alex de Waal, 'The Nazis Used It, We Use It', London Review of Books, vol. 39, no. 12, 15 June 2017.

Conflict Expansion to Cities

Rapid urban growth in the developing world has become a source of vulnerability and a key driver in the perpetration of armed conflict. Regions already struggling with poverty, weak political institutions and conflict have been further destabilised by the growing demands and social complexity stemming from sprawling urban areas. Far from being solely a local issue, unmanaged urban growth has been recognised as a key global challenge within the United Nations' Sustainable Development Goals for 2030. The pressures unleashed by this process are heaviest upon poor countries. They are, however, potentially devastating in areas facing armed conflict.

In sub-Saharan Africa, which hosts half of the UN's peacekeeping operations, the urban population will grow by 132% between 2019 and 2043, when it is forecast to surpass the 1 billion mark. Afghanistan's urban population is forecast to almost triple from 9 to 25 million in 30 years.[1] The International Committee of the Red Cross estimated in 2016 that 50m people worldwide were affected by urban armed conflict.[2] But the roles of cities in armed conflicts go beyond that of sites for urban warfare. Cities often receive significant numbers of people displaced by conflicts, and local authorities frequently lack the necessary infrastructure and institutions to properly manage sudden and large inflows.[3]

Cities have also come to play a key role in armed conflict, supporting non-state armed groups in achieving political and economic goals beyond battlefield victories. In Iraq, the successful occupation of the country by US-led forces in 2003 was followed by a civil war starting 'as a primarily urban guerrilla struggle'.[4] Mogadishu remains a hotspot in the armed conflict between clan-based militias, al-Shabaab and international forces – seven years after the radical Islamist group was driven out of the Somali capital by African Union troops.[5] As the case studies below show, Colombia's Medellín and Pakistan's Karachi hosted armed groups and sustained war economies despite not seeing the bulk of combat.

Some urban centres in fragile or conflict-affected countries have become sites of 'conflict expansion' – convergence points for illicit economies, non-state armed groups and displaced populations. In other words, cities become tightly integrated into the broader dynamics of an armed conflict by sustaining, magnifying and transforming its dynamics, and sometimes leading to new conflict. The three main conflict-expansion mechanisms – population displacement, illicit economies and non-state group activities – can combine in different ways to transform or prolong a conflict. Rapid urban population growth facilitates this process, for instance, by exacerbating pre-existing sectarian divides, creating political and economic strain and providing opportunities for criminals and rebels to establish territorial presence and erode state control.

Cities also provide opportunities for armed groups from outside the urban area to secure finance by working with criminal organisations, raise recruits from marginalised populations or hide from government operations in rural areas. In this way, cities can become hubs for political violence and its perpetrators, supporting non-state armed groups in achieving their political and economic goals beyond battlefield victories.[6] Given the presence of rival groups interested in the same opportunities, armed actors may also develop more ruthless tactics, potentially exacerbating the severity of conflict in cities. The two scenarios are not mutually exclusive: cities may both prolong and transform the dynamics of conflict by offering rural-based armed groups access to funds, recruits and control, while simultaneously intensifying urban violence.

Growing awareness of the urban dimension

Understanding how urban dynamics drive conflict (and vice versa) is crucial in tailoring specific policies to address their related challenges. Many current political and security policies to prevent or resolve conflict are centred around concepts such as state sovereignty or prioritise national governments

– despite the fact that most conflicts are driven by sub-national and local dynamics.[7] However, awareness of the need to address the role urbanisation plays in conflict has grown. According to a 2010 study by the London School of Economics, cities have become 'primary sites of state erosion and crisis across much of the developing world'. In 2017, the United Nations recognised its 'failure ... to adequately acknowledge the pace, scale and implications of urbanisation'.[8] Several Western militaries have also identified urbanisation as a key factor affecting the future shape of wars. The US Army has intensified its study of the topic since a 2014 report by its Megacities Concept Team. In 2018, General Stephen Townsend, head of the US Army's Training and Doctrine Command, acknowledged that combat in an increasingly urban world will lead to a 'scale of devastation beyond our comprehension'. As counter-insurgency scholar David Kilcullen has prominently pointed out, although military strategy places armed threats into single categories (such as guerrilla, piracy and terrorism) and makes a neat division between governments and their foes, 'in the world of complex, adaptive social systems such as cities, trading networks, and licit or illicit economies', single-threat environments do not exist.[9]

Armed conflict has added security challenges to the profound socio-economic and institutional problems ubiquitous in developing-world cities. These security effects can perhaps best be understood through an analysis of the historical effect of conflict expansion. This essay will examine the encroachment of conflict dynamics in Medellín, Colombia, and Karachi, Pakistan, over the second half of the twentieth century. Despite the different contexts, the two cities illustrate how the three mechanisms of population displacement, illicit economies and non-state group activities combined to both transform pre-existing conflict dynamics and incite new violence.

Karachi: conflict expansion in a megacity

The port city of Karachi is Pakistan's largest agglomeration as well as its financial and industrial heart. It is also the site of numerous armed clashes and terrorist attacks along sectarian, ethnic, political and criminal lines. Karachi is one of the world's largest megacities, with 14m inhabitants in 2015 according to the UN and more than 20m according to the local government.[10] Its growth in the second half of the twentieth century was extraordinary: in 1950, three years after the partition of British India that created the state of Pakistan, Karachi had just over 1m inhabitants. Taking into account the conservative estimate of 14m residents in 2015, its population mushroomed by 1,300% in 65 years.

Karachi illustrates how displaced populations, illicit economies and armed groups altered the urban environment and overwhelmed security and governance mechanisms. As well as providing safe haven for armed groups from outside the city, the city's vast marginalised areas also facilitated the emergence of armed criminal organisations, with newcomers such as the Tehrik-e-Taliban Pakistan (TTP) exploiting the erosion of state presence and intensifying existing local rivalries.

Displacement leads to fractured urban growth

Since independence, mass population flows to the megacity have destabilised political and territorial relationships between sectarian groups, intensifying local rivalries. The first large conflict-related population flow occurred in 1947, when hundreds of thousands of Muslims living in India (commonly known as *muhajir*) moved to what was then Pakistan's first capital, causing a dramatic shift from a predominantly Hindu population to an almost exclusively Muslim one.[11] The second large population flow occurred in the 1980s, when nearly a million Afghans fled the violence resulting from the Soviet invasion of Afghanistan. More Afghans fled into Pakistan and its largest economic centre after the rise of the Taliban regime in 1996 and the US-led invasion of Afghanistan in 2001. Military operations during the 2000s in Khyber Pakhtunkhwa and the Federally Administered Tribal Areas (FATA) caused a significant flow of ethnic Pashtuns to Karachi, causing 'persistent concerns' among ethnic parties and civil-society organisations native to Sindh, the province where Karachi is located. This third population inflow, often taking place in bursts prompted by intense armed violence or political shifts in nearby provinces and countries, not only caused rapid and unplanned urban growth, but also dramatically shifted the city's ethnic composition – Sindhis went from 60% of the population in 1947 to 7.22% in 1998.[12]

The influx from these displacements exacerbated Karachi's ethnic and sectarian rivalries. Like other metropolitan centres, Karachi hosts a multitude of cultural, religious and ethnic groupings, but unlike other metropolises, it has not forged a deep coexistence between these communities. This division also manifests in the political space, with frequent clashes between three parties representing different communities: the *muhajirs* under the Muttahida Qaumi Movement (MQM), the Sindhis represented by the Pakistan People's Party (PPP) and the Pashtuns rallying around the Awami National Party (ANP). This often translates into competition for resources – the *muhajir* community, for instance, has used its numerical superiority in Karachi to gain 'greater control of transport links and commercial activity'. Tensions over local resources, distribution of government jobs and funds related to extortion activities have also triggered bouts of violent clashes between these communities and armed groups linked to them.[13] With parties capturing state institutions and providing public services in accordance with sectarian or political allegiances, Karachiites came to suffer from patchy access to public services. Piped water is inaccessible in 24% of households, public transport receives some of the lowest scores among Pakistani major cities and 99% of the population in a recent survey stated that the police serve the interests of selected influential groups.[14] This has implications for conflict dynamics: with a very young population (67% of Pakistanis are under the age of 25), young men in impoverished areas come under risk of recruitment by armed groups.

Rise of organised crime

The unmanaged and conflictive population growth has paved the way to a second major conflict-related source of instability in Karachi: the illicit economy. Organised criminal groups fill gaps left by the state in the provision of public services such as housing and water supplies, even if only on a rudimentary level.[15] Only one-third of housing units needed each year in the fast-growing megacity are provided by legal economic entities, with the remainder being developed by land-grabbing groups known as 'land mafias'.[16] Land grabbers intimidate people into selling their land for a fraction of the market value and use political connections to convert the land into commercial or residential properties. Land grabbing by armed actors associated with one ethnic group has often led to spiralling violence as their evicted rivals sought retaliation. Land is important not only for money but also for politics: areas under dispute

contain voters that are placed into 'vote banks' in order to help factions in their fight (literally and via elections) for political control of the city.[17]

Armed conflict has been at the centre of the thriving organised-crime scene in Karachi – as have the factional disputes for resources and votes between the different political groups. The opium transit route through Karachi took off in 1979 with the Soviet invasion of Afghanistan. Both drugs and weapons began to be processed and stockpiled by previously small criminal groups based in some of the marginalised areas of the city that were suddenly connected to a global illicit economy. This was the case, for instance, in the areas of Lyari and Sohrab Goth in Karachi. The trend accelerated under the rule of the Taliban in Afghanistan and the impact of the US-led invasion of Afghanistan in 2001. According to the Pakistan representative at the UN Office on Drugs and Crime, 'Karachi is the largest transit hub of drugs', with around 42–43% of Afghan-produced opiates passing through the country. This has strengthened revenue streams for armed groups and, for some of them, encouraged political and criminal activities to merge.

> Understanding how urban dynamics drive conflict is crucial in tailoring specific policies

Armed groups move to Karachi

The third major, and potentially most violence-inducing, conflict-related flow into Karachi has been that of non-state armed groups. One of the most violent currently operating in the city is also one of its newest residents: the TTP, the Taliban movement of Pakistan, which established a base in Karachi around 2009 partially due to the city's lucrative illicit economies and partially because it had been driven out of the northwestern provinces by military operations.[18] Senior members of the Afghan Taliban have also sought sanctuary in the city. More recently, in 2015, Karachi became part of the expansion of the Islamic State, also known as ISIS or ISIL, in Pakistan, with a local terrorist cell responsible for 'multiple attacks' in the city in 2015.[19] Religious schools in the megacity have been frequently cited as sources of radicalisation for ISIS terrorist attacks in Pakistan, with some 94 madrassas under surveillance in Karachi and southern Sindh province in 2018.[20] In September 2014, al-Qaeda in the Indian Subcontinent (AQIS) burst into the militant underworld with a failed raid on a naval dockyard in Karachi in an attempt to hijack a frigate. Whereas some of these newcomers, such as AQIS, had little impact on local violence, others such as the TTP challenged existing local powers, altered the invisible boundaries established by pre-existing groups and clashed.

Violence ensued, not only due to the brutally violent nature of the militant armed groups themselves, but also because of the tactics they adopted to operate in the hyper-competitive territorial struggles between so many armed actors in Karachi. By 2013, the TTP had 8,000 members in the Pakistani megalopolis, taking advantage of the poor state presence and the illicit economy by forging links to criminal groups and conducting its own extortion rackets. The arrival of such a violent (and ambitious) actor also inevitably set a collision course with another major Pashtun group, the ANP, whose grip on neighbourhoods such as the Sindh Industrial Trading Estate and Qasba Colony was violently challenged. As a Karachi journalist told the International Crisis Group, the well-demarcated geographical division of Karachi along ethnic lines was disrupted, as the TTP and other newcomers 'had no geographic limits'.[21]

The competitiveness and shifting allegiances between armed and political groups in Karachi has also encouraged interactions and even mergers between the three conflict-related flows. For instance, the D-Company is considered a crime-terror group, blending the less militarised approach of criminal groups that need a level of political order in place and more 'purely' terrorist groups such as al-Qaeda and the TTP that benefit from criminal finances but are not crucially interested in state stability. A sectarian group, the Sipah-e-Sahaba-e-Pakistan, formed in the 1980s as a Sunni response to the Iranian revolution, has been reported to assist, cooperate and train with Islamist terror groups such as the Afghan Taliban.[22]

Be it through the direct action of insurgent and militia groups or through a gradual migration of illicit economies and populations, conflict expansion has had a profound effect on the security and political dynamics in Karachi. Still, the urban space has not passively hosted conflict originating elsewhere, but also altered its character. Given the political importance and economic connectivity of a megacity such as Karachi, these changing conflict dynamics – along with local geography and politics – acquire critical roles in national and regional stability.

Medellín: a hub for guerrillas and paramilitaries

Colombia's second-largest city, Medellín, has been a critical site for armed actors that contributed to Colombia being considered, during part of the 1990s, 'on the verge of becoming a failed state'.[23] Almost all of the main players of Colombia's conflict in the 1990s and 2000s were present in the city, in addition to local criminals and militias. These included not only the fabled Medellín Cartel, which supplied an estimated 70% of the cocaine consumed in the US during that time, but also leftist guerrillas and right-wing paramilitary groups. The city's enduring linkage with the armed conflict shows how urban vulnerabilities and politics play a critical role in broader security dynamics.

Conflict expansion in Medellín revolves around displaced populations, illicit economies (through Colombia's long-standing cocaine industry) and a range of non-state armed groups of varying ideological and criminal orientations. As in the case of Karachi, local sources of vulnerability facilitated the arrival and prolonged stay of such conflict dynamics. These vulnerabilities included marginalised communities such as Comuna 13, pre-existing armed groups that could be co-opted, and weak governance mechanisms incapable of coping with population growth and crime.

Displaced populations move to Medellín

The transition from a small city with fewer than 200,000 people in the late 1930s to Colombia's second-largest population centre with 2.5m inhabitants challenging for Medellín. The urbanisation process was tightly linked to Colombia's experience of armed conflict. *La Violencia*, a period of conflict between supporters of the Conservative and the Liberal parties that took place between 1948 and 1958, sparked intense violence in the countryside. A combination of direct armed conflict and violent disputes for land between peasants and traditional landowners resulted in forced population displacement 'of huge magnitude' from the rural to urban areas.[24] By 1963, when Colombia for the first time become a majority-urban country, Medellín had established itself as an important industrial centre, a further pull factor for struggling peasants.[25]

Armed conflict would resume in the 1960s, when the Marxist-Leninist guerrilla movements FARC and ELN emerged. Medellín's population grew by four and a half times from 1938 to 1964, and broke the 1m mark in 1973, in large part due to migration and displacement from rural areas.[26]

Forced displacement led to a *descampesinización* (de-ruralisation) of Colombia, according to the 2015 report on forced displacement published by the National Centre of Historical Memory. However, with insufficient economic and job opportunities and unable to afford housing anywhere near the centre, the recently arrived communities built informal settlements in the hills surrounding the city, often with precarious materials and without access to public services. Hillside slum-like communities, especially the one called Comuna 13, would later become hotbeds of armed activity by gangs, guerrillas and paramilitaries.[27]

FARC targets Medellín

The Revolutionary Armed Forces of Colombia (FARC) and the smaller National Liberation Army (ELN), both established in 1964, followed the *foquista* model successfully used in Cuba by Fidel Castro and Ernesto 'Che' Guevara, based on initiating popular upheaval in rural areas and only later going against the government's urban bastions. Starting in the late 1970s, FARC began to increase its urban footprint, in part to counterbalance military pressure by the government in rural areas. This move was not only justified according to the political economy of the conflict, but also as a reflection of Colombia's transition from a rural to a predominantly urban country. In its seventh national conference (1982), the FARC leadership stated that 'the urban work' had acquired a 'strategic status' and decided to transition towards 'the organisational structure of the military in the cities that allows, in conjunction with other revolutionary organisations, the conduct of insurrectional actions'.[28]

In looking more towards cities, FARC was following in the footsteps of the M-19, which in the 1970s gained public attention by 'conducting audacious urban actions and employing an attractive language for the medium- and lower-[income] sectors of Colombian cities'. On top of the political and economic significance of cities, Medellín also possessed strategic military importance. It was a crucial hub for highways connecting to the north and east

of the country, a prized avenue to transport fighters, weapons and other assets. To a lesser extent, the ELN also focused more on cities during the 1980s, partly in order to adapt its strategy of 'Prolonged Popular Warfare' to Colombia's new urban-majority society.[29] The ELN also saw the deployment of urban militants as part of a reactive strategy to prevent its 'dissolution' after severe blows during 1970s and 1980s, which included a more decentralised structure.[30]

Local militias and gangs co-opted

One of the tools FARC hoped to draw from were urban militias, which would feature strongly in Medellín from the 1980s onwards.[31] At the turn of the 1980s, a new type of criminal structure appeared in the city: youth gangs that would not only commit petty crimes but also engage in drug trafficking.[32] Some of these gangs were assimilated as 'armed wings' of larger drug-trafficking organisations. In reaction to the growing violence and armament of the gangs, popular militias were formed in some marginalised communities to protect the population in face of an absent state authority.[33]

The appearance of the militias, with their aims of popular protection and distance from government authority, presented an opportunity for leftist guerrillas to implement their plans to 'urbanise' themselves. At a time when the gangs were proliferating through the popular neighbourhoods, demand for the security and control offered by the militias also grew. There were ten militia groups in the city in 1993, compared with just one in 1988.[34]

The same informal settlements formed by populations fleeing the conflict waged by FARC and ELN guerrillas in the countryside became a beachhead in the urbanisation plans of these conflict actors. Comuna 13 was among the hardest hit by the guerrillas and their rules. The guerrillas were initially well received by locals due to their stated aim of establishing order, as well as organising cultural events and parties. However, soon both FARC and ELN started enforcing strict rules (FARC was reportedly stricter), such as a night-time curfew, and even executing those accused of theft. They also imposed 'revolutionary taxes' on small businesses and transportation companies.

The right-wing paramilitary group United Self-Defence Groups of Colombia (Autodefensas Unidas de Colombia, AUC) reacted to the guerrilla plan for urban environments with their own. Around the time of the first conference of the AUC in 1997, the group decided to follow the guerrillas and challenge them in Medellín through the Urban Self-Defence Groups (Grupos de Autodefensa Urbana, GRAU) and the moving of rural combatants from inner areas of Antioquia department to the departmental capital. In 1998, the paramilitaries decided to subcontract some of the small gangs, known locally as *bandas* or *combos*, in their strategy to fight the guerrilla-linked militias.[35] The Bloque Metro gave ideological and military training to gang members, especially those that did not adapt well to the strict rules of the leftist guerrillas.[36] From 1995 to 2005 was the period of the most intense confrontation between political armed actors in the city, and a time when criminal gangs lost a great deal of their autonomy in face of intense pressure and co-optation by politically motivated actors linked to the armed conflict.[37]

> The two cities came to play a critical role in the political economy of the armed conflicts

Cocaine boom fuels conflicts

FARC's move to Medellín was not solely motivated by ideological reasons. In the 1970s, cocaine began arriving in Medellín. The drug industry was initially not directly linked to the armed conflict, since Colombia was a convenient processing post for the coca base imported from Peru and Bolivia en route to the United States. However, guerrilla groups quickly realised they could benefit from the increasingly lucrative trade. FARC used its armed presence in remote rural areas, in which the state was largely absent, to regulate the transactions between coca-growing peasants and buyers in the international drug trade. FARC protected the largest cocaine-refining laboratory in the country (reportedly owned by Pablo Escobar's Medellín Cartel) in a jungle area of Caquetá department, in exchange for a tax of 10–20% of the profits, according to police reports in 1984, when the laboratory was dismantled.[38]

Local thinking for a global problem

The histories of political violence in Karachi and Medellín illustrate the three main destabilising mechanisms behind conflict expansion in urban centres. Urban dynamics related to the wider armed conflict, such as illicit economies and unmanaged population growth, facilitated further conflict, while conflict actors exploited existing vulnerabilities and communal rifts. The two cities also came to play a critical role in the political economy of the armed conflicts taking place in their vicinities or connected areas: Afghanistan's opium economy continues to rely on Karachi's port and criminal actors, while Colombia's drug-trafficking networks were directed from Medellín, and FARC's rural insurgency was financed in part by drug money.

Conflict expansion poses difficult problems for those seeking to develop strategies to alleviate it. The three main mechanisms through which this expansion takes place – the flows of displaced populations, illicit economies and non-state armed groups – have placed the cities in a grey zone between peace and warfare. Karachi is located relatively far from the key battlefields in the northern provinces and areas bordering Pakistan, whereas in Colombia the internal armed conflict of the last half-century has long been associated with the country's jungles and mountains. Yet even as the main battles took place in rural areas, population hubs were gradually exposed to increasing levels of the conflict-related flows.

Awareness of the specificities of this phenomenon is crucial for the design of government policy, as a city's protracted, long-term spiral into violence and the sudden outbreak of war require different responses. Similarly, stabilisation or conflict-prevention work in a city requires specific tools and knowledge to tackle local political trends that are often different from those taking place at the national level. The concentration of violence and sectarian divides in marginalised areas in Karachi and Medellín illustrates how conflict dynamics find openings in specific spaces.

Due to the multidimensional aspect of conflict expansion in cities, appropriate responses will need to go well beyond military tools or any individual policy area. Medellín itself has countered with some success, as many of the violent actors left after demobilisation agreements with the paramilitary groups in the 2000s. Interventions in the urban space, via infrastructure and social policies that integrate marginalised areas to the broader urban economy and society, were part of the city's improvements. The cable car now linking Comuna

13 to the rest of the city has come to symbolise the progress made in the past 15 years (even if much remains to be done).

Cities themselves may be the best arbiters of both the problem and the solution. In recent years, regional and global groupings of cities have shown their ability to voice concerns and coordinate local solutions, with potentially global effects. A recent example is the C40 group of globally connected cities, which was instrumental in the planning of the Paris Agreement on climate change, and its implementation. The inclusion of cities and their networks in international organisations, regional groupings (such as the African Union), post-conflict development mechanisms, conflict-prevention discussions and UN peacekeeping, political and peacebuilding strategies can infuse local thinking into this century's urbanised conflicts.

Notes

1   United Nations, Department of Economic and Social Affairs, Population Division (UNDESA), 'World Urbanization Prospects: The 2018 Revision', custom data acquired via website.

2   'War in Cities', *International Review of the Red Cross*, vol. 98, no. 901.

3   Jo Beall, Tom Goodfellow and Dennis Rodgers, 'Cities, Conflict and State Fragility', Crisis States Research Centre, January 2011, p. 9.

4   James Fearon, 'Iraq's Civil War', Foreign Affairs, vol. 86, no. 2, March/April 2007.

5   See, for instance, International Crisis Group, 'Managing the Disruptive Aftermath of Somalia's Worst Terror Attack', 20 October 2017; Muhyadin Ahmed Roble, 'Mogadishu's Dilemma: Who's in Control?', *Terrorism Monitor*, vol. 11, no. 12, 14 June 2013.

6   The concept of urban hubs for violent trends was first developed by Daniel Esser in 'The City as Arena, Hun and Prey – Patterns of Violence in Kabul and Karachi', *Environment & Urbanization*, vol. 16, no. 2, October 2004, pp. 31–8.

7   Antônio Sampaio, 'Before and After Urban Warfare: Conflict Prevention and Transitions in Cities', *International Review of the Red Cross*, vol. 98, no. 1, 2016, p. 94.

8   United Nations, 'Report of the High Level Independent Panel to Assess and Enhance Effectiveness of UN-Habitat', 1 August 2017, p. 2.

9   David Kilcullen, *Out of the Mountains: The Coming Age of the Urban Guerrilla* (London: Hurst, 2013), p. 17.

10 UNDESA, 'World Urbanization Prospects: The 2018 Revision'. Karachi figure is from 2015; 'Residents in Karachi', Karachi Metropolitan Corporation website, December 2018.

11 Laurent Gayer, *Karachi: Ordered Disorder and the Struggle for the City* (Oxford: Oxford University Press, 2014), p. 27–28, 42–3.

12 Zia Ur Rehman, 'Karachi: A Pashtun City?' in *Cityscapes of Violence in Karachi*, ed. Nichola Khan (London: Hurst, 2017), pp. 64–9.

13 Huma Yusuf, 'Conflict Dynamics in Karachi', United States Institute of Peace, 2012, p. 3–12.

14 Haroon Jamal and Zia-ul-Haque Khan, 'Citizens' Perceptions of Urban Public Services', Social Policy and Development Centre, May 2016.

15 Nazia Hussain and Louise Shelley, 'Karachi: Organised Crime in a Key Megacity', *Connections: The Quarterly Journal*, vol. 15, no. 3, 2016, p. 6.

16 World Bank, 'Transforming Karachi into a Livable and Competitive Megacity', 2018, p. 71.

17 Yusuf, 'Conflict Dynamics in Karachi', p. 12; Taimur Khan, 'Karachi Mafia Seek Political Clout with Land Grabs', *National*, 30 December 2010.

18 International Crisis Group, 'Pakistan: Stoking the Fire in Karachi'.

19 Zoha Waseem, 'Daesh in Pakistan's Militant Landscape and the Allure for Urban Extremists', *Strife*, no. 6, May/June 2016, p. 21.

20 Kathy Gannon, 'IS Deadly New Front in Pakistan's decades-old Terror War', Associated Press, 18 August 2018.

21 International Crisis Group, 'Pakistan: Stoking the Fire in Karachi', ibid.

22 Christine Fair, 'Urban Battle Fields of South Asia Lessons Learned from Sri Lanka, India, and Pakistan', RAND, 2004, pp. 109–11.

23 Juan Carlos Pinzón, 'Colombia Back from the Brink: From Failed State to Exporter of Security', *Prism*, vol. 5, no. 4, p. 3.

24 No reliable numbers exist for forced displacement during this period, but Colombia's National Centre of Historical Memory cites estimates that up to two million people fled the countryside to cities during La Violencia. 'Una Nación Desplazada: Informe Nacional del Desplazamiento Forzado en Colombia', Centro Nacional de Memoria Histórica, September 2015, pp. 41–2.

25 'Población Urbana (% del Total): Colombia', Datos, Banco Mundial, 2018.

26 Carlos Alberto Patiño Villa, *Medellín: Território, Conflicto y Estado* (Bogotá: Planeta, 2015), p. 128–30.

27 This issue would come back to haunt local authorities decades later when the issue of precarious living and unplanned urbanisation would be taken up by drug lord Pablo Escobar. He built a hillside community in 1984 called 'Medellín without Slums' as one of the popular projects he designed to benefit poor people in his hometown (since then the area has been renamed 'Barrio Pablo Escobar'). Nahuel Gallota, 'Moravia, el barrio colombiano en el que Pablo Escobar "hizo obra"', *Clarín*, 4 October 2015.

28 FARC-EP, Secretariado del Estado Mayor Central, 'Planteamiento Estratégico', VII Conferencia Nacional, p. 117. Cited in: Centro Nacional de Memoria Histórica, 'Guerrilla y Población Civil Trayectoria de las FARC 1949–2013', May 2014.

29 Ralph Rozema, 'Paramilitares y Violencia Urbana en Medellín, Colombia', Foro Internacional, vol. XLVII, no. 3, July–September 2007, p. 541–3.

30 Luis Miguel Buitrago Roa and Miguel Esteban Suarez Gutierrez, 'Historia de la interacción político-militar entre guerrillas

colombianas, 1964–2015', *Anuario Colombiano de Historia Social y de la Cultura*, vol. 44, no. 2, 2017, pp. 199–225.

[31]   Mario Aguilera Peña, 'Las Guerrillas y las Construcciones de Poder Popular', CEDEMA, 2010, p. 346.

[32]   Ramiro Ceballos, 'Violencia Reciente en Medellín: Una Aproximación a los Actores', *Bulletin de l'Institut Français d'Études Andines*, vol. 29, no. 3, 2000, p. 388.

[33]   Ralph Rozema, 'Paramilitares y Violencia Urbana en Medellín, Colombia', Foro Internacional, vol. XLVII, no. 3, July–September 2007, p. 541–3.

[34]   Manuel A. Alonso Espinal et al., 'Medellín: El Complejo Camino de la Competencia Armada', in *Parapolítica: La Ruta de la Expansión Paramilitar y Los Acuerdos Políticos*, ed. Mauricio Romero (Bogotá: Corporación Nuevo Arco Iris, 2007), p. 117–8.

[34]   Espinal et al., 'Medellín: El Complejo Camino de la Competencia Armada', pp. 109–164.

[36]   'La Alianza entre el Bloque Metro y las Bandas de Medellín', Verdad Abierta, 20 October 2011.

[37]   Elsa Blair et al., 'Conflictividades Urbanas vs "Guerra" Urbana: Otra "Clave" para Leer el Conflicto en Medellín', *Universitas Humanistica*, no. 67, January–June 2009, pp. 36–7.

[38]   'El Narcotráfico que Incendió el Conflicto Armado', *Verdad Abierta*, 25 September 2013.

Armed Conflict and Forced Displacement

According to the Office of the United Nations High Commissioner for Refugees (UNHCR), the number of people both within countries and across borders who have been forcibly displaced due to persecution, armed conflict or violence has grown by more than 50% in the past ten years. In 2007, there were 42.7 million forcibly displaced people, but this number had risen to 68.5m by the end of 2017 – more than the population of France.

Both refugee and internally displaced person (IDP) populations are now at record levels for the post-Second World War period. One out of approximately 110 people on the planet is forcibly displaced as a result of conflict or persecution, with 31 people displaced every minute. Notably, while much international coverage focuses on refugees, the refugee population has been rapidly outpaced by the growth in IDP populations (see **Figure 1**). Indeed, two-thirds of all displaced persons remain in their home country.[1]

The majority of displaced individuals flee their homes due to the belief that the risks associated with remaining are too great. They move to escape the atrocities of violence and find safe haven, to be able to establish a livelihood and gain access to economic opportunities, and to join their kin elsewhere. All too often, however, displacement is strategically motivated and not simply a by-product of violence. Armed combatants in conflicts in Colombia, Sri Lanka, Uganda, Syria and many other countries have purposefully employed violence with a view towards clearing specific populations from a territory.[3] By available estimates, this strategic use of violence to displace has been employed in between one-third and half of civil wars in the post-1945 period. While rebels have also often engaged in these activities, governments likely account for 85% of strategic uses.[4]

Whether a by-product of violence or driven by strategic motivations, displacement has significant and lasting economic, political and security implications for the displaced individuals, as well as for the communities that subsequently host them. The majority of refugees are hosted by developing countries, which have themselves often been affected by conflict and therefore struggle to carry the additional economic burden associated with rapid and large refugee influxes. The arrival of displaced populations often has the effect of challenging established bargains between governments and opposition actors along social, religious and political lines.

It is also the case that the movement of displaced populations out of conflict zones can provide cover for militants and their arms to enter new territories and cross international boundaries, placing host communities at risk of conflict diffusion. As a result these risks, refugees are often the target of violence in host states.[5]

Forced displacement in 2018

In 2018, five of the deadlier conflicts in the world – Syria, Afghanistan, Nigeria, Yemen and Somalia – were also associated with some of the highest rates of displacement of both refugees and IDPs. As of mid-June 2018, the conflicts in Syria, Afghanistan and

Figure 1: Global population of IDPs and refugees, 1993–2017[2]

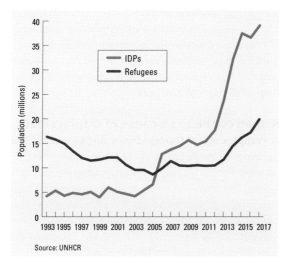

Source: UNHCR

Figure 2: Top ten host countries for refugees and IDPs, 2017

Refugees Hosted (Number)	Rank	IDPs Hosted (Number)
Turkey (3,480,348)	1	Colombia (7,677,609)
Pakistan (1,393,143)	2	Syria (6,150,005)
Uganda (1,350,504)	3	DRC (4,351,276)
Lebanon (998,890)	4	Iraq (2,615,988)
Iran (979,435)	5	Somalia (2,116,705)
Germany (970,365)	6	Yemen (2,014,062)
Bangladesh (932,216)	7	Sudan (1,997,022)
Sudan (906,599)	8	South Sudan (1,903,953)
Ethiopia (889,412)	9	Afghanistan (1,837,079)
Jordan (691,023)	10	Ukraine (1,800,000)

Source: UNHCR

South Sudan accounted for some 57% of the refugees worldwide (6.3m, 2.6m and 2.4 m, respectively).

Neighbouring countries have accommodated the majority of this displacement (see **Figure 2**). Turkey hosts almost 3.5m Syrian refugees, while Lebanon's population of 6m includes approximately 1m registered Syrian refugees. Jordan also hosts almost 700,000. (Germany is the only developed Western nation that hosts a relatively large number of Syrian refugees.)

Pakistan and Iran host significant numbers of refugees from the long-running conflict in Afghanistan, while Sudan and Uganda are the primary hosts of refugees fleeing violence in neighbouring South Sudan. Bangladesh currently hosts the bulk of people displaced from Myanmar. Finally, Ethiopia is host to refugees from a number of countries including, primarily from neighbouring Somalia.

Syria, with more than 6m IDPs, has seen more than 12m of its citizens forcibly displaced by the conflict – more than half of its pre-war population. Syria is now rapidly approaching the level of internal displacement observed in Colombia as a result of its decades-long civil war between the government and various rebel organisations, including the Revolutionary Armed Forces of Colombia (FARC) and the National Liberation Army (ELN).

The original remits of international agencies and actors did not address displacement that occurred exclusively within sovereign political boundaries, meaning that the plight of IDPs has often been ignored. In recent years, however, the UNHCR has come to believe that IDPs are indistinguishable from refugees in terms of their plight and ambitions, and are perhaps more vulnerable than refugees as they remain subject to the rules and protection of a government that may actually be the cause of their original displacement. Accordingly, the UNHCR has expanded its scope to provide support for humanitarian agencies working with IDPs.

This is a crucial improvement in international responses to forced displacement, because the dynamics underlying internal displacement are fundamental to understanding the subsequent movement of refugees across borders. Often, affected individuals first become IDPs and then refugees. This sequential process is evident in the case of the civil war in Syria. Like many other refugee situations, this case began with mass internal displacement. A clear majority – 85% – of those interviewed recently after arriving in Greece stated that they were IDPs within Syria before fleeing that country and acquiring refugee status.[6] Many had been displaced internally up to 12 times before finally leaving the country.

While as many as 17m refugees across the world are now informally integrated within the fabric of local host communities, more than 3m still reside in camps that were intended to house them for brief stays. This situation is exacerbated by the fact that forcibly displaced people are, on average, displaced from their homes for increasingly longer periods of time. For refugees in protracted displacement situations, where they remain away from their home for more than five years, the average length of displacement abroad is now approaching 20 years.[7] Protracted displacement poses a significant challenge to the paradigm of emergency humanitarian interventions, extends the period of burden-sharing for host communities and makes eventual return and reintegration of the displaced more precarious.

Armed conflict as a cause of displacement

A complex set of factors drives displacement. The decision to move, as well as where and when, is affected by geographic location, transportation networks, communication technologies, former colonial relationships, interventions by great powers and poverty and economic hardship.[8] Social networks and a desire to reunite family and kin networks are also crucial in migration decision-making.[9]

Violence during armed conflicts remains the single most important determinant in migration decision-making, but rather than simply being passive recipients of humanitarian assistance, refugees often occupy key roles in the dynamics of conflicts.[10] Civilians exposed to violence during conflicts make reasoned assessments about the decision to remain loyal to the government, join combatant groups, flee to safer areas within their home country or emigrate across national borders.[11]

The empirical evidence about decision-making is still limited, however, and research on the effects of exposure to violence on the decision to flee is still at a preliminary stage. Importantly, not all evidence reports the same relationship between individual exposure to violence or victimisation during war and taking the decision to flee. On the one hand, in Kosovo in 1999 there appeared to be a very strong correlation between the movement of violence into new areas and the subsequent movement of individuals out of those same areas in the immediate aftermath.[12] Recent evidence from Syria demonstrates, on the other hand, that exposure through social and communication networks to information about violence may drive decisions to flee prior to any direct exposure to the violence itself.[13]

Yemen and Syria: differing displacement processes

Two ongoing wars illustrate the varying processes of displacement triggered by armed conflict. The civil war in Yemen broke out in 2015 as a contest between the Yemeni government of Abd Rabbo Mansour Hadi and the Houthi militia and their allies loyal to the previous leader, Ali Saleh. After Hadi fled the country, Saudi Arabia launched airstrikes against the Houthis and large parts of the Yemeni population in an attempt to restore his government. In the subsequent years, tens of thousands of individuals have been killed by conflict and many more by the consequences of war, such as famine and the cholera outbreak. In the face of overwhelming and abject hardships, Yemeni civilians have opted to leave their home areas in large numbers, but a considerable majority remain within the borders of the country. Crucially, this situation does not reflect a preference to remain in their homeland so much as it demonstrates the paucity of exit options. Yemeni civilians cannot flee north to Saudi Arabia, which is the source of much of the violence. The trek east

to Oman is too long and arduous across unpassable desert conditions. The final exit option is to cross the Gulf of Aden to Eritrea, Djibouti or Somalia, none of which offer dramatically improved conditions, besides the perilous sea crossing.

More than half of Syria's pre-war population of 22m has been displaced by the civil war, but in contrast to Yemen, a significant proportion of the displaced population have been able to find relatively safe haven abroad. Indeed, this case is the focal point of contemporary displacement processes precisely because large numbers of displaced people have been able to exit the country to nearby Turkey, Lebanon, Jordan and beyond, provoking a wider debate surrounding how to manage the humanitarian implications of displacement. In this instance, beyond merely having greater access to exit options through geographic proximity and social ties to kin abroad, the Syrian population also arguably had greater economic means by which to complete the journey to these neighbouring countries and beyond.

Strategic displacement

Displacement is not simply an unintended consequence or by-product of armed conflict. In many instances, state security forces and armed non-state actors strategically displace populations in order to gain military or political advantage.[14] The targeted repression of individuals and groups of citizens – most often active opposition movements and members of ethnic-minority populations – is shown to be a consistent predictor of displacement.[15] In Myanmar, for example, the government of the predominantly Buddhist country has targeted the 1m members of the Muslim minority Rohingya population of Rakhine State. While discrimination against this population is far from new in Myanmar, recent years brought an escalation in state action. The Rohingya were excluded from the country's census in 2014 and subjected to more violent forms of repression beginning in late 2016, precipitating the mass movement of the Rohingya into neighbouring Bangladesh.

Recent research is unveiling three broad strategies of displacement that are deployed during civil wars: 'cleansing', depopulation and forced relocation.[16] Cleansing involves the collective targeting of a group based upon ethnic, social or political ties and is aimed at permanently expelling those individuals from an area.[17] Depopulation involves the indiscriminate rather than collective targeting of militant and civilian opponents. This form of targeting results in the mass movement of entire towns and villages rather than subsets thereof.[18] Finally, forced relocation implies that violent actors are interested not only in expelling opponents from a particular space but also in directing where those displaced populations go.[19]

Strategic displacement is sometimes used in areas where the electoral loyalties of the local population threaten the territorial control of the state or armed groups. Since the 1980s, more than 6m Colombians have been internally displaced by the conflict between the government and non-state armed groups. At the heart of these displacements lies an explicit strategy of political cleansing in which specific groups are expelled from their home territories in order to effect control of these spaces. Such a strategy requires being able to accurately identify the loyalties of local residents. Over a 30-year period in the Apartadó municipality of Colombia, political cleansing was used to target and displace residents in areas with higher levels of electoral support for rebel-affiliated parties.[20]

> Violence is the most important determinant in migration decision-making

The Lebanese civil war (1975–90) resulted in the deaths of more than 144,000 individuals and the destruction of nearly 175 towns. At its core, this war was fuelled by strategic uses of violence by armed ethnic groups designed to displace populations. More than 30% of the pre-war population (1.2m) were uprooted from their homes, with about 40% of the towns (379 of 1,000) experiencing some population displacement. Christian militias attempted to cleanse Muslim populations from areas of their own control, while the Palestinian Liberation Organization (PLO) in turn targeted Christian populations.[21]

In Iraq, the displacement of ethnic groups – especially in neighbourhoods within Baghdad – in the aftermath of US intervention in 2003 led directly to increases in violence, which was targeted against those specific populations.[22] In Burundi, Hutus suspected that displaced-person camps were being used by Tutsi militias as bases, and justified the use of violence against them as a means of eradicating the Tutsi threat.[23]

Armed conflict as a consequence of displacement?

While population displacement is often a by-product or an intentional strategic outcome of violence and other dangers associated with conflict, this relationship may also operate in the opposite direction. Large population movements may affect both sending and receiving states, the local communities that host displaced people and the dynamics of an ongoing armed conflict.[24]

The vast majority of refugees never directly engage in violence. Armed groups, however, may take advantage of refugee flows to facilitate the spread of arms, combatants and ideologies across new territories and international boundaries. The Hutu militiamen who fled Rwanda in 1994 among the 2m civilians escaping the Rwanda Patriotic Front took control of the refugee camps in Zaire (now the Democratic Republic of the Congo) and from there continued their war against the new Tutsi government. Members of the Tamil Tigers assassinated Indian prime minister Rajiv Gandhi in a suicide bombing in May 1991. They were able to do so in part by taking advantage of the cover provided by a large local population of Tamil refugees in India.[25]

Rather than showing a direct relationship between the number of refugees crossing a border and the risk of the diffusion of violence, these examples indicate that such relationships exist only under specific and rare conditions and highlight the importance of not treating refugees as a homogeneous group. The relationship is instead indirect. Firstly, ethnic ties between refugee groups and local populations in host states may lead refugee populations to provide resources or support to domestic opposition groups, often in exchange for protection and livelihood. Somali refugees have collaborated with ethnic Somali separatists in the Ogaden region of Ethiopia, for example. This dynamic is likely when refugees share ethnicity with domestic groups that are explicitly excluded from local politics.[26] Secondly, in situations where a delicate demographic balance exists or supports a political bargain between the government and the opposition, host governments may see refugees as a threat to that balance and act accordingly against them, leading to violent repression.

Countries receiving refugees may initiate interstate disputes to prevent additional arrivals. In doing so, they may violate sovereign claims. This logic appears to have been present when the US intervened in Haiti in 1994 and India invaded East Pakistan in the 1970s with the intention of stemming the flow of Haitian and Bangladeshi refugees, respectively. Vietnam invaded Cambodia in December 1978 in part as retaliation against Cambodian aggression but also in response to mounting numbers of refugees who were fleeing Pol Pot's regime and heading to Vietnamese territories. Alternatively, the state from which refugees originate (i.e., the state experiencing conflict, violence or persecution) is likely to initiate an interstate dispute when violating international borders in pursuit of dissidents who may be travelling among refugee populations fleeing the country. In 1996, the Rwandan government invaded eastern Zaire in an attempt to clear militants from refugee camps in the aftermath of the genocide in Rwanda.[27]

Finally, refugees may have an actual or perceived negative economic impact on the host country, which can provoke a backlash from local populations. The influx of refugees from Kosovo into Macedonia, for example, led to the widespread perception that refugees were responsible for declining local economic conditions. These often unfounded perceptions may themselves heighten the risk of conflict diffusion by isolating refugees as the targets of violence in host states. Accordingly, an empirical correlation between refugees and violence may actually reflect growth in attacks against refugee populations amid largely exaggerated accusations of the problems caused by refugees.[28]

Economic and political consequences of displacement

The current massive displacement of Syrian refugees has placed the issue of forced migration at the heart of political debates throughout the world – a minority of states have advocated for more openness, but a majority have sought to close their borders. Just a decade or so ago, the idea that European Union member states would close their borders and eschew the principles of the Common European Asylum System (CEAS) and the Schengen Agreement was unthinkable; in 2006, there were just three controls at internal borders within the EU.[29] By 2017, however, there were 20 checkpoints and controls at borders internal to the EU, including on each of France's borders, Germany's border with Austria, and Austria's borders with Slovenia and Hungary, among others. Since the Berlin Wall fell in 1989, EU member states have constructed almost 1,000 kilometres of physical walls, with construction accelerating in 2012 and especially after 2015.[30] These wall-building efforts have notably been focused upon closing off access to the EU from the Middle East via the Balkan route.

Efforts to fortify borders and restrict the movement of refugees and asylum seekers have taken place across the world. US President Donald Trump is adamant that a physical wall must be constructed along the United States' southern border with Mexico to control migration from Central America. Australia continues to house thousands of would-be asylum seekers offshore. Turkey has recently completed the construction of a border wall covering almost the full length of its border with Syria. Actions of this kind may be justified by claims of risks associated with the diffusion of conflict and violence, but their rationale is rooted in concerns regarding the economic impacts of and broader political responses to the arrival of refugees and asylum seekers.

Host countries often struggle to manage the burden associated with hosting refugees for long periods of time. While a great deal of generosity has been shown by populations hosting Syrian refugees during this crisis, attitudes towards and support for hosting appear to have frayed in many countries.[31] The arrival of large numbers of refugees can certainly place strains on the economies of receiving countries, such as employment losses among native informal workers and increase in the rents of higher-quality housing units.[32] Lebanon hosts the greatest per capita number of refugees in the world, a considerable burden that has been associated with a doubling in the unemployment rate (to 20% in 2017), economic losses thought to total in excess of US$7bn and a public debt that continues to grow.[33] Data from a survey of 2,400 residents in Lebanon in 2017 suggests that more than 80% of Lebanese citizens attribute some amount of blame to the Syrian refugees for exacerbating their national economic woes. More than 90% highlight concerns about competition in the labour market and almost two-thirds cite fears of higher rent at the top of their concerns regarding hosting Syrians.[34]

While cases such as Lebanon suggest that there may be real economic costs associated with hosting displaced populations in the short term, a large body of research reflects the potential for net-positive outcomes over longer time frames.[35] In the longer term, both high- and low-skilled migrants appear to have a positive influence on the economies of host countries. Refugees in the US are more likely to start small businesses than native-born citizens and in 2015 paid US$20.9bn in tax.[36] In Rwanda, the influx of Congolese refugees over the past two decades has prompted an influx of international aid, which has significantly boosted the local economy.[37]

More broadly, it appears that a 1% increase in the size of immigrant populations may be associated with (on average) an increase in GDP of up to 2%. Moreover, through remittances sent back to their low- and middle-income countries of origin, migrants provide a much-needed source of support to people who stay behind, often much higher than official aid disbursements. As much as three-quarters of the more than US$600bn remitted to home countries in 2017 went to low- and middle-income countries.

> Negative attitudes in host communities may have more to do with scapegoating and poor management

The relative optimism of the longer-term economic case is further supported by evidence regarding the positive role of contact between host and refugee communities. Focusing once again upon Lebanese citizens, research suggests that attitudes towards hosting refugees are strongly conditioned by whether the respondents have Syrian friends in Lebanon and whether or not they have knowledge of any Syrians displaced by the current refugee crisis. Findings suggest that Lebanese respondents are more tolerant of hosting refugees when they know personally or have contact with a Syrian.[28] Some 46% of respondents said that they personally knew a Syrian who had been displaced, and among these 69% said they were acquaintances and 16% said they were friends. Individuals with Syrian friends were 47% more likely to support hosting Syrian refugees than were individuals without any Syrian friends. Just as importantly, the percentage of Lebanese who see refugees as a threat to themselves and their family drops by 17% when they state that they have a Syrian friend. Individuals with Syrian friends are

also more supportive of accepting a Syrian refugee as a daughter/son-in-law (a percentage increase of 263%); more willing to have a Syrian refugee as a business partner (a percentage increase of 288%); to hire a refugee (a percentage increase of 158%); more willing to live next door to a Syrian refugee (a percentage increase of 114%); and more willing to rent their apartment to a Syrian (a percentage increase of 174%).

In sum, negative attitudes towards hosting refugees and other displaced persons may have less to do with the displacement itself and the actual burden placed upon host communities and more to do with scapegoating and poor management of the situation. Given a healthy combination of human capital that these populations bring with them, forward-thinking host-country policy responses, and actions taken by the international community, it may be possible for these populations to make positive contributions to host countries.

The road ahead

Armed conflicts displace populations from their homes and sometimes across international borders. Sometimes this is an unfortunate by-product of the violence at the heart of armed conflicts, other times it is an intentional strategy of the armed actors. When displaced across borders, refugees can place burdens on local host communities which may affect security, the economy or the politics of the local area. The arrival of refugees may also provide opportunities for the diffusion of violence, depending upon the nature of the hosting arrangements.

Refugees and other migrants frequently face backlash from local host communities. Rising populism is tilting the political calculus in many Western countries, leading to tighter immigration restrictions and border fortifications that reflect a new narrative in which refugees and migrants in general are viewed as a threat to the way of life of Western nations.[39] These negative policy responses have, in turn, worsened conditions on the ground for these vulnerable populations. Since 2013, perhaps as many as 30,000 individual migrants are known to have died or gone missing during their journeys.[40] Many of these deaths may be attributable to deterrence-based border policies in the West.

Governance is crucial to the successful transition of refugees from initial displacement to integration within host communities. The key to successfully facilitating the cross-border movements of refugees lies in providing for their safe and secure transit, while sufficient opportunities once in local host areas would ease burden-sharing. Importantly, these actions incur costs, which should be shared across the international community and not simply borne by neighbouring countries, which inevitably host the majority of refugees. Recognising these challenges, the UNCHR proposed a new global compact on refugees in 2018 that outlines a framework for response by member states, as well as a programme of action to ensure implementation by member states and relevant stakeholders. The compact specifies key objectives to ease pressure on host countries, enhance refugee self-reliance, expand access to third-country solutions and support conditions in countries of origin to facilitate safe returns.

Notes

1   United Nations High Commissioner for Refugees (UNHCR), 'Global Trends 2017: Forced displacement in 2017', 25 June 2018. United Nations High Commissioner for Refugees (UNHCR), 'Global Trends 2017: Forced displacement in 2017', 25 June 2018. UNHCR monitors and supports individuals displaced by armed conflict, persecution, famine and/or natural disasters. This essay uses the terms 'refugee' and 'internally displaced persons (IDPs)' as defined by the UN Convention on the Status of Refugees, Article 1 (1951) and the UN's 'Guiding Principles on Internal Displacement' respectively.

2   UNHCR, 'Global Trends 2017'. Refugee data series taken only from 1993 onwards in order to make it more directly comparable with the IDP series, which UNHCR only began monitoring after the conclusion of the Cold War.

3   Stathis N. Kalyvas, *The Logic of Violence in Civil War* (Cambridge: Cambridge University Press, 2006); Abbey Steele, *Democracy and Displacement in Colombia's Civil War* (Ithaca, NY: Cornell University Press, 2017).

4   Yuri M. Zhukov, 'Population Resettlement in War: Theory and Evidence from Soviet Archives', *Journal of Conflict Resolution*, vol. 59, no. 7, 2015, pp. 1155–85; Adam Lichtenheld, 'Explaining Population Displacement Strategies In Civil Wars: A Cross National Analysis', Paper presented at the Annual Meeting of The Peace Science Society, Austin, TX, November 2018.

5   Ato Kwamena Onoma, *Anti-Refugee Violence and African Politics* (Cambridge: Cambridge University Press, 2013); Burcu Savun and Christian Gineste, 'From protection to persecution: Threat environment and refugee scapegoating', *Journal of Peace Research*, vol. 56, no. 2, December 2018.

6   Heaven Crawley, Franck Duvell, Katharine Jones, Simon McMahon and Nando Sigona, *Unravelling Europe's 'Migration Crisis': Journeys Over Land and Sea* (Bristol: Policy Press, 2017).

7   Jennifer Hyndman and Wenona Giles, *Refugees in Extended Exile: Living on the Edge* (Abingdon: Routledge, 2016).

8   Leon Gordenker, 'Early Warning of Disastrous Population Movement', *International Migration Review*, vol. 20, no. 2, 1986, pp. 170–89; Susanne Schmeidl, *From Root Cause Assessment to Preventive Diplomacy: Possibilities and Limitations of the Early Warning of Forced Migration*, PhD Dissertation, Ohio State University, 1995.

9   Duncan Maclaren, Susan Mcgrath and Ei Phyu Smith, '"Living with the Community is More Safe": Settlement Experiences of the Karen in Australia', in *After the Flight: The Dynamics of Refugee Settlement and Integration*, ed. Morgan Poteet and Shiva Nourpanah (Newcastle upon Tyne: Cambridge Scholars Publishing, 2016).

10   Sarah K. Lischer, *Dangerous Sanctuaries: Refugee Camps, Civil War, and the Dilemmas of Humanitarian Aid* (Ithaca, NY: Cornell University Press, 2006).

11   Will H. Moore and Stephen M. Shellman, 'Whither Will They Go? A Global Study of Refugees' Destinations, 1965–1995', *International Studies Quarterly*, vol. 51, no. 4, 2007, pp. 811–34; Christian Davenport, Will H. Moore and Steven C. Poe, 'Sometimes You Just Have To Leave: Domestic Threats and Refugee Movements', 1964–1989', *International Interactions*, vol. 29, no. 1, 2003, pp. 27–55; Prakash Adhikari, 'Conflict-Induced Displacement: Understanding the Causes of Flight', *American Journal of Political Science*, vol. 57, no. 1, 2013, pp. 82–9.

12   P. Ball and J. Asher, 'Statistics and Slobodan: Using Data Analysis and Statistics in the War Crimes Trial of Former President Milosevic', *Chance*, vol. 15, no. 4, 2002, pp. 17–24.

13   Benjamin Laughlin, 'Information cascades and refugee crises', Working paper, University of Rochester, 2018; Justin Schon, 'Motivation and opportunity for conflict-induced migration: An analysis of Syrian Migration Timing', *Journal of Peace Research*, vol. 56, no. 1, 2019.

14   Kelly Greenhill, *Weapons of Mass Migration: Forced Displacement, Coercion, and Foreign Policy* (Ithaca, NY: Cornell University Press, 2010); Nils Hägerdal, 'Ethnic Cleansing and the Politics of Restraint: Violence and Coexistence in the Lebanese Civil War', *Journal of Conflict Resolution*, vol. 63, no. 1, 2019; Steele, *Democracy and Displacement in Colombia's Civil War.*

15   Moore and Shellman, 'Whither will they go?'; Davenport, Moore and Poe, 'Sometimes You Just Have To Leave'; Adhikari, 'Conflict-induced displacement'.

16   Lichtenheld, ibid.

17   Kalyvas, ibid.; Steele, ibid.

18   Laia Balcells, 'Rivalry and revenge: Violence against Civilians in Conventional Civil Wars', *International Studies Quarterly*, vol. 54, no. 2, 2010, pp. 291–313.

19   Alexander Downes, *Targeting Civilians in War* (Ithaca, NY: Cornell University Press, 2008).

20   Abbey Steele, 'IDP resettlement and collective targeting during civil wars: Evidence from Colombia', *Journal of Peace Research* (in press).

21   Hassan Charif, 'Regional development and integration' in *Peace for Lebanon?*, ed. Deirdre Collings (Boulder, CO: Lynne Rienner, 1994), pp. 151–61; Faten Ghosn and Amal Khoury, 'The case of the 2006 War in Lebanon: Reparation? Reconstruction? Or both?', *International Journal of Human Rights*, vol. 17, no. 1, 2013, pp. 1–17.

[22] Sarah Kenyon Lischer, 'Security and Displacement in Iraq: Responding to the Forced Migration Crisis', *International Security*, vol. 33, no. 2, 2008, pp. 95–119; Nils B. Weidmann and Idean Salehyan, 'Violence and Ethnic Segregation: A Computational Model Applied to Baghdad', *International Studies Quarterly*, vol. 57, no. 1, 2013, pp. 52–64.

[23] US Committee for Refugees, 'Burundi: A patchwork of displacement', in *The Forsaken People: Case Studies of the Internally Displaced*, ed. Roberta Cohen and Francis M. Deng (Washington DC: Brookings Institution Press, 1998).

[24] Idean Salehyan and Kristian Skrede Gleditsch, 'Refugees and the Spread of Civil War', *International Organization*, vol. 60, no. 2, 2006, pp. 335–66; Daniel Milton, Megan Spencer and Michael Findley, 'Radicalism of the Hopeless: Refugee Flows and Transnational Terrorism', *International Interactions*, vol. 39, no. 5, 2013, pp. 621–45; Gina L. Miller and Emily H. Ritter, 'Emigrants and the Onset of Civil War', *Journal of Peace Research*, vol. 51, no. 1, 2014, pp. 51–64; Michael K. Miller and Margaret E. Peters, 'Restraining the Huddled Masses: Migration Policy and Autocratic Survival', *British Journal of Political Science*, 2018, pp. 1–31.

[25] Robert Muggah, *No Refuge: The Crisis of Refugee Militarization in Africa* (New York: Zed, 2006); Beth Elise Whitaker, 'Refugees in Western Tanzania: The Distribution of Burdens and Benefits among Local Hosts', *Journal of Refugee Studies*, vol. 15, no. 4, 2002, pp. 339–58; Gérard Prunier, *Africa's World War* (Oxford, Oxford University Press, 2010).

[26] Seraina Rüegger, 'Conflict Actors in Motion: Refugees, Rebels and Ethnic Groups'. Unpublished PhD dissertation, ETH Zürich, 2013; Seraina Rüegger, 'Refugees, Ethnic Power Relations and Civil Conflict in the Country Of Asylum', *Journal of Peace Research*, vol. 56, no. 1, 2019.

[27] A. Dowty and G. Loescher, 'Refugee Flows as Grounds for International Action', *International Security*, vol. 21, no. 1, 1996, pp. 43–71; B.R. Posen, 'Military Responses to Refugee Disasters', *International Security*, vol. 21, no. 1, 1996, pp. 72–111; I. Salehyan, 'The Externalities of Civil Strife: Refugees as a Source of International Conflict', *American Journal of Political Science*, vol. 52, no. 4, 2008, pp. 787–801.

[28] David Benček and Julia Strasheim, 'Refugees Welcome? A Dataset On Anti-Refugee Violence in Germany', *Research & Politics*, vol. 3, no. 4, 2016; Teo Kermoliotis, 'Hoaxmap: Debunking false rumours about refugee "crimes"', Al-Jazeera, 16 February 2016.

[29] Markus Crepaz, *Trust Beyond Borders: Immigration, the Welfare State, and Identity in Modern Societies* (Ann Arbor, MI: University of Michigan Press, 2008).

[30] Ainhoa Ruiz Benedicto and Pere Brunet, 'Building Walls: Fear and Securitization in the European Union', Report no. 35 of the Centre Delas D'Estudis Per La Pau, Barcelona, Spain, 2018.

[31] Faten Ghosn and Alex Braithwaite, 'Could Contact Stem the Rising Tide of Negative Attitudes Towards Hosting Syrian Refugees in Lebanon?' *Oxford Monitor of Forced Migration: Field Monitor*, vol. 7, no. 2, 2018, pp. 69–74.

[32] Semih Tumen, 'The economic impact of Syrian refugees on host countries: Quasi-experimental evidence from Turkey', *American Economic Review*, vol. 106, no. 5, 2016, pp. 456–60.

[33] International Labour Organization, 'ILO Response to Syrian Refugee Crisis in Lebanon'; World Bank, 'Lebanon Overview', 2018.

[34] Ghosn and Braithwaite, 'Could Contact Stem the Rising Tide of Negative Attitudes Towards Hosting Syrian Refugees in Lebanon?'.

[35] Jennifer Alix-Garcia, Sarah Walker, Anne Bartlett, Harun Onder and Apurva Sanghi, 'Do refugee camps help or hurt hosts? The case of Kakuma, Kenya', *Journal of Development Economics*, vol. 130, January 2018, pp. 66–83; Jean-François Maystadt and Philip Verwimp, 'Winners and losers among a refugee-hosting population', *Economic Development and Cultural Change*, vol. 62, no. 4, 2014, pp. 769–809. While quantitative research on economic effects of refugees on host countries is relatively new, there is a larger and more established literature on the impact of voluntary migrants on host economies. George Borjas, 'The Economics of Immigration', *Journal of Economic Literature*, vol. 32, no. 4, 1994, pp. 1,667–717; Saul Lach, 'Immigration and Prices', *Journal of Political Economy*, vol. 115, no. 4, 2007, pp. 548–87; Marios Zachariadis, 'Immigration and international prices', *Journal of International Economics*, vol. 87, no. 2, 2012, pp. 298–311.

[36] New American Economy, *From Struggle to Resilience: The Economic Impact of Refugees in America* (New York: NAE, 2017).

[37] J. Edward Taylor, Mateusz J. Filipski, Mohamad Alloush, Anubhab Gupta, Ruben Irvin Rojas Valdes and Ernesto Gonzalez-Estrada, 'Economic Impact of Refugees', *Proceedings of the National Academy of Sciences*, 20 June 2016.

[38] Faten Ghosn, Alex Braithwaite and Tiffany S. Chu, 'Violence, displacement, contact, and attitudes toward hosting refugees', *Journal of Peace Research*, vol. 56, no. 1, 2019.

[39] Rogers Brubaker, 'Between Nationalism and Civilizationism: The European Populist Movement in Comparative Perspective', *Ethnic and Racial Studies*, vol. 40, no. 8, 2017, pp. 1,191–226; Andrew Geddes, *Immigration and European Integration: Beyond Fortress Europe?* (Manchester: Manchester University Press, 2008).

[40] Missing Migrants portal (https://missingmigrants.iom.int).

The Security Implications of Climate Change

Climate change is a high-probability, high-impact security threat that will continue to accelerate over the coming decades, with a wide range of implications for the geostrategic environment. Climate change works as a 'threat multiplier' – it exacerbates the drivers of conflict by deepening existing fragilities within societies, straining weak institutions, reshaping power balances and undermining post-conflict recovery and peacebuilding. Projections of the speed and the magnitude of climate change vary, but both long-term climate trends (such as sea-level rise and desertification) and short-term irregularities and extremes (known as 'climate variability', e.g., seasonal variations) can influence social and political stability, particularly in already fragile contexts. The science of how the climate will continue to change over the coming decades provides a sound basis for risk assessment – far more so than information used to assess other factors affecting global security, such as nuclear threats or changes in the balance of geopolitical power.

Climate change can affect stability both directly and indirectly. Storms and droughts damage livelihoods, while changes in precipitation patterns or increases in groundwater salinity due to rising sea levels can cause water insecurity and drive resource competition, which in turn may fuel local conflicts. Drought and shifting growing seasons can mean poor harvests or price fluctuations for food commodities on international markets, undermining food security and increasing grievances domestically. Climate-related forced displacement and migration can create tensions in destination areas, particularly when much of this movement is to, from or through already fragile regions. At the same time, human mobility is also an important adaptation mechanism that can reduce the negative impacts of climate change. Climate change can lead to economic contraction by disrupting agricultural exports or damaging coastal economic infrastructure.

These direct and indirect effects can, in turn, have political and security repercussions – changing water availability complicates transboundary water management, as along the Tigris, Euphrates, Nile, Indus, Mekong and other river systems that support large populations, as well as transboundary aquifers. Food insecurity can be a trigger for demonstrations, which may lead to the expression of broader political grievances that threaten regimes, as in Egypt during the Arab Spring in 2011[1] and in Sudan since December 2018. The political reverberations of climate-linked migration and refugee movements can create geopolitical challenges far from migrants' origin countries. Elsewhere, as climate change shifts the viability of countries' key economic sectors (such as agriculture), non-inclusive regimes that reinforce discriminatory behaviours (for example, against historically marginalised ethnic groups) are particularly ill-positioned to accommodate new demands, such as implementing climate-smart agriculture or supporting community-level conflict-resolution measures, for example between farmers and pastoralists.

Many countries highly exposed to climate-change hazards also face underlying security fragilities, and where these respective vulnerabilities compound each other they are more likely to have a destabilising effect – although whether or not these difficulties contribute to violent conflict is highly context-specific. Countries where this combination of climate-hazard exposure and state fragility is highest include much of central Africa (such as Nigeria, Sudan, Somalia and the Democratic Republic of the Congo); countries in West, South and East Asia (such as Yemen, Iraq, Syria, Afghanistan, Pakistan and Myanmar); as well as Colombia and Central America.[2] States facing fiscal and capacity challenges may struggle to implement climate-adaptation measures to manage such risks. Analysis of countries' progress towards the 'Leave No One Behind' agenda of the United Nations' Sustainable Development Goals (a framework of 17 goals adopted by UN member states designed to address global challenges related to climate, inequality and poverty, among others) indicates that a majority of countries still fall short of including, prioritising or adequately financing inclusive-resilience planning.[3]

Responses to climate change can also drive security risks unintentionally. Climate-adaptation projects that are not responsive to relevant social and political dynamics can exacerbate resource and power competition, or deepen fault lines within societies. For example, hydropower projects that favour energy security, industry or export agriculture over traditional users can increase livelihood insecurity, forced displacement and migration, leading to grievances against the state and within societies. The dams on Ethiopia's Omo River that support biofuels and sugarcane cultivation, for example, are seen as oppressive state-building measures by downstream communities.[4] New climate-finance flows, such as those being channelled through the Green Climate Fund, can create negative dynamics if they are not designed to avoid new resource competition and intercommunal conflict. Transitions to renewable energy or bioenergy also bring risks. There are no governance measures for climate-change geo-engineering in place at present, and unilaterally deployed technologies such as solar-radiation management and carbon dioxide removal could prove geopolitically contentious. Bioenergy with carbon capture and storage (BECCS) may compete for land and water with food crops, while stratospheric aerosol injection could affect global hydrological cycles, leading to chronic flooding or droughts.[5]

Despite the wide-ranging ways in which climate change can and will affect the security environment, it is important not to overstate or oversimplify the role of climate in conflict causality. In many places, climate impacts and extremes do not result in conflict. Where climate change does play a role, it is in concert with a host of other causal factors. Overemphasising the role of climate may risk deflecting blame from more pertinent causes or perpetrators, or misdirect conflict-prevention efforts. Governance is the primary factor in determining resilience to climate impacts, and good governance will be vital in peacefully managing competition

> Governance is the primary factor in determining resilience to climate impacts

and conflicts of interest that arise as climate change brings further disruption to ecological and human systems.

It is also important not to limit the assessment of climate-security risk to the question of the causal relationship between climate change and violent conflict. Whether or not climate impacts influence the onset of a conflict, they will certainly make conflicts in climate-exposed regions more difficult to resolve, and increase the risk of recurrence.

While climate change is not the direct cause of the conflicts active in 2018, many regions facing security challenges have weather extremes in line with climate projections, which likely influenced important aspects of their violent dynamics. Climate-related factors centring on water and agriculture, forced migration and displacement illustrate how the climate–security nexus interacts with these situations.

Afghanistan

The severe drought that affected 22 of Afghanistan's 34 provinces in 2018 led to a 45% reduction in domestic food production, displaced 263,000 people within Badghis and Herat provinces between June and August alone and created the country's worst food-insecurity emergency since 2011, with 10.6 million people (43.6% of the population) facing severe food insecurity.[6] Regions where rural livelihoods are dependent on rain-fed agriculture were hardest hit, particularly the West and North West regions. Over the course of the year, many households relocated to provincial capitals in pursuit of basic needs and income-generating opportunities. This rapid influx created sprawling informal settlements at the city margins, particularly in Herat city and Qala-e-Naw in Herat and Badghis provinces, whose population grew by a quarter of a million in the first half of the year. Those displaced internally by the drought were joined by more than 670,000 returnees from Iran (who were driven in part by the economic downturn there following the US withdrawal from the Iran nuclear deal) – the highest number since the International Organization for Migration began tracking population movements in the context of the Afghan conflict in 2007. As of November, the conditions in these informal settlements remained dire, with 141,000 people still living in self-erected, temporary shelters and 207,000 in need of urgent winterisation support.[7]

While meteorological data for Afghanistan are often patchy, anecdotal reports of the 2018 drought's impact indicate that it was the most severe in living memory for Afghan farmers and pastoralists. Several years of low precipitation was compounded by a 'La Niña' event that resulted in a deficit in precipitation of more than 70% in most parts of the country during the winter planting season.[8] Controlling access to water supplies became a conflict tactic, with both government forces and Taliban fighters reportedly restricting irrigation water in Greater Kandahar to pressure civilians to, respectively, force out insurgents or accede to their demands.[9]

The kind of environmental disruption Afghanistan is experiencing increases the incidence of negative coping strategies. These included distress-selling livestock for well below market rates (under US$300 per head of cattle compared to a pre-drought price of US$1,400);[10] consuming the following year's seed grain (as of November, 92% of farmers reported having insufficient or no seeds for the winter planting season); withdrawing children from school for labour; and selling or marrying off daughters. Of the 161 pledged or married children identified in Badghis and Herat provinces in 2018, 90% were girls between 4 and 15 years old.[11] These have both near- and longer-term social and economic consequences that can damage development and security trajectories. For example, in 2011 nine out of ten recruits to the Afghan Security Forces were illiterate, necessitating additional training programmes to enable them to write their names and count numbers, creating an additional challenge to establishing an enduring security force in the country.[12]

In Afghanistan, water scarcity can also strengthen the economic case for growing opium poppy instead of wheat or other crops. Poppy requires less irrigation and provides significantly higher economic returns than other crops per unit of land. Accordingly, many farmers grow poppy as a temporary coping strategy, with 54% of those who cultivated opium poppies in recent years classed as infrequent poppy growers.[13] However, while the total area under poppy cultivation has fluctuated, with a 56% and 43% drop in 2018 in the North and West regions (those hardest hit by drought), poppy cultivation remains widespread and continues to be a crucial component of the Afghan economy, securing livelihoods for cultivators, agricultural labourers and those involved in the illicit drug trade. The opium trade is a key source of revenue for non-state armed groups, particularly the Taliban, which taxes poppy cultivation and processes around half of all domestically produced opium into morphine and heroin for domestic and international markets. Afghan opiates reach all continents except South America, via the Balkan route (towards Europe), the Northern route (to Central Asia and Russia) and Southern route (Africa, Asia, Oceania and North America).[14] The opium economy is an expanding part of Afghanistan's economy, accounting for 20–32% of GDP in 2017, which was a record year for opium production.[15]

The drought in 2018 was in line with future climate-change projections, which anticipate reduced spring rainfall and river flow (due to reduced snowmelt in Afghanistan's highlands), flooding from both extreme rainfall events and rapid snowmelt in years with high snowfall and spring temperatures, as well as generally warmer weather and long-term aridification. Increasingly severe weather-related disruptions are therefore likely to exacerbate Afghanistan's ongoing humanitarian crisis and increase the burden of disaster response, which will compete with other fiscal priorities, including development and reconstruction. Additional poppy cultivation in the context of climate-related water-supply uncertainties may fuel instability by increasing the funding sources of violent extremist organisations, which will in turn impede licit economic development. These effects will only increase, as observed climate change and variability continues to accelerate faster than projected a decade ago.

Yemen

Yemen was the world's worst humanitarian crisis in 2018. As of December 2018, more than 20m people faced food insecurity in Yemen. Around 90% of Yemen's food is imported, in part due to having only 3% arable land. The country's dependence on food imports and rising food costs due to supply disruption and currency depreciation have contributed to the risk of famine. Some 16m people lacked access to safe water or sanitation in 2018, a situation that contributed to Yemen's historic cholera outbreak, the largest in epidemiologically recorded history with more than 1.2m cases and 2,556 reported deaths since April 2017, along with high levels of malnutrition, which increased vulnerability to disease.[16]

The humanitarian crisis has been precipitated by flagrant violations of international humanitarian and human-rights law by the Houthi rebels and the Saudi-led coalition.[17] Since the beginning of the war in 2015, the different parties to the conflict have made strategic use of water control and access. The Saudi-led coalition has repeatedly targeted or destroyed water infrastructure, such as the al-Nahdin Dam and reservoir and a sanitation facility and water station that supplies the majority of the water to the city of Hudaydah, while Houthi rebel forces blocked the delivery of aid to Yemen's third city, Ta'izz, including water and fuel needed to pump water. The Saudi-led coalition's blockade of Hudaydah port, which handles 60–70% of Yemen's imports, has cut off fuel, food and medicine supplies. Water infrastructure (including wastewater-treatment facilities) has been directly targeted and indirectly damaged by the fighting, and some facilities have stopped operating due to the rising costs of fuel, driven in part by the Yemeni rial's depreciation. In the absence of adequate infrastructure, most Yemenis' basic water needs have been met by private tanker trucks, the cost of which has risen with fuel costs.[18] Health infrastructure has also been damaged in the fighting, complicating efforts to mitigate the humanitarian crisis.

The actions of conflict parties have compounded the effect of Yemen's history of water insecurity, which is linked to chronic aridity, resource mismanagement, poor water infrastructure and growing demand from a soaring population, which nearly quadrupled between 1975 and 2010.[19] Yemen is one of the world's most water-stressed countries, with an estimated 125 cubic metres of water per capita, compared to a global average of 7,500 m³ – by 2030, this is projected to drop to 55 m³ per capita.[20] Prior to the current conflict, the Yemeni government struggled to implement water-governance measures on fiercely independent household users, while an estimated 70–80% of the country's rural conflicts were water-related, with tribal and village fighting destroying wells and pumps and inflicting fatalities.[21] Intercommunal violence and tribal disputes have been interwoven with water-access issues. Prior to the current conflict, the prevalence of small arms helped make Yemen one of the countries whose local water disputes most often turned violent, and many other political disputes had water resources at their core.[22]

Climate change will continue to impact water availability and agricultural production in the region as the Arabian Peninsula heats up, with annual mean temperature projected to increase 2–2.5 °C by mid-century and from 2.5–4.9 °C by 2100 depending on the emissions pathway.[23] Much of the Persian Gulf/Arabian Peninsula area is projected to become uninhabitable by 2100 under a business-as-usual emissions scenario as summer heat and humidity exceed the threshold for human survival.[24] While there is some ambiguity in the global climate models regarding future rainfall patterns in Yemen, more rainfall is unlikely to increase water availability due to warmer temperatures driving increased evaporation.[25] While a political solution to the current fighting may be achieved, this climate-sensitive resource will remain a key conflict driver. Armed conflict would become more difficult to solve, while grievances and intercommunal disputes would be more likely to continue.

Syria

The popular uprising that escalated into the current Syrian civil war was preceded by the country's deepest and most prolonged drought on record – a drought made two to three times more likely by climate change.[26] The drought decimated agricultural communities and pushed 1.5m mainly Shi'ite Syrians from eastern communities to migrate to Sunni-dominated cities in the west of the country. The Assad regime's indifference to and obstruction of the international response to the severe humanitarian crisis created the background against which the frustrations of the Arab Spring developed.

The disruption the drought caused to Syria's economy took place in the context of water-resource mismanagement and sectarian tensions, for example, around the provision of well licences. It was not the drought on its own, but rather the political context in which it took place, that influenced the onset of conflict. The provincial town of Daraa, where the protests against the regime started, was a receiving area for those displaced by the drought, but also an agricultural economy where livelihoods had plummeted as employment opportunities dried up.

Developments in and around Syria in 2018 included ongoing competition for water around the Za'atari and Azraq refugee camps in Jordan, which together house 139,000 refugees out of the total number of 670,000 to 1.3m Syrian refugees in the country. Jordan already has low water availability per capita (less than 150 m³ annually), which is projected to decrease due to climate change and population growth – groundwater is extracted at twice the rate at which it can be recharged.[27] Boreholes dug to supply the Za'atari camp that over-extract from Jordan's largest aquifer – pumping 3.2m litres of water per day – are creating friction with Jordanian host communities, while trucks that fill the camp's water tanks from nearby municipal wells have increased the price for local users. Citing refugee overburden and security concerns, Jordan closed its border with Syria in June to those newly displaced by a government offensive aimed to drive rebels from the territories in the southwest. In July, when 20,000 civilians amassed at the Nasib border crossing (closed since 2015) to escape fighting in Daraa region, Jordanian soldiers either fired on them, or fired warning shots (reports denied by the Jordanian military). The border crossing was reopened in October.

Syria's exposure to climate-change hazards could impact its long-term stability. Prior to the drought, Syria's agricultural sector employed up to 40–50% of the national workforce (including the informal economy) and accounted for 25% of GDP.[28] With increasing temperatures and aridity projected for the region, medium and long-term post-conflict stabilisation efforts aimed at restoring this sector are likely to take place in an increasingly challenging environment. In deciding whether to return home, Syrians will consider economic opportunities, safety and, in smaller cities and rural areas, the availability of water and the infrastructure for agriculture. In the short term, as Syria's neighbours seek to repatriate Syrian refugees to ease the strain on their own public services, the presence of refugees will continue to be central to political debate in the host countries (as it was in Turkey's June presidential election).

Lake Chad region

The Boko Haram/Islamic State West Africa Province (ISWAP) insurgency takes place in the Lake Chad region, which has some of the highest population growth rates and lowest human-development indices in the world, with Niger ranked 189th out of 189 countries, Chad 186th, Nigeria 157th and Cameroon 151st.[29] The area also suffers from weak governance institutions. Climate change in these territories aggravates natural-resource degradation and causes internal and cross-border displacement, thus fuelling ongoing inter-ethnic and intercommunal conflicts.

Lake Chad is located at the junction of the borders of Cameroon, Chad, Niger and Nigeria, providing a water source in the otherwise arid/semi-arid environment of the Sahel, and supporting livelihoods with water for crops and livestock, fertile land and fish. The shallow, marshy lake has shrunk by 90% since the 1960s, although the degree to which this has been driven by climate change is uncertain.[30] Over the past 40 years the population around the lake has tripled, from 700,000 in 1980 to more than 2m in 2014, and is likely to double again in the next 20 years.[31] The resulting pressure on natural resources has driven competition and confrontation between groups such as farmers and pastoralists, or people displaced by the conflict and host communities. Future climate-driven warming in the Sahel will further dry out the region and complicate these grievances.

Boko Haram originated in the capitol of Borno State, which borders the remnants of Lake Chad on the Nigerian side. Violence perpetrated by extremist groups, the Nigerian armed forces and the Civilian Joint Task Force formed to oust Boko Haram has harmed and displaced civilians, contributing to a humanitarian crisis. In 2018, the Multinational Joint Task Force, comprised of the armed forces of Lake Chad's bordering states plus Benin, successfully pushed back against violent extremist organisations, regaining territorial control and improving security in some areas. Intense fighting and Boko Haram attacks targeting military bases and civilians in other areas continued to displace thousands of people (totalling 2.5m across the Lake Chad region as of December), prevent IDP and refugee return and disrupt humanitarian-aid delivery. By the end of 2018, 10.7m people in the Lake Chad region relied on humanitarian assistance to survive.[32] As with other crises in climate-change-affected areas, the ongoing conflict has disrupted livelihoods and the economy. Access to the lake has been restricted and fishing banned in order to facilitate military patrols and operations on and around the lake. Trade has also suffered as a result of border closures. Fighting has impeded humanitarian-aid operations, as well as development and climate-adaptation initiatives, increasing the region's vulnerability to the impact of climate change and exacerbating the humanitarian situation.

Long-term climate trends and near-term climate variability are also making livelihoods from fishing, agriculture and livestock herding more uncertain and less tenable. Coping strategies based on flexibly combining fishing, agriculture and livestock herding are increasingly harder to sustain, as natural resources to support these economic activities may not be reliably available from season to season. In this context, young men in particular have higher incentives (including but not limited to financial gain) to join violent or extremist organisations.[33] Climate variability and climate change are also relevant to stabilisation efforts that seek to, for example, reintegrate demobilised fighters by providing them with support to take up fishing or farming. If these livelihoods fail to be viable, for example due to declining lake-water levels or inadequate rainfall, such stabilisation efforts will ultimately prove counterproductive when ex-combatants' raised expectations are unmet in the context of a changing natural-resource landscape.

The UN Security Council has now formally recognised (Resolution 2349 (2017)) the climate-change dimensions of the Lake Chad crisis as part of an effort driven by non-permanent members to raise the profile of climate security and establish a permanent home for the issue within the UN system. More integrated solutions to complex emergencies in climate-change-affected settings may follow in the region, for example by the UN supporting the development of comprehensive resilience strategies such as that between the African Union and Lake Chad Basin Commission. Risk assessments of climate security informed by local, national and regional-level reporting can improve the UN's early-warning and conflict-prevention responses in the context of foreseeable climate-change-related threats.

Central America

Central America is highly exposed to the impacts of climate change, which includes tropical storms and more irregular or extreme rainfall patterns, as well as ocean warming and acidification along its coasts. These factors can exacerbate the drivers of instability, such as internal and transboundary migration, and compound other security challenges, for example by further straining weak governance systems and strengthening the position of organised criminal groups, including gangs and drug cartels.

Agriculture accounts for a significant portion of GDP in the region: 13.3% in Guatemala, 14.2% in Honduras and 12% in El Salvador.[34] A significant percentage of the respective populations are employed in agriculture: 29.4% in Guatemala, 28.5% in Honduras and 18.8% in El Salvador.[35] Some 90% of the coffee traded from the region is produced by smallholder farmers, who maximise their earnings by growing a labour-intensive, high-value export crop, but one which is highly sensitive to increasing temperatures and rainfall variations.[36] An outbreak of the climate-related pathogen 'coffee rust' fungus in 2012–13 followed a season of above-average rainfall and warmer night-time minimum temperatures, and led to Honduras, El Salvador and Guatemala declaring national emergencies after the total value of their export coffee crops declined from about US$3.4 billion in 2011/12 to US$1.6bn in 2013/14.[37] Resulting food insecurity led to warnings of a Crisis-level famine (IPC Phase 3) from the World Food Programme and Famine Early Warning System. This crisis was in turn an important factor contributing to the 2014 surge in unaccompanied minors seeking to enter the United States, almost all of whom came from Guatemala, El Salvador or Honduras.[38]

While 2018 was not a year of significant climate-related stress on agriculture in Northern Triangle countries, the outlook for the coffee sector indicates that by 2050 almost 80% of areas currently cultivated in Central America will become unsuitable due to climate change.[39] Migration (both internal urban migration and transboundary) is a routine coping strategy in Northern Triangle countries for livelihood diversification and food security, including among agricultural workers in the coffee sector. Increased migration can in turn exacerbate fragility and instability dynamics, as licit formal and informal urban labour markets struggle to absorb influxes of rural migrants. Urban poverty, unemployment and economic stagnation enlarge the ranks of gangs, whose armed violence and intimidation tactics in turn drive out-migration.[40] Rural or urban migrants use human smugglers, in turn strengthening the power and influence of organised crime.

In 2018, members of the 'caravan' that reached the southern US border cited growing urban violence as a push factor for migration. Depending on population growth and climate and development scenarios, the World Bank projects between

1.4m and 2.1m internal 'climate migrants' in Central America and Mexico by 2050. Most of this migration is rural–urban and would likely increase transboundary migration too. Globally, the number of climate-driven internal migrants could reach 143m by 2050, with up to two-thirds of these in sub-Saharan Africa.[41]

Rohingya crisis

In a densely populated and highly climate-vulnerable location, a population influx driven by conflict and instability can drive maladaptive responses that further threaten human security and risk loss of life. While climate change did not play a role in the onset of the ethnic cleansing that drove more than 900,000 Rohingya refugees into Bangladesh, it illustrates how such crises occurring in climate-vulnerable areas can compound vulnerability and complicate effective response. The refugee camps in Cox's Bazaar, particularly Kutupalong and Balukhali camps and expansion areas, were constructed in a hilly area that was rapidly deforested as the camp grew into the world's largest refugee settlement between May and August 2017.[42] Residents continue to use nearby trees for fuelwood and construct makeshift shelters on slopes to avoid flooding in flat areas, making the camp and its inhabitants more vulnerable to flooding and landslides during monsoon season.[43] Demands on fuel and groundwater have increased resentment among locals as well as overall vulnerability in the area to extreme weather events. With repatriation agreements between Bangladesh and Myanmar stalled due to the unwillingness of the Rohingya to return to Rakhine State under the current security conditions, the refugee situation is likely to continue to add pressure to Bangladesh's environmental and human-security challenges through 2019.[44]

Future trends

Climate-related drivers for armed violence and conflict will increase as climate change progresses. Minimising these risk factors will require adapting existing conflict-resolution measures, the UN system, donors' policies and aid and development programming to the nature, scale, dynamics and security implications of climate change.

Climate change may also shape evolving geostrategic competition on a number of fronts. The South China Sea and the Arctic are particularly relevant regions that are being reshaped by climate. In the former, China is already adopting measures to address climate change as a way to compete for allies and partners and establish itself as a global leader in climate response, particularly in the context of the recent US withdrawal from climate leadership. This dynamic was cited, albeit without naming China specifically, in New Zealand's December 2018 'Defence Climate Assessment' as a reason for the New Zealand ministry of defence to engage with climate matters.

The transition from fossil fuels to low-carbon energy sources necessary to limit climate change will also bring economic disruption and potentially transformative geo-economics implications. If the global energy mix (the balance of oil, gas, coal, nuclear and renewables used to meet energy needs) transitions away from fossil fuels, it will radically change the global geopolitics of energy. States whose oil and gas exports comprise a significant portion of GDP – such as Venezuela, Russia and Middle Eastern countries – may face significant economic challenges in a reshaped energy economy. In a energy landscape shaped by competition to lead in renewable-energy technology, the relative power and influence of key exporting countries may shift in unpredictable ways.[45]

> Climate change causes displacement, thus fuelling ongoing inter-ethnic conflict

Ongoing global political developments suggest cause for concern about mustering the necessary international coordination to prevent more extreme climate-change scenarios. As substantial action on climate change needs to be taken before the effects are more clearly felt, and because the economics of addressing the challenge require significant changes, progress is being made more slowly than climate science makes clear is necessary. Global emissions continue to rise while political trends in some countries reinforce climate inaction. In June 2017, US President Donald Trump announced the world's second-largest emitter's intention to withdraw from the Paris Climate Agreement, and while Brazilian President Jair Bolsonaro walked back his threat to do the same, increased deforestation under eroded environmental-protection policies could prove as impactful for Brazil's emissions and global carbon sequestration.

Climate science continues to provide stark warnings of a system that may be more sensitive than previously understood, increasing the risk of self-reinforcing feedback loops that could push Earth systems past a 'Hothouse Earth' tipping point, posing severe risks for economies, political stability and, ultimately, the habitability of the planet for humans.[46] The politics of managing some of the early tremors of climate change, such as the outflow of Syrian refugees into Europe, have already proven counterproductive to building the necessary political consensus to put solutions in place, as political parties opposed to both refugee resettlement and implementing effective climate-change and energy policies have been empowered.[47] Germany's 2017 general election, for example, saw the far-right, anti-immigrant Alternative for Germany (AfD) win 12.6% of the vote, in part as a reaction to the influx of Syrian refugees and other migrants in 2015. As the wide-reaching geopolitical, economic and security repercussions of climate change increase, there is a risk that they may erode the international community's ability to act preventatively in a way that is commensurate with the threat. As efforts are under way to adapt the liberal international order to a range of new stresses, climate science provides a relatively clear picture of upcoming challenges, and even more reason for it to address underlying fragilities in the international system.

Notes

[1]   Troy Sternberg, 'Chinese drought, bread and the Arab Spring', *Applied Geography*, vol. 34, no. 4, May 2012, pp. 519–24.

[2]   Ashley Moran et al., 'The intersection of global fragility and climate risks', USAID, September 2018.

[3]   Marcus Manuel, Francesca Grandi, Stephanie Manea, Amy Kirbyshire and Emma Lovell, '"Leave no one behind" index 2018', Overseas Development Institute, July 2018.

[4]   Harry Verhoeven, 'The politics of African energy development: Ethiopia's hydro-agricultural state-building strategy and clashing paradigms of water security', *Philosophical Transactions of the Royal Society*, vol. 371, no. 2002, 13 November 2013.

[5]   Janos Pasztor, 'The Need for Governance of Climate Geoengineering', *Ethics and International Affairs*, Carnegie Council, no. 31.4, December 2017.

[6]   Famine Early Warning Systems Network, 'Central Asia: Afghanistan: Food Security Outlook', October 2018 to February 2019; Food and Agriculture Organization of the United Nations, 'Afghanistan: Drought Response: November 2018', 23 November 2018.

[7]   UN Office for the Coordination of Humanitarian Affairs (OCHA), 'Afghanistan 2019 Humanitarian Needs Overview', November 2018.

[8]   Food and Agriculture Organization of the UN, 'Afghanistan Drought Response', November 2018.

[9]   Sharifullah Sharfat and Abubakar Siddique, 'In Rural Afghan War, Irrigation Water Is Tool', *Gandhara*, 4 April 2018.

[10] Mustafa Sarwar, 'Almost Two-Thirds Of Afghanistan Hit By Drought', *Gandhara*, 5 June 2018.

[11] UN International Children's Emergency Fund, 'Geneva Palais briefing note on the situation of children in Afghanistan', 27 November 2018.

[12] Lieutenant General William B. Caldwell, 'Education Key to Building Afghan Security Forces' Capacity', Council on Foreign Relations, 7 June 2011.

[13] Defined as having grown opium poppy in fewer than four years of the five-year period between 2012 and 2016. For these farmers, opium makes up around half of household income. UN Office on Drugs and Crime, Islamic Republic of Afghanistan Ministry of Counter Narcotics, 'Afghanistan opium survey 2017: Challenges to sustainable development peace and security', May 2018.

[14] UN Office on Drugs and Crime, 'Afghan Opiate Trade Project' website.

[15] 'Afghanistan opium survey 2017'.

[16] Frederik Federspiel and Mohammad Ali, 'The cholera outbreak in Yemen: lessons learned and way forward', *BMC Public Health*, vol. 18, article 1338, 2018; World Bank, 'The World Bank in Yemen – Overview', 11 October 2018.

[17] UN Office of the High Commissioner for Human Rights (OHCHR), 'Yemen: United Nations Experts point to possible war crimes by parties to the conflict', 28 August 2018.

[18] Naif Mohammed Abu-Lohom et al., 'Water supply in a war zone: A preliminary analysis of two urban water tanker supply systems in the Republic of Yemen', Water Global Practice discussion paper, World Bank Group, 2018.

[19] UN Population Fund Yemen, 'Population Development'.

[20] George O. Odhiambo, 'Water scarcity in the Arabian Peninsula and socio-economic implications', *Applied Water Science*, vol. 7, no. 5, September 2017, pp. 2479–92.

[21] World Bank, 'Future Impact of Climate Change Visible Now in Yemen', 24 November 2018; UN Educational, Scientific and Cultural Organization, 'United Nations world water development report 4: managing water under uncertainty and risk', 2012.

[22] Republic of Yemen, 'Intended Nationally Determined Contribution (INDC) under the UNFCCC', 21 November 2015; Environment, Conflict and Cooperation Library, 'Local Violence over Water Resources in Yemen' website.

[23] Mansour Almazroui, 'Assessment of CMIP5 global climate models and projected changes in surface air temperature over the Arabian Peninsula in the twenty-first century', *Arabian Journal of Geosciences*, vol. 11, no. 21, article 650, 2018.

[24] Jeremy S. Pal and Elfatih A.B. Eltahir, 'Future temperature in southwest Asia projected to exceed a threshold for human adaptability', *Nature Climate Change*, vol. 6, 2016, pp. 197–200.

[25] Clemens Breisinger et al., 'Climate Change, Agricultural Production and Food Security: Evidence from Yemen', Kiel Institute for the World Economy, Kiel Working Paper no. 1747, November 2011.

26   Colin P. Kelley, Shahrzad Mohtadi, Mark A. Cane, Richard Seager and Yochanan Kushnir, 'Climate change in the Fertile Crescent and implications of the recent Syrian drought', Proceedings of the National Academy of Sciences of the United States of America (PNAS), vol. 112, no. 11, 17 March 2015, pp. 3241–6.

27   United States Agency for International Development, 'Jordan: Water Resources & Environment', data updated 30 July 2018.

28   H. Harding, 'Working in the Grey Zone', *Syria Today*, no. 61, May 2010.

29   UN Development Programme, 'Human Development Index and its components', 2018 Statistical Update, Human Development Indices and Indicators.

30   Although much of the lake's shrinkage in the 1980s and 1990s was driven by severe and prolonged drought, current surface-area variations are primarily determined by north-flowing river systems whose basins are influenced by the West African Monsoon, the climate-change impact on which remains uncertain; Géraud Magrin, 'The disappearance of Lake Chad: History of a myth', *Journal of Political Ecology*, vol. 23, no. 1, December 2016.

31   Magrin, 'The disappearance of Lake Chad: History of a myth'; 'Demographic Dynamics and the Crisis of Countries around Lake Chad', UN Population Fund West and Central Africa Regional Office, 2018.

32   OCHA, 'Lake Chad Basin: Crisis Update, November–December 2018', no. 26, January 2019; OCHA, 'Global Humanitarian Overview 2019', December 2018.

33   Chitra Nagarajan et al., 'Climate-Fragility Profile: Lake Chad Basin', adelphi, 2008; International Crisis Group, 'Fighting Boko Haram in Chad: Beyond Military Measures', Africa Report no. 246, 8 March 2017.

34   CIA World Factbook, 2017 figures.

35   UN Development Programme, Human Development Reports, 'Global Human Development Indicators', September 2018.

36   Christian Bunn et al., 'Multiclass Classification of Agro-Ecological Zones for Arabica Coffee: An Improved Understanding of the Impacts of Climate Change', PLoS One, 2015.

37   Peter Baker, 'The "Big Rust": an update on the coffee leaf rust situation', Coffee & Cocoa International, January 2014.

38   United States Congressional Research Service, 'Unaccompanied Alien Children: Potential Factors Contributing to Recent Immigration', CRS Report, July 2014.

39   Higher-altitude areas may become more suitable as the optimal coffee zone 'climbs up the mountain'. World Coffee Research, 'Climate Change: Pinpointing the World's Most Vulnerable Coffee Zones', October 2015.

40   El Salvador and Honduras have the two highest intentional homicide rates in the world, while Guatemala is tenth-highest. The World Bank, 'Intentional homicides (per 100,000 people); UN Office on Drugs and Crime's International Homicide Statistics database'; David James Cantor, 'The New Wave: Forced displacement caused by organized crime in Central America and Mexico', *Refugee Survey Quarterly*, vol. 33, no. 3, 2014, pp. 34–68.

41   Migration is inherently multi-factorial and climate-related displacement and migration are far more likely to be internal rather than cross-border. Kanta Kumari Rigaud et al., *Groundswell: Preparing for Internal Climate Migration*, World Bank, 2018.

42   'The Rohingya Crisis, Life in the camps', Reuters Graphics, 4 December 2017.

43   In response to the overcrowding, the Bangladeshi government is constructing facilities to relocate 100,000 Rohingya refugees to Bhashan Char, a sediment island 30 kilometres from the mainland that emerged in the Bay of Bengal over the past two decades, which itself floods at high tide and during monsoon season, and is vulnerable to cyclones and sea -evel rise. Somini Sengupta and Henry Fountain, 'The Biggest Refugee Camp Braces for Rain: "This Is Going to Be a Catastrophe"', *New York Times*, 14 March 2018.

44   Amnesty International, 'Myanmar: Fresh evidence of violations amid ongoing military operation in Rakhine State', 11 February 2019.

45   Global Commission on the Geopolitics of the Energy Transition, 'A New World: The Geopolitics of the Energy Transition', International Renewable Energy Association, January 2018.

46   Will Steffen, et al., 'Trajectories of the Earth System in the Anthropocene', *PNAS*, vol. 115, no. 33, 14 August 2018.

47   Stella Schaller and Alexander Carius, 'Convenient Truths: Mapping climate agendas of right-wing populist parties in Europe', Adelphi, 2019.

CONFLICT REPORTS

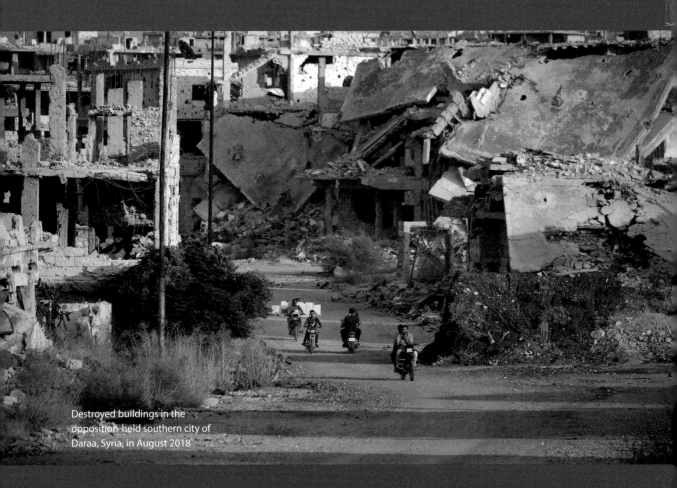

Destroyed buildings in the
opposition-held southern city of
Daraa, Syria, in August 2018

1 Americas

MS–13 gang members at a detention centre in San Salvador, El Salvador

Regional Introduction

The five armed conflicts currently active on the American continent share various characteristics and one key driver. In Colombia, El Salvador, Honduras, Mexico and Rio de Janeiro, organised criminal groups fight one another and the state to control the production, distribution routes and sale of illicit drugs, both within the countries where they operate and across their borders. Commonly referred to as drug-trafficking organisations (DTOs), criminal syndicates or cartels, the non-state armed actors in these conflicts are in fact neither monolithic nor hierarchical organisations. Instead, they compete and use armed violence to control territory rather than coordinating to fix market prices (as economic oligopolies do). They engage in various illicit activities, diversifying their portfolios beyond the drugs trade (including arms trafficking, people smuggling, kidnapping for ransom and protection rackets), or enter the narcotics business having evolved from their insurgent origins (as in the case of the National Liberation Army (ELN) in Colombia). Urban militias establish sophisticated extortion systems to exploit local resources and businesses (as in the case of Red Command (CV) in Rio de Janeiro's slums).

Although the criminal bands (BACRIMs) in Colombia, the *maras* in Central America and the cartels in Mexico depend on international networks for their main sources of business and income, their activity is deeply rooted in local dynamics. The drivers and consequences of these armed conflicts are closely intertwined with local communities and institutions and shaped by specific national policies and politics. Crucially, while seeking to maximise profit, Latin America's criminal organisations establish sophisticated systems of social control and capture state structures. Armed groups recruit foot soldiers locally and exploit poverty, marginalisation and limited state reach. They also penetrate enforcement institutions at every level, through bribery, collusion, intimidation and violence.

The conflicts in Latin America also expose the limits of the analytical distinction between political and criminal wars. Rather than fighting the state to challenge, change, substitute it or secede from it, the armed groups in Colombia, Central America, Mexico and Rio – with the (mostly nominal) exception of the ELN – are criminal organisations without a political agenda. Instead, they seek profit, of which the international narcotics trade offers a virtually limitless source. If this key objective sets them apart from traditional, politically motivated insurgencies, it is their organisational capacity and willingness to engage the state in sustained armed confrontation that establishes them as parties to armed conflicts – if anything, ones with particularly formidable resources to fight their enemies. Similarly, just like ideologically or politically motivated groups, armed criminal groups distort social behaviour, hollow out democratic practices, erode the rule of law, disrupt local and national economies, hamper development in marginalised areas, force displacement and victimise civilians.

No official statistics exist on the casualties of these conflicts, yet there are indications that they are high. The Office of the Prosecutor General in Colombia estimates that around half of the homicides in 2018 were a result of clashes between criminal groups or were perpetrated by hitmen working for these organisations. In Mexico, media and civil-society organisations estimate cartels-mandated executions to be in the thousands. Approximately 1,000–1,500 people were killed in Rio de Janeiro this year during security operations. The United Nations Office on Drugs and Crime (UNODC) consistently ranks El Salvador's and Honduras's homicide rates among the highest in the world. Although intentional homicides form the basis of these statistics and are therefore not comparable as such to the metrics of conflict-related fatalities (including those used in this publication), they offer a sense of the magnitude of the problem and the impact of violence on the people living in the crossfire of criminal organisations.

Decades-long efforts to defeat these groups have failed and at times even escalated violence (as in the case of Mexico's decapitation strategy to eliminate the cartel leaders, or Central America's *Mano Dura* ('Iron Fist') policies). Law enforcement in the region faces two main challenges. Firstly, human-rights violations against the civilian populations are widespread. In Colombia's rural districts, with the realisation that the demobilisation of the Revolutionary Armed Forces of Colombia—People's Army (FARC–EP) would not bring the hoped-for peace dividends, dissident groups have returned to disappear civilians and tax the sale of coca paste. Secondly, throughout 2018, thousands of people from El Salvador, Guatemala and Honduras embarked on the perilous journey to the US border to escape rape and sex slavery, constant death threats, extortion and forced recruitment by the gangs. They reported, however, to be often more scared of the police back home. Lacking the capacity and viable intelligence to confront the gangs effectively, Honduran and Salvadoran security forces harass the small fish, targeting youth who fit the profile of gang recruits.

At the policy level, state responses have focused on increased militarisation and ever-harsher measures. In 2018, politicians who promised a strong approach to organised crime won the presidential elections in three of the region's countries. In Brazil, presidential candidate Jair Bolsonaro pledged to wage war on violent crime in Rio's favelas and to grant immunity for crimes committed by on-duty police. President Iván Duque campaigned against a peace agreement with the ELN – Colombia's last remaining Marxist–Leninist guerrilla group that

> Criminal organisations seek to maximise profit and establish systems of social control

Americas

controls much of the country's coca-growing regions – cancelling talks a month after his inauguration. Duque also delivered on promises to roll back certain provisions of the peace agreement with the FARC–EP, including lenient judicial measures for former armed-group members who submit to the truth and reconciliation process. The campaign tone of Mexico's President Andrés Manuel López Obrador (AMLO) was different. Since his inauguration in December, however, he has proceeded to create a National Guard – an elite military police focused on combatting drug cartels. While hybrid forces and joint operations have shaped the responses to armed groups in Brazil, Colombia and Mexico, and the armed forces have taken on an increasing number of national-security roles, police resources have been neglected. Positive results from military measures are still to materialise, but their potential to weaken the discredited law-enforcement institutions is easy to foresee.

Although not fully fledged armed conflicts, Guatemala and Venezuela are the situations to monitor in 2019. President Nicolás Maduro's government has responded violently to peaceful demonstrations demanding an end to its rule, with the proportion of deaths due to police and military action on the rise in 2018, according to local organisations. The humanitarian crisis continues to deteriorate, with medicine and food shortages, spiralling child mortality and malnutrition, and increasing displacement to neighbouring countries. Civil militias have supported the recent military repression of anti-government protests, beating demonstrators while passing through the crowds on motorbikes. The opposition's loose organisation and peaceful stance, and the armed forces' cohesiveness, have so far prevented the situation from escalating into an armed conflict, but it is unclear how long they will continue to do so. Meanwhile, Guatemala faces many of the same challenges as El Salvador and Honduras: gang-dominated trafficking, weak security forces and dysfunctional judicial institutions. Although the *maras* operating there have not reached the organisational sophistication of those in the neighbouring countries, they may soon pose a similar threat to the Guatemalan state.

Brazil (Rio de Janeiro)

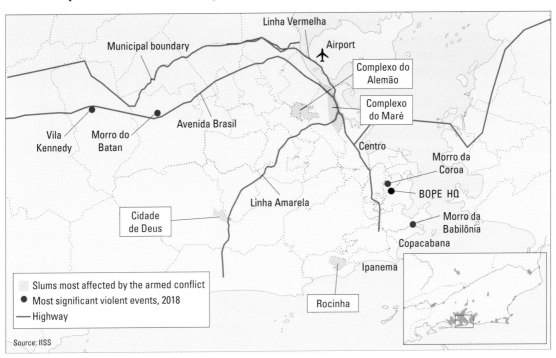

Slums most affected by the armed conflict
● Most significant violent events, 2018
— Highway

Source: IISS

Overview

The conflict in 2018

The metropolitan area of Rio de Janeiro experienced another violent year in 2018, with a new military intervention and increased gunfights between gangs, militias and the state's Military Police (PMERJ, or simply PM). The political aspiration of 'pacifying' and bringing socio-economic development to slum areas in order to prevent gang violence was abandoned in political discourse and significantly reduced in practice, with the closing of several Pacifying Police Units (UPPs). The policy known as 'pacification' had helped to significantly reduce criminal violence in the five years following its creation in 2008. Its decline from 2013 came at a time of political turmoil in Brazil, with rising support for security policies centred on lethal force against suspected criminals.

On 16 February 2018, President Michel Temer announced that the military would assume responsibility for security in the state of Rio. The president's announcement was triggered by the wave of robberies and gunfights that occurred during Carnival (Rio's main annual festival), but the gradual increase in homicides in recent years and the constant gunfights between criminal groups were also factors. The measure was supported by the governor of Rio de Janeiro state and placed all local security institutions under the command of Army General Walter Souza Braga Netto until 31 December 2018.

The initial months of the intervention saw no progress in security indicators such as robbery and homicides, while intentional homicide numbers increased. Overall security indicators improved in the second half of the year, but the intensity of the armed confrontation between rival criminal groups and between them and the security forces was still high at the end of the year.

Key statistics

Type:	Internal
IDPs total (2017):	not applicable
IDPs new (2018):	not applicable
Refugees total (2018):	not applicable
Refugees new (2018):	not applicable
People in need (2018):	not applicable

The conflict to 2018

Armed violence in Rio de Janeiro is due to the clashes between organised criminal groups against each other and the security forces. Rival gangs fight to conquer territory or to gain control over illicit economies, including drugs, extortion and unlicensed services (such as public transportation, natural-gas provision and cable TV). Armed criminal groups publicly patrol the streets and violently oppose the arrival of rival groups or security forces, although they do not oppose the entrance of some government services such as schools and health facilities. Armed groups' territorial control does not therefore equate to a complete absence of the state.

In 2008, then-security secretary José Mariano Beltrame announced a new policy, which became known as 'pacification'. It centred on establishing a more permanent state presence in the slums, to be supported – but not entirely consisting of – police interventions. Part of Beltrame's motivation was to create a stable environment in preparation for Rio's staging of the football World Cup in 2014 and the Olympic Games in 2016. The policy envisioned an approach whereby the PM, sometimes with support from the armed forces, would enter gang-dominated territories, take control and establish a UPP base that would regularly patrol the area and build relations with the local communities. The next step of the strategy consisted of the arrival of other state institutions and infrastructure investment to provide better health, education, sanitation, transportation, financing and jobs – but this component fell short of expectations, hampered by political rivalries inside the state government and a long-standing silo mentality among public agencies.

The programme led to a significant reduction in violence (see **Figure 1**). According to state-government figures, from 2007 (the year before the

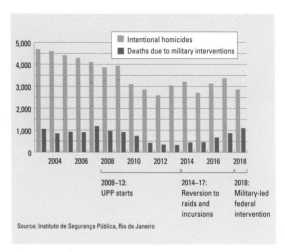

Source: Instituto de Segurança Pública, Rio de Janeiro

Figure 1: Violence trends, 2003–18

beginning of the UPPs) to 2014, intentional homicides plunged by 65.5% in areas with UPP bases, whereas in the municipality as a whole the number fell by 42.5%.[1] The overall metropolitan numbers registered similar improvements. Deaths due to security forces' intervention, which reflects violence during police operations and armed opposition by gangs, fell by 62.5%, from 1,185 deaths in 2007 to 444 in 2014. The initial success of the programme led the state government to open several new UPP bases, including in some of the city's largest slums such as Rocinha and Alemão. From 2015, however, the programme gradually declined. Its rapid expansion to more slums without a corresponding increase in personnel, training and budget led to an over-stretching of the limited resources available at a time when Rio was hit by the decline in international oil prices and Brazil's economic downturn.[2] Finally, human-rights abuses by UPP officers, accompanied by a gradual increase in homicide numbers, sapped support for the UPP project both from the public and government authorities.

Forces

Three main gangs operate in the slums of the city of Rio de Janeiro: Red Command (CV), Pure Third Command (TCP) and Friends of Friends (ADA).

Military Police (PMERJ/PM)

The main public security force tasked with fighting organised criminal groups is the Military Police

(PMERJ, or simply PM). The agency answers to the Rio state government and is officially responsible for patrolling and enforcing public order. Its hierarchy is similar to that of the army and its members are an automatic reserve force for the armed forces. As of late 2018, the PM had 43,500 members.[3] It is the force usually tasked with entering slum territories dominated by criminal factions and enforcing arrest warrants or searching for suspects based on intelligence by other public bodies.

In order to enforce arrest warrants or intervene in a gang-on-gang confrontation or other violent episode, the PM has developed a militarised approach. It is armed with rifles and handguns, and often enters gang territory inside armoured vehicles known as *caveirões* ('big skulls'), which allow them to respond to gunfire from gangs. The PM also includes the Special Police Operations Battalion (BOPE), an elite group specialising in high-risk urban operations in the style of the US SWAT forces.

The state government also oversees the Civilian Police (PCERJ). The PCERJ is responsible for investigations in support of the criminal-justice system and intelligence collection, but in recent years it has taken part in direct clashes with criminal suspects (to a much lesser extent than the PM). As of December 2018, the PCERJ had approximately 9,100 active members.[4]

Red Command (CV)

The Red Command (CV) is the oldest and largest organised criminal group operating in Rio de Janeiro. It has been involved in transnational drug trafficking since the 1980s, mainly through cocaine coming from Colombia. It also operates in arms trafficking and the sale of cocaine to local consumers. It operates in other Brazilian states, sometimes in association with local, smaller criminal groups. In Rio, CV controls several slums where state institutions and legal economic opportunities have long been absent, imposing rules on behaviour, limiting locals' freedom of movement and forcing small businesses to pay extortion fees. It is equipped with large numbers of handguns and increasingly high-calibre rifles such as the AK-47. In November 2018, the Argentinian authorities announced that it had seized weapons destined for CV, including AK-47, FAL and parts for AR-15 rifles, some with telescopic targeting systems.[5]

CV's headquarters have traditionally been in the Alemão slum complex in the northern area of Rio. Its activity was greatly reduced (at least publicly) after local authorities occupied the area with the Pacifying Police Units (UPPs) in November 2010. However, the group has gradually recovered its ability to operate in the slums as government control declined from 2013 and 2014. Its leader is Luiz

Fernando da Costa, also known as 'Fernandinho Beira-Mar', who continues to issue orders despite being in prison.

CV was formed in the Cândido Mendes Penal Institute, a maximum-security prison in Ilha Grande off the southern coast of Rio de Janeiro. Common criminals met political prisoners from leftist guerrilla groups fighting the military regime in power in Brazil during the 1970s. CV founders later published accounts of how they learned organisational techniques from the guerrillas in order to better protect themselves from rival groups (inside the prison) and demand better conditions. Some books that were seized with CV's founders, such as Carlos Marighela's *Manual of the Urban Guerrilla*, explained basic urban-insurgency techniques. CV members also had some contact with leftist-revolutionary literature and some theoretical-communist readings, although the group never developed any revolutionary or ideological orientation.

Several founding members of CV (which was initially called Red Phalanx) either escaped or were released after serving their time. Once out of prison, CV prospered, exploiting a thriving cocaine economy and the availability of sanctuaries and recruiting pools in Rios's impoverished slums. During the 1990s and 2000s, other criminal factions emerged to take advantage of the increasing profits of the cocaine industry, including CV's most formidable opponents, the TCP and the ADA, both of which derive from a prior group known as Third Command.

Pure Third Command (TCP)

Since 2016, the Pure Third Command (TCP) has acquired partial territorial control over several slums and firmly established itself as the second-most powerful criminal organisation in Rio after CV (excluding the vigilante militias). The TCP formed in 2002 in small to medium-sized slum areas in northern and western Rio. The rise of vigilante groups, known as 'militias', during the 2000s significantly weakened the TCP in western areas (though it retained the Senador Camará area). The TCP's traditional stronghold in the northern area of Rio is still the Parada de Lucas slum, and it has withstood repeated attempts by CV to wrest control of Vigário Geral slum.

During 2017 and 2018, the rapid decline of a rival group, ADA, led many ADA members to defect to the TCP and the TCP to conquer seven of ADA's slums.

Friends of Friends (ADA)

The criminal group Friends of Friends (ADA) has suffered heavy losses in recent years in clashes with CV and, to a lesser extent, the TCP. Large areas of Rocinha, for instance, transferred their allegiance to CV. The group's decline accelerated in 2011, when Nem da Rocinha was arrested fleeing his territory when security forces entered to establish a UPP base. From prison, Nem forged an alliance with the TCP in 2017, forming a new organisation called Friends' Third Command (TCA). The TCA was short-lived: a key ADA member, Carlos da Silva Fernandes, also known as 'Arafat', announced a few months later that he was defecting to the old TCP. Several ADA members in prison requested to be transferred to cells closer to the TCP. This is a long-standing practice in Brazilian prisons, which house criminals according to their factions in order to maintain their safety and minimise the risk of fights. This mass transfer signalled that ADA was reduced and weakened.

By the end of 2018, ADA retained control of only two areas in the city of Rio: Vila Vintém in the west and Morro do Dezoito in Água Santa.[6] Celsinho da Vila Vintém was still a top leader in ADA, showing unusual longevity by the standards of Rio's criminal underworld. Despite its declining territorial presence, ADA still maintains communication with São Paulo's First Capital Command (PCC), Brazil's largest and wealthiest criminal organisation.[7] The PCC shares ADA's approach, including a focus on business expansion and less armed confrontation. An alliance with the PCC may be the only way for ADA to survive.

Militias (Justice League)

The term 'militias' is used in Rio to describe armed self-defence groups claiming to provide security to impoverished communities and slums against drug-trafficking organisations. These groups have a strong presence in the impoverished western areas of the metropolitan area of Rio, where they first emerged (Rio das Pedras). They were formed by off-duty or retired police officers (especially from the MP), firefighters and prison guards and expanded rapidly through the metropolitan area during the 2000s.

The most organised of these militias is the 'Justice League', led by Wellington da Silva Braga, also known as 'Ecko', one of the most wanted men in Rio de Janeiro by the end of 2018. He inherited the command of the organisation from his brother Carlos Alexandre Braga, also known as 'Carlinhos Três Pontes', who was killed in April 2017. The Justice League is particularly strong in the areas of Campo Grande, Paciência and Santa Cruz, in western Rio, as well as Seropédica and Nova Iguaçu in Baixada Fluminense, immediately to the north of the city of Rio. In the second half of 2018, the group assumed control of two more slums in the western area of Rio city (Antares and Rola) after intense clashes with the Red Command, a long-standing presence in those areas. At the end of July and beginning of August, gunfights in Antares and Rola lasted seven days, with militia members posting videos on social media to celebrate some victories. With this expansion, the militia consolidated its position as the dominant armed criminal actor in western Rio.

The militias are more involved in extortion and the provision of illicit services than drug trafficking, although there are reports of increasing drug dealing in some militia territories. The Public Prosecutor's Office and the State Legislature determined that they also wield influence in politics and the police through corruption rings. For instance, a wide-ranging investigation conducted by the State Legislature, concluded in 2008, denounced several members of the city council, a former head of the Civilian Police, a former state lawmaker and 67 military-police officers for involvement with the militias.

Drivers

Unmanaged urbanisation

The rapid urbanisation of Brazil in the second half of the twentieth century played an important role in the evolution of organised crime. Some 46% of Brazil's population lived in urban areas in 1960, but this rose to 74% in 1990. In the same period, the total urban population more than tripled, reaching 110 million.[8] The country's economy expanded as well:

GDP per capita grew by 1,372% during those four decades.[9] The country, however, remained ranked 'among the most unequal in the world', something that began to change only in the mid-1990s.[10] This inequality is clear in the urban space, where the slums expanded in size and population.

Rio municipality was already struggling in 1960, when 335,000 people (10% of its population) were living in slums, but by 2000 the slum population passed the 1m mark.[11] The absence of public services and permanent state security in these areas provided space for criminal organisations to operate and prey on the local communities.

Criminal organisations provide sporadic assistance to local inhabitants, for instance by helping them improve homes, assisting them in accessing medicine or health care, resolving disputes and barring their members from conducting robberies in their own territories. They also impose rules that frequently place locals at odds with state security forces, such as demanding that locals hide drugs, weapons or even fighters in their homes and keeping silent during police operations, while also imposing curfews and other limitations. As a result, criminal organisations are mostly feared, even if sometimes they may help locals with the simple services that are hard to access in marginalised communities.

Transnational drug trafficking
The hubs of illicit smuggling and marijuana sale migrated to marginalised slum areas in the 1940s and 1950s in order to escape the prohibition policies. In the 1980s, the transnational empire of Pablo Escobar's Medellín Cartel lowered prices for cocaine, making it available to a much larger pool of customers. The large ensuing revenues, in conjunction with the proximity of some slums (such as Rocinha) to the wealthy areas in the South Zone of Rio, helped the rise of rival criminal organisations involved in the drug trade. In order to take and control territory – meaning more drug-selling points and more negotiating power with

international smugglers – the gangs began to fight more frequently and more violently.

Clashes between CV and its main drug-trafficking competitor, the TCP, have been a major source of gang-on-gang violence over the past decade. The two groups' funding, armed tactics and territorial-control styles share many similarities, so betrayals, rebellions and shifting alliances are relatively common, fragmenting a group's hierarchy in a particular slum, or, as in the case of the ADA, in the entire organisation. Fragmentations leave groups vulnerable to attempts by rival organisations to seize territory, leading to more violence.

Militarised security policies
The PM – the main agency responsible for security operations in gang-controlled areas – is a highly militarised police force, dating back to the military-regime era (1964–85), when it supported the persecution of political opponents. The PM's approach to combatting gangs in the slums has resulted in frequent gunfights in densely populated areas, which created a complicated relationship with local communities. Community leaders and civil-society organisations accuse the PM of abuses and indiscriminate shootings in the pursuit of criminal suspects. In particular, the Special Police Operations Battalion (BOPE), the tactical unit of the PM, has been accused of killing civilians.

Recurring incursions into slum territories for short-term tactical objectives (to enforce arrest warrants, stop a local gang dispute or simply show force) often triggers armed opposition by gangs. In many territories controlled by CV, TCP or ADA, the PM is immediately received by bullets. This, in turn, reinforced the PM militarised response, including the use of armoured vehicles. Over the years, this confrontation came to dominate the security 'strategy' and substitute efforts to create institutions, provide services and offer stable governance in marginalised areas.

Political and Military Developments

Federal intervention
Rio's Carnival celebration in mid-February 2018 was marred by chaotic scenes, including a wave of mass robberies that affected wealthy districts and gunfights that resulted in the deaths of three

police officers. Claiming that 'organised crime had nearly taken over the state of Rio de Janeiro', on 16 February Temer announced a federal intervention in the public security of Rio de Janeiro State, a constitutional tool that had not been used since the transition from the military regime in the mid-1980s. The decree placed all security agencies and institutions in Rio under the authority of the head of the intervention, Army General Walter Souza Braga Netto, including the Security Secretariat, the military and civilian police forces, the fire brigades and state-administered prisons.

Civil-society organisations and local experts criticised the measure, arguing that it was a political manoeuvre to prop up Temer's unpopular government and lacked a long-term strategy. States and cities in Brazil's northeast facing severe security crises did not benefit from a corresponding federal response. Despite the criticism, 76% of Rio State's inhabitants supported the federal intervention, according to a March poll by Datafolha.

Throughout the year, Braga Netto and his team repeatedly stated that the aims of the intervention were not primarily directed at a military confrontation with criminals or the occupation of slum areas. The mission was related to the administrative overhaul of Rio's public-security bodies, aimed at improving their management and equipment.

The armed forces did support the PM in interventions in Vila Aliança, Coreia and Vila Kennedy. The intervention in the latter, a slum in the western area of the city, was described by the authorities as a 'laboratory' for future territorial interventions. On 23 February, 3,2000 army soldiers entered Vila Kennedy, some of whom remained stationed in the community for more than a month to deter armed activity by gangs and militias. No major criminal investigation followed, however, and gang violence quickly returned: the area registered the highest number of shots fired in the metropolitan area of Rio during the ten-month-long federal intervention in Rio, with 343 individual reports of gunfights or shots. The direct presence of military officers in slum areas was not repeated, with the exception of short operations to support ad hoc police incursions.

Closing of UPP bases

Ten years after the inauguration of the first UPP base, 2018 marked the lowest point of the pacification strategy that was once Rio's most prominent security policy. On 26 April, the state government's Security Secretariat announced plans to deactivate 12 UPP bases and merge seven other bases with nearby units. This represented precisely half of the 38 UPP bases operational at the beginning of the year. Then-minister of public security Raul Jungman explained that the decision was taken because the programme had 'expanded beyond the capacities of the state', especially in terms of providing socio-economic development and infrastructure investment. The first two deactivations took place in May, affecting the UPPs in Batan and Vila Kennedy slums in western Rio. On 31 May, officers left Mangueirinha – the only UPP base located in the Baixada Fluminense region, an agglomeration of cities that is part of the Rio metropolitan area. On 20 July, authorities announced the closure of the unit in Cidade de Deus (west Rio). In September, the UPP in the northern slum of Camarista-Meier was closed. On 7 November, 1,000 members of the armed forces and PM officers were deployed to support the withdrawal of the UPP forces responsible for the slums of Coroa, Fallet and Fogueteiro (central Rio).

Election of hardline governor

In October's elections, former judge and newcomer to politics Wilson Witzel was elected as governor of Rio de Janeiro state, taking office from 1 January 2019. One of his promises was the formation of 'sniper teams' in helicopters who would 'take down' armed criminals in slums at a distance. His government plan includes 'authorisation to shoot down criminals bearing weapons of exclusive use by the armed forces' and aims to improve the UPP idea with the 're-urbanisation' of slums under a programme entitled 'City Community'. He has also announced the closure of the state's Security Secretariat, responsible for the coordination of all security agencies, including strategy and intelligence, in order to enable security agencies to coordinate more effectively with federal agencies such as the Federal Police.

ADA decline

The events in Rocinha slum (located near the wealthy neighbourhoods of Gávea and São Conrado), where armed clashes broke out in the second half of 2017, shaped the fates of Rio's criminal organisations in 2018. Rocinha has traditionally been one of the most profitable slums for drugs sales (due to the affluent consumer base nearby) and one of the most stable when Antônio Bonfim Lopes, alias Nem, was the local criminal boss. Nem, who belonged to the ADA faction, was arrested in 2011. His successor, known as Rogério 157, destabilised the local criminal underworld in 2017 by shifting his allegiance from ADA to CV. Also in 2017, a long-standing alliance between ADA and the TCP broke down due to internal disputes, leading ADA to lose several territories to the TCP, CV and militia groups, via invasions or defections.

ADA's geographical reach was at its smallest in 2018. The first large-scale confrontation linked to ADA's decline took place in June, when the TCP invaded two slums with strong ADA presence. The closing of the UPP in Batan on 14 May was followed, on 7 and 8 June, by the entrance of the TCP to dispute ADA's criminal operations there, resulting in intense gunfights. Later, during 16 and 17 July, ADA also lost control of Coroa slum, near the financial district. With these losses, ADA went from controlling the criminal economies in 19 slums at the beginning of 2017 to being present in just two by the end of 2018.

| Violent Events

In 2018, there were 83 instances of gunfights lasting two hours or more – a strong indication of clashes between rival criminal organisations for territorial control of slums or police operations facing resistance from armed groups.[12] Notable clashes took place from 7–8 June 2018, when an attack by TCP on ADA members in Coroa slum resulted in intense gunfights, and between 5 and 11 June, when several gun battles erupted as CV members attempted to expel the TCP from Chapéu Mangueira and Babilônia slums, near areas frequented by tourists in Rio's South Zone. This incident followed clashes in April, when the TCP took over some areas of Babilônia from CV. Between 15 and 19 July, five suspected criminals were killed in clashes with the MP in Alemão slum complex.

Increased intensity in armed clashes
Although authorities do not reveal details about violence specific to organised crime, some numbers point to increased intensity in armed clashes. Security authorities from the Rio state government consider multiple homicides as highly likely to be connected to clashes between organised armed groups.[13] The number of individual cases of multiple homicides (with three or more dead) increased by 62.3% in 2018 in comparison to the previous year, according to local civil-society organisation Fogo Cruzado.[14] Furthermore, according to Fogo Cruzado, clashes between armed groups more than doubled, going from 337 incidents of gun violence in 2017 to 735 in 2018. This number relates to a subsection of 2,541 gun-violence reports for which Fogo Cruzado was able to identify a motivation according to press and official reports.

More people killed by security forces
Another key indicator showing increased intensity of armed clashes is the number of people killed in interventions by state security forces, which saw an 18.6% jump in 2018, according to official numbers.[15] A total of 1,032 people were killed during these operations.[16] Rio's Public Ombudsman stated on 27 September 2018 that it had received 'dozens' of reports of moral and physical abuse by the police and armed forces during the federal intervention.[17] All those killed in security interventions are not directly affiliated with criminal groups opposing the police intervention. On 20 June 2018, seven people, including a 14-year-old boy, were killed during an operation by the army and the Civilian Police in Maré. A local non-governmental organisation said that shots were fired from helicopters hovering close to residential areas.

Murder of Councillor Marielle Franco
On 14 March, Marielle Franco, a prominent member of the Rio de Janeiro City Council and an activist for human rights, and her driver Anderson Gomes were shot dead by gunmen in the central district of Estácio. The murders sparked protests due to suspicions that Franco had been killed by militia groups dissatisfied with her political work. After months of silence from the authorities regarding the investigation, Rio's Security Secretary General Richard Nunes said in December that a militia group had killed Franco due to fears she would interfere with their illicit acquisition of land in western areas.[18]

Impact

Human-rights violations

The Defender's Office, a public watchdog in Rio, reported at the end of 2018 an increase in police operations in slums, 'especially those triggered by the so-called "revenge operations"'.[19] During these 'revenge' operations – launched in response to the death of an officer in a slum – PM personnel act with brutality against locals, entering houses without search warrants and verbally and sometimes physically abusing civilians.[20] A common complaint during these operations is the practice of beating young black men, regardless of whether they are linked to crime.

Radical political ideas

Rio is no stranger to candidates promising to increase repression of suspected criminals, but Governor Witzel went a step further by promising to 'shoot down' suspects and wage 'war on organised crime' as well as suggesting that ships could be used as prisons if necessary. His election reflects a broader, nationwide, shift in public perceptions of crime-fighting strategies towards favouring repressive tactics while criticising human-rights defenders. The victory of Jair Bolsonaro, a right-wing former military officer, in the 2018 presidential election was the most prominent outcome of this general inclination.

Trends

Growing militarisation

The new governor of Rio de Janeiro, Wilson Witzel, promised to increase the use of firepower against suspected criminals, stating in a November interview that 'the police will do the correct thing: it will aim at the [criminal's] little head and fire!'[21] It is unclear what will be the balance between the 'urbanisation' and the 'shoot-down' aspects of his security propositions, but his discourse clearly emphasises the repressive and militarised aspects of public security.[22]

Weak UPP programme

The dismantlement of the UPP programme indicates that a significant reduction in violence is highly unlikely in 2019. Witzel's reduced focus on the UPP programme means that there is little chance of recovering, at least in the short term, the core proposition of the strategy: the perma-nent presence of police forces accompanied by socio-economic development and infrastructure investment to stabilise violent slums. With the decreased credibility of the state's commitment to a permanent presence in slums, criminal gangs and militias (already bold and well armed) will continue to exert control over these marginalised urban spaces. This does not mean that state institutions are completely absent from slums, even the most violent ones. In fact, a major cause of armed clashes in the city is the ad hoc security incursions by the PM into gang-controlled territories – often resulting in armed opposition by criminals and gunfights that may last for hours. These types of security operations are very likely to continue, but Rio's history shows that a significant reduction of violence has only been achieved when the UPPs managed to recover urban territories via a perma-nent institutional presence.

Notes

[1] Laís Carpenter, 'Número de homicídios por intervenção policial em áreas com UPP cai 85,3% em sete anos', *O Globo*, 11 May 2015.

[2] Antônio Sampaio, 'Out of Control: Criminal gangs fight back in Rio's favelas', *Jane's Intelligence Review*, December 2014, pp. 44–8.

[3] 'História da PMERJ', PMERJ website (http://www.pmerj.rj.gov.br/historia-da-pmerj/).

[4] 'Polícia Civil em Números', Polícia Civil RJ, November 2018.

[5] Gustavo Carabajal, 'Modificaban fusiles AR-15 para venderlos en favelas de Río de Janeiro', *Nacion*, 3 November 2018.

[6] Cecília Olliveira, 'Yuri Eiras, 'Death of a Rio Cartel', *Intercept*, 13 December 2018.

[7] Luís Adorno and Flávio Costa, '"Apoiamos o Nem": PCC confirma aliança pelo domínio do tráfico de drogas na maior favela do Rio', *UOL*, 12 July 2018.

[8] World Bank (https://data.worldbank.org).

[9] World Bank's data on GDP per capita (https://data.worldbank.org).

10 'World Social Science Report 2016, Challenging Inequalities: Pathways to a Just World', ISSC, IDS and UNESCO, 2016.

11 Valéria Grace Costa, 'Traços e Tendências Recentes da Expansão das Favelas no Município do Rio de Janeiro', *Revista do Arquivo Geral da Cidade do Rio de Janeiro*, no. 5, 2011, p. 162.

12 The number was released by civil-society organisation Fogo Cruzado, which monitors gunfights in the metropolitan area of Rio. See Fogo Cruzado, '2018 Report'.

13 Interview in Instituto de Segurança Pública (ISP), Rio de Janeiro, 20 September 2018.

14 Managed by journalists, Fogo Cruzado maintains a widely used mobile-phone application that allows users to report shootings. These reports are then cross-referenced with official and press reports to determine the number of people killed and to confirm locations.

15 Authorities do not provide a breakdown of people killed in high-intensity gunfights. It is likely that bystanders are part of this count.

16 'Visualização de Dados – Morte por Intervenção de Agente do Estado', Instituto de Segurança Pública.

17 'Comunidades do Rio Sofrem 30 Tipos de Violações Durante Intervenção', Defensoria Pública do Estado do Rio de Janeiro, 27 September 2018.

18 Marcelo Godoy, 'Milicianos Mataram Marielle por Causa de Terras, Diz General', *O Estado de São Paulo*, 14 December 2018.

19 Defensoria Pública do Estado do Rio Janeiro, 'Circuito de Favelas por Direitos: Relatório 2018', December 2018, p. 102.

20 'Vingança de policiais é um crime que se repete, diz Anistia Internacional', *Jornal Nacional*, 31 July 2017.

21 Renata Pennafort, '"A Polícia Vai Mirar na Cabecinha e... fogo"', diz novo governador do Rio', *O Estado de São Paulo*, 1 November 2018.

22 PSC-PROS, 'Plano de Governo Wilson Witzel', p. 8.

Colombia

| Overview

The conflict in 2018

In 2018, the implementation of the 2016 peace agreement between the government and the Revolutionary Armed Forces of Colombia (FARC) continued in Colombia. While the country's security situation improved after the signing of the peace agreement, multiple criminal groups involved with drug trafficking and other illegal activities remain active and continue to threaten both the civilian population and government institutions. The conflict no longer unfolds under the logic of an ideological struggle for political power – what persists of the decades-long civil war are instances of regional and localised violence, mostly but not limited to rural areas, in the departments of Antioquia, Arauca, Chocó, Nariño, Norte de Santander, Putumayo and Valle del Cauca. The challenge now facing the Colombian state is a highly sophisticated criminal network of several large-scale criminal drug-trafficking organisations either cooperating or fighting for the control of territories and drug-trafficking routes. In 2016, 69% of the total hectares under coca cultivation worldwide were located in Colombia. Most of the world's cocaine comes from Colombia, which produced some 866 tonnes of the drug in 2016, or 43% of total global production.[1] Regionally, political instability in Venezuela and weak border monitoring in 2018 created safe-haven areas for guerrillas and criminals expanding their operations across the border.

On 7 August 2018, Iván Duque was sworn in as the new Colombian president. A right-wing politician and hardline critic of the peace agreement with FARC, Duque promised a stronger approach towards guerrillas and criminal organisations. Duque ended peace talks with the left-wing National Liberation Army (ELN) in September 2018 after the group refused the government's preconditions to stop all criminal activities, including a unilateral ceasefire and the liberation of all hostages.

The conflict to 2018

FARC and the ELN were founded in the 1960s after a decade of political violence known as *La*

Key statistics	
Type:	Internationalised
IDPs total (2017):	6,500,000–7,500,000
IDPs new (2018):	30,000
Refugees total (2018):	not applicable
Refugees new (2018):	not applicable
People in need (2018):	7,000,000

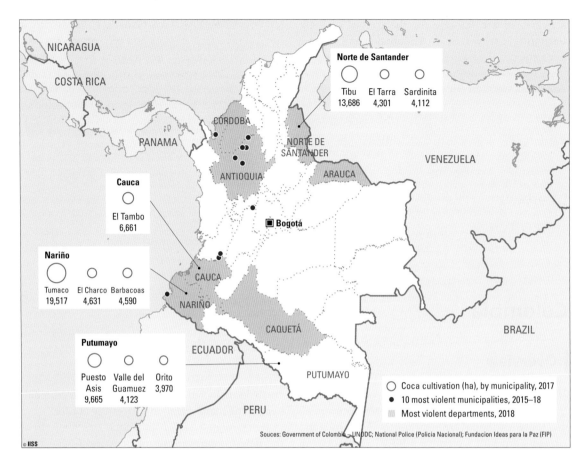

Norte de Santander
Tibu 13,686
El Tarra 4,301
Sardinita 4,112

Cauca
El Tambo 6,661

Nariño
Tumaco 19,517
El Charco 4,631
Barbacoas 4,590

Putumayo
Puesto Asis 9,665
Valle del Guamuez 4,123
Orito 3,970

○ Coca cultivation (ha), by municipality, 2017
● 10 most violent municipalities, 2015–18
▦ Most violent departments, 2018

Souces: Government of Colombia; UNODC; National Police (Policia Nacional); Fundacion Ideas para la Paz (FIP)

© IISS

Violencia (1948–58). *La Violencia* was a civil war between Colombia's Conservative and Liberal parties that resulted in the deaths of at least 200,000 civilians, most of whom peasants and rural workers. The civil war ended when the parties agreed to alternate in government by presenting a joint National Front candidate to each election and restricting the participation of other political movements. Political exclusion, social and economic problems and the international Cold War context generated the bases for the guerrilla movements and the appeal of their Marxist-Leninist revolutionary message. In 1964, the FARC guerrilla group was born, followed by the ELN in 1965 and the Popular Liberation Army (EPL) in 1967. The guerrillas were motivated by leftist ideals of social revolution and common objectives, including the fight against the privatisation of natural resources and the representation of the rural poor.

In the 1980s, rural landowners began organising right-wing paramilitary groups to protect themselves from the guerrillas. The largest paramilitary group was the United Self-Defence Forces of Colombia (AUC), an umbrella organisation formally disbanded in 2006, but the splinter groups that emerged from the dissolution of the AUC formed large criminal organisations, including the Gulf Clan and the Popular Revolutionary Anti-Terrorist Army of Colombia (ERPAC).

Peace negotiations between the Colombian government and FARC began in September 2012 and took place mostly in Havana, Cuba, resulting in a peace agreement on 24 August 2016. The referendum to ratify the deal in October was unsuccessful (50.2% of voters voted against). The parties signed a revised peace deal in November that was then ratified by both houses of Congress, thereby ending 52 years of civil war. FARC completed its demobilisation in August 2017, with 11,000 fighters and collaborators delivering more than 8,000 weapons to United Nations monitors. Despite the successful peace process, the state still does not control former insurgent zones, where several large-scale criminal organisations have assumed the control of illegal activities or are fighting for the control of those territories, particularly in Putumayo and Arauca departments, the south of Chocó department and in the Bajo Cauca and Northern Antioquia regions of Antioquia department. Additionally, several splinter groups from FARC remain active in the country. The dispute between the ELN – the last remaining guerrilla group – and criminal groups for territorial control also increased in 2018 in the territories left behind by FARC, particularly in areas rich in natural resources, cocaine and coca production and where the Colombian government has no reliable presence. These confrontations produce direct and indirect effects on the local populations, such as forced displacement, with serious humanitarian consequences. Consequently, Colombia's security and defence policies continue to focus on counter-insurgency and counter-narcotics operations.

Forces

Criminal organisations in Colombia not only are in conflict with the state security forces but also fight each other for control of drug-trafficking territories and routes. ELN attacks are directed mostly against the security forces, but they are also in open conflict with the EPL over the control of the Catatumbo region, Norte de Santander department, and with the Gulf Clan in Chocó department. The Gulf Clan, originally a paramilitary group, is in conflict with the left-wing guerrillas, including the ELN, EPL and FARC dissident groups. The Gulf Clan also clashes with other, smaller criminal organisations (such as the Aguilas Negras, Caparrapos, Rastrojos and Puntilleros). Though none of the criminal groups poses an existential military threat to the Colombian state, they undermine the presence and control of the national, regional and local authorities in Colombia's 32 departments.

State forces

The Colombian armed forces consist of the National Army of Colombia, the Navy, the Air Force and the Naval Infantry, which combined have 470,634 active personnel. The Colombian Army has been the main military branch involved in the armed conflicts and in 2018 had 240,000 active personnel.

The National Police (PNC) is in charge of public security. Albeit not technically part of the armed forces, the PNC has been controlled and administered by the Ministry of Defence and has a highly militarised structure since 1953. In 2018, it comprised approximately 180,000 uniformed personnel.

As a strategy to curb drug trafficking, the government is heavily involved in the substitution and eradication of coca-crop production, the latter with the support (dating back to the 1980s) of the United States as part of the US 'war on drugs'.

The Colombian government has programmes to eradicate coca by mechanical means (burning or cutting) or with herbicides sprayed by airplanes and helicopters.

In 2017, Colombia's armed forces began a significant transformation process to a post-conflict military force and began shifting their counter-insurgency focus towards a multi-mission one. Colombia has the third-largest defence expenditure in the Americas, after the US and Brazil. The Minister of Defence has proposed increasing the defence budget from US$10 billion in 2018 to US$11.2bn in 2019, an increase which would bring defence spending to approximately 3.3% of Colombia's GDP. Of the additional US$1.2bn, US$466 million will be invested in strengthening Colombia's military capacities and improving security policies.

FARC dissidents

Between 2,000 and 2,500 FARC fighters spread across 16 departments rejected the 2016 peace agreement, labelling those that accepted it as traitors. These fighters have rebranded themselves as the 'true FARC', while the Colombian government refers to them as FARC dissidents. In 2018, 19 illegal armed groups were identified to have split from the demobilised FARC.

The First Front, commanded by Néstor Gregorio Vera Fernández (also known as 'Iván Mordisco'), has 450 members and a horizontal leadership structure. The group operates in the Amazonas, Arauca, Caquetá, Guainía, Guaviare, Meta, Vaupés and Vichada departments, where it controls territory and coca cultivation and maintains several laboratories that transform coca paste into cocaine. It also controls the arms- and drug-trafficking routes through the jungle to the borders with Brazil and Venezuela.

The Front Oliver Sinisterra (FOS) has 400 fighters and in 2018 was commanded by Walter Patricio Artízala Vernaza (also known as 'Guacho'). It controls territory in Nariño department, which has one of the highest concentrations of coca cultivation in the country. The group also controls several key drug-trafficking corridors towards Ecuador and the Pacific Ocean. The kidnapping and murder of several Ecuadorian citizens in March–April 2018 brought the group into conflict with the Ecuadorian government and also led to a response from the Colombian government. In December 2018, Colombian security forces killed Guacho, the main point of contact with the Mexican cartels (particularly the Sinaloa Cartel) and arrested other leaders of the group over the year. It is not clear whether the rebel group will be able to recover from these major blows.

National Liberation Army (ELN)

Founded in 1964 by a group of Catholic priests, left-wing intellectuals and students embracing liberation theology and trying to emulate Fidel Castro's Cuban revolution, the National Liberation Army (ELN) is the last active guerrilla group in Colombia with a significant presence, having approximately 2,000 fighters.[2] Today, the ELN's main activities and sources of revenue are extortions, kidnappings and drug trafficking. The Central Command (COCE) directs the strategy of the group and is composed of five commanders and divisions that operate independently, making it harder for the government to bring down the group's leadership. The most notorious commander is Nicolás Rodríguez Bautista (also known as 'Gabino'). The ELN operates in nine of Colombia's 32 departments, with a particularly strong presence in the northeast. Since the government's peace agreement with FARC, the ELN has taken over areas previously under FARC control, particularly in the departments of Cauca and Chocó. The ELN began peace talks with the government of Juan Manuel Santos in 2017, but failed to reach an agreement.

Gulf Clan (Urabeños)

The Gulf Clan (also known as the Urabeños) emerged from the demobilisation of the AUC paramilitary group in 2006. It has become one of the dominant criminal forces in the country, with a presence in at least 17 departments, approximately 4,000 men

and the armed capability to challenge other armed groups and state security forces. The group's leader is Dairo Antonio Úsuga (also known as 'Otoniel'), and the group's base and territorial stronghold is centred around the Gulf of Urabá in the departments of Antioquia and Chocó. The group's main revenues come from controlling the cocaine market, although the network as a whole is less a drug cartel and more a service provider to independent drug traffickers. The Gulf Clan escorts shipments along international-trafficking corridors, ensures access to or protection for processing laboratories and provides storage and dispatch services on the Atlantic coast and border regions. Additionally, the group charges other traffickers for permission to cross areas under its control.

The Gulf Clan remains one of the most powerful organised-crime groups in Colombia, but has suffered several setbacks, with Otoniel's command circle decimated by arrests or deaths. Otoniel's second-in-command, Roberto Vargas Gutiérrez (also known as 'Gavilán'), and Manuel Arístides Meza Páez (also known as 'El Indio'), Otoniel's third-in-command, were killed in September 2017 and March 2018 respectively. In response, Otoniel has promoted a group of young lieutenants more motivated by criminal intent than the older generation and with little connection to the Gulf Clan's original paramilitary roots.[3] These changes led to internal dispute and fragmentations within the group's leadership. Los Caparrapos, a group of 180, split from the Gulf Clan in 2018 and now fights it for territorial control in Bajo Cauca.

Popular Liberation Army (EPL)/Los Pelusos

The Popular Liberation Army (EPL)/Los Pelusos is a dissident faction of the former armed wing of the Colombian Communist Party, which emerged in 1967 and demobilised in 1991. The EPL presence is concentrated in the Catatumbo region, Norte de Santander department, along the border with Venezuela. The group has between 200 and 250 fighters. Following the demobilisation of FARC in 2017, the EPL has been trying to recruit dissident FARC guerrillas and expand out of its historical communities into areas formerly controlled by FARC, such as the Norte de Santander and Cesar departments. The group funds its operations partly by kidnappings, extortions, cattle raiding, money laundering and the distribution of illegal drugs.

Armed Group	Strength	Presence (Departments)
FARC dissidents	2,500	Guainía, Guaviare, Meta, Nariño, Vaupés
ELN	1,500–2,500	Antioquia, Arauca, Bajo Cauca, Bolívar, Boyacá, Casanare, Cauca, Cesar, Chocó, Nariño, Norte de Santander, Santander
Gulf Clan	3,000–4,000	Antioquia, Atlántico, Bolívar, Boyacá, Casanare, Cesar, Chocó, Córdoba, Cundinamarca, La Guajira, Magdalena, Meta, Nariño, Santander, San Andrés, Providencia, Sucre, Tolima, Quindío
EPL	250–350	Cesar, Norte de Santander
Puntilleros	450	Casanare, Guaviare, Meta, Vichada

Puntilleros

The origin of the Puntilleros can be traced back to the demobilisation of the Popular Revolutionary Anti-Terrorist Army of Colombia (ERPAC) paramilitary force in 2011. Its operations are concentrated in the region of the Orinoquía, mainly in the departments of Casanare, Guaviare, Meta and Vichada. According to authorities, the group has approximately 450 men.[4] The Puntilleros control the strategic points of the main drug-trafficking route through the eastern plains, from the department of Meta to the border with Venezuela.

Drivers

Ideology and crime

For the past four decades, ideology and criminal activities have coexisted in the internal conflicts of Colombia, as both guerrillas and paramilitary groups used drug trafficking to finance their activities and warfare. Since the demobilisation of FARC, criminal activities and competition for territory previously under FARC control have driven the violence. Organised crime groups are active in 274 municipalities in 28 of 32 departments in the country. The EPL and ELN retain some remnants of ideological motivation and have an underlying objective of creating a socialist state, but are also heavily involved in criminal activities.

Drug trade

Colombia's relationship with the drug trade began in the 1970s when poor farmers began planting marijuana as a far more lucrative alternative to the legal crops. Cartels, paramilitary and guerrilla groups became involved in drug trafficking in the 1980s. In the late 1990s and early 2000s, much of the fighting between the FARC and the AUC was for control over coca plantations and trafficking routes.

Drug trafficking continues to be the main driver of violence in Colombia. Direct and indirect participation in the drug trade and the taxation, administration and control of areas of production and trafficking are the main source of revenue for guerrilla, paramilitary and

organised-crime groups. According to the UN Office on Drugs and Crime (UNODC), cocaine production in the country has risen since 2013, increasing 31% in 2016 from 1,053 tonnes to a record 1,379 tonnes in 2017 (with an estimated market value of US$2.7 billion).[5] The predominant trafficking route is along the Pacific coast where coca-leaf production and cocaine manufacture is concentrated. The vast majority of coca cultivation takes place in the departments of Antioquia, Caquetá, Guaviare, Meta, Nariño, Putumayo and Vichada, with two-thirds of coca cultivation taking place in southern Colombia. The department of Nariño has the largest area under cultivation, with approximately 19,500 hectares around the port city of Tumaco. The cocaine is trafficked from Colombia to Central America and

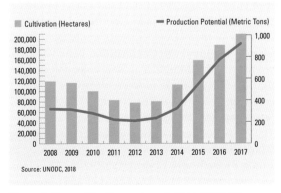

Source: UNODC, 2018

Figure 1: Coca cultivation and production, 2008–17

Mexico, using planes, ships and semi-submersible vessels, and then from Mexico across the border into the US, mostly by Mexican organised-crime groups. Colombia is also the main supplier of cocaine for the European market, with the drug mainly trafficked through Spain and the Netherlands.

Society and the state

Colombia's social, economic and political challenges have historically facilitated criminal activities. Colombia is a middle-income country with a GDP of US$6,760 per capita and Latin America's second-most unequal country after Brazil, with a GINI coefficient of 50.8 in 2016. Some 14.5 million Colombians lived below the poverty line in 2017, one-third of whom live in the countryside, where most criminal activities take place.

In addition, the country faces several structural challenges related to corruption, including the collusion of the public and private sectors; the influence of organised crime on policy and institutions; weak state presence in remote areas; and an inefficient criminal-justice system. In Transparency International's Corruption Perceptions Index of 2017, Colombia was ranked 96th out of 180 countries. Corruption is considered the main problem facing the country by 20% of Colombian citizens, with the police forces generally considered to be highly corrupt.[6]

The absence of state institutions in many parts of the country, particularly in rural areas, has left poor and marginalised populations unprotected from criminal and guerrilla groups, although some armed groups have achieved a certain amount of social legitimacy within those communities.[7]

Regional instability

Venezuela's economic, political and social crisis and the demobilisation of Colombia's largest guerrilla group have shifted criminal dynamics on the Colombia–Venezuela border, transforming the region into a major organised-crime hub. Venezuela serves as a trans-shipment point for drug cargo trafficked by Colombian armed groups and destined for markets in the US and Europe. Contraband smuggling is another a highly lucrative criminal activity along the Colombia–Venezuela border.

Political and Military Developments

Presidential and legislative elections

Colombia held parliamentary and presidential elections in 2018. The congressional elections of 11 March 2018 marked FARC's debut on the political scene. Although the party performed poorly, receiving only 0.28% of the overall vote, the Common Alternative Revolutionary Force (the political successor of the former rebel FARC group) was guaranteed five seats in the Senate and five in the lower House as per the 2016 peace agreement. The election results were fragmented, with no party achieving more than 16% of the vote. The three largest conservative parties – Democratic Centre (CD), Radical Change (CR) and the Conservative Party – collectively secured more than 40% of votes for seats in the Senate and House of Representatives.[8] The CD emerged as the largest party with 19 seats in the Senate and 33 in the lower House of Representatives. The conservative bloc has a majority in Congress, which ensures governability.

On 8 March 2018, Rodrigo Londoño (also known as 'Timochenko'), the candidate of the Common Alternative Revolutionary Force, withdrew from the presidential race, citing the absence of electoral and security guarantees. The presidential elections of Colombia were held on 27 May 2018. No candidate reached more than 50% of turnout and a second round of elections between right-wing candidate Iván Duque and left-wing candidate Gustavo Petro was held on 17 June. With 53.98% of the votes, Duque won the race and took office on 7 August. During his presidential campaign, Duque promised to modify, but not revoke, the peace deal with FARC. The rise to power of Duque and the conservative bloc foresees a more repressive approach towards criminal organisations that is reflected by an increase in the coordination and actions of the security forces.

Transitional justice

Colombia's transitional justice system, the Special Jurisdiction for Peace (JEP), followed the signing of the peace agreement with FARC to try former fighters for crimes committed during the country's decades-long armed conflict. Crimes committed after demobilisation remain subject to regular judicial procedure, which includes the possibility of extradition. The JEP plays a central role in determining in which category former guerrillas are classified.[9]

The most emblematic case of the challenges facing the JEP is that of Seuxis Paucis Hernández Solarte (also known as 'Jesús Santrich'), a lead FARC negotiator in the peace talks. Colombian authorities arrested Santrich in April 2018 after the US charged him with drug-trafficking crimes committed after the 2016 peace agreement. Former FARC guerrilla commander Iván Márquez, one of the main figures in the peace process, protested against Santrich's arrest, calling it a 'judicial setup' and blaming the JEP for endangering the peace agreement. Márquez went into hiding in August 2018 and his current whereabouts are unknown.

Talks with the ELN break down
The negotiations between the government and the ELN encountered many difficulties in 2018 following the expiration of the bilateral ceasefire on 10 January. Not all factions of the ELN supported the decision to negotiate with the administration of former president Manuel Santos, who suspended peace talks on 29 January 2018 after the ELN killed seven police officers and injured more than 40 in three separate attacks.

Duque, who criticised the agreement with FARC as being too lenient, is adopting a tougher stance. On 1 August 2018, the sixth round of talks between the government and the ELN concluded in Havana without an agreement. The kidnapping of seven uniformed personnel (four soldiers and three police officers) and two civilians in early August halted prospects for further talks. The hostages were released, but Duque demanded that the ELN suspend any criminal activity in order for the talks to continue – a precondition that the ELN refused to accept. The government also rejected the appointment of a top ELN commander, known as 'Gabino', as a delegate in peace talks and ordered his capture in November, a move which put the process at a critical crossroad.

| Violent Events

Violence on the borders with Ecuador and Venezuela
Attempts by Ecuadorian and Colombian authorities to crack down on cross-border drug-trafficking groups sparked a wave of retaliatory violence in Ecuador's northwestern Esmeraldas province in 2018. On 26 March, three Ecuadorian journalists were kidnapped by the Front Oliver Sinisterra (FOS), generating international media attention. Despite negotiations and joint military operations of the Colombian and Ecuadorian governments, the journalists were found dead on 13 April.

The ELN and the EPL operated on the Colombia–Venezuela border and have increasingly clashed for control of territory. The ELN is already operating in 12 Venezuelan states. Homicides increased by 95% in the Arauca border department between August and October 2018, compared to the same period in 2017.[10]

Attacks on human-rights defenders
Murders and threats against human-rights defenders increased substantially in 2018. Since December 2016, 295 human-rights defenders have been killed.[11] Most of the victims are members of local action boards, the most basic form of association officially recognised by the constitution; leaders of indigenous communities and communities of Colombians of African descent; and leaders of coca-substitution programmes. On 2 December 2018, two leaders and one minor of the Awá people were killed by an unidentified armed group.

Only 70% of the activists' murders are under investigation, and no perpetrator has been identified in the vast majority of cases.[12] The impunity rate of murders that occurred between 2009 and 2017 is 91.4%.[13] In August 2018, Duque announced the adoption of a broad pact to protect social leaders and human-rights defenders and instructed the Ministry of the Interior to urgently formulate a policy based on these commitments.

Impact

Forced displacements

Clashes between armed groups have had a significant humanitarian impact. Between January and November 2018, more than 30,500 Colombians were forcibly displaced due to the violence, adding to the 7.7m people who have been displaced since 1985. Colombia's rural communities are disproportionally affected by these displacements. According to 2017 data from the UN Office for the Coordination of Humanitarian Affairs (OCHA), seven out of ten displaced people belong to rural communities, with the departments of Antioquia (Bajo Cauca region), Chocó, Nariño (Pacific region) and Norte de Santander (Catatumbo region) accounting for 95% of the forced displacements.

Coca cultivation

The number of hectares under coca cultivation rose by 17% from 2016 (146,000 hectares) to 2017 (171,000). The government's effort to eradicate or substitute coca crops in 2018 was largely unsuccessful, with only 24,891 hectares of coca plantations eradicated by September 2018 (which nevertheless represented a substantial increase from the 1,175 hectares eradicated in 2017).[14]

The dramatic resurgence of coca-crop cultivation (which almost halved from 2000 to 2013) was facilitated not only by market dynamics and the strategies of trafficking organisations, but also by ineffective substitution strategies. The Colombian state has little or no presence in the rural areas where farmers grow coca leaves. Most farmers do not necessarily choose to cultivate coca, but are obliged or persuaded to do so either by armed groups who watch over the trade or because other crops are simply not profitable. Under the peace agreement, the government has pursued crop-substitution and alternative development programmes to pull farmers away from coca production, but a lack of resources has delayed the implementation of those programmes and the expectations in some rural communities of receiving compensation for replacing coca have not been fulfilled.

Trends

Venezuela: the border and the migration

Instability in Venezuela and the resultant migration will continue to affect Colombia's security situation in 2019. The porous border between the two countries makes it easy for criminal organisations to move in and out of Venezuela, which provides a safe haven for several Colombian criminal organisations. Criminal organisations, particularly the ELN and dissidents from the FARC, are also recruiting those fleeing Venezuela. Colombia is also the main recipient of Venezuelan migrants, with Colombia's Migration Authority reporting that more than 1m Venezuelans had entered the country between 2015 and September 2018.

The future of the ELN

The ELN is one of the most powerful criminal organisation in Colombia, both in terms of revenues and number of fighters. A peace agreement with the group is critical for the pacification of the country. The future of peace talks between the ELN and the Duque administration remains uncertain as the parties continue to deeply mistrust each other.

If they fail, the ELN will continue to increase its criminal activities and attack the security forces as well as infrastructure and companies in Colombia and Venezuela, while victimising local communities along the border and continuing to hamper socio-economic development.

Coca cultivation

Duque has stated several times that the substitution of coca cultivation is one of the main objectives of his administration. In his presidential term, Duque hopes to eradicate 70% of the illicit crops, which would amount to 120,000 hectares of coca cultivation. Defence Minister Guillermo Botero has promised a return to aerial fumigation, but the long-term sustainability and efficacy of this strategy has been criticised.[15] Botero has also argued that eradication should be mandatory for farmers and be accompanied by assistance from the state to the local population. Forced eradication and programmes for the substitution of illegal crops will continue in 2019, but will encounter several challenges. The success of Colombia's eradication policy depends largely on the ability of the government to tackle the coca production with a comprehensive strategy, supporting the farmers and communities and extending state presence to rural areas.

Violence

In 2017, Colombia's homicide rate reached its lowest level since 1975, with 24 homicides per 100,000 inhabitants. According to the country's chief prosecutor, however, Néstor Humberto Martínez, in 2018 homicides rose again for the first time since 2009, with 8,475 people were murdered from January to November 2018.[16] The homicide rate was 24.1 per 100,000 inhabitants in 2017, but 25.4 in December 2018.[17] Homicides increased in 306 municipalities located in regions where illicit crops (coca, marijuana and poppies) are cultivated, as well as in the cities of Medellín and Cali. The new criminal dynamics and the fighting over territories and trafficking routes previously controlled by FARC, coupled with the inability of the state to control those areas, indicate that violence will keep rising in 2019.

The reintegration process

The reintegration process will pose several challenges in 2019, including the impact of illegal economies and efforts by armed groups to lure former FARC members into their ranks, exposing the fragility of the peace process. The process of demobilising and reintegrating former FARC combatants will remain a pressing issue in 2019. Of the 26 initial reintegration camps, 24 remain in operation. They were established to incorporate FARC back into civilian life, in line with the 2016 peace deal, and are due to close in August 2019. Economic reintegration remains a subject of serious concern, with the fundamental goal of providing income-generating opportunities to some 14,000 former combatants still far from being realised. The vast majority of those in the process of reintegration still have no clear economic prospects beyond the monthly stipend, which is due to end in August 2019. Although the government's budget proposal for 2019 provides that public spending on reintegration be maintained at the same level as 2018, it is not clear whether this will suffice to implement the reintegration process fully.

Independently, several former FARC commanders have voiced concerns about their physical and legal security and have left reintegration areas. There is a stark contrast between the situation of those former guerrillas who are under protection provided by the state and those who are outside their scope; as of October 2018, 74 FARC members were killed outside the government security umbrella.

| Notes

1   'World Drug Report 2018', UN Office on Drugs and Crime (UNODC), June 2018.

2   'The Missing Peace: Colombia's New Government and Last Guerrillas', International Crisis Group, 12 July 2012.

3   Nelson Matta, 'El nuevo círculo de confianza de "Otoniel"', *El Colombiano*, 21 September 2018.

4   'Puntilleros', *Colombia Reports*, 23 October 2018.

5   'Coca Crops in Colombia at all-time high', UNODC, September 2018.

6   'Informe 2018', Corporación Latinobarómetro, November 2018.

7   Joel Gilin, 'Understanding the causes of Colombia's conflict: Weak, corrupt state institutions', *Colombia Reports*, 13 January 2015.

8   Nicholas Casey, 'Colombian Election Brings Divided Congress to Power', *New York Times*, 12 March 2018.

9   Parker Asmann, '3 Obstacles for Transitional Justice in Colombia', *Insight Crime*, 19 October 2018.

10   'Los primeros 100 días del Presidente Iván Duque', Fundacion Ideas para la Paz (FIP), November 2018.

11   'Informe especial de Derechos Humanos Situación de lideresas y líderes sociales, de defensoras y defensores de derechos humanos y de excombatientes de las Farc-EP y sus familiars', Indepaz, Fundación Heinrich Böll, no. 8, June 2018.

12   Fabio Diaz and Magda Jimenez, 'Colombia's murder rate is at an all-time low but its activists keep getting killed', *Conversation*, 6 April 2018.

13   Tristan Ustyanowski, 'En 2018 empeoró la situación de los líderes sociales en Colombia', *France24*, 17 December 2018.

14   'Colombia: Monitoreo de territorios afectados por cultivos ilícitos 2017', UNODC, September 2018.

15   Juan Camilo Montoya, 'Ministro de Defensa pide fumigación aérea para erradicar cultivos', *El Colombiano*, 28 October 2018.

16   Adriaan Alsema, 'Homicides in Colombia up 7%: chief prosecutor', *Colombia Reports*, 20 April 2018.

17   'Sin política pública contra los homicidios no es posible proteger la vida en Colombia', FIP, 15 December 2018.

El Salvador

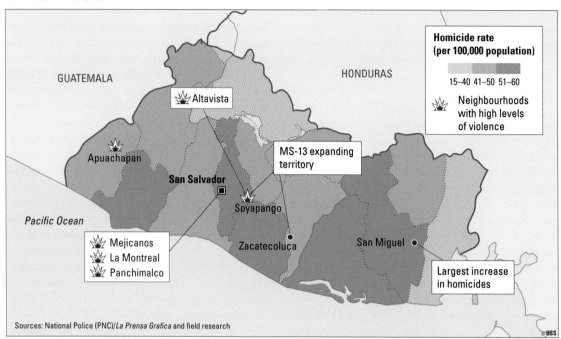

Sources: National Police (PNC)/*La Prensa Grafica* and field research

Overview

The conflict in 2018

The conflict in El Salvador grew in complexity and sophistication in 2018, with the Mara Salvatrucha (MS-13) transnational gang remaining the primary offensive actor. In 2018, the MS-13 continued to expand its territorial control along El Salvador's coastal region, making modest inroads in the cocaine-transport business.[1] Cocaine seizures in 2018 exceeded any other year in Salvadoran history, highlighting the country's growing role as a transit country.[2] The MS-13 also broadened its financial sources and gained access to more sophisticated weaponry. The increase in revenue was evidenced by the number of businesses acquired, including car lots, hotels, brothels, buses and bus routes, and night-clubs.[3] The increased access to the formal market was coupled with more sophisticated money-laundering operations.

The conflict to 2018

In recent years, the conflict in El Salvador centred on fighting between the two main gangs, the MS-13 and

Key statistics	
Type:	Internal
IDPs total (2017):	300,000
IDPs new (2018):	no data
Refugees total (2018):	not applicable
Refugees new (2018):	not applicable
People in need (2018):	not applicable

the Barrio 18, as well as both gangs fighting against the state. This dynamic fundamentally changed during and following the 2012–14 'truce' between the two gangs, which was negotiated in an opaque fashion by the current Minister of Defence David Munguía Payés.[4] While the MS-13 used the time since the truce to restructure into a tier-one threat to the state, the Barrio 18 remained relatively stagnant and has since significantly weakened.

Forces

The two primary forces fighting in El Salvador are the MS-13 and the National Civil Police (PNC). Gangs such as the Barrio 18 and other small groups maintain a presence in the country, but do not have the capacity to threaten the state. Both factions of the Barrio 18 (the Sureños and the Revolucionarios) lost significant territory and influence in the country during 2018.

The Mara Salvatrucha (MS-13)

The Mara Salvatrucha (MS-13) is a transnational gang, operating (with differing degrees of sophistication and development) in El Salvador, Guatemala, Honduras and the United States. The gang maintains a relatively hierarchical structure, although local-level members have a significant amount of autonomy, particularly in generating revenues. The El Salvador branch of the gang is led by *la ranfla*, or national leadership, who set the overall policies and strategies. Below *la ranfla*, *programas* operate as larger, semi-autonomous structures that combine approximately 30 local-level (neighbourhood) *clicas* made up of approximately 10–25 members. Individual *programas* and *clicas* make decisions on how to fund activities or devise local military strategies within the parameters set by the *ranfla*.

The national *ranfla* makes all major operational decisions, mostly from within prison. The imprisoned gang leadership, *la ranfla histórica,* is primarily constituted of older gang members who have been in prison for years or decades. This group communicates with the *ranfla libre*, or unimprisoned leadership, through illicit mobile phones and through the use of *wilas*, written encrypted instructions in a mixture of English, Spanish and gang argot.

Gang secrecy makes estimating the number of active gang members difficult. Credible estimates of MS-13 membership in El Salvador range from 17,000 (with some 9,000 in prison) to 60,000.[5] In 2018, the MS-13 acquired more sophisticated weaponry, primarily from Nicaragua but also from the US. While still using ageing AK-47 and M-16 assault rifles, the gang now boasts a growing number of new weapons, including Dragunov sniper rifles, new AK-47 assault rifles, Uzis, rocket-propelled grenades, a small number of light anti-tank weapons and C4 explosives. The improved weaponry is unevenly distributed across the *clicas*: the groups that transport cocaine or control local distribution have the financial resources to purchase higher-grade weapons, while others do not. The MS-13 also conducted experiments with improvised explosive devices and car bombs in 2018, though on a limited basis.

The MS-13's primary objective is to undermine the state's control of the country. In 2018, it was estimated that the gang was active in some 205 of the nation's 262 municipalities. This figure will probably grow as the MS-13 implements a rural-expansion strategy, broadening out from its urban strongholds to control drug-transport routes and other illicit highways. The gang also has a rudimentary political arm used to finance the municipal campaigns of members or sympathisers. This effort first came to light in the 2014 electoral cycle and became more operational and widespread in 2018.

National Civil Police (PNC)

The National Civil Police (PNC), created in 1992, maintains approximately 17,500 members under the Ministry for Public Security. The armed forces, numbering 24,500, are primarily responsible for external threats but assume some responsibility in combatting gangs and organised crime with the aim of reinstating a strong state authority over areas with gang domination.[6] The security forces tasked with countering the MS-13 are three anti-gang units comprised of approximately 600 special-forces personnel and 600 PNC officers. These specialised units use helicopters, armoured cars and assault rifles, compensating for the PNC's lack of heavy weapons. Specifically, anti-gang units are tasked with targeting the non-incarcerated MS-13 leadership to restrict the communications capacity and capabilities of the prison leadership.

Drivers

Gang violence, rampant corruption and economic stagnation are the primary drivers of the conflict in El Salvador, along with widespread impunity, which undermines the legitimacy of the state. El

Salvador is among the countries with the highest levels of impunity in the world, with an estimated 95% of murders going unpunished, which is significant in a country with one of the highest homicide rates in the world.[7]

National security policy

An immediate cause of rising violence is the government's pursuit of more draconian measures. In 2017, the Salvadoran government extended the 'extraordinary measures' for holding gang members in prison, including prolonged isolation in detention, suspension of hearings and visitation, lack of access to telephones or any communications with the outside world and mixing of gang members from different gangs in the same prisons. In February 2018, the United Nations declared these measures a violation of human rights, but the government has maintained them largely due to the population's demands to reduce violence. The degree of the measures' application varied – depending on external circumstances and the political necessity of each side – but overall the measures infuriate the imprisoned gang leadership.

Porous borders

In the regional context, the porous Central American borders offer enormous advantages for the MS-13's survival and growth. The MS-13 is not constrained by borders, while state authorities are. This limitation on state control is exacerbated by a lack of functional multi-state cooperation efforts among the law-enforcement agencies and armed forces of El Salvador, Guatemala and Honduras. If an MS-13 member is threatened or in danger, the MS-13 can move this member to safe harbour in neighbouring Honduras or Guatemala, where the gang also maintains a significant presence. The MS-13 can also easily move money, weapons and drugs among the three countries with relative impunity at the same time as increasing revenue and sharing political and military lessons learned. This tendency accelerated in 2018 and provided the MS-13 a significant strategic advantage over both the state and rival gangs in controlling territory.

Returning Salvadoran nationals

The usually constant flow of deportations of Salvadoran nationals from the US (primarily for those individuals overstaying visas) has been increasing. In 2018, approximately 24,000 Salvadorans were deported back, although fewer than 20% of them had criminal records.[8] This process creates a two-pronged effect. Many recent deportees are unacquainted with their country of birth. Placed into an environment with limited job opportunities and almost non-existent community bonds, they become easy targets for extortion or forced recruitment by the MS-13. This dynamic in turn destabilises communities and forces more individuals to attempt to migrate again. Deportations also significantly reduce the amount of remittances sent back to family members in El Salvador, thus exacerbating an already bleak economic situation.

Political and Military Developments

MS-13 territorial expansion

As a result of its successes in fighting the state, the MS-13 is expanding its territorial control and bringing violence to previously non-violent regions. In particular, the gang's strategy of expansion to rural areas from its urban enclaves means expanding into traditional drug-trafficking routes, including El Salvador's Pacific coast or La Libertad and Ahuachapán. In 2018, the areas were the gang sought to expand were also some of the most violent.

Political participation and negotiations

While not as mature as similar efforts by the MS-13 in Honduras, the MS-13's political pay-to-play activity in El Salvador grew significantly in 2018. Making use of its growing financial resources, the MS-13 financed and supported candidates running in municipal elections across the political spectrum.

In response, the state cracked down on politicians affiliated with the MS-13, arresting several government officials in 2018. In April 2018, the major of the municipality Concepción Batres was detained after allegedly taking bribes and paying the MS-13 in exchange for votes. The arrest and conviction of Raúl Mijango – a key negotiator of the 2012 gang truce and trusted interlocutor of the MS-13 – in October 2018 was viewed by the gang as a sign that

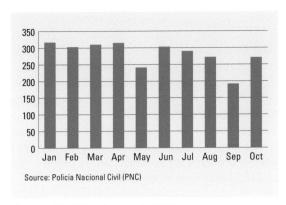

Source: Policia Nacional Civil (PNC)

Figure 1: Homicides by month, 2018

the state was after the gang's political allies, significantly limiting the possibility of further broad negotiations.

Still, the MS-13 did negotiate with the government (albeit in a clandestine manner) in 2018, as attested by spikes in killings (visible as a rise in bodies on the streets) when the gang was pressuring for concessions. The violence dropped sharply when the gang's demands were met.[9] On its part, the government was anxious to demonstrate control over gang violence and negotiated with the gang to cease the killings in exchange for improved prison conditions for the gang's leadership. Such shifting crime rates demonstrated the control that the MS-13 maintains. The sharp drop in homicides from March to May (see **Figure 1**), for example, coincided with negotiations with the major political parties immediately prior to and after the 19 March legislative and municipal elections as all sides sought gang votes. The sharp drop from July to August coincided with El Salvador's negotiations to open diplomatic relations with China.

Erosion of government legitimacy

In 2018, the gangs in general, and the MS-13 in particular, created both the perception and reality that they were an effective parallel government, especially as confidence in El Salvador's security forces remained low. Rogue elements of the National Civil Police (PNC) and the security forces have been accused of (and in some cases charged with) carrying out extrajudicial executions of suspected gang members. In a 2017 survey by the Institute of Public Opinion (IUDOP), 60% of respondents believed that

some or all of the PNC used excessive force.[10] The state, having lost the monopoly on the use of force, is viewed as having abandoned the population or being too incompetent and corrupt to combat the gang. In some cases, when MS-13 territorial control ensures a drop in violence and insecurity, the gang is perceived as the legitimate governing force and is often trusted more than the police.

Further diminishing trust in public institutions, security forces also frequently work with the MS-13. In 2018 alone, the Salvadoran Ministry of Defence removed at least 23 members of the security forces with ties to the gangs.[11]

MS-13's internal tension

The MS-13 displayed signs of internal tension in 2018. A dissenting *ranfla libre* faction, known as the MS-13 503, challenged the MS-13's internal cohesiveness for the first time. The challenge was relatively short-lived as the historic leadership of the MS-13 in prison, fearing a full-scale split, quickly reasserted control. The showdown culminated in the assassination of the faction's leader, Carlos Humberto Rodríguez Burgos (also known as 'Shyboy'), in Mexico City in March 2018 – reportedly by the Mexican transnational criminal organisation, the Sinaloa Cartel – further demonstrating the MS-13's transnational reach. The MS-13 503 faction appeared to have dissolved after Burgos's death, but the possibility of internal splits remains.

MS-13's reduced online visibility

While the reach of the MS-13 grew in 2018, there is one major area where Salvadoran security forces limited the gang's presence. In 2017, the MS-13 released a series of videos on YouTube and other online media issuing threats to the government and rival gangs alike. Members also bragged about attacks and denounced what they called police abuses of the MS-13's human rights. The videos were far less frequent in 2018, in part because its members appearing in the videos became easily identifiable targets. The anti-gang units also reported significant success in 2018, more than in previous years, in targeting the leadership of the MS-13, thanks to improved intelligence and electronic monitoring of gang communications via mobile phones and walkie-talkie channels.

Americas

Violent Events

In 2018, the homicide rate in El Salvador was 48 people per 100,000 (or 3,340 total homicides) – approximately a 10% decrease from 2017, though such figures are not necessarily indicative of an improving security situation.[12] Forced disappearances increased in 2018, with 3,015 reported cases, suggesting that violent crimes, and specifically homicides, were not decreasing but simply being carried out in more clandestine ways. The gang used the same tactic as during the 2012–14 truce, making the homicides appear to drop sharply when in fact the rate remained relatively constant. During that time, rather than throwing bodies on the street, the gang buried victims in clandestine cemeteries, thus keeping them out of public view and making them difficult to count in official statistics.

Homicide spike in gang-affected areas

Homicide rates are not distributed evenly across El Salvador. In 2018, the departments with the highest homicide rates per 100,000 inhabitants included La Paz (59.4), Usulután (55.7), San Miguel (55.2) and San Salvador (54.4).[13] San Miguel and Usulután are located along the key maritime cocaine-transportation route. The MS-13 is seeking to expand its territorial control there in order to enter the drug-transport business and thus comes into conflict with local drug gangs. La Paz is a key transit point for human trafficking and drug flows, and is also a high-conflict area due to violence over territorial control. San Salvador is the political and economic capital of the country, where the MS-13 has operated the longest and where it has waged its fight against other gangs most effectively. While homicides rates differed among departments, such figures only represent murders reported to officials. Though not all homicides are committed by gang members, the majority are. Homicides are reported at higher rates than other crimes such as extortion or rape, and can therefore give a better sense of the gang's violent activities – even if not all homicides are linked to the conflict between the MS-13 and the state.

State crimes

The PNC's interaction with the Salvadoran population, both in and around areas of gang control, is limited to armed incursions in affected neighbourhoods to arrest specific gang members or disrupt particular gang activities. During surge operations where the PNC or special anti-gang units stay in a neighbourhood for a day or more, civilians report an increase in crimes committed against residents.

According to data provided by the PNC, in 2017 there were 251 reports of crimes committed by the PNC and an additional 65 reports against the Salvadoran armed forces. Between January and June 2018, citizens reported an additional 73 crimes – including extrajudicial executions and robberies – committed by PNC officers. As most Salvadoran residents do not report crimes to the police, these numbers probably only represent a fraction of the total and residents are even less likely to report a crime to the police if the police committed the crime. The crippled judicial system in El Salvador almost ensures that these incidents are seldom investigated through formal channels.

Impact

A climate of fear

According to the 2017 IUDOP survey, 80.7% of the respondents felt that the government was of little or no benefit to Salvadoran residents.[14] This lack of confidence means that those affected by crime rarely report it and the number of victims is impossible to accurately ascertain. Additionally, internal displacement and relocations by civilians out of gang-controlled territories often occur in the middle of the night to avoid reprisals, and are therefore not registered. Victims of sexual violence and forced recruitment either join the gang, remain silent or migrate. The violence thus largely remains in the shadows, with no viable options for victims to seek redress or justice.

Gang members use violence, or the threat of violence, to maintain control over neighbourhoods and sometimes entire municipalities. In areas of MS-13 control, the civilian population is constantly navigating between forces which they feel neither loyalty to nor protected by. In this environment, the gangs operate through a strong show of force and intolerance for disobedience or perceived signs of disrespect. The MS-13 is ruthless in imposing its rules for local behaviour, which extend to what shoes people can own, the types of clothes they can wear and what products they can consume, buy or sell (such as Coca Cola versus Pepsi).[15]

Threats and violent acts manifest in several different ways. In El Salvador, small-business owners or lower- and middle-class residences are the main victims of extortion. Women and girls frequently experience gendered and family violence, including gang rapes and sex slavery for the gangs. Boys and young men are often forcibly recruited. Assaults and homicides are frequent across the demographic spectrum, especially for individuals who do not pay extortion fees.

Mass displacement

The gang's structural reliance on violence as the primary instrument of social control is a main driver of both internal and external migration. While MS-13 territorial control often brings a drop in homicides, the gang usually remains a predatory force in the community and brings other types of violence that drive people to leave. In some instances, family members left after children in middle school and high school were forcibly recruited by the MS-13. In other instances, women and children fled after becoming victims of sexual abuse. Often, owners of small community businesses escape when they can no longer pay fees.

In 2017, there were some 296,000 internally displaced persons, or 4.6% of the population. This number was likely much higher at the end of 2018. Interviews with human-rights-monitoring groups conducted between May and August 2018 in the

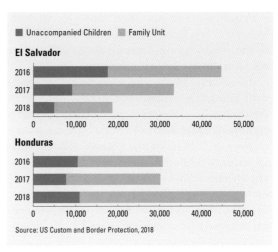

Figure 2: Migrants apprehended at US southern border, 2006–18

three main Salvadoran cities indicated that the phenomenon of people abandoning their homes due to gang occupation and human-rights abuses grew significantly in 2018. Additionally, more than 49,000 Salvadoran migrants were apprehended along the southern US border in fiscal year 2017.[16] For fiscal year 2018, approximately 5,000 unaccompanied children and 14,000 family units from El Salvador arrived at the southern US border (see **Figure 2**).[17]

Economic impact

The conflict has suppressed both foreign and domestic investment and job creation in key economic sectors such as tourism, complicating an already dire situation. The MS-13's increasing willingness to invest resources in the electoral process will likely further undermine the local and national body politic.

Trends

MS-13 influence in 2019 elections

By the end of 2018, the conflict in El Salvador had worsened, with both sides increasing their combat capabilities but neither with the ability to win decisively. The likelihood of negotiations between the government and the MS-13 is limited.

Informal negotiations, usually denied by the government, will likely increase in the run-up to the February 2019 presidential elections. If the trends observed in the past two electoral cycles continue, all

major political parties will negotiate with the gang to buy their votes as a bloc in this election as well.

Further expansion of the MS-13

The MS-13 will continue to pursue more territorial control and revenues. The most likely areas of geographical expansion are the Pacific coast – where the maritime drug-trafficking networks operate – and the northern corridor from Morazán to the Guatemalan border – where the land routes for transporting cocaine run. These routes service both the external and internal markets for crack cocaine, cocaine, marijuana and a more potent and lucrative form of marijuana known as 'krispy'.

If the MS-13 is successful in displacing the traditional, locally based transportation networks – some with deep political ties to the major political parties – that move cocaine, weapons and humans, the gang's revenues will significantly expand. While previous expansion efforts failed, the group's military capacity and sophistication have grown. Enhanced revenues will allow the MS-13 to continue purchasing better weapons, hire additional military trainers and improve their communications by using more secure technologies.

Chinese security aid

The PNC is unlikely to receive more resources and funding in the near term, particularly given the growing strains with the US government – the main provider of security funding and training. However, El Salvador's diplomatic recognition of

China – and China's willingness to supply weapons and training – could have a significant impact on the conflict, conditional on the winner of the 2019 presidential elections and the new president's attitude towards China and the MS-13. China has already demanded that areas of potential Chinese investment in El Salvador – largely along the Pacific coast and surrounding areas where a Special Economic Zone is proposed under the current government – be cleared of gang activity before the investments take place, thus providing a strong incentive for a major offensive by the government.

Deepening humanitarian crisis

While migrant caravans have, for years, characterised Central American migration to the US, such a migration tactic will likely increase. This migration, coupled with the increasing deportation of Salvadorans living in the US, will only complicate an already difficult situation in El Salvador and deepen the humanitarian crisis and consequences of gang violence.

Notes

[1]   Interview with US Drug Enforcement Administration agents and National Civil Police (PNC) gang specialists, September 2018. This report also draws upon interviews with MS-13 members and Salvadoran gang experts between March and June 2018.

[2]   Francisco Hernández, 'Histórico decomiso de cocaína durante 2018', *La Prensa Gráfica*, 17 November 2018.

[3]   For each bus that the MS-13 owns or controls, they also control the route and receive the transportation money that accompanies that route. As transportation costs are conducted in cash, the acquisition of the buses and routes is useful for money laundering.

[4]   Douglas Farah and Pamela Phillips Lum, 'Central American Gangs and Transnational Criminal Organizations', *International Assessment and Strategy Center*, February 2013.

[5]   Higher estimates include gang members who serve as paid lookouts, messengers and retail crack and cocaine vendors. The lower estimates include only full-fledged members, or *hommies* (less than one-third of the total).

[6]   IISS, *The Military Balance 2018* (Abingdon: Routledge for the IISS, 2018), p. 406.

[7]   Christine Wade, 'El Salvador's Legacy of Impunity Hampers Its Ongoing Fight Against Corruption', *World Press Review*, 12 July 2018.

[8]   Acan-Efe, '4,645 salvadoreños deportados en 2018 poseen antecedentes penales', *La Prensa Gráfica*, 23 November 2018.

[9]   Reports of the negotiations between the MS-13 leadership and the government first came from the dissident MS-13 503

leadership in a series of YouTube videos released at the end of 2017 and early 2018, who denounced the talks as treason. Oscar Iraheta, 'Mareros de la MS-503 denuncian que las MS y el Gobierno negocian tregua''', *Diario de Hoy*, 4 December 2017.

[10]   'Los Salvadoreños evalúan el tercer año de Gobierno de Salvador Sánchez Cerén', Instituto Universitario de Opinión Pública, 2017.

[11]   Francisco Hernández, 'Ejército separó a 638 militares por vínculos con pandillas desde 2010', *La Prensa Gráfica*, 29 November 2018.

[12]   Francisco Hernández and Edwin Segura, 'La Paz, el Departamento más violento de 2018', *La Prensa Gráfica*, 7 January 2019.

[13]   Homicide rates are indicated by homicides per 100,000 as reported to El Salvador's National Police (PNC). These figures represent public data from the PNC for registered homicides in 2017.

[14]   'Los Salvadoreños evalúan el tercer año', Instituto Universitario de Opinión Pública.

[15]   Types of shoes, such as blue Nikes, can signal loyalty to a rival gang. Food and sodas may be banned if a company does not pay the necessary 'toll' to transit and sell their goods in the gang territory.

[16]   'U.S. Border Patrol Nationwide Apprehensions by Citizenship and Sector in FY2017', FOIA request to US Customs and Border Protection, 2017.

[17]   'U.S. Border Patrol Southwest Border Apprehensions by Sector FY2018', US Customs and Border Protection, 2018.

Honduras

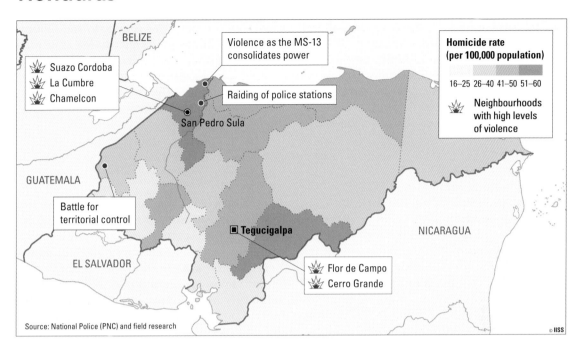

Source: National Police (PNC) and field research

© IISS

Overview

The conflict in 2018

The Honduras branch of the Mara Salvatrucha (MS-13) transnational gang significantly expanded its territorial control in 2018, particularly around the city of San Pedro Sula and throughout the nearby Atlantic coastal regions. With the help of former police officers, who provided the gang with training and leadership, the MS-13 evolved into a major player in the regional cocaine-transportation business while consolidating its hold on the internal crack, cocaine, marijuana and 'krispy' (a marijuana derivative) markets.[1]

The expansion of the MS-13 led to one of the gang's most recent and innovative changes – the decision to halt its policy of extorting local businesses and individuals in communities under gang control. Instead, the MS-13 increased its other criminal activities, including money-laundering operations through the purchase of small hotels.[2] The limiting of small-scale extortion allowed the MS-13 to generate greater social acceptance and political capital, while more revenues allowed the gang to purchase new weapons, acquire enhanced military training and improve its security and communications protocols. A decrease in homicides

rates seems to coincide with the internal restructuring that the MS-13 is undergoing in Honduras, rather than necessarily indicating security forces' success against the gang's control.

The conflict to 2018

The MS-13 began operations in Honduras and the rest of Central America in the mid-1990s following the mass deportation of gang members from California. Until recently, the gang's Honduran branch had few ties to significant drug-trafficking operations, little political acumen, relatively stable territorial divisions and no discernible military strategy. Since 2016, however, the Honduran MS-13

Key statistics	
Type:	Internal
IDPs total (2017):	200,000
IDPs new (2018):	no data
Refugees total (2018):	not applicable
Refugees new (2018):	not applicable
People in need (2018):	not applicable

has become the most innovative and successful of the MS-13 branches in the region, developing significantly more sophisticated political and military structures than other regional affiliates. While the Salvadoran branch of the MS-13 is gaining territory and acquiring more sophisticated weapons, the MS-13 in Honduras is not only developing militarily but also using its increased control to engage in direct political participation. This new political confidence is due in part to the gang's recruitment of highly trained police officers expelled from of the national police force over corruption and human-rights abuses. These officers enter the MS-13 with the rank of *palabrero* (a local leader) and provide high-level tactical and strategic planning and weapons training to the gang.[3] This is a significant shift from the gang's traditional practices.

Forces

The two primary forces in Honduras are the MS-13 gang and the Honduran state. Barrio 18 holds some territory in the capital Tegucigalpa, but the MS-13 has largely eliminated it in the rest of the country. Smaller groups – such as Los Chirizos and Los Ponce – continue to operate locally, but have been pushed to the margins of the conflict.

The Mara Salvatrucha (MS-13)

The Mara Salvatrucha (MS-13) both enhanced its military capabilities and expanded its size and territorial control in 2018. Field interviews indicate that recruits are seeking to join the MS-13 in such numbers that many are turned away or made to wait for several months before beginning initiation. Estimates of gang-member participation range from 6,000 to 36,000. The variation in these estimates arises from differences in participation definitions, including level of involvement in the gang and active versus inactive participants, such as lookouts.[4]

The MS-13 reorganised in two important ways in 2018. Firstly, the gang began operating in a less centralised manner, while maintaining its traditional hierarchical structure. The *ranfla nacional* (national leadership) make collective decisions for the organisation as a whole, which are then passed to local leaders (heads of *programas* and *clicas*). Each *clica* is made up of between 15 and 30 members that operate within one neighbourhood, as is the case in El Salvador. However, with the compartmentalisation of the command-and-control structure over 2018, local members now operate with greater flexibility and adaptability with less risk of exposure for the leadership. They can exchange lessons learned among different neighbourhood structures.

Secondly, the gang has professionalised its lower-level members to improve working conditions. Traditionally, the *chistas* and *banderas* – the two types of lookouts that fall to the youngest people aspiring to join the gang – were given one meal a day and some marijuana to smoke, and could be left on duty for days at a time. The new structure pays the lowest-ranking members about US$150 a month, in addition to fixed schedules, free time, allotments of 'vacation days' (with the permission of the *jefe de clica*) and two marijuana joints a day when on duty. These adjustments have resulted in more formal field units. The MS-13 has also instituted strict communications protocols to enhance the gang's ability to share information between members on a need-to-know basis only.

The MS-13's primary objective is to gain control of key cocaine-trafficking and human-smuggling routes, to dominate the local drug-retail business and to create a parallel state with increasingly sophisticated political participation. To achieve these goals, the gang focused on upgrading its weapons from handguns and outdated AK-47s and M-16s to newer, more sophisticated weapons, including new AR-15 and AK-47 assault rifles, Dragunov sniper rifles, light anti-tank weapons and Uzi pistols and submachine guns for urban combat. The MS-13 also increasingly uses commercially purchased drones to carry out surveillance on police patrols and rival gangs in and around San Pedro Sula.

State forces

The Honduran state maintains a combined armed force of 14,950 members, including army (7,300), navy (1,350) and air force (2,300). Despite continuous upgrades, Honduran military equipment remains old and unreliable. The civilian police force consists of approximately 8,000 members,[5] but is among the most corrupt in the hemisphere. In 2012 surveys by the United Nations Development Programme (UNDP) and the Latin American Public Opinion Project (LAPOP), the Honduran police ranked as the worst both in terms of the perception of the police participating in crimes and in citizens' trust.[6] In recent years, at least 2,500 members of the police have been expelled from the force for corruption and human-rights abuses.[7] Despite ongoing attempts to professionalise the police force, there have been few signs of improvement.

In an attempt to mitigate these challenges, the government created a hybrid force, known as the Military Police for Public Order (PMOP), with about 4,000 members, under the direct control of the executive branch.[8] The PMOP is the lead organisation in combatting the MS-13 and is specifically tasked with eliminating gang leadership, re-establishing state control over contested or gang-controlled territory and ensuring citizen security. This unit operates in coordination with the police and under the anti-crime task force known as FUSINA, but the effort has largely failed. The PMOP has experienced several corruption scandals, and numerous senior officials were arrested for being on the payroll of the MS-13.

To address the transnational facets of the MS-13, in 2015 Honduras and Guatemala established the joint inter-agency Maya-Chortí Task Force on the Honduras–Guatemala border, tasked with coordinating the increasingly overlapping counter-narcotics and anti-gang efforts across the Northern Triangle (El Salvador, Guatemala and Honduras). Funded by the United States, this 1,500-strong task force combines police, military and intelligence units and prosecutors to attack drug trafficking and gang operations, but in reality the unit faces numerous challenges. The task force has scarcely any functioning equipment, little operational capacity and no communications with its inter-agency partners in neighbouring countries.

| Drivers

The conflict's root causes lie endemic poverty, corruption and political disenfranchisement, further complicated by impunity, which is the norm for the crimes that Honduras's weak judicial system attempts to prosecute.[9] These factors, combined with an overall weak state capacity and the electoral crises of 2006, 2013 and 2017, led to a legitimacy crisis of democratic institutions.[10] Only 20% of the respondents to the 2017 Latinobarómetro indicated that they had confidence in the Honduran electoral institutions.[11] Honduran residents are caught between an ineffective state and a violent – though increasingly less brutal – gang, without alternative options. Electoral controversy and political corruption continue to strengthen the MS-13 both politically and militarily as the group establishes itself as an effective political counterpart to the Hernández administration.

Poverty
Poverty and lack of economic opportunities continue to drive the conflict. In 2016, approximately 60% of the population in Honduras lived in poverty, while in rural areas approximately 20% lived in extreme poverty.[12] Around 74% of Hondurans work in the informal economy, without security or benefits.[13] The failure of the state to provide legal and stable job opportunities or economic growth exacerbates the conflict. As jobs become increasingly scarce in rural areas, people, particularly youth, move to urban areas, where they encounter the MS-13 for the first time. Internal migrants are more easily targeted and extorted given their lack of ties to the community. In many cases, and for young men specifically, working with the MS-13 is one of the few viable employment and career options.

Corruption and impunity
High levels of corruption and impunity are key drivers of the conflict. Increasingly, high-profile corruption cases fail to result in sentences, while lower-level cases are often not fully investigated. In December 2015, the Inter-American Commission on Human Rights reported that the impunity rate in Honduras is between 95% and 98%.[14] At least 130 attorneys were murdered between 2010 and 2018, while many more have received death threats while attempting to prosecute cases.[15] At least 60 Honduran journalists were killed during the same time period.[16]

Electoral crises

The recurrence of electoral crises eroding the state's political legitimacy also fuel the conflict. Disputed results in 2006 and a *coup d'état* in 2009 preceded fraudulent results in 2013. The electoral process has therefore been widely discredited. Another electoral crisis and controversy enveloped Honduran President Juan Orlando Hernández's victory in the November 2017 presidential elections – likely the result of significant fraud – further delegitimising both the state and the current administration and enhancing the attractiveness of the MS-13 as an alternative governance structure. In November 2018, Hernández's brother – who exercised significant influence with the president – was arrested in Miami on charges of international drug trafficking, providing further evidence of the Hernández family's involvement in illicit activities.

Disputed borders

At the regional level, the MS-13's efforts to control key informal border-crossing points has fuelled the conflict. The gang's expansion in 2018 was aimed at gaining control of key routes for the transit of illicit products (from cocaine to weapons and migrants) on the southern border with Nicaragua and the northern and western borders with Guatemala and El Salvador. The strategy necessitated the forcible eviction of either the state or other armed groups from those crucial nodes, which led to a sharp rise in violence in all three border regions. This violence further displaced residents, exacerbating already difficult economic and security conditions, particularly for those living along the Atlantic coastal region.

Political and Military Developments

Increased engagement with politics

Under the tutelage of former police officers and populist political leaders, the MS-13 continued to engage in both political participation and targeted attacks against security forces in 2018, making the gang a more viable political actor. In late 2017, the MS-13 – for the first time in its history – actively engaged against the police in support of the left-wing political party (Libre) as the party protested against the results of the presidential election. As the votes were being counted, vote tallies gave the coalition opposition leader, Salvador Nasralla, a significant lead until a sudden blackout stopped the count; when the blackout ended hours later, Hernández emerged with a significant lead. Amid fraud accusations by the international community, the populist left-wing coalition backing Nasralla paid the MS-13 to take to the streets. The gang subsequently manned barricades across San Pedro Sula and other commercial centres; burned and looted police stations; captured hundreds of police weapons and significant amounts of police anti-riot gear; and directed the burning and looting of tractor-trailer trucks, highway toll-houses and businesses.

Increased engagement with society

In parallel to its direct involvement in political violence, the MS-13 paid significant attention to building a larger social base in Honduran communities, particularly around San Pedro Sula and the Atlantic coast. Since 2016, the MS-13 has increasingly offered social services to local residents, including providing work programmes for single mothers on a limited basis (primarily by providing equipment to sew garments at home); instituting weekly neighbourhood courts where the local MS-13 leader rules on grievances (such as theft, spousal abuse and the unsanctioned sale of drugs); and reducing the abuse of non-gang members in MS-13-controlled areas (including forced recruitment and systematic rape). The gang has also halted the practice of small-business extortion.

To bring about needed changes in gang-member behaviour, the gang leadership issued new guidelines that instructed members to refrain from rape, to pay for food rather than demand it for free from local merchants, to greet the elderly with respect and to ban the use of alcohol or drugs while on duty. Those that violate the new rules are first beaten, then executed if they continue to disobey. As a consequence of such measures, the MS-13 is now referred to as 'La Mara Buena' ('The Good Gang') in the northeastern region of Honduras. Although the MS-13 has attempted to rebrand itself as 'La Gran Familia' ('The Big Family') – i.e., not a gang at all – La Mara Buena still represents a significant psychological victory, as it is supposed that the gang's 'goodness' stands in contrast not only to other gangs but also to the government.

Expansion of MS-13 control

The MS-13's constant and ongoing quest for expansion prioritises the geographic spaces vital to the movement of illicit products as well as areas of political clout. While control of key areas has traditionally shifted from gang to gang, in 2018 the shifts went almost entirely in favour of the MS-13. The gang's effort to expand its drug-transportation business was also aided by the arrests and extraditions of many rival gang leaders by the United States Drug Enforcement Administration (DEA). Between 2013 and 2017, the DEA arrested and extradited the leaders of the Cachiros, Valle Valle, the Rosenthals and Atlantic drug-trafficking organisations, allowing the MS-13 to move into the territories controlled by those groups.

In 2018, the MS-13 focused on gaining control of the city of San Pedro Sula and the overland corridor to Puerto Cortés in the Atlantic coastal region, a key zone for drug trafficking and human smuggling. The gang also focused on expanding its control of territory from Puerto Cortés along the coastal region to Omoa Beach, a key transit route for illicit products to Guatemala and Belize. To a lesser degree, the MS-13 also expanded its presence at the informal crossing on the Nicaragua border, an historically strategic route for weapons smuggling, which explains the MS-13's possession of upgraded military weapons. By controlling the territory along most international borders as well as the coast, the MS-13 is now capable of moving larger (several-hundred-kilo loads) of cocaine and operating beyond its traditional urban bases.

The Honduran branch of the MS-13 also continued to expand – though still in a limited capacity – into Belize and Mexico and might soon enter into new conflicts with Belizean gangs, Mexican drug-trafficking organisations and more local drug-dealing gangs.

Violent Events

Rather than fixed and predictable combat fronts, violent events in 2018 in Honduras were largely single-victim homicides or assassinations of three or four people over broad swathes of the country. In the first nine months of 2018, there were 34 instances of assassinations of three or more people, almost all of them in the San Pedro Sula region and along the Honduras–Guatemala border. This figure does not include the many unreported killings by gangs, police and criminal groups where the victims are dismembered and clandestinely buried or dumped in rivers. This widespread, seemingly unpredictable violence creates an atmosphere of uncertainty and instability over broad areas. This contributes to the sense that the MS-13 provides security in areas under gang control, while areas where control is contested are subject to violence.

The more social facet of the MS-13 in Honduras has resulted in the continued decrease of the homicide rate in the country. In 2018, the homicide rate was approximately 42 deaths per 100,000 residents.[17] By contrast, in 2011 it was approximately 85 deaths per 100,000 residents – among the highest in the world.[18] A drop in homicides, however, does not indicate an improved security situation. In the areas of MS-13 control, the rates of homicides and other violent crimes often drop because the gang has achieved its objectives and no longer needs to kill to occupy the territory.

Violence in Choloma

The largest sustained violent event in 2018 occurred in January in the Choloma district of San Pedro Sula – the economic heart of Honduras – and was a continuation of the electoral violence following the November 2017 presidential elections. Sustained hit-and-run fighting took place across shifting street barricades as the MS-13 outfought police forces and held territory until March. The violence culminated with the gang burning and looting dozens of tractor-trailer trucks and firebombing of toll booths along major highways, but declined in frequency after January.

Violence also spiked during June and July when a significant number of multiple assassinations occurred, related to territorial control and the drug trade. On 17 June, four individuals died in Choloma during a battle between the police and the MS-13 as the police tried to take a safe house suspected of being a cocaine repository. On 16 July, four gang members died in a surprise attack by the MS-13 on a Barrio 18 safe house in San Pedro Sula. Finally, on

31 July, four individuals died in La Entrada, Copán (along the Guatemala border), when the MS-13 and a local drug-trafficking organisation fought a battle over control of the nearby border crossing.

Impact

Weakening of state legitimacy

The state lost significant legitimacy in 2018. The contested electoral results followed by corruption scandals polarised politics and fuelled feelings of despair among the population. The electoral violence highlighted the inability of the state to hold even their own fortified positions and its inability to protect civilians from widespread looting and destruction. The overarching success of these attacks demonstrated the power of the MS-13 in driving politics (including the financing of favoured candidates in municipal and regional elections). Now able to offer social services – however rudimentary – the MS-13 continues to build a solid social base. Through these efforts, the group is becoming a viable alternative to the state, often with more legitimacy than the formal government. According to Latinobarámetro, only 18% of Hondurans were satisfied with their government in 2017.[19] In some cases, and in particular with young men, this dissatisfaction led to more people attempting to join the MS-13.

The success in limiting the violence from spreading widely throughout the country was likely just the result of the MS-13's decision to become a more social and political organisation rather than simply one of brute, violent force. The state eventually forced the retreat of the MS-13 from the streets in San Pedro Sula and defused the immediate threat to the Hernández presidency. In Tegucigalpa, the violence and demonstrations remained limited, police and military presence were high, and the rival Barrio 18 gang maintained a significant presence that counterbalanced the MS-13. The Honduran state was also successful in keeping the media away from the events taking place in San Pedro Sula, which prevented a larger international backlash over the contested election results.

Climate of violence and fear

The expansion of the MS-13 in 2018 came with significant humanitarian implications and affected many local communities. While homicides were down overall, certain towns and neighbourhoods were completely ravaged by violence. The perception that the MS-13, rather than the state, is winning the conflict is a significant push factor in both internal displacement and outward migration. The Internal Displacement Monitoring Centre estimated that as of December 2017, approximately 190,000 Hondurans had been internally displaced (approximately 2% of the population). Honduras is the second-largest sending country to the US, behind only Guatemala. In 2018 fiscal year, US immigration officials apprehended 11,000 unaccompanied Honduran children and 40,000 family units at the US southwest border.[20]

Trends

The MS-13's territorial expansion

The MS-13 will likely maintain a stronghold over many of the illicit markets operating in Honduras and beyond, and continue to gain significant revenues from its almost complete domination of the growing internal drug market. In 2018, the MS-13 demonstrated an increasing sophistication and participation in transporting cocaine, 'krispy' and migrants. It only needs to be moderately successful in any of these endeavours to be able to buy more and better weapons, increase its military training and technological capacities, and expand its nascent social-services efforts.

If the gang can successfully establish permanent footholds in key transportation nodes along the Honduran coast and into Mexico and Belize, it could evolve into a truly transnational drug-trafficking organisation. Whether the MS-13 can compete with other hemispheric actors remains to be seen. The main obstacle to its continued expansion will likely come from other criminal groups from Brazil, Colombia and Mexico, which are now establishing beachheads on the Atlantic coast of Honduras. So far, these groups have negotiated the movement of loads of cocaine with the MS-13, but such arrangements tend to be short-lived and often end in violence. A second obstacle will be the state. Given that the MS-13 maintains significant control of the northeastern region of the country, any effort by the state to dislodge the group would come at a high military cost for residents and a significant territorial cost for the MS-13.

Erosion of trust in the state

The combination of more resources and restructured operations will likely increase the view by significant portions of the population that the MS-13 is the real power in the country, with more legitimacy than the government. This, in turn, will likely lead the MS-13 to attempt to create new methods of direct participation in the government, further eroding citizen trust and increasing corruption. Such political participation will likely occur across municipal, state and congressional elections. The gang has already demonstrated an ability to coerce, threaten and buy certain behaviours from the civilian population and such participation would only be an extension of these current efforts. As such, the MS-13 will have the ability to deliver important vote counts to whichever candidate it chooses to support.

Limited state capacity

Given the widespread perception that the Honduran government is no longer able to contain the growth of the MS-13 and the government's own corruption and weakness, the state is likely

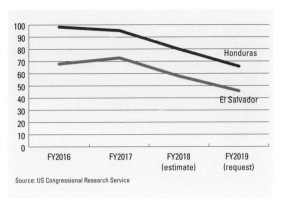

Source: US Congressional Research Service

Figure 1: US aid (US$m)

to implement a more hardline security policy over a part of the national territory. From a rule-of-law perspective, the Mission to Support the Fight Against Corruption and Impunity in Honduras (backed by the Organization of American States) has had some success in bringing corruption to light, though few prosecutions have followed, signalling that this instrument will fail to fully meet its mandate of countering corruption and strengthening institutions.

The growing tensions between the Hernández administration and the US administration over migration, the MS-13 expansion and the arrest of the Honduran president's brother all signal that the Honduran government will likely receive significantly less US aid in 2019 than in previous years (see **Figure 1**), limiting its options for improving equipment and training.

| Notes

[1] 'Krispy' is a marijuana derivative sold in blocks and laced with chemicals. It is favoured by criminal groups because it is more addictive and sells at much higher prices.

[2] Extortion remains an important source of gang revenue, but is now targeted at larger companies and businesses and individuals from outside gang-controlled communities (such as bus owners, natural-gas companies and drinking-water wholesalers).

[3] This report draws upon interviews with MS-13 members and elite police units in San Pedro Sula, Honduras, December 2018.

[4] Higher estimates include gang members who serve as paid lookouts, messengers and retail crack and cocaine vendors. The lower estimates do not include those who are not *hommies* (fully-fledged members). Less than one-third of gang members are *hommies*. See Elyssa Pachico, 'The Problem with

Counting Gang Members in Honduras', *InSight Crime*, 17 February 2017.

[5] IISS, *The Military Balance 2018* (Abingdon: Routledge for the IISS, 2018), pp. 410–11.

[6] Mimi Yagoub, 'From Chile to Mexico: Best and Worst of LatAm Police', *Insight Crime*, 20 March 2017.

[7] Felipe Puerta, 'Arrests of Honduras Police Reveal Setbacks in Purge', *Insight Crime*, 16 October 2018; 'Honduran Police Chief José David Aguilar Morán helped drug trafficker Wilter Blanco', *El Heraldo*, 1 January 2018.

[8] IISS, *The Military Balance 2018*, pp. 410–11.

[9] 'Violence, Inequality, and Impunity in Honduras: Situation of Human Rights in Honduras', Inter-American Commission on Human Rights (IAHCR), 2015.

[10] In 2006, the Venezuela-aligned Mel Zelaya won the presidential

elections and was forcibly removed from office in June 2009 in a military coup, plunging the nation into a prolonged political crisis; see Elisabeth Malkin, 'Honduran President is Ousted in Coup', *New York Times*, 28 June 2009. The following election cycle in 2013 was also marked by credible allegations of fraud. The losing candidate was Xiomara Castro, ex-president Zelaya's wife; Nick Miroff, 'Honduras election bring risks of more instability', *Washington Post*, 23 November 2013.

11 Corporación Latinobarómetro, 'Informe 2017', 2017.

12 'Honduras Overview', World Bank, 2018.

13 'Informal employment (% of total non-agricultural workers)', World Bank, 2018.

14 'Violence, Inequality, and Impunity in Honduras', IAHCR.

15 'Honduras: 151 abogados han sido asesinados entre 2002 y 2018', *La Prensa*, 7 August 2018.

16 'Periodistas asesinados en Honduras', Pasos de Animal Grande and Comisionado Nacional de los Derechos Humanos (CONADEH), 2017.

17 Héctor Estepa, 'Como el país más violento en el mundo ha reducido la cifra de homicidios a la mitad', *El Confidencial*, 13 November 2018.

18 'Intentional Homicides (per 100,000), Honduras', World Bank, 2018.

19 'Informe 2017'.

20 'U.S. Border Patrol Southwest Border Apprehensions by Sector FY2018', US Customs and Border Protection, 2018.

Mexico (Cartels)

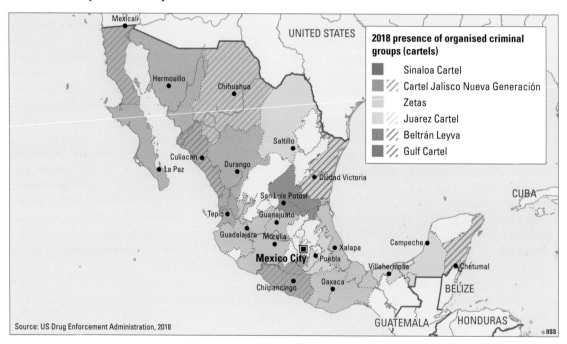

Source: US Drug Enforcement Administration, 2018

Overview

The conflict in 2018

In 2018, the armed conflict among the drug cartels and between them and the Mexican state continued to drive high levels of violence. In the campaign leading up to the presidential vote on 1 July 2018, the candidates openly discussed the security crisis in the country and proposed different strategies to address it. Militarisation was one suggested approach, accompanied by a proposal for an Interior Security Law in Congress that would legitimise the use of the armed forces for public-security tasks. The presidential candidate of the leftist Morena party, Andrés Manuel López Obrador (also known as 'AMLO'), who campaigned on a different security policy, including amnesty and truth commissions, won the election and took office in December.

The conflict to 2018

Historically, organised crime in Mexico has been linked to illegal drug trafficking, although the existence of illegal drug markets has not always been associated with violence. During the twentieth century, large drug-trafficking groups were in control of specific regions of the territory, and operated under a common Pax Mafiosi that limited violent contestation. The political party in office, the Institutional Revolutionary Party (PRI), had agreements and protection rackets in place with drug traffickers – especially the Sinaloa Cartel – in exchange for money and political favours. When the PRI lost local and national elections in 2000 after 70 years in office, these agreements were no longer valid and confrontations between the government and organised crime in Mexico emerged.

The opposition political party (the National Action Party – PAN) won both the elections in 2000 and 2006, led by Vicente Fox and Felipe Calderón respectively. Both administrations (but mainly the Calderón administration) designed security strategies based on attacking organised crime. The main pillar of security strategy since December 2006 has been the militarisation of public security by implementing several military operations in different regions of Mexico. This militarisation, accompanied by a decapitation strategy (where leaders of the criminal organisations were detained or subdued) fragmented the criminal groups. While four drug-trafficking organisations were active in the 1990s (the Gulf Cartel, the Tijuana Cartel, the Juárez

Key statistics	
Type:	Internal
IDPs total (2017):	345,000
IDPs new (2018):	no data
Refugees total (2018):	not applicable
Refugees new (2018):	not applicable
People in need (2018):	not applicable

Cartel and later the Sinaloa Cartel, which splintered from the Tijuana Cartel), at the end of the Calderón administration in 2011, there were more than 100 organisations (including armed wings, local bands and gunmen). This increase was accompanied by more violence (between and within groups, and towards the government) and human-rights violations.

The increasing violence is not solely due to the government's security strategies, which continued after Calderón left office and the PRI regained power with Enrique Peña Nieto in 2012. Several events also occurred at the international level that exacerbated the security situation in Mexico, including the closing of the Caribbean route used by Colombians to traffic cocaine to the US, the rise in drug consumption in the US and increasing gun trafficking from the US to Mexico.

Forces

Criminal groups in Mexico fight against each other and against the state to control strategic territories and drug routes. In 2018, the US Drug Enforcement Administration (DEA) identified six main criminal groups, each with several splinter or associated groups, operating in different territories.[1] The activities and violent tactics of these groups differ, depending on their financial capacities, but all had the capacity to fight the state using long-range weapons and military equipment such as rocket launchers, grenades, AK-47 and AR-15 rifles and Uzi machine guns, among others.

State forces
Mexico is divided into 12 military regions, all with a permanent army presence. In these regions, the armed forces have a remit to conduct activities

related to national security. The deployment of military personnel throughout the Mexican territory increased from 34,529 in 2013 to 52,807 in 2017. The military zones with the greatest number of personnel deployed were zone IV (Nuevo Leon, Tamaulipas and San Luis Potosi) and zone IX (Guerrero).[2]

The Mexican Marines in particular are heavily involved in operations against organised crime. According to the Navy Report of Accountability (2013–18),[3] the Marines participated in 101,991 operations against organised-crime groups from 2013 to 2017, mostly in 16 states (including Baja California, Guerrero, Jalisco, Michoacán, Colima, Sinaloa, Sonora, Tamaulipas and Veracruz).

The budget assigned to the army was MX$81 billion (US$4.3bn), expected to grow by 15.6% to MX$93.7bn (US$4.9bn) in 2019, while the budget for the navy was reduced by 5.5%, from MX$31.3bn (US$1.6bn) to MX$29.6bn (US$1.5bn).[4] The extra funding for the army in 2019 will be used for the National Guard (to be put under army command) and would be generated by its participation in several activities (including real estate, the building of the new Mexico City airport and managing the road transportation of gasoline). However, Mexico is still investing less in national defence compared to other countries. According to the Stockholm International Peace Research Institute (SIPRI), Mexico invested only 0.58% of its GDP in national defence, while average global military expenditure in 2016 was 2.2% of GDP.[5]

Sinaloa Cartel

The Sinaloa Cartel has been active since 1994 and was one of the strongest criminal organisations in the country until its leader, Guzmán Loera, better known as 'El Chapo', was captured in 2016 (after two spectacular prison escapes, in 2001 and 2014). The cartel's main activity is trafficking drugs from Mexico to the US, including cocaine, methamphetamine, marijuana and heroin, through the checkpoints of El Paso and Tijuana. The DEA reports that the cartel, besides having a presence in several Mexican states, has international operations in 40 countries in South America, Central America and Africa. The Sinaloa Cartel has diversified its activities in recent years, although not as much as other cartels, to include extortion and illegal imports of minerals and other products from China, including synthetic opioids such as fentanyl. After El Chapo's arrest, his sons have tried to maintain leadership of the organisation, but clashed for control of the territory with the CJNG and a new organisation identified as the Baja California Cartel.[6] Ten criminal groups are associated with the Sinaloa Cartel, including armed wings (Gente Nueva, Los Ms), gunmen or operators (El Aquiles, El Ondeado), and locally operating bands (Artistas Asesinos, Los Mexicles, La Barredora, among others).[7]

Jalisco New Generation Cartel (CJNG)

The Jalisco New Generation Cartel (CJNG) operates in the centre and south of the country and on the Pacific coast.[8] Led by Nemesio Oseguera Cervantes, also known as 'El Mencho', the cartel has expanded significantly since it was created in 2011 after splintering from the Millennium Cartel. Its members formerly acted as an armed wing of the Sinaloa Cartel, when they were known as the 'Mata Zetas', or 'Killing Zetas'. The cartel clashes with the Sinaloa Cartel in Chihuahua, Jalisco and Baja California states; against the Gulf Cartel and Los Zetas in Tabasco, Veracruz and Guanajuato states; and against the Knights Templar in Guerrero State. Although its main activity is the international trafficking of illegal drugs (cocaine, heroin, methamphetamine and fentanyl), the CJNG has diversified its activities and engaged in the national commercialisation of illegal drugs, the extortion of local producers of fruits (avocados and lemons in Michoacán), and oil theft in Guanajuato, where it clashes frequently with a local band called Santa Rosa de Lima. The trafficking of illegal drugs to the US is conducted through the border cities of Tijuana, Ciudad Juárez and Nuevo Laredo, reaching drug-distribution hubs in Los Angeles, New York, Chicago and Atlanta.[9] In a YouTube video uploaded in July 2018, the cartel showed off its weaponry, including military vehicles, M82 rifles (known as 'killing police' rifles) and bulletproof vests. The group has used heavy weaponry in the past, shooting down an army helicopter in Jalisco State in 2015 with a rocket-propelled grenade, killing six soldiers.[10] Particularly gruesome tactics, including mass graves and disappearances of civilians, have gained them a reputation that allows them to control the population.[11]

Juárez Cartel

The Juárez Cartel was created in 1990 under the command of Amado Carrillo, who took advantage of agreements with public servants, from the municipal police and the armed forces, to traffic drugs to the US. Although the expansion of the cartel has not been significant (its operation is concentrated in Chihuahua State, mainly in Ciudad Juárez), it was one of the most violent cartels during the Calderón administration due to a turf war with the Sinaloa Cartel for the control of the city of Ciudad Juárez, one of the main drug-smuggling entry points to the US. Clashes with the Sinaloa Cartel, as well as the governmental development initiative 'Todos Somos Juarez' (We Are All Juarez) implemented from 2012 to 2013, weakened the cartel's capacity, although in 2018 it retained the ability to challenge the state and distribute drugs (marijuana and cocaine) to the US.[12] Two armed wings are associated with the Juárez Cartel (La Linea and Los Aztecas), although the cartel might have fragmented further in recent years.[13]

Gulf Cartel

The Gulf Cartel is one of Mexico's oldest criminal organisations, active since 1976. Its leadership has undergone many changes, and fragmentation has destabilised its internal structure, particularly the violent separation of Los Zetas in 2010. The cartel still controls some territories in Tamaulipas State used for trafficking heroin and methamphetamine to the US, although some are disputed with Los Zetas. The cartel has also diversified its activities to include extortion and kidnapping of migrants.[14]

Beltrán Leyva Organisation (BLO)

Although the Beltrán Leyva brothers worked as allies of the Sinaloa Cartel, they became independent in 2008 when they suspected that El Chapo had betrayed them when the authorities captured Alfredo Beltrán Leyva. According to the DEA, in 2018 the Beltrán Leyva Organisation (BLO) had a presence in Guerrero, Morelos, Nayarit and Sinaloa states, but there was no clarity about the number of criminal groups working for them. The cartel's main activity, in common with other criminal organisations in Mexico, is the distribution of illegal drugs to the US (with hubs in Los Angeles, Phoenix, Chicago and Atlanta) including marijuana, cocaine, heroin and methamphetamine. The activities of the BLO have been diminished because of internal fragmentations and the killing in 2017 of Juan Francisco Patrón, also known as 'H2', a high-ranking leader.

The main operations of the BLO in 2018 took place in Guerrero State through the trade of heroin by one of its subgroups, Los Guerreros Unidos.

Los Zetas

Los Zetas, formed in 2000 to provide protection for the Gulf Cartel, is comprised of former members of the Mexican armed forces. As an armed wing of the Gulf Cartel, it was responsible for territorial expansion, also across Mexico's southern border. After several leaders of the Gulf Cartel were arrested or killed, Los Zetas became independent in 2010, declaring that the Gulf Cartel was now its enemy.[15] Los Zetas has been the group with the greatest territorial expansion and diversification of activities, although in 2018 it lost control in several states. According to the DEA, Los Zetas has a presence in Campeche, Tabasco, Puebla, Quintana Roo, Coahuila and Tamaulipas states.[16] Contrary to other organised-crime groups, Los Zetas has not focused its activities on the drug business. Rather, it has developed an extractive business model including fuel theft, extortion, human trafficking and kidnapping. In 2017, the Atlantic Council suggested that Los Zetas was responsible for 40% of the stolen oil in Mexico.[17] The group's violent tactics include the use of narcomessages (messages left next to the executed bodies), or the posting of *narcomantas* (messages left in public places for everyone to see) to communicate with the government or civilians. Several massacres have been linked to the organisation, including the killing of 72 migrants in Tamaulipas State in 2011 and the firebombing of a casino in Monterrey that killed 53.

| Drivers

Corruption and institutional weaknesses

Corruption and weak governmental institutions have been constant drivers behind the growth of organised crime in Mexico. The weakness of police institutions is also the main reason the army has taken up public-security tasks in Mexico. According to the think tank México Evalúa, corruption, institutional weaknesses and impunity were prevalent not only in poorer states (such as Tamaulipas and Chiapas), but also in large cities such as Mexico City.[18]

At both the local and national levels, corruption networks are fed by impunity and money obtained

illegally. Corruption mostly takes place at the subnational level, where local police forces and attorney offices do not have the human or economic resources to fight organised crime. Mexico has more than 330,000 municipal police officers and 32 state police forces, but their salaries are lower than those of federal police. These disparities and the lack of institutional capacity and police training have allowed organised crime to influence and corrupt local governmental institutions by offering money or involving them in criminal activities. In 2014, 43 trainee teachers were kidnapped (in collaboration with the city major) by the municipal police of Iguala, Guerrero State, and handed to a criminal group. The disappearance of these 43 students reached the attention of the international media and, although the government has been under pressure to clarify the facts, the location of the students is still unknown.

In general, the state's response to combatting institutional weakness and corruption has been ineffective or lacking: the National Anti-Corruption System was created in 2015, but it has not been fully implemented; witness-protection programmes are not in place; and there are no consequences for public officers involved in corruption scandals.

Poverty

López Obrador attributes the violent situation in the country to poverty. According to a 2017 report prepared by the National Council for the Evaluation of Social Development Policies (CONEVAL), in December 2016, 43.6% of the Mexican population (53.4m people) lived in poverty, of which 7.6% (9.4m) lived in extreme poverty and the percentage of the population in living poverty increased from 2014 to 2016 in five states: Veracruz, Oaxaca, Tabasco, Chiapas and Campeche.[19]

Given the current lack of social programmes and education opportunities, the only way youth living in poverty can change their destiny is through joining a gang, working for drug-trafficking organisations or committing illegal activities. For this reason, in September 2018, the new government announced an investment of more than MX$110m (US$5.5m) in a social programme called 'Youth Building the Future' directed at young adults between 18 and 25 years old who were not studying or working.

Militarisation of public security

Since the Calderón administration (2006–12), military operations have been implemented all over the country to fight organised crime: 15 operations took place between 2006 and 2014. In 2017, the army deployed 150,311 military personnel to address public-security threats with the objective of reducing violence. According to information presented to Congress by the Office of the President in April 2018, the Mexican armed forces participated in 748 daily operations (31 operations per hour). However, evidence suggests that violence, instead of going down, has increased.[20]

In response to the militarisation of public security, criminal groups began to increase their weaponry to fight the government and defend themselves. Although in some places military operations were successful in 'beheading' criminal groups (arresting or subduing kingpins), the mid-term effect of the government's strategy was the fragmentation of criminal groups and an explosion of turf wars to control specific territories. The multiplication of criminal groups and human-rights violations by the army (including forced disappearances and extrajudicial executions) has exacerbated violence, rather than reducing it.

Access to the US

Mexico shares more than 3,000 kilometres of border with the US, which is the biggest drug-consumption market in the world according to the United Nations Office on Drugs and Crime (UNODC). Mexico is the main supplier of heroin and marijuana to the US and has become the most important trafficking country for smuggling other drugs such as cocaine, methamphetamine and, lately, fentanyl into the US, leading to clashes between organised-crime groups (and between organised-crime groups and the armed forces) over the territory required to smuggle illegal drugs into the US.

Besides the logic of supply and demand, regional prohibition policies have also refocused the conflict on access to the US border, increasing drug trafficking through Mexico and raising levels of violence in the country. In Colombia, the eradication of illegal crops and cocaine laboratories and confrontations with the main drug cartels have taken place since the 1980s. When the US took control of the Caribbean route (which was used by Colombian drug traffickers to smuggle cocaine to the US through Miami) in the early 2000s, Colombian criminal groups partnered with Mexican criminal groups to negotiate trafficking options.

The US–Mexican border, with its 48 border crossings, became the best option for smuggling drugs to the US. Mexican criminal groups were paid both in cash and with product (cocaine), allowing them to develop local markets in Mexico. In this way, Mexican cartels became important players in the regional drug business, not only smuggling cocaine and other drugs to the US but also developing military strategies for controlling territory, fighting the state and protecting their financial business through money laundering. Drug-related revenues for Mexican organisations triggered and were used to finance violence.

The shared border with the US has also increased violence by enabling the smuggling of weapons and military equipment from the US to Mexico (aided by the lack of strict gun-control policies in the US).

Legalisation of marijuana in US
As of May 2017, medicinal marijuana was legal in all but six US states, and eight states had approved the use of recreational marijuana. Legal suppliers in the US are limited in their capacity to cover the increasing demand, opening an opportunity for Mexican criminal groups to smuggle marijuana through the black market and taking advantage of the shared border between Mexico and the US. As yet, however, there are no estimates of how much of the product is supplied through the black market.[21]

Political and Military Developments

Confrontations between armed forces and criminal groups[22]
The number of confrontations between the armed forces and organised crime has decreased over time.[23] Information about the total number of confrontations is only up to date to December 2017, but figures about military personnel killed or injured in confrontations are available to October 2018. According to these figures, the majority of confrontations between the armed forces and criminal groups in 2018 took place in six states (Guerrero, Jalisco, Michoacán, Nayarit, Sinaloa and Tamaulipas) with high presence of organised crime (the Gulf Cartel and Los Zetas in Tamaulipas; the CJNG in Jalisco, Michoacán and Nayarit; the Sinaloa Cartel in Sinaloa; and the BLO in Guerrero, among others).[24]

Two of the main objectives of the security forces' operations are drug eradication (marijuana and poppy crops) and drug seizures (marijuana and cocaine). Information for 2018 is available up to September 2018, during which time the marines participated in 12,098 operations. In one operation in August 2018, the marines seized 2,250 kilograms of cocaine from a ship transporting 66 bags of narcotics along the Pacific coast near Oaxaca. Eight criminals were detained, including a Canadian and two Colombians. Also in August, the marines seized 50 tonnes of methamphetamine in Culiacán, Sinaloa State, with an estimated value of US$5bn, making it one of the biggest synthetic drug seizures ever in Mexico.

The navy collaborated in 2018 (January to September) in 4,563 joint operations with other governmental dependencies such as the army, the federal police and the Office of the General Attorney, but in only 36 specific confrontations with organised-crime groups, in Tamaulipas, Michoacán, Veracruz, Jalisco and Mexico City.[25]

Confrontations between the federal police and criminal groups
From December 2012 to December 2017, the federal police participated in 722 operations to fight organised crime with the objective of disarticulating criminal groups and seizing illegal drugs. According to the Federal Police Report of Accountability (2012–18),[26] 707 members of criminal groups were detained during this period, of which 21 were in the federal government's List of Priority Individuals, and significant quantities of cocaine, methamphetamine, marijuana, ecstasy and fentanyl were seized.

In 2018, the federal police participated (up to August) in 124 operations, detaining 109 alleged criminals. According to data obtained by an information request,[27] from January to October 2018, 82 alleged criminals were detained, 23 were injured and 38 were killed in operations with the participation of the federal police in Chihuahua, Puebla, Tamaulipas and Veracruz states. Except for Puebla, all these states have a presence of organised crime (the presence of Los Zetas was reported for Puebla in 2018, but no group was identified in previous years). Surprisingly, the number of detainees in Puebla was much higher than in the other states: while 27 alleged criminals were detained there, only five were detained in Chihuahua, seven in Tamaulipas and four in Veracruz.

Presidential elections
Presidential elections took place in June 2018. For the first time during a presidential campaign, the security situation was a topic discussed by the different candidates. The winning candidate, López Obrador, proposed a change in the security paradigm, mentioning alternative solutions to the military intervention such as amnesty, transitional justice and truth commissions in territories most

affected by violence and the presence of organised crime. His discourse changed, however, after taking office. By the end of the year, Congress was discussing a proposal to approve a National Guard with a military structure under the command of the army.

Civil-society organisations, international organisations and academics were invited to Congress to discuss the proposal, and provided empirical evidence of the negative effect that the militarisation of public security has had on levels of violence and human-rights violations. Notably, the controversial 2017 Interior Security Law, intended to formalise the armed forces' role in fighting crime, was declared unconstitutional by the Supreme Court in November 2018.

Violent Events

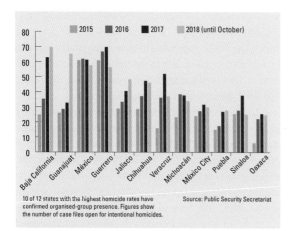

10 of 12 states with the highest homicide rates have confirmed organised-group presence. Figures show the number of case files open for intentional homicides.

Source: Public Security Secretariat

Figure 1: Homicide rates by state per 100,000 people, 2015–18

The states with the highest rates of intentional homicides per 100,000 inhabitants in Mexico are those with the presence of at least two criminal groups (see **Figure 1**).[28] For instance, the highest rate of intentional homicides in 2018 (up to October) was recorded in Baja California, which is also the state with the highest number of criminal groups and where the navy has undertaken operations to fight organised crime.[29]

Executions

Homicides include a broader range of violence beyond that solely related to the armed confrontation of armed criminal groups among themselves and with the state. Executions are a better proxy for organised-crime-related violence because they evolve similarly to the temporal and spatial evolution of the Mexican conflict, and indicate the homicides committed by criminal groups against members of the government, civilians or other criminal groups. According to the national newspaper

Milenio, which gathers information from public and official sources, executions increased in 2018 compared to 2017: 15,877 executions were reported in 2018, representing a 27% increase compared to 2017 (12,532). Every month of 2018 was more violent than the same month in 2017, with growth rates ranging from 1.2% (in December and March) to 5.3% in January. (January was the most violent month of the year, with 1,562 executions reported.)

Most of the executions in 2018 were concentrated in four states: Guanajuato, Guerrero, Baja California and Chihuahua (see **Figure 2**). The targets differed depending on the region and the criminal group involved in the violent event and were driven by confrontations between the state and criminal groups; clashes between criminal groups to control specific turfs or local markets; attacks on reporters or political candidates; or attacks on civilians (usually in their private properties or vehicles).

In August 2018, 53 people were killed in different events in Guanajuato State, mostly in municipalities located in the state border line (adjacent to Queretaro and Michoacán), while 11 people

77% of the executions in 2018 occurred in 10 states

Source: *Milenio*

Figure 2: States with highest incidence of executions, 2018

were killed in Chihuahua State in August 2018 in a safe house located in the city of Juarez. In Guerrero, seven dismembered bodies were found in plastic bags close to Chilapa in January 2018, while in April 2018, six State Police officers were attacked and killed by a criminal group when they were driving back from attending nine families who had been threatened by criminal groups in the municipality of Petalán. The massacre was filmed by one of the criminals and uploaded to the internet.

Political violence

Two political candidates for the local elections in Guerrero were killed by criminal groups in May 2018 while travelling in their private vehicles. The Democratic Revolutionary Party (PRD), the strongest political party in the state, argued that it was too dangerous to get involved in electoral campaigns in many municipalities of the state. More than 20 candidates resigned from their candidacy due to threats received from criminal groups.

The electoral process of 2018 was considered the most violent in the history of the country. According to the newspaper *Excelsior*, 112 politicians were murdered in 2018 and more than 400 aggressions to politicians took place since September 2017. Of the 112 politicians killed, 28 were pre-candidates, 14 were candidates and the remainder were public officers, such as majors, aldermen, militants and deputies, among others.[30]

Impact

Civilian population

Several civil-society organisations have complained that the participation of the armed forces in the fight against organised crime has affected civilians, increased human-rights violations and exacerbated the security situation in their communities. Data Civica, a civil-society organisation, published a dataset in January 2018 with information about missing persons in Mexico, according to which, 33,964 individuals were reported missing between 2006 and 2017. The locations of these individuals are still unknown. Many journalists have also been kidnapped, tortured or killed. The Human Rights National Commission in Mexico reported 3,899 complaints regarding human-rights violations from 2006 to 2018 (184 in 2018 up to October), including arbitrary detentions, torture, forced disappearances and extrajudicial executions, among others.

Socio-economic impact

The war against organised crime in Mexico has had a negative impact on socio-economic indicators as well. According to data gathered by the National Survey of Urban Public Security for the second trimester of 2018, four out of ten households were the victims of theft or extortion, the two criminal offences that most affect the population. Insecurity perceptions also increased in 2018: while 74.9% of the population considered their city unsafe in June 2017, this figure increased to 75.9% in June 2018. In 2018, 85.6% of Mexicans thought that the security situation had deteriorated compared to previous years (this figure was 80.7% in 2017 and 74.6% in 2016).

Trends

Expansion of cartels and increase in violence

Criminal groups in Mexico will continue to grow over 2019 – not only in size but also in military capacity, violent tactics, activity diversification and territorial control. The violence has increased steadily from 2014, in most cases due to fights over the control of illegal-drug markets (production, trafficking or retail markets). Not only has organised crime become more violent, but governmental strategies to fight it have also provoked an increase in violence: violence has increased more in regions where military operations have been implemented than in regions without a military operation. A continued heavily militarised response will exacerbate these trends. The ongoing fragmentation of organised-crime groups suggests also that criminal violence will continue and evolve. Without measures to counter money laundering and financial structures, criminal groups will continue to benefit from revenue derived from drug trafficking and other illegal activities.

State strategy likely to remain unchanged

Although presidential candidates discussed the security situation during their campaigns and proposed alternatives to the current military approach, there are no concrete indications that the new administration will change the current strategy in 2019. Congress is in the process of approving the National Guard under the military command, a situation that would ensure the participation of the armed forces in public-security activities. These measures are likely to bring the same results as previous policies – an intensification of violence in the territories controlled by criminal groups without a corresponding weakening of such control.

In 2018, civil-society organisations such as Seguridad sin Guerra (Security without War) proposed alternatives to the militarisation of public security, stressing the positive democratic implications of returning public-security tasks to civil institutions. The proposal with the most probability of being considered in Congress in 2019 is that of strengthening the National System of Public Security with the objectives of designing evidence-based security policies and centralising police development training (for municipal, state and federal police forces), as well as providing social security for all police officers.

Legalisation of prohibited drugs

Former Mexican president Ernesto Zedillo, in collaboration with some academics, published a report in 2018 that questioned the effectiveness of prohibitionist policies and proposing new alternatives for legalising prohibited drugs, including cocaine, heroin and methamphetamine.[31] According to the report, the legalisation of drugs is an important step toward reducing violence in Mexico.

Although some states in the US have legalised the use of recreational marijuana in recent years, the Mexican federal government has been more conservative in approving law proposals to regularise illegal drugs. López Obrador's new government has been more open to discussing a law proposal to regularise marijuana, following two rulings by the Supreme Court in late October that helped reach the number of rulings (five) required to establish a precedent for the legal consumption of marijuana. If this proposal is not discussed during the first semester of 2019, however, the replacement of the current Supreme Court ministers who voted in favour of the recreational use of marijuana would delay the discussion and no policy change would occur in 2019. Still, as criminal groups in Mexico diversify their activities to include oil theft, extortion and kidnapping of migrants, policies centred on eradicating drug trafficking are unlikely to suppress the profits of criminal groups entirely.

| Notes

[1]   Evolution of territorial control by organised crime according to information provided by Mexican Office of the Attorney General (PGR) and US Drug Enforcement Administration (DEA) for the years 2005, 2013 and 2015 (PGR) and 2018 (DEA).

[2]   Information request no. 0000700118418 to the SEMAR in 2018.

[3]   'Informe de Rendición de Cuentas de Conclusión de la administración 2012–2018, Secretaría de Marina', 29 October 2018.

[4]   Ricardo Moya, 'Incrementa el presupuesto para Sedena en 2019; reducen el de Semar', El Universal, 15 December 2018.

[5]   Iñigo Guevara, 'Presupuesto militar para 2018', El Heraldo, 12 September 2018.

[6]   Lino González Veiguela, 'Los cárteles más fuertes de México 2018', Esglobal, 28 June 2018.

[7]   Laura Atuesta and Yocelyn Samantha Pérez-Dávila, 'Fragmentation and cooperation: the evolution of organised crime in Mexico', Trends in Organised Crime, vol. 21, no. 3, February 2017, pp. 235–61.

[8]   González, 'Los cárteles más fuertes', although the DEA report confirms the presence of the CJNG in 22 of the 32 Mexican states.

[9]   DEA, '2018 National Drug Threat Assessment', October 2018.

[10] Christopher Woody, 'Mexico says it caught gunmen who shot down an army helicopter – and it may signal trouble for the country's most powerful cartel', Business Insider, 2 August 2018.

[11] González, 'Los cárteles más fuertes'.

[12] June S. Beittel, 'Mexico: Organized Crime and Drug Trafficking Organizations', Congressional Research Service, 3 July 2018.

[13] Atuesta, 'Fragmentation and cooperation'.

[14] González, 'Los cárteles más fuertes'.

[15] Atuesta, 'Fragmentation and cooperation'.

[16] González, 'Los cárteles más fuertes'.

[17] Beittel, 'Mexico: Organized Crime and Drug Trafficking Organizations'.

[18] Panel with Marco Fernández, 'Debilidad institucional y combate a la corrupción', Mexico Evalua, 11 May 2018.

[19] CONEVAL, 'Coneval Informa La Evolución De La Pobreza 2010–2016', 30 August 2017.

20 Leticia Robles De La Rosa, 'Militares hicieron 31 operativos cada hora', *Excelsior*, 4 April 2018.

21 For a more detailed discussion of the issue, see Luis Alonso Pérez, 'Legalización de marihuana en Estados Unidos no ha resuelto problemas de seguridad', *Huffington Post*, 12 November 2018; Alejandro T. Ramírez, 'La marihuana legal en EU y la violencia en México', *Forbes*, 2 May 2014; Jonathan P. Caulkins et al., 'High Tax States: Options for Gleaning Revenue from Legal Cannabis', *Oregon Law Review*, vol. 91, no. 4, 2012–13, p.p 1041–68.

22 Official data on confrontations between the armed forces and criminal groups are no longer available since the government stopped gathering information about civilians and military personnel killed and injured in these clashes, as well as the number and the geographical location where these confrontations took place, after April 2014.

23 Information request no. 0000700005118 to the SEDENA in 2018.

24 Information request no. 0000700213918 to the SEDENA in 2018.

25 Information request no. 0001300108418 to the SEMAR in 2018.

26 'Informe de Rendición de Cuentas de Conclusión de la Administración 2012-2018 de la Policía Federal', Policía Federal, 27 November 2018.

27 Information request no. 0413100129618 to the Federal Police in 2018.

28 A dataset of homicides allegedly related to organised crime from 2006 to 2010 was published on the presidential webpage in January 2011. Met with criticism from local attorney offices and the press, the federal state stopped publishing official data on homicides related to organised crime in the country. Mexico has two official data sources on homicides: the first, gathered by the National Institute of Statistics and Geography, provides the total number of homicides (dataset up to date to December 2017); the second, gathered by the Public Security Secretariat, provides open case files for intentional homicides and is available up to October 2018. Additionally, some newspapers (such as *Reforma* and *Milenio*) and civil-society organisations have collected information and released their own estimates of executions and homicides related to organised crime.

29 Exceptions were in Mexico City and the State of Mexico. Although both federal entities had high rates of intended homicides in 2018, they had no presence of criminal groups or federal operations to fight organised crime. The trend of homicides in these states confirm that, historically, they have high homicide rates not necessarily related to the presence of organised crime.

30 'Elecciones en México 2018: 112 políticos asesinados', *Excelsior*, 6 September 2018.

31 Alejandro Madrazo Lajous, Catalina Pérez Correa González and Ernesto Zedillo, 'La política de drogas en México: causa de una tragedia nacional', Programa Política de Drogas, CIDE, 2018.

2 Asia-Pacific

Thai bomb-squad members inspect the site of a motorcycle-bomb attack

Regional Introduction

The armed conflicts in the Asia–Pacific region are discrete theatres with no significant connections, and remained so throughout 2018. Accordingly, Myanmar, the Philippines and southern Thailand all addressed their respective internal-security situations with tailored military and political approaches, without relying on any dedicated regional instruments or security-cooperation mechanisms. The three conflicts also have vastly different levels of projections and varying potentials to affect broader geostrategic dynamics. Myanmar and the stabilisation of its conflicts are crucial to China's geostrategic interests, as they occur in the territories of major Belt and Road Initiative (BRI) projects, where two of its economic corridors pass. The Philippines' internal conflicts have important implications for national security and politics as the insurgents advance redistributive and self-determination claims. Aside from sporadic engagements across the Celebes and Sulu seas and still-limited links to international jihad, the Moro and the Maoist conflicts in the archipelago have no larger implications for the region, however. Similarly, the armed insurgency in southern Thailand has virtually no influence outside the provinces in which it occurs, failing even to feature in political debates in Bangkok.

The security situation in Myanmar is set to deteriorate in 2019 and armed violence to increase, following the effective collapse of the peace process. Two major ethnic armed organisations (EAOs) are not party to it and others, suspicious of the military's intent, have shown little intention of honouring the Nationwide Ceasefire Agreement (NCA). A new unilateral ceasefire announced by the Myanmar Armed Forces (the Tatmadaw) in December will not prevent the EAOs in Kachin and Shan states from fighting each other. There are indeed few reasons to believe that the military's motives for peace are sincere. The Tatmadaw continues to deal with one group at a time, committing major atrocities and creating mass displacement, while the civilian government remains unwilling or unable to appreciate the scale of the problem.

This strategy has already had negative implications in Rakhine State, where violence will likely escalate in 2019, leading to further mass displacement and human-rights abuses, and potentially to a full-fledged armed conflict between the Tatmadaw and the Arakan Army (AA) (ethnically Rakhine), and possibly the Arakan Rohingya Salvation Army (ARSA) too. The resistance movement in the state has become increasingly more organised, more capable and better funded, and the recruitment and training of young pupils is on the rise. No political solution is in sight for the Rohingya population, while their abysmal humanitarian conditions, systematic victimisation and entrenched discrimination may create inroads for radical extremism. Expectations remain low for the Myanmar government to investigate or prosecute senior generals for genocide, crimes against humanity and war crimes as recommended in the September 2018 report by the United Nations Fact-finding Mission on Myanmar.

Most insurgents in the region do not share the ideologies or objectives of international jihadism and pursue separatist and self-determination agendas, claiming autonomy or independence for the territories in which they operate. In Thailand's southernmost provinces, in the Mindanao and Sulu provinces of the Philippines and along Myanmar's northeastern border with China, grievances against a central state seen as excluding or repressing local populations drive the conflicts, together with quests for fairer redistribution of resources and more political representation for ethnic or religious minorities. Even when

not explicitly declared, armed groups in Southeast Asia are interested in obtaining international legitimacy rather than challenging the international order.

There has been no conclusive evidence to date of connections between the long-standing Malay-Muslim or the historical Filipino-Moro insurgencies either with the Islamic State, also known as ISIS or ISIL, or with al-Qaeda. For separatist nationalist groups, such as the National Revolutionary Front (BRN), the MARA Patani and the Patani United Liberation Organisation (PULO) in southern Thailand, the aim is to create an independent state in the historical Patani region at the border with Malaysia. The EAOs in northeastern Myanmar seek greater civic, political and cultural rights, more inclusive development, and more equal access to land and public revenues, without challenging the existence of the Burmese state. Through armed struggle and peace negotiations with the government in Manila this year, the Moro Islamic Liberation Front (MILF) succeeded in creating an autonomous region in Mindanao, the Philippines' only Muslim-majority province, and was vocal in distancing itself from the coalition of ISIS-affiliated jihadist groups that laid siege to Marawi city in 2017.

> Most insurgents pursue separatist and self-determination agendas

The Abu Sayyaf Group (ASG), Ansar Khalifah Philippines (AKP), Bangsamoro Islamic Freedom Fighters (BIFF) and the Maute Group in the Philippines, along with the Gerakan Mujahidin Islam Patani (GMIP) in southern Thailand, are the notable exceptions to this trend. Their affiliates overtly commit to international extremist doctrines or aim to establish a caliphate in the areas over which they extend their political claims. In these cases, the penetration of transnational jihadism has been a bottom-up phenomenon, by which ISIS or al-Qaeda have inserted themselves into pre-existing militant groups and infiltrated social networks (most notably via familial ties). Even when these groups have proclaimed their allegiance to radical Islamism, however, these connections have remained limited. In the Philippines, where the majority of jihadists in the Asia-Pacific region are active, the direct involvement of ISIS and al-Qaeda militants is still small compared to other global regions, with evidence of direct financial and personnel transfers being often inconclusive or anecdotal. This tenuous engagement is likely to continue, particularly as jihadist groups are still to recover from being decimated in the battle for Marawi.

In the short to medium term, armed violence will likely continue to decrease in southern Thailand and in the Philippines, even though political solutions are unlikely to materialise for some of the conflicts. The martial law imposed in Mindanao in 2017 and extended in 2018 has proved effective in containing violence and should continue to do so through 2019, when it is scheduled to end. The full implementation of the peace agreement between the government and the MILF to establish the Bangsamoro Autonomous Region in Muslim Mindanao (BARMM) will remain key in addressing the conflict's drivers as opposed to its symptoms. The Bangsamoro Transitional Authority (BTA) – the interim local government for western Mindanao and the Sulu archipelago – is set to begin its works by the spring of 2019, and in principle allows for the participation of the Moro National Liberation Front (MNLF). This framework creates incentives for committing to democratic rules and inclusive governance, and may limit the appeal of extremist ideologies.

The government will continue to struggle to eradicate the highly resilient and decentralised Maoist insurgency in the larger Philippines (particularly in eastern Mindanao, where its hold is strongest). Although the incidence of violent attacks will likely remain in check, appetite for a political solution to this conflict's underlying causes is unlikely to emerge in 2019. Bangkok's commitment to a political solution to Patani demands for autonomy will also continue to be ambiguous. Even if the government appointed by the March 2019 election were to seek a new approach to resolving the conflict, the military will likely continue to lead on the matter.

Myanmar (EAOs)

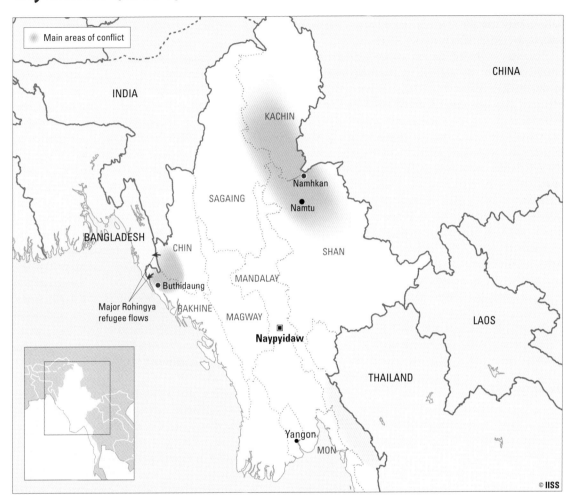

Overview

The conflict in 2018

More than a third of Myanmar's 330 townships are affected by conflict.[1] Active fighting continued in 2018, in particular in the country's northeast in Kachin State and northern Shan State. The latter months of the year also witnessed significant operations in northern Rakhine and southern Chin states.

Fighting decreases during the wettest months of the year (June to October). The months either side of the wet season tend to be the most violent. Between January and April 2018 during the first fighting season, clashes between the Tatmadaw (Myanmar armed forces) and the Kachin Independence Army (KIA) were the most prominent, according to data collected by the Myanmar Institute for Peace and

Security (MIPS), followed by clashes with the Ta'ang National Liberation Army (TNLA), the Arakan Army (AA) and the Karen National Union (KNU). There were dozens of improvised explosive device (IED)

Key statistics

Type:	Internal
IDPs total (2017):	240,000
IDPs new (2018):	30,000
Refugees total (2018):	1,125,000
Refugees new (2018):	15,000
People in need (2018):	1,245,000

attacks during the first four months of 2018, with a peak in May. The last month before the monsoon season, May was the most violent month of the year, with 92 armed clashes recorded.[2]

The first fighting season concentrated in the northeast, with the second in Rakhine State and southern Chin State. From October, heavy fighting occurred between the AA and the Tatmadaw. The Tatmadaw offered a unilateral four-month ceasefire to northeastern ethnic armed organisations (EAOs) in order to concentrate forces on operations against the AA, which were still ongoing at the end of the year.

Two more EAOs joined the Nationwide Ceasefire Agreement (NCA). While this was largely symbolic – both groups are small and poorly armed – it gave a much needed victory to the government. After this minimal progress at the beginning of the year, however, two large NCA signatories (NCA–S) suspended their participation in the process in November.

In 2018, both EAOs and the Tatmadaw targeted civilian areas. Although this was most evident in Rakhine State, IEDs were also laid along Lashio–Muse road and in front of two banks (Inwa and Yoma) in Muse. There was also a significant surge in the frequency and intensity of inter-ethnic armed clashes, particularly in Shan State, which accounted for approximately 15% of all recorded clashes in 2018.

In 2018, Myanmar's government strove to counter the international isolation that followed the fallout from the Rohingya crisis. It did so by building closer relations with China, India and Russia, among others, in 2018.

The conflict to 2018

Debate over power-sharing arrangements between the ethnic Bamar majority and dozens of minority groups preceded independence in 1948. The Panglong Agreement, signed in 1947, laid out a blueprint for ethnic autonomy and financial arrangements, but founding father Aung San – who signed for the Burmese government – was assassinated just five months later. Dissatisfaction with the execution of these arrangements and lack of central control over the periphery of the country led to the establishment of EAOs, beginning with the KNU in 1949. After a military *coup d'état* in 1962, General Ne Win's regime sought to 'Burmanise' the country. A backlash against these policies led to the rise of dozens

of other EAOs in the ensuing decades. Though elections were held in 1974, Ne Win maintained control through his Burmese Socialist Programme Party (BSPP).

Protests against economic conditions and BSPP rule in 1988 unnerved the military, which launched a further coup. The new junta, concerned about the prospects for further unrest, instituted market-oriented reforms and sought ceasefire agreements with a number of EAOs, allowing these groups to exert some independence over their territories and retain their weapons. Nevertheless, fighting between the Tatmadaw and non-ceasefire EAOs continued throughout the 1990s and 2000s.

A new constitution was approved in a referendum in 2008, and elections were held for new national and regional legislatures in 2010, and a new presidential administration in 2011. Though the main opposition party, the National League for Democracy (NLD), boycotted the vote, many ethnic parties participated in national and local polls, providing an opening for political participation by previously marginalised ethnic groups. At the same time, however, the Tatmadaw sought the incorporation of EAOs with which it had long held ceasefires into a Border Guard Force under Tatmadaw command. Several groups, including the Kachin Independence Organisation (KIO), rejected this proposal, seeing it as tantamount to surrender, and hostilities resumed between these groups and the Tatmadaw.

Once in office, the new administration under then-president Thein Sein reached out to the NLD and civil-society groups to invite them to participate in the political process, and to the EAOs to participate in a nationwide peace process. This opening led to the negotiation of the NCA, signed in 2015 prior to national elections that year. Though negotiated by nearly all the EAOs in the country, with a draft agreed on by all groups, only eight EAOs signed the final document: the All Burma Students' Democratic Front (ABSDF), the Arakan Liberation Party (ALP), the Chin National Front (CNF), the Democratic Karen Benevolent Army (DKBA–5), the Karen National Liberation Army–Peace Council (KPC), the KNU, the Pa-O National Liberation Organisation (PNLO) and the Restoration Council of Shan State (RCSS).

The NLD, led by Aung San Suu Kyi, the daughter of founding father Aung San, won elections in a landslide in 2015. The NLD's initial approach to the peace process focused on attracting further signatories to the NCA, and the establishment of a series of 21st Century Panglong Conferences (21CPCs), beginning in August 2016. The 21CPC process was established in an attempt to draw upon the credibility of Aung San Suu Kyi with ethnic minorities, but the power-sharing agreement between the elected NLD government and the Tatmadaw hampered progress in the current peace process, causing it to stall.

Forces

There are more than 100,000 armed personnel from approximately 40 non-state armed actors in Myanmar.[3] They vary in size, capability and current ceasefire status. Militias play an important role in the conflict and some estimates, which vary widely, suggest that there could be up to 5,000 militia groups operating at local levels in the country, with a total strength of more than 180,000.[4] Other estimates suggest a fraction of this number; indeed, the exact strength may be 'unknowable'.[5] Estimates below vary widely but are based on various independent sources.

Tatmadaw (Myanmar armed forces)

The Tatmadaw has held the central role in the country's affairs since 1962. The military-drafted 2008 constitution places primacy of the Tatmadaw over the civilian government, rendering it 'free from any civilian control or oversight'. Importantly, the commander-in-chief of the armed forces appoints the ministers of defence, border affairs and home affairs. Other security services, such as the Myanmar Police Force, report to the minister for home affairs. The 2008 constitution also reserved 25% of seats in parliament for members of the armed forces, granting veto power over parliamentary decisions. The progress since the 2010 transition is the result of a carefully managed and permitted process by the Tatmadaw, and not (as is sometimes alluded to) of charismatic leadership or popular pressure.

Since 2011, Senior General Min Aung Hlaing has aimed to modernise the Tatmadaw. In line with this goal, its force strength has been trimmed and, although exact information is not publicly released, is estimated at between 300,000 and 350,000 personnel.[6] The Tatmadaw has procured – and continues to procure – aircraft, naval vessels and armoured vehicles, primarily from China and Russia but increasingly from other countries too, including India, Israel and Ukraine. A long history of faulty or poor-performing materiel has led to greater diversification of defence contractors.[7] In 2018, the Tatmadaw took delivery of six JF-17 *Thunder* fighters and 15 K-8 trainer/light attack aircraft from China, six Yak-130 light attack aircraft from Russia and received six HJT-16 *Kiran* trainer aircraft as a gift from India. Myanmar also took delivery of *Shyena* ASW torpedoes from India (a contract worth US$38 million), and *Super Dvora* patrol boats from Israel.[8] Acquisitions of the latter have garnered some international criticism as the patrol boats were used in operations in Rakhine State in 2018; K-8s have also recently been used against EAOs in Kachin State and northern Shan State.

Ethnic armed organisations (EAOs)

There are 135 recognised ethnic groups in Myanmar. Since independence and throughout the country's modern history, most of these groups have been involved in some form of armed struggle.[9] Similarly, different ethnic groups have formed tactically significant alliances with or against the Tatmadaw, and in some cases against other EAOs. Some of these organisations have been disbanded or have reformed into the Border Guard Force or militia, while others continue to fight against the Tatmadaw. Importantly, most current EAOs have territorial disputes both with the Tatmadaw as well as with neighbouring EAOs or militias.

There have been many blocs that have represented EAOs over the previous decades, including the National Democratic Front (NDF) and the Ethnic Nationalities Council. Repeatedly, they have been superseded by new alliance structures led by large EAOs pushing their interests – such as the KIO, KNU, RCSS or UWSP – or they have been effectively divided by the Tatmadaw.

The collapse of the United Nationalities Federal Council (UNFC)

The United Nationalities Federal Council (UNFC) was formed in 2011 by 12 EAOs to negotiate with the government as a bloc. The KNU left in 2014, reportedly due to internal power struggles, and the bloc was dealt a significant blow in 2017 when another founder, the KIO/KIA, pulled out following the departure of the MNDAA, SSPP, TNLA and WNO. Without the support of large EAOs backed by armed forces, such as the KIO, the government has been targeting remaining EAOs as the next Nationwide Ceasefire Agreement (NCA) signatories.

It is in this environment that two smaller UNFC member EAOs – the LDU and the NMSP – signed the ceasefire agreement in February 2018. Significantly, the EAOs did so without the Tatmadaw ceding to earlier UNFC demands under the bloc's nine-point proposal. The two groups became the first signatories to the ceasefire under the National League for Democracy (NLD) government – earlier

Overview of ethnic armed organisations active in Myanmar

EAO	Umbrella group	Date NCA signed (if signed)	Previous ceasefires (if any)	Strength (approximate)	Alliances (current)	Opposition (active)	Activity location
All Burma Students' Democratic Front (ABSDF)	NCA–S	2015	2013	400	KIA, KNU	Tatmadaw	Kachin State, Karen State, Shan State
Arakan Liberation Party/Arakan Liberation Army (ALP/ALA)	NCA–S	2015	2012	<100	KNU	Tatmadaw	Karen State, Rakhine State
Chin National Front (CNF)	NCA–S	2015	2012	200		Tatmadaw	Chin State
Democratic Karen Benevolent Army/Klo Htoo Baw Battalion (DKBA–5)	NCA–S	2015	2011	1,500	KNU, KPC	Tatmadaw	Karen State
Kachin Independence Organisation/Kachin Independence Army (KIO/KIA)	FPNCC		1994	12,000	AA, MNDAA, NDAA, SSA–N, TNLA, UWSA	Tatmadaw	Kachin State
Karen National Union/Karen National Liberation Army (KNU/KNLA)	NCA–S	2015 (suspended participation in 2018)	2012	5,000	DKBA–5, KPC	MNLA, Tatmadaw	Karen State, Bago Region, Tanintharyi Region
Karen National Union/Karen National Liberation Army–Peace Council (KPC)	NCA–S	2015	2007	200	DKBA–5, KNU	Tatmadaw	Karen State
Karenni National Progressive Party (KNPP)			2005, 2012	600		Tatmadaw	Kayah State
Lahu Democratic Union (LDU)	NCA–S	2018		<200		Tatmadaw	Shan State
Myanmar National Truth and Justice Party/Myanmar National Democratic Alliance Army (MNTJP/MNDAA)	FPNCC			2,000	AA, KIA, NDAA, SSA–N, TNLA, UWSA	Tatmadaw	Shan State
National Socialist Council of Nagaland–Khaplang (NSCN–K)			2012	500	National Socialist Council of Nagalim–Isak-Muivah (India) (NSCN–IM)	Tatmadaw	Sagaing State, northeast India (Manipur, Nagaland)

ceasefires were negotiated by the Union Solidarity and Development Party (USDP) military-backed government.

As well as the threat of attack from the Tatmadaw, the KNU (a signatory of the NCA) has increased its presence in and around NMSP-held territory. Any KNU–NMSP violence may have seen the NMSP fighting both the KNU and Tatmadaw. This increased threat environment led the NMSP to sign the NCA in February. Despite this move, the KNU and the MNLA clashed several times in 2018.

Other UNFC parties were hamstrung in joining the NCA by their own internal politics. For the KNPP, widely touted to be on the verge of signing the NCA, the incident in December 2017 which saw several Karenni deaths at the hand of the Tatmadaw and led to subsequent protests, made it virtually impossible for the leadership to sign the agreement in February. The KNPP were subsequently engaged in low-intensity clashes with the Tatmadaw in October.

Overview of ethnic armed organisations active in Myanmar

EAO	Umbrella group	Date NCA signed (if signed)	Previous ceasefires (if any)	Strength (approximate)	Alliances (current)	Opposition (active)	Activity location
New Mon State Party/ Mon National Liberation Army (NMSP/MNLA)	NCA–S	2018	1995, 2012	800		KNU, Tatmadaw	Mon State
Palaung State Liberation Front/Ta'ang National Liberation Army (PSLF/TNLA)	FPNCC			6,000	AA, KIA, MNDAA, NDAA, SSA–N, UWSA	Pansay militia, SSA–S, Tatmadaw	Shan State
Pa-O National Liberation Organisation/ Pa-O National Liberation Army (PNLO/PNLA)	NCA–S	2015	2012	400		Tatmadaw	Shan State
Peace and Solidarity Committee/National Democratic Alliance Association–East Shan State (PSC/NDAA)	FPNCC		2011	4,000	AA, KIA, MNDAA, SSA–N, TNLA, UWSA	Tatmadaw	Shan State
Restoration Council of Shan State/Shan State Army–South (RCSS/ SSA–S)	NCA–S	2015 (suspended participation in 2018)	2012	8,000		SSA–N, Tatmadaw, TNLA	Shan State
Shan State Progress Party/Shan State Army– North (SSPP/SSA–N)	FPNCC		1989	8,000	AA, KIA, MNDAA NDAA, TNLA, UWSA	SSA–S, Tatmadaw	Shan State
United League of Arakan/Arakan Army (ULA/AA)	FPNCC			1,500	KIA, MNDAA, NDAA, SSA–N, TNLA, UWSA	Tatmadaw	Chin State, Kachin State, Rakhine State, Shan State
United Wa State Party/ United Wa State Army (UWSP/UWSA)	FPNCC	2011	1989, 2011	30,000	AA, KIA, MNDAA, NDAA, SSA–N, TNLA	Tatmadaw	Wa State
Wa National Organisation/Wa National Army (WNO/ WNA)			1997	<200	UWSA (as of 2017)	Tatmadaw	Shan State

Asia-Pacific

The rise of the Federal Political Negotiation Consultative Committee (FPNCC)

The Federal Political Negotiation Consultative Committee (FPNCC) formed in 2017. Led by the powerful UWSP/UWSA, it includes the AA, KIO/KIA, MNDAA, PSC/NDAA and TNLA. The FPNCC rejects the current path to peace set out in the NCA and seeks to negotiate an alternative agreement based on a new constitution. The Myanmar government has in turn rejected the FPNCC's agenda and authority as an umbrella organisation and remains adamant in its refusal to change the constitution.

When the KIO-led Northern Alliance joined with the UWSP-led (and widely viewed as China-backed) FPNCC, it formed one of the most powerful backed alliances in recent history, both politically and militarily. The Northern Alliance has frustrated the Tatmadaw, particularly with its seemingly coordinated attacks in the first half of 2018.

Despite the apparent unity of the FPNCC, with all EAOs attending the third 21st Century Panglong Conferences (21CPC), internal divisions remain. The TNLA clashed with the SSPP over territorial disputes in 2018, and throughout the latter half of the year there were suggestions that some EAOs were seeking to negotiate independently with the Tatmadaw, using their membership to the group as leverage.

The Tatmadaw's willingness to sit with the FPNCC demonstrates the strength of the alliance and China's strong backing of the group. Beijing's role as peace broker is significant and is key to any lasting agreement. Significantly, the Tatmadaw yielded to holding dialogue with three smaller, and in recent years the most violent, EAOs – the AA, MNDAA and TNLA – following numerous trips to Naypyidaw by Sun Guoxiang, China's special envoy for Asian affairs, to mediate between the two.

United Wa State Party/United Wa State Army (UWSP/UWSA)

With its origins in the now-defunct Communist Party of Burma (CPB), the United Wa State Party (UWSP) has maintained its long-standing political, defence and economic ties with China. This was demonstrated in 2018 with China's engagement in the peace process and the relationship with the UWSP-led FPNCC. While no military engagements were recorded in 2018, UWSA troops moved west of the Salween to Mansi township, where they joined the KIA's Brigade 3 and the MNDAA, provoking the ire of the Tatmadaw. Towards the end of 2018, not dissimilar to that seen in China proper at the same time, the UWSA began a campaign of repression against Christians in their areas of control, closing and looting churches and jailing Christian Wa citizens.

Shan State Progress Party/Shan State Army–North (SSPP/SSA–N)

The Shan State Progress Party/Shan State Army–North (SSPP/SSA–N) continued to cooperate with other EAOs, such as the TNLA, in 2018, leading to repeated clashes between the TNLA–SSPP and the RCSS that caused civilian deaths and displacement. The SSPP left the UNFC in late 2017 and joined the FPNCC. Clashes early in the year between the generally allied TNLA and SSPP showed tensions over contested territory.

Restoration Council of Shan State/Shan State Army–South (RCSS/SSA–S)

The Restoration Council of Shan State/Shan State Army–South (RCSS/SSA–S) operates primarily in southern Shan State, and in recent years has been engaged in monthly clashes with the TNLA due to territorial disputes and the former's alleged involvement in the drug trade. In 2018, joint SSPP and TNLA offensives against the RCSS continued. The RCSS, an NCA signatory, has clashed several times with the Tatmadaw since 2015, including in 2018. These clashes have been the subject of ceasefire monitoring patrols overseen by the Joint Ceasefire Monitoring Committee (JMC). The group also clashed in a territorial dispute with another NCA signatory, the PNLO, in October. Most importantly, in a major blow to the peace process, the RCSS suspended its involvement in the NCA-mandated peace process in November.

Kachin Independence Organisation/Kachin Independence Army (KIO/KIA)

Since 2011, the Kachin Independence Organisation (KIO) has been in a 'state of strategic indecision', debating whether to go to war, negotiate peace or do both.[10] As a result, the group has effectively been waging a defensive campaign, holding its positions and territory while avoiding large-scale actions against the Tatmadaw that might trigger counter-attacks. An effective and persistent offensive by the Tatmadaw on strategic Kachin Independence Army

(KIA) positions in the first half of the year saw the EAO lose several key bases. As a result, the KIA employed more guerrilla-style tactics, harassing the Tatmadaw's extended supply routes and allegedly launching improvised explosive device (IED) attacks on the Mandalay–Myitkyina railway. If true, the latter demonstrates a significant escalation in tactics that have not been employed since 2013, and that could have severe impacts on tourism and local popular support.

Karen National Union/Karen National Liberation Army (KNU/KNLA)

The Karen National Union (KNU) was founded in 1947. Its armed wing is the Karen National Liberation Army (KNLA). The KNLA Brigade 7 split with the KNU in 2007 and formed the KPC, a separate group and signatory of the NCA. As the largest NCA signatory group, the KNU's withdrawal from the NCA-mandated peace process in November has been a significant blow to the prospects of the agreement. Clashes in Hpapun in Karen State between the KNU's Brigade 5 and the Tatmadaw in April, May and August 2018 were a worrying development. One of the key complaints was the construction of a road through contested territory, which the KNU believe to be for military rather than commercial purposes.

Palaung State Liberation Front/Ta'ang National Liberation Army (PSLF/TNLA)

The Ta'ang National Liberation Army (TNLA) began military operations in the Palaung area in 2011 with arms and training assistance from the KIA, which continues to deliver support in their joint campaign against the Tatmadaw. The TNLA also conducts joint operations with the SSPP, and other Northern Alliance partners, including against the RCSS. In recent years, the TNLA has been one of the most active EAOs, involved in hundreds of low-intensity skirmishes with the Tatmadaw, and this continued in 2018.

United League of Arakan/Arakan Army (ULA/AA)

Excluded from the peace process by the Tatmadaw, the Arakan Army (AA), the armed wing of the United League of Arakan (ULA), has in recent years established itself primarily in Kachin State for training and strategic purposes, despite its main aim being the representation of the interests of the Buddhist Rakhine people. After years of training and combat experience with northeastern EAOs, the AA returned in force to Rakhine State in 2018. Its units have operated in the majority-Buddhist townships of Kyauktaw, Min Bya, Mrauk-U and Ponnagyun, close to the state capital of Sittwe. From Paletwa and Kyauktaw, the AA has also been able to infiltrate west into the majority-Rohingya townships of Buthidaung and Rathedaung. The group was at the centre of some of the most intense fighting in the last quarter of 2018.

National Socialist Council of Nagaland–Khaplang (NSCN–K)

In August, the National Socialist Council of Nagaland–Khaplang (NSCN–K) replaced its Indian Naga leader with a Myanmar Naga leader, a move possibly driven by a willingness to abandon demands for a cross-border autonomous Naga homeland. During the third 21CPC, the government urged the EAO to join the peace process and later that month, a contingent of Tatmadaw troops were dispatched to Sagaing, reportedly leading to the withdrawal of the NSCN–K from the area.[11] In August, India and Myanmar opened land borders in Chin and Sagaing states. At the beginning of June, the NSCN–K twice attacked the Assam Rifles in India, killing up to five people. Later that month, Indian special forces Para 21 unit, killed five NSCN–K soldiers. The strengthening of India–Myanmar relations bodes poorly for the NSCN–K and escalation is likely in 2019.

New Mon State Party/Mon National Liberation Army (NMSP/MNLA)

After several years in the UNFC and following the collapse of the bloc, the New Mon State Party (NMSP) was faced with little choice but to sign the NCA – which it did in February 2018 – to avoid potential onslaught from both the Tatmadaw and the KNU. Regardless, since the signing, clashes between the KNU and Mon National Liberation Army (MNLA) have occurred in contested territory in Yebyu and Mudon townships.

Drivers

Various and overlapping causes drive Myanmar's web of armed conflicts. While some are uniquely historical, others are emerging as a result of the country's transition to civilian government and broader economic development. Among the main drivers are contested territory and resources, unequal access to services including health and education, illicit traffics, endemic corruption and weak governance.

Vestiges of colonialism

The tension between the centre of Myanmar and its periphery that drives today's conflict was instituted in colonial times and reinforced through subsequent political structures. A strong central administration, mainly based in the Buddhist urban areas, characterised British rule from 1824 to 1948. During the Second World War, occupying Japanese forces allied with Buddhist Burmese in the centre of the country, while groups of the frontier areas (including the insurgent Burmese Communist forces) were generally loyal to the Allied powers. As colonisation came to an end, the Communist Party of Burma (CPB) established itself as the main insurrectionary force and 'protector of the people'. Under its leadership, the Anti-Fascist People's Freedom League (AFPFL) formed, and was eventually elected to the constituent assembly following a national vote that relented colonial control. The non-communist elements within the AFPFL expelled the CPB in 1958 and a civil war ensued. Multiple ethnic groups situated in the frontier regions revolted against the new AFPFL central government. The Mon and Karen people were among the first to revolt against the central government in 1948 and 1949, respectively. Other ethnic groups followed, including the Arakanese, Chin, Kachin, Karenni and Shan, demanding greater political rights or self-determination. These local geopolitical formations have foreshadowed discordance between the centre and periphery in contemporary Myanmar.

Power of the armed forces

The 2008 constitution, which reserved a quarter of seats in parliament for members of the armed forces and grants military officials veto power over parliamentary decisions, has so far hindered any meaningful peace negotiations outside the Tatmadaw-mandated NCA structure. It has also further entrenched the power of the military in civil society and domestic politics. The Tatmadaw's economic and political power defines the extent of state control in Myanmar. Constitutional provisions and other laws provide for a civilian government with limited autonomy from the Tatmadaw. This 'state capture' is the primary explanation for the persisting challenges of contested state authority, limited state capacity and legitimacy.

Economic insecurity

One of the key problems in these areas is limited budget for public services. States and districts are dependent on central-government funding, but state and regional allocations make up only 8% of the central-government budget.[12] To offset this dependence and the limited transfers, communities, with the assistance or direction of EAOs, take responsibility for public services, particularly in areas not controlled by the government, levying taxes and managing access to infrastructure such as farms, mines and roads. There has been renewed interest in 2018 in how a decentralisation of governance may work within the confines of the 2008 constitution, and increased discussion on the subject among policy experts in the country.[13] Effective decentralisation is key both during political dialogue and to improve sub-national institutional capacity, which is constantly labelled as weak and inefficient.

More broadly, a weak banking sector and a limited institutional capacity that contribute to political instability have reduced the country's resilience and were cited by the International Monetary Fund (IMF) in 2018 as possible high-impact risks for Myanmar. The body also deemed natural disaster, which has the potential to devastate livelihoods and the larger economy, a high-impact risk. These risks are exacerbated by the ongoing violence and could act as accelerators to the conflict in 2019.

Structural influence of EAOs

The electoral victory of the NLD government, and the lack of progress in the current peace process, have divided many groups, with different factions wanting to join the NCA and others wanting to continue fighting for better terms. EAO internal divisions also add to the challenges of the negotiation process.

Corruption

Endemic corruption in some EAOs – and within the state security services – as well as a history of bartering for peace, increases the complexity of negotiations and often sustains conflict. Forced recruitment of soldiers, extortion and other forms of harassment are widespread in contested areas by both the EAOs and the Tatmadaw. This often drives fear and resentment of all conflict actors among local populations. At the central-state level, democratic reforms are largely cosmetic, and at best shallow, with the military still controlling key positions of power.

Political and Military Developments

In 2018, the spotlight was on the ageing leadership of the NLD and its reluctance to include younger members. The resignation of President U Htin Kyaw for health reasons was the most visible example of this problem. Another NLD stalwart, U Win Thein, stepped aside for the same reason; and nonagenarian and co-founder of the party U Tin Oo has long been ill. There are many reports of young NLD hopefuls becoming disgruntled following the replacement of such figures by others of a similar age. Unlike her Tatmadaw colleagues, Aung San Suu Kyi, 73, does not have an obvious successor nor a publicly available legacy document (or speech) for a successor to follow, and the party may find itself rudderless were she to pass.[14]

Failure of peace talks

The third 21CPC, which took place from 11–16 July 2018, failed to generate progress with the non-signatories of the NCA and achieved only limited gains with signatories. Again in 2018, EAOs expressed concerns that the 21CPC and the NCA were instruments of political control over ethnic ambitions, rather than honest attempts at peace-building. With little progress and continuing conflict, these views are becoming harder to refute.

In February, the New Mon State Party (NMSP) and the Lahu Democratic Union (LDU) signed the NCA, bringing expectations of progress to the third 21CPC session. The government, the armed forces and the NCA signatories adopted 14 additional basic principles at the conference, four of which related to political issues, one to economic, seven to social and two to land and environmental matters. During the conference, the United Wa State Party (UWSP), the de facto leader of the Federal Political Negotiation Consultative Committee (FPNCC), stated that it would only consider signing the NCA if the government and the Tatmadaw subscribed to a written commitment allowing the EAOs to change the NCA after signing it.[15] On the sidelines of the conference, the Tatmadaw conducted informal discussions with the AA, the Myanmar National Democratic Alliance Army (MNDAA) and the TNLA, encouraging the groups to sign the ceasefire agreement, conditional on their disarmament – a proposal that they rejected. Regardless, the Tatmadaw's discussions in 2018 with these three EAOs were significant as they had previously refused to acknowledge the groups.

The demand of a number of EAOs to put the rights of 'ethnic nationalities' on the agenda continued to be ignored.[16] The signatory EAOs also expressed concern at the slow implementation of political agreements, with the vice-chair of the NMSP publicly complaining about the political process. The United Nationalities Federal Council (UNFC) held an executive meeting to discuss their continuing participation in the peace process on 26 August. The leaders of these NCA signatories then jointly stated on 11 September that urgent meetings with the Tatmadaw were required, as the peace process had not progressed sufficiently. The two largest signatories, the KNU and the RCSS, withdrew from the peace talks, suspending their official participation in the process.

The Rohingya crisis

The situation in Rakhine State deteriorated further in 2018. In 2017, the Tatmadaw engaged in a campaign ostensibly to root out Arakan Rohingya Salvation Army (ARSA) insurgents after a series of attacks. What resulted was a campaign of grave human-rights abuses, which led to Rohingya civilians fleeing en masse. As of August 2018, there were nearly one million Rohingya in refugee camps in

Cox's Bazar, Bangladesh. Myanmar and the United Nations signed a memorandum of understanding (MoU) at the start of June allowing the Office of the UN High Commissioner for Refugees (UNHCR) access in Rakhine State to assess local conditions and to help refugees to make informed decisions on voluntary return. Naypyidaw did not meet the requirements of the MoU, however, and Rohingya refugees refused to return, fearing for their safety. In June and August 2018, Canada, the European Union and the United States independently imposed sanctions on several Tatmadaw commanders and units for their role in the 2017 violence. At the end of August, the UN Independent International Fact-finding Mission on Myanmar confirmed that the Tatmadaw had systematically targeted civilians and employed sexual violence, including rape, during the crackdown in Rakhine State in 2017.[17] The report recommended that senior generals should be 'investigated and prosecuted' in an international criminal tribunal for genocide, crimes against humanity and war crimes. The International Criminal Court (ICC) has launched a preliminary examination into the Rakhine violence, asserting jurisdiction in the matter in September on behalf of Bangladesh (as Myanmar is not a member).

Violent Events

According to data collected by the MIPS, violent clashes were significantly down in the second half of 2018. Still, most dry-season months recorded clashes in approximately 20 townships across the country.[18]

Kachin State assault

In the first half of the year, Kachin State was the most active and significant battleground in Myanmar. The Tatmadaw launched an assault on KIA bases, in particular those that were not part of a 1994 ceasefire agreement. In April, breaking with an informal agreement, a video was released showing the carnage of a KIA ambush and dead Tatmadaw soldiers. On 11 April, the Tatmadaw launched a major offensive against KIA positions in Mogaung, Mohnyin, Momauk, Tanai and Waingmaw townships. Artillery and airstrikes were reported against several KIA battalions in Mogaung and Tanai. More than 3,000 people were displaced from Hugawng, Injangyang, Sumprabum and Tanai townships. The offensive and the months that preceded it marked the most intense fighting in Myanmar during 2018.

Muse city attack

Hostilities between the TNLA and the Tatmadaw increased in early May 2018. On 10 May, the TNLA clashed with the Tatmadaw in Namtu township, Shan State, with four Tatmadaw soldiers were reportedly killed. This attack was followed two days later by a large assault led by approximately 100 TNLA combatants on Tatmadaw outposts on the outskirts of Muse city, along the Myanmar–China border, killing 19 people, including 15 civilians. The TNLA released a statement that said that the attack was part of its ongoing campaign against drug production and distribution, as well as retaliation for a previous attack by the Tatmadaw against the KIA. Other analysis suggests that the TNLA's increased clashes were part of a larger Northern Alliance effort to relieve pressure on the KIA and draw Tatmadaw forces away from the organisation. The TNLA's attacks coincided with similar guerrilla-style activity by other Northern Alliance actors, the MNDAA and AA.

Arakan Army offensive

As a glimmer of hope appeared that a dialogue between the AA and the Tatmadaw could finally gain traction, fighting erupted in southern Chin and Rakhine states – perhaps under the pretence of improving leverage at the negotiating table. The first significant clash took place on 14–15 October, where the AA engaged the Tatmadaw in Paletwa township, Chin State, and then again on 23 October. A second surge of violence began when on 22 November, AA troops ambushed and killed three Tatmadaw soldiers. Another ambush on 3 December resulted in four AA deaths. Violent clashes then occurred between the Tatmadaw and the AA between 3 and 7 December, with seven Tatmadaw troops and four AA soldiers confirmed dead. On 16 December, a heavily armed force of masked men, allegedly from the AA, confronted military logistics trucks, causing extensive damage. Confrontations between the two groups again occurred on 18 and 19 December in

Kyauktaw and Ponnagyun townships, Rakhine State, with more than 900 villagers fleeing the violence. On 25 December, after declaring a unilateral ceasefire to EAOs in the northeast of the country, the Tatmadaw concentrated its efforts on an offensive against the AA, using heavy artillery, limited naval patrol boats and airstrikes in Paletwa township, Chin State, and northern Rakhine State.

Other violent events

Violent events were less frequent in 2018 but increased in intensity during the latter part of the year between the RCSS, Shan State Progress Party (SSPP) and TNLA. Fighting between these groups around Hsipaw, Kyaukme and Namtu townships intensified in the last few months of the year and appear set to continue. Fighting between NCA signatories was significant throughout the year, particularly between the Pa-O National Liberation Army (PNLA) and RCSS, and between the KNU and Mon National Liberation Army (MNLA), shortly after the latter signed the agreement.

Impact

Vulnerable townships

According to the 2018 report by the Humanitarian Assistance and Resilience Programme Facility and the Myanmar Information Management Unit exploring risk and vulnerability in Myanmar, the 36 most critically vulnerable townships were located in areas of conflict or natural disaster. The 36 townships had the worst educational attainment in Myanmar (51% were illiterate and 59% had no education), suffered from poor sanitation (only 35% had safe sanitation) and had poor access to services (only 19% had electricity and less than half had identity documents allowing for access to government services). The most critically vulnerable townships had witnessed 40% of all violent conflict in the years of study (2015–16) and, according to conflict data from 2018, they also experienced some of the most frequent incidences of violent clashes.

The human toll

The conflict has led to mass displacement. The Tatmadaw, EAOs and militias are known to demand food, finance, intelligence and recruits from local villagers. If villagers refuse to cooperate, they risk being accused of treason. Local populations therefore fear all armed groups entering their communities, and displacement is often favoured over remaining in areas where there is active troop movement.

The UN Office for the Coordination of Humanitarian Affairs (OCHA) reported that as of December 2018, 97,000 people were displaced in Kachin State, 9,000 in Shan State, 10,000 in Kayin State and 128,000 in Rakhine State. Of those displaced in Kachin and Shan states, some 28,000 were displaced in 2018. More than 725,000 Rohingya refugees have fled to Bangladesh since August 2017. OCHA also reported that up to 600,000 Rohingya remain in Rakhine State and face serious hardships due to continuing intercommunal tensions. Access by humanitarian actors and the conditions in camps for internally displaced persons (IDPs) deteriorated significantly in 2018. Moreover – highlighting the wider problems of vulnerability in Myanmar – some 268,000 people were temporarily displaced due to seasonal floods in 2018.

Trends

Increased violence in Rakhine State has shifted the country's conflict dynamics and offered space for greater ceasefire dialogue with northeastern EAOs. Meanwhile, as the West reels from realising the extent of the Rohingya crisis, China has stepped into the void left both in the peace process and in the slowing economy.

Shifting area of conflict

On 21 December 2018, the Tatmadaw declared a unilateral, four-month ceasefire in the Northern Command in Kachin State, the Northeastern, Eastern and Central Eastern commands and the Triangle Command in Shan State, covering most active hostilities in the country except for those of the AA in Rakhine State. The December–April fighting season, traditionally a period of greater intensity for the Tatmadaw, demonstrates that their focus during these months will be on combatting the AA in Rakhine and southern Chin states. This offers a possible period of greater, lasting ceasefire dialogue with northeastern and eastern EAOs. Despite the prospect, this will be difficult to achieve and the current unilateral ceasefire is unlikely to last, particularly if the campaign against the AA is successful. The response of other Northern Alliance EAOs during this time may be important for the unity and solidarity of the coalition.

Shifting tactics

The KIA's move away from fixed-position bases towards guerrilla tactics, in cooperation with other Northern Alliance actors, suggests conflict could spread across further townships in 2019. Previous Tatmadaw offensives on fixed positions in 2013 led to a similar dispersion. If other Northern Alliance groups, such as the TNLA, follow similar tactics this would bode poorly for the safety of civilian and IDP populations, as EAOs attempt to operate from within them. Given the tactics employed by the Tatmadaw in Rakhine State in late 2017, the safety of civilians in 2019 – particularly in what the Tatmadaw assesses to be areas of operation – should be of the utmost concern. Some reports of the Tatmadaw arming northern militias, the Lisu and Rawang, may indicate a redoubling of old tactics of divide and rule.[19] The increase in IED attacks in 2018, including a worrying trend of targeting non-military targets, is likely to continue and could worsen in 2019. This is in part a response to the changing capabilities of the Tatmadaw, which has increased the use of airstrikes, including the use of Chinese-made CH-3A armed drones and mobile artillery on fixed positions under Senior General Min Aung Hlaing. Unconfirmed reports of EAOs, other than the United Wa State Army (UWSA), possessing man-portable air-defence systems (MANPADS) are probably overblown, particularly when viewed with their capability to effectively use them. But such a development should not be dismissed in the medium term given the recent evolution of tactics and the obvious deterrent potential.

Geopolitical influences

One of the most interesting and important aspects of the conflict in 2018 was Myanmar's geopolitical manoeuvring following the fallout from the Tatmadaw's 2017 offensive in Rakhine State. The Rohingya crisis led to a freeze of aid funding from several countries and soured diplomatic ties with the EU, US and important regional players Indonesia and Malaysia. China, and to a lesser extent Russia and India, filled the gap. In August, commander-in-chief Senior General Min Aung Hlaing visited Moscow to purchase arms, while in December, Indian President Ram Nath Kovind conducted his first state visit following the opening of the land border crossing in May.

China–Myanmar relations remain the most crucial for Naypyidaw to manage. Beijing has attempted to maintain its strong pre-transitional presence in Myanmar and as a result, Chinese investment is significant, including through large-scale Belt and Road Initiative (BRI) infrastructure projects. Chinese investment in Myanmar is near impossible to accurately quantify, however. Aid and investment is provided from different levels in China – central, provincial and local – to similar national and subnational levels in Myanmar, while ties between cross-border ethnic Chinese in Myanmar, such as the Ta'ang and Kokang, are also prominent.

Data from the IMF puts the value of Myanmar's debt to Chinese creditors at US$4.3 billion in the 2015/16 financial year, and according to the most recent IMF 2016/17 figures, the number remained steady. The long-held concerns of high interest rates of Chinese loans continued in 2018 and were the subject of debate around the proposed deep-sea port in Kyak Phyu. The initial plan for a US$7.3bn ten-berth port was significantly resized, according to Deputy Finance Minister Set Aung, to a US$1.3bn two-berth port.[20] There continues to be concern in government and in the Tatmadaw of an overreliance on China. Regardless, Beijing's role in the peace process both as a funder and as an envoy between the FPNCC and Naypyidaw has cemented its central role in Myanmar's future. The signing in September of an MoU on the China–Myanmar Economic Corridor (CMEC) – which runs through townships in the northeast where conflict is significant – may suggest Beijing is confident it can control EAOs operating in the area and in the FPNCC. Regardless, the long history of China's interference in Myanmar's domestic affairs and support of ethnic armed organisations has left deep suspicions of Beijing.

Tensions between Bangladesh and Myanmar have worsened throughout the Rohingya crisis in 2018. Dhaka was frustrated at the inflow of refugees, while Naypyidaw believes that Bangladesh is hosting ARSA and AA bases, providing strategic depth and sanctuary, as leverage in negotiations on Rohingya returns. There is no indication that their positions will change in 2019.

Increased international scrutiny, stalemate in peace talks

International funding for the peace process has been in the hundreds of millions of US dollars, yet less than half has been disbursed, due to poor coordination.[21] In 2018 many international donors slowed further the release of pledged money in response to the state-led violence in Rakhine State.

The NLD will be looking to achieve some success in peace talks ahead of the 2020 elections. The increasing power of the FPNCC, following the joining of the KIO in 2018, and the disintegration of the UNFC are two major factors hindering the process. With the prolonged withdrawal in 2018 of the KNU and RCSS, the NCA has lost its two major EAOs and looks weak. Intense fighting in Rakhine State has offered new opportunity for a ceasefire with northeastern EAOs, but the Tatmadaw will be reluctant to sign bilateral agreements outside the NCA. Progress is needed further afield too, while elections add renewed pressure to demonstrate the NLD has improved the provision of services, including education and healthcare.

Asia-Pacific

| Notes

[1]   The Asia Foundation, 'The Contested Areas of Myanmar: Subnational Conflict, Aid and Development', October 2017; Humanitarian Assistance and Resilience Programme Facility and the Myanmar Information Management Unit, 'Vulnerability in Myanmar: A Secondary Data Review of Needs, Coverage and Gaps', June 2018.

[2]   Myanmar Institute for Peace and Security, 'Peace and Security Brief', vol. 2, no. 6, June 2018.

[3]   Maung Aung Myoe, 'The Soldier and the State: The Tatmadaw and Political Liberalization in Myanmar since 2011', *South East Asia Research*, vol. 22, no. 2, 2014, pp. 244–5.

[4]   Min Zaw Oo, 'Understanding Myanmar's Peace Process: Ceasefire Agreements', Catalyzing Reflection, Swiss Peace Foundation, February 2014, p. 33.

[5]   John Buchanan, 'Militias in Myanmar', The Asia Foundation, July 2016.

[6]   Andrew Selth, '"Strong, Fully Efficient and Modern": Myanmar's New Look Armed Forces', Griffith Asia Institute, Regional Outlook, no. 49, 2016.

[7]   Jeff M. Smith, ed., *Asia's Quest for Balance: China's Rise and Balancing in the Indo-Pacific* (Lanham, MD: Rowman & Littlefield, 2018).

[8]   The Stockholm International Peace Research Institute (SIPRI), Arms Transfers Database, accessed on 20 March 2019.

[9]   Elliot Brennan and Min Zaw Oo, 'Peace, Alliance and Inclusivity, Ending Conflict in Myanmar', Brookings Institution, 1 April 2016.

[10] Anthony Davis, 'A Vision for War Without End in Myanmar', *Asia Times*, 30 May 2018.

[11] Myanmar Institute for Peace and Security, 'Peace and Security Brief', vol. 2, no. 9, September 2018.

[12] Humanitarian Assistance and Resilience Programme Facility and the Myanmar Information Management Unit, 'Vulnerability in Myanmar'.

[13] See Tinzar Htun and Mael Raynaud, 'Schedule Two of the 2008 Constitution: Avenues for Reform and Decentralization and Steps Towards a Federal System', Konrad-Adenauer Stiftung, 2018.

[14] Elliot Brennan, 'Myanmar: No Country for Young Men', *Interpreter*, Lowy Institute, 26 March 2018.

[15] Htet Zaw, 'UWSA Still Concerned over Implications of Signing NCA', *Irrawaddy*, 17 July 2018.

[16] Ashley South, 'Protecting Civilians in the Kachin Borderlands, Myanmar', Humanitarian Policy Group Working Paper, December 2018; and Asian Development Bank, UN Development Programme, UN Population Fund, and the UN Entity for Gender Equality and the Empowerment of Women, 'Gender Equality and Women's Rights in Myanmar: A Situation Analysis', 2016.

[17] UN Human Rights Council, 'Myanmar: UN Fact-Finding Mission Releases Its Full Account of Massive Violations by Military in Rakhine, Kachin and Shan States', 18 September 2018.

[18] Myanmar Institute for Peace and Security, 'Peace and Security Brief', vol. 2, no. 5, May 2018.

[19] Myanmar Institute for Peace and Security, 'Peace and Security Brief', vol. 2, no. 3, March 2018.

[20] Kanupriya Kapoor and Aye Min Thant, 'Exclusive: Myanmar Scales Back Chinese-Backed Port Project Due to Debt Fears – Official', Reuters, 2 August 2018.

[21] Thomas Carr, 'Supporting the Transition: Understanding Aid to Myanmar Since 2011', The Asia Foundation, February 2018.

Philippines (ASG)

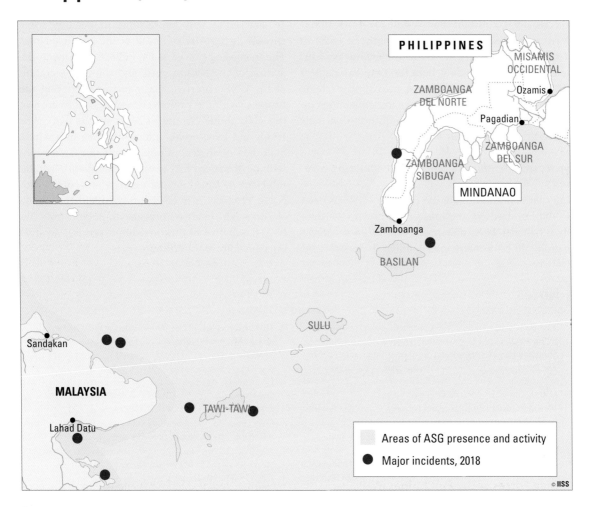

Overview

The conflict in 2018

Under the strain of martial law and repeated military offensives, the Abu Sayyaf Group (ASG) struggled to revive its faltering insurgency in 2018. The strength of the ASG diminished during 2018 as a result of a sustained counter-insurgency campaign waged by the Armed Forces of the Philippines (AFP). The losses sustained by the group followed the decimation of its largest faction and the death of its leader, Isnilon Hapilon, during the Marawi siege in 2017. Since Hapilon's death, the ASG no longer has an established presence on mainland Mindanao and has retreated to its remote island hideouts of Basilan, Sulu and Tawi-Tawi. The group has no central leader and its factions have different affili-

ations. ASG fighters based in Basilan, commanded by Furuji Indama, remain affiliated to the Islamic State, also known as ISIS or ISIL. Sulu-based factions led by Radullan Sahiron and the group's fighters in the Tawi-Tawi islands are not aligned with ISIS. Its remaining factions, restricted to islands off western Mindanao, have engaged in low-level violence.

The Moro peace process in Mindanao, between the government and the Moro Islamic Liberation Front (MILF), proceeded in 2018 without the involvement of the ASG and other radical ISIS-aligned groups. In the absence of peace talks, clashes between the ASG and the AFP erupted frequently in Basilan, Sulu and Tawi-Tawi. The ASG continued its campaign of kidnappings and piracy attacks in the

Sulu Sea, albeit on a smaller scale compared with previous years due to regional naval and air patrols by the Philippines, Indonesia and Malaysia. On 31 July, an ISIS-claimed suicide bombing in Lamitan city, carried out by a Moroccan national linked to the ASG, killed 11 people, but such a major attack was an outlier in 2018.

The conflict to 2018

The ASG was founded in 1991 by the radical Islamist preacher Abdurajak Abubakar Janjalani as a splinter when the Moro National Liberation Front (MNLF) dropped its call for independence in favour of autonomy for Mindanao's Moro Muslim minority. The ASG was initially hierarchical with a centralised leadership structure and in the 1990s it received financial support from Jemaah Islamiah (JI) and al-Qaeda, enabling it to launch major attacks. The ASG committed the deadliest terror attack in the Philippines' history in 2004 when it bombed a passenger ferry in Manila Bay, killing 116 people.

The ASG's capabilities declined in the mid-2000s after the deployment of more than 600 US special forces to Mindanao as part of the global 'war on terror'. Several of the group's leaders were killed in military operations, yet by the late 2000s the ASG

Key statistics	
Type:	Internal
IDPs total (2017):	5,000
IDPs new (2018):	no data
Refugees total (2018):	not applicable
Refugees new (2018):	not applicable
People in need (2018):	not applicable

had re-emerged after splintering into a network of factions spread across Basilan, Sulu and Tawi-Tawi. Since then, the ASG has transitioned from an ideologically inspired jihadi group into a predominantly criminal enterprise, launching a wave of piracy attacks and kidnappings-for-ransom in the Sulu and Celebes seas. In the early 2010s, the ASG enriched itself through ransom pay-outs amounting to tens of millions of US dollars. It became notorious for abducting Westerners and beheading hostages when no payment was made.

In 2014, the ASG reverted to an extremist outlook when its leader, Isnilon Hapilon, pledged allegiance to ISIS. From May–October 2017, the ASG laid siege to Marawi, in the Mindanao province of Lanao del Sur, alongside the ISIS-linked Maute Group (MG).

| Forces

Armed Forces of the Philippines (AFP)

The Armed Forces of the Philippines (AFP) has 125,000 regular combatants serving in the army, navy and air force. An additional 50,000 reservists serve in Citizen Armed Forces Geographical Units (CAFGUs). The AFP is divided into six area-unified commands, with the Western Mindanao Command (WMC) bearing responsibility for fighting the ASG. Joint task forces in Basilan, Sulu and Tawi-Tawi coordinate operations against the group at the local level. In Sulu, where the ASG is most active, the AFP maintains 11 battalions, totalling around 5,500 troops.[1] On 4 December 2018, Lieutenant-General Benjamin Madrigal was appointed as the new AFP commander and on 23 May 2018 Lieutenant-General Arnel dela Vega as the new WMC commander.

The AFP employs aerial and ground offensives against ASG hideouts in Basilan, Sulu and

Tawi-Tawi and also conducts intelligence-led operations to rescue hostages. On 16 May 2018, then-Joint Task Force Sulu commander Brigadier-General Cirilito Sobejana said that the armed forces were 'looking at a two-year window to completely wipe-out the group', and aimed to rescue all hostages by the end of 2018;[2] a target which has not been met. In the maritime domain, the AFP has built permanent installations on outlying islands and conducts trilateral naval patrols with Indonesia and Malaysia to contain the ASG and deter kidnapping incidents.

Abu Sayyaf Group (ASG)

The Abu Sayyaf Group (ASG) was formed in 1991 to fight for an independent Islamic state in the southern Philippines. The group is based in the island provinces of Basilan, Sulu and Tawi-Tawi, located off Mindanao's western coast, and operates along the coast of the Zamboanga Peninsula and in Malaysia's eastern state of Sabah. The group has no central command-and-control structure and no overall figurehead, and is split into dozens of factions and cells arranged along clan and family lines. The factions in Basilan are loosely led by Furuji Indama, while those in Sulu are commanded by veteran militant Radullan Sahiron.

Since the mid-2000s, estimates put the group's strength at around 400–500 fighters, yet more recent government estimates suggest a drop to fewer than 150 by September 2018.[3] The ASG remains rhetorically committed to establishing an Islamic state, but operates as a criminal organisation that pursues profit to ensure its survival. The ASG has access to rifles looted from AFP bases and smuggled from neighbouring countries, uses grenades and improvised explosive devices (IEDs), and deploys speedboats in kidnapping operations at sea. These attacks have targeted commercial vessels, tourists and local fishermen, while on land the ASG launches ambushes and engages in gun battles with the AFP in its island strongholds.

Drivers

Roots in the Moro insurgency

The roots of the ASG's violent uprising lie in the wider Moro separatist insurgency, waged by the MNLF and MILF since the 1970s. The two Moro fronts originally fought for full independence for Mindanao's Moro Muslims, but later dropped this demand in favour of pursuing autonomy via peace talks. The ASG's founders disapproved of this strategy and opposed the peace process between the Philippine government and the MILF that resulted in a new Bangsamoro region to replace the existing Autonomous Region in Muslim Mindanao (ARMM) in July 2018. The new region is set to encompass the ASG's maritime territories of Basilan, Sulu and Tawi-Tawi.

The ASG rejects the idea of autonomy and holds anti-government grievances over the perceived historical oppression of the Moros. Despite being present in Mindanao since the arrival of Arab traders in Sulu in the 1300s, Muslims were oppressed first by Spanish and US colonialists and later by the Philippine state. Christian migration southward has eroded Moro culture and fuelled resentment over lack of political rights. The Moros have long argued for greater administrative control of their communities and access to revenues from natural resources including hydropower, timber, gold and mineral deposits.

The continuation of the mainstream Moro conflict on Mindanao alongside the ASG's separate uprising has contributed to a climate of instability in the region, in which armed Islamist rebel movements have thrived. A culture of clan warlordism, tribal politics and corruption among local politicians in areas of jihadist influence has further fuelled lawlessness in the southern Philippines.

Tactical advantages

The ASG's remote maritime areas of operation make the group resilient and hard to defeat with conventional tactics. Militant hideouts in the isolated island provinces of Basilan, Sulu and Tawi-Tawi are far from mainland Mindanao and the centre of state power in Manila, 950 kilometres to the north. The waters of the Sulu and Celebes seas, in which the islands are located, have historically been underpoliced, allowing the free movement of militants in the region's waterways. On land, the group operates out of rugged and mountainous terrain, with many of its fighters based in the mountains surrounding Patikul town, Sulu. The advantage of the ASG's guerrilla tactics and small fighting units has served to prolong the insurgency.

For much of its three-decade existence, the ASG has not taken the form of a hierarchical organisation, instead operating as a network of loosely affiliated factions spread across Basilan, Sulu and Tawi-Tawi. Its decentralised structure has also made the ASG difficult to combat and intelligence gathering an arduous task for the AFP. The ASG is insular and secretive, while its factions operate along clan and family lines with members linked by blood or intermarriage, making it highly resistant to infiltration.[4] Children are recruited into the group from a young age, making membership of the ASG a way of life.

Poverty and underdevelopment in Mindanao

Poverty in the ASG's strongholds drives recruitment for the group. Western Mindanao and the islands of Basilan, Sulu and Tawi-Tawi have long been plagued by weak governance, poor service provision and high youth unemployment, and access to water and electricity remains limited in the poorest areas. Eleven of the 20 most impoverished provinces in the Philippines are in the Mindanao region, which contains 25 of the country's 81 provinces.[5] The poverty rate in the ARMM in 2015 (the latest year for which figures are available) was 59%, compared to 26.3% at the national level.[6] In the ASG's main stronghold of Sulu, 65.7% live below the poverty line, making it the second-poorest province in the Philippines.

Political and Military Developments

ASG presence limited to island provinces
The ASG's fractured nature and lack of a main figurehead post-Marawi has damaged its ability to act coherently as a single organization. The group remained confined largely to its traditional strongholds in the island provinces of Basilan, Sulu and Tawi-Tawi during 2018. The defeat of Hapilon's faction in Marawi in October 2017 marked the end of the ASG's presence on mainland Mindanao, where it had collaborated with the MG and the Bangsamoro Islamic Freedom Fighters (BIFF) to lay siege to the city. In 2018, the ASG was infrequently active along the coasts of the Zamboanga Peninsula and Malaysia's Sabah State, but did not establish a permanent presence there.

Duterte's response to Marawi
President Rodrigo Duterte's response to the Marawi siege facilitated a military crackdown on the ASG during 2018: Mindanao and the Sulu archipelago have been under martial law since the siege began in mid-2017. On the advice of the AFP and Philippine National Police (PNP), on 12 December 2018 Duterte extended the martial law until the end of 2019, enabling the AFP to launch sustained offensives against the ASG and set up road checkpoints to prevent militants from moving freely.[7] The government has sought to further degrade the ASG's capabilities through its Program Against Violent Extremism (PAVE), formally launched on 18 April after a two-year trial. The initiative aims to integrate former ASG militants back into society through economic, educational and psychological support. At its launch, ARMM governor Mujiv Hataman described PAVE as a 'sustainable' solution to the growth of Islamist extremism. Earlier in the year, Defence Secretary Delfin Lorenzana voiced support for the continuation of PAVE, revealing it had helped 173 former ASG militants in the past two years.

ASG remains excluded from Moro peace process
The ASG remained opposed to the Moro peace process and committed to its violent campaign, while the government quickly rowed back on suggestions that it might attempt to engage the ASG in political talks. Duterte's cooperative rhetoric, which was a departure from his long-standing 'no negotiation' policy, was short-lived. After the ASG carried out a suicide bombing on 31 July, the government accused the group of 'war crimes' and called on the army to launch 'intensive military operations', thereby ending any prospect of a peace dialogue.[8]

Violent Events

AFP offensives
The majority of ASG encounters took the form of clashes with the AFP. During 2018, 161 fatalities resulted from 63 armed clashes and violent incidents involving the ASG (see **Table 1**). The vast majority of those killed – 106 – were ASG militants, compared to 28 AFP troops and 27 civilians. In addition, 91 ASG members were arrested and 168 surrendered to the authorities.

Most fighting during 2018 centred on Sulu's Patikul town, while brief encounters frequently occurred in rural areas of Basilan, Sulu and Tawi-Tawi. On 11 February, an AFP–ASG clash in Panamao, Sulu, left five ASG fighters dead and seven AFP soldiers wounded. On 24 February, an encounter in Maluso, Basilan, resulted in the deaths of seven militants. On 13 March, fighting in Patikul, Sulu, killed five militants and left six AFP soldiers injured. On 2 May, the army launched a combined air and ground offensive targeting Indama's faction in Sumisip, Basilan, killing nine jihadists. From 13–14 May, major clashes in Patikul left 15 militants

Table 1: Highest-fatality incidents, 2018			
Date	**Location**	**Fatalities**	**Incident Type**
2 May	Sumisip, Basilan	9 (9 ASG militants)	AFP ground and aerial offensive against ASG
13 May	Patikul, Sulu	12 (10 ASG militants, 2 AFP troops)	ASG–AFP clash
31 July	Lamitan, Basilan	11 (1 ASG militant, 6 AFP troops, 4 civilians)	ASG suicide-bomb attack on AFP checkpoint
26 October	Patikul, Sulu	10 (7 ASG militants, 3 AFP troops)	ASG–AFP clash
13 Dec	Minis island, Sulu	8 (7 ASG militants, 1 AFP soldier)	ASG-AFP clash

and three soldiers dead. On 16 November, militants ambushed a group of AFP soldiers attempting to locate hostages in Patikul, Sulu, leaving five government troops dead and 23 wounded. On 13 December, fighting on Minis island, Sulu, left seven militants and one soldier dead.

At the beginning of 2018, General Sobejana said the ASG had between 300 and 400 fighters, but on 28 August, Defence Secretary Delfin Lorenzana said the ASG had suffered a 'significant drop' in its membership due to sustained military operations. He estimated the ASG to have only 100 fighters in Sulu and 35 in Basilan, yet did not provide figures for the number of ASG members active in Tawi-Tawi and other areas. The ASG's declining activity at the end of the year suggests that its strength has significantly reduced.

Lamitan bombing

In a year which saw few major ASG attacks, one incident served as an outlier. On 31 July, a powerful bomb hidden in a van exploded at an army road checkpoint on the outskirts of Lamitan city, Basilan, killing the driver, six AFP troops and four civilians. The attack, later revealed to be a suicide bombing, was claimed by ISIS and was carried out by a Moroccan national linked to the ASG. The attack showed that links between Basilan-based ASG fighters and ISIS have persisted after the death of Hapilon. The attacker's identity also raised alarm over whether foreign jihadis were fighting alongside the ASG in the Sulu archipelago. The incident followed the arrest of a Spanish ASG member in Maluso in January, and the detention of an Egyptian man at Zamboanga city port in February suspected of trying to join the group. While the full extent of ASG–ISIS relations remains unclear, the attack indicates cooperation between ISIS and Indama's Basilan-based group. No ASG attacks in Sulu or Tawi-Tawi were claimed by ISIS in 2018.

Piracy and kidnappings

The ASG continued to launch piracy attacks and kidnappings at sea, yet at a reduced rate. Eight incidents occurred at sea during 2018, compared to dozens of attacks per year at the height of the ASG piracy epidemic between 2015 and 2017. In February, militants aboard three motorboats tried to hijack a large cargo ship in waters off Sigabo island, wounding two crew members before a Philippine Coast Guard (PCG) vessel forced them to retreat. A second piracy attack occurred on 10 August when militants boarded a Malaysian-owned tugboat off Tawi-Tawi, yet failed to seize hostages after crew members locked themselves inside a secure room. Five incidents occurred in Malaysian waters. On 27 February, Malaysian troops killed three ASG militants in Tawau, while on 8 May, soldiers killed four militants on board a speedboat off Lahad Datu. On 11 September, the ASG abducted two Indonesian fishermen from a vessel off Sabah. On 6 December, the ASG opened fire on a tugboat off Pegasus Reef before kidnapping three Indonesian fishermen from a fishing trawler in the same area.

Outside the group's usual strongholds, on 31 August ASG militants raided the coastal town of Sirawai, Zamboanga del Norte province, killing four and abducting two civilians before retreating. Earlier in August, intelligence from the local government in Palawan warned that an ASG cell was plotting kidnappings in the province, north of its usual area of operation. In response, the navy continued to hold regular trilateral naval and air patrols in the Sulu Sea alongside Indonesian and Malaysian sailors, while Malaysian authorities implemented a dusk-to-dawn curfew for civilian vessels off the coast of the Eastern Sabah Security Zone (ESSZ). The AFP established a new outpost on Panguan island near the Malaysian sea border to prevent the ASG from using the area as a 'safe haven'. The PCG also deployed several additional patrol vessels off Palawan and Zamboanga. This combination of measures was successful in limiting ASG piracy attacks and kidnappings-at-sea.

Aside from attacks at sea, the ASG kidnapped 18 hostages in 2018, including government workers, teachers and the relatives of local officials. No hostages were killed, and most were either rescued by the army or freed unharmed after their families paid ransom. (The government maintained its long-held policy of not paying ransoms.) The ransoms demanded for Filipinos ran into tens of thousands of US dollars, in contrast to the multi-million-dollar amounts demanded by the group for Western victims in previous years.

Impact

Civilian victimisation

Civilians in Basilan, Sulu and Tawi-Tawi faced the risk of death and injury in targeted and indiscriminate attacks carried out by the ASG in 2018. However, the threat was lower than in previous years. Four civilians were killed in the 31 July suicide blast at an army checkpoint on the outskirts of Lamitan city. The intended target was likely to have been a parade involving schoolchildren in the city centre,[9] but the bomber detonated the device early when the AFP stopped his vehicle.

A small number of other deliberate ASG attacks on civilians occurred in 2018. On 4 January, militants beheaded two civilians in a village near Sumisip, Basilan. Two construction workers were killed when the ASG ambushed their vehicle in Basilan on 31 January, while the next day two civilians were killed during an ambush in Sulu. On 24 February, a village chief was assassinated in Mohammad Ajul town, while a public-health official was shot dead on 12 April in Jolo. On 18 August, militants killed a village peacekeeper in Ungkaya-Pukan, before killing four civilians during a raid on Sirawai later that month.

Civilians were also at risk of being injured in the crossfire during encounters between the AFP and the ASG, which caused minor localised displacement. On 7 August, some 5,000 members of the indigenous Yakan tribe fled their homes amid an AFP offensive in Basilan. Unexploded ordnance left over from historical clashes also posed a threat. On 3 January, a buried mortar shell exploded, killing eight and injuring five people at a rubber plantation in Sirawai, an area that witnessed intense AFP–ASG fighting in the 1990s.

Civilians in areas of ASG activity were also at risk of being mistakenly targeted during army offensives. On 14 September, the AFP claimed to have killed seven ASG militants near Patikul, yet a local human-rights group said the men were civilians from the local Tausug community harvesting fruit in the area. Local non-governmental organisation Suara Bangsamoro described the men as 'victims of a summary execution' at the hands of troops, yet the AFP denied the accusation and maintained the men were ASG members.

Hostages prevent AFP from full-scale offensive

The ASG is thought to still hold at least eight hostages in unknown locations across Basilan and Sulu. The AFP sighted captives in a mountainous area near Patikul in March. According to then-WMC chief Lieutenant-General Carlito Galvez, uncertainty over the location of hostages was preventing the AFP from launching an all-out offensive, in particular aerial-bombing campaigns, while they focused on rescuing the victims.

ASG attacks delay infrastructure projects

The government maintains it will struggle to bring development to areas where the ASG operates, due to the risk of attacks on contractors. The ASG targeted workers on state-run infrastructure projects in early 2018. On 4 February, the Department of Public Works and Highways (DPWH) said construction projects scheduled for Basilan would face lengthy delays due to the risk of extortion and ambushes by the ASG. A string of attacks on workers followed the announcement. An engineer was abducted in Jolo on 14 February, while on 16 April, a DPWH warehouse sustained damage in a grenade attack.

Trends

Despite the ASG's capabilities being degraded after sustained military offensives, the group still poses a significant threat to government soldiers and the civilian population in its traditional island hideouts of Basilan, Sulu and Tawi-Tawi. The ASG also poses a threat to coastal communities on the Zamboanga Peninsula and along the east coast of Malaysia's Sabah State, where it has engaged in shoot-outs with security forces and launched piracy attacks. Yet without a central leadership or hierarchical command-and-control structure, the ASG does not represent a coherent or organised fighting force as it did to a greater extent in past decades. The ASG operates more as a network of loosely affiliated factions, sub-factions and cells, based along clan and family lines. Most of these groups, with the exception of Indama's ISIS-linked faction in Basilan, appear to be shifting away from large-scale attacks motivated by ideology and towards criminal activities such as kidnapping to boost profits and bolster their ranks.

Attempts to revive piracy and kidnapping in the Sulu Sea on a large scale are proving unsuccessful, due primarily to trilateral naval patrols and the AFP's land-based crackdown under martial law. The ASG is under increasing pressure, not only under siege by the military, but also facing declining revenues from kidnappings-for-ransom and reduced support from ISIS, as the global jihadist group loses territory and influence in the Middle East. In 2019, Duterte will expect to build on recent gains and crack down further on the ASG, aided by the renewed extension of martial law in Mindanao. With neither side open to peace talks, the ASG is likely to continue its violent campaign, although on a somewhat reduced scale. The ASG has developed a reputation for resilience over the past three decades, having survived many repeated army offensives under six presidents. The group may reduce its visible presence and focus on recruiting in its areas of influence.

Notes

[1]   Roel Pareño, '11 battalions back in Sulu to go after Abu Sayyaf leaders', *Philippine Star*, 5 January 2018.

[2]   Jaime Laude, 'Finish off Abu Sayyaf in 2018, soldiers told', *Philippine Star*, 18 May 2018.

[3]   Francis Wakefield, 'Government troops still chasing 150 Abu Sayyaf terrorists – Lorenzana', *Manila Bulletin*, 28 August 2018.

[4]   Jamela Alindogan, 'Inside Abu Sayyaf: Blood, drugs and conspiracies', Al-Jazeera, 24 July 2016.

[5]   'Mindanao has 11 of 20 Poorest Provinces in the Philippines', *Summit Express*, 26 March 2016.

[6]   Jodesz Gavilan, 'Poverty in Mindanao', *Rappler*, 28 May 2017.

[7]   Mara Cepeda, 'Congress extends martial law in Mindanao to end of 2019', *Rappler*, 12 December 2018.

[8]   'Pres. Duterte Orders Soldiers to Destroy Abu Sayyaf Terrorists', *Zamboanga Today*, 15 August 2018.

[9]   John Unson, 'Basilan bomber appears to be targeting school children in Lamitan', *Philippine Star*, 3 August 2018.

Philippines (Moro)

Overview

The conflict in 2018

The peace process between the Philippine government and the Moro Islamic Liberation Front (MILF) made major strides forward in 2018. In July, President Rodrigo Duterte and MILF chair Al Haj Murad Ebrahim signed the Bangsamoro Organic Law (BOL), paving the way for a new self-governing region to replace the existing Autonomous Region in Muslim Mindanao (ARMM). The law still needs to be ratified in a plebiscite scheduled for early 2019. The 1993 and 1997 ceasefires between the Moro National Liberation Front (MNLF), the MILF and the Armed Forces of the Philippines (AFP) continued to hold in 2018.

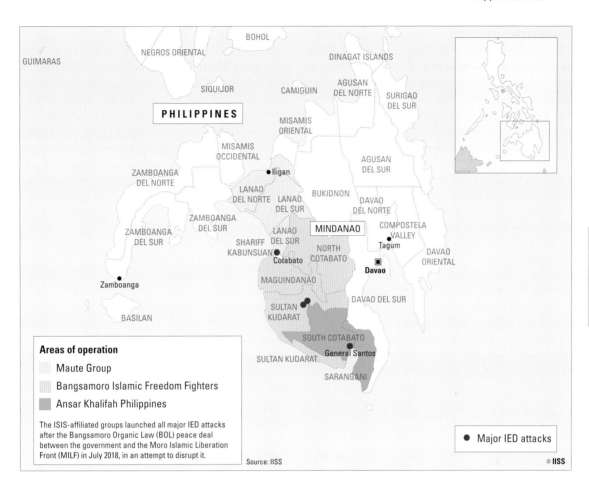

Areas of operation

Maute Group

Bangsamoro Islamic Freedom Fighters

Ansar Khalifah Philippines

The ISIS-affiliated groups launched all major IED attacks after the Bangsamoro Organic Law (BOL) peace deal between the government and the Moro Islamic Liberation Front (MILF) in July 2018, in an attempt to disrupt it.

Source: IISS

● Major IED attacks

© IISS

Several groups linked to the Islamic State, also known as ISIS or ISIL, remained opposed to the peace process and continued to fight government forces. The Bangsamoro Islamic Freedom Fighters (BIFF) were the most active, engaging in major clashes with the AFP in Maguindanao and North Cotabato. The Maute Group (MG) clashed with troops on a smaller scale in Lanao del Norte and Lanao del Sur, while Ansar Khalifah Philippines (AKP) remained active in Sarangani and South Cotabato. After the BOL was signed, the BIFF and AKP launched a series of mass-casualty bomb attacks targeting civilian areas.

The conflict to 2018

The Moro insurgency began in 1972, following earlier armed uprisings by Moro Muslim rebels against Spanish, American and Japanese colonisers. The MNLF was the first group to fight for an independent homeland for western Mindanao's Moro Muslim population. The MILF emerged as a splinter in 1977. The two groups have battled government forces for much of the past five decades.

Both the MNLF and MILF have signed previous peace agreements with the government (see **Table 1**). The 1976 Tripoli Agreement between the MNLF and the government of Ferdinand Marcos promised autonomy, but collapsed amid a dispute over which areas should be covered. A major breakthrough came in 1989 with the establishment of the ARMM, encompassing the provinces of Lanao del Sur, Maguindanao, Sulu and Tawi-Tawi. MNLF founder

Key statistics

Type:	Internal
IDPs total (2017):	92,000
IDPs new (2018):	no data
Refugees total (2018):	not applicable
Refugees new (2018):	not applicable
People in need (2018):	300,000

Nur Misuari served as governor of the ARMM for five years after his group signed a Final Peace Agreement with Manila in 1996. The MILF became the dominant Moro rebel group in the mid-1990s after the MNLF splintered and declined in strength. In 2014, the MILF signed the Comprehensive Agreement on the Bangsamoro (CAB) under then-president Aquino's administration, vowing to decommission in return for an upgraded autonomous region. The CAB has reduced violence on the ground while talks over the proposed new region have continued to progress under Duterte.

In recent years, the MILF and MNLF have largely avoided clashing with the AFP, with two notable exceptions. MNLF fighters laid siege to Zamboanga city for three weeks in 2013, before a 2015 joint MILF–BIFF ambush killed 44 police officers, briefly souring relations with the government. In 2017, a coalition of ISIS-affiliated jihadist groups composed of the MG, the AKP, BIFF and the Abu Sayyaf Group (ASG) laid siege to Marawi city between May and October, threatening the BOL-centred peace process. The MILF responded by voicing its opposition to ISIS and restating its commitment to peace.

Forces

Armed Forces of the Philippines (AFP)
The Armed Forces of the Philippines (AFP), which appointed Lieutenant-General Benjamin Madrigal as its commander in December 2018, has 125,000 combatants serving across the army, navy and air force and a 50,000-strong reserve force organised in Citizen Armed Forces Geographical Units (CAFGUs). The AFP's Western Mindanao Command (WMC) is charged with maintaining peace with the MILF and MNLF while combatting ISIS-linked groups. Since repelling the 2017 Marawi siege, the AFP has attacked ISIS-linked groups in their rural western Mindanao strongholds through coordinated ground and air offensives.

Moro Islamic Liberation Front (MILF)
Although it no longer attacks government troops, the Moro Islamic Liberation Front (MILF) retains 30,000 armed fighters stationed at bases across western Mindanao and has access to an arsenal of high-powered rifles. The group is led by its chairman, Al Haj Murad Ebrahim and retains a significant degree of public support. In past decades, the MILF launched ambushes against government forces as

Table 1: Peace agreement timeline

Peace agreements between the government and the two main Moro insurgent groups, the MNLF and MILF

Date	Agreement	Signatories	Goals	Result
1976	Tripoli Agreement	Government–MNLF	Create autonomous region in the south	Collapsed. Hostilities resumed
1989	Autonomous Region in Muslim Mindanao (ARMM)	Government–MNLF	Give autonomy to the Moro population of western Mindanao	Established – covers Basilan, Sulu, Tawi-Tawi, Maguindanao and Lanao del Sur. MNLF leader Nur Misuari served as ARMM's Governor, 1996–2001
1996	Jakarta Accord	Government–MNLF	End conflict between government and MNLF. Facilitate implementation of Tripoli Agreement	Final Peace Agreement successful
2014	Comprehensive Agreement on the Bangsamoro (CAB)	Government–MILF	Create new region to replace ARMM. MILF to disarm and transition into a political party	Failed
2018	Bangsamoro Organic Law (BOL)	Government–MILF (signed by President Duterte on 26 July 2018)	Create new region to be led by senior MILF figures. The Bangsamoro Autonomous Region in Muslim Mindanao (BARMM) covers existing ARMM provinces, Cotabato city and at least 21 villages in North Cotabato province	Ratified. Public vote to be held in January 2019

part of its campaign for an independent Moro state. In recent years, the MILF has dropped its demand for full independence in favour of autonomy and is preparing to disarm and transition to a political party with a central role in governing the new Bangsamoro region.

Moro National Liberation Front (MNLF)

The Moro National Liberation Front (MNLF) was founded in 1972 with the aim of creating an independent Moro state. Initially a centralised organisation, it splintered after signing a 1996 peace deal. Its founder, Nur Misuari, still leads a 3,000-strong faction and serves as de facto leader. Yusop Jikiri leads another major faction and represents the group as its chair. The MNLF no longer attacks the AFP, but used high-powered firearms in the past. At its peak in the 1970s the MNLF had around 30,000 fighters, but this has now fallen to fewer than 10,000, mostly based in western Mindanao and the Sulu islands. Like the MILF, the MNLF dropped its call for independence in favour of autonomy, but has not been involved in the BOL-centred peace process, raising concerns it could prove disruptive.

Bangsamoro Islamic Freedom Fighters (BIFF)

The Bangsamoro Islamic Freedom Fighters (BIFF) broke away from the MILF in 2010 after its founder, Ameril Umbra Kato, grew frustrated with the group's reduced demands. Kato died in 2011 and the group is now led by Abu Toraife. The BIFF seeks the establishment of an independent Moro state and is divided into three main factions active in Maguindanao, North Cotabato and Sultan Kudarat. The group pledged allegiance to ISIS in 2014 and participated in the 2017 Marawi siege. Among its 300–500 fighters are dozens of jihadists from Indonesia and Malaysia trained in bomb-making. The group attacks AFP troops and civilians using rifles and improved explosive devices (IEDs), launching ambushes in rural areas and orchestrating bombings in cities.

Maute Group (MG)

The Maute Group (MG), founded by brothers Abdullah and Omar Maute between 2010 and 2011, espouses a radical form of Islam centred on Salafi-Wahhabi ideology. The group is aligned to ISIS and aims to forge an Islamic caliphate in the Philippines. The Maute brothers played a central role in orchestrating the 2017 Marawi siege, in which most of the MG's fighters and senior leaders were killed. The surviving members, thought to number fewer than 100, are based in Lanao del Norte and Lanao del Sur provinces and engaged in sporadic gunfights with government forces in 2018. The AFP claims that the MG is actively recruiting again under its new leader Abu Dar, whom the AFP considers the leader of ISIS in Southeast Asia.[1]

Ansar Khalifah Philippines (AKP)

Ansar Khalifah Philippines (AKP) formed in 2014 and aims to establish an ISIS-style caliphate in Mindanao. It is not known who leads the AKP today after its founder, Mohammad Jaafar Maguid, was killed in a police shoot-out in 2017. The AKP is the least active of Mindanao's ISIS-affiliated groups and has around 50 members in the provinces of Sarangani and South Cotabato, where it infrequently clashes with state security forces.

| Drivers

Oppression of Moro Muslim population

The roots of the conflict lie in the oppression of the Moro Muslims, who account for more than one-fifth of residents on the Catholic-majority island of Mindanao.[2] Moro rebels led uprisings against Spanish, US and Japanese foreign rule in the nineteenth and twentieth centuries, having lived in the area since the arrival of Arab traders in Sulu in the 1300s. Past colonial rulers and the modern-day Philippine state have denied the Moros an independent homeland and full political control over their communities, and a sense of historical injustice has persisted for generations. A key cause of resentment has been Christian migration to Mindanao, which allegedly threatens traditional Moro identity and culture.[3]

Poverty and underdevelopment

Economic marginalisation has long been a driver of recruitment for Moro rebel groups. Moro-majority provinces are among the most deprived in the Philippines, despite being rich in natural resources such as hydropower, timber, gold and mineral deposits. The ARMM also has some of the most fertile soils in the country, with agriculture accounting for 56.4% of the region's economy.[4] However, most profits are accrued by the government and large firms operating in the region. Western Mindanao is plagued by poor infrastructure and limited service provision. Figures from the Philippine Statistics Authority (PSA) reveal that 59% of ARMM residents were living in poverty in 2015 compared to a national average of 26.3%.[5] The poverty rate in Lanao del Sur was 74.3%, making it the country's poorest province.

State fragility and a fractured separatist movement

The absence of state authority and rule of law, and a history of warlordism and clan politics in western Mindanao have all contributed to sustaining the conflict. Fracturing within the rebel movement has had a similar effect. Ideological disputes have resulted in the formation of splinter groups and sub-factions within the two Moro fronts. These divisions have centred on whether the movement should be more secular or Islamist in nature, and whether the Moros should pursue full independence or accept autonomy.

The emergence of the Islamic State

The emergence of ISIS in Iraq and Syria in 2014 has served as a more recent trigger for violence in the southern Philippines, transforming what was for decades a local separatist movement into a conflict linked to transnational jihadism. ISIS's ideology inspired militants in Southeast Asia to seek to carve out a regional caliphate. Mindanao, already home to armed Islamist groups, was viewed as an ideal target. This threat materialised in 2017 when Filipino militants took over Marawi with the help of jihadis from Indonesia and Malaysia. This attempt was defeated after five months, but Mindanao's ISIS-aligned groups – the AKP, BIFF and the MG – remain active and retain the ambition to establish a caliphate.

Political and Military Developments

Government–MILF peace process nears completion

The peace process between the government and the MILF made significant progress during 2018, with several major steps taken toward the creation of a new autonomous region in western Mindanao. In February, the BOL was presented to the Senate by Juan Miguel Zubiri, chair of the Senate subcommittee on the bill. A crucial breakthrough came on 15 May, when three House of Representatives (HoR) committees approved the text of the BOL without any further amendments. On 30 May, the HoR voted in favour of the BOL with a majority of 227–11, while the 22-member Senate voted unanimously in favour. The BOL was signed into law by Duterte on 26 July.

Duterte and MILF Chair Ebrahim held a ceremonial signing on 6 August, with hopes that the BOL would 'finally end the decades-old conflict'. Attention soon turned to the implementation phase, with a regional plebiscite to ratify the BOL set to be held on 21 January and 6 February 2019 in all areas due to be included in the new Bangsamoro Autonomous Region (BAR). Thousands of current and former MILF rebels registered to vote. In July 2018, Ebrahim said the MILF's 30,000 fighters would be decommissioned before the BAR is established, while its six largest camps would be converted into 'productive civilian communities' to help ex-rebels integrate into society. In August, the MILF confirmed that Ebrahim will be chief minister of the BAR transition government. Over the next two years, the MILF is set to transition from a rebel group to a political party, enabling its participation in future elections in the new region.

Senior government and MILF leaders support BOL

As the peace process gained momentum, the government expressed its commitment to the BOL, and Duterte of his desire to correct 'historical injustices' against the Moros. On 18 April, then-AFP chief Lieutnant-General Carlito Galvez said he hoped for a 'final, peaceful and equitable resolution of the conflict', stating the need to 'address grievances' and 'set the conditions for a just and lasting peace'. The BOL received a positive reception from rebel leaders too. MILF vice-chair Ghazali Jaafar said that the BOL would result in a political entity 'above' the level of the ARMM and that its provisions were acceptable to the MILF's leadership and the MILF-led Bangsamoro Transition Commission (BTC) Both sides campaigned for a 'yes' vote in the plebiscite.

The make-up of the proposed Bangsamoro region
The BAR is set to cover the existing five provinces of the ARMM – Basilan, Lanao del Sur, Maguindanao, Sulu and Tawi-Tawi – along with six municipalities in Lanao del Norte and 39 villages in North Cotabato. The new region will have its own 80-member elected parliament able to pass laws and appoint a chief minister, and will receive an unconditional annual grant of US$1.3 billion from the central government, in addition to 75% of taxes collected from its territories. The Bangsamoro administration is also set to receive 100% of profits from most natural resources, while separate revenue-sharing deals have been agreed for fossil fuels, uranium and inland water resources.[6] Manila will retain control over defence and security, with Duterte having already ruled out the creation of a separate Bangsamoro military or police force. However, the AFP and Philippine National Police (PNP) have confirmed they are open to accepting Moro recruits – including former MILF and MNLF rebels – once the BOL has been ratified.

Radical groups oppose the peace process
Radical groups affiliated to ISIS remain opposed to the BOL and intent on disrupting the peace process. On 6 June, BIFF spokesperson Abu Misri Mama said, 'we are not in favour of autonomy; that's the reason why we left the MILF in the first place' and added that BIFF would 'continue to fight for independence'. The AKP and the MG hold a similar view, but the position of the more moderate MNLF is mixed. MNLF chair Jikiri said he was optimistic the bill would bring 'peace, hope and development', and pledged to reach out to unsupportive groups, yet the faction led by Misuari has not voiced support. On 6 September, MILF chief negotiator Mohaqher Iqbal said initial talks with the MNLF and two BIFF factions had been 'positive', but warned that the most powerful BIFF faction commanded by Abu Toraife was refusing to engage on the issue.

Maute Group and AKP show signs of activity
The MG and the AKP remained active in 2018. The MG engaged in gun battles with AFP–PNP forces in the Lanao del Sur towns of Marantao, Masiu, Piagapo and Tubaran. According to military-intelligence reports, the MG recruited from impoverished settlements around Lake Lanao to rebuild its ranks after suffering huge losses in Marawi city in 2017. Further south, the AKP was active in Sarangani and South Cotabato provinces, but kept a low profile, clashing infrequently with security forces.

Violent Events

AFP–BIFF fighting escalates in western Mindanao
Fighting between the AFP and BIFF intensified in 2018, with clashes erupting in Maguindanao and North Cotabato provinces. The BIFF launched ambushes against AFP troops using firearms and improvised explosive devices (IEDs), while the army targeted militant hideouts in large-scale ground and aerial offensives. Several encounters were notable for their intensity, prolonged nature and high number of fatalities. On 8–11 March, the AFP attacked BIFF positions in Datu Saudi town, leaving 44 militants dead and 26 wounded. On 10 June, the military launched a combined aerial and ground assault against the BIFF in Liguasan Marsh, killing 15 and wounding eight militants. Clashes in Maguindanao and North Cotabato over the next few days left another 14 militants dead. On 3 July, BIFF attempted to take over buildings in the Maguindanao town of Datu Paglas, sparking clashes that killed 15 militants and one soldier.

Aside from these major outbreaks of violence, small-scale encounters occurred on a weekly basis. Clashes between the AFP and BIFF decreased in frequency toward the end of the year, reflecting a reduction in BIFF activity and resources due to earlier battlefield losses. Most violent incidents involving the group occurred in an area the AFP labels the 'SPMS box': the closely clustered Maguindanao towns of Mamasapano, Pagatin, Shariff Aguak and Shariff Saydona Mustapha.

Bombings targeting civilians after BOL peace deal
In the weeks after the BOL was signed, IEDs exploded in several urban centres. On 28 August, a bomb went off at a street festival in Isulan town, Sultan Kudarat province, killing three and injuring 34 civilians. On 2 September, a second device detonated outside an internet café in the town, killing two and injuring 15. Both attacks were perpetrated by BIFF. On 16 September, a blast blamed

on the AKP hit a shopping street in General Santos, South Cotabato, wounding seven people. BIFF struck again on 31 December, when an explosion at a shopping mall in Cotabato city, Maguindanao province, left two people dead and 34 injured. The incidents formed part of a wider trend of rising ISIS-linked IED attacks, with 28 taking place in western Mindanao in 2018. The majority of explosions were blamed on BIFF, while most were small-scale and targeted military vehicles by the roadside, resulting in between one and five casualties. The MILF and the MNLF repeatedly stated their opposition to extremist ISIS-linked groups in 2018, and pledged to cooperate with government forces.

Low-level violence involving the MILF and MNLF

While the MILF and the MNLF did not attack government forces in 2018, members of the two Moro fronts were involved in minor skirmishes in Lanao del Sur, Maguindanao and North Cotabato provinces, including clan disputes and gunfights between rival factions. In most cases, violence subsided upon the intervention of rebel commanders. On 25 May, a joint AFP–PNP anti-drug raid resulted

in the killing of nine MILF fighters in Matalam, North Cotabato province, sparking tension between the government and the MILF at a crucial stage of the peace process. The MILF claimed the victims were disarmed before being shot, whereas the AFP said it came under fire. A Malaysian-led International Monitoring Team (IMT-13) mandated to oversee the ceasefire launched a probe into the incident, reducing tensions. (The findings are yet to be released.)

The AFP's sustained anti-ISIS campaign

The AFP maintained pressure on ISIS-aligned groups under martial law in Mindanao. The measure was first imposed after the jihadi takeover of Marawi in May 2017, and then extended by Congress until 31 December 2019.[7] The government also sought to damage ISIS-aligned groups through its Program Against Violent Extremism (PAVE), launched by ARMM governor Mujiv Hataman in April to reintegrate former jihadists through the offer of education, training and financial support.[8] The initiative led several small groups of BIFF and MG militants to surrender in 2018.

Impact

AFP–BIFF clashes lead to mass displacement

Fighting between the AFP and BIFF affected residents in Maguindanao and North Cotabato. Localised displacement often occurred near clash sites, particularly during large-scale government offensives. In mid-March, 500 families fled from central Maguindanao as the army launched aerial attacks targeting BIFF positions. On 10 April, more than 1,600 people were displaced amid gun battles in Shariff Saydona Mustapha, Maguindanao province. An additional 2,300 civilians fled in the following days as airstrikes pounded the BIFF in the adjoining towns of Datu Salibo, Datu Saudi, Mamasapano and Shariff Aguak. On 10 June, the ARMM recorded the displacement of 15,000 people from 1,793 families in Liguasan Marsh after heavy fighting. On 13 June, 10,000 civilians were displaced amid clashes between the AFP and BIFF in Pikit, North Cotabato. In early July, the ARMM said 50,000 people (12,040 families) were displaced amid heavy fighting between the AFP and BIFF in Maguindanao province. Civilians were also forced

to flee from clan disputes between rival MILF and MNLF factions.

In August, the United Nations said that 69,000 residents of Marawi city were still displaced following the 2017 siege. On 28 November, Finance Secretary Carlos Dominguez said the government had received a total of PHP35.1bn (US$670 million) in aid from international organisations and donor nations to rebuild the city.

ISIS-affiliated groups threaten civilian life

Civilians remained at risk of harm from ISIS-linked groups in 2018, which saw at least 25 civilian deaths as a result of the conflict. Civilians were at risk of being caught in crossfire during AFP–BIFF clashes, and were also sometimes targeted by the AKP, BIFF, and the MG in indiscriminate attacks. Bombings in Cotabato, General Santos and Isulan cities in the aftermath of the BOL signing left seven civilians dead and 90 wounded. Civilians were also at risk of being hit by stray bullets during localised disputes between the MILF and the MNLF.

Livelihoods affected in rural areas

Clashes between the AFP and BIFF affected liveli-hoods in the countryside. In mid-June, fishermen were unable to fish in Liguasan Marsh for almost a week due to a sustained government anti-BIFF offensive. In July, clashes between the AFP and BIFF in the Maguindanao towns of Datu Paglas, Rajah Buayan and Shariff Saydona Mustapha pre-vented 16,590 students from attending school for more than a week. The indigenous Teduray tribe was particularly affected due to the proximity of BIFF to its settlements in Maguindanao. In January, 1,600 Teduray families were trapped in their homes in Datu Saudi and Datu Unsay due to BIFF activity. The ARMM provided shelter to 421 Teduray fami-lies after their villages were burned down by BIFF in a series of raids in late 2017. On 2 September, BIFF abducted and killed two tribespeople in Datu Hoffer before setting fire to houses, forcing more than 300 villagers to flee.

Trends

The signing of the BOL by President Duterte and MILF Chair Ebrahim in July marked a signifi-cant breakthrough in the Moro peace process. If the deal is implemented, leading to the creation of a new Bangsamoro region, it will likely end the insurgency waged by the MILF and MNLF. This scenario would leave only smaller radical elements – ISIS-affiliated groups such as the AKP, BIFF and the MG – to battle government forces. Despite not being able to launch an attack on the scale of the Marawi siege the previous year, these groups still presented a major obstacle to peace in 2018, but they are now geographically isolated from each other and coming under increased pressure as the AFP's sus-tained offensives under martial law squeeze their areas of activity. The current situation is in marked contrast to the build-up to the Marawi siege, when these groups and an ISIS-affiliated ASG faction were able to join forces to launch a combined assault. Yet despite the efforts of the MILF, it remains unlikely that any of the radical groups will be persuaded to sever their ties with ISIS. With martial law extended in Mindanao until the end of 2019, Duterte will aim to crush the remnants of ISIS and ensure they cannot regain enough strength to threaten the stability of the region.

The BIFF under the command of Abu Toraife, and the MG under the leadership of Abu Dar, retain their aim to forge an Islamic caliphate in Mindanao and disrupt the peace process through recruiting marginalised youth and launching attacks. Yet with the BOL unifying the government and the MILF – and to an extent the MNLF and the public – against radical elements, jihadi groups face a declining recruitment pool.

The ultimate success or failure of the BOL-centred peace process will depend on the immediate next steps and the implementation of the peace deal in the coming years. The first test will be the plebiscite set for early 2019, when voters in BAR-included areas are expected to ratify the deal at the ballot box. Once this hurdle has been overcome, harder tasks lie ahead. The MILF faces a challenge to transition from an armed rebel group to a political party, with more than 30,000 fighters to decommission. It is likely that rebel leaders set to play a central role in governing the new Bangsamoro region will find the adjustment easier than ordi-nary insurgents, who will have to integrate back into mainstream society and find employment. The key long-term test will be the ability of the new regional administration to reduce the grievances of the Moro population, and bring much-needed eco-nomic development and job opportunities to the impoverished provinces of western Mindanao. If this is achieved, it will likely smooth the transition to civilian life for former MILF and MNLF fight-ers while dealing a significant blow to the ongoing recruitment efforts of ISIS-affiliated groups still seeking to disrupt the peace process.

Notes

1 'Philippine military identifies new leader of ISIS in South-east Asia', *Straits Times*, 6 March 2018.

2 Philippine Statistics Authority, 'Factsheet on Islam in Mindanao', 28 September 2017.

3   B.K. Schaefer, 'Moro Separatism in the Philippines: The Strategic Failure of a Promising Counterinsurgency', *Small Wars Journal*.

4   'ARMM's GRDO Growth Rate Hits Record-High 7.3% in 2017', Government of the Philippines, Autonomous Region in Muslim Mindanao website, 26 April 2017.

5   Jodesz Gavilan, 'Poverty in Mindanao', *Rappler*, 28 May 2017.

6   Ver Marcelo, 'The Bangsamoro Organic Law: Everything you need to know', CNN Philippines, 24 July 2018.

7   Mara Cepeda, 'Congress extends martial law in Mindanao to end of 2019', *Rappler*, 12 December 2018.

8   Ali G. Macabalang, 'Reintegration set for ex-rebels', *Tempo*, 19 April 2018.

Philippines (NPA)

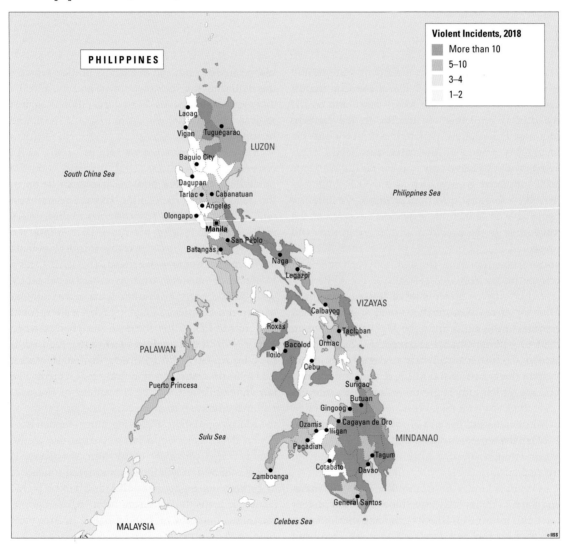

| Overview

The conflict in 2018

Fighting between the government forces of the Philippines and the New People's Army (NPA) intensified during 2018 as the peace process stalled following President Rodrigo Duterte's termination of formal talks in November 2017. Clashes between the NPA and the Armed Forces of the Philippines (AFP) were most intense in eastern Mindanao where the NPA is strongest, with sporadic fighting in rural areas across the country. In line with historical trends, most incidents in 2018 took the form of small-scale clashes, ambushes and improvised explosive device (IED) attacks. The rebels continued to collect 'revolutionary taxes' in their areas of influence and attacked firms that failed to comply. The NPA also targeted a broad range of local opponents including village chieftains, tribal leaders, politicians and alleged military informants.

Talks to restart the peace process collapsed abruptly in mid-June, when the government and the National Democratic Front of the Philippines (NDFP) – which represents the NPA and the Communist Party of the Philippines (CPP) – disagreed on the conditions for resuming negotiations, in particular on whether to hold them in the Philippines or a neutral country. Relations between the government and the CPP deteriorated in the second half of the year, with Duterte accusing the CPP of plotting to overthrow him and CCP leader-in-exile José Maria Sison declaring that the CPP–NPA–NDFP would not engage in any further dialogue during Duterte's tenure.

The conflict to 2018

The long-running communist rebellion in the Philippines began with the formation of the NPA – the armed wing of the CPP – in 1969. Left-wing student activist Sison founded the CPP–NPA as the successor to the Hukbalahap communist movement, which had led an armed uprising against US colonialists and Filipino elites after the Second

Key statistics	
Type:	Internal
IDPs total (2017):	8,000
IDPs new (2018):	no data
Refugees total (2018):	not applicable
Refugees new (2018):	not applicable
People in need (2018):	not applicable

World War. Driven by Marxist–Leninist ideology, the CPP–NPA has waged a guerrilla war – or a 'Protracted People's War' – for the last five decades with the aim of overthrowing the Philippine state and replacing it with a socialist government led by the working classes. The NPA was at its strongest in the mid-1980s during the dictatorship of Ferdinand Marcos, with around 26,000 fighters. The Marcos era witnessed large-scale clashes between government forces and NPA rebels.

Public support for the NPA has declined in the democratic era and the conflict has fluctuated, with periods of rising violence interspersed with peace talks. The NDFP, established in 1973, represented the CPP–NPA in talks with successive governments led by Ramos, Aquino, Estrada, Arroyo and Aquino II, but to little avail. After Duterte's election in 2016, both sides declared separate unilateral ceasefires and several rounds of formal negotiations were held in Oslo and Rome (see **Table 1**). The peace process collapsed in February 2017 when a dispute over a prisoner amnesty coincided with insurgent attacks. Violence has since flared, and all attempts to revive talks have failed.

Forces

Armed Forces of the Philippines (AFP)

The Armed Forces of the Philippines (AFP) has 125,000 combatants serving in the army, navy and air force and a reserve force of 50,000 in Citizen Armed Forces Geographical Units (CAFGUs). The AFP appointed Lieutenant-General Benjamin Madrigal as commander in December 2018, replacing the retiring Lieutenant-General Carlito Galvez. The AFP is divided into six area-unified commands, with the Eastern Mindanao Command (EMC) responsible for fighting the NPA. The AFP pursues a mainly reactive

strategy against the NPA, but also launches targeted offensives and engages NPA rebels when on patrol in remote areas. In September, army spokesperson Colonel Edgard Arevalo said the AFP was 'on the right track to destroy the NPA' by mid-2019.

The recent emergence of ISIS-aligned groups in Mindanao has displaced the NPA insurgency as a priority for the armed forces. Given the threat posed to the territorial integrity of the Philippines when jihadis laid siege to Marawi city in 2017 in the hope of carving out an Islamic caliphate, the small-scale dynamics of NPA violence led the group to be viewed as more of a criminal nuisance. With the AFP still battling ISIS remnants in the region, the armed forces' attention remains diverted.

New People's Army (NPA)

The New People's Army (NPA) is the armed wing of the Communist Party of the Philippines (CPP). The two groups are closely connected and are represented in peace talks by the National Democratic Front of the Philippines (NDFP). The three are often referred to collectively as the CPP–NPA–NDFP. The NPA has around 3,900 fighters nationwide, according to AFP estimates in June 2018.[1] The group's arsenal consists predominantly of high-powered firearms looted from army bases. The NPA also deploys improvised explosive devices (IEDs) to target army and police vehicles. The NPA is strongest in eastern Mindanao, but remains active in rural areas across the country. The group does not control territory, but extends considerable influence and de facto administers its rural strongholds by collecting 'revolutionary taxes'. Unsupportive firms and local-level opponents are intimidated into compliance and targeted in raids and ambushes.

The CPP–NPA's ideology and objectives have remained unchanged since its founding. The CPP deploys frequent anti-colonial and anti-US rhetoric, denouncing the 'bureaucratic capitalism' and 'feudalism' of the governing Filipino elite. The Maoist movement – still led by José Maria Sison from self-imposed exile in the Netherlands – aspires to overthrow the government and replace it with a proletariat-led socialist system that would redistribute land and reduce inequalities. The NPA's strategy of survival is to dampen the government's resolve by inflicting repeated losses on the AFP.

| Drivers

The NPA's nationwide presence

The NPA is active in 70 of the Philippines' 81 provinces, making it difficult for the AFP to contain and ultimately defeat the group, especially as the Philippines is an expansive maritime nation with more than 7,000 islands. The NPA's choice to operate in densely forested, mountainous and inaccessible terrain is a deliberate and strategic one, with Sison having outlined the necessity of geographical decentralisation in his 1974 book, *Specific Characteristics of Our People's War*. Sison wanted the NPA to be difficult to defeat via conventional means, avoiding detection and major offensives by operating in hostile jungle environments. NPA fighters frequently move between a network of temporary bases to maximise these advantages.

The CPP–NPA's enduring ideology

Unlike other rebel groups, the CPP–NPA's ideology has remained remarkably consistent since its formation. Through a campaign of armed resistance, the CPP–NPA aims to overthrow the government, which it describes as semi-colonial and semi-feudal, and replace it with a socialist system. Sison outlined the movement's core principles in *Philippine Society and Revolution* (1970), which laid the foundations for the CPP's anti-capitalist and anti-imperial stance, and he still serves as the organisation's main leader. While its ideological unity has made the CPP–NPA resistant to fracturing, enabling its endurance, its refusal to compromise on its primary aims has limited its ability to negotiate with the government.

Rural poverty

Poverty and underdevelopment have long fuelled grievances against the government, sustaining the NPA's support and recruitment in rural areas. Lack of access to land and resource revenues are key drivers of the conflict. In Mindanao, weak governance, limited infrastructure and inadequate service provision have created an environment in which armed groups flourish and recruit. Many rural residents see the NPA as fighting for their interests.

The inequalities within Philippine society are high. In 2015, 11.5% of urban dwellers lived in poverty, while rural residents faced greater hardship, with 34.3% of farmers and 34% of fishermen living below the national poverty line.[2] State-led development initiatives in the past decade have reduced rural poverty only marginally.

Lack of trust under Duterte

After five decades of conflict, deeply ingrained positions and a lack of trust have developed between the government and the CPP–NPA–NDFP. The peace process has failed under six administrations, both sides have broken promises and ceasefires have routinely collapsed. Failed talks with the Duterte administration triggered the recent violence. Initial hopes – Duterte is a left-leaning politician who vowed to pursue a negotiated end to the conflict – were soon dashed, fuelling anger from the CPP–NPA–NDFP and inflaming rhetoric on both sides, which led to more violence on the ground.

Political and Military Developments

Failure to revive the peace process

Attempts to revive the peace process between the government and the CPP–NPA–NDFP failed in 2018. In April, hopes were raised after Duterte said the NPA were 'not enemies' and Sison responded that the NDFP was 'willing and ready' to engage in dialogue. On 21 April, Duterte set a 60-day deadline for the process to resume, and on 8 May, Presidential Advisor on the Peace Process Jesus Dureza confirmed back-channel talks had produced positive results. On 6 June, Sison said 'many issues had been resolved' ahead of an expected ceasefire and the restart of formal talks in Oslo. However, on 15 June the government suspended the talks for three months after a spate of rebel attacks. The peace process did not resume as the parties failed to agree over whether talks should be held in the Philippines, as proposed by the government, or in a neutral foreign country, as preferred by the CPP. The CPP also rejected the government's list of pre-conditions, including a full cessation of hostilities, the encampment of rebels and assurances the CPP would not seek to enter a coalition government.

With the national peace process stalled, the government sought to initiate localised peace talks in July and September, allowing province-level politicians to engage with NPA commanders. However, the government stipulated that any such talks must adhere to the same set of preconditions outlined for the national-level peace process. The CPP rejected the offer, claiming NPA field commanders across the country were unanimously opposed to the new proposal.[3]

Table 1: Timeline of the peace process

Peace talks between the government and the NPA since President Duterte came to power in 2016

Date	Event
Jun 2016	Rodrigo Duterte inaugurated as President of the Philippines, after campaigning to revive peace talks with the National Democratic Front of the Philippines (NDFP) – the representative of the New People's Army (NPA) and Communist Party of the Philippines (CPP) – in formal negotiations with Manila.
Aug 2016	First round of peace talks between the government and the NDFP held in Oslo, Norway. Both sides implement separate unilateral, indefinite ceasefires and agree to hold further negotiations.
Oct 2016	Second round of peace talks between the government and the NDFP in Oslo, Norway. The parties agree on a framework for social and economic reforms aimed at reducing poverty and inequality in rural areas.
Jan 2017	Third round of peace talks between the government and the NDFP held in Rome, Italy. Discussions of a joint ceasefire break down, but both sides agree to maintain separate unilateral ceasefires ahead of further talks.
Feb 2017	The NDFP criticises Duterte's refusal to release political prisoners. Clashes between the NPA and Armed Forces of the Philippines (AFP) resume. Both the NDFP and the government terminate their separate unilateral ceasefires.
Apr 2017	Fourth round of peace talks between the government and NDFP held in Amsterdam, the Netherlands. No ceasefire announced.
May 2017	President Duterte cancels a fifth round of peace talks with the NDFP amid continued NPA attacks on government forces and collection of 'revolutionary taxes'.
Nov 2017	President Duterte signs proclamation No. 360, terminating the peace process between the government and the NDFP amid continuing violence, and announces intention to list the NPA and CPP as 'terrorist organisations'.

Asia-Pacific

Worsening government–CPP relations

After back-channel talks faltered, Duterte and Sison embarked upon a public war of words, reversing the conciliatory tones of earlier in the year, intensifying divisions and fuelling violence. In July 2018, Duterte described NPA rebels as 'robots' fighting for a 'bankrupt mind'. Sison retorted in August, calling Duterte a 'crazy guy in power … very capable of violence'. By the end of 2018, relations between the government and the CPP–NPA–NDFP had sunk to their lowest point in the Duterte era. Sison announced the NDFP would not engage in formal talks for the remainder of Duterte's time in office. In September, the government accused the CPP of orchestrating a coordinated plot (dubbed 'Red October') to overthrow Duterte, involving nationwide mass strikes by rebel-infiltrated workers groups and intensified rebel attacks. The CPP denied the accusations but said it promoted a 'broad united front' against Duterte 'open to all patriotic forces'.

Government crackdown on the CPP–NPA–NDFP

The Duterte administration continued to crack down on the CPP–NPA–NDFP in the courts, aiming to discredit the communist movement and its allies. In late February 2018, the Department of Justice (DoJ) filed a petition before the Manila Regional Trial Court seeking to legally designate the CPP–NPA–NDFP as a 'terrorist organisation'. The case stalled when back-channel talks began, but when negotiations broke down in June, the DoJ confirmed that it would proceed with the case. In August, the DoJ filed a petition seeking the rearrest of NDFP peace consultants – including senior CPP leaders Benito Tiamzon, Wilma Tiamzon and Rafael Baylosis – who had previously been freed to participate in talks. In July, Defence Secretary Delfin Lorenzana said Sison would be detained should he return home from self-imposed exile. The government also released a list of more than 600 individuals it sought to designate as terrorists, including left-wing political activists and a UN human-rights representative. The list drew criticism from activists concerned about a widening crackdown on leftist organisations.[4]

Violent Events

Violence escalates nationwide

Violent encounters between the NPA and AFP took place throughout the year (see **Figure 1**). The period immediately following the failure of back-channel talks in mid-June led to a significant spike in violence and the highest number of deaths. While June 2018 saw 24 deaths as a result of armed encounters involving the NPA, this number rose to 31 in July and 39 in August, before falling to 20 in September. Most incidents took the form of small-scale encounters and ambushes perpetrated by the NPA, while gun battles were initiated by both sides. Most were chance encounters, as neither the armed forces nor the NPA launched large-scale or coordinated offensives during the year. The AFP's reactionary strategy against the NPA is in stark contrast to the offensive strategy it employed against ISIS-aligned groups in western Mindanao during 2018, which was centred on large-scale ground offensives coordinated with airstrikes. In the NPA conflict, violence followed a familiar pattern, replicating the jungle warfare and guerrilla tactics long associated with the Maoist insurgency. Most violence occurred in rural areas, but occasionally the NPA shot dead AFP troops and Philippine National Police (PNP) officers in urban areas in ambushes carried out by 'sparrow units' – small rebel hit squads operating in towns and cities.

NPA–AFP clashes in the countryside

The NPA's battlefield tactics in 2018 fell in line with historical trends, with the group ambushing state security personnel in the countryside. While maintaining a presence in rural areas nationwide, the NPA was most active in the Mindanao administrative regions of Caraga, Davao and Northern Mindanao, with rebel attacks frequently taking place in the provinces of Agusan del Norte, Agusan del Sur, Bukidnon, Compostela Valley, Davao del Norte, Davao del Sur, Davao Occidental, Davao Oriental, Misamis Occidental, Misamis Oriental, Surigao del Norte and Surigao del Sur. The majority of rebel attacks made use of firearms, involved small bands of fighters and resulted in one to four fatalities. Several high-casualty incidents also occurred. On 25 June, AFP troops opened fire on a group of PNP officers in a densely forested area of Santa Rita, Samar province, having

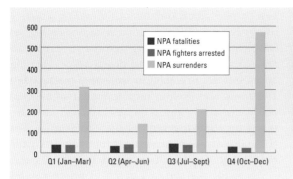

The AFP made significant inroads against the NPA in 2018, as martial law remained in place in the Mindanao region. In total 1,499 insurgents were removed from the battlefield during 2018: 142 were killed in clashes with the AFP, 136 were arrested and 1,221 surrendered. Fatalities and arrests declined because the NPA engaged in fewer armed encounters as its strength dwindled. In October–December, rebel surrenders rose sharply, as the NPA came under increasing strain under martial law and the government's Comprehensive Local Integration Programme (CLIP) offered livelihood support to former rebels.

Figure 1: AFP counter-insurgency campaign against NPA, 2018

mistaken them for NPA insurgents. The incident left six police officers dead and another seven wounded. On 15 August, joint AFP–PNP forces killed seven rebels during a raid on an NPA camp in San Jose de Buenavista, Antique province. On 20 October, a suspected rebel ambush on farmers in Sagay, Negros Occidental, left nine people dead.

NPA's raids and IEDs

Aside from unintended clashes and spontaneous outbreaks of violence, the NPA launched a few more audacious, pre-planned attacks on AFP bases and PNP stations in the countryside. In one such incident in August, around 100 heavily armed rebels raided a police station in Lapinig, Northern Samar province, seizing firearms and injuring three police officers. Most attacks of this nature were smaller-scale, with the NPA often retreating after being outmatched by the superior firepower of government forces. IEDs were also deployed by the NPA during 2018, forming part of a wider trend of rising IED attacks in Mindanao, mostly carried out by Islamist groups.[5] The NPA used roadside IEDs to attack army and police vehicles in the provinces of Agusan del Sur, Compostela Valley, Davao del Sur, Iloilo, Masbate, Rizal and Surigao del Sur. The port in Masbate was targeted twice: an explosion on 1 August destroyed a bridge and a blast on 3 September damaged two Philippine Coast Guard (PCG) vessels.

Limited progress in the AFP's anti-NPA campaign

The AFP's anti-NPA counter-insurgency campaign made some progress in 2018, though not to the extent hoped for by senior military leaders. In January, General Rey Leonardo Guerrero estimated the NPA to have 3,700 fighters and aimed to reduce its strength by 50% during 2018.[6] Yet in June, senior army spokesperson Arevalo estimated the NPA's strength at 3,900. The NPA has maintained the capacity to clash with government forces regularly despite the deaths of 142 of its fighters and the arrest of 136 during the year. In 2018, at least 1,221 NPA fighters voluntarily surrendered through the government's Comprehensive Local Integration Programme (CLIP), which offers PHP65,000 (US$1,200) livelihood assistance to ex-rebels as well as payments for returned firearms.[7] The defection rate rose sharply in the final three months of the year, during which 507 rebels surrendered to AFP troops, contributing to a slight reduction in the level of violence during the last quarter of 2018.

The declining frequency of violent clashes involving the NPA during October–December also indicates that the AFP's campaign has started to dent the NPA's capabilities under martial law in Mindanao, where the group is most active. Martial law has been in place on the island since the ISIS-led siege of Marawi city in 2017. On 12 December, Congress approved a request from Duterte to extend it until 31 December 2019, amid the continued threat posed by the NPA and ISIS-linked groups.

| Impact

Worsening security situation in rural areas

The failure to restart peace talks led to escalating violence in rural areas during 2018. Small-scale rebel ambushes, attacks on government troops and gun battles between the AFP and the NPA took place regularly. The failure to agree a ceasefire compounded the fragile security situation in communities already blighted by poor governance and weak rule of law. While the majority killed in clashes were NPA rebels and AFP troops, civilians were also affected, with 75 killed during 2018. In addition to the risk of being injured by stray bullets, civilians faced the threat of displacement. Displacement was often localised and temporary in nature, with civilians returning home once violence subsided, but on several occasions was more substantial. On 29 January, 758 civilians (161 families) fled their homes amid an anti-NPA military offensive in the Surigao del Sur towns of Lianga and San Augustin. In early February, around 1,000 people fled after rebels entered a residential area in Maragusan, Compostela Valley province. Later that month, 812 civilians fled clashes in Lanzuna, Surigao del Sur province. On 8 May, a series of encounters between the NPA and the AFP in North Cotabato and South Cotabato provinces forced 957 residents to flee.

The NPA's de facto control of populations

The failure of the AFP to substantially degrade the NPA's strength allowed the rebels to maintain de facto control over rural populations. The NPA continued to collect 'revolutionary taxes' from wealthy individuals and businesses based in the countryside. In September, AFP spokesperson Arevalo said the NPA had accrued PHP5.3 billion (US$97 million) in illegal taxes nationwide between 2015 and 2017 and claimed that such extortion 'cripples agriculture, drives away investors and stunts economic growth' in affected areas.[8]

The NPA launched raids and arson attacks on firms that failed to pay, targeting mining firms, banana-plantation owners, agricultural business and construction companies. In 2018, it killed at least 53 local opponents including village chiefs, army informants, ex-rebels and town councillors. Aided by weak state presence in Mindanao, the NPA acts

as a parallel administration. After raiding a quarry site in Negros Oriental province in September, an NPA statement condemned 'destructive small-scale mining' and 'environmental degradation', warning businesses not to engage in 'anti-people activities'.[9] The group sees itself as responsible for administering justice according to its ideology and interests, punishing firms that fail to adhere to its rules. The NPA also handed down verdicts against a wide range of opponents in its so-called 'People's Courts'.

Indigenous groups caught between the NPA and the AFP

Indigenous people, referred to as Lumads, were often among those worst affected by the insurgency in 2018 due to the geographical proximity of their communities to NPA hideouts in remote mountainous areas. Lumads often suffered higher levels of displacement than other groups. On 15 July, 1,607 Manobo tribespeople were forced to flee from sustained AFP–NPA clashes in Lianga, Surigao del Sur province, marking the highest single incidence of displacement during 2018. Lumads were often suspected by the army of being NPA sympathisers, while the NPA accused them of being AFP informants. Lumads also were caught in the escalating propaganda war between the NPA and the AFP that followed the collapse of the back-channel talks in June. In September, the armed forces accused the NPA of 'blatant and glaring violations of international humanitarian law' against the Lumad, describing the NPA as 'oppressors' of indigenous people.[10] The NPA denied the accusations, instead blaming the army and the government for the oppression of rural communities. Human-rights groups have frequently raised concerns that Lumads, student activists and environmental campaigners have been targeted under Duterte's widening crackdown on left-leaning groups since the peace process collapsed in 2017.

Trends

Although rebel attacks decreased towards the end of 2018, the insurgency waged by the NPA showed little sign of abating as efforts to restart the peace process failed. The revival of talks looks unlikely, as the government and the CPP remain divided on several key issues, including whether talks should be held in the Philippines or a neutral country; whether

CPP leader Sison should return to the Philippines from exile in the Netherlands to participate in talks; and whether the NDFP will agree to meet the government's preconditions for negotiations to restart. While the peace process remains suspended, rebel attacks and ambushes against government forces look set to continue in 2019. Rural residents and businesses will likely remain under the insurgents' de facto control in eastern Mindanao and other areas where the NPA maintains the relative freedom to recruit, collect taxes and target opponents.

The AFP will miss its stated target to eradicate the NPA by mid-2019, especially given its priority of combatting the ISIS-affiliated militant groups in western Mindanao. If the AFP does manage to defeat these groups, it may then be able to pursue its campaign against the NPA with greater vigour. The extension of martial law in Mindanao until the end of 2019 is designed to aid the armed forces in this

regard. However, the structural and organisational nature of the NPA will make it difficult to inflict a decisive defeat upon the group will be a difficult task. Since its formation in the late 1960s, the CPP–NPA has demonstrated remarkable resilience in the face of repeated military offensives, and the current form of the NPA insurgency appears as challenging as at any point over the last five decades. As long as the conflict continues, the communities affected by the insurgency will live in fear of human-rights abuses and suffer from the lack of much-needed economic development.

Notes

[1] 'AFP: Focused-military ops vs. NPA successful', *Philippine News Agency*, 25 June 2018.

[2] Philippine Statistics Authority, 'Farmers, Fishermen and Children consistently posted the highest poverty incidence among basic sectors – PSA', 30 June 2017.

[3] 'CPP: Localized peace talks rejected by local revolutionary groups', *GMA News*, 18 July 2018.

[4] 'PH "terror" list a "gov't hit list" – Human Rights Watch', *Rappler*, 9 March 2018.

[5] Michael Hart, 'Mindanao's Insurgencies Take an Explosive Turn', *Diplomat*, 1 June 2018.

[6] 'AFP vows to reduce by half NPA's 3,700 fighters', *Rappler*, 9 January 2018.

[7] Department of the Interior and Local Government, 'Revised Guidelines for the Implementation of the Comprehensive Local Integration Program (CLIP)', 3 March 2016.

[8] 'Military: NPA rebels amass over P5M from extortion', *Sunstar Manila*, 25 September 2018.

[9] 'NPA torches quarry equipment in Sta. Catalina', *Panay News*, 21 September 2018.

[10] 'NPAs scored for harassment of highland people', *Manila Bulletin*, 3 September 2018.

Southern Thailand

Overview

The conflict in 2018

Although most of 2018 followed a trend of decreasing attacks and fatalities, the main active insurgency group, the Barisan Revolusi Nasional (BRN), carried out a string of bombings at the end of December. The surge in attacks was the BRN's response to efforts by the Thai armed forces and Malaysia to force it into negotiations, with Kuala Lumpur threatening BRN leaders to join talks or lose their safe havens in Malaysia. During the same period, BRN leaders refused to meet with Thai government negotiators and reportedly went into hiding.

The relaunch of Thailand's negotiations strategy followed a major military reshuffle at the beginning of October, including the promotion of the conservative royalist General Apirat Kongsompong

to commander-in-chief of the Royal Thai Army, Lieutenant General Pornsak Poonsawas to head of the Fourth Army Region (responsible for the South) and General Udomchai Thammasaroraj to lead negotiations in the peace talks. The reshuffle put a

Key statistics	
Type:	Internal
IDPs total (2017):	not applicable
IDPs new (2018):	not applicable
Refugees total (2018):	not applicable
Refugees new (2018):	not applicable
People in need (2018):	not applicable

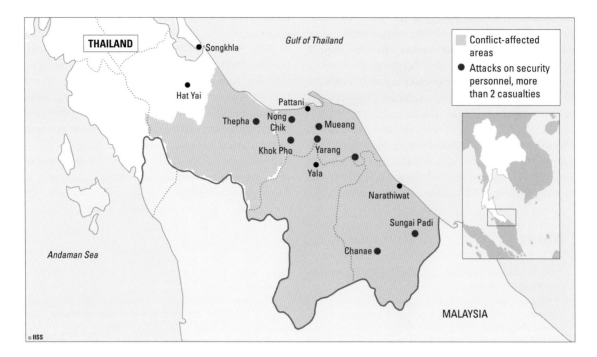

new face on the counter-insurgency policy ahead of the expected election in early 2019, but the armed forces remained firmly in control of both the security and diplomatic response.

From the outset, Udomchai appeared to abandon the negotiating strategy of his predecessor, which had been based on establishing ceasefire 'safety zones' through talks with Majlis Syura Patani (MARA Patani), an umbrella group of insurgent factions that does not have command of active militants on the ground. The new lead negotiator began to emphasise that the BRN should be included in peace talks, despite the latter's reticence. The lack of progress in talks and the failure of the safety-zone initiative marginalised MARA Patani, which withdrew from the talks in December.

Despite the spike in violence at the end of December, attacks overall declined, reaching the lowest level since 2004. The strengthened security presence, government peace efforts, the internal migration of Buddhists out of conflict zones and a strategic BRN shift were the main factors credited for the lessening attacks. BRN representatives described the group's new strategy as relying on more targeted attacks that would avoid civilian casualties and maintain community support, while showing that areas in southern Thailand are 'ungovernable'.[1]

If there was an insurgent policy to minimise civilian casualties, there were also exceptions, with improvised explosive device (IED) attacks inflicting indiscriminate fatalities. At the end of 2018, estimates put the number of fatalities since 2004 at 7,000, with those directly attributable to the insurgency at below 5,000.

The conflict to 2018

The Malay ethno-nationalist insurgency and its rejection of assimilation into the Thai state has driven decades of conflict in southern Thailand. Separatists seek independence of the region covered by the former kingdom of Patani, spanning the Thai provinces of Narathiwat, Yala and Pattani, and parts of northern Malaysia. Violence erupted in the 1940s and again in the 1960s, continuing through the 1980s before mostly subsiding, in part because of a government amnesty programme. Violence re-emerged in 2001. The current phase of the armed conflict was triggered by an insurgent raid in January 2004 on an army base in Narathiwat province that killed four soldiers. The rebels also stole hundreds of light weapons, which they have used in attacks up to the present day.

The draconian security response (directed by then-prime minister Thaksin Shinawatra) to the 2004 raid resulted in mass killings that became memorialised in the insurgent narrative. Counter-insurgency policy and peace negotiations then underwent wide fluctuations as Thailand experienced two military coups in 2006 and 2014 and a succession of elected and unelected governments.

Militant attacks peaked in 2007, with an average of four people killed each day in the month of May, resulting in massive internal migration, particularly of Buddhist civilians, to relatively safe areas such as Songkhla's provincial capital of Hat Yai. At about the same time, Thai authorities began to acknowledge that the BRN was behind most of the violence, not the Patani United Liberation Organisation (PULO),

which previous intelligence and security efforts had targeted.

The militant violence following the 2004 raid disproportionately targeted Buddhist civilians, particularly monks and teachers, but shifted in recent years to include more Muslim civilians and local army 'collaborators', as well as security personnel and paramilitary soldiers recruited from the region. Militant attacks and fatalities have declined annually since 2016. Recent attacks have mostly been concentrated in the three provinces of Narathiwat, Pattani and Yala, as well as five districts of Songkhla province, although militants have carried out attacks across the country.

Forces

State forces

The Royal Thai Armed Forces has historically played a prominent role in Thailand's politics and often dominated defence policy, including the counter-insurgency campaigns in the south and control of the negotiations process under the current government. The Royal Thai Armed Forces has carried out more than a dozen coups in Thailand, the most recent in May 2014 by former army chief and subsequent and current Prime Minister General Prayut Chan-o-cha. Though the government has backed peace talks with insurgents and promoted human-rights training, the security forces continue to be accused of torture and unlawful detentions.

Most of Narathiwat, Pattani and Yala provinces have been under a state of emergency since 2005, and the already extensive security presence across the countryside has increased since the return of military rule. The Fourth Army Region is responsible for security in the south, with counter-insurgency strategy largely conducted by the Internal Security Operations Command (ISOC), the political arm of the military.

By the standards of armed forces in Asia, the Royal Thai Army (RTA) is well armed and relatively professional. According to an ISOC statement at the beginning of the year, 3,000 regular soldiers were to be withdrawn from the south over the course of 2018, leaving a garrison of 58,000 regular army personnel, mostly armed with light weapons such as M16s, and increasingly equipped with body armour and hardened vehicles, which provide more effective defence against improvised explosive devices (IEDs).

Thailand also fields 20,000 border-patrol police and 21,000 *thahan phran* (hunter/soldier) rangers (although not all these forces are deployed to the south), with the latter including locally recruited paramilitary soldiers known as the Volunteer Defence Corps. Both forces are equipped with a variety of arms, including military-grade automatic rifles and shotguns. Local police and officials are often equipped only with handguns. The increased reliance on local recruits, including both soldiers and a network of informants, reflects the armed forces' evolving counter-insurgency strategy. Upon assuming command of the Fourth Army Region, Pornsak announced a further extension of the military's presence into rural areas including rolling patrols deployed in villages for longer periods of time.

Barisan Revolusi Nasional (BRN) (National Revolutionary Front)

The Barisan Revolusi Nasional (BRN) is the largest active armed militant group currently conducting attacks in southern Thailand. The group was founded in 1963 and subsequently split into the BRN–Coordinate (BRN–C), the BRN–Congress and the BRN–Ulema by 1984, the first of which is the most dominant and best organised and resourced. A network of religious teachers leads the BRN–C and draws recruits from *pondok* Islamic religious schools. The BRN also includes non-violent supporters such as *ulema* religious teachers and members of the *pemuda* youth wing advocating for regional independence or autonomy, with an overlapping membership with the group's armed wings.

Thai authorities have identified former school headmaster Doonloh Wae-mano, also known as Abdullah Wan Mat Noor, as the new chair of the BRN's executive council, known as the Dewan Pimpinan Parti (DPP) (Party Leadership Council), but the BRN denies having a single commander. Doonloh is considered to be a hardliner opposed to peace talks in their current form and BRN attacks are often timed to affect negotiations or in response to other developments. The BRN operational structure is based on semi-independent and loosely organised cells, with militants and the leadership typically well integrated and often able to assume ordinary lives in communities when not militarily active. Cells comprising small groups of relatively young fighters (known as *juwae* and recruited locally from schools and communities) operate relatively independently after training and respond to strategic directives rather than tactical command and control from senior leaders. The armed forces estimates that the group's armed combatants number about 3,000, while BRN tells the media that there are militant cells in nearly every district in the deep south.

Runda Kumpulan Kecil (RKK) (Small Patrol Units)

Founded in the early 2000s by members of the BRN–C, Runda Kumpulan Kecil (RKK) includes militant cells across Thailand's southernmost provinces and is composed of about 500 members. RKK 'sleeper units' are among the most active of BRN-affiliated cells that have recently carried out attacks. DPP operational decisions are generally carried out at the cell level, with considerable autonomy for individual units.

Malaysian authorities have claimed that Uzman Jeh-umong, a militant allegedly linked to the Islamic State, also known as ISIS or ISIL, is an RKK leader. In February 2017, Jeh-umong was arrested in possession of bomb-making materials in Kelantan State, Malaysia. The claim was the strongest association of Thailand's insurgency with ISIS to date.

Majlis Syura Patani (MARA Patani) (Patani Consultative Council)

The umbrella group Majlis Amanah Rakyat Patani was formed in 2015, and renamed shortly thereafter as Majlis Syura Patani (Patani Consultative Council, while keeping the acronym MARA Patani), at the initiative of members who favoured negotiations with the Thai government. The grouping includes BRN members (who do not have direct control over combatants), as well as factions of groups that previously had prominent roles in the armed insurgency such as PULO. Influential members of the BRN withdrew from the peace process in 2015, expressing doubt about the government's willingness to make concessions.[2]

MARA Patani is the most inclusive of the insurgent groupings and, for most of 2018, was the primary contact for ongoing negotiations with the Thai government. MARA Patani's inability to control militants on the ground threatened the credibility of the peace process, however, and the group appeared increasingly marginalised at the end of the year.

Spokesperson Abu Hafez is the most publicly visible representative of the grouping. In 2016, he said that southern insurgents were considering shifting their goals from outright independence to autonomy and self-rule.[3] At the end of 2018, Thailand's negotiating chief Udomchai explicitly endorsed discussions about autonomy while ruling out any form of independence.

In October, Abu Hafez said the umbrella group had expanded its membership by three unidentified participants and rebranded as 'MARA Patani Plus', but there was little indication that the expansion had been formalised or would have a substantive effect on negotiations.

Patani United Liberation Organisation (PULO)

Founded in Saudi Arabia in 1968, the Patani United Liberation Organisation (PULO) was a major separatist force in southern Thailand for decades and retains a public presence, although the BRN is now the most active militarily. Some PULO leaders were trained in Syria and Libya in the 1980s.

The group was largely dormant during the 1990s, but widely seen as resurgent following the January 2004 attack on a Thai army base that signalled the rekindling of the conflict. After a series of splits within the group, most factions are believed to have reunified after 2004, although different wings are represented in the MARA Patani negotiations with Thai authorities. The group was associated with attacks against civil servants and teachers in subsequent years, but has not taken credit or been blamed for any recent attacks. Since 2011, PULO has been led by Kasturi Mahkota, who has expressed support for the 'inclusivity' of MARA Patani in the context of peace talks.

Gerakan Mujahidin Islam Patani (GMIP)

Formed in 1985 by Thai national and Afghanistan war veteran Nasoree Saesaeng, the Gerakan Mujahidin Islam Patani (GMIP) – also known as the Pattani Islamic Mujahideen Movement – has the stated aim of establishing an Islamic state in Thailand's south and is considered the most closely affiliated with international extremist doctrines espoused by al-Qaeda and Jemaah Islamiah. The

group has rejected the religious practices of most Malays as un-Islamic.

Following the 9/11 attacks in New York, the Malaysian group Kumpulan Mujahidin Malay, based in Terengganu State, assisted GMIP in carrying out attacks and conducting a propaganda campaign in southern Thailand. The GMIP has not been definitively linked to more recent attacks. Members of the group are reported to be involved in criminal activities including extortion and kidnap-for-ransom. In August 2018, Nasoree turned himself in to army rangers in Pattani province, a major turning point in counter-insurgency efforts and the 'Bring People Home' rehabilitation programme.

Drivers

Malay ethno-nationalist identity

The ethno-nationalist insurgency in southern Thailand is ideologically rooted in the historical Kingdom of Patani, which was formally absorbed into the Kingdom of Siam by the Anglo-Siamese Treaty of 1909. The Malay identity for the majority in the region predates the union with Siam by hundreds of years. Although data on area demographics is incomplete, with undocumented cross-border migration to and from Malaysia common, 2018 estimates stated that 85% of residents in Narathiwat, Pattani and Yala self-identified as ethnically Malay.

Islamic religious identity is also integral to conceptions of Patani-Malay ethnicity across the region and perceived threats to that combined identity take on a religious dimension.[4] As a result, any policy of assimilation into the 'Thai' identity involves a perceived surrender of faith as well as cultural and ethnic identity. Most Muslims in the region adhere to the Shafi'i school of Islam, although religious study abroad and madrassas have contributed to a growing subscription to Salafism, accounting for about 20% of the region's Muslims.[5]

Insurgent demands have traditionally centred on the establishment of an independent state in southern Thailand, although the historical Kingdom of Patani also included areas of present-day Malaysia. While the possibility of establishing such a state is limited, the appeal continues to act as a rallying cry, with the cause of an independent Patani, or 'Patani Merdeka', invoked in propaganda materials, including on a banner rigged to an IED in November.

That demand has been modified in various forms, with the civil-society group known as the Federation of Patani Students and Youth (PerMAS) advocating for 'self-determination'. Most other civil-society groups in the region, such as Justice of Peace and Civil Society for Peace, privilege human-rights issues over political demands in public statements. MARA Patani representatives demand self-determination, with the possibility for residents of the area to choose between independence, autonomy or remaining part of Thailand.

Assimilation efforts

Over decades, various governments in Bangkok have pursued parallel, mutually reinforcing narrative and assimilation policies, including state-sponsored migration of Thai-Chinese to the region and the promotion of Buddhism as the state religion. Government-school curricula have been traditionally taught in the Thai language rather than pupils' native Malay, holding back learning outcomes and provoking local resentment.[6] Only about 25% of students over 15 years old stay in government schools, with many instead attending *pondoks*, while student achievement in multiple subjects consistently falls short of national standards.[7]

Dress code also became a point of contention in 2018 after a school in Pattani banned female students from wearing headscarves, eliciting protests from the Muslim community and a national-level debate about freedom of religion. In November, a provincial administrative court issued an injunction against schools enforcing the ban pending further court action.

The army and the current military-led government have supported efforts to build relations with Muslim leaders in the region, but since the 2014 coup, senior leaders have also reinforced the concept of 'Thainess' to define national unity, portraying themselves as protectors of Buddhism, the monarchy and a conception of citizenship based on mono-cultural traits. This messaging has been particularly prevalent in schools, with plans announced in 2018 to expand lessons about the history of the Thai monarchy in creating present-day Thailand.

Human-rights abuses

Two major incidents in 2004 are frequently cited as motivations for insurgents to resume violence and remain powerful rallying symbols for the insurgency: the storming of the Krue Se Mosque in April and the Tak Bai massacre in October. In the former case, security forces killed 32 militants who had retreated to the mosque in Pattani province, violating the sacrality of a place of worship. In the latter, 85 protesters were killed in Narathiwat's Tak Bai

district, most of whom suffocated in lorries while being transported to detention.[8]

Although senior defence officials have emphasised human-rights training for security personnel, civil-society and human-rights groups still accuse the armed forces of enforced disappearances, secret detentions and abuses at facilities in the south. Critics of the government have accused it of covering up past detentions, forced disappearances and murders, including that of prominent Muslim lawyer Somchai Neelapaijit in 2004.

Economic and political marginalisation

Insurgent spokespeople consistently cite alienation from the state because of discrimination by local government, particularly in education and employment opportunities. Residents in the region are on average significantly poorer than their counterparts in Bangkok, although the data does not support a direct correlation of poverty rates with violent incidents. The Malay Muslim population faces disproportionately high unemployment and educational disadvantages and is under-represented in the public sector in comparison to the Thai Buddhist population.[9]

Political and Military Developments

A disrupted negotiating strategy

In the last three months of 2018, Thai authorities and Malaysian facilitators relaunched their negotiations strategy with insurgent groups, pushing the BRN to join talks while reframing the format as a 'dialogue process' that would solicit all points of view instead of seeking an immediate ceasefire. As part of those efforts in December, the new Malaysian facilitator Abdul Rahim Noor, appointed by Mahathir Mohamad's administration in the previous quarter, told the Thai government that he would pressure BRN leaders to attend talks by threatening their safe havens in Malaysia. In response, the BRN signalled that it would not be forced to the table by launching a series of attacks, while its senior leaders went into hiding.

Different generals pursued separate and sometimes conflicting pacification policies over the course of 2018 (see **Table 1**). General Aksara Kerdpol, the government's chief negotiator in peace talks with MARA Patani until he was replaced in October, led an effort to create 'safety zones', where insurgents

were to cease hostilies in return for amnesty and limited autonomy. In January, Aksara claimed that both MARA Patani and the BRN had agreed to a safe house that would host further negotiations and a trial of the plan in Narathiwat's Cho-airong district.

The initiative, however, was repeatedly derailed by public comments by Piyawat, the then-commander of the Fourth Army Region, and then by Prayut. In March, MARA Patani released a rare public statement, rejecting Piyawat's earlier comments and insisting that peace talks were not about 'safety zones' or his signature 'Bring People Home' amnesty programme. Then in May, the umbrella insurgent group accused Prayut of breaching protocol by making unilateral comments about the process, leading to a halt in talks. The safety-zone plan was further damaged when the deputy chair of Pattani's Islamic Committee, which was supposed to host the safe house for negotiations, was shot and killed in June in Pattani's Sai Buri district. The assailant remained unidentified amid speculation that the killing was meant to derail the process.

Table 1: Timeline of major developments in the peace process

Date	Development	Date	Development
17 Jan 2018	Thai chief negotiator announces 'safe houses'	24 Aug 2018	Malaysia appoints new Peace Facilitator Abdul Rahim Noor
2 Feb 2018	'Bring People Home': 288 militants turn in weapons	17 Sep 2018	Regional army chief threatens to detain insurgents' families
15 Feb 2018	MARA Patani agrees to 'safety zones'	11 Oct 2018	Thailand appoints new Chief Negotiator General Udomchai Thammasararoj
21 Feb 2018	BRN attacks linked to 'Bring People Home'		
15 Mar 2018	Thai chief negotiator dismisses talk prospects with BRN	16 Oct 2018	MARA Patani announces expansion including three new unspecified groups
23 Mar 2018	MARA Patani rejects talks to 'Bring People Home'	22 Oct 2018	BRN issues statement backing 'sincere' peace talks
17 Apr 2018	PM Mahathir identifies first 'safety zone' in Joh Rong district	21 Nov 2018	Thai Defence Minister Prawit Wongsuwan backs talks with BRN
1 May 2018	Hundreds protest 'Bring People Home' resettlement in Narathiwat	18 Dec 2018	PM Mahathir suggests Thailand consider autonomy for deep South
10 May 2018	Peace talks break down		
10 May 2018	PM Mahathir wins re-election in Malaysia	27 Dec 2018	Malaysian peace facilitator says BRN pressured to join talks
8 Jun 2018	Patani's Islamic Committee's Deputy Chairman killed	28 Dec 2018	BRN carries out a series of attacks in reaction to pressure
14 Aug 2018	GMIP senior leader surrenders		

The 'Bring People Home' programme

In the first half of the year, Piyawat continued to promote the 'Bring People Home' programme. In January 2018, police said 158 insurgents had laid down their weapons and authorities opened a centre in Pattani to process defectors. Anonymous sources associated with the programme said in February that nearly 2,000 insurgents were ready to surrender, but ultimately only 288 men publicly turned themselves in, with some criticising the initiative as a public-relations stunt involving inactive former militants.[10] The most high-profile surrenders occurred in May when the armed forces announced the surrender of a 'core' member of the insurgency and in August when Gerakan Mujahidin Islam Patani (GMIP) leader Nasoree turned himself in. The scheme suffered a setback, however, when the planned resettlement of former insurgents in Narathiwat's Sukhirin district was cancelled after local residents objected, citing economic concerns and the proposal to relocate the ex-militants close to the villages.

Malaysian election

On 10 May, the coalition of former prime minister Mahathir Mohamad won an historic election in Malaysia, signalling a significant shift in Kuala Lumpur's role as a facilitator for Thailand's peace negotiations. Mahathir returned to office in May after defeating the ruling party, which he had previously led as prime minister for 20 years until 2003. The 93-year-old premier quickly expressed determination to broker peace in southern Thailand. In August, he appointed a new mediator, Abdul Rahim, a former senior police officer and prominent figure in the region who played a significant role in ending Malaysia's communist insurgency in the 1980s. Immediately after the election, Thailand's National Security Council stated that the future of peace talks depended on Kuala Lumpur's new policy.

Mahathir's visit to Bangkok in October, followed by a visit by his presumed successor Anwar Ibrahim in November, reaffirmed Kuala Lumpur's commitment to the peace process and raised hopes of progress, particularly because of the insurgents' reliance on Malaysia as a safe haven. At the end of the year, Abdul Rahim's cooperation with Thai authorities and threats to expel key BRN leaders from Malaysia led to a breakdown in the peace process.

ISIS connections

While there is still little evidence that transnational jihadist groups have gained traction in recruitment in Thailand's south, there were signs in 2018 of tentative connections to ISIS amid the group's reorganisation in Southeast Asia. In February, Thai police announced they were monitoring 50 websites linked to ISIS for activity in southern Thailand. They did not find that the online materials were responsible for motivating attacks. In April, Thai authorities arrested and then released a suspect wanted by Malaysia for alleged ties to ISIS. The testimony of a militant tried in Jakarta, Indonesia, detailed cross-border coordination, including a trip to Thailand, allegedly to meet an ISIS-linked Uighur with the help of a cleric in Pattani.

Violent Events

Attacks on civilians

Most victims of the violence in 2018 were once again civilians. Despite stated intentions to avoid civilian casualties for fear of losing popular support, many insurgent attacks over the course of the year were indiscriminate. A bombing on 22 January killed three civilians at a market in Yala, while an IED attack on 11 February at a market in Pattani's Yarang district was part of a coordinated series of attacks across the province. On 9 April, three bombs hidden in motorbikes injured 13 civilians in Sungai Golok district in Narathiwat, with coordinated attacks across four provinces in May injuring three. Five civilians in Yala were injured by antipersonnel mines planted in rubber plantations to 'disrupt the daily life of people'.

The motive behind many of the attacks remained unclear, such as a shooting in June that killed four family members panning for gold in Narathiwat's Sukhirin district. Police suspected that insurgents perpetrated the attack because military-grade weapons were used, but also raised the possibility of rival gold prospectors being responsible. In other incidents, authorities suggested unrelated criminality in the region as a possible motive, with the most prominent example being the murder of five men in Yala's Bannang Sata district. An attacker shot a former village leader with an M16 in a suspected insurgent attack, but police linked the killing to the drug trade.

Other attacks on civilians and infrastructure seemed to substantiate the theory that violence was intended to send the message that the region was ungovernable. In February, an arson attack at a department store in Narathiwat, involving small IEDs placed near flammable products and detonated during closing hours, seemed designed to prevent casualties. The attack occurred just before a visit by an Organisation of Islamic Cooperation (OIC) delegation to the region, who praised authorities for their handling of the conflict. High-profile attacks on infrastructure such as utility poles throughout the year, the bombings of ATMs in May and assaults on the offices of the Provincial Electricity Authority in August made headlines but did not harm people. In the last case, station staff were temporarily taken hostage and then released unharmed.

Paramilitaries and other security forces targeted

There was an increase in the number of insurgent ambushes beginning in August targeting military outposts and patrols, with most of the fatalities being paramilitary soldiers. In August and September alone, 14 security personnel were killed in shooting incidents, most of which occurred in Pattani. Those attacks included the killing of two rangers in an ambush in Pattani's Nong Chik district, which spurred a tough security crackdown across the district.

At the beginning of the year, suspected insurgents targeted individuals associated with the security forces and their families. In January, militants killed three relatives of a former paramilitary soldier in Pattani's Thung Yang Daeng district, ending a period of relative quiet. Later in the month, suspected insurgents killed a paramilitary soldier in Pattani's Mueang district whose parents and sibling had been killed in the previous two years.

Impact

Allegations of abuse continued into 2018, including in connection to the high-profile trial for an alleged bomb plot in Bangkok in October 2016, in which seven defendants claimed that they had been forced to make false confessions.[11] In August 2018, the detention of Malay Muslim human-rights activist Burhan Buraheng in Pattani's Sai Buri district also elicited allegations of abuse of power by the security forces.[12] In September, residents of Pattani's Nong Chik district reported living in a climate of fear after the implementation of draconian martial-law measures in response to an ambush in the district that killed two army rangers. Piyawat, then the commander of the Fourth Army Region, also threatened collective punishment of insurgents' families. At the end of the year, the family of a young man who died in Narathiwat Hospital while serving a prison sentence requested an investigation. There were signs of progress, however, with the armed forces-appointed legislature deliberating a bill that would ban the use of torture in December 2018.[13]

Trends

Challenges to the peace process

Even before the attacks at the end of December, the prospects for the peace process seemed limited. The Thai government consistently pushed for peace negotiations in 2018, even appealing to the BRN towards the end of the year. The format and substance of the talks remains ambiguous, however, with the focus on 'safety zones' having an unclear relevance to long-term solutions. Even after the October reshuffle, the government and military's willingness to make substantive concessions to bring the BRN to the table remained in considerable doubt. Additionally, the election set for early 2019 could see a major reorganisation of political power, even if junta leaders maintain their grip on power. Past peace negotiations, such as those initiated by the previous government in 2013, have fallen apart amid the lack of substantive concessions. If the current round falters, violence could increase.

While the BRN–C and RKK have been associated with most attacks, questions remain about the ability of the Supreme Council to control units on the ground, given their considerable operational latitude. Developments in the peace process or a lessening of the BRN's influence could open opportunities for transnational groups to expand their influence.[14]

Counter-insurgency policy

The announcement in December 2018 of a much-delayed general election scheduled for 24 February 2019 sparked hopes of a 'return to democracy' and a renewed peace initiative. Prayut, however, made clear his intention to retain his position after the election, suggesting that the current counter-insurgency policy and negotiating strategy would continue regardless of the electoral results.[15] The formation of the pro-armed forces Palang Pracharath Party, including four sitting members of the current cabinet, further indicated the armed forces' plan to continue in power.

Growing sympathy for extremist ideology

Recent surveys show that there is growing sympathy for extremist ideology in Thailand, while violent attacks in Southeast Asia (such as the Marawi siege in the Philippines in 2017 and the series of bombings in Indonesia in 2018) have shown ISIS's ambitions in the region, following its territorial collapse in the Middle East.[16] Thailand's south has seen relatively little transnational extremist activity, however, compared to Indonesia, Malaysia and the Philippines.

Whether the number of attacks continues to decline, or if the surge at the end of December 2018 marks the beginning of a new, more violent cycle, depends on multiple factors, including the BRN's willingness to engage in talks, the success of security operations and the outcome of nationwide elections. Without government concessions on some forms of autonomy, however, core grievances will persist, making a political solution unlikely and leaving military progress subject to reversal.

Notes

1   Don Pathan, 'Southern Thai Peace Talks Hit Snag Over Rebel Group's Demand', *Benar News*, 19 March 2018.

2   Sheith Khidhir, 'Is the insurgency ending?', *Asean Post*, 13 September 2018.

3   Razlan Rashid, 'Thai Deep South: A Need to "Review" Independence Demands', *Benar News*, 28 November 2018.

4   Interview with Don Pathan, 'Thailand's Forgotten Extremists', United Nations Development Programme, Asia and the Pacific website.

5   Krithika Varagur, 'Preaching the Peace', Pulitzer Centre, 27 October 2018.

6   Adam Burke, Pauline Tweedie and Ora-orn Poocharoen, 'The Contested Corners of Asia: The Case of Southern Thailand', The Asia Foundation, 2013.

7   Darunee Jumpatong, 'Bilingual Education in the Deep South', Ministry of Education, 20 January 2008.

8   'Thailand: No Justice 10 Years After Tak Bai Killings', Human Rights Watch, 25 October 2014.

9   Neil J. Melvin, 'Conflict in Southern Thailand: Islamism, Violence and the State in the Patani Insurgency', Stockholm International Peace Research Institute Policy Paper no. 20, September 2007, p.18.

10 Mariyam Ahmad, 'Thai Military Revamps Program to Entice Deep South Rebels to Surrender', *Benar News*, 9 February 2018.

11 'Thai court convicts 9 young Muslim men in Bangkok bomb plot – after defendants say they were tortured into making false confessions', Associated Press, 29 September 2018.

12 'Thailand: Rights Activist Detained in Deep South', Human Rights Watch, 2 August 2018.

13 Chularat Saengpassa, 'Bill on torture to go before NLA', *Nation*, 5 December 2018.

14 Hara Shintaro, 'Conflict and Islamic radicalism in Patani', *Prachtai*, 8 January 2018.

15 'Thai PM Prayut keeps options open, avoids joining any party in run-up to election', *Strait Times*, 27 November 2018.

16 'Merdeka Center New Poll Show Malaysia and Thailand Are Now at the Highest Levels of Sympathy Towards Jihadist & Terrorism', Terrorism Research & Analysis Consortium, November 2018.

Asia-Pacific

3 Europe and Eurasia

The eastern part of the town of Shushi/Shusha, Nagorno-Karabakh, which was completely destroyed in 1992

Regional Introduction

The armed conflicts in Nagorno-Karabakh and eastern Ukraine are the only two currently active on the Eurasian continent. Russia has a prominent role in both theatres. In the Armenian–Azerbaijani dispute, its positions are virtually identical to the West's, maintaining a rhetorical commitment to similar peacemaking and conflict-resolution agendas. In Ukraine, however, Russia's goals are diametrically opposed to the West's and actively destabilising. In both situations, Moscow is interested in retaining influence over former Soviet territories and presence in areas of geostrategic relevance in the power competition with the West. As a result, in Nagorno-Karabakh, Russia seeks to balance established military and economic cooperation in Armenia with arms deals and plans to expand trade ties in Azerbaijan. In Ukraine, Russia aims to limit a drift towards the West by supporting separatist sentiments and armed groups in the Donbas region and by asserting its control over the Kerch Strait (located off the Crimean peninsula it annexed in 2014).

Stalemate continued in both conflicts in 2018, with no substantial changes to the parties' military positions, and no movements in the lines dividing the contested territories from the countries (re)claiming them. The contestations that remain at the root of the two conflicts, however, have different implications for the countries involved. The political and military crisis exposed by the Maidan Revolution, and exemplified by the introduction of martial law in November 2018, still directly affects Ukraine's social and political relations on a daily basis. Fighting over the territory of Nagorno-Karabakh, while featuring prominently in the nationalist rhetoric of both Armenia and Azerbaijan, has instead become somewhat normalised after 30 years of conflict, with limited consequences for social and political life in Baku and Yerevan.

Low-level violence characterises both conflicts. Besides a major naval incident in the Sea of Azov in November that seemed to precipitate the confrontation between Russia and Ukraine, the main form of violence in both conflicts this year has been shelling and exchanges of fire across the Lines of Contact, and across the international border between Armenia and Azerbaijan. The total fatalities are higher in the Ukrainian conflict than in Nagorno-Karabakh (with more than 10,000 deaths recorded since 2014), but in 2018, casualties remained relatively low in both conflicts. Daily ceasefire violations continued to have direct humanitarian and economic effects on the civilian population, particularly in eastern Ukraine, from where more than a million people have been displaced since 2014. Armenian official figures are outdated, but we know that internally displaced persons (IDPs) from Nagorno-Karabakh have resettled mainly in the capital.

Prospects for peace will remain limited for both conflicts in 2019. Political developments, particularly Ukraine's repeated reference to Russia as the 'aggressor state', heightened tensions between the two countries in 2018. As a result, the Friendship Treaty due to expire in March 2019 will not be renewed. The unexpected democratic transition in Armenia may also lead to increased tensions over Nagorno-Karabakh in 2019. Armenian President Nikol Pashinyan's openness to dialogue is unlikely to ease tensions if it continues to be accompanied by an uncompromising rhetoric on territorial concessions. Though an equilibrium has so far held, by which the conflict parties seek to minimise military incidents, the possibility of fighting (such as an event like the 'four day war' in 2016) cannot be ruled out.

Besides these two active conflicts, at least two unresolved conflicts in Eurasia – Kosovo and Cyprus – have the potential to affect politics in the region. The former in particular might destabilise immediate neighbours as well as the larger Balkan region, and the possibility of renewed violence in 2019 should not be ruled out. Kosovar–Serbian tensions heightened over the course of this year, with the assassination of a prominent Kosovar Serb politician and the decision of the Kosovar government to implement an import tax on goods from Serbia and Bosnia-Herzegovina. Furthermore, in December, Kosovo resolved to form a national army without the vote of ethnic Serbian members of parliament, some of whom have been boycotting the Assembly since the spring. It is unlikely that the vote will materialise as a danger to stability and peace in the region, despite Serbia's show of force at the border; however, the security situation in Kosovo is fragile and the potential for violence remains. With the border demarcation still disputed, discussions of territory swaps also create concerns in neighbouring countries about the implications for the broader region.

> Daily ceasefire violations have direct humanitarian and economic effects on civilians

A political settlement to the Cyprus question will likely continue to remain elusive in 2019. While the United Nations (UN) resumed efforts to revive the negotiations soon after the collapse of the peace process in 2017, reunification talks will not start until at least June 2019 – after municipal elections in Turkey in March and European Parliament elections in May. The UN is set to focus on an agreement over a common road map, and although expectations remain low, according to a recent bipartisan survey (including international partners), most respondents in both communities said they want a settlement. Two new crossing points between the Turkish-run and Cypriot government-run areas opened in November (as agreed in 2015) and local political leaders agreed to more confidence-building measures. The extent of their implementation, however, remains limited.

Armenia–Azerbaijan (Nagorno-Karabakh)

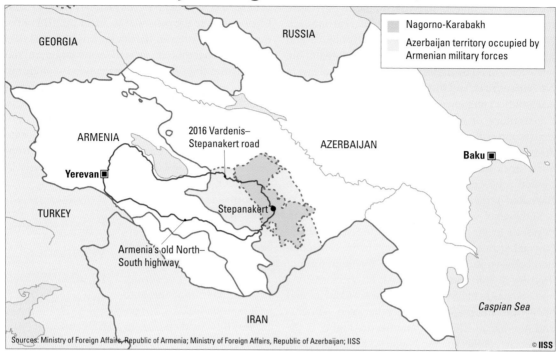

Sources: Ministry of Foreign Affairs, Republic of Armenia; Ministry of Foreign Affairs, Republic of Azerbaijan; IISS   © IISS

Overview

The conflict in 2018

The dynamics of the conflict between Armenia and Azerbaijan have changed significantly since Armenia's surprise democratic transition in May 2018, which followed weeks of anti-government protests and the resignation of then-prime minister Serzh Sargsyan. While relations between the conflict parties remain tense, Armenian Prime Minister Nikol Pashinyan and Azerbaijani President Ilham Aliev met in late September 2018 at the Commonwealth of Independent States (CIS) summit in Dushanbe, Tajikistan, and pledged to de-escalate tensions along the borders. As a result, the volume of ceasefire violations dropped significantly.

The conflict to 2018

The Nagorno-Karabakh conflict is a conflict between Armenia and Azerbaijan over the disputed region of Nagorno-Karabakh, as well as seven surrounding districts. These territories, *de jure* part of Azerbaijan, are de facto controlled by ethnic Armenians of the Republic of Artsakh (Nagorno-Karabakh).

In 1988, Karabakh Armenians, who made up the majority of the republic and were increasingly subjected to discriminatory policies by Baku, demanded that Nagorno-Karabakh be transferred from Soviet Azerbaijan to Soviet Armenia. In the same year, the Nagorno-Karabakh legislature passed a resolution to join Armenia. In response, strikes and protests erupted in Azerbaijan against the possible unification of Nagorno-Karabakh with Armenia, which escalated to pogroms against ethnic Armenians in Sumgait and Baku, Azerbaijan's two largest cities, in 1988 and 1990 respectively. The Soviet Union was caught off guard by the violence and had neither the mechanisms nor the will to lead a meaningful conflict-resolution process with the two groups.

Key statistics	
Type:	Internationalised
IDPs total (2017):	400,000
IDPs new (2018):	no data
Refugees total (2018):	not applicable
Refugees new (2018):	not applicable
People in need (2018):	not applicable

Competing claims and lack of effective communication between the two sides resulted in the early 1990s in a full-scale war and population exchange of Armenians residing in Azerbaijan and Azerbaijanis residing in Armenia. As the war progressed, the majority of Armenians in Nagorno-Karabakh and Armenia shifted their aims to push for Nagorno-Karabakh's independence.

In 1992, the Organization for Security and Co-operation in Europe (OSCE) Minsk Group, led by France, Russia and the United States, engaged in peace negotiations and brokered a ceasefire agreement in 1994 that fell short of a comprehensive agreement on the final status of Nagorno-Karabakh but ensured 20 years of relative stability.[1] This relative calm broke down with Azerbaijan's discontent around the status quo and in early April 2016, the conflict escalated with the most intense fighting since 1994, killing approximately 350 people on both sides. While the current situation has largely reverted back to the relative calm present throughout the 2000s, the possibility of resumed large-scale fighting has increased, given Azerbaijan's military build-up in certain areas.

Forces

Armenian armed forces

Armenian Prime Minister Nikol Pashinyan is the commander-in-chief of the Armenian armed forces. The political leadership of the armed forces is represented by the Armenian Ministry of Defence, headed by Davit Tonoyan. The Armenian armed forces are comprised of five army corps and an air force, which is predominantly engaged in air defence. The overall number of Armenian service personnel in the army and air force is 42,950.

The Armenian armed forces are a conscript force with an increasing number of professional officers. Armenian men between the ages of 18 and 27 are required to register at local commissariats. Armenia's defence expenditure in 2018 rose significantly by around 17% to US$506 million. Over the course of 2018, the armed forces greatly improved combat readiness and defence capabilities, including the installation of modern command, control, communications, computers, intelligence, surveillance and reconnaissance (C4ISR) cameras on the front-line.

Since the start of the conflict, the armed forces have focused on supporting the Artsakh Republic Defense Army (Nagorno-Karabakh Defense Army) to maintain control over the territory of Nagorno-Karabakh as well as the surrounding territories, the latter of which are widely seen as a bargaining chip.

Artsakh Republic Defense Army (Nagorno-Karabakh Defense Army)

The Artsakh Republic Defense Army is comprised of an army, air force and air defence. The commander-in-chief is Nagorno-Karabakh President Bako Sahakyan and the minister of defence is Lieutenant General Levon Mnatsakanyan. Estimates of the number of active service personnel range between 18,000 and 20,000.[2] Despite its small size, the Artsakh Defense Army is a skilled and professional force, comprised of veterans experienced in insurgency and guerrilla-warfare tactics who are able to exploit the mountainous terrain.[3]

There is a high degree of integration between the Armenian and the Nagorno-Karabakh armed forces, and at times it is difficult to distinguish which military equipment belongs to Armenia and which to Nagorno-Karabakh. Despite the close ties between the Artsakh Republic Defense Army and the Armenian armed forces, there is still an important separation in the operational command of the Artsakh Republic Defense Army, which controls the disputed territories as well as surrounding areas.[4] The objective of the Artsakh Republic Defense Army is predominantly defence, maintaining control over Nagorno-Karabakh and the surrounding territories, and repelling attacks and incursions from Azerbaijan.

Armed forces of Azerbaijan

Azerbaijani President Ilham Aliev is the commander-in-chief of the armed forces of Azerbaijan, with Colonel-General Zakir Hasanov heading the Defence Ministry. In 2018, there were 66,950 active personnel in the Azerbaijani armed forces, with 300,000 in reserve. The Azerbaijani armed forces have three branches – army, air force and air defence, and navy. Azerbaijan has an 18-month mandatory military-

Europe and Eurasia

service requirement for all able-bodied men at 18 years of age.

The objective of the armed forces of Azerbaijan overall is to liberate the territories occupied by Armenian forces. The types of violent tactics used include ceasefire violations along the Line of Contact (LoC), sometimes with tanks, as well as periodic incursions into territory controlled by the Artsakh Defense Army in order to increase Azerbaijan's political leverage in the peace process.[5]

Although this strategy did not change in 2018, Baku has attempted to widen the conflict in more subtle ways, taking advantage of the fact that Azerbaijan's military capabilities have been upgraded along the LoC, as well as in its exclave of Nakhichevan. In 2018, this was evident in the expansion of the area of fighting beyond the LoC between Karabakh and Azerbaijan to the more frequent targeting of civilian areas along the international border between Azerbaijan and Armenia.[6]

Drivers

Failed Soviet nationalities policies

The roots of the current conflict date back to February 1988, when Nagorno-Karabakh Armenians, with the backing of Armenia, decided to secede from Azerbaijan – an attempt that was met with resistance from Azerbaijan. While there were instances of pre-Soviet Armenian–Azerbaijani intercommunal conflict in 1905–06 and 1918–20, the current conflict is predominantly the result of failed Soviet nationalities policies. In particular, the Soviet state failed to manage the antagonistic national narratives that began to emerge in the 1960s, which framed Nagorno-Karabakh as 'rightfully' belonging to either Armenians or Azerbaijanis; it neglected to address the disputed national boundaries of Nagorno-Karabakh; and it was oblivious to the lack of intercommunal dialogue between Armenians and Azerbaijanis.[7] Despite the fact that Soviet nationalities policies allowed for both ethnic groups to live side by side in peace in one Soviet state for 70 years, these same policies failed to resolve the ethnic-based grievances that growing between Nagorno-Karabakh Armenians and Baku. When intercommunal violence between Armenians and Azeris broke out in 1988, Moscow had no system for resolving such strife through consensus. This crisis of management exhausted all possible channels of negotiation and the aggrieved parties escalated to all-out war in late 1991.

Strong regional interests

Following the ceasefire agreement brokered by the OSCE in 1994, there have been no international monitoring missions on the ground and the ceasefire is left to the conflict parties to manage. The OSCE Minsk process has slowed to a near halt. Two regional players maintain significant geostrategic influence on the conflict: Russia and Turkey. Russia and Armenia are considered strategic allies: Russia maintains troops along Armenia's borders with Turkey and Iran, while Armenia is a member of the Russia-led Eurasian Economic Union (EEU) and Collective Security Treaty Organization (CSTO). Russia is also selling arms to Azerbaijan, however, calling into question Russia's status as an ally in Armenian public discourse.

Turkey – Azerbaijan's main regional ally – cooperates with Azerbaijan in military matters (by selling weapons and being party to treaties making Turkey and Azerbaijan guarantors if either is attacked) and has economically blockaded Armenia since the 1990s. Turkey demands that Armenia withdraw from Nagorno-Karabakh and the seven surrounding districts as a condition for re-establishing diplomatic relations.

Azerbaijan's growing discontent with the status quo as well as its rapid economic growth (thanks to gas and oil exports) has boosted its military power and increased its ability to dictate the dynamics of military escalations. Armenia's military capabilities have also grown, albeit more modestly, and its security alliance with Russia has deepened. This relative balance of power and the marginalisation of the peace negotiations have converged to keep the violence somewhat contained and the conflict mostly 'frozen', even as ceasefire violations occur on both sides every day.

Political and Military Developments

Aliev consolidates control in Azerbaijan

On 11 April, snap presidential elections were held in Azerbaijan, some six months ahead of schedule. Aliev, who has ruled Azerbaijan since 2003, won his fourth consecutive term in office, which is expected to run until 2025. In May 2018, mechanisms for state control of information in Azerbaijan were strengthened, with the parliament voting to allow state censorship of the media in the event of renewed open conflict.

Armenia's 'Velvet Revolution'

In Armenia, protests erupted in mid-April after Serzh Sargsyan, whose term limit as president was coming to an end, attempted to extend his rule by assuming the post of prime minister. These protests resulted in Sargsyan's resignation and a peaceful change of government, which saw opposition MP Nikol Pashinyan take up the post of prime minister.

Armenia's so-called 'Velvet Revolution' and the subsequent democratic shift has added a degree of uncertainty to the political trends of the conflict. For the first time in 20 years, Armenia is not being led by a native of Nagorno-Karabakh. Concerns within Armenia and expectations within Azerbaijan that Russia would work against the new Armenian leadership did not materialise. The Velvet Revolution demonstrated that Armenia was politically strong enough to undergo internal change, making untenable the Azerbaijani narrative that Armenia is too weak to defend itself and kept the status quo relatively unchanged only through Russian patronage.

Moreover, Pashinyan has taken a different approach to the conflict than his predecessor Sargsyan. While seemingly more open to and more proactive in initiating dialogue, Pashinyan has also taken a rather hardline stance to the conflict, pledging not to give any territory to Azerbaijan, not even in exchange for Azerbaijan's recognition of Nagorno-Karabakh's independence.

In July 2018, Pashinyan's son Ashot Pashinyan enlisted in the Armenian army, where he is now serving in Nagorno-Karabakh in a unit near the Line of Contact (LoC). While Prime Minister Pashinyan stated that it was his son's personal decision to join the military, he framed the development as a 'peace loving' gesture demonstrating his personal stake in the conflict and his commitment not to 'spare anything to defend [his] country and people'. He called on Aliev to send his son to the army to show a similar indication of goodwill, and Aliev enlisted his son Heydar in September 2018.

Azerbaijan's military capability increases

The Azerbaijani government continued to build its military advantage in the conflict in 2018, with reports from the beginning of the year stating that the capital assets of the Azerbaijani Armed Forces Assistance Fund – the body that maintains the development of the armed forces – exceeded US$51.77 million.[8]

In June, Azerbaijan announced its acquisition of a new missile system obtained from Belarusian and Israeli companies. Azerbaijan claims that the missiles of this system have a range of 300 kilometres, making them capable of reaching targets anywhere in Armenia, but also northern Iran, most of Georgia and much of the Russian North Caucasus. The missile system is also able to counteract the *Iskander* missile systems acquired by Armenia from Russia. The impact of this build-up of capabilities on both sides means that any new confrontation may escalate beyond what was possible before.

In addition, over the course of much of April and up until mid-May 2018, the Nagorno-Karabakh defence ministry reported new movements of Azerbaijani troops and a build-up of military equipment and personnel at the LoC. Combined with the steady military build-up in the Azerbaijani exclave of Nakhichevan since 2012, a resumption of violence would potentially both intensify and broaden the scope of conflict.

CIS meeting between Pashinyan and Aliyev

In late September 2018 during the CIS summit in Dushanbe, Tajikistan, Pashinyan and Aliyev met for the first time and agreed to work towards preventing ceasefire violations and to start direct communication. The news came as a surprise to observers as there were no official indications that such a plan was being prepared. Pashinyan stated that the two leaders had recommitted to the negotiation process and agreed to establish a direct line of communication, though the specifics had not yet been decided. Despite the lack of a concrete plan, the informal commitment immediately reduced ceasefire violations from the start of October. According to data from the Azerbaijani Ministry of Defence, Armenian ceasefire violations dropped from more than 100 per day to approximately 25 per day. Even as both sides remain at odds on important aspects of the conflict's regulation, serious steps from the leaders of both sides have a high capacity for quick and significant changes in the conflict's dynamics.

Protests in Nagorno-Karabakh

Protests broke out in Nagorno-Karabakh in June 2018 after an incident in the capital Stepanakert in which national-security officers beat two civilians. Nagorno-Karabakh citizens, seemingly inspired by the events in Armenia, blocked roads and gathered to demand the resignation of the police and national-security heads. Such protests are a first in Nagorno-Karabakh, where opposition voices have long been silenced by the de facto Nagorno-Karabakh government, which has cited the necessity for unity and loyalty given the context of war. Protesters ended their demonstrations only after Pashinyan urged them to do so, promising that a parliamentary commission would investigate the incident.

Violent Events

Overall, 2018 saw less fighting than the previous four years. Violence was limited to ceasefire violations along the LoC, the number of which remained at stable levels before dropping in October 2018. No fatalities were caused by major offensives, but rather were the result of isolated ceasefire violations.

There were approximately 13 fatalities in total for 2018, compared to around 50 in 2017, 200 in 2016, 60 in 2015, and 55 in 2014.[9] Most of the violence was centred along the LoC between Nagorno-Karabakh and Azerbaijan, although sporadic shelling by Azerbaijan of positions in the northeast of Armenia – a trend that began in 2014 – continued in 2018. While these attacks resulted in damage to civilian property, no fatalities were recorded in 2018.

Impact

Impact on civilians

The conflict continues to negatively impact civilians on both sides. On 29 March, three staff members of the landmine-clearing charity HALO were killed when their vehicle hit an anti-tank landmine in Nagorno-Karabakh. On 13 April, three residents were injured in a landmine explosion in the Tavush district of Armenia while collecting plants near a military-defence outpost. There were no reports of injuries or casualties on the Azerbaijani side in 2018.

Trends

Democracy in Armenia

The Velvet Revolution in Armenia has transformed the conflict into one between an authoritarian state and a democratic state, which may impact the way the international community perceives the legitimacy of their respective claims. Pashinyan, highlighting this change in July, stated that any attack by Azerbaijan against Armenia would be considered an attack on democracy as well. He travelled to Nagorno-Karabakh less than 24 hours after taking office on 8 May and held his first press conference as prime minister there, signalling the importance of Nagorno-Karabakh for the new Armenian government. He criticised the current format of peace negotiations, which excludes Nagorno-Karabakh as a party, and signalled he might take a more hands-on approach to the conflict compared to Sargsyan.

Stability in the near future

The conflict will likely remain stable in 2019. However, the build-up of military equipment in Azerbaijan's exclave of Nakhichevan in 2018 might open a new front there, which would widen the conflict zone far beyond what exists today, potentially reaching the Armenian district of Vayots Dzor.

Notes

1   Sabine Freizer, 'Twenty years after the Nagorny Karabakh ceasefire: an opportunity to move towards more inclusive conflict resolution', *Caucasus Survey*, vol. 1, no. 2, 2014, pp. 109–22.

2   IISS, *The Military Balance 2019* (Abingdon: Routledge for the IISS, 2019), p. 184–7.

3   Richard Giragosian, 'Armenia and Karabakh: One Nation, Two States', Armenian General Benevolent Fund, 1 May 2009.

4   Ron Synovitz, '"Open Secret": Experts Cast Doubt On Yerevan's Claims Over Nagorno-Karabakh', *Radio Free Europe/ Radio Liberty*, 5 April 2016.

5   'Armenia accuses Azerbaijan of all-out "war"', Al-Jazeera, 22 December 2015.

6   Richard Giragosian, 'Is war imminent in the Caucasus?' *Al Jazeera*, 24 December 2015.

7   Thomas de Waal, 'The Nagorny Karabakh conflict: Origins, dynamics and misperceptions', *Accord*, no. 17, 2005.

8   Rashid Shirinov, 'Armed Forces Assistance Fund's assets exceed 88M manats', *Azernews.Az*, 4 January 2018.

9   Emil Sanamyan, 'Karabakh: More (Relative) Calm Ahead in 2018?', Eurasianet, 12 January 2018.

Ukraine

Overview

The conflict in 2018

The stalemate in eastern Ukraine continued in 2018, while relations between Russia and Ukraine deteriorated further when the Ukrainian parliament ratified a decree on the reintegration of the Donbas region in February. Passing the decree – which officially identified Russia as the aggressor and occupying power in the Donbas – helped the Ukrainian government domestically as it placated the anti-Russian demonstrators who protested in favour of the bill in January. It also allowed the Ukrainian armed forces to broaden their influence in the region and move towards launching a Joint Forces Operation (JFO), headed by the armed forces, to replace the Anti-Terrorist Operation (ATO).

February marked the third anniversary of the Minsk II Agreement – a set of measures agreed upon by the leaders of Ukraine, France, Germany and

Russia on 11 February 2015 to ease the war along the 457 kilometre contact line running through Donetsk and Luhansk oblasts. Casualty rates continued to rise in 2018, however, with more than 3,000 civilian deaths and more than 4,000 military casualties. Although ceasefire violations reached their lowest level in two years in March, they had risen again by the end of 2018.[1] Information warfare, the closeness of the front-lines, similarity in some weapons systems and the inaccessibility around the war zone complicate apportioning the ceasefire violations, with each side blaming the other, further exacerbating the deteriorating relationship. Political and military tensions between the two countries reached their peak in November during the Sea of Azov crisis, when Russia attacked and captured two Ukrainian gunboats and a tug travelling through the Kerch Strait to Mariupol, causing Ukraine to declare martial law in ten regions for 30 days.

The issues of internally displaced persons (IDPs), human-rights violations and other consequences of the ongoing conflict remained pronounced in 2018. Although civilian casualties decreased in 2018, especially compared to 2017, as of July 2018, the Ministry of Social Policy had registered more than 1.5 million IDPs in total.

The conflict to 2018

Then-president Viktor Yanukovych's failure to sign the Association Agreement with the European Union in late November 2013 prompted major protests and political turmoil in Ukraine. Beyond this trigger, the Revolution of Dignity (November 2013–February 2014) was deeply rooted in mass discontent with Yanukovych's repressive policies and his highly corrupt regime. The protests turned violent on 19–20 February 2014, with more than 100

Key statistics	
Type:	Internationalised
IDPs total (2018):	1,500,000
IDPs new (2018):	30,000
Refugees total (2018):	not applicable
Refugees new (2018):	not applicable
People in need (2018):	3,500,000

demonstrators dying during the bloodiest days of political violence since Ukraine's independence in 1991. Yanukovych was eventually ousted from power on 22 February.

These events reinforced the pro-Western sentiment of some segments of Ukraine society, but not all Ukrainians drew the same conclusions and a significant ethnic Russian minority kept supporting close relations with Russia. The armed conflict in eastern Ukraine broke out in April 2014. According to Kiev, the onset of the hostilities was precipitated by Russia's annexation of Crimea on 27 February and the seizure of government buildings in Donetsk, Kharkiv and Luhansk by pro-Moscow activists. According to Moscow, the conflict followed the provocation of the Maidan Revolution.

Pro-Moscow activists in Donetsk and Luhansk declared independence on 11 May 2014 and appealed to Russian President Vladimir Putin for assistance, prompting Ukraine to launch an ATO in the region. The separatists gained significant ground in the initial stages of the conflict, as the Ukrainian army consisted mostly of volunteer battalions and was unprepared to deal with a separatist challenge. The Ukrainian armed forces reorganised and began to launch counter-offensives in 2016 against the pro-Russian separatist forces.

| Forces

Ukrainian armed forces

In 2018, the Ukrainian armed forces had approximately 209,000 active military personnel, with 145,000 in the army, 45,000 in the air force and 11,000 in the navy.[2] Since 2014, the Ukrainian armed forces have been modernising their existing military equipment, purchasing abroad and investing in Ukrainian factories to produce new and supe-

rior military equipment, with the specific intent of defending Ukraine's territorial integrity.

The desire to join NATO has dictated the course of Ukraine's military-reform process in the past four years as Ukraine strives to meet key NATO standards, including restructuring the general staff. Other reforms have centred on improving command and control and standardising unit establishments.

Volunteer units have been incorporated into the army and the national guard. The number of training exercises has also increased, both on the national and international levels, with strengthened cooperation between Ukrainian and NATO soldiers through exercises such as *Rapid Trident* 2018, *Sea Breeze* 2018 and *Combined Resolve X*.

The Ukrainian armed forces still face challenges such as corruption, institutional weakness and lack of clear-cut strategic targets for the development of military institutions. Nevertheless, Ukraine has been successfully testing new weapons, such as the 155 mm self-propelled howitzer *Bogdana*, and the *Vilkha* missile system. The state has also purchased 55 Airbus helicopters from France: 21 H225 helicopters, ten H145 helicopters and 24 H125 helicopters, with the first four H225s due to arrive in Ukraine by the end of the year. The state has also received the FGM-148 *Javelin* anti-tank missile from the United States. In contrast to Russia's rapid support of separatist forces, US military support to Kiev arrived slowly.

Donetsk People's Republic (DNR) and Luhansk People's Republic (LNR)

The two main separatist forces in eastern Ukraine are the Donetsk People's Republic (DNR) and the Luhansk People's Republic (LNR). It is difficult to allocate equipment ownership to either or to get an accurate estimate of personnel numbers and force composition. Most information originates from official reports by the Ukrainian armed forces, according to which the DNR and LNR possess a large number of tanks, artillery and air-defence systems. Personnel numbers are estimated at around 34,000 (20,000 in DNR and 14,000 in LNR) and divisions include the Vostok and Oplot brigades and the Sparta battalion.

Separatist forces tried to regain and maintain key towns along the contact line by shelling the Ukrainian armed forces, which have been successful at counteracting such offensives. Fighting is focused around the cities of Horlivka, Avdiivka and Slavyansk.

Russian armed forces

According to the Ukrainian Ministry of Defence (MoD), the Russian armed forces have been supplying weapons and personnel to the separatist forces in eastern Ukraine. President Poroshenko stated that up to 50% of those involved in the fighting against Ukraine are Russian soldiers, with numbers fluctuating between 2,500 and 10,000. Russia has supplied weapons such as the 9M133 *Kornet* anti-tank guided missile, T-72B1 and B2 main battle tanks, as well as various Man-Portable Air Defence Systems (MANPADS) and self-propelled air-defence systems.

Besides supporting the separatist forces in eastern Ukraine, Russia has progressively modernised its armed forces and improved its arsenals with new-generation military equipment. Increased military activity in Russia's Southern Military District (which now includes Crimea) through the *Zapad* 2017 and *Vostok* 2018 exercises sent alarming signals to Ukraine and the West. The military exercises in early December used the *Pantsir* missile system and further alarmed the Ukrainian MoD.

Drivers

Russian versus Western influence

Ukraine's desire to join NATO and become an EU member has long been a point of contention, with Russia perceiving Ukraine's drift towards the West as a provocation. The West has supported Ukraine's declared aspirations, though sluggish reforms have hampered the process. For Russia, Ukraine is a key partner and an important buffer with Europe. The West's interest in Ukraine, its involvement in the 2004 Orange Revolution and its reaction to the annexation of Crimea threaten Russia's interests and stability in the region.

The West's military and financial assistance has helped counteract Ukraine's political instability and economic decline after 2014, but the EU's dependence on Russian gas (37% of gas imports) and the dramatic increase of Russia's exports to Europe have sent mixed signals to Ukraine about Western support.[3] The activities of the Donetsk People's Republic (DNR) and Luhansk People's Republic (LNR), has complicated the situation, with the large ethnic-Russian minority in eastern Ukraine and Crimea welcoming Russia's intervention and support. This divide threatens Ukraine's territorial integrity, especially in cities such as Kharkiv and Odessa, where there are large ethnic Russian populations.

Economic development

The imbalances in wealth across Ukraine are an important driver of the conflict. The eastern region of the country is poorer, struggling with a declining industrial base and feeling increasingly alienated from Kiev. The global recession of 2008 aggravated Ukraine's economic situation, already marred by corruption and inefficiencies.

The cost of war and rapid inflation have made Ukraine reliant on external support. IMF funds come with demands for active and successful economic reforms. The World Bank has stated that Ukraine has sufficient potential to improve its situation, but its economic growth depends heavily on the implementation of necessary reforms.[4] Ukraine's close economic links with Russia pose difficulties for the Ukrainian government, especially after it officially proclaimed Russia as the aggressor in eastern Ukraine in February 2018.

Religious tensions

The Ukrainian Orthodox Church has answered to the Moscow patriarchate for centuries, but since Ukraine gained its independence in 1991, church tensions have been mounting, with Russia accusing the Ukrainian Orthodox Church of meddling in Ukraine's domestic politics. In response, the Ukrainian Church has blamed the Moscow patriarchate for not playing a peace-building role in the conflict in the Donbas. When the conflict in eastern Ukraine erupted in 2014 and relations with Russia soured, talks of an independent Orthodox Church became prominent in Ukraine and led to the Ecumenical Patriarchate of Constantinople's recognition of an independent Ukrainian Orthodox Church.

This development came at a very heated time for Russian and Ukrainian relations in October–December 2018, during the Sea of Azov crisis and while the martial law was being introduced in Ukraine. As a consequence of the development, Russia could lose a large proportion of its parishes in Ukraine, which would reduce its involvement in local and domestic politics.

Political and Military Developments

Martial law

The Sea of Azov clashes between Ukrainian gunboats and the Russian coastguard on 25 November 2018 prompted the Ukrainian government to take security measures. The National Security and Defence Council (NSDC) and Poroshenko proposed a 60-day martial law to begin on 28 November. Parliament approved a 30-day martial law in ten regions in eastern and southern Ukraine along the Russia–Ukraine and Moldova–Ukraine borders, deemed to be the most vulnerable to Russian aggression. Shortly after these decisions, the Ukrainian armed forces reported that Russia had stationed T-62M tanks 11 miles from the Ukrainian border. The escalatory behaviour played into the hands of Russia, demonstrating its power and capabilities, while allowing Ukraine to justify the martial law and the increase in its own capabilities along the contact line.

Joint Forces Operation in the Donbas

On 30 April 2018, the Ukrainian Army officially launched a new campaign in eastern Ukraine, the JFO, marking the end of the ATO begun in 2014. The change shifted the responsibility for operations from Ukraine's Security Service, in charge of the ATO, to the Ukrainian armed forces. The name change also carried symbolic and practical connotations, as it officially indicated that the Ukrainian armed forces were fighting an external aggressor.

Under these changes, all law-enforcement agencies in the Donbas (including the Border Guards Services, the National Guard, the Security Service, the police and the Fiscal Service) are to report to the Joint Forces Headquarters.[5] The shift towards a more serious and consolidated military operation in eastern Ukraine benefitted the Ukrainian government politically as it demonstrated to the public that the state was taking necessary measures to safeguard territorial integrity and defend Ukraine's independence.

Termination of 'Friendship Treaty'

On 10 December, the Ukrainian parliament passed a law terminating the 1997 Friendship, Cooperation and Partnership Treaty with Russia, sparking further tension and threatening the negotiations on the Donbas. In response, Russia's Ministry of Foreign Affairs emphasised the long-standing historical and cultural ties between the two countries, the need for good neighbourliness and the detrimental impact of the decision not only on Russian–Ukrainian relations, but also on Ukraine's national interests. Ukraine, however, used the passing of the law to consolidate the new official rhetoric of Russia being the aggressor. The respective media promoted these lines of argument, intensifying the divide among the civilian population.

MH17 developments

In May 2018, there was a development in the investigation of the Malaysian Airlines Flight MH17, shot down over eastern Ukraine on 17 July 2014. The international joint investigation team (JIT) concluded that MH17 was shot down by a Russian *Buk* surface-to-air missile supplied by the Russian 53rd Anti-Aircraft Brigade. Australia and the Netherlands stated that they held Russia responsible for the downing.[6] Russia, in turn, blamed Ukraine for the incident, releasing a serial number that (Russia claimed) confirms that the missile belonged to Ukraine.[7]

Violent Events

Kerch Strait incident (Sea of Azov)

The clash in the Sea of Azov on 25 November was the most prominent violent event in the Ukrainian conflict in 2018. Two Ukrainian gunboats, *Berdyansk* and *Nikopol*, and one tug, *Yani Kapu*, were travelling to Mariupol through the Kerch Strait, linking the Black Sea with the Sea of Azov, over which Russia opened a bridge in May that connected annexed Crimea with mainland Russia. Russian boats reportedly attacked the Ukrainian ships, as (according to Russia) the latter ignored the demands of the coastguard to halt. Russia subsequently captured the vessels and took 23 soldiers into custody, and sent two Su-25 aircraft to patrol the area.

Unlike the dynamic of the conflict in eastern Ukraine, this confrontation occurred between the military forces of the two countries. The Ukrainian Navy stated that the damage caused to the Ukrainian tug constituted an act of aggression according to United Nations Resolution 3314. The detainment of the sailors also sparked international condemnation. During an emergency meeting of the UN Security Council, five EU countries – United Kingdom, The Netherlands, France, Poland and Sweden – called on Russia to release the ships and crew.

The killing of Aleksandr Zakharchenko

On 31 August 2018, Aleksandr Zakharchenko, the self-proclaimed head of the DNR, was killed in an explosion in a Donetsk café. Russia blamed Kiev for the assassination and claimed that Ukraine was trying to disrupt the Minsk agreement, while Ukrainian intelligence services claimed to possess information showing Russian involvement in the incident. The explosion happened at a time when the separatist forces were suffering from losses on the front-lines, especially around Horlivka, a strategically important area in the conflict. The Ukrainian media speculated that the bombing was intended to draw attention away from the front-line.

Impact

Internal tensions

The most important political implication of the conflict for Ukraine remains the safeguarding of its territorial integrity. Pro-Russian sentiment in the annexed Crimea, war-torn Donbas and southern and eastern cities (where support for Russia has historically been higher due to Soviet internal migration) poses a political problem for the Ukrainian government, as it creates domestic ethnic tensions which could erupt in Russia's favour. The Ukrainian government's pro-Western stance has also exacerbated the divide between regions that would favourably move towards the West and those that lean towards Russia.

For Russia, the situation in Ukraine poses a conundrum. Russia justified its actions domestically by blaming the Ukrainian government for alienating ethnic Russian minorities and shaping its rhetoric around the duty to protect its citizens abroad. At the same time, it has been hit hard by political and economic sanctions in the wake of its occupation of Crimea.

Humanitarian impact

The conflict in eastern Ukraine has continued to affect the political and social landscape in Ukraine, albeit to a lesser extent than in previous years. According to the Ministry of Social Policy of Ukraine, as of 3 December 2018 there were 1,514,690 registered IDPs in Ukraine, with the share of employed IDPs decreasing by 6% from March to June.[8] Food insecurity doubled in the year to May 2018, aggravating the situation and challenging the Ukrainian government to deliver supplies to civilians living in non-government-controlled areas.[9] Wellbeing among IDPs also declined in 2018, mostly due to the decrease in average monthly income – in June 2018, the reported salary was UAH2,090 (US$79.80), compared to UAH2,446 (US$87.15) in December 2017. The only important improvement regarded the elderly. On 4 September, the Grand Chamber of the Supreme Court made the landmark decision to protect the pension rights of IDPs.

The Office of the United Nations High Commissioner for Human Rights (OHCHR) recorded a number of human-rights violations and produced a detailed report on the effects of the war on civilians, particularly the 600,000 people living within 5 km of the contact line. OHCHR recorded 105 casualties between 16 May and 15 August 2018 (12 deaths and 93 injured). Of the 160 human-rights violations recorded in the occupied and conflict-affected areas, 53 were committed by the government of Ukraine, ten by armed groups and 22 by Russia.

The martial law imposed in late November carried numerous domestic implications for civilian life, including curfews, suspension of civil rights and seizure of property and businesses.

Economic impact

Although Ukraine's economic problems are mostly due to the political instability in 2014, they are also the result of the lack of reform and a history of corruption dating back to 1991. Inflation rates saw a drastic increase from 12.1% in 2014 to 48.7% in 2015, and although this decreased to 10.9% in 2018 from 14.44% in 2017, the economy remains volatile.[10] The World Bank predicts that if Ukraine does not reform its economy, 2019 will see a decline in investor confidence, and a consequent 2% decline in overall growth.

The economy has seen some positive trends. In the first six months of 2018, Ukraine repaid UAH104.73 billion of state debt (US$4bn), which included UAH23.77bn of foreign debt (US$91m).[11] The country has also seen a 3.5% GDP growth, compared to 2.52% in 2017, resulting in GDP rising to US$126bn. The state remains heavily reliant on the IMF tranches, however, and the lack of substantial financial and anti-corruption reforms have put a strain on the relationship between Ukraine and the West. Income stagnation and an unstable currency affect the civilian population. Grave discontent in 2018 led to protests outside the parliament, and will probably be exploited in the electoral campaign ahead of the 2019 presidential elections.

Trends

Stalemate to continue

The military stalemate is likely to continue, with ceasefire violations increasing. It is highly unlikely that the two countries will be able to conduct productive negotiations on the Donbas region. It is also unlikely that Poroshenko will convince parliament to extend martial law, as such an action would interfere significantly with election campaigns.

The 2019 presidential vote is unlikely to prompt a clear resolution of the conflict, or a thawing of Russian–Ukrainian relations. Ukraine will not elect a pro-Russian president, given that all the presidential candidates appear unwilling to cooperate with Moscow. If Poroshenko returns to office for a second term, no significant policy changes will occur, and the relations will continue without significant change.

Show of power for political ends

The increased Russian naval activity in Crimea is a power stance, yet Ukraine may view it as a grave threat and use it domestically to justify increased military spending and other governmental actions. Although Ukraine may interpret the Russian deployment of the *Pantsir* missile system as raising the risk of a possible attack on the mainland, such an event is unlikely to happen at this stage. Russia would not risk alienating its allies and attracting more Western activity in the region. Ukraine, however, could use the build-up on the peninsula for political purposes, especially during the election season. Aside from the exploitation of this factor by both Ukrainian and Russian media, it is unlikely that the *Panstir* missile system will be used for anything other than show-casing Russia's power.

Notes

1   Organization for Security and Co-operation in Europe (OSCE) figures.

2   IISS, *The Military Balance 2019* (Abingdon, Routledge for the IISS, 2019), pp. 213–14.

3   Ivana Kottasová, 'Europe is still addicted to Russian gas', CNN Business, 5 June 2018.

4   'Ukraine: Economic Growth Depends on Reforms and Financing', press release, World Bank, 4 October 2018.

5   'The operation of the United Forces: what is it and what is different from ATO', 24tv.ua, 30 April 2018.

6   'MH17: The Netherlands and Australia hold Russia responsible', Government of the Netherlands website, 25 May 2018.

7   'The Ministry of Defense of the Russian Federation determined the number of the missile MH17 that shot down. According to the agency, it belonged to Ukraine', TASS, 17 September 2018.

8   'National Monitoring System Report on the Situation of Internally Displaced Persons', International Organization for Migration, Mission in Ukraine, June 2018, p. 6.

9   'Six things you need to know about the crisis in Ukraine', United Nations in Ukraine, 7 May 2018.

10 IMF Data Mapper, 'Ukraine – Inflation rate, average consumer prices', International Monetary Fund, December 2018.

11 'Ukraine government preparing to get next IMF tranche', Ukrinform, 23 August 2018.

Europe and Eurasia

4 Middle East and North Africa

Houthi loyalists rally
in support of the UN
ceasefire in Sana'a, Yemen,
on 19 December 2018

Regional Introduction

In 2018, the Middle East remained the world's most volatile region: none of its seven active conflicts saw any serious prospect of settlement, while de-escalation efforts were both tentative and incomplete. Fuelled by the combination of state weakness, repressive governance and regional rivalries, these conflicts emphasised the unsettled and complex nature of politics in the Middle East. Though they varied considerably in nature and intensity, most armed conflicts in the region involved a tangled mixture of local, transnational, governmental and external actors, with the battlefields sharing several trends.

The targeting of civilians, deliberate or not, characterised the major conflicts. In Syria, civilian communities were the primary target of the Syrian government's bombing campaign, which strived to punish and displace rebel-friendly constituencies. Nonetheless, the end to major fighting did not translate into better conditions for civilians: access to basic services and United Nations humanitarian assistance remained curtailed even after capitulation. In rebel-controlled Idlib, civilians suffered from the strengthening of the jihadi Hayat Tahrir al-Sham (HTS) group, resulting in a number of foreign donors withholding or cancelling humanitarian assistance over concerns that extremist groups would divert it. Ethnic cleansing was also deployed in Turkish-occupied territory in the northwest, where Kurdish residents were often ousted and replaced by Arab internally displaced persons (IDPs). Even the US-led campaign against the Islamic State, also known as ISIS or ISIL, which neared its end in 2018, caused considerable damage to major urban centres in Syria and Iraq. The coalition relied on airstrikes and heavy artillery to counter the jihadi group's deployment of improvised explosive devices (IEDs) and mines, as well as the use of human shields, driving away large numbers of civilians without adequate efforts to mitigate the consequences. In Iraq, millions, including those displaced by the fighting between ISIS and the Iraqi forces, remained dependent on humanitarian support and unable to return home. In Egypt, the government's campaign in the Sinai prioritised military means over development and outreach to the civilian population. In Yemen, civilians suffered from the rapid collapse of infrastructure and the economy due to airstrikes, Houthi restrictions and the blockade imposed by the Saudi-led coalition. The income famine that followed caused more indirect casualties than direct ones, weakening entire communities and prompting the world's worst humanitarian crisis. At the end of 2018, more than 20 million people were in need of humanitarian assistance. In Gaza, Hamas infiltrated peaceful demonstrations of Palestinian civilians against the Israeli-imposed blockade to further its political objectives, leading to an Israeli crackdown that killed over 150 civilians and injured at least 10,000 (including 1,849 children), according to Amnesty International.

The risk of escalation remained high in the both crowded and volatile battlefields. In February 2018, US forces responded with massive airpower to an advancing force of Russian mercenaries and allied Syrian forces in eastern Syria, killing hundreds. Later in the year, Syrian air defences mistakenly downed a Russian spy plane while seeking to hit an Israeli aircraft that had just bombed a Syrian base hosting Iranian personnel. In southern Syria, Iran sought to retaliate against sustained Israeli strikes in May by launching drone strikes across the Golan Heights, which failed. International pressure and intense Russian–Turkish diplomacy delayed an expected campaign by the Syrian government to capture the rebel enclave of Idlib, but there was widespread expectation that it would happen in 2019. In Yemen,

fears persisted that a successful Houthi missile strike would inflict significant damage in Saudi Arabia, prompting a massive Saudi retaliation. In all these cases, the reluctance to engage in direct, all-out confrontation reduced the potential for an accidental escalation that could pit conventional militaries against each other, although the possible triggers remain numerous.

The regionalisation of these conflicts entrenched divisions, making it harder to reach settlements. Most conflicts in the Middle East attracted regional interference, fuelling the fighting, pushing warring parties into uncompromising positions and thus obstructing mediation efforts. In Libya, the forces of Marshal Khalifa Haftar obtained steady Egyptian and Emirati support that helped its military to advance, but also made

> The regionalisation of these conflicts entrenched domestic divisions

the powerful commander less inclined to enter good-faith negotiations. Similarly, the Syrian government found no reason to compromise due to unconditional Iranian and Russian political and military assistance, which rendered its reconquering campaign successful.

Peace processes and diplomatic initiatives designed to de-escalate or settle conflicts failed or stalled. A global crisis of governance and multilateralism affected the standing and efforts of the UN, just as the armed conflicts in the Middle East required further peacemaking support. This left various UN envoys tasked with brokering settlements using limited leverage and tools, and hostage to the will of powerful international and regional actors. Plans to hold a national vote in Libya in 2018 were delayed to 2019 due to deteriorating circumstances on the ground, the factions' incompatible agendas and divisions among external players. UN diplomacy in Syria faced even harder obstacles with the failure of UN envoy Staffan de Mistura to obtain concessions on humanitarian access, secure commitments from regional and international powers on boosting the peace process, and appoint a constitutional committee. In late 2018, a new (and fourth) envoy replaced de Mistura, who resigned. In Israel–Palestine, US moves rendered multilateral efforts moot. Expectations were low that a much-touted peace plan devised by President Donald Trump's son-in-law Jared Kushner would relaunch negotiations. In fact, US decisions to cut aid to the UN Relief and Works Agency (UNRWA), move the embassy to Jerusalem and close the Palestinian Authority office in Washington DC aggravated an already dire situation.

As a corollary to this trend, no systemic and comprehensive reconstruction efforts were launched in 2018, despite financial pledges and declarations of intent. In Syria, talk about reconstruction faced difficult realities: the imperative of humanitarian assistance and the desire to repatriate refugees clashed with the lack of a political settlement and widespread concerns that financial assistance would prop up the Assad government. In Yemen, reviving the economy remains essential to prevent a famine, but disputes over the central bank, a destroyed infrastructure and the blockade have so far precluded this possibility. Despite pledges upon defeating ISIS, the Iraqi government was unable to rebuild vital infrastructure in Fallujah, Mosul and Ramadi, fuelling the resentment of local communities.

There was also some rare good news in late 2018 that concluded an otherwise gruelling year. The UN envoy Martin Griffith brokered an agreement over the vital port and city of Hudaydah between the Houthi forces that controlled it and the Saudi-supported Yemeni government, aiming to avoid a showdown that would prevent vital humanitarian aid from transiting through the port. The implementation of the agreement – establishing a ceasefire and mandating a mutual pullback of forces to facilitate UN humanitarian operations – faced immediate operational difficulties and further political obstacles, however, created by the Houthis and the forces operating under the Saudi-led coalition. Deep distrust between the parties stood in the way of progress, with each side coming up short on their commitments.

The outlook for the region in 2019 remains dire. Levels of violence are likely to decrease in the short term as Assad's forces claim victory and frontlines stabilise in Yemen, but these conflicts will remain unsettled, generating perverse incentives and opportunities for local and regional players. Prospects for a regional showdown resulting from the escalation of proxy wars remain low, however, with regional powers acutely aware of the costs of such brinkmanship.

Egypt (Sinai)

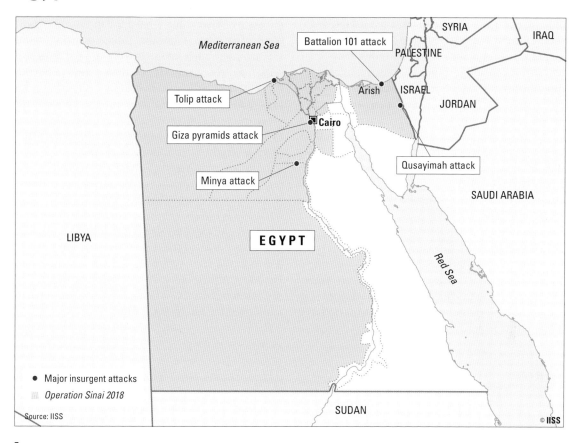

Source: IISS

Overview

The conflict in 2018

In February 2018, Egypt launched *Operation Sinai 2018* to combat terrorism across the country. With an estimated 60,000 security personnel deployed and covering an area that extended to the Nile Delta and the Western Desert (the vast region along Egypt's porous border with Libya) in addition to the Sinai Peninsula, the scale of the operation represented a significant escalation in the country's counter-terrorism strategy. The operation entailed the mobilisation of the army, navy and air force, as well as other entities under the Ministry of Interior, such as the Central Security Forces, Border Guard, National Guard and the police. Security officials described the operation as 'comprehensive', integrating military operations with economic-development programmes and efforts to counter violent extremism, although it also entailed severe restrictions on movement in and out of the North Sinai governo-

rate. In Sinai, military activity was concentrated in central and North Sinai, particularly the area between Arish, the capital of North Sinai governorate, and Rafah, on the border with the Gaza Strip.

While terrorist attacks did not cease as a result of the operation, they did become significantly less frequent. Wilayat Sinai (Sinai Province) – the Sinai affiliate of the Islamic State, also known as ISIS or

Key statistics

Type:	Internal
IDPs total (2018):	no data
IDPs new (2018):	no data
Refugees total (2018):	no data
Refugees new (2018):	no data
People in need (2018):	no data

ISIL, and the main perpetrator of large-scale acts of violence – launched numerous sporadic attacks in 2018, but it was unable to execute multiple high-profile attacks as in previous years. The largest attack this year was in mainland Egypt, rather than Sinai, where ISIS claimed responsibility for an ambush on three buses carrying Christian pilgrims in Minya governorate in November 2018 that killed seven people. The security forces and Wilayat Sinai also contested the narrative in Sinai, with both entities releasing propaganda about their activities. There remains little information about the events in North Sinai beyond official channels, as independent observers and foreign media are barred from entering the region.

The conflict to 2018

Since 2013, armed groups have carried out large-scale deadly attacks against the Egyptian armed forces in Sinai, with Wilayat Sinai as the key actor in the insurgency. Although the government declared a state of emergency in 2014, deploying troops to Sinai, and launching frequent airstrikes and raids, it has not been able to end the insurgency. Recurring attacks by Wilayat Sinai have killed dozens of soldiers at a time, with the group growing more sophisticated since 2014. In July 2015, the group seized control (albeit for less than a day) of Sheikh Zuweid, the third-largest city in North Sinai, in an operation that targeted numerous checkpoints and other locations. Wilayat gained international notoriety in 2015 when it downed the Russian plane MetroJet Flight 9268, killing 224 people.

Although insurgency attacks initially focused on the armed forces, they have increasingly shifted to target civilians, reflecting ISIS's methods elsewhere. In November 2017, an attack on a mosque in Sinai left 235 civilians dead, the deadliest attack in Egyptian history. (The attack remains unclaimed.) It was in the aftermath of this attack that Egyptian President Abdel Fattah Al-Sisi declared the launch of *Operation Sinai 2018* to stabilise Sinai, and publicly authorised the use of 'brute force'.

Forces

Egyptian security forces

In July 2013, then-defence minister General Sisi led a *coup d'état* against then Egyptian president Muhammad Morsi and immediately declared a 'war on terror' against the Muslim Brotherhood (the president's party), which he blamed for jihadi activity. Sisi mobilised various branches of the army, the interior ministry and intelligence agencies. Egypt has three intelligence agencies: the General Intelligence Service under the office of the president, the Military Intelligence Service attached to the Ministry of Defence, and the State Security Investigations under the Ministry of Interior.

Egypt's war on terror has targeted jihadi groups and the Muslim Brotherhood, as well as other political opponents and dissidents. Since Sisi became president in 2014, he has empowered the security branches of the state by expanding their mandates. For example, he expanded the jurisdiction of military courts in October 2014.

The Egyptian government has attempted to enlist the support of tribesmen in Sinai in the fight against jihadi groups, but with mixed success. The government has declared publicly on numerous occasions that it has cooperated with tribesmen who provide the military with intelligence, but the information about such collaboration is incomplete. Local sources suggested that the security forces began arming tribesmen in 2018.[1]

The United States is a key ally of and donor to Egypt's war on terror. In September 2018, the US approved the sale of 56,000 tank rounds to Egypt for use in operations in Sinai and released US$195 million in military aid, previously withheld due to Egypt's poor human-rights record.[2] Egypt is the second-largest recipient of US military aid after Israel, receiving approximately US$1.3 billion per year.[3]

Egypt has cooperated closely with Israel in Sinai: since 2016, Israel has carried out at least 100 clandestine airstrikes in North Sinai governorate using unmarked drones, helicopters and jets, with the approval of the Egyptian security forces.[4] While Egypt and Israel officially deny this cooperation, armed groups in Sinai have claimed that Israel has been operating in the region since 2014. Forces from the United Arab Emirates were reportedly present in Sinai as well, training and assisting Egyptian troops, but also conducting counter-terrorism operations.[5]

An international peacekeeping force, the Multinational Force & Observers (MFO), has been present in Sinai since 1981, with the original aim of upholding the 1978 peace treaty between Egypt and Israel. As of October 2017, the MFO comprised 1,163 military personnel from 12 countries.

Wilayat Sinai (Sinai Province)

Wilayat Sinai is the main non-state armed group operating in Sinai. It evolved from the Ansar Bayt al-Maqdis group, which first emerged in 2011 before changing its name in November 2014 to Wilayat Sinai when it declared allegiance to ISIS. Estimates of Wilayat Sinai's ranks vary from a few hundred fighters to up to 1,000. The group's leader is Muhamad al-Isawi (*nom de guerre* Abu Usama al-Misri), who succeeded Abu Duaa al-Ansari upon his death in August 2016. Wilayat Sinai's main area of operation is in north and central Sinai, but it has claimed attacks elsewhere, indicating successful coordination between multiple regional cells. It typically relies on suicide attacks, improvised explosive devices (IEDs) and vehicle-borne IEDs, but since 2015, it has also procured sophisticated weaponry, including anti-aircraft and anti-tank missiles. The group has also carried out beheadings, including one in November 2018, as punishment for 'collaborators' suspected of working with the security forces.

The group initially targeted Israel, but since 2013 has shifted its focus toward the Egyptian security forces and government targets. It has also launched sporadic attacks against the MFO base in Sinai. Since 2016, Wilayat Sinai has attacked members of Egypt's Coptic Christian minority and Sufi Muslims. The group utilises social media effectively and frequently to publicise its attacks, using it to claim responsibility for at least eight large attacks in 2018.

Wilayat Sinai has remained the dominant armed group in Sinai, despite reports of groups affiliated with al-Qaeda seeking to challenge ISIS's near-monopoly on jihadi activity in Sinai. Previously, Wilayat Sinai had engaged in a pragmatic arrangement with Hamas, the Palestinian group that controls the Gaza Strip; however, a rapprochement between the Egyptian government and Hamas has undermined that relationship. In January 2018, Wilayat Sinai released a video criticising Hamas and urging attacks on its members, courts and security positions, as well as on minority groups in Gaza.

Muslim Brotherhood

The Muslim Brotherhood governed Egypt from June 2012 until June 2013, but its leaders and members faced persecution in the aftermath of Sisi's military coup and the group was designated a terrorist organisation after being ousted from power. Former president Muhammad Morsi was jailed along with the majority of the Brotherhood's leadership, while many fled the country. The security forces killed nearly 1,000 people in their attempt to break up sit-ins by supporters of the Brotherhood in two squares in Cairo (Rabaa al-Adawiya and al-Nahda) in August 2013. Since then, some of the younger Brotherhood cadre have challenged the leadership and turned to violence, carrying out attacks against police stations and military installations or sabotaging state infrastructure. Although such attacks are mostly small scale and conducted by 'lone wolves', there have been attempts at organising these individuals, leading to the formation of small 'revolutionary' groups, such as Hassm and Lewaa al-Thawra. The violence launched by Brotherhood-affiliated groups fundamentally differs from the violence carried out by groups such as Wilayat Sinai, not only in terms of the methods used but also in its core objectives. Members of the Muslim Brotherhood do not seek to overthrow the state and establish an Islamic 'caliphate', but rather to participate in the political process, or in some cases, to avenge the persecution of the group.

| Drivers

Marginalisation and economic insecurity

The violence in Sinai originates from the peninsula's long-standing marginalisation and neglect. Israel captured Sinai in 1967, and the region returned to Egyptian control only in 1981 after the Camp David Peace Accords. The agreement included a clause for Sinai to remain de-militarised, which left the region vulnerable to the establishment of smuggling routes and other illicit activities. Networks of underground tunnels between North Sinai and the

Gaza Strip flourished after 2007 when Egypt and Israel began imposing a blockade against the occupied territory.

The Bedouin population in Sinai has been systematically discriminated against and deprived of the rights enjoyed by other Egyptians. For instance, Bedouins have been barred from serving in the army or holding other specific governmental posts.[6] Restrictions on their right to vote and on their ability to own land were only lifted in 2007.[7] North Sinai has also suffered from decades of economic neglect and is the country's poorest governorate (according to outdated official statistics).[8] Government investment has been concentrated in the south of the peninsula, where a lucrative tourist industry has flourished, but the rest of the province has not benefited from private capital flows or public development programmes. Since the closure of the region to outsiders in 2013, the situation has deteriorated further, with residents unable to move around freely or conduct business. This situation may have resulted in initial collaboration between Bedouins and armed groups, based on a convergence of interests, but public sympathy for jihadis remains limited.[9]

Political exclusion

When the Arab Spring protests began in Egypt in January 2011, leading to the withdrawal of the police from the streets, armed groups in North Sinai governorate took advantage of the security vacuum. The first attack after the Arab Spring targeted a controversial pipeline near Arish that supplied gas to Israel. Armed groups launched at least four cross-border attacks into Israel, mostly using rockets, though one shooting in 2012 killed an Israeli soldier (before the completion of the fence along the border). After the *coup d'état* in 2013 reinstated military rule in Egypt, armed groups in the Sinai Peninsula began targeting more aggressively both military positions (e.g. killing soldiers at checkpoints) and state interests such as tourism (e.g. targeting a bus with Korean tourists in South Sinai governorate in 2014 and in 2015 downing a Russian MetroJet plane). The ultimate objective for jihadi groups such as Wilayat Sinai is to overthrow the state and establish an Islamic caliphate, in line with the ideology of jihadi groups generally, including ISIS, which perceive modern nation-states as lacking legitimacy. Wilayat Sinai has accordingly depicted security forces and the president as apostates.

Notwithstanding this ideological stance, the insurgency in Sinai is based on domestic grievances, particularly against the armed forces. Wilayat Sinai frequently refers to the armed forces' violent tactics as a justification for its activities. It has conducted numerous attacks as a way to avenge prisoners, acts of torture or deaths. Hostility towards the armed forces among the population emerged in response to their 'eradicationist approach', based on using military means to remove dissent and any opposition, which the armed forces have pursued since their return to power in 2013.[10] Such grievances are exacerbated by the view that the armed forces and political leadership are serving US and Israeli interests, while neglecting the local population.

| Political and Military Developments

Presidential elections

Sisi ran virtually unopposed in the election of 26–28 March 2018 (see **Table 1**). Earlier contenders included two former military commanders, Sami Anan (the former second-in-command of the Supreme Council of Armed Forces) and Ahmed Konsowa (an army colonel) as well as former prime minister Ahmad Shafik and Mohamed al-Sadat, nephew of former president Anwar al-Sadat. Both Anan and Konsowa were disqualified and detained after declaring their bids for presidency, while Shafik was deported from the UAE (where he was living) back to Egypt and pressured to drop out of the race. Sadat withdrew, citing an environment of fear and harassment.

Sisi's only opponent – Moussa Mustafa Moussa – was a relatively unknown figure who had himself endorsed Sisi. Sisi won the election with around 97% of the vote. Spoiled ballots, which are not included in the overall tally of votes, received 7% of the vote – higher than in any previous election. Sisi immediately took steps to strengthen his grip on power by appointing loyalists to prominent positions, including the ministers of defence and interior. He purged senior army officers whose loyalty he doubted – some were threatened with corruption

	Candidate	Profile	Result
	Abdel Fattah Al-Sisi	President since 2014. Former Defence Minister	Elected. Won with 97% of the vote
	Moussa Mostafa Moussa	El-Ghad Party. Known as a Sisi supporter and seen as a symbolic candidate	Defeated. Received 3% of the vote
	Sami Anan	Lieutenant General. Former Chief of Staff of Armed Forces (2005–12)	Arrested. As member of the Supreme Council of the Armed Forces, the military gave him the choice to either resign or receive permission to run, but he did neither
	Ahmad Konsowa	Army Colonel	Arrested. Sentenced to six-year prison term for violating military code (expressing political views while actively enlisted)
	Ahmad Shafiq	Former Air Force Senior Commander. Former prime minister under President Mubarak (January–March 2011). Ran for president in 2012 (lost to Morsi)	Withdrawn (and undeclared arrest). Announced intention to run from the UAE, where he lived. Deported to Egypt and forced to withdraw candidacy under threat of corruption charges
	Khalid Ali	Human Rights Lawyer & Activist. Recipient of the 'Egyptian Corruption Fighter' Award (2011)	Withdrawn. After announcing his intention to run, he renounced citing concerns over safety.
	Mohamad Anwar El-Sadat	Former member of Parliament. Nephew of assassinated President al-Sadat	Withdrawn. After announcing his intention to run, he renounced citing concerns over safety

Table 1: Contenders for Egypt's presidential election, 26–28 March 2018

charges, while others were arrested. He shuffled top positions, including members of his inner circle and the military leadership, including the head of the General Intelligence Service. Meanwhile, the revenues of commercial ventures linked to the Ministry of Military Production, the Ministry of Defence and the government-owned Arab Organization for Industrialization rose sharply.[11]

President Sisi is constitutionally barred from seeking a third term in power, but loyalists have already sought to bypass this restriction and supporters have launched a campaign to extend the two-term limit.

State repression

The security forces cracked down heavily on dissidents in 2018, particularly individuals affiliated with the Muslim Brotherhood, but also secular and liberal activists who sought to organise protests or other political activity. Around 50,000 political activists are imprisoned in Egypt and solitary confinement is regularly used to punish political prisoners.[12] Hundreds have been forcibly disappeared, including at least 12 children, of whom six were tortured. In September 2018, a court sentenced 75 demonstrators to death for taking part in a protest in support of deposed president Morsi in 2013 (although the

sentence is not final). Egypt also extended its state of emergency for another three months in October 2018, citing ongoing insecurity and terrorism. (The state of emergency was imposed in April 2017 after attacks on two churches killed 45 people, and has been since renewed every three months.)

The security forces and intelligence services further consolidated their power by forcibly acquiring media networks. Well-known media figures have faced dismissal for making unwelcome comments on air. The authorities created a hotline for reporting any media that spreads 'false news' or undermines national security. After legislation on 'cyber crime' was passed in May 2018, more than 500 websites, including international media, were blocked. The Supreme Media Regulatory Council announced in October that online news outlets needed to register under a new media law, pay a EGP50,000 registration fee (approximately US$2,800) and fill in an application about the website's founder, editor-in-chief, editorial policy, sources of funding, audience and other information. A new law requires social-media accounts with a large following to register with the government, and a new government controlled social-media platform (similar to Facebook) might soon be created. Bloggers, satirists and human-rights activists faced arrest.

Operation Sinai 2018

The decision to launch *Operation Sinai 2018* in February 2018 followed several large-scale attacks in Egypt in 2017. Its tactical approach is very similar to previous operations that failed to put an end to the insurgency, such as *Operation Martyr's Right*, launched in 2015. The armed forces claimed that *Operation Sinai 2018* was 'comprehensive', including a focus on post-conflict projects for the region. It also aspires to promote 'moderate' thought – a project that has included Egypt's top Islamic institution, al-Azhar and a cornerstone of the government's response to jihadism.

As of the end of October 2018, the security forces had reportedly killed 450 militants and arrested nearly 4,000 as part of *Operation Sinai 2018*.[13] In mid-June, the government said the operation was a success and announced that the armed forces were withdrawing 70% of the 60,000 soldiers deployed at the start of the operation.[14] This partial withdrawal resulted in loosened security measures, such as permits for travel on the international coastal road along the Mediterranean Sea, previously restricted.

Operation Sinai led to a clear decline in Wilayat Sinai's activities, with many of its attacks resulting in no fatalities. This reduced operating capacity may be a result of the death of the group's leaders and commanders. Egypt's army spokesperson announced the death of an 'emir' in April, while the group itself acknowledged the death of key figures, such as Abu Hamza al-Maqdisi and Nasser Abou Zaqul. However, as the leadership of the group has remained shrouded in secrecy, the precise significance of these individuals is unknown. Despite the decline in its larger-scale attacks, Wilayat Sinai continued to release propaganda material stating that it has not been defeated and that it continues to pose a significant threat to the security forces in Sinai.

Violent Events

Sinai attacks

In February, Wilayat Sinai attacked the headquarters of the Armed Forces Battalion 101 in Arish, North Sinai governorate. The group claimed that the attack resulted in fatalities (though it did not specify a figure), and released photographs of the operatives who carried out the attack wearing soldiers uniforms taken from the victims.[15] In April, Wilayat Sinai released photographs of its operatives controlling checkpoints in North Sinai in broad daylight, challenging the security forces' claims that it is in control of the area. In November the group released a video featuring former police and military personnel who had allegedly joined the group.

One of Wilayat's largest attacks in 2018 was in Qusayimah in central Sinai in mid-April. At least 14 fighters attacked an army base with machine guns, rifles, rocket-propelled grenades and suicide attacks. Egyptian security forces initially announced the deaths of eight soldiers, but Wilayat Sinai reported 22 via its news site Amaq (subsequent sources corroborated the higher number). The group also killed dozens of soldiers and police personnel in other attacks in Sinai throughout the year.

Minya governorate attack

The most visible attack by Wilayat Sinai in 2018 took place outside Sinai, possibly as a result of the group's limited capacity in the peninsula. Gunmen affiliated with the group attacked a bus carrying Christian worshippers returning from a monastery in Upper Egypt, killing eight people. Wilayat Sinai described it as revenge against the Egyptian government's imprisonment of female supporters of the group. Egyptian police subsequently declared that they had killed 19 attackers during a shoot-out in the governorate of Minya. In August, a suicide attacker attempted to enter a Coptic church but only killed himself.

Giza pyramids attack

On 28 December, Wilayat Sinai also claimed an attack against a tourist bus near the Giza pyramids that killed three Vietnamese tourists and one Egyptian tour guide. The attack highlighted the group's ability to inflict damage despite the increased security operations. The attack near the pyramids was highly symbolic, coming at a time when Egypt is struggling to revive tourism, its main source of revenue. The government subsequently announced that it had killed 40 suspected militants in three raids.

Western Desert and Libyan border

Egypt's security forces ramped up extensive security operations in the Western Desert in an attempt to secure the border with Libya. In October, the Ministry of Interior announced that it had killed 11 alleged militants in Farafra oasis in the Western Desert who were planning 'hostile attacks'. Egypt has continued to support and coordinate operations with the Libyan National Army (LNA), led by General Khalifa Haftar, in east Libya. Libyan special forces working with the LNA announced in October the capture of Hisham al-Ashmawi (whose *nom de guerre* is Abu Omar al-Muhajir), one of Egypt's most-wanted fugitives – Sisi requested his extradition. Ashmawi headed an al-Qaeda-linked group, al-Mourabitoun, and his capture was portrayed as a further unravelling of armed networks in Egypt. However, the extent of Ashmawi's involvement in armed attacks in Egypt remained unsubstantiated, and his capture may represent little more than a symbolic victory.

Assassinations and assassination attempts

In 2018, there were also several failed assassination attempts on prominent figures that remained unclaimed. In July, Egypt's security forces announced they had thwarted plans by Wilayat Sinai to assassinate Sisi, including a potential operation to kill him during a pilgrimage in Mecca. An attack on 23 March 2018 targeted the security chief of Alexandria, Mustafa al-Nimr, by detonating an IED outside the Royal Tolip Hotel. The explosion killed two police officers. The attack remained unclaimed, although Egyptian security forces attributed it to the Muslim Brotherhood-affiliated group Hassm.

Impact

Effects on civilian life

The effects of the violence on residents of the North Sinai governorate have been severe. On numerous occasions, Wilayat Sinai targeted economic and health infrastructure, besides kidnapping and killing civilians. Military activity under the auspices of *Operation Sinai 2018* has reduced the number of attacks by Wilayat Sinai against civilians but has also had negative effects. The first phase in particular, which lasted until June, put civilians under conditions resembling collective punishment. According to a report by Human Rights Watch, 420,000 residents of North Sinai were in urgent need of humanitarian assistance and restrictions on movements of goods and people caused shortages of food, fuel and medical supplies. Security activity interfered with everyday life. For example, the assassination of an army officer in Arish in early September resulted in the deployment of troops around the city and a shutdown of shops and the central market.[16] The government also suspended schools and universities in North Sinai from February to September.

Residents are trapped between the armed forces and jihadi groups. The extent of their support for groups such as Wilayat Sinai is weak but jihadis have killed residents who cooperated with the armed forces, whether as informants or as labourers, leaving some residents unsure whether the security forces can protect them.

Demolitions and evictions

HRW also reported widespread demolitions of homes and forced evictions in the area close to Rafah. Based on an analysis of satellite imagery, HRW found that the army demolished 3,600 buildings between January and April 2018, of which at least 3,000 were homes. This is the largest number of demolitions since the government created a buffer zone along the Rafah border in 2014. Soldiers have conducted house-to-house searches in Arish and seized but never returned private possessions such as mobile phones, computers and other electronic devices. Communication outages left mobile-phone networks disconnected for days. This trend intensified later in the year when explosions destroyed electricity-transmission towers in Arish in mid-September and the three main cities of North Sinai remained with no electricity for five days.

Seeking to improve their image among civilians, Egyptian security forces have released photographs of soldiers distributing humanitarian assistance to residents of North Sinai. They also sought to detract attention from the humanitarian implications of *Operation Sinai 2018* by emphasising developmental projects, which they described as a key part of their role in Sinai. In November, the security forces announced that they had completed the first phase of building a village in central Sinai, working with the North Sinai provincial authorities and the Sinai Development Authority.

Economic impact

Five years of heavy military operations in North Sinai have left the region's economy debilitated. Military activity in the area has resulted in the destruction of commercial buildings and farms. The North Sinai Agriculture Directorate stated that 90% of farms in the three main cities of Rafah, Sheikh Zuweid and Arish have been destroyed, reducing olive production by 80%.[17] Unofficial sources believe that unemployment rates may have reached 60%.

The economic situation in Egypt more generally also deteriorated in 2018. Since the floating of the Egyptian pound in 2016, there have been consistent price hikes that affected fuel, drinking water, electricity and other basic goods, such as potatoes, which doubled in price in September 2018. A significant increase in the price of metro fares in May – which in some cases tripled – triggered protests in Cairo, to which the government responded by detaining dozens of people and deploying heavy security around metro stations.

Trends

Wilayat Sinai regroups

Wilayat Sinai was not able to wage large-scale or high-profile attacks in 2018, indicating a decline in its capability. With the defeat of ISIS in Iraq and Syria, the 'provinces' – especially Sinai – may represent the only chance for the group's survival. As the group loses control over territory, individuals and funds may be channelled into the surviving outposts in an attempt to keep the group afloat. The insurgency in Sinai, however, is focused on a struggle against Egypt, and does not control territory in a stable manner. It would thus struggle to become a new 'base' for ISIS.

Violence continues

Although the government heralded *Operation Sinai 2018* as a success, stability is likely to remain tenuous in 2019. There are no plans for disarmament, demobilisation and reintegration of former Wilayat Sinai operatives or discussions about a potential cessation of hostilities. The Egyptian government is also unlikely to offer amnesty to individuals who participated in the insurgency, seeking instead a military victory. Based on the strategies it has pursued over the past five years, the government is more likely to continue to use executions and prison sentences as deterrents. Even if Wilayat Sinai is militarily weakened in North Sinai, however, violence is unlikely to disappear. The region is set to remain fertile ground for violent activity and armed groups that have proven to be resilient and capable of adapting to new conditions, including decreased mobility in Sinai.

Government investment in Sinai

The Egyptian government has increasingly discussed development projects in Sinai as an immediate priority in both the current and an eventual post-conflict environment. The Armed Forces Engineering Authority, an agency of the Ministry of Defence, is involved in the implementation of 290 projects in Sinai at a cost of EGP175bn (approximately US$10bn), with 134 reportedly completed. From a political and military standpoint, the army is keen to demonstrate that it is adopting a counter-insurgency strategy in Sinai and is able to maintain a strategic presence in the region. For this reason, the government's strategy centres on mega-projects and on supporting the armed forces' expanded economic footprint. A new development plan, scheduled to be completed in 2022, aims to attract around US$15bn in local and international investment and turn Sinai into a lucrative region.

Operation Sinai 2018 is unlikely to alter the patterns of violence in Sinai in the near future, particularly as political reform do not materialise and the space for political participation narrows. In his second term, Sisi demonstrated a continuation of the same priorities and approaches of his previous tenure and called for greater international support for his government's counter-terrorism activities in Egypt. Counter-terrorism operations have succeeded in reducing armed attacks, but not in addressing the root causes of the violence, which include political alienation, an oppressive security apparatuses and economic marginalisation.

Notes

[1] Brian Rohan, 'Egypt arming Sinai tribesmen in fight against Islamic State', Associated Press, 27 September 2018.

[2] United States Department of Defense, Security Cooperation Agency, 'News Release: Egypt – 120MM Tank Rounds', 27 November 2018.

[3] See https://www.foreignassistance.gov/explore/country/Egypt.

[4] David D. Kirkpatrick, 'Secret Alliance: Israel Carries Out Airstrikes in Egypt, With Cairo's O.K.', *New York Times*, 3 February 2018.

[5] Adam Entous, 'Donald Trump's New World Order', *New Yorker*, 18 June 2018.

[6] 'Egypt's Bedouins began to demand equal citizenship rights', *Guardian*, 17 June 2011.

[7] Iffat Idris, 'Sinai Conflict Analysis', K4D, 2 March 2017, p. 9.

[8] Giuseppe Dentice, 'The Geopolitics of Violent Extremism: The Case of Sinai', *Euromesco*, February 2018, p. 15.

[9] Emma Graham-Harrison, 'How Sinai became a magnet for terror', *Guardian*, 8 November 2015.

[10] Omar Ashour, 'Sinai's Stubborn Insurgency: Why Egypt Can't Win', *Foreign Affairs*, 8 November 2015.

[11] 'From war room to boardroom: Military firms flourish in Sisi's Egypt', Reuters, 16 May 2018.

[12] Amnesty International, 'Egypt: The use of indefinite solitary confinement against prisoners amounts to torture', 7 May 2018.

[13] '450 jihadists killed in Egypt Sinai offensive: Army', *France24*, 16 October 2018.

[14] International Crisis Group Crisis Watch, 'Egypt', June 2018.

[15] 'Province of Sinai claims attack on military battalion headquarters in North Sinai', *Mada Masr*, 23 February 2018.

[16] 'Week of violence in Arish prompts heightened security measures', *Mada Masr*, 3 September 2018.

[17] Mohannad Sabry, 'Egypt's Sinai, war on terror, and the "deal of the century"', Al-Jazeera, 3 July 2018.

Iraq

Overview

The conflict in 2018

In December 2017, then Iraqi prime minister Haider al-Abadi announced the defeat in Iraq of the Islamic State, also known as ISIS or ISIL. The US-led Combined Joint Task Force (CJTF) also announced that it had successfully pushed ISIS from nearly all its territorial holdings in Iraq and Syria.

In the course of 2018, however, ISIS adapted to its loss of territory by reforming as a covert-network organisation, a process that was most advanced in Iraq.[1] Consequently, the Iraqi government and its international partners shifted to a counter-terrorism strategy combined with a focus on reconstruction and economic development. Localised conflicts and endemic corruption threatened to delay and distort these reconstruction efforts, which ISIS exploited by launching attacks in rural and mountainous regions and mixed demographic areas, particularly in the triangle stretching across the provinces of Diyala, Kirkuk and Salahuddin. ISIS also continued to probe Baghdad's defences, targeting its western belt (Fallujah, Karma, Abu Ghraib) and Jurf al-Sakhar and Arab Jabour to the south. These attacks mirrored ISIS's pre-2014 insurgency strategy, targeting local-government officials and tribal chiefs, capturing electricity and oil infrastructure, setting up fake checkpoints and hijacking trucks.

Iraq's national parliamentary elections, held in May 2018, saw Iran-backed militias make significant political gains on the back of their role in the war against ISIS. These forces were grouped together in the Fatah (Conquest) alliance headed by Badr Organisation leader Hadi al-Amiri, which emerged as the second-largest political group, cementing the status of the Popular Mobilisation Units (PMU) as a political as well as a military reality.[2]

Key statistics	
Type:	Internationalised
IDPs total (2018):	2,000,000
IDPs new (2018):	150,000
Refugees total (2018):	370,000
Refugees new (2018):	no data
People in need (2018):	8,700,000

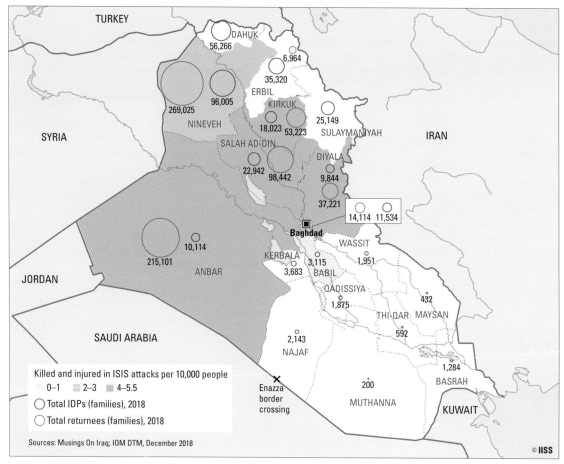

Killed and injured in ISIS attacks per 10,000 people
- 0–1
- 2–3
- 4–5.5

◯ Total IDPs (families), 2018
◯ Total returnees (families), 2018

Sources: Musings On Iraq; IOM DTM, December 2018

© IISS

The conflict to 2018

Iraq has been the site of multiple overlapping conflicts since the US-led invasion in 2003. A sectarian civil war, anti-government insurgencies, intra-Shi'ite militia violence and Kurdish paramilitary forces have all challenged the authority of the Iraqi government and its international partners. Since 2014, however, the war with ISIS, the Sunni jihadist insurgent group, has been the main conflict in the country.

On 4 June 2014, ISIS launched a major offensive in northern Iraq and took Tikrit and Mosul (Iraq's second-largest city) within days. The Iraqi security forces partially disintegrated as a result, allowing the Kurdish paramilitaries (Peshmerga) to take control of Kirkuk, the strategically vital and oil-rich province at the heart of the territorial dispute between the Iraqi government and the Kurdistan Region of Iraq (KRI).

In October 2014, the rapid advance of ISIS prompted the US, along with more than 30 other coalition partners, to form the CJTF and launch *Operation Inherent Resolve* to 'degrade and destroy' ISIS in both Syria and Iraq. *Operation Inherent Resolve* has supported the Iraqi security forces and the Peshmerga to retake territory from ISIS by providing air support, materiel, intelligence cooperation and training. By the end of November 2017, the Iraqi security forces, with international support, had successfully recaptured all major towns and cities in Iraq that had fallen to ISIS.

The rout of the Iraqi security forces by ISIS in 2014 prompted Iraq's leading Shi'ite religious figure, Ayatollah Ali al-Sistani, to issue a religious edict calling on Iraqis to volunteer for the Iraqi security forces. Various pre-existing Shi'ite militias used this fatwa to expand their recruitment and operational role and became an important auxiliary force in the war against ISIS. These militias, many of whom have close ties to Iran's Islamic Revolutionary Guard Corps (IRGC), acquired a legally recognised status as the PMU.

In September 2017, the Kurdish leadership attempted to capitalise on territorial gains by holding an independence referendum. The pro-independence camp won a decisive victory, but the Iraqi security forces and PMU launched operations against Peshmerga positions, retaking territory lost in 2014 including Kirkuk. The Iraqi security forces also took control of the KRI's external borders and ports of entry, securing Kurdish capitulation and the resignation of President Masoud Barzani.

Forces

State forces
The Iraqi security forces have three main components deployed in the conflict with ISIS: the Army (Ministry of Defence); Federal Police (Ministry of Interior); and Counter-Terrorism Service (CTS; under the Office of the Prime Minister). ISIS's June 2014 offensive led to a severe reduction in the operational capacity of the Iraqi army and Federal Police. Front-line strength for each fell from 110,000 and 60,000 respectively in May 2014, to 54,000 and 36,000 by January 2015. Since then, the Iraqi armed forces have gradually been consolidating and rebuilding their brigades, which are supplemented by auxiliary forces from Sunni tribes and local militias. The Iraqi Army is deployed to all the main battlefronts, while the Federal Police are mainly deployed in Baghdad and the Tigris River Valley north of Samarra.[3]

The CTS, a special-operations force created by the US post-2003, is the most effective fighting unit. An independent security agency reports directly to the Office of the Prime Minister, it has about 10,000 men, trained and equipped by the US, and has taken the lead in almost all major operations against ISIS since 2014. The CTS has suffered heavy losses (40–60%), particularly during the Mosul offensive.[4] Rebuilding the CTS's fighting strength, and reorienting it back towards counter-terrorism operations, will be crucial for maintaining security gains in post-ISIS Iraq.

Combined Joint Task Force (CJTF)
The US leads on the Combined Joint Task Force (CJTF), which brings together more than 30 coalition partners to conduct airstrikes in Iraq and Syria and provide air support to Iraqi and Kurdish forces fighting ISIS. Coalition air support has been crucial to the success of the Iraqi security-forces operations against ISIS, particularly in close coordination with the CTS. The US, along with other international partners, has deployed forces in Iraq to advise, assist and train Iraqi forces. As of March 2018, more than 138,000 Iraqi personnel had received training, including the Iraqi security forces, the police, the Kurdish Peshmerga and Sunni tribal fighters.[5]

Kurdish Peshmerga
The Peshmerga are a Kurdish paramilitary force of an estimated 150,000 personnel. Split between two main political factions, the Kurdish Democratic Party (KDP) and the Patriotic Union of Kurdistan (PUK). Following ISIS advances in June 2014, the Peshmerga deployed to disputed territory abandoned by the Iraqi security forces but proved a less effective fighting force than previously thought. ISIS overran Kurdish positions in Nineva and Diyala in August 2014, while the Iraqi security forces retook all territory lost to the Peshmerga in 2014 with limited fighting.

Popular Mobilisation Units (PMU)
The Popular Mobilisation Units (PMU) are a collection of predominantly Shi'ite militia forces. Their total manpower is estimated at approximately 140,000 men who mobilised to fight ISIS in 2014.[6] The PMU were officially integrated into the Iraqi security forces as an 'independent' security organisation through the so-called 'Hashd law' in November 2016. Many of the PMU's most powerful groups (such as the Badr Organisation, Asa'ib Ahl al-Haq, Kataib Hezbollah, Kata'ib Sayyid al-Shuhada, Harakat Hezbollah al-Nujaba and Saraya al-Khorasani) are closely linked to Iran's Islamic Revolutionary Guard Corps (IRGC). The PMU also has units from non-Shia sects (including Sunni units) and Shia units loyal to the Iraqi *hawza* and Ayatollah Ali al-Sistani (the Abbas Combat Division), and to the cleric Moqtada al-Sadr (Saraya al-Salam).

Islamic State (ISIS)
The Islamic State, also known as ISIS or ISIL, grew out of networks connected to Abu Musab al-Zarqawi's al-Qaeda in Iraq (AQI) during the Syrian

civil war. Led by Abu Bakr al-Baghdadi, ISIS developed into a transnational Salafi jihadist terrorist organisation aimed at establishing a caliphate. The group controlled extensive territory in Syria and Iraq between 2014 and 2017. At its peak between 2014 and 2015, ISIS was estimated to have a force of around 35,000 fighters in Iraq and Syria and to govern more than eight million people.[7] By the end of 2017, the group had been pushed out of nearly all territory conquered in Iraq and the influx of foreign fighters to Iraq essentially stopped.

ISIS has now reverted from a proto-state to a covert terrorist network. Its bureaucratic structures, its organisational discipline, and its general security, financial and logistics bureaus all remain intact.

ISIS is still assessed to be more capable than AQI at that group's peak in 2006–07.[8] As of June 2018, estimates put the total number of ISIS fighters in Iraq at 15,500–17,100.[9]

Jaysh Rijal al-Tariqa al-Naqshbandia (JRTN)

Among the non-ISIS Sunni groups, Ba'thist Jaysh Rijal al-Tariqa al-Naqshbandia (JRTN) is the most prominent. JRTN is led by Izzat Ibrahim al-Douri, formerly a senior Ba'athist in the Saddam Hussein regime. Despite ideological differences, JRTN and ISIS have cooperated militarily on several occasions. However, in May 2015, Douri released a statement dissociating his group from ISIS and condemning its treatment of religious minorities.[10]

Drivers

Patronage, corruption and sectarianism

Iraq has a patronage-based system of government that relies on the country's vast oil reserves. Rents from the oil extractions are used by the political elite to reward allies, pursue personal projects and disburse funds to resolve disputes, rather than funding public goods and services. Jobs in the public sector, with better pay and benefits, are awarded based on connections to political parties. As a result, incompetence and corruption are systemic and exacerbated by the country's underdeveloped banking sector. Transparency International ranked Iraq 168th out of 180 countries in its corruption-perception index for 2017.

Patronage and corruption have created marginalised groups – minority religious and ethnic groups and those without the right connections to established political factions have been cut out of employment opportunities and denied access to public services, including clean drinking water and stable electricity supply. These dynamics erode the legitimacy of central government and encourage people to join militias and insurgent groups in order to gain both dignity and a livelihood.

This patronage system has also exacerbated antagonism between Iraq's main sects. Since most political parties are organised on a sectarian basis, political patronage channels jobs, contracts and services towards certain groups and away from others, encouraging sect-based political mobilisation. Sunni grievances at what is perceived as sect-based

discrimination and socio-economic marginalisation – unemployment levels in Sunni areas was estimated in 2014 to be twice as high as the national rate – have facilitated recruitment for insurgent groups.[11]

ISIS has exploited these sectarian divisions. A breakdown in the relationship between Iraq's Sunni community and the Iraqi government allowed the group to gain a foothold in Sunni-majority cities in Iraq's western Anbar province in 2012–13, when widespread civil unrest broke out in these areas, and to use these positions to launch its attack in 2014.

Regional and ethnic disputes

The Kurdish regional question, and Kurdish demands for independence, have repeatedly sparked conflict with the Iraqi state, most recently following the independence referendum in 2017. However, the intra-Kurdish rivalry between the Kurdish Democratic Party (KDP) and the Patriotic Union of Kurdistan (PUK) has also led to conflict, as it did in the mid-1990s.

In addition to the Kurdish dispute, there are also more localised conflicts over resources and political representation revolving around other ethnic and religious minorities. Shi'ite Turkmen forces have played an important role in security dynamics in Salahuddin and Kirkuk; Shabak forces played a similar role in Nineva; while Christian, Assyrian and Chaldean militias are active in Nineva Plains.

Socio-economic challenges

Iraq has gone through a period of economic hardship linked to the ISIS insurgency and falling global oil prices (oil accounts for 90% of government revenues and over half of Iraq's GDP). Austerity measures have particularly affected the country's bloated public sector. The country is also experiencing a demographic youth bulge and struggles to provide employment opportunities for young people, particularly graduates. Rapid urbanisation, internal displacement and high unemployment all contribute to socio-economic dislocation that feeds alienation and radicalisation, in turn driving the conflict.

Geopolitical rivalries

Multiple overlapping geopolitical rivalries intersect with Iraq's local conflict dynamics. Iran provides materiel and training, and has close political ties to numerous Shi'ite militias and political parties, including Islamic Dawa Party, Badr Organisation and Asa'ib Ahl al-Haq, as well as the Kurdish PUK. Turkey has established a military camp at Bashiqa, Nineva governorate, and has trained a 3,000-strong force under former Nineva governor Atheel al-Nujaifi. At various times since 2003, both Syria and the Gulf states have provided support to Sunni insurgents in Iraq. Meanwhile, the US and Iran have competed for influence over Iraq's political institutions and security forces, and even run competing organisational networks within the Ministry of Interior.

Geopolitical rivalries have eroded Iraq's capability to build a coherent unified state and armed forces. They also contributed to the proliferation of non-state paramilitaries that continue to challenge the government's monopoly on the legitimate use of force in its territory. The Saudi–Iran rivalry in particular has dragged Iraq's sectarian conflicts into wider regional confrontations, with several of Iraq's Iran-backed Shi'ite militias having deployed to Syria to fight for the Assad regime.

Environmental factors

In recent years, Iraq has suffered from an escalating water-shortage that has affected irrigation and agricultural land usage. This crisis is partly a result of rising temperatures but mainly a consequence of damming projects in Turkey and Iran that have limited downstream flows and increased salinity levels in Iraq, exacerbated by decades of mismanagement of Iraq's water and irrigation systems.

These environmental conditions have been a factor in the radicalisation of young men and the rise of ISIS because they have contributed to rural poverty and internal displacement as farmers abandon agricultural lands and move to the cities and their growing slum districts in search of work. For example, water shortages in 2011–12 led to mass deaths of livestock, and ISIS was subsequently able to recruit many of the desperate farmers.

Displacement and returnees

The politics of displacement are also a driver of conflict. Local authorities and militias use administrative pressures and violence at checkpoints and within camps, and sometimes block returning displaced persons, to effect demographic change. In many cases, ethnic or religious minorities have lost confidence in state security forces to protect them, leading to the mobilisation of self-protection forces and militias on ethno-sectarian bases.

Political and Military Developments

A new phase of ISIS insurgency

In December 2017, then prime minister Abadi declared victory on ISIS after Iraqi forces retook Qaim, a strategic town on the Iraqi–Syrian border. Already in October 2017, however, ISIS indicated that it was switching to an insurgency strategy instead of seeking to hold territory and fight conventional battles. It therefore put up little fight for its residual territory between October and December.

ISIS remains operational in Iraq via sleeper cells and continues to probe Baghdad's defences, targeting districts in its western belt (Fallujah, Karma, Abu Ghraib) and to the south of the city (Jurf al-Sakhar and Arab Jabour). The Baghdad–Kirkuk highway has seen a high number of kidnappings and assassinations, leading to its closure for periods of several weeks.

May elections

On 12 May 2018, Iraq held parliamentary elections in which Sairoon (Marching Forward), an electoral coalition uniting the Moqtada al-Sadr Shi'ite

Islamist Sadrist movement and the Iraqi Communist Party (ICP), won the most seats. The second-largest bloc was Hadi al-Amiri's Fatah (Conquest), a coalition constituted by Badr Organisation and Iranian-aligned elements of the PMU. Incumbent prime minister Abadi's electoral bloc, Nasr (Victory), came in third with 42 seats and subsequently underwent a series of splits.

Given his weakened position, Abadi was unable to muster enough support to secure a second term in office. Following months of negotiations over government formation, a compromise candidate was found in Adel Abdul Mahdi, previously a senior figure in the Islamic Supreme Council of Iraq (ISCI), recently refashioned as an independent and credited for a strong understanding of economics.

In October and November, Abdul Mahdi began the process of forming a new cabinet and set out a programme of reforms for the public administration and the national economy, as well as consolidating a strategy for the security gains against ISIS. He faces an entrenched system of political patronage and factionalism that will make implementing his reforms extremely challenging. While the appointments of Thamir Ghadhban and Louai al-Khatib, for the oil and electricity portfolios respectively, were widely welcomed as fitting Abdul Mahdi's new 'technocratic' ethos, other appointments have led to disappointment. For example, the key cabinet position of finance minister went to Fuad Hussein, who spent more than a decade as chief of staff to former Kurdish president Barzani. The attempt to appoint Hasan al-Rubai, a senior figure in Asa'ib Ahl al-Haq, to the ministry of culture also raised criticism.

Abdul Mahdi is supported by an unstable and fragmented coalition between the Sadrists and Amiri's Construction bloc. Tensions have already arisen between the two as the Sadrists moved to block Amiri's pick of Faleh al-Fayyed for the interior ministry. Abdul Mahdi has struggled to get his cabinet approved by parliament: as of 24 October 2018, only 14 of his 21 cabinet nominations had been approved by parliament, leaving key ministerial positions, including defence and interior, unfilled.

US Iran sanctions

In 2018, the US reimposed economic sanctions on Iran following the former's withdrawal from the Joint Comprehensive Plan of Action (JCPOA) on Iran's nuclear programme. Given the close economic ties between Iraq and Iran, the US sanctions could have important economic and political implications: Iraq imported Iranian goods (including food and agricultural products) worth US$6 billion in the year to March 2018, comprising 15% of Iraq's total imports in 2017. Iraq also relies on Iran for energy, with contracts between the two countries totalling US$12bn in 2017.

There is also a potential for US–Iran rivalries to result in violent actions inside Iraq if Iranian-backed militias seek to retaliate against US targets inside Iraq or threaten the Iraqi government if it agrees to implement the sanctions.

In November, the US de-escalated tensions by granting Iraq a series of tiered exemptions from the sanctions on energy imports conditional on setting out a road map to energy independence from Iran.

Instability and protests in south Iraq

The importance of improved governance to long-term stability in Iraq was underlined in July and September 2018 when large-scale unrest broke out in Iraq's southern provinces, particularly the strategically vital and oil-rich province of Basra, which accounts for 90–95% of Iraq's oil and gas production. Protesters demanded improved public services – especially water and electricity – and employment opportunities. In several instances, the protests turned violent, with widespread attacks on political party and militia offices, many of which were set on fire. On 7 September, the Iranian consulate in Basra was ransacked and burnt. These eruptions of civil unrest indicate the extent to which the relationship between the political elites and their core constituency in the Shi'ite south has been frayed by years of corruption and inefficiency.

Instability and unrest in the south, and Basra in particular, are intimately related to the underlying drivers of conflict in Iraq and its future trajectories. Most of the manpower which the Iraqi security forces and PMU have deployed against ISIS has been drawn from these southern provinces. At the same time, the war against ISIS has sucked political and material resources away from the south, allowing long-standing problems in governance and administration to fester.

Violent Events

In 2018, ISIS militants were active in Anbar governate along the Iraq–Syria border and the Fallujah–Ramadi corridor, from where the group launched attacks into Iskandiriya and Jurf al-Sakhar in Babil governorate. Other areas of ISIS activity included rural areas of Diyala governorate and in and around Hawija and Kirkuk.

The Iraqi security forces and the PMU, with support from the international coalition, continued operations against ISIS, particularly in Diyala, Kirkuk and Anbar governorates. In November, a major deployment of the Iraqi security forces and the PMU to western Anbar governorate began clearing vast desert spaces from ISIS militants and secure the border with Syria. The operation also involved Iraqi forces targeting ISIS positions on the Syrian side of the border.

Suicide attacks and VBIEDs
ISIS continued to use suicide bombings and vehicle-borne improvised explosive devices (VBIEDs) in its efforts to degrade physical and political security in Iraq. The group's success with this tactic has, however, declined in 2018. No mass-casualty civilian attacks occurred on the scale of the Nasiriyah checkpoint attack in Dhi Qar province in September 2017, in which more than a hundred civilians were killed or injured. Nevertheless, ISIS was able to penetrate defences on several occasions both in Baghdad and in Sunni-majority cities in the north and west of the country. On 15 January, the group carried out a double suicide-bombing attack on Baghdad's Tayaran square, killing 35 and injuring 90. ISIS car bombings killed six people on 23 October in the town of Qayyara near Mosul and five people (with 16 injured) on 18 November in Tikrit.

Targeted assassination
Targeted assassinations of tribal leaders and members of the security forces have long been a key tactic in ISIS's campaign of intimidation seeking to drive a wedge between the local leadership and the Iraqi state, and to demonstrate the inability of the latter to provide security for those who reject ISIS. These attacks depend on high levels of operational intelligence and consequently indicate that ISIS has developed an advanced capability in a given area of operations.

This strategy re-emerged in 2018. In the course of a week in October–November, ISIS assassinated three tribal chiefs in rural villages in Kirkuk governorate, taking the men from their homes and executing them in front of the local populations. On 14 April, ISIS attacked the funeral of Sunni tribal fighters killed by ISIS in the village of Asdira near the northern Iraqi town of al-Shirqat – killing 25 and injuring 18.

Fake checkpoints, ambushes and kidnapping
Another sign of ISIS's growing ability to operate in remote areas has been the prevalence of fake checkpoints used to ambush Iraqi security forces, the PMU and civilian targets. These attacks have spread from remote locations to more strategically important sites. Of particular note in 2018 were the repeated attacks on the Baghdad–Kirkuk highway, leading to the road's closure for weeks at a time. In one of these attacks in March 2018, ISIS killed 35 civilians. On 24 March, it used a fake checkpoint on a main road in the Hamrin Mountains region to kidnap and execute eight police personnel. On 28 October, it killed an Iraqi police officer in an attack on a police patrol in the al-Tarfawi region of the Hamrin Mountains in Kirkuk. On 11 October, ISIS attacked a military vehicle in Qaim district in Anbar governorate, killing one member of the Iraqi security forces and kidnapping two.

Iraqi forces, the PMU and the international coalition
Throughout 2018, the Iraqi security forces, the PMU and the CJTF continued to launch small-scale operations against remaining ISIS positions in order to prevent the group from regaining a presence in key towns and cities and to dislodge ISIS militants from their hiding places in remote locations.

On 22 February, a planned ISIS attack against the Enazza border crossing into Saudi Arabia was disrupted. In October, the Iraqi security forces dismantled some 40 ISIS positions in eastern Diyala governorate, killing two ISIS militants. On 31 October, the security forces and air support conducted clearing operations in Salahuddin governorate, killing four ISIS militants and destroying tunnels and materiel. In November, the security forces targeted ISIS positions in Nineva and Kirkuk governorates, killing 19 ISIS militants in a raid on

2 November. On 4 November, coalition airstrikes in Dibris, northern Kirkuk governorate, killed 25 ISIS militants.

On 3 November, the Iraqi security forces launched artillery strikes on ISIS targets who were ten kilometres inside Syrian territory, signalling the start of a major operation. With PMU support, Iraqi security forces advanced westward towards the Syrian border in order to drive out ISIS militants from vast desert regions in Anbar, Nineva and Salah ad-Din governorates. The operation involved two Iraqi Army brigades, each with 3,000–5,000 men. The PMU deployed some 20,000 fighters.

Tensions between PMU and US/CJTF

Although tacitly operating on the same side in the war against ISIS, the Iranian-backed Shi'ite militias of the PMU and US/CJTF forces are also competing for influence in Iraq in the context of the broader geopolitical struggle between the US and Iran. In 2018, PMU forces claimed to have been attacked by coalition forces in several incidents around the town of Qaim, strategically located on the Iraq–Syria border. On 18 June, an airstrike on Shia militias affiliated with the PMU operating near Qaim killed 22 militiamen. The PMU publicly blamed the US and its allies and warned against a possible escalation of tensions between the two sides (the US denied responsibility for the attack). On 24 September, PMU leaders accused Danish forces (operating as part of the US-led coalition) of shelling their base near Qaim.

Turkish and Iranian actions

Iraq's weakened state and the presence of non-state armed factions on its territory makes the country a target for military actions by neighbouring states, particularly Turkey and Iran. On 8 September, Iran's IRGC stated that it had fired seven missiles into the KRI targeting two Iranian Kurdish opposition groups, the Kurdistan Democratic Party of Iran (KDPI) and the Democratic Party of Iranian Kurdistan (PDKI). The missile strikes in the town of Koya, 300 km north of Baghdad, killed 11 and injured more than 50. Meanwhile, Turkey continued to target the Kurdistan Workers Party (PKK) in airstrikes targeting the Haftanin, Hakurk and Zap regions of northern Iraq. An escalation in such strikes caused Iraq's Foreign Ministry to summon the Turkish ambassador in mid-December to complain about the repeated violations of Iraqi airspace.

Impact

Geopolitical and regional impact dynamics

The conflict with ISIS has allowed Iraq's neighbours to exert greater influence in the country's politics. Iran in particular has used the expansion of Shi'ite militias and their integration into Iraq's security apparatus (via the PMU structure) to increase its power in the country. The political success of the PMU in the May 2018 elections has allowed Iran to penetrate deeper into Iraq's political field, but Iran's influence networks are not limited to Shi'ite groups. Iran's influence over the PUK was an important factor in the group's withdrawal from disputed territories following the independence referendum in 2017, which helped to precipitate the collapse of the Peshmerga in the face of the Iraqi security forces and PMU advances.

Iran's growing influence in Iraq plays into wider regional and geopolitical rivalries. Under President Donald Trump, the US has taken a more aggressive posture vis-à-vis Iran. Saudi Arabia, meanwhile, has moved diplomatically to broaden its engagement with Iraqi political actors across the sectarian spectrum to exploit intra-Shi'ite rifts, to increase its influence and to contain, or roll back, Iranian influence.[12] Turkey, which has political ties to the Nujaifi political family (whose power base is in Mosul), has also deepened its involvement in Iraq and improved its relations with the government thanks to the ISIS conflict. Turkey's primary interest in the region is combatting the PKK, and its military deployment in Bashiqa in northern Iraq to combat the PKK has been controversial. The retaking the Kirkuk oilfields, which accounted for over half of the Kurdistan Regional Government's oil production, however, helped Baghdad to reassert control over its oil exports and removed the contentious issue of Kurdish oil exports through Turkey from Iraqi–Turkish relations.

Victory against ISIS, the fallout from the Kurdish independence referendum and the international isolation of the KDP that followed have strengthened the position of the Iraqi government vis-à-vis the KRG. Not only have the Kurds lost control over Kirkuk's oilfields, but the KRG is also in dire need of funds to pay public-sector salaries. Internal divisions between the KDP and PUK have also helped the Iraqi government to impose its will, although enduring disputes over territory and natural resources remain to be resolved.

Humanitarian impact

The war on ISIS has come at a significant humanitarian cost. Ethnic and sectarian cleansing have been part of ISIS's modus operandi, but other armed factions, including the PMU, have exploited the war to target specific groups or prevent them from returning to their homes in the hopes of shifting demographic realities on the ground. Population surveys of internally displaced people (IDPs) suggest a complex picture of humanitarian needs, including shelter, education, health, food and security. The issue of returnees remains crucial for future political stability and whether ISIS can, once again, exploit sectarian divisions and ethnic grievances to sway marginalised communities.

In 2018, the International Organization for Migration (IOM) and the United Nations High Commissioner for Refugees (UNHCR) estimated the total number of IDPs as a result of the conflict in Iraq at 1.8 million, with 4.2m returnees. However, in September 2018 the UN Office for the Coordination of Humanitarian Affairs (OCHA) registered a slow-down in the rate of returns.[13] IDPs mainly come from provinces most affected by the ISIS conflict: Anbar (1.2m; 38%), Nineva (975,000; 30%) and Salahuddin (460,000; 14%).[14]

Human trafficking

Iraq is a source and destination country for men, women and children subjected to sex trafficking and forced labour. The war with ISIS has exacerbated the vulnerability of various groups, particularly women and children. ISIS militants have kidnapped thousands of women and children, especially Yazidis, and trafficked and sold them in Iraq and Syria, where they are subjected to forced marriage, sexual slavery, rape and domestic servitude. Non-

ISIS forces, including PMU militias, have repeatedly used child soldiers. The US State Department's 'Trafficking in Persons Report 2018' criticised the Iraqi government for failing to hold anyone criminally accountable for such violations and also for continuing to punish some trafficking victims for crimes committed as a direct result of being subject to trafficking, for example, child soldiering, prostitution and immigration violations.[15]

Economic impact

Iraq's economy, highly dependent on oil production and global oil prices, has suffered much from the war. In 2015, oil accounted for 54% of Iraq's GDP, 99% of exports and 93% of government fiscal revenues. The rise of ISIS coincided with a major fall in global oil prices, and the combination of the two factors exacerbated Iraq's challenging economic circumstances. The International Monetary Fund (IMF) found that Iraq's non-oil real GDP fell by 3.9% in 2014, 9.6% in 2015 and 8.1% in 2016 before gradually returning to growth in 2017. In 2018, Iraq's non-oil real GDP was projected to grow at 2.0% (2.9% when oil was included).[16]

The ISIS offensive disrupted oil exports through the northern route (25% of total exports), not through the southern route through Basra (which accounts for 75% of Iraq's total). Between 2014 and 2017, ISIS also held several small oilfields, from which it reportedly produced approximately 20,000–30,000 barrels per day in 2015.[17] In 2016, the Iraqi government had to seek support from the IMF and World Bank to service loans and reduce its budget deficit. Under the US$5.34bn agreement, the government stated that it would restore fiscal balance, retrench inefficient capital expenditure and improve the country's credit rating.[18]

In 2018, the Iraqi government announced 60 reconstruction projects collectively costing US$85bn, but an international donor conference in February pledged only US$30bn, mostly as investments and credit facilities. The new government has already run into difficulties with its initial programme, which failed to give sufficient attention to reconstruction in Sunni provinces, prompting the Sunni Speaker of Parliament Mohamed al-Halbousi, from Anbar governorate, to submit a motion with Sunni demands.

Middle East and North Africa

Trends

In 2018, the conflict with ISIS in Iraq moved into a counter-terrorism and counter-insurgency phase. Since March 2018, ISIS has proved increasingly capable of launching attacks, carrying out kidnappings, setting up fake checkpoints and ambushing Iraqi security forces and PMU forces. This pattern is likely to continue in 2019, particularly in ungoverned spaces and rural locations. The governorates of Anbar, Diyala, Nineva and Salahuddin will all continue to be hotspots for ISIS activity, as will Baghdad and its western belt.

Countering ISIS effectively will depend on several factors. Firstly, the CTS must be restaffed and reorientated towards counter-terrorism and intelligence-gathering operations. Secondly, the US and coalition partners must continue to support military operations and training. Thirdly, progress needs to be made in reconstruction and economic development and the return or integration of IDPs.

These objectives depend on the emergence of a strong central government capable of securing and improving Iraq's economy and public services. However, serious doubts linger over the ability of the new Iraqi government to deliver. Pressure is building from Iran-aligned factions to curtail US military involvement in Iraq and to reduce the power and effectiveness of the US-aligned CTS within Iraq's security apparatus. Meanwhile, reconstruction and resettlement of IDPs will continue to be hampered by endemic corruption. Abdul Mahdi's new government is sustained by a fractious and tenuous accommodation among Shi'ite factions who continue to struggle over control of key security ministries. Geopolitical rivalries, particularly the ramping up of US–Iranian tensions, will only further exacerbate these divisions. In 2019, ISIS, other Sunni insurgent groups and non-state actors from Shi'ite and other ethnic and sectarian groups will continue to exploit the weakness of the Iraqi state and drive the centrifugal dynamics of conflict in Iraq.

Notes

[1]   United Nations Security Council, 'Letter dated 16 July 2018 from the Chair of the Security Council Committee pursuant to resolutions 1267 (1999), 1989 (2011) and 2253 (2015) concerning Islamic State in Iraq and the Levant (Da'esh), Al-Qaida and associated individuals, groups, undertakings and entities addressed to the President of the Security Council', 27 July 2018, p. 5.

[2]   Renad Mansour and Christine van den Toorn, 'The 2018 Iraqi Federal Elections', LSE Middle East Centre Report, July 2018, pp. 13.

[3]   Michael Knights, 'The Future of Iraq's Armed Forces', Al-Bayan Center for Planning and Studies, March 2016, pp. 23–5.

[4]   David M. Witty, 'Iraq's post-2014 Counter-terrorism service', Washington Institute for Near East Policy, October 2018, p. 70.

[5]   Christopher M. Blanchard and Carla E. Humud, 'The Islamic State and U.S. Policy', CRS Report, Congressional Research Service, 25 September 2018, p. 9.

[6]   Inna Rudolf, 'From Battlefield to Ballot Box', International Centre for the Study of Radicalisation, 2018, p. 9.

[7]   Paul D. Shinkman, 'ISIS By the Numbers in 2017', U.S. News, 27 December 2017.

[8]   Defense Department Spokesman Sean Robertson quoted in Jeff Seldin, 'Islamic State "Well-Positioned" to Rebuild Caliphate', Voice of America, 16 August 2018.

[9]   Blanchard and Humud, 'The Islamic State and U.S. Policy', p. 2.

[10]   'Jaysh Rijal al-Tariqa al-Naqshbandia (JRTN)', Mapping Militant Organizations, Stanford University, 27 July 2015.

[11]   Mohsin Khan, 'ISIS and the Iraq Economy', Atlantic Council, 6 August 2014.

[12]   Renad Mansour, 'Saudi Arabia's New Approach in Iraq', CSIS Analysis Paper, November 2018.

[13]   'Humanitarian Bulletin Iraq', United Nations Office for the Coordination of Humanitarian Affairs (OCHA), September 2018.

[14]   'Number of Returns Exceeds Number of Displaced Iraqis: UN Migration Agency', International Organization for Migration, 1 December 2018.

[15]   'Trafficking in Persons Report', US State Department, 28 June 2018.

[16]   'Iraq: IMF Country Report no. 17/251', International Monetary Fund, August 2017, pp. 13, 32.

[17]   Kenneth Katzman, 'Iraq: Politics, Security, and U.S. Policy', CRS Report, Congressional Research Service, 22 June 2015, p. 34.

[18]   Harith Hasan, 'Beyond Security: Stabilization, Governance, and Socioeconomic Challenges in Iraq', Atlantic Council Issue Brief, July 2018.

Israel–Palestine

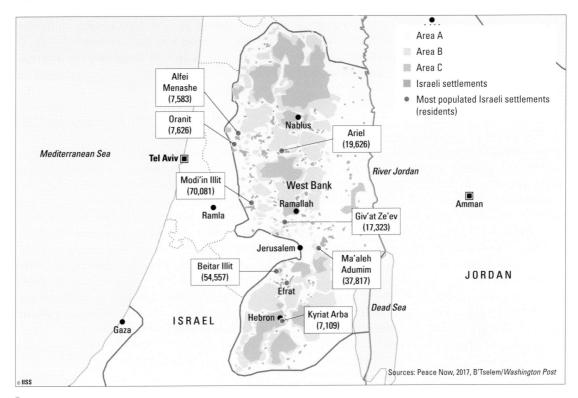

Sources: Peace Now, 2017, B'Tselem/*Washington Post*

| Overview

The conflict in 2018

The conflict between Israel and Palestine continued unabated throughout 2018. Violence peaked in the Gaza Strip, where the socio-economic situation deteriorated sharply. Between March and July 2018, protests against land expropriations and the Israeli blockade, as well as demands for the return of Palestine refugees, led to a six-week border protest known as the 'Great March of Return'. In November 2018, an Israeli covert operation in the southern Gaza Strip led to the deaths of seven Hamas militants and one Israeli soldier, resulting in exchanges of fire for two days before a ceasefire was reached.

In addition to intermittent clashes between Israelis and Palestinians, the West Bank spiralled into several days of violence in December after a shooting outside a settlement resulted in the death of a baby and the subsequent killing of two Palestinian suspects. Against the backdrop of the United States' decision to recognise Jerusalem as the capital of Israel and the move of the US Embassy there on 14 May, the prospects for a solution to the conflict remained slim.

The conflict to 2018

The Israel–Palestine conflict began in 1947–48. The first Arab–Israeli war resulted in the creation of the state of Israel on 14 May 1948 and the expulsion of more than 700,000 Palestinians from the territories that constituted the new state. In two successive wars (1967 and 1973), Israel defeated a coalition of Arab states led by Egypt and Syria and occupied the rest of the Palestinian Territories (East Jerusalem, the West Bank and the Gaza Strip). The unsolved conflict led subsequently to the outbreak of two Palestinian

Key statistics	
Type:	Internal
IDPs total (2018):	no data
IDPs new (2018):	no data
Refugees total (2018):	5,000,000
Refugees new (2018):	no data
People in need (2018):	2,500,000

revolts in Jerusalem, the West Bank and the Gaza Strip, known as intifadas (1987–93; 2000–05), three Israeli military operations in Gaza (2008–09; 2012; 2014) and intermittent waves of violence and terrorist attacks. Since the 1993 Oslo Accords, the situation has gradually worsened following the acceleration of Israel's settlement policy in the West Bank and Jerusalem and the isolation of Gaza following the Hamas takeover in 2007. Hamas seeks to impose itself as a legitimate political actor, but continues to acquire arms, partly with the support of Iran, and launch attacks against Israel.

Forces

Israel Defense Forces (IDF)

The Israel Defense Forces (IDF) is the most capable military force in the Middle East, with equipment and training that considerably overmatch the conventional capability of other regional armed forces. Israel has a highly capable and modern defence industry, with aerospace, intelligence, surveillance and reconnaissance (ISR), missile and armoured-vehicle sectors, counter-rocket systems (*Iron Dome, David's Sling, Arrow*) and active-protection systems for armoured vehicles. Around 40,000 soldiers serve in the standing army, which is organised in regional commands. The Southern Command is responsible for all units intervening in the south, including the protection and the crossing of the border with Gaza.

Israel's defence policy prioritises homeland defence but with the ability to intervene in its vicinity, especially in Lebanon, Syria, the Sinai Peninsula and the Palestinian Territories (West Bank and the Gaza Strip). Currently addressing threats posed by Hizbullah and Iran's proxies in Lebanon and Syria, and by Hamas in Gaza, the IDF retains the capability to operate simultaneously on the northern and southern fronts. The IDF has conducted several counter-terrorism operations in Gaza, including destroying smuggling tunnels connecting the Gaza Strip with the Sinai Peninsula. It has launched similar operations in December 2018 against Hizbullah's tunnels at the Israel–Lebanon border.

Hamas

Hamas is the largest Palestinian militant Islamist group, formed in 1987 at the start of the first intifada against Israel's occupation in the West Bank and Gaza. It has been designated a terrorist group by the US and the European Union, but many Palestinians view it as a legitimate resistance group. In 2017, Ismail Haniyeh replaced Khaled Meshal at the helm of the central Political Bureau. The military wing, Izz al-Din al-Qassam Brigades (IDQ), is estimated to consist of around 15,000–20,000 fighters trained in urban warfare and live-fire exercises in built-up areas. The IDQ has sophisticated capabilities, including artillery rockets, mortars and anti-tank systems. Israel's military actions in recent years have periodically degraded the command and the physical infrastructure of Hamas but seemingly had little effect on the long-term ability of the IDQ to import and produce rockets, partly thanks to a decade of Iranian transfer of arms and technology. In late 2016, Hamas announced a new maritime-police force, separate from other security forces in Gaza.

Hamas's ultimate goal is the defeat of Israel. Since its inception, Hamas has tried to institute itself as a legitimate resistance force while maintaining an offensive role against Israel. In recent years it has been increasingly concerned with preserving its superiority over other Gazan armed groups (al-Quds Brigades and Salafi-jihadi groups such as Jaysh al-Islam, Jaysh al-Umma and Jund Ansar Allah). In 2006, Hamas won the Palestinian parliamentary elections with 44.5% of the vote, taking 74 of the 132 seats of the Palestinian Legislative Council. Amid the refusal of Fatah (the party leading the Palestinian governing bodies including the Palestinian Authority and the Palestinian Liberation Organization) to join a Hamas-led coalition, Hamas formed a government alone and Ismail Haniyeh was nominated prime minister. The two parties eventually agreed to form a national unity government, but latent tensions between Fatah and Hamas led to a military conflict in June 2017, known as 'the battle of Gaza', that ended with Hamas taking complete control of the Gaza Strip.

Palestinian Islamic Jihad (PIJ)

Palestinian Islamic Jihad (PIJ) is a small, armed, Palestinian militant group that split from the Muslim Brotherhood in Cairo in the late 1970s. Unlike other Palestinian groups, PIJ refuses to negotiate and engage in diplomatic process with Israel, and does not seek political representation within the Palestinian Authority (PA). From October 1995 to September 2018, the group was led by Ramadan Abdullah Shallah. The new appointed secretary general, Ziad al-Nakhalah, lives in Lebanon. The armed wing of the PIJ is known as the al-Quds Brigades. The PIJ was involved in suicide-bombing operations during the second intifada in 2000 and was designated a terrorist organisation by the US in 1997. Over the last decade, the group has deployed its own rocket system in Gaza and periodically surfaced to claim responsibility for several attacks against Israel. It is supported, both financially and materially, by Iran but remains less popular and less well equipped than Hamas.

Drivers

Land and settlement issues

The origins of the conflict can be traced back to inter-communal violence in Mandatory Palestine (1920–1948) between Jews and Arabs. Beyond religious, ethnic and confessional dimensions, the Israel–Palestine conflict is mainly a territorial dispute between two peoples claiming the same territory, including the holy city, Jerusalem, as their capital. Since the 1967 war that resulted in the Israeli occupation of East Jerusalem, the West Bank, the Gaza Strip and the Golan Heights, Israel has strived to keep the Palestinian Territories under its control. The 1993 Oslo Declaration of Principles aimed to establish interim governance arrangements and a framework to facilitate further negotiations for a final agreement, to be concluded by the end of 1999. This process led to the creation of the Palestinian Authority (PA) in 1994 and formalised the two-state solution, but it did not halt the expansion of Israeli settlements, and the transfer of control and power to the PA never took place.

The 1995 Oslo II Accord divided the West Bank into three regions: Area A was placed under full Palestinian sovereignty (18% of the territory and 50% of the Palestinian population today); Area B was administered by both the PA and Israel (18% of the territory and 40% of the population); and Area C, which contains the Israeli settlements, was administered by Israel (over 60% of the West Bank territory and 6% of the population). Since 1967, 250 Israeli settlements and settlement outposts have been established across the West Bank and East Jerusalem, along with at least 600,000 people, in contravention of international law.[1] The territory foreseen for an independent Palestinian state has thus been fragmented and dramatically reduced. East Jerusalem has been entirely annexed and the city recognised as the 'complete and united' capital of Israel under the nation-state law voted in July 2018. The two-state solution based on pre-1967 borders has therefore become nearly impossible to achieve.

The lack of a Palestinian sovereign state, the civil and military occupation of the West Bank and Jerusalem, the five million Palestine refugees scattered across the Middle East, and the treatment of Israeli Arabs (20% of Israel's population) as second-class citizens all perpetuate the Palestinians' sense of displacement and dispossession. The inter-Palestinian divide and the isolation of the Gaza Strip following the 2007 Hamas takeover has aggravated these challenges further.

Failed peace negotiations

Since the 1990s peace negotiations undertaken under the auspices of the US in Madrid and Oslo, there has been a succession of failed talks (see **Table 1**). The 1993 Oslo Accords ended with the assassination of then Israeli prime minister Yitzhak Rabin in 1995. The implementation of the 1998 Wye River Memorandum remained unfinished as both parties accused each other of not fulfilling their share of responsibilities, and the 2000 Camp David Summit ended without an agreement. The 2001 negotiations in Taba failed as then US president Bill Clinton left office and then Israeli prime minister Ehud Barak lost elections to Ariel Sharon. The two major 2003 peace plans (the US-sponsored Roadmap and the Geneva Accord) failed due to the intifada and a hawkish Likud government in Israel. PA President Mahmoud Abbas refused to accept the 2008 peace offer from then Israeli prime minister Ehud Olmert. The 2010 direct negotiations between Israeli Prime Minister Benjamin Netanyahu and Abbas failed because Israel refused to temporarily halt construction of settlements, and the 2013–14 negotiations led by then US secretary of state John Kerry collapsed due to both parties' unwillingness to compromise.

While the US has been a central mediator for a long time, it is today perceived as a biased broker due to its recognition of Jerusalem as the capital of Israel in December 2017. Although US President Donald Trump has promised to unveil his 'deal of the century', nothing substantial and realistic has been proposed over the year. The peace process is now in a stalemate that is likely to fuel further violence and political radicalisation in both Israeli and Palestinian societies.

Palestinian economic malaise

After more than 70 years of conflict that resulted in an Israeli restrictive regime in the Palestinian Territories and internal divide between the West Bank and Gaza, the Palestinian economy is devastated. It relies on a combination of foreign aid, local resources and custom revenues governed by the 1994 Paris Economic Protocol between Israel and the PA. The Palestinian trade deficit has grown substantially over the last two decades. Israeli products have free access to the Palestinian markets, while Palestinian exports to Israel are subject to a wide range of restrictions. Israel forces Palestinian imports (and to some extent its exports) to go via its territory, while the Palestinian trade taxes are collected by Israel and transferred to the PA. Within the West Bank, all goods are routed by Israel via military checkpoints and crossings through the Israeli West Bank barrier.[2] As the trade tax represents a major source of Palestinian public income, this renders the PA particularly vulnerable to unilateral suspension of clearance-revenue transfers by Israel. Israel has long used the withholding of tax payments for political purposes, such as in 2015 in retaliation for the Palestinians' move to join the International Criminal Court (ICC) in The Hague.

The economic situation in Gaza is different due to the land, sea and air blockade imposed by Israel and Egypt after the Hamas takeover in 2007. The embargo caused a shortage of basic products, especially food, construction materials, fuel and medical supplies, leading to the proliferation of smuggling tunnels under the border with Egypt. Some of these underground passages were also used for smuggling weapons, drugs and cash to Gazan armed groups (primarily to Hamas). When General Abdel Fattah Al-Sisi ousted Egypt's president Muhammad Morsi, he dismantled most of the tunnel complex that supplied Gaza, destroying almost 1,500 tunnels between 2013 and 2014. The collapse of the 'tunnel economy' (controlled and taxed by the Hamas government), the embargo (combined with circulation and exploitation restrictions imposed by Israel on Gazan farmers and fishermen) and Hamas' bad governance reportedly affected the local economy and the population's well-being.

Political and Military Developments

Israel's settlement policy

The Israeli government's settlement policy represents a serious obstacle to a peace dialogue. The PA sees it as proof of its lack of commitment to a two-state solution and as a strategy to creating further hostilities between Israeli settlers and Palestinians.

In late 2018, 413,000 Israeli settlers were living in Jewish settlements in the West Bank,[3] mostly in Area C on illegally confiscated/appropriated Palestinian private lands and state property. Plans for housing units approved reached record numbers, with 3,808 housing units throughout the West Bank, compared with 3,154 housing units in 2017 (also higher than in the previous two years). In addition to these tenders, the Higher Planning Committee of the Civil Administration approved settlement plans for 2,191 units, bringing the units approved in 2018 to 5,618.[4] Meanwhile, 459 Palestinian structures were demolished or seized by the Israeli authorities across the West Bank, mostly in Area C and East Jerusalem, displacing 472 Palestinians, including 216 children and 127 women.[5]

Since 2017, the Israeli government has tried to accelerate and expand its settlement policy by passing the 'Regularisation Law' that allows Israel to retroactively expropriate Palestinian land on which settlements have been built. Its implementation has so far been frozen as part of an agreement between the government and the petitioners (Palestinian regional councils and human-rights organisations) until the High Court of Justice rules on the constitutionality of the law.

Inter-Palestinian conflict

The relationship between Fatah and Hamas remained tense and fragile in 2018, making it difficult to unify Palestinian claims under a coherent voice and fuelling

Table 1: Timeline of previous peacemaking initiatives

Peace Talks and Official Accords	Date	Negotiators/Mediators	Achievements
Madrid Conference	1991	Co-sponsored by US and USSR. Hosted by Spain. Participation of Israeli and Palestinian–Jordanian delegations.	Palestinians were part of a joint Palestinian–Jordanian delegation. Direct and multilateral negotiations followed the conference.
Oslo Accords	1993–95	Israel prime minister Yitzhak Rabin and chairman of the Palestinian Liberation Organization (PLO), Yassir Arafat. Mediation of US president Bill Clinton and Norwegian Ministry of Foreign Affairs.	Declaration of Principles on Interim Self-Government Arrangements (Oslo I) signed in Washington DC on 13 September 1993. Interim Agreement on the West Bank and the Gaza Strip (Oslo II) signed in Taba, Egypt, on 24 September 1995 and then in Washington DC on 28 September 1995. Mutual recognition of State of Israel and PLO. Palestinian Authority (PA) created and tasked with limited self-governance over West Bank and Gaza Strip.
Wye River Memorandum	1998	Israel Prime Minister Benjamin Netanyahu and PLO chairman and PA president Yassir Arafat. Mediation of US president Bill Clinton.	Negotiation held in Maryland, US, 15–23 October 1998, aimed to resume the implementation of the 1995 Interim Agreement on the West Bank and the Gaza Strip (Oslo II Accord). Agreement signed in Washington DC on 23 October 1998.
Sharm el-Sheikh Memorandum	1999	Israel Prime Minister Benjamin Netanyahu and PLO chairman and PA president Yassir Arafat. Overseen by US secretary of state Madeleine Albright. Witnessed and co-signed by Egyptian president Hosni Mubarak and King Abdullah II of Jordan.	Sharm el-Sheikh Memorandum on the Implementation Timeline of Outstanding Commitments of Agreements Signed and the Resumption of Permanent Status Negotiations signed on 4 September 1999.
Camp David Summit	2000	Israel prime minister Ehud Barak and PLO chairman and PA president Yassir Arafat. Peace meetings brokered by US president Bill Clinton.	No solution reached that could satisfy both Israeli and Palestinian demands. Talks ended without an agreement.
Taba Summit	2001	Israel minister of foreign affairs Shlomo Ben-Ami and Palestinian diplomat Saeb Erekat. Mediation of US president Bill Clinton.	Held in Taba, Egypt on 21–27 January 2001, following the collapse of the Camp David talks. US president proposed 'The Clinton Parameters' (including the 'Land Swap' principle). Talks ended without an agreement.
Roadmap for Peace	2002	Proposed by the Quartet on the Middle East (US, EU, UN and Russia). Discussed between PA Prime Minister Mahmoud Abbas and Israel prime minister Ariel Sharon. Mediation of US president George W. Bush.	The Quartet outlined the principles of a Roadmap for peace including an independent Palestinian state. The final text of the Roadmap, mainly drafted by the US administration, was released on 30 April 2003. The process reached a deadlock and the plan was never implemented.
Sharm el-Sheikh Summit	2005	Series of meetings between Israel prime minister Ariel Sharon, PA President Mahmoud Abbas, Egyptian president Hosni Mubarak and King Abdullah II of Jordan.	Israelis and Palestinians reconfirmed their commitment to the Roadmap.
Annapolis Conference	2007	Organised and hosted by US president George W. Bush. Israel prime minister Ehud Olmert and PA President Mahmoud Abbas. Foreign delegations included the European Union, the Arab League, Russia and China.	Middle East Peace Conference held on 27 November 2007 at the US Naval Academy of Annapolis, Maryland, US, to revive the peace process and implement the Roadmap for Peace. Negotiations continued after the conference but ended in September 2008 without an agreement.
Direct Talks	2010	Israel Prime Minister Benjamin Netanyahu and PA President Mahmoud Abbas. Mediation of US president Barack Obama represented by US secretary of state Hillary Clinton.	Talks held in Washington DC and Sharm el-Sheikh to revive the peace process. They ended in September 2010 when the Israeli partial moratorium on settlement construction in the West Bank expired and the Palestinian leadership refused to continue the negotiations.
Direct Talks	2013–14	Israeli minister of justice Tzipi Livni and Palestinian diplomat Saeb Erekat. Mediation of US secretary of state John Kerry and US special envoy Martin Indyk.	Held in Washington, Jerusalem and Hebron were given nine months to reach a final status agreement. On the day of the deadline, 29 April 2014, negotiations collapsed.

Middle East and North Africa

further violence between the two competing factions and militants. Since the 2006–07 Fatah–Hamas
clashes, both parties have attempted to reach reconciliation agreements. These all failed, including
the October 2017 accord brokered by Egypt and
signed in Cairo that stipulated that Hamas give full
civilian control of the Gaza Strip to the PA and that
legislative, presidential and local elections should
be conducted within one year of its signing. PA
President Mahmoud Abbas (elected in 2004 following
Yassir Arafat's death) has refused reconciliation until
Hamas cedes control of Gaza and agrees to discuss
its disarmament. Tensions surged in March 2018
when Palestinian Prime Minister Rami Hamdallah
avoided what Fatah considered an assassination
attempt when an improvised explosive device (IED)
exploded along his convoy route in northern Gaza.
Fatah accused Hamas of planning the attack, but the
group denied any involvement. The security situation in Gaza remains highly volatile as armed groups
such as the Izz al-Din al-Qassam Brigades (IDQ), the
Palestinian Islamic Jihad (PIJ) and other small Salafi-
jihadi groups seek to attack and fight against Israel.

Divisive US strategy
The United States' decision to recognise Jerusalem
as the capital of Israel irremediably undermined the
credibility and capacity of the Trump administration
to foster the resumption of an Israeli–Palestinian
peace process. The US decision to move its embassy
to Jerusalem on the 14 May caused great tension
within the West Bank and the Gaza Strip. Palestinians
were infuriated with the decision as East Jerusalem
was to be the capital of the future Palestinian state
in the event a two-state solution was agreed and
implemented. The Gazans resorted to what began
as a peaceful protest to express their opposition to
the US decision through the so-called 'Great March
of Return' that quickly turned violent. Abbas turned
to international forums and institutions (the United
Nations, European Union and the International
Criminal Court (ICC)) for support after losing hope
in the possibility of impartial and fair US mediation.

While the US has yet to produce the long-awaited
peace plan, Palestinian representatives have already
stated that they will refuse everything coming from
Washington given its assumed bias towards Israel.

In 2018, the US also diverted US$230m of bilat-
eral economic assistance intended for the West Bank
and Gaza for other purposes; cut aid to the UN Relief
and Works Agency for Palestine Refugees in the Near
East (UNRWA) from US$360m in 2017 to US$65m in
2018; and ended the US Agency for International
Development's aid programme for Israelis and
Palestinians (approximately US$10m annually). The
US also conditioned any future funding to the PA on
the PA's willingness to negotiate a peace agreement,
which the PA rejected following the US recognition
of Jerusalem as the capital of Israel.

Limited details presented by Trump's adviser Jared
Kushner in June fuelled harsh criticisms. He admitted
that the plan would not endorse the two-state solution;
it did not intend to convince the Palestinians to accept
political losses in exchange for economic assistance; it
counted on Arab states (most expressed scepticism);
and said that Abbas was an obstacle to peace.

Israel–Gulf rapprochement
Significant changes came from the Gulf since tensions
heightened between Qatar, which continues to fund
the Hamas government in Gaza, and Saudi Arabia,
the United Arab Emirates and Bahrain, which instead
have shown growing signs of openness towards
Israel. Regional tensions have also increased between
Saudi Arabia and Iran, which has strived to portray
itself as the sole defender of the Palestinians.

Oman's Sultan Qaboos bin Said has sought to
demonstrate Oman's openness and utility towards
peace by hosting and meeting with Netanyahu in
Muscat in October 2018. Two previous Israeli prime
ministers visited Oman but this was the first trip
since 1996. During the 2018 IISS Manama Dialogue
in Bahrain, Oman's Minister of Foreign Affairs
Yusuf Alalawi justified Qaboos's decision, stating
that a rapprochement with Israel was integral in
advancing the Palestinian cause.

Violent Events

The 'Great March of Return'
In March of 2018, following the United States' recognition of Jerusalem as the capital of Israel and

its cutting aid to UNRWA, Palestinians began a
series of protests along the fence with Israel, initially planned to last for six weeks from 30 March

(Land Day, commemorating the killing of six Israeli Arabs by Israel's security forces during demonstrations over Arab land confiscation in Galilee in 1976) to 14 May, the 70th anniversary of the creation of Israel. The Palestinian objective was to demand an end to the 11-year blockade on Gaza and to allow Palestinian refugees to return to their villages and towns. The protests quickly turned violent with protesters resorting to burning tyres and throwing stones, incendiary kites and Molotov cocktails, while Israel used live ammunition, high-velocity bullets and tear gas aimed at thwarting the protest and maiming rather than killing the protesters. Israel blamed Hamas for orchestrating the wave of violence.

On 20 April, Israel dropped leaflets in Gaza calling on Palestinians to stay away from the fence as the Israeli Army was prepared to take all measures to prevent any border breaches, but Palestinians continued to appear in large numbers every Friday. Israel faced intense criticism from the UN and other international organisations for its excessive use of force against civilians, with estimates placing the Palestinian death toll at more than 150, with at least 10,000 injured, including 1,849 children, 424 women, 115 paramedics and 115 journalists.[6]

November clash in Gaza

Following the cycle of violence that started in March and several attempts at achieving a truce and a ceasefire, on 11 November Gaza witnessed its most intense clash since the 50-day war in 2014. Seven Hamas militants and one Israeli soldier were killed during an undercover Israeli operation. Hamas and the PIJ responded to the operation by firing around 400 rockets into southern Israel. The Israeli Army declared that the *Iron Dome* missile-defence batteries had intercepted more than 100 rockets, and the IDF responded with more than 100 airstrikes. After mediation efforts by the UN, Egypt, Norway and Switzerland, Israel and Hamas agreed on a ceasefire, but the situation in Gaza remained tense at the end of the year.

Daily violence

During the year, violence occurred on a daily basis in the Palestinian Territories due to the radicalisation of some parts of both Israeli and Palestinian societies. Since 2015, the conflict has been characterised by Israeli settler violence against Palestinian civilians, and by Palestinian lone-wolf knife, vehicle and gun attacks against Israeli civilians (mostly settlers) and security forces. Violence has been mainly located in the West Bank and East Jerusalem, though terror attacks have also occurred in the past in Israeli cities such as Tel Aviv). The UN Office for the Coordination of Humanitarian Affairs (OCHA) reported a total of 295 Palestinians killed and more than 29,000 injured (the highest death toll since the 2014 conflict in Gaza) over the year, with 60% of the fatalities and 80% of the injuries occurring in the context of Gaza's 'Great March of Return'.[7] OCHA also recorded 280 incidents where Israeli settlers killed or injured Palestinians or damaged Palestinian property, marking a 77% increase compared to 2017. In total, 14 Israelis were killed in 2018 by Palestinians and at least 137 injured.[8]

On 9 December, seven Israelis were wounded in a drive-by shooting attack near the settlement of Ofra in the West Bank. One of those wounded was a 21-year-old pregnant woman whose baby died. On 11 December, two attempted car-ramming attacks took place against the Israeli security forces, one near Hebron and one near the village of Jiftlik in the northern area of the West Bank. On 13 December, an armed Palestinian opened fire on soldiers and civilians at a hitchhiking stop near the Givat Assaf outpost east of Ramallah. Two soldiers from the Netzah Yehuda Battalion (the ultra-Orthodox Nahal unit) were killed, while another soldier and an Israeli woman were seriously wounded. The same day, two Israeli police officers were wounded after a Palestinian stabbed them in the Old City of Jerusalem, and the Israeli Army reported two suspected car-ramming attacks, one near Ramallah and one near the settlement of Kochav Yaacov. These attacks came a few hours after the Israeli Army killed two Palestinians, one suspected of having carried out the attack on 9 December and the other for an attack perpetrated in October. Hamas and the PIJ released similar statements calling on Palestinians to escalate confrontations. However, the PA security forces, which have been coordinating operations with Israel for years, cooperated with Israeli raids and manhunts into Palestinian towns and arrested many Hamas militants in late December.

Impact

Israeli government crisis

In November, Israel's Defense Minister Avigdor Lieberman resigned over the security cabinet's decision to accept a ceasefire with Palestinian militants in Gaza. Lieberman declared that the military response had been insufficient and inappropriate; that the government was making a mistake by negotiating with Hamas; and that he opposed decisions that would allow Qatari fuel and money into Gaza. His party, Yisrael Beiteinu, left the ruling coalition and called on other parties to agree on an early date for a general election (originally scheduled for November 2019). The political crisis, compounded by several years' of allegations of corruption, weakened Netanyahu, who by late 2018 controlled just 61 of the 120 parliamentary seats.

Amid controversy over a new law extending the military draft to Jewish ultra-Orthodox men, Netanyahu announced in late December that elections would be held in April 2019. As the issue of the conscription of ultra-Orthodox Jews has for years divided Israeli political life and society (with religious parties opposing military conscription), Netanyahu preferred to call for early elections rather than risking the coalition's division and downfall. The same month, the Israeli police recommended indicting him on charges of bribery and corruption on suspicion that he had eased business regulations for the country's largest telecommunications company in exchange for favourable coverage for him and his wife on a popular news website owned by the firm.

Economic and humanitarian strain in Palestine

Palestinian real GDP growth amounted to 2% in the first half of 2018. However, this percentage masks the fact that all growth comes from the West Bank, (real GDP growth of 5%), while Gaza's economy shrunk by nearly 6% in the first quarter of 2018, according to World Bank data. At the same time, food insecurity in Palestine affected nearly a third of the population (about 1.7m people), driven by high poverty and unemployment rates. Poverty (13.9%) and food insecurity (11.6%) were less widespread in the West Bank than in Gaza, where seven out of ten people were food insecure and more than half of the population lived in poverty and without a job.[9]

Situation in Gaza

In February 2018, Gaza declared a state of emergency, citing the impact of cuts in foreign aid on sanitation and fuel. The West Bank's strained relationship with Gaza decreased the total funding and services available to Gazans in 2018, leading Qatar to deliver US$15m in cash to Hamas in November, in addition to the US$60m fuel donation supervised by the UN. The conflict with Israel has also damaged Gaza's infrastructures and capabilities, including water and electricity supplies. There is a shortage of potable water in Gaza as well as a lack of treatment of wastewater, which results in more than 108,000 cubic metres of raw sewage flowing daily from Gaza into the Mediterranean Sea.[10] For most of 2018, electricity was only available for approximately five hours per day (although this rose to approximately 15 hours in November and December, thanks to Qatar's payment).[11]

Education has also been severely impacted by the conflict, the blockade and the inter-Palestinian divide, despite 1,200 civil servants paid by the PA returning to work, including 800 teachers,[12] as part of the reconciliation process signed in October 2017. More than 450,000 basic, secondary and kindergarten students and teachers were identified as 'people in need' in the 2018 Humanitarian Response Plan of the UN, while some 50% of students aged between five and 17 years old did not achieve their full educational potential. Schools in Gaza continued to be chronically overcrowded in 2018: 70% of UNRWA schools and 63% of schools run by the Ministry of Education operated on a double-shift system, reducing instructional hours on core subjects and foundation learning.

Political uncertainty in the West Bank

With no elections held since 2006, Abbas remained the primary decision-maker and interlocutor with the international community in 2018. This situation has undermined the Palestinian government's legitimacy and efficiency and exacerbated tensions with Hamas. Abbas's popularity declined in 2018, especially after a year of visible support for Israeli raids in Palestinian towns and waves of arrests in the ranks of Hamas in the West Bank. Moreover, Abbas is in ill health, leading many Palestinians and observers to discuss his political succession and the potential consequences for the Israeli–Palestinian conflict. Several names have circulated (such as Marwan Barghuti, in jail in Israel; Jibril Rajub, former commander of the Preventive Security force in the West Bank; Majed Farah, head of intelligence; and Mohammed Dahlan, former commander of the Preventive Security force in Gaza, now exiled in Abu Dhabi). Some analysts and observers predict a dramatic power struggle once Abbas vacates office.

Israel–Palestine conflict still a strategic issue in the Middle East

The impact of US decisions and the strategic realignments at work between some Gulf states in 2018 proved the continued strategic importance of the Israel–Palestine conflict in the region. Arab governments condemned the US decision on Jerusalem because they feared for their own stability and credibility. Demonstrations in support of the

Palestinians were organised in Amman, Jordan, in December 2017, during which they also denounced Saudi Crown Prince Muhammad bin Salman's collusion with the US and Israel. The same criticism was violently expressed in Gaza, where a Saudi flag was burned during demonstrations. Saudi authorities had to give guarantees of their pro-Palestine stance, with King Salman bin Abdulaziz pledging US$200m in aid to the Palestinians and reasserting support to the Palestinian struggle at the Arab League summit in April and his annual address to the kingdom's Shura Council in November. At the same time, Iran and Hizbollah increased their criticisms of an alleged Israeli–Saudi rapprochement and called on the Palestinians to start a new intifada. Amid worsening regional tensions. Tehran has used this narrative to portray itself as the leader of the 'resistance axis'.

| Trends

No imminent prospect of peace

By the end of the year, in the wake of the fragile ceasefire agreed upon by Hamas and Israel, and a US regional diplomacy that exacerbated the divisions between the conflict parties, the Israel–Palestine peace process was mired in a hazardous stalemate.

Uncertainty remains over the US peace plan that could be presented in 2019. In any case, the two-state solution is likely to continue to be threatened, leading more and more observers and activists to support the one (democratic) state solution. This alternative solution, however, remains all the more complicated to implement in the near future, given that the Israeli government does not want to assume the security, economic and demographic consequences of a unified state. Some argue that in the long run the continuation of the settlement policy and the security deterioration in the West Bank could force Israel to reoccupy partly or entirely the Palestinian territories.[13]

More economic and security challenges

Violence between Hamas and Israel could escalate again in 2019. The economic and humanitarian situation in Gaza will continue to deteriorate in spite of external assistance. Under a baseline scenario that assumes persistence of the Israeli restrictions (linked to the blockade) and the internal divide between the West Bank and Gaza, the World Bank projects real GDP growth of the Palestinian economy to hover around 1.9% (essentially in the West Bank) over the next two years, which means a decline in real per capita income by more than 2% and an increase in unemployment to 35%. Mounting frustrations could in turn lead to more uprisings.

Israeli elections

The evolution of the conflict may also depend on the results of the Israeli parliamentary elections planned to take place in April 2019. Netanyahu's political career (amid criminal investigations) and the inclination of the next Israeli government to promote peace with the Palestinians will have important repercussions on the direction of the conflict in 2019.

Middle East and North Africa

Notes

1 'Humanitarian Impact of Settlements', United Nations Office for the Coordination of Humanitarian Affairs (OCHA) website; 'Statistics on Settlements and Settler Population', Israeli Information Center for Human Rights in the Occupied Territories website.

2 OCHA reported the existence of 140 checkpoints (64 permanent) in the West Bank in 2018. 'Over 700 road obstacles control Palestinian movement within the West Bank', OCHA, 8 October 2018.

3 'Settlements Data: Population', PeaceNow website.

4 'Tenders for 641 Units Published in Record Year', PeaceNow, 27 December 2018.

5 '2018: More casualties and food insecurity, less funding for humanitarian aid', OCHA, 27 December 2018.

6 'Six Months On: Gaza's Great March of Return', Amnesty International, October 2018.

7 'Overview: December 2018', OCHA, 16 January 2019.

8 '2018: More casualties and food insecurity, less funding for humanitarian aid'.

9 'WFP Palestine Country Brief: December 2018', World Food Programme, December 2018.

10 Shira Efron, Jordan R. Fischbach, Ilana Blum, Rouslan I. Karimov and Melinda Moore, *The Public Health Impacts of Gaza's Water Crisis: Analysis and Policy Options* (Santa Monica, CA: RAND Corporation, 2018), pp. ix–x, 19.

11 'Gaza Strip electricity supply', OCHA website.

12 'Education undermined by deteriorating humanitarian situation in Gaza', The Humanitarian Monthly Bulletin, OCHA, April 2018.

13 United Nations, 'Israeli Practices towards the Palestinian People and the Question of Apartheid', *Palestine and the Israeli Occupation*, no. 1, 2017.

Libya

Overview

The conflict in 2018

Violence continued in Libya in 2018, though the impact of the conflict between the Government of National Accord (GNA) and the Libyan National Army (LNA) – the two power brokers in the country – remained relatively contained. Clashes between rival militias in the capital Tripoli undermined the GNA and exposed an untenable status quo. The LNA launched military operations in Derna and terrorist organisations carried out a series of attacks. Clashes also affected the impoverished and marginalised south and the strategic oil-crescent region.

The conflict considerably delayed the timetable of the United Nations' 'action plan' (launched in 2017 with the intention of breaking the political stalemate in Libya), which had already been obstructed by the meddling of foreign powers. Worried about the return of terrorism in Libya, Egypt continued to promote an anti-Islamist agenda, supported by the United Arab Emirates but opposed by Turkey. Russia demonstrated an increasing interest in Libyan affairs, while competition between France and Italy over the leadership of the mediation process intensified. As a result, elections originally scheduled for December 2018 have been postponed to spring 2019, though it remains unclear whether adequate security and political conditions will be in place by then.

Internally, however, the year saw significant steps made towards reconciliation, with agreements between rival communities. New security arrangements for Tripoli, although fragile, appeared to be effective. Oil production rose, and the chairman of the National Oil Corporation Mustafa Sanalla said that Libya oil output had reached 1.28 million barrels per day.[1]

The conflict to 2018

In 2011, mass protests and an international intervention precipitated a regime change in Libya that ousted Muammar Gadhafi, who had ruled the country for 42 years. The inability of the transitional authorities to rebuild state institutions left Libya in a state of transition, exacerbating existing tensions. The increasing insecurity and proliferation of armed groups and militias led to a second civil war in 2014 that forced the House of Representatives (HoR, the parliament that resulted from the election that year) to leave the capital Tripoli and move to Tobruk.

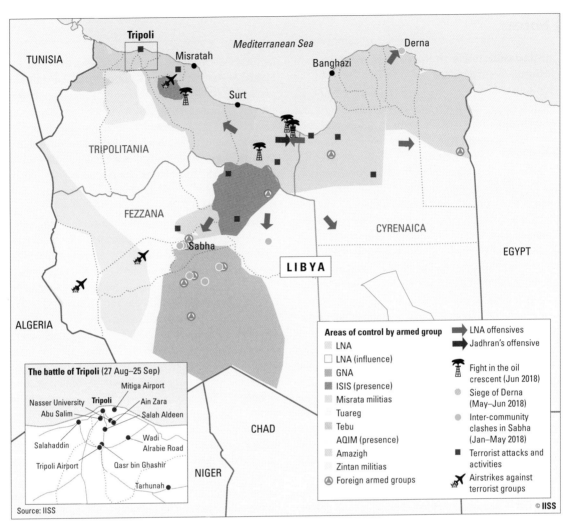

The battle of Tripoli (27 Aug–25 Sep)

Source: IISS

Areas of control by armed group
- LNA
- LNA (influence)
- GNA
- ISIS (presence)
- Misrata militias
- Tuareg
- Tebu
- AQIM (presence)
- Amazigh
- Zintan militias
- Foreign armed groups

- LNA offensives
- Jadhran's offensive
- Fight in the oil crescent (Jun 2018)
- Siege of Derna (May–Jun 2018)
- Inter-community clashes in Sabha (Jan–May 2018)
- Terrorist attacks and activities
- Airstrikes against terrorist groups

© IISS

This second wave of violence has polarised the country, deepened its fragmentation and created a breeding ground for terrorist organisations. It pitted revolutionary and counter-revolutionary forces against each other, effectively splitting the country in two. Tripoli and the western region have been under the control of revolutionary groups and militias from the capital and the cities of Misrata and Zintan. In the eastern part of the country, the LNA (under the command of General Khalifa Haftar and supported by Egypt and the UAE) has gradually extended its influence to the entire Cyrenaica region. The Libyan Political Agreement (LPA), signed in Skhirat, Morocco, in December 2015, established the GNA (led by Prime Minister Fayez al-Sarraj) with the goal of uniting a divided country, but three years after the agreement, the GNA is still struggling to maintain control in Tripoli.

Libya's division is reflected in parallel institutions in the east and the west – the National Oil Corporation (NOC), the Central Bank of Libya (CBL) and the Libyan Investment Authority (LIA). This fragmentation poses a major challenge to the reconciliation process and revives centrifugal forces present since the second phase of the Libyan civil war.

Key statistics

Type:	Internationalised
IDPs total (2017):	190,000
IDPs new (2018):	no data
Refugees total (2018):	13,000
Refugees new (2018):	no data
People in need (2018):	820,000

Forces

Militias affiliated with the Government of National Accord (GNA)

The establishment of the Government of National Accord (GNA) in 2015 was a watershed moment for western Libya. While some militias affiliated with the now-defunct Government of National Salvation (GNS) of Khalifa al-Ghwell (created after the launch of *Operation Libya Dawn* in 2014) opposed the new national unity government, several armed groups in Tripoli shifted their allegiances towards the GNA. Among these groups are the Abu Salim Brigades, also known as Abu Salim Central Security Forces (ASCSF) led by Abdul-Ghani al-Kikli (also known as 'Ghneiwa'); the Nawasi Brigade (also known as Eight Force), led by Mustapha Qaddur; the Special Deterrence Force (SDF), an armed group of 500–1,500 militiamen previously known as RADA and led by Abdelrauf Kara; and the Tripoli Revolutionaries Brigade (TRB), one of the largest militia groups in Tripoli with 3,000 militiamen, led by Haithem Tajouri.[2] Other militias from western Libya also backed the GNA, including the Halbous Brigade from Misrata and the Special Operations Force (SOF) from Zintan, led by Emad Trabelsi. In addition, the GNA attempted, unsuccessfully, to establish its own security force, the Presidential Guard (PG).

Most of these groups, especially the TRB, the SDF, the Nawasi Brigade and ASCSF, took advantage of their support for the GNA to secure more funds and increase their ranks. Labelled 'super-militias', they became more influential and powerful than the government itself. Their main goal is to preserve a dominant position and thwart attempts to challenge their authority in the capital, whether from outsiders or armed groups that have been expelled from Tripoli. Since the end of the battle for Tripoli in September 2018, armed groups under the GNA umbrella have resisted attempts to disarm and demobilise them.

Libyan National Army

In 2015, the House of Representatives (HoR), the parliament based in Tobruk in the east of the country, legitimised *Operation Dignity* (launched in 2014 by Haftar in eastern Libya to combat Islamist militant groups), paving the way for the establishment of the Libyan National Army (LNA). Since then, the LNA has been fighting terrorist organisations, a broad category which includes Islamist and revolutionary groups. *Operation Dignity* is not, however, limited to eastern Libya, and Haftar has frequently vowed to take control of Tripoli and the entire country. For this reason, the LNA is seen by Islamist and revolutionary groups as a counter-revolutionary force and its leader a military-coup plotter. Haftar's nationalistic ambitions contrast with the federalist forces in the HoR, causing frictions between the two bodies.

The LNA includes the Saiqa Special Forces, as well as tribal groups in eastern Libya and affiliated militias in southern and western parts of the country. In total, the LNA comprises approximately 25,000 fighters.[3] It receives substantial support from regional powers, such as Egypt and the UAE (the latter operates a military air base in al-Khadim, near Benghazi).[4] Saiqa officers have also graduated from military academies in Jordan.

Misrata militias

The city of Misrata in western Libya has been a revolutionary stronghold since the beginning of the uprising against Gadhafi. More than 200 militias, with a combined strength of approximately 40,000 fighters, operate in the city without a unified stance or chain of command.[5] The establishment of the GNA in Tripoli exacerbated divisions in the city, with some groups supporting the national unity government – such as the Halbous Brigade, the al-Majoub Brigade and the Abu Bakr Siddiq Brigade – while others oppose it, such as the Samoud Front of Salah al-Badi, the Salah al-Burki Brigade, the Libyan National Guard (LNG) and the Misrata Military Council. Most of these groups have an Islamist background or are close to the Muslim Brotherhood's Justice and Construction Party (JCP), and therefore are considered part of the Libyan political Islam factions supported by Qatar and Turkey.

Drivers

A lucrative war economy

The war economy and the predatory behaviour of local armed groups are powerful drivers of the conflict in Libya.[6] Sarraj and his cabinet rely on the supermilitias to retain power, which has resulted in militia-cartel members securing executive positions and controlling sovereign institutions, banks and government offices. The supermilitias also benefit from illicit revenues, such as selling hard currency on the black market, issuing letters of credit and smuggling fuel and people. Disputes over state resources and economic activity erupt frequently, leading to intense fighting. In August 2018, allegations of corruption against the militia cartel in Tripoli led to the most intense violence in the city since 2014. The 7th Infantry Brigade (from the city of Tarhouna) accused the ASCSF, the Nawasi Brigade, the SDF and the TRB in Tripoli of profiting from their support to the GNA, launching military operations to cleanse the capital of corrupt militias.

Internal fragmentation

Since the end of the revolution, the proliferation of militias and armed groups, and the failure to disarm and demobilise them, has led to increasing instability and insecurity in Libya, in turn fuelling the conflict between revolutionary and counter-revolutionary forces. The approval of the Political Isolation Law in 2013 (which prevents members of Gadhafi's regime from holding office) and, more importantly, the launch of *Operation Dignity* (*Karama*) and *Operation Libya Dawn* (*Fajr Libya*) in 2014, represented major escalations that exacerbated the country's regional and political divide.

Persistent tensions between rival groups since 2014 has further deprived national institutions of authority, forcing them to rely on armed groups and militias to implement decisions, leading to increasing lawlessness. The fight has also assumed a more religious character. The recent expansion of the Saudi-imported Madkhalism doctrine (a quietist approach to Islam whose influence has grown both in eastern and western Libya, even inside secular armed groups) has added a further dimension to the conflict.[7] Since then, the rivalry between Madkhalist and Salafist factions on one side and groups affiliated to political Islam parties on the other has become a constant feature of the conflict, adding further fissures to an already fragmented social fabric and creating unexpected commonalities between rival groups.

Foreign meddling

In 2014, Egyptian President Abdel Fattah Al-Sisi welcomed the launch of Haftar's *Operation Dignity* as an important contribution to Cairo's fight against the Muslim Brotherhood and political Islam more generally. Since then, Cairo's support for Haftar has deepened the divide between revolutionary and counter-revolutionary forces in Libya as well as between eastern and western Libya.

The rivalry between Qatar and the UAE has also affected the Libyan conflict. While Doha, together with Turkey, backed the GNS and cultivated strong relations with the Misrata militias, the UAE gave full support to Haftar, joining Egypt and Saudi Arabia in their fight against the Islamist factions. In 2017, Qatar allegedly violated a 2014 Gulf Cooperation Council (GCC) agreement by providing assistance to Islamist groups in the region. In response, the LNA severed diplomatic ties with Doha, accusing it of supporting terrorist groups.

The stance of Western powers towards the Libyan crisis has also been divisive. Since the election of President Emmanuel Macron in 2017, France has tried to assume a leading role in the reconciliation process, hosting two meetings in Paris and attempting to legitimise Haftar on the international scene. France's activism has caused resentment in Italy, Libya's former colonial ruler, which has been supportive of Sarraj and the GNA. Wary of France's move in Libya, Italy has sought support from Washington and Moscow to undermine Macron's initiatives. The Italian government has also frequently blamed the UK and France for the 2011 military intervention in Libya. Rome suspects that Paris hides economic plans that could be detrimental to the interests of the Italian national oil company ENI, one of the few multinational oil companies with a prominent role in the Libyan oil sector.

Political and Military Developments

A faltering UN action plan

On 20 September 2017, Ghassan Salamé, the UN Special Representative and head of the UN Support Mission in Libya (UNSMIL), presented a UN action plan for Libya. The plan was based on four main points: discussions between the HoR and the Tripoli-based High Council of State (HCoS, which succeeded the General National Congress in 2016) to amend the 2015 LPA; a National Conference involving a wide range of political actors that would be a 'synthesis of the hopes of the Libyan people'; a referendum on the draft constitution approved by the Constitution Drafting Assembly (CDA) in July 2017; and parliamentary and presidential elections.

Although Salamé's plan received broad international support, it also became a point of tension between France and Italy. On 29 May, the French government convened Libya's main political figures in Paris and brokered a Joint Declaration, which was agreed upon but not signed by all. The document provided for general and presidential elections to be held on 10 December 2018, as well as a 'constitutional basis' to regulate relations between institutions by 16 September. It was, however, unclear what this basis was, with some assuming it referred to the 2011 Interim Constitutional Declaration, others to the draft constitution or even the two documents combined.

Fighting in the oil-crescent region in June 2018 and the battle of Tripoli in August and September forced a postponement, while international pressures piled up. The new Italian government repeatedly expressed its objections to the Joint Declaration, rallying support from international partners to hinder France's diplomatic activism.[8] The International Conference on Libya – held in Palermo, Italy, on 12–13 November 2018 and attended by the main international and regional powers (including the main Libyan factions) – expressed support for Salamé's action plan, which had been slightly revised in the meantime to include a postponement of the elections to spring 2019, and the National Conference to be held in February 2019.

Delays to reform

Talks between the HoR and the HCoS to amend the LPA, reducing the number of Presidency Council (PC) members and establishing a separate government, continued in 2018. The election of JCP member Khaled Mishri as head of the HCoS surprisingly re-launched negotiations in late April. Mishri and HoR President Agila Saleh agreed to reduce the PC from nine members to three, with a separate prime minister heading the government. The move aimed at revitalising the PC, which has been weakened by defections and boycotts.

Disputes over the mechanism to select PC members persisted until October, when the HoR and HCoS negotiating teams approved a solution. Salamé's cautious welcome to the breakthrough was interpreted by HoR members as a reluctance to move forwards with the reform of the PC, which would have meant reshuffling the body and possibly replacing Sarraj a few weeks before the International Conference on Libya in Palermo, an outcome not favoured by Italy, which has backed Sarraj since he took office.

HoR obstructionism

Preparations to approve a draft constitution and end the transitional phase in Libya continued throughout 2018. The resistance of Haftar's supporters, concerned about provisions banning the general from running for president, and federalist forces in Cyrenaica, opposed to the centralised system established by the draft constitution, continued to undermine the process. In July 2017, the CDA approved a draft constitution, but the Court of Appeal in Bayda invalidated the vote. On 14 February 2018, the Supreme Court overturned the Court of Appeal's ruling, thereby allowing the HoR to legislate on the referendum law.

Pressure mounted in the HoR, however, when a group of MPs rejected the Supreme Court's ruling and the authority of the CDA and called for the adoption of the 1951 Constitution instead, which provided Libya with a monarchy and a federalist system. On 24 September the HoR passed the referendum law with 135 votes in favour (out of 200), dividing Libya into three regional constituencies and establishing the procedures for holding the constitutional referendum – a 50% + 1 person quorum in each region for the referendum to be valid and a two-thirds majority nationwide for the draft to be approved.

The HoR's adoption on 26 November of a constitutional amendment to the 2011 Interim

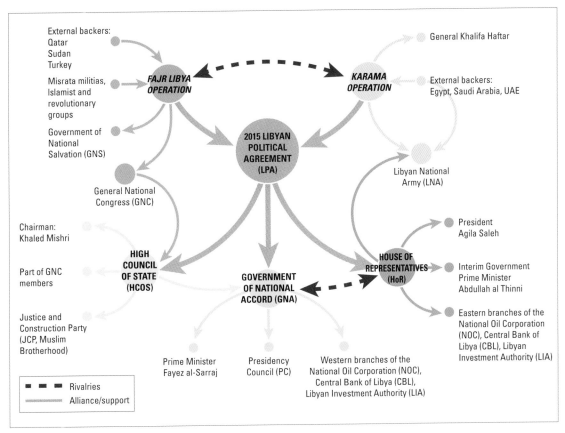

Figure 1: Political relations in Libya

Constitutional Declaration also paved the way for a referendum on the draft constitution. If the referendum takes place and the draft constitution is approved before elections, Libya's unfinished transition could terminate, finally opening a new page in the country's history.

Tensions inside the LNA

Reports that Haftar was suffering health problems emerged on 10 April 2018. Presumably affected by a stroke, the LNA commander was hospitalised in Paris for three weeks, raising doubts about his ability to lead and increasing tensions within the LNA, especially after the press started discussing the succession process. While HoR President Saleh and UN Special Representative Salamé were reassuring the Libyan public and the international community of Haftar's recovery, Saleh was put under pressure to appoint a temporary commander of the LNA. Amid rumours about possible successors to the general, armed groups and tribal actors began presenting their candidates. The Furjan tribe,

which Haftar comes from, reportedly insisted on appointing another member of the tribe, confirming the suspicion that the LNA is not a proper army but a coalition of tribes and militias in eastern Libya.

The UAE allegedly favoured the appointment of Oun al-Furjani, while Egypt and France backed General Abdul Salam al-Hassi, a senior LNA commander. On 18 April, Major-General Abdul Razzak al-Nazhuri, chief of staff of the LNA and another candidate to Haftar's office, survived an assassination attempt in Benghazi. He was apparently excluded from the race due to his proximity to Saleh. Haftar's return to Libya on 26 April averted the risk of a dissolution of the LNA and coincided with the launch of the LNA offensive on Derna, a show of force aimed to achieve full control of Cyrenaica, ease pressure on Egypt's western front and confirm that Haftar was still in control of his fighters.

Tribal clashes in southern Libya

The Rome reconciliation agreement of March 2017 between the Arab Awlad Suliman tribe and the

Tebu and Tuareg minorities established a peaceful coexistence between the three groups in the Fezzan region in southern Libya after three years of large-scale conflict. The delicate balance collapsed in January 2018 when clashes between the Awlad Suliman and the Tebu resumed. The fighting intensified in the following months in and around Sabha,[9] offering Haftar the opportunity to extend the LNA's influence in southern Libya. As he did with local armed groups in Sabratha in September 2017, Haftar tried to co-opt militias fighting in Sabha, offering the LNA's backing and enlisting local affiliates. On 20 February, the LNA appointed a commander to the 6th Brigade, an armed group based in Sabha and composed mainly of Awlad Suliman tribesmen,

claiming it was operating as part of the LNA. The 6th Brigade initially denied the claim, saying it was operating under the GNA's defence ministry. The National Tebu Assembly (NTA) took the occasion to criticise the GNA, saying it was biased in favour of the Awlad Suliman. The competition between the GNA and the LNA intensified in April after the 6th Brigade unexpectedly announced that it was joining Haftar's forces. However, the 6th Brigade's move quickly backfired. After repeated attempts, on 10 May Tebu militiamen finally took control of Fort Elena, the 6th Brigade's headquarters in Sabha, ousting the armed group from the southern city and foiling Haftar's attempt to extend the LNA's influence in southern Libya.

Violent Events

The fall of Derna
Unable to make inroads in southern Libya, the LNA reverted to a more consolidated theatre of operations, moving towards Derna, the only city in eastern Libya not under its control. Sporadic clashes, shelling and occasional airstrikes took place in the first part of 2018, but the fighting intensified in May following Haftar's return from Paris. On 7 May, Haftar announced the start of the offensive to oust the Derna Protection Force (DPF) from the city. Despite international outcry, neither the GNA nor the international community were able to prevent the fighting and relieve the humanitarian pressure on Derna. With support from Egypt, France and the UAE, the LNA gained control of Derna in June, although sporadic clashes continued in the following months. The LNA neutralised prominent jihadists in the city and exposed the collusion between the DPF and terrorist organisations active in North Africa, including al-Qaeda in the Islamic Maghreb (AQIM).

The fighting in the oil crescent
The LNA's offensive on Derna was delayed in mid-June by Ibrahim Jadhran's surprise attack on the oil-crescent region (Jadhran had controlled the oil crescent until 2016, when Haftar ousted him). Jadhran – the former leader of the Petroleum Facilities Guard (PFG) – led a coalition which included the Magharba tribe, Tebu militiamen, the Benghazi Defence Brigades (BDB) and Chadian mercenaries. The coalition seized the Es Sider and Ras Lanuf oil terminals on 14 June, forcing the LNA to withdraw 120 kilometres east of Ajdabiya.

As occurred on previous occasions, Jadhran was not able to rally support for his offensive. On 21 June, the LNA launched a counter-attack and retook Es Sider and Ras Lanuf, forcing Jadhran and his forces to retreat. The LNA's offensive reached the edges of Sirte, where the Misrata militias, who were part of *Operation Solid Structure* (launched by the GNA in May 2016 to oust the Islamic State, also known as ISIS or ISIL, from Sirte), declared a state of emergency. The LNA's aircraft pounded Jadhran and his allies in Ghadahiya and Saddadah, raising the risk of a major confrontation between Haftar's forces and the Misrata militias, until the LNA decided to refocus on Derna.

The battle for Tripoli
The war economy and the predatory behaviour of the main militias in Tripoli were the main causes of the fighting that erupted in the capital on 26 August. The 7th Infantry Brigade (also known as the Kani Brigade) from Tarhouna launched an offensive in southern Tripoli against ASCSF and other groups of the militia cartel. The fighting affected the area around the airport and drew in militias from outside the capital. Some of them, including the Samoud Front of Salah Badi from Misrata, came in support of the Kani Brigade; others, such as the SOF and the Amazigh Mobile Forces, backed the GNA.

A ceasefire was agreed on 4 September in Zawiya but the fighting continued, forcing the armed groups of the militia cartel to ally and establish the Tripoli Protection Force (TPF). On 25 September, the TPF took control of the Qasr Ben Ghasir district and the Naqliya barracks, forcing the attackers out of southern Tripoli. Sporadic clashes between rival militias continued while the GNA made attempts to establish regular police and security forces and end the militias' rule in the capital.

The return of the Islamic State

The inability of Libyan authorities to provide security enabled the return of ISIS in 2018. After being pushed out of Sirte in 2016, the remnants of ISIS regrouped on the outskirts of the city, establishing a significant presence in central-southern Libya along the front-line between the LNA and *Operation Solid Structure*. In 2018, ISIS carried out frequent attacks against LNA fighters, but also extended its reach to Tripoli with spectacular attacks, such as those against the High National Elections Commission (HNEC) building on 2 May; the NOC's headquarters on 10 September; and the GNA foreign ministry on 25 December. The attack against the NOC's headquarters occurred in the midst of the battle for Tripoli, confirming how the continuation of the conflict favoured the expanding activity of terrorist groups in the country. To counteract the revival of ISIS, the United States launched frequent airstrikes against ISIS militants and positions in southern Libya.

| Impact

Humanitarian consequences

The ongoing conflict in Libya has had major humanitarian consequences. The violence in Sabha in the first half of 2018 directly affected civilians, with the remoteness of the location representing a serious obstacle to the delivery of humanitarian aid. In May, the opening of a new front in Derna represented another challenging development. The LNA's offensive in a highly populated urban environment brought the eastern city to the brink of humanitarian collapse. As the fighting between the LNA and the DPF intensified, local authorities reported shortages of food, water and hard currency, describing the situation as catastrophic.

As in Derna, the fighting in August in Tripoli took place in a dense urban theatre. According to the GNA's estimates, by the end of September the clashes had led to 117 people dead and 581 injured, while 20 people were reported missing. UNSMIL reported that 16 civilians were killed, though the actual number of civilian casualties was believed to be higher. According to UNICEF, the fighting also displaced 25,000 people, half of whom were children.

Internally displaced persons (IDPs) are gradually returning to their homes. However, difficulties and challenges persist, including the need to provide essential services and secure a safe return for all. According to the UN High Commissioner for Refugees (UNHCR), 403,978 IDPs had returned to their homes between 2016 and April 2018, while 187,423 people remained internally displaced as of December 2018.

Even though the flow of migrants along the Central Mediterranean Route (which passes through Libya) significantly decreased compared to previous years, the death rate at sea increased in 2018, while migrants, refugees and asylum seekers continued to be abused in Libya's detention centres.[10] In October, the International Organization for Migration (IOM) identified 669,176 migrants in Libya.

Increasing levels of lawlessness and impunity

Rampant abuses and human-rights violations were common in 2018. The outburst of violence aggravated the lawlessness of the country, weakening its central institutions and contributing to its sociopolitical fragmentation. In June, videos emerged which suggested that civilians were being summarily executed in Derna. These developments highlighted the continued impunity of militias and armed groups in Libya, just a few months after the International Criminal Court (ICC) urged the LNA to cooperate in arresting and handing over Major Mahmoud al-Warfali for war crimes. The fact that Warfali, a member of the Saiqa Special Forces who escaped from prison in July, is still at large raises serious doubts about the LNA's willingness to cooperate with the ICC.

Kidnappings and abductions were also frequent, in particular in southern Libya where the lack of rule of law favoured the presence of criminal groups and rebel forces from neighbouring countries. The Chadian Military Command Council for the Salvation of the Republic (CCMSR) and the Sudanese Justice and Equality Movement (JEM) were responsible for most of the kidnappings, aimed to acquire funds via ransoms.

Oil production falls

Jadhran's offensive in the oil crescent in June forced the NOC to declare *force majeure* and pull out its workers from the Es Sider and Ras Lanuf oil terminals. Two oil tanks in Ras Lanuf were also set alight, reducing the storage capacity by 400,000 barrels. More than half of the tanks had already been damaged or destroyed in previous clashes in the area. As a result, Libya's total oil output dropped from about one million barrels per day (bpd) to 600,000–700,000 bpd at the end of June.

The LNA immediately retook the oil terminals, but Haftar's decision to hand them over to the eastern NOC brought the country to the brink of partition. Haftar accused the Tripoli-based and internationally recognised NOC of funding militias and terrorist groups responsible for the offensive in the oil crescent, including the PFG and the BDB. Only intense international pressure forced him to return the terminals to the internationally recognised NOC based in Tripoli in July.

Trends

Attempts to broker security arrangements

The new security arrangements for Tripoli produced encouraging results in 2018, returning the control of sovereign institutions to the state and starting a gradual process of disarmament, demobilisation and reintegration (DDR) of the main militias in the capital. However, it is likely that armed groups will continue to resist any measure that curbs their influence and it is unclear whether the same process could be applied outside Tripoli.

The reunification of the Libyan armed forces is also part of the international plan to rebuild effective security and military institutions. Successive negotiations in Cairo brokered by the Egyptian government have not produced tangible results so far. The GNA has also started talks with Turkey with a view to re-establishing security and military cooperation, motivated in part by the Egyptian regime's support for Haftar.

Economic reforms

Fees on foreign-currency exchanges are helping stabilise the Libyan dinar exchange rate, reducing the profits of militias engaged in illicit activities and corrupt practices. Sanctions imposed by the UN against human smugglers and militiamen responsible for violence in Tripoli and the oil crescent are also helping restore the rule of law, but it is not yet clear if they can deter criminals and militiamen. Despite travel bans and asset freezes, militiamen and criminals are still operating in Libya, holding a considerable sway on political and military developments.

Elections

The main political development of 2019 will be the presidential elections in Libya, Algeria, Mauritania and Tunisia, the outcome of which will shape the future of the Maghreb region in the medium term. The obvious contenders in Libya are Haftar and Sarraj, but the former has so far refused to announce his candidacy and regularly threatens to take control of Tripoli by force. The first to announce his candidacy was Aref Nayed, the former ambassador to the UAE. Accordingly, his objectives are thought to align with those of the UAE and Haftar: combatting political Islam and eradicating Islamist factions from the country. Saif al-Islam Gadhafi, son of the late dictator Muammar Gadhafi, reportedly announced his candidacy in controversial circumstances (the announcement was made by a spokesperson). His whereabouts are not known and he has not appeared in public since his alleged release from prison in Zintan. But he is still considered influential and could represent a wild card in the elections, especially if he receives Russian support.[11]

While the HNEC has already laid the groundwork for elections to take place in the first half of 2019, the National Conference in February will represent the first important test to understand the real intentions of the main Libyan factions. The constitutional referendum could give the Libyan people the opportunity to move towards statehood. However, given the polarised political landscape, the resurgent terrorist threat and the

conflicting agendas of the major powers, a political solution still seems unlikely. Indeed, holding
an election in such a divisive context could further
destabilise Libya.

Notes

1   Benoit Faucon, 'Libya's Oil Production Has More Than Doubled
    Since June, Oil Chief Says', *Wall Street Journal*, 14 November
    2018.
2   Erin Neale and Yousouf Eltagouri, 'Tripoli: A Kaleidoscope',
    Atlantic Council, 22 June 2018.
3   Amanda Lapo, 'Libya: The challenge of unifying factions in
    a fragmented state', Military Balance Blog, IISS, 17 December
    2018.
4   UN Panel of Experts on Libya, 'Final report of the Panel of
    Experts, S/2017/46', UN, 1 June 2017.
5   Cameron Glenn, 'Libya's Islamists: Who They Are – And What
    They Want', Wilson Centre, 8 August 2017.
6   Tim Eaton, 'Libya's War Economy: Predation, Profiteering and
    State Weakness', Research Paper, Chatham House, April 2018.
7   Carlos Zurutza, 'The Sect Quietly Uniting a Divided Libya –
    Under Salafism', Ozy, 29 June 2018.

8   Maryline Dumas and Mathieu Galtier, 'La Libye prise en otage
     par la France et l'Italie', *Orient XXI*, 17 October 2018.
9   Michel Cousins, 'Mounting strife in southern Libya adds to the
     country's instability', *Arab Weekly*, 4 March 2018.
10   The central Mediterranean route is one of the world's deadliest
     sea crossings. According to the UN High Commissioner for
     Refugees (UNHCR), 1,095 died along it between January and
     July 2018, or one out of every 18 arrivals. UNHCR, 'Desperate
     journeys: Refugees and migrants arriving in Europe and at
     Europe's borders ', 6 August 2018. Francesca Mannocchi, 'They
     can't sail for Europe – so what's happening to migrants trapped
     in Libya?', *Middle East Eye*, 15 September 2018.
11   Henry Meyer, Samer al-Atrush and Stephen Kravchenko,
     'Russia Has a Plan for Libya – Another Qaddafi', Bloomberg, 20
     December 2018.

Syria

Overview

The conflict in 2018

Control of territory in Syria changed considerably in
the course of 2018. The Assad regime made further
substantial territorial gains in the former rebel strongholds of Eastern Ghouta and areas of southwestern
Syria, including Daraa province, known as the birthplace of the revolution. The regime advance was
facilitated by the use of airstrikes and sieges that
forced rebel groups into surrender and evacuation
deals. Many prominent rebel groups suffered heavy
losses and by the end of the year were concentrated
in the northwest, having formed coalitions to survive.

By the end of the year, a demilitarised zone in
northwestern Syria, designed to avert a full-scale
regime offensive, was largely holding, although
in light of previous regime actions and comments
from regime officials, a future offensive in the area
seemed likely. Islamic State, also known as ISIS or
ISIL, also continued to suffer significant territorial
losses to the Syrian Democratic Forces (SDF), who
were supported by the US-led coalition, as well as
to the regime and its allied forces. By the end of the

year, ISIS controlled only small villages and pockets
of territory in the country, largely limited to eastern
Deir ez-Zor province.

By December 2018, the regime held more territory than any other group in Syria and continued
to show a lack of meaningful commitment to peace
talks, while a number of regional powers began to
resume relations with the regime. The United States'
announcement in mid-December that it would withdraw its troops from Syria highlighted the waning
interest in the country in some quarters.

Key statistics	
Type:	Internationalised
IDPs total (2018):	6,600,000–6,800,000
IDPs new (2018):	1,630,000
Refugees total (2018):	5,700,000–6,500,000
Refugees new (2018):	no data
People in need (2018):	13,100,000

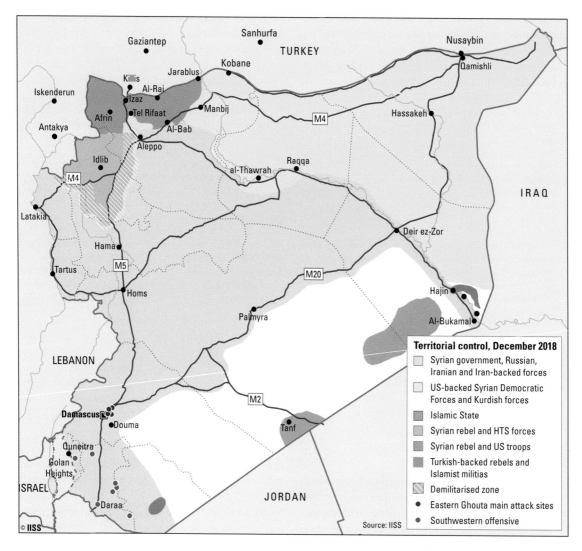

Territorial control, December 2018
- Syrian government, Russian, Iranian and Iran-backed forces
- US-backed Syrian Democratic Forces and Kurdish forces
- Islamic State
- Syrian rebel and HTS forces
- Syrian rebel and US troops
- Turkish-backed rebels and Islamist militias
- Demilitarised zone
- Eastern Ghouta main attack sites
- Southwestern offensive

Source: IISS

© IISS

The conflict to 2018

In March 2011, a wave of peaceful demonstrations erupted in Syria following the detention and torture of boys who had written graffiti in support of the Arab Spring. Long-term discontent with human-rights abuses committed by the Assad regime, and long-standing social and economic inequalities fuelled the protests. The regime violently suppressed the protests and many civilians were detained, imprisoned, tortured and killed. The crackdown led to the formation of both moderate and hardline rebel groups, who launched military operations against the regime, and the situation escalated into a civil war. The Free Syrian Army, one of the largest groups, was formed primarily by defectors from the regime's Syrian Arab Army.

Initially, the regime suffered heavy losses in manpower (casualties and defectors), equipment and territory. Moderate opposition groups received financial, political, logistical and often military support from Arab states and Western nations, particularly Saudi Arabia, Qatar, Turkey, the US, the United Kingdom and France.

As the conflict progressed, Islamist groups grew in number and strength, most notably Hayat Tahrir al-Sham (HTS), Syria's al-Qaeda offshoot, and ISIS, who proclaimed the establishment of a caliphate in areas of Syria and Iraq in June 2014, but had lost most key areas of the territory it once controlled in Syria by the end of 2017 after the coordinated Western and regime offensives.

The course of the conflict changed in September 2015 when Russia intervened on the side of the regime. This development, together with the Iranian intervention, led to substantial losses for both moderate and hardline rebel groups and allowed the regime to reassert control over increasing swathes of the country. Despite a number of attempts at brokering ceasefires, the conflict has largely continued uninterrupted since 2011, with extremely high levels of violence, including the use of chemical-weapons and mass displacement (with one of the biggest refugee flows in recent times).

Forces

Syrian government
The Syrian Arab Army (SAA), under the command of President Bashar al-Assad's government, has been fighting to defend areas under its control and retake rebel-held areas since the conflict began in 2011. The volunteer National Defence Forces was formed in late 2012, with the military training from the Iranian Islamic Revolutionary Guard Corps, to support the SAA. Many trained fighters subsequently moved to the Local Defence Forces (LDF), an Iranian-backed umbrella group of pro-regime militias, established in 2013–14. Russian and Iranian support has greatly increased the capabilities of the regime's forces and their ability to hold territory.

Hizbullah
Hizbullah, originally founded with Iranian backing in 1982 to resist the Israeli occupation of Lebanon, has likely been involved in the Syrian conflict since 2011 (though confirmed only in 2013). The exact number of its fighters in Syria is unclear. The US government estimates that at least 7,000 are active in the country.[1] The organisation's military wing is highly trained, and possesses both a regular and reserve force and a wide variety of land weapons, including small arms, heavy machine guns, anti-tank missiles, as well as vehicles including Humvees and mobile artillery pieces.

Throughout 2018, Hizbullah continued to fight alongside the regime and other allied forces to take control of opposition-held areas, including the Eastern Ghouta area, Deir ez-Zor province and southwest Syria. Through its involvement in the conflict, the organisation seeks to restore key supply routes through Syria and deflect the possibility of a Sunni state on the Lebanese border.

Russia
Russia's military involvement in Syria in support of the regime began in 2015 and has been key to the regime's widespread territorial gains since. Exact numbers of Russian troops in Syria are unknown but in August 2018 the country's Ministry of Defence said that more than 63,000 military personnel had fought in Syria since 2015. Russia has tested an extensive number of weapons in Syria, including aircraft and advanced missiles and provided the regime with advanced military equipment such as the BTR-82A armoured vehicle and the S-300 air-defence system.[2]

Throughout 2018, the Russian Army continued to support regime offensives as part of its efforts to uphold the regime and build regional influence. Russia fought and carried out airstrikes in the year's major battles in the Eastern Ghouta region and other areas of Rif Damashq province; Daraa and Quneitra provinces; and in the northwest.

An unknown number of Russian private military companies (PMCs) are also active in Syria, the most well-known being the Wagner Group. Estimates of Russian PMCs' strengths vary between 2,000 and 3,000, and they are thought to play an integral role in many regime offensives. The country had long denied reports that Russian contractors in Syria had any connection to Syria's armed forces. However, a US-led coalition attack on SDF headquarters in Deir ez-Zor province in February 2018, led to numerous reports of PMC contractors with links to the Kremlin being killed. Later in the month, the Russian Foreign Ministry confirmed that dozens of Russian citizens had been killed in the incident, the first confirmation of non-military Russian deaths in Syria.

Iran and other regime-allied forces
The Islamic Revolutionary Guard Corps (IRGC), Iran's elite force, founded after the Iranian Revolution to protect and continue the revolution's aims, has supported the Syrian regime since 2012 as a way to strengthen Iran's presence in the Levant. With an estimated 2,000 personnel in operational

and training roles, the IRGC has played a significant role in many of the regime's key battles. It also commands a number of Shia militias operating in Syria (Liwa Fatemiyoun and Liwa Zaynabiyoun), as well as Artesh, the conventional military of Iran, deployed in Syria since 2016.

The Shia militias Liwa Fatemiyoun and Liwa Zaynabiyoun are the most notable among many pro-regime forces and militias operating in Syria. Liwa Fatemiyoun is composed of Afghan nationals, and Liwa Zaynabiyoun of Pakistani nationals, with an estimated 8,000–10,000 and 1,000–2,000 fighters, respectively.

National Liberation Front; Free Syrian Army remnants; Syrian National Army

The Free Syrian Army (FSA) is the umbrella designation of moderate opposition factions who have been fighting the Assad regime since 2011. Established by defecting SAA soldiers, the FSA has since included different groups and is primarily funded by Gulf and Western states. Sustained regime offensives and surrender deals have drastically reduced its strength and territorial control to northwest Syria. Other moderate groups and alliances have seen their manpower greatly reduced, with many rebel fighters having been evacuated to areas of the northwest throughout 2018. The majority of remaining moderate opposition groups, including remnants of the FSA, now operate under the National Liberation Front in northwest Syria.

Hayat Tahrir al-Sham (HTS)

Currently the main Salafi-jihadist group in Syria and one of the strongest remaining rebel groups, Hayat Tahrir al-Sham (HTS) was formed in 2017 following a merger between Jabhat Fatah al-Sham (Syria's al-Qaeda offshoot, founded in 2012) and a number of other Islamist and jihadist groups. In light of regime offensives in many former rebel strongholds, fragmentation and defections, the group has lost much of its power and control, but still retains a significant presence in the northwest, and controls much of Idlib province. HTS often engages also in fighting with moderate opposition groups.

Turkey

Turkey has been indirectly involved in the Syrian conflict since its beginning by funding and training rebel groups. Direct military involvement began in late 2016 with *Operation Euphrates Shield*, aimed to expel ISIS from the city of Jarablus and halt the territorial expansion of the Kurdish YPG in the northwest – Turkey's primary objective, along with securing its border with Syria (see next chapter for more on Turkey's role in the Syrian civil war).

Syrian Democratic Forces (SDF)

The Syrian Democratic Forces (SDF) is a multi-ethnic, yet primarily Kurdish, coalition of militias and fighters, founded in October 2015 with the aim of creating a democratic, federal and secular Syria. The majority of the group's operations are against ISIS. In conjunction with the US-led CJTF–OIR it conducted successful offensives against the group in Raqqa, Deir ez-Zor, Hasakah and Aleppo provinces. It is estimated to have between 60,000 and 75,000 fighters and has received financial and military support from the US and CJTF–OIR, through extensive air cover and training. In July 2018, the SDF engaged in talks with the regime regarding the future of areas under its control, with no discernible developments.

Kurdish People's Protection Units (YPG)

The Kurdish People's Protection Units (YPG), formed in 2004, is the military wing of the Kurdish Democratic Union Party and has been the primary component of the SDF since the SDF was established in 2015. The YPG's strength is estimated at between 20,000 and 30,000 fighters. The group is predominantly Kurdish, and has fought in northern and eastern Syria against the regime and allied forces, Turkish armed forces, Islamist groups, the Free Syrian Army and ISIS. As part of the SDF, the YPG receives financial and military support from the US-led CJTF–OIR and has access to mostly light weaponry including AK-47s.

Combined Joint Task Force–*Operation Inherent Resolve* (CJTF–OIR)

Combined Joint Task Force–*Operation Inherent Resolve* (CJTF–OIR) was established in October 2014 by the US Central Command to coordinate military operations against ISIS in Syria and Iraq. Besides the US, it includes members of the armed forces of more than 30 allied countries, including the UK, France, Jordan and the United Arab Emirates. Current estimates report that around 2,000 US troops are deployed in Syria. The CJTF–OIR mainly

Table 1: Main warring parties in Syria	
Pro-regime and allied forces	• Syrian government: Syrian Arab Army; Local Defence Forces; National Defence Forces • Russia: Russian armed forces and private military contractors • Iran: Islamic Revolutionary Guard Corps Ground; Artesh • Hizbullah • Shia militias: Liwa Fatemiyoun; Liwa Zaynabiyoun
Rebel groups	• National Liberation Front; Free Syria Army; Syrian National Army • Jihadist groups: Hayat Tahrir al-Sham; Hurras al-Din; Turkestan Islamic Party • Islamic State, also known as ISIS or ISIL
Kurdish groups	• People's Protection Units: YPG • Syrian Democratic Forces: SDF
International forces	• Turkey: Turkish armed forces • Israel • US-led coalition: Combined Joint Task Force–*Operation Inherent Resolve*

conducts operations against ISIS through airstrikes (more than 11,000 since its inception), but has also given ground assistance and training to a number of Syrian opposition groups, particularly the SDF.

In 2018, the task force continued to focus on operations to degrade ISIS, but the US, UK and France also launched isolated, limited targeting of Syrian government positions in 2017 and 2018. In December, US President Donald Trump announced that US forces would be withdrawing from Syria, placing the future of the coalition and the SDF in doubt.

Islamic State, also known as ISIS or ISIL

The Islamic State is a jihadi militant group originating in the late 1990s and present in numerous countries. The group's primary aim is the establishment of a global Sunni caliphate. The group evolved from Islamic State of Iraq (ISI), which came to prominence during the US occupation of Iraq. Its subsequent leadership was constituted of a number of former Saddam Hussein-era officers and Sunni extremists. Following the outbreak of the Syrian conflict in 2011, the group's current leader, Abu Bakr al-Baghdadi, sent ISIS fighters to garner support and establish cells in the country. In 2014, the group established a de facto state in parts of Iraq and Syria, controlling vast areas in northern and eastern Syria.

The group is known for its highly violent tactics, including public beheadings. ISIS acquired much of its weaponry from capturing Syrian military bases, gaining access to weapons and systems including artillery, armoured vehicles, anti-tank missiles and small arms. It also procured many weapons through the black market.

The offensives of the SDF, supported by the CJTF–OIR and regime and allied forces, have regained most of ISIS-held territory in Syria. Exact numbers of remaining fighters are unclear, with the US Congress estimating that there were about 14,000 in August. (A UN report published in August estimated that more than 20,000 ISIS fighters remained in Syria and Iraq.) The group's small pockets of territory are now largely confined to eastern areas of Deir ez-Zor province. In light of significant territorial losses, ISIS's strategy in 2018 has largely been based on survival. However, it continues to mount an effective and violent underground insurgency.

Israel

Reportedly involved in the conflict since 2012, Israel confirmed only in 2017 that the Israel Defense Forces (IDF) had carried out attacks against the Syrian regime and its allies Hizbullah, the Iranian forces and Shia militias. Throughout 2018, Israel continued to conduct airstrikes against the regime, Hizbullah and Iranian-linked positions, weapons-storage and other military sites, and convoys, aiming to reduce the Iranian presence in Syria.

Drivers

Persecution under Assad regime

The underlying cause of the conflict lies in the deeply rooted opposition to the Assad regime in Syria, due to widespread human-rights abuses and entrenched economic and social inequalities. Human-rights abuses were reported in the country long before the outbreak of conflict, including unlawful detentions and torture, mainly of individuals opposing the Assad regime, as well as violent repression of ethnic minorities and un-investigated deaths of individuals held in custody. Protests against harsh regimes and inequalities occurred in many of the region's countries during the Arab Spring in 2011. In Syria, protests were violently repressed, with many civilians imprisoned, tortured and killed, despite the protests' peaceful nature. The harsh regime crackdown fuelled further opposition and the eventual military organisation and response by the opposition.

Rise of ISIS

The rise of ISIS in 2014 further complicated the dynamic of the conflict in Syria. Facilitated by the ongoing conflict, as well as its own size and capabilities, ISIS quickly took control of vast swathes of the country, imposing a brutal Islamist regime on the population under its control, torturing and killing thousands of civilians that opposed or disobeyed it. ISIS's extensive propaganda further fuelled violence by calling for thousands of foreign fighters to travel to Syria to fight for a global caliphate. By seizing key oil reserves, ISIS not only amassed significant revenues, but also severely impacted the Syrian economy. Likewise, by taking control of military bases and appropriating the weapons and supplies of other groups, the group rapidly gained a strategic foothold in many areas of the country. The group's insurgent origins have allowed it to continue to launch violent attacks across Syria, even after the loss of most of its territory.

Geopolitical influences and rivalries

Since the outbreak of war Syria has witnessed the involvement of many regional and international actors seeking to influence the course of the conflict and assert their presence and influence in the region. Russia, Turkey, Iran, Israel and the US have been the main countries involved on the ground, through the direct deployment of their armed forces, while Gulf states including Qatar and Saudi Arabia, have indirectly fuelled the conflict through military and economic support for Syrian proxies or a combination of both.

The aims of each country involved in the war are diverse, reflecting the wide range of strategic agendas, domestic pressures and historical ties. Given its commitments in Afghanistan and Iraq, as well as domestic pressure to avoid another protracted involvement in the Middle East, the US attempted to limit its on-the-ground role in Syria and to fighting ISIS as part of its regional counter-terrorism strategy. However, its alliance with the mainly Kurdish SDF, as well as its initial funding of moderate opposition groups, has demonstrated the multifaceted nature of its involvement.

Russia, a long-standing ally of the regime, supports Assad as part of its wider strategy to establish a permanent influence in the region. Israeli aversion to Iran's involvement in Syria also continued to drive violence, with the country conducting strikes on Hizbullah and Iranian-linked sites in attempts to weaken the Iranian presence. Israel's diplomatic relations with Russia prevented Russia's interference with Israeli actions. Russia reportedly assured Israel that Iranian militias would not be deployed to southern border areas following regime territorial gains.

Turkey's involvement in Syria is rooted in its long-standing campaign against the Kurdish ethnic minority in Turkey and desire to secure the Turkey–Syria border to prevent the migration of fighters into Turkey. Its offensives against the Kurdish YPG are mostly due to fears of links between the YPG and the Kurdistan Workers' Party (PKK), a Turkish group proscribed as a terrorist organisation by Turkey and the US, among others.

Iran's involvement stems from its aims to ensure the survival of the Ba'athist Assad regime, as well as to create a 'land bridge' from Iran to Lebanon. The country's Shia forces also seek to combat the largely Sunni opposition in Syria.

This patchwork of actors has led to both a complex battlefield and rising international tensions as the strategies and agendas of different states come into opposition.

Political and Military Developments

Ceasefires and demilitarisation

Two parallel tracks of peace talks continued in 2018, with the Astana process, sponsored by Russia, Turkey and Iran, again overshadowing United Nations-led talks. In growing moves to control the peace process, Russia also hosted two rounds of talks in Sochi.

In January, UN talks in Vienna were attended by regime and opposition delegations, but failed to produce a comprehensive ceasefire to address growing violence in Eastern Ghouta. The Russian-led Syrian Congress of National Dialogue in Sochi, held at the end of January, also failed to make any major breakthroughs. The only notable development from the congress was an agreement to establish a committee to draft a new constitution with UN involvement, although progress remained slow in 2018. Around 1,500 delegates attended, mainly representatives of the regime, allied groups and regime-tolerated opposition factions. The anti-regime Syrian Negotiations Commission (SNC) voted not to attend the congress, which was also boycotted by YPG-linked Kurdish groups due to Turkey's co-sponsorship of the event.

Despite the intensity of the Eastern Ghouta offensive, ceasefire attempts were continuously postponed, due to sharp disagreements at the UN Security Council. On February 24, a 30-day ceasefire was unanimously passed, but did not include operations against ISIS or 'terrorist groups'. It was almost instantly broken, with the violations receiving widespread international condemnation. Further rounds of Astana process talks were held in March and May, although with little discernible progress, as was the case with trilateral talks between Russian, Turkish and Iranian officials in April.

In light of indications that the regime was planning a full-scale offensive in Idlib province, in September, Turkish officials held talks with Russia and Iran. On 17 September, a deal was announced between Turkey and Russia to create a 15–20 kilometre 'demilitarised zone' in Idlib province, designed to avoid a full-scale offensive in the area. While a reduction of violence was reported, shelling and clashes continued, while regime statements indicated that the zone merely postponed the intended offensive.

Chemical attacks

The regime's suspected chemical-weapon attack on Douma in Eastern Ghouta on 7 April – which reports estimated to have caused 40–80 casualties and more than 500 injured – caused further strain on US–Russian relations. In response, the US, France and UK launched more than 100 missiles at three sites associated with chemical-weapons production and storage (a scientific-research centre and storage facility and command post near Damascus, and a chemical-weapons storage facility in Homs). The Pentagon later announced that the Syrian regime still had the capacity to carry out chemical attacks, but its capacity had been reduced. In November, the regime accused rebel groups of launching a chemical attack in Aleppo city – allegations that were denied. The regime has previously made such allegations before conducting chemical-weapon attacks.

Rojava region seeks autonomy

The Democratic Federation of Northern Syria, known as Rojava (comprising the areas of north and northeast Syria under Kurdish control), sought to solidify its de facto autonomy in late 2018 against a backdrop of doubts regarding continued US support. On 27 July, a delegation from the Syrian Democratic Council (SDC), the SDF's political wing, travelled to Damascus for talks with regime officials. A statement from the SDC said that the regime had agreed to create a road map for eventual negotiations regarding a 'decentralised democratic Syrian state'. A second round of talks on 14 August reportedly discussed issues of local administration and decentralisation. However, in September a regime minister commented that Kurdish areas would not be given special autonomy in a future peace agreement. Assad echoed such sentiments, saying he would use force to take control of Kurdish-held areas if negotiations were unsuccessful.

Withdrawal of Western support

In May, the US withdrew assistance to rebel forces in northwest Syria, shifting its focus to security and reconstruction in areas taken from ISIS by the SDF. Cuts did not affect humanitarian assistance, but rather projects supporting independent media, policing and education initiatives. Similar withdrawals occurred in August and September, by the

US, UK and Israel. On 17 August, the US said that it would redirect US$200 million of funding originally intended for stabilisation efforts in SDF-held areas in northeastern Syria. The administration reasoned that other coalition partners, including Saudi Arabia, had pledged around US$300m for such projects. The UK Department for International Development (DFID) also announced financial withdrawals, saying that it would end a number of aid schemes in opposition-held areas, citing increasing difficulties in the implementation of non-humanitarian programmes. DFID also ceased funding of the Syrian Free Police, an opposition force of around 3,000 mostly unarmed officers. In September, due to regime territorial gains in southern Syria, Israel ceased its humanitarian assistance to Syrian civilians in the Israeli-occupied Golan Heights, where around 12,000 civilians in Israeli hospitals and a field hospital in the Golan Heights, the country had reportedly treated.

In an unexpected move, President Trump announced on 19 December that ISIS had been defeated in Syria and that subsequently US troops would be withdrawn from the country. The SDF and Western states criticised the move and rejected the idea that ISIS had been defeated, while US Secretary of Defense Minister James Mattis and US special envoy to the anti-ISIS coalition Brett McGurk separately announced their resignations. Russia and Turkey praised the withdrawal, however, with Turkish President Recep Tayyip Erdogan announcing Turkey would prevent a power vacuum in Syria following the withdrawal. The SDF attempted to find reassurances by engaging in talks with French officials, as well as agreeing for regime troops to be deployed to the outskirts of Manbij for assistance in the event of a Turkish offensive.

Downing of Russian plane strains Russia–Israel relations

Relations between Russia and Israel worsened following an incident in September when Syrian air defences mistakenly shot down a Russian reconnaissance plane off the Syrian coast, killing all 15 on board. Due to Israel having conducted airstrikes in Latakia province shortly before, both Russia and Syria blamed Israel for the incident, with Russian officials threatening retaliations. While Putin later alleviated tensions, the incident highlighted the precariousness of the countries' relationship.

Violent Events

Launch of Operation Olive Branch

On 14 January, Turkey launched *Operation Olive Branch* against the YPG in the Afrin region, deploying thousands of Turkish-backed FSA fighters to the region. The regime strongly condemned the Turkish incursion, and on 20–22 February pro-regime fighters entered the Afrin region and deployed to the front-lines. To counter the Turkish advance, the SDF redeployed more than 1,700 fighters from anti-ISIS operations in Deir ez-Zor province to Afrin, but on 24 March Turkish security forces had full control of the Afrin region.

Regime takes control of Eastern Ghouta

Fighting intensified in the Damascus suburb of Eastern Ghouta between January and April 2018. More than 200 casualties were reported in the first four days of February in Irbin, Douma and Harasta, while more than 260 rockets were launched by regime and allied forces on 18 February alone. The regime was also accused of launching a chlorine-gas attack in Douma on 1 February and another in Shayfouniya on 25 February. Despite a UN resolution calling for 30-day ceasefire on 24 February and Putin's request for daily 'humanitarian pauses', regime airstrikes and shelling continued (while Russia accused rebel groups of shelling civilians attempting to leave the area).

In March, the regime made substantial territorial gains, leading to a wave of surrenders and evacuation deals, causing mass displacement. By mid-March, Douma was the last main rebel-held area. On 7 April, the regime launched another chlorine-gas attack in Douma, killing 40–80 civilians. The powerful rebel group Jaysh al-Islam was forced to surrender and more than 40,000 fighters and civilians evacuated from Douma to Jarablus. On 12 April, the Russian Ministry of Defence announced that the regime had taken full control of Eastern Ghouta.

Eastern Qalamoun and Southern Damascus

Following the fall of Eastern Ghouta, the regime focused on the remaining rebel-held areas in and around Damascus. Heavy fighting in Eastern Qalamoun resulted in 8,500 civilians and Jaysh al-Islam fighters agreeing on 19–20 April to be evacuated from Dumayr, Jayrud, Nasriya and Ruhayba.

In the southern areas of Damascus under the control of ISIS and HTS, heavy shelling and fighting were reported daily from 19 April to 19 May. On 3 May, the regime agreed an evacuation deal with HTS that saw 5,000 HTS fighters and civilians evacuated from Babila, Beit Sahem and Yalda, east of the Yarmouk camp, to Idlib province, while a ceasefire between the regime and ISIS resulted in further evacuations. By 21 May, the regime was in control of all areas in and around Damascus.

Southwestern Syria

Since July 2017, the regime and allied forces had largely adhered to the de-escalation zone brokered by the US, Russia and Jordan in the southwestern provinces of Daraa, Quneitra and Suweida. However, regime airstrikes reported on 12 and 13 March in areas of Daraa province, signalled an impending offensive. US officials pledged that the US would take action against an escalation of the violence in the region, but such promises proved to be empty. The US government communicated to FSA rebels on 24 June that they should not expect any assistance or intervention.

On 15 June, heavy shelling, rocket strikes and ground offensives began, and the first Russian airstrikes in the region in over a year were reported on 23 June. By late June, regime forces had begun to encircle the city and captured Busr al-Harir and Mlehat al-Atash, splitting the remaining rebel-held territory in Daraa province.

The culmination of the offensive saw the FSA-affiliated Southern Front, which had been in control of much of southwestern Syria, particularly Daraa province, for over three years, either agreeing to surrender deals or evacuated to Idlib province. The regime flag was raised in Quneitra city on 26 July, with remaining rebel-held areas reduced to small amounts of territory held by ISIS-affiliated Jaysh Khalid Ibn al-Walid.

Northwestern Syria

Fighting occurred across northwestern Syria throughout 2018, both between regime and rebel forces and among rebel groups. Violence took the form of assassinations, improvised explosive device (IED) and vehicle-borne IED (VBIED) explosions, and shelling. On 3 February, a rebel group shot down a Russian jet, killing the pilot, the first such incident since Russian intervention began in 2015. In response, Russia briefly escalated airstrikes in Idlib province, with 68 reported on 4 February alone. Apart from January, regime attacks on the region were less frequent and intense throughout most of the first half of 2018, than in southern Syria.

In August, there were indications of an impending offensive in the northwest as regime forces dropped leaflets over Binnish, Kefraya and Taftanaz and fortified positions in Latakia, Hama and Idlib provinces. Russia mobilised its largest military deployment to the Mediterranean since its intervention began in 2015. Ahrah al-Sham, Nour al-Din al Zinki and a number of other rebel groups formed a coalition – the Syrian Liberation Front – that also became part of the wider Turkish-backed FSA-affiliated National Liberation Front (NLF). Regime airstrikes and shelling followed in September before Russia and Turkey announced a 'demilitarised zone' in northwest Syria on 17 September that mandated the withdrawal of all 'radical fighters' (i.e., jihadist groups), and the removal of all heavy weaponry, from a 15–20 km area by 15 October.

The NLF accepted the deal and withdrew weaponry from the area by the specified date. However, HTS and other jihadist groups did not withdraw, raising doubts as to the future of the agreement. Similarly, shelling from regime and allied forces, as well as rebel groups, was regularly reported, while regime officials continued to state that the area would eventually be under the control of the regime.

ISIS offensives

Operations to take control of remaining ISIS-held territory continued throughout 2018 in separate offensives from regime and allied forces, and from the SDF and the US-led CJTF–OIR. Iraqi forces also conducted a number of strikes against the group throughout the year in Deir ez-Zor province.

Regime operations against ISIS primarily occurred in Deir ez-Zor, Suweida and Rif Damashq provinces. On 12 August, regime forces announced they had taken control of all ISIS-held areas in Suweida province, with only small pockets of fighters remaining. By 17 November the regime controlled the Tulul al-Safa area between Rif Damashq and Suweida provinces after heavy fighting.

Anti-ISIS offensives from the SDF were mainly focused on eastern areas of Hasakah and Deir ez-Zor provinces. In June, the SDF took control of Dshisha, Hasakah province, and announced that ISIS no longer held significant territory in the province. On 10 September, the SDF launched an offensive on Hajin, Deir ez-Zor province, the last major ISIS stronghold in the country and took control of the city on 14 December.

Attacks from ISIS throughout the year highlighted its continued ability to launch attacks and affect the country's stability despite its loss of territory. On 25 July, the group carried out a spate of coordinated attacks in Suweida province that killed more than 250 people.

Impact

Humanitarian implications

While battlefront fighting and civilian casualties reduced later in the year, offensives in 2018 had enormous effects on Syria's human security situation. Levels of displacement reached new highs, with a total of 6.2m people in Syria internally displaced as of October 2018,[3] and the UN High Commissioner for Refugees (UNHCR) recording more than 1m displacements between October 2017 and October 2018. Severe shortages of medical supplies and aid exacerbated the situation, with civilians still subject to indiscriminate attacks and an estimated 12m–13m people in need of humanitarian assistance as of October 2018.[4]

The regime offensive in Eastern Ghouta was one of the most violent of the conflict, with more than 1,600 civilian casualties, numerous reports of banned munitions use and chemical attacks, and severe shortages of food and medical supplies. The intense violence and evacuation deals caused mass displacement, with estimates of 130,000–150,000 displaced through the offensive.[5] Offensives in April and May in other areas of Damascus and Rif Damashq province again saw fatalities and caused the displacement of around 9,000. The regime offensive in June and July in Daraa, Quneitra and Suweida provinces had similar consequences, with the UNHCR reporting the displacement of 300,000 people.

Violence from other forces also had severe humanitarian consequences. Turkey's offensive to take the Afrin region led to the reported deaths of more than 200 and the displacement of more than 137,000. Substantial gains at the expense of ISIS by the regime and allied forces in Rif Damashq, Suweida and Deir ez-Zor provinces and by the SDF and CJTF–OIR in Deir ez-Zor province caused further displacement, more than 500 civilian casualties due to US-led coalition airstrikes.[6] Civilians also continued to be vulnerable to ISIS attacks, with a number of suicide bombings and gun attacks conducted by the group killing more than 250 people in Suweida province in July.

Many of those displaced throughout 2018 fled to northwestern Syria, placing further strain on the worsening humanitarian situation in the region, which itself was facing violence throughout the year. As of December 2018, there were an estimated 3m people in Idlib province and nearby areas, half of whom had been displaced previously, some as many as nine times. Levels of and access to clean water, working medical facilities and food were also very low, highlighting the dangers that civilians will face in the event of a full-scale offensive in the region.

Aid deliveries have been scarce, with many Syrians suffering from a severe shortage of food and medical supplies, including in regime-held areas. Civilians have also become vulnerable to the breaking of surrender deals and the conditions of living under an 'authoritarian peace'. Deals included stipulations protecting against arrest and conscription, but mass arrests and forced conscriptions have occurred regularly, particularly in areas of Eastern Ghouta and Daraa province. There have also been numerous reports of violence and intimidation by regime forces against the population. Civilians also remain vulnerable to unexploded landmines, particularly in former ISIS-held areas in Raqqa, Hasakah and Deir ez-Zor provinces.

Refugee returns and reconstruction

The pressure on Lebanon, Jordan and Turkey, that are hosting the highest numbers of Syrian refugees, as well as regime territorial gains, resulted in more politicians calling for refugee returns. In May, the Syrian regime announced Law 10, a new law on property rights that stipulates that residents must return to prove ownership of property in areas where redevelopment zones have been declared, otherwise the property would be seized by the regime. The law was widely criticised as many Syrians have lost documents proving ownership of their properties or are unable or unwilling to return to their homes due to security concerns. The deadline for claims was initially set at 30 days, but has since been extended to a year.

Despite statements from local activists, the UN, Western countries, officials from the regime and neighbouring countries, and Russia, stated consistently that it was safe for refugees to return to some areas of Syria. A number of returns, mainly from Lebanon, occurred throughout 2018, with an announcement in August that the regime had established a coordination committee focusing on repatriation. Turkey stated its intentions to create further 'safe zones' in the country for returnees. As of the end of September, the UNHCR reported that 28,251 refugees had returned to Syria.

Trends

Likely regime offensive in northwest Syria
While the Russia- and Turkey-brokered demilitarised zone in northwest Syria was largely holding by the end of 2018, prospects for a future regime offensive in the area in 2019 are highly likely. A full-scale offensive would have huge humanitarian implications for the estimated 3m people present in the region, while access to clean water, medical facilities, food and other basic supplies is already perilously restricted. Turkey has said that it will not accommodate more refugees, while Lebanon, Jordan and the European Union have also made similar comments.

Attacks against ISIS to continue
Offensives to take control of remaining ISIS-held areas will continue in 2019, mainly in desert areas of Homs province, while the SDF will continue to fight remaining pockets of ISIS territory in villages in Deir ez-Zor. At the end of 2018, US officials said that ISIS only held an estimated 1% of territory in Syria, but the group has shown enduring ability to launch large, violent attacks, including in areas no longer under its control. Despite its major territorial losses, the group's definitive defeat is far from certain in 2019.

Humanitarian situation will remain severe
The humanitarian situation will remain severe. Aid access in many areas captured by the regime has not improved, with widespread lack of aid and basic humanitarian supplies, damaged infrastructure and too few equipped health facilities. Humanitarian appeals for Syria remain substantially underfunded, with the 2018 Syria response plan of the UN Office for the Coordination of Humanitarian Affairs (OCHA) only 64.8% funded. Funding shortfalls will likely continue in 2019.

Reconstruction and stabilisation projects will likely increase in 2019. With around one-third of Syria's pre-war housing and infrastructure destroyed, current reconstruction costs are estimated between US$200 billion and US$350bn. Russia, China and Iran have made some reconstruction investments in the country, while European and Western states have regularly insisted that any contribution to reconstruction must run in tandem with a credible UN-led political process.

Little prospect of peace talks
Prospects for a comprehensive peace process in 2019 remain unlikely. In light of its increased territorial control, the Assad regime no longer needs to make meaningful political concessions. The Kurdish administration's indication that it is willing to strike a deal with the regime also demonstrates the regime's primacy. Similarly, the dominance of Russia, Iran and Turkey over the peace process, combined with the continued lack of progress and relevance on the part of the UN process, demonstrates the increasing inability of the UN and Western states to pressure the regime into making meaningful political change. The leverage of Western states now lies solely with the provision of funds for reconstruction.

The US troop withdrawal, announced in mid-December, will greatly affect developments in Syria. Russia, Turkey and Iran will likely vie for control of areas that the US evacuates, due to the presence of key oil and gas fields as well as fertile land and water resources, while Israel will likely face difficulties in the absence of a key ally. The withdrawal will also likely lead to further Turkish offensives on Kurdish forces, in particular the city of Manbij, with relations with the US having been a key feature in Turkish restraint to date. The SDF and regional analysts have also expressed anxiety that the withdrawal will allow ISIS to regroup and launch counter-attacks.

Notes

1 'Country Reports on Terrorism 2016', Bureau of Counterterrorism, United States Department of State, July 2017.
2 'S-300 missile system: Russia upgrades Syrian air defences', BBC News, 2 October 2018.
3 United Nations High Commissioner for Refugees (UNHCR), 'Syria Factsheet: January – October 2018', 2018.
4 UN Office for the Coordination of Humanitarian Affairs (OCHA), 'Syrian Arab Republic' portal, December 2018.
5 'After the death of about 1650 citizens in the shelling of the Russian and the regime forces on it … the Eastern Ghouta witnesses the largest organized displacement in Syria during which more than 144 thousand persons have been displaced', Syrian Observatory for Human Rights, 30 March 2018; Peter Beaumont, 'Conflict displaces almost 700,000 Syrians in deadly first months of 2018', Guardian, 10 April 2018; 'The failure of Eastern Ghouta', Pax for Peace, 25 June 2018.
6 Syrian Observatory for Human Rights, 31 December 2018.

Turkey (PKK)

Overview

The conflict in 2018

In 2018, clashes between Turkey and Kurdish units escalated considerably after Turkey launched *Operation Olive Branch* in northern Syria in January. The operation aimed to clear the Afrin district of the forces of the People's Protection Units (YPG), which is considered to be an affiliate of the Turkey-based guerrilla organisation Kurdistan Workers' Party (PKK). In Syria, Turkish armed forces fought alongside the Free Syrian Army (FSA), a group directly armed, trained and equipped by Turkey. In March, the Turkey–FSA coalition completed its objective by gaining control of the Afrin district.

In mid-2018, two new Kurdish insurgent groups, Wrath of Olives (named in response to *Operation Olive Branch*) and the Afrin Liberation Forces, began carrying out ambushes against Turkish and FSA military targets, assassinating political figures and civilians backing the Turkish occupation and launching indiscriminate bombings of FSA targets in civilian areas. Meanwhile, in Turkey, clashes between the PKK and Turkish security forces continued on a regular basis, as did the Turkish government's repression of Kurdish political movements both at the local and the national level.

The conflict to 2018

The low-intensity conflict between Turkey and the PKK – which is still formally recognised as a terrorist organisation by Turkey, the European Union and the United States – has persisted for more than three decades, ranging from ambushes against Turkish armed forces and skirmishes between the two sides to full-fledged military operations targeting the Kurdish organisation. Since the 1980s, the PKK has called for the recognition of Turkey's Kurdish minority, inspired by its imprisoned founder and leader Abdullah Ocalan's vision of separation from Turkey. The organisation then readjusted its objectives to seeking autonomy and ethnic recognition

Key statistics	
Type:	Internal
IDPs total (2018):	950,000–1,100,000
IDPs new (2018):	no data
Refugees total (2018):	65,000
Refugees new (2018):	no data
People in need (2018):	no data

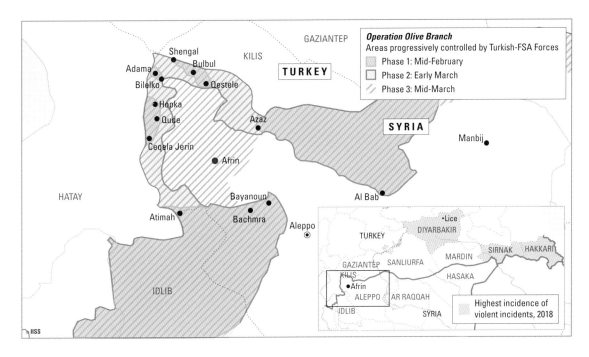

within Turkey, but the changing political situation of Kurdish minorities in Iraq and Syria has revitalised ambitions for a Kurdish national state.

Historically, clashes have taken place mainly around southeast Turkey, where most of the Turkish Kurdish minority lives, and northern Iraq, where the PKK has its main bases and training camps. In 2016, however, the conflict extended into Syrian territory, as Turkey fought against the YPG, the PKK's Syrian Kurdish affiliate, and the main fighting force of the Syrian Democratic Forces (SDF).

Forces

Turkish security forces

Turkey's objective is to eliminate the YPG (and, by extension, the SDF) from northern Syria in order to secure its southern border. This, in turn, would facilitate achieving its domestic objective of eradicating the PKK by further isolating the organisation. Turkey has deployed elements of its Second Army both in southeastern Turkey and as part of *Operation Olive Branch*, supported by Turkish Air Force squadrons, as well as units from its gendarmerie force, police special units and teams from its National Intelligence Organisation. Official figures for Turkey's deployment in southeastern Turkey are not available, and there is only scant official information on Turkish troops involved in *Operation Olive Branch*, which might number between 6,000 and 8,000. On both fronts, Turkish armed forces rely on infantry and commando units, supported by artillery units (and, in Syria, armoured units),

as well as fixed- and rotary-wing airframes, including the Turkish Army's AH-1W *SuperCobra* and T129 attack helicopters and the Turkish Air Force's F-16s. Turkish security forces are usually equipped with light weapons and armoured personnel carriers (APCs).

Free Syrian Army (FSA)

Directly armed, trained and equipped by Turkey, the Free Syrian Army (FSA) aspires to be a dominant political and military force in northern Syria (and, potentially, in Syria at large). The FSA is formed of a myriad of different armed groups – including Syrian Turkmen, Syrian Arabs and a minor component of Turkish ultranationalist units – and was formally reorganised in December 2017 around four main 'legions', built, in turn, upon several existing autonomous or semi-autonomous battalions. The FSA's total size is unknown, but estimated to be around

15,000. With the launch of *Operation Olive Branch*, between 4,000 and 5,000 FSA troops deployed between Azez and Kilis, and in the west of Afrin, equipped with light and anti-tank weapons, mortars and APCs.

Kurdistan Workers' Party (PKK)

The main objectives of the Kurdistan Workers' Party (PKK) revolve around obtaining political and legal recognition of the Kurdish minority in Turkey. With the YPG's military and political expansion in Syria, however, the long-standing objective of creating an autonomous Kurdish entity and, eventually, a Kurdish state, seem to have resurfaced. There are no reliable estimates on the size of the PKK in Turkey. While its founder and ideological leader Abdullah Ocalan has been imprisoned in solitary confinement since 1999, PKK senior field commanders based in northern Iraq's Qandil Mountains are the de facto leaders of the organisation. The PKK operates mainly by carrying out ambushes and hit-and-run attacks against Turkish patrols and military outposts, usually organised around small units. PKK units rely on light and anti-tank weapons, as well as improvised explosive devices (IEDs).

Syrian Democratic Forces (SDF)

The Syrian Democratic Forces (SDF) aims at maintaining territorial and political control of northern Syria, as it did during the advance of Islamic State, also known as ISIS or ISIL, in 2014, and during the current Turkish offensive. The SDF's commander Mazlum Kobane (formerly known as Ferhat Abdi Sahin) was previously a high-ranking member of the PKK. The strength of SDF troops is estimated between 40,000 and 80,000. While the SDF includes Syrian Kurdish, Syrian Arab and Assyrian elements, the vast majority of its units belong to the Kurdish People's Protection Units (YPG) and Women's Protection Units (YPJ). YPG forces were crucial in protecting northern Syria from the advance of ISIS and in creating the Kurdish-led Democratic Federation of Northern Syria, better known by its Kurdish name Rojava.

Despite their large size, SDF units are mostly armed with light and anti-tank weapons, and possess some APCs provided by the US. International partners (the US, France and the United Kingdom) have provided equipment, supplies, training and mentoring since the beginning of ISIS's advance in northern Syria in 2014, and some of their units are deployed alongside SDF forces in SDF-controlled territories.

Wrath of Olives

Wrath of Olives emerged as an active force in the conflict in 2018. While information is sparse, it has been established that it is an Arab-Kurdish platform sharing common goals with (but with no direct ties to) the YPG and the SDF, who have denied it being an offshoot formation of their organisations.[1] Pursuing a more aggressive and indiscriminate offensive strategy than the SDF, Wrath of Olives has been calling on the Afrin civilian population to relocate to other areas to avoid being caught up in their actions, which mainly target elements belonging to the FSA, but the group does not shy away from indiscriminate attacks or targeted assassinations against individuals cooperating with Turkish forces.

| Drivers

Turkey and Kurdish self-determination

The root cause underpinning and exacerbating the conflict between Turkey and the PKK lies in the incompatibility of their respective political goals, namely the Kurdish quest for self-determination, the PKK's pursuit of political autonomy and Turkey's opposition to the recognition of minority rights of its Kurdish population. Turkey sees any expansion of Kurdish political influence in the region as a potential threat to its own national security and, ultimately, as a threat to the unity of the country. While the PKK only represents one, albeit prominent, platform linked to the Kurdish issue, the Turkish government tends to conflate most forms of Kurdish political activism with PKK or terrorism-related activities, further compounding tensions between the two sides.

The fate of pro-Kurdish parties in Turkey is one of the most prominent examples of this dynamic. Since the 1990s, all Kurdish parties that ran for parliamentary elections have been disbanded by the Constitutional Court for alleged ties with the PKK. The People's Democratic Party (HDP, Turkey's current pro-Kurdish party) focuses on a social-democratic political agenda in which the Kurdish issue is but one of the items, rather than being its defining element. In spite of that, and despite a track record of electoral successes, its leaders and many of its MPs are currently imprisoned.

Influence of regional developments

Before the outbreak of Syria's civil war, the Kurds, who live as a divided minority across national boundaries between Turkey, Syria, Iraq and Iran, reached a breakthrough achievement towards self-determination with the constitutional recognition of the Kurdistan Regional Government (KRG) as a federal government in northern Iraq in 2005. Despite deep political divisions among Iraqi Kurds and between the Iraqi Kurdish minority and the rest of the Kurdish political world, for many Kurds this

development was still a milestone towards the creation of a Kurdish state.

The political progress of Iraqi Kurds, coupled with the turmoil caused by the ongoing US-led invasion of Iraq, also bolstered the PKK's ambitions for Kurds in Turkey, leading to a resumption of hostilities in 2010 after a five-year-long ceasefire. The PKK launched a continuous stream of attacks against Turkish forces from strongholds based in the Qandil Mountains of northern Iraq, and the Turkish security forces retaliated with operations against the PKK in both Turkey and northern Iraq. Syria's civil war (which began in 2011) and particularly the advance of ISIS in Syria between 2013 and 2014 further aggravated the Turkey–PKK conflict, opening a cross-border front in northern Syria on top of the long-established domestic front in southeastern Turkey.

Political and Military Developments

Turkey's Operation Olive Branch

Turkey's decision to intervene militarily in northern Syria with *Operation Olive Branch* stood out as the single most important development of 2018. Launched in January, the operation saw Turkish armed forces and the FSA entering Syria to obtain control of Afrin, a district within the Aleppo governorate, which, due to its geographic location and the loss of other important urban areas, had become of strategic interest for the SDF. The main combat phase of the operation lasted until March and ended with Turkish and FSA forces entering and occupying Afrin city. Turkish forces remained in control of Afrin at the end of the year, effectively depriving the SDF of one of its last remaining cities after the fall of Al Bab and Azaz during *Euphrates Shield*.

US involvement in northern Syria

Turkey and the US are effectively on opposing fronts in the Kurdish chapter of the Syrian conflict, with Washington sustaining, arming and deploying military units in support of the SDF, the organisation Turkey is attempting to eradicate. In an effort to mend bilateral relations, but also to keep an eye on each other's moves, the US and Turkey agreed in June 2018 on the so-called 'Manbij Roadmap', a document based on the common understanding

that both sides would cooperate to clear the district of Manbij of 'all terror organisations' – which in Turkey's interpretation includes the SDF.[2]

The SDF had held Manbij, a district of 400,000 inhabitants located 100 kilometres east of Afrin, since mid-2016, when the group captured it from ISIS after a US-supported two-month offensive. Although US, UK and French security forces continued to operate in and around Manbij, the US withdrawal announcement led SDF personnel to vacate the district's northwestern outskirts in mid-December 2018 and allow Syrian regime forces to enter in order to prevent a possible Turkish full-scale incursion. Russian military-police units were also seen patrolling central areas of Manbij, further increasing the international troops presence around the city, and making a Turkish military advance more difficult to launch.

The Kurdish issue in election campaigning

The campaign for June's parliamentary and presidential elections in Turkey temporarily focused the political debate on the Kurdish issue. Without moving from his nationalist position, President Recep Tayyip Erdogan attempted to stress how the 'war against the PKK' should be seen as the main obstacle to a resolution of the issue, while opposition leaders from the Republican People's Party

(CHP, Turkey's second-largest party) courted Kurdish voters (who represented approximately 10 million votes) by promising the recognition of minority rights. The political situation, however, remained deadlocked. Selahattin Demirtas and Figen Yuksekdag, two of the most prominent figures of HDP, campaigned from their prison cells where they have been detained since 2016, accused of disseminating propaganda for the PKK.

Turkey increases border security

Turkey made further progress in fortifying its southeastern border, both through the construction of a security wall along the Turkish–Iranian border and by increasing the number of operational military stations along the border with Syria. Both projects, together with the wall along the Turkish–Syrian border that was completed in 2017, were developed to hamper the movement of PKK units across the border.

Violent Events

Clashes in southeastern Turkey

In 2018, the majority of violent events on Turkish soil took place in the provinces of Diyarbakir, Hakkari and Sirnak, all located in southeastern Turkey. Claims made by the Turkish government about peace finally descending upon the provinces stood in stark contrast with fatality figures, which numbered more than 200 in 2018. The actions of the PKK and Turkish security forces followed what has become a fairly standard pattern, with the PKK launching seemingly disconnected surprise attacks and laying ambushes against Turkish patrols and military outposts, and Turkish security forces responding mainly with targeted operations and airstrikes.

Almost 200 people were killed in the provinces of Sirnak and Hakkari in 2018. The majority of these belonged to the PKK, while approximately a quarter were members of Turkish security forces. The most prominent attacks included the June airstrikes by Turkey in the Bestler-Dereler area (Uludere district) that killed seven PKK members, while in April, a PKK attack killed three soldiers and wounded one. In November, the PKK launched its first recorded attack with an uninhabited aerial vehicle (UAV) filled with explosives and nails, which however crashed without causing any casualties.

Many of the clashes between the PKK and Turkish security forces in Diyarbakir province took place in Lice, one of Diyarbakir's smallest districts, also considered the PKK's birthplace. In February, a PKK senior commander and his three bodyguards were killed during a security operation, while in April, a PKK attack killed one Turkish soldier and wounded four. In late June, in two separate actions, a Turkish soldier was killed by a rocket-propelled grenade (RPG) attack while conducting a patrol in the district, while another one was killed while returning home. Between July and August, Osman Gulen, a PKK senior figure, and four other PKK militants were killed in three separate operations. Finally, the Turkish security forces killed three more PKK members between September and December.

The battle for Afrin

Turkey's *Operation Olive Branch* began on 20 January 2018 with two days of artillery and mortar fire and airstrikes against SDF positions in and around Afrin city and the broader district. During the operation's first week, Turkey and the FSA took control of a few villages in the outskirts of the Afrin district, but Kurdish units either successfully defended or quickly recaptured several key objectives. The FSA also lost Ahmad Fayyadh Al-Khalaf, commander of its Samarkand Brigade. The capture of Mount Barsaya at the end of January brought Turkey its first operational breakthrough after a week of fighting and led it to control all routes and movements between Afrin and FSA-controlled Azaz.

In early March, the capture of Rajo, a town located in the northwestern part of Afrin district, brought a second, important breakthrough for Turkish and FSA troops; once a major SDF stronghold, the town capitulated in a few days as SDF units withdrew to defend Afrin city. Meantime, Turkish forces were manoeuvring to encircle Afrin, which by mid-March was effectively surrounded. The fight led to the death, among others, of a second high-ranking FSA figure, Waed al-Mousa, commander of FSA's First Legion. Turkish forces had, however, effectively captured Afrin by 18 March.

After the fall of Afrin

With Turkish forces firmly in control of Afrin, SDF leaders pledged to continue fighting in Afrin and elsewhere with irregular tactics. Among countless clashes, a series of SDF operations launched in July led to the deaths of nine Turkish soldiers and three FSA members, while another major attack in late August killed a commander of the FSA's al-Sham Division and 19 of its members. At the same time, a new organisation called Wrath of Olives emerged in Afrin. The group officially announced its formation in August after killing a senior figure of FSA's Levant Front in June and three civilians accused of collaborating with Turkey. In its announcement, the group warned Afrin's population to distance itself from Turkish and FSA units and installations, as these would be targeted.[3] Over the following months, Wrath of Olives conducted various attacks, including an ambush that led to the killing of a commander of FSA's Sultan Murad Division and an improvised explosive device (IED) attack that left three Turkish soldiers and two FSA members dead. The group has also been eager to publicise its action by publishing videos in which it executed prisoners accused of treason, and claimed responsibility for the bombing of a marketplace in Afrin in December, in which nine people were killed and dozens were wounded.

Impact

Humanitarian impact
According to the United Nations, the operation in Afrin has led to the displacement of more than 100,000 civilians, while dozens were killed. In June, the UN Office for the Coordination of Humanitarian Affairs (OCHA) reported the presence of explosive remnants of war (ERW) around Afrin as well as the destruction of key infrastructure, the lack of access to health services for the local population and the disruption of commercial supply lines into Afrin.[4]

From a political perspective, Turkey's operation has seriously hindered the SDF's ambitions to carve out a secure living space in northern Syria for the Kurds and other ethnic groups. As the last pockets of ISIS resistance fell, the SDF now firmly controls northern Syria's territory east of the Euphrates, while the western areas of the country, along the border with Turkey, remain under Turkish/FSA control. As areas formerly under ISIS control are liberated, approximately 50,000 of the 80,000 internally displaced persons (IDPs) estimated to have left Raqqa, Deir ez-Zor and Al-Hasakeh have begun returning to their areas of origin.[5]

Trends

Tensions with Assad regime
With the support of Turkey, the FSA progressively expanded its clout in northern Syria in 2018. As it gains more ground, the organisation clashes not only with SDF's interests, but also with those of the Assad regime, which is wary of Turkey's agenda for the future of Syria, and is involving itself more directly in the Turkey–SDF fight. During the siege of Afrin, troops belonging to the Syrian regime tried and failed to reach the city in an attempt to deter Turkey from capturing it. The interposition of forces from the Syrian regime between Turkey/FSA and SDF units might become a recurrent, if risky, strategy.

From the Syrian regime's perspective, Turkey's advance in northern Syria, left unchecked, could significantly empower the FSA (and, by extension, Turkey itself), from both a military and a political perspective – something Western powers are also wary of. Given the extremist ideologies that move many of the FSA sub-groups, NATO countries (other than Turkey) involved in Syria have so far been firm in their support for the SDF. As news of the US decision to withdraw its troops emerged in mid-December, the French Ministry of Defence released a statement stressing its role alongside the SDF would not change, while French patrols around Manbij continued.

Fighting may expand to Manbij
The increasing presence of non-SDF units in the Manbij area (including French and Russian patrols) made it more complicated for Turkey to launch an offensive on the city in 2018. As a consequence, what

Erdogan declared in mid-December was an operation due to be launched 'in a matter of days' had to be postponed.

Turkey's ultimate objectives remain the control of northern Syria and the elimination of SDF's military and political presence, making a new eastward offensive in Syria inevitable. Erdogan refused to meet with US National Security Advisor John Bolton to discuss the matter and rejected requests for reassurances that Turkey would not attack SDF forces after US troops leave Syria.

With Afrin under control, both commanders within the FSA and, more recently and tellingly,

Turkish officials, including Erdogan, have made comments that suggest a new, eastbound Turkish offensive towards the districts of Manbij and Kobane may be launched early in 2019. This would allow Turkish forces to clear two of the remaining SDF strongholds in the region, paving the way for the FSA to be fully in control of the area. By the end of the year, the FSA was reported to have several divisions on standby, preparing for military operations in Manbij. Should fighting reach Manbij, a city of 100,000 people, the number of IDPs will increase significantly.

Notes

[1]   Wladimir van Wilgenburg, 'YPG rejects involvement in attacks by mysterious groups in Afrin', *Kurdistan 24*, 22 August 2018.

[2]   Tuvan Gumrukcu and Ece Toksabay, 'Turkey, U.S. agree roadmap to avert crisis in Syria's Manbij, few details', Reuters, 4 June 2018.

[3]   Wladimir van Wilgenburg, 'Mysterious armed group warns

Afrin residents of "new battle"', *Kurdistan 24*, 16 August 2018.

[4]   'Syrian Arab Republic: Humanitarian situation update in Afrin District and for IDPs in surrounding communities (as of 15 June 2018)', United Nations Office for the Coordination of Humanitarian Affairs (OCHA), June 2018.

[5]   'IDPs Tracking', Humanitarian Response portal, OCHA.

Yemen

Overview

The conflict in 2018

Efforts to find a military solution to the Yemen conflict continued in 2018. After initial progress, the renewed advance of the Saudi-led coalition and the Popular Resistance Forces (PRS) on Hudaydah city came to a halt in June 2018, and the front-lines running approximately along the border of the two former Yemeni states barely moved. Airstrikes by the Saudi-led coalition on Sa'dah and Hudaydah and the capital Sana'a intensified in early November after the US government called for the resumption of peace talks, then decreased in mid-November.

After a failed attempt in September, the United Nations Special Envoy Martin Griffiths (appointed on 16 February 2018) brought together representatives of the internationally recognised government (led by President Abd Rabbo Mansour Hadi) and Ansar Allah (led by the al-Houthi family) to the negotiating table in December. The representatives

agreed to a ceasefire for three ports including Hudaydah, to exchange 15,000 prisoners and to a statement of understanding for Ta'izz to improve the humanitarian situation. No consensus was reached on the reopening of Sana'a airport and the reconstitution of the Central Bank of Yemen (CBY).[1] The UN Security Council unanimously backed these agreements with Resolution 2451 on 21 December.

Key statistics	
Type:	Internationalised
IDPs total (2018):	2,300,000
IDPs new (2018):	no data
Refugees total (2018):	28,000
Refugees new (2018):	no data
People in need (2018):	24,000,000

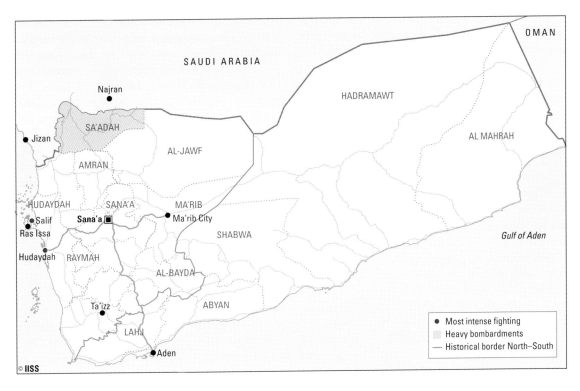

While the United Arab Emirates increased its political influence and military control in Aden and most of the other southeastern coastal governorates in 2018, Saudi Arabia focused on Mahrah governorate, ostensibly to stop arms smuggling. Despite US and UK military advice on targeting, Saudi-led coalition airstrikes continued to hit civilians and seemed to violate end-user agreements, increasing the international public scrutiny of Western governments' arms sales to the Saudi-led coalition.[2] Several European countries took steps to halt arms sales to coalition members, and in December the US Senate passed a resolution calling for an end to US military support for the coalition.

The humanitarian situation in Yemen remained catastrophic, with the majority of the population of 28 million Yemenis in need of humanitarian assistance at the end of 2018.

The conflict to 2018

Yemen's history as a unified state with a central government is relatively short. The two predecessors of the Republic of Yemen only emerged in the 1960s: the Yemen Arab Republic (YAR/North Yemen) in 1962 and the People's Democratic Republic of Yemen (PDRY/South Yemen) in 1967, succeeding the Mutawakkilite Kingdom and British-controlled territories (including the Colony of Aden) respectively. The two Yemeni states were integrated in 1990, but the process was left incomplete, and failed attempts at democratic transformation in the 1990s and 2010s produced many political grievances.

In November 2011, domestic protests and international pressure forced long-term president Ali Abdullah Saleh to abdicate in favour of his vice-president Hadi. Saleh was granted immunity and kept his position as chairman of the General People's Congress (GPC) and his relatives retained control of important parts of the security forces. The Gulf Cooperation Council (GCC) Initiative and its Implementation Agreement of 2011 organised the transfer of power from Saleh to Hadi and called for a National Dialogue Conference (NDC), which convened from March 2013 to January 2014. The NDC laid the groundwork for a democratic and federal Republic of Yemen, but did not reach consensus over the demarcation of the federal states and political violence continued throughout the process. When Hadi ignored NDC recommendations (such as those concerning membership of the Constitution Drafting Committee), repeatedly violated the law in appointing senior civil servants and finally lifted fuel subsidies (as demanded by the International Monetary Fund) without improving social safety nets, the Houthi-led Ansar Allah rebels seized the opportunity. The group called for demonstrations and brought its militias to Sana'a in summer 2014 to 'protect' government institutions. In 2015, it became public that Ansar Allah had also forged an alliance with the ex-president Saleh, their former adversary whom they had fought between 2004 and 2010.

Ansar Allah signed a UN-brokered agreement with the government in September 2014 but kept control of the capital and seized the port city of Hudaydah in October. In early 2015, Hadi went ahead with the constitutional draft, including the controversial division of the country into six federal states. Ansar Allah reacted by abducting the president's chief of staff and laying siege to the presidential palace. Hadi resigned but escaped to Aden to revoke his resignation. When Ansar Allah militias took Ta'izz and Aden, Hadi fled to Saudi Arabia.

On 26 March 2015, a Saudi-led coalition launched *Operation Decisive Storm*, which aimed to reinstall Hadi quickly. UN Security Council Resolution 2216 retroactively provided international backing on 14 April 2015. When the rebels did not surrender as easily as expected, the Saudi-led coalition relabelled the military intervention *Operation Restoring Hope* on 22 April 2015.

Both Saudi-led coalition operations relied heavily on airstrikes and land, aerial and maritime blockades, with devastating consequences for the population. The Saudi-led coalition destroyed the Yemeni air force and retook sparsely populated southern Yemen from Ansar Allah in summer 2015. However, the majority of the population remains under the control of Ansar Allah, while Hadi is still in exile in Riyadh.

On 6 June 2015, Ansar Allah began to retaliate by launching their first missile attack on Saudi border areas. In 2016, the group attacked UAE and US vessels in the Red Sea, and by 2017, the first of Ansar Allah's missiles was intercepted over the Saudi capital Riyadh – in total, Ansar Allah is said to have launched around 200 missiles to Saudi Arabia between June 2015 and August 2018.[3]

Saleh tried to regain power for his family by using Ansar Allah and military units still loyal to him, but the alliance broke down when Saleh shifted towards the Saudi-led coalition in late 2017. He was killed during clashes in Sana'a on 4 December 2017. Ansar Allah proceeded to dismantle the GPC, executing its military commanders, imprisoning its political leaders, threatening prominent individuals and suppressing opposition. Saleh's death in 2017 and the final collapse of the Saleh–Houthi alliance have cost Ansar Allah access to important financial and military resources, however, and driven important troops and commanders who were loyal to Saleh to change sides.

Forces

Saudi-led coalition

The Saudi-led coalition originally comprised all GCC states except Oman: Saudi Arabia, the UAE, Kuwait, Bahrain and Qatar (until 2017) as well as Jordan, Egypt, Morocco and Sudan. Pakistan was expected to join but declined, while Senegal announced in 2015 that it would send troops but backtracked due to domestic opposition.

Saudi Arabia and the UAE, led by the crown princes Muhammad bin Salman and Muhammad bin Zayed Al Nahyan respectively, are the two leading forces within the Saudi-led coalition. The coalition is dominated militarily and financially by Saudi Arabia, which is the largest contributor, providing 100 fighter jets. The UAE, the second-largest contributor, has provided around 30 fighter jets, but has also led operations on the ground in Yemen with Emirati special forces, military advisers and military trainers playing a major role. The UAE also contracted mercenaries and military companies such as Acadimi (the successor of Blackwater) for ground fights and assassinations. Sudan has provided ground forces (Sudanese Rapid Support Forces) while Egypt has sent warships.

US and UK experts advise the Saudi-led coalition command. The United States is the main supplier of arms to Saudi Arabia, provides military training and until November 2018 also carried out mid-air refuelling of aircrafts.

Saudi Arabia and UAE thus have sophisticated weapons, including the F-15, F-16E/F, *Typhoon* and *Mirage* 2000-9 fighter jets and *Patriot* PAC-2 and -3 surface-to-air missile systems. Saudi Arabia is in the process of acquiring the Terminal High-Altitude

Area Defense (THAAD) missile system (worth US$15 billion), which the UAE already possesses. Saudi Arabia has admitted that it has used cluster bombs, and there are unconfirmed reports that it has used white phosphorus.

Although there are differences within the coalition, the overarching goals for Saudi Arabia and the UAE are to force the Houthis into a political settlement of the Gulf states' choice, to secure the Saudi–Yemeni border, to eliminate Iranian influence in the country and to influence or control Yemeni infrastructure (especially ports and pipelines).

The UAE is establishing an overarching political and security structure in the southern governorates, with Security Belt Forces in Aden, Lahj and Abyan governorates as well as Elite Forces in the governorates of Shabwah, Hadhramaut and more recently Mahrah. As part of this process, the UAE claims to have trained and equipped approximately 60,000 Yemenis to fight al-Qaeda in the Arabian Peninsula (AQAP), the Islamic State–Yemen (ISIS–Y) and Ansar Allah. To secure its dominance, the UAE complements these paramilitary forces with arrests (18 UAE-run prisons were discovered in 2017), the targeted killings of Islahis and support for those parts of the Southern Movement that seek the independence of South Yemen.[4]

Ansar Allah (Houthis, Shabab al-Muminin)

Ansar Allah developed into the dominant political and military force in the northwest after 2011, leveraging popular demands for revenge and compensation as well as more inclusive and transparent governance. Ansar Allah opposes Saudi-supported Wahhabi-Salafi proselytism, the Islah party, AQAP – which Ansar Allah considers a US invention – and US interventions. The group is currently led by Abdulmalik al-Houthi and is also known as the Houthis, from the name of the al-Houthi family at its helm. The family adheres to the Zaidi branch of the Shia and claims descent from the son-in-law of Muslim prophet Muhammad.

The Houthis' mix of religious and Arabnationalist ideology (also tapping into the YAR's national-identity narrative) and their demands for transparency and inclusion initially appealed to many in Yemen, including those from the mainly non-Zaidi majority (Shafi'i Sunni) in Ta'izz and Hudaydah. Until its alliance with Saleh became public, Ansar Allah also benefited from never having been part of Saleh's corrupt regime.

Ansar Allah's slogan 'Allah Is Great, Death to America, Death to Israel, Curse on the Jews, Victory to Islam' began to appear in many parts of the country after 2011. These slogans, reminiscent of the Iranian Revolution – together with Ansar Allah's animosity towards Saudi Arabia – explain why the Iranian leadership and media frequently express their support for the group.[5] Since 2015, Iran seems to have moved from political advice (not necessarily adopted by Ansar Allah) and 'moral support' to supplying military advisers and equipment, such as uninhabited aerial vehicles (UAVs) and missile parts (which are smuggled into Yemen and reassembled into missiles).

To achieve its aims, Ansar Allah utilises a short-term tactical approach rather than a long-term strategic view. They use civil–political means (such as participating in the NDC, organising demonstrations, forging tactical alliances and carrying out provocations) as well as military means (expelling the Salafis from their centre in Dammaj, fighting tribal militias in Amran, invading the capital and large parts of Yemen in 2014 and launching missile attacks on Saudi territory) in order to secure immediate gains. They have a record of violating agreements whenever they detect a quick-win situation.

After looting military equipment between 2004 and 2010, Ansar Allah have subsequently gained access to more sophisticated weapons (including missile systems) from government forces since 2014. Iranian support is obvious but indirect, most likely via associates of the Islamic Revolutionary Guard Corps (IRGC), and very limited compared to the expenses of the Saudi-led coalition. The Iranian leadership has repeatedly denied any involvement in the conflict and has offered its support to negotiations.

By 2018, the arsenal of Ansar Allah comprised missiles of Soviet, North Korean, Chinese and Iranian origin, some of them originating from the 1990s, some of them of more recent production.[6] Ansar Allah also make use of UAVs, as well as planting land and naval mines, using snipers and shelling in residential areas.

Popular Resistance Forces

The Popular Resistance Forces comprises an estimated 100,000 fighters and is a conglomerate of Yemeni army units supportive of President Hadi, various militias (such as the Elite Forces, Security Belt

Forces, Islah militias) and, since 2018, the National Resistance Forces. The latter were set up in spring 2018 to fight Ansar Allah after the alliance between Ansar Allah and Saleh ended with Saleh's death. They comprise 3,000–10,000 former members of the Republican Guard (until 2012 under the command of Saleh's son Ahmed) and the Central Security Forces (until 2012 under the command of Saleh's nephew Yahya). Both forces received training and equipment from the US during Saleh's presidency. The National Resistance Forces fought alongside the Saudi-led coalition in 2018 in *Operation Golden Spear* under the command of Tariq Muhammad Saleh, a former leader of the Presidential Guard and nephew of Saleh.

Popular Resistance fighters receive salaries, operational support and equipment (including vehicles, artillery, communications equipment and minesweeping equipment) from the Hadi government and the Saudi-led coalition. However, what unites the Popular Resistance is their fight against Ansar Allah and/or Sunni militants, not loyalty to President Hadi.

Yemeni Congregation for Reform (Islah)

The Yemeni Congregation for Reform (Islah) is a political party founded after the unification of YAR and PDRY in 1990. It is a heterogeneous organisation which brings together many actors including the Muslim Brotherhood, Salafis, conservatives and tribal leaders, some of which have received (and continue to receive) external support (e.g., from Saudi Arabia and Qatar), or even reside in Saudi Arabia. Parts of the Islah party are also well connected to Vice-President General Ali Mohsen al-Ahmar, who led the wars against Ansar Allah prior to 2011 and who has close links to Sunni militants. Due to the strong representation of tribal leaders, the Islah party can mobilise armed tribesmen, especially in the north where its tribal militias fought Ansar Allah in the 2000s.

In spite of the UAE and Saudi Arabia listing the Muslim Brotherhood as a terrorist organisation, Saudi Arabia retains good relations with the Islah party, which is in control of Marib governorate, has a strong position in Ta'izz and officially supports Hadi. By contrast, the UAE ordered the murder of Islah politicians, hindering Saudi efforts at rapprochement between the Islah party and the UAE in late 2017. A new attempt, supported by the UK Foreign Secretary Jeremy Hunt, led to a meeting between the UAE crown prince and senior Islah officials in November 2018.

Southern Movement (Al-Hirak Al-Janubi)

The Southern Movement (Al-Hirak Al-Janubi) emerged from the protests against the mismanaged unification of the YAR and PDRY in 1990. Unification was based on a power-sharing agreement between the two ruling elites, but the regime in Sana'a quickly disposed of the former PDRY leadership. The Southern Movement is split into several factions, most of which refused to participate in the NDC. The faction led by Ali Salim al-Baidh, one of the architects of the unification in 1990, is one of the most vocal in demanding independence. The Southern Transitional Council (STC), which is dominated by (former) southern governors who defected from Hadi in 2017, follows the same line. It seeks independence and a return to the pre-unification status, without Hadi as president. Although the STC receives substantial support from the UAE, the relation between the STC and the UAE-sponsored militias has not as yet been officially defined. The STC's relationship with the UAE is in sharp contrast to other southern secessionist groups who oppose Saudi Arabia or UAE interventions, which they equate to the government in Sana'a and accuse of being occupying forces.

Militant jihadi groups

The two main militant jihadi groups in Yemen are al-Qaeda in the Arabian Peninsula (AQAP), which rebranded itself in Yemen as Ansar al-Sharia in 2011, and the Islamic State in Yemen (ISIS–Y), which became known in Yemen in 2014. The groups have their strongholds in areas not controlled by Ansar Allah and compete with each other for recruits and media coverage. Clashes between the groups were reported in 2018 for the first time. Unlike ISIS–Y, AQAP has developed a long-term strategy aimed at winning over local communities. They control smaller areas, especially in Bayda and Abyan governorates, and held the port city of Mukallah, Hadhramaut governorate, from April 2015 to April 2016. The Popular Resistance Forces compete with AQAP for recruits in the south by offering opportunities for unemployed men. While Saudi Arabia focuses on the fight against Ansar Allah, a de facto anti-AQAP front has emerged as Ansar Allah, UAE-supported militias and the US military (which launched at least 26 uninhabited aerial vehicle (UAV) strikes in 2018) fight AQAP and ISIS–Y.

This combination of factors has reduced AQAP's capacity considerably. However, with an estimated strength of up to 4,000 full-time fighters and easy access to weapons, AQAP is far from being defeated.[7] In 2018, it attacked UAE-supported paramilitary forces in Bayda and Abyan, indicating that the presence of UAE-sponsored militias can attract AQAP activity.

Table 1: Conflict parties' relations

	KSA	UAE	STC	Ansar Allah	Hadi government	Al-Islah	AQAP	ISIS–Y	UAE-supported militias	National Resistance Forces
KSA		allied	competing	fighting	allied	allied (informal)	fighting	fighting	competing	indirectly allied (since 2018)
UAE	allied		allied	fighting	competing	fighting (but negotiating)	fighting	fighting	allied	indirectly allied (since 2018)
STC	competing	allied		no regional overlap but hostile	competing	allied or competing	not known	not known	probably allied	no regional overlap, otherwise conflict to be expected
Ansar Allah	fighting	fighting	no regional overlap but hostile		fighting	fighting	fighting	fighting	fighting	fighting (since 2018)
Hadi government	allied	competing	competing	fighting		allied	fighting	fighting	competing, sometimes fighting	allied (since 2018)
Al-Islah	allied (informal)	fighting (but negotiating)	allied or competing	fighting	allied		not known	not known	competing, sometimes fighting	indirectly allied (since 2018)
AQAP	fighting	fighting	not known	fighting	fighting	not known		competing, sometimes fighting	fighting	not known
ISIS–Y	fighting	fighting	not known	fighting	fighting	not known	competing, sometimes fighting		fighting	not known
UAE-supported militias	competing	allied	probably allied	fighting	competing, sometimes fighting	competing, sometimes fighting	fighting	fighting		no regional overlap, otherwise conflict to be expected
National Resistance Forces	indirectly allied (since 2018)	indirectly allied (since 2018)	no regional overlap, otherwise conflict to be expected	fighting (since 2018)	allied	indirectly allied (since 2018)	not known	not known	no regional overlap, otherwise conflict to be expected	

Drivers

In light of the Saudi–Iranian competition for regional hegemony, it is tempting to frame the Yemen conflict as a sectarian conflict. However, the war in Yemen is about local and regional influence, with almost all armed local conflict parties being directly or indirectly linked to external power centres. Although there are many grievances that are increasingly being framed in sectarian terms, the conflict drivers are political and economic.

Mutual threat perceptions

In spite of Saudi support for the Yemeni (Zaidi) Imam in the 1960s, the main driver of violence between Ansar Allah and Saudi Arabia is their perception that each threatens the other's existence. Ansar Allah opposes Wahhabism, the political movement based in the radical Islamic doctrine prevalent in Saudi Arabia. Like al-Qaeda, Wahhabis do not recognise the different Shia strands but rather consider them all as infidels. Conversely, convinced that the Wahhabis aim at extinguishing Zaidism, Ansar Allah perceive their fight against Saudi (Wahhabi) intervention as a form of self-defence.

Regional strategic interests

The intervention of the Saudi-led coalition in Yemen is meant to counter Iranian influence in the region (Saudi Arabia believes that Ansar Allah is Iran's proxy), but it also aims at a diversification of transportation routes to Saudi Arabia, the world's largest oil exporter. Control over some parts of Yemen would allow Saudi Arabia direct access to the Indian Ocean, thus reducing its dependence on the waterways of the Red Sea and the Arabian/Persian Gulf. Mahrah governorate, which borders Saudi Arabia, Oman and the Arabian Sea, is of particular strategic importance to Saudi Arabia, as well as to the UAE. Likewise, control over Yemeni ports and islands fits well into the expansion strategy of the UAE, which has deployed security forces to these areas which are far away from the front-lines.

Patronage and lack of transparency

Even before the war, and even more so now, corruption and nepotism flourish in Yemen. For example, the numbers of regular government forces and militias are likely inflated to generate extra income for the commanders.[8] Attempts to eliminate names of those who draw upon multiple sources of state income and non-existing workers/soldiers from the public payrolls date back to pre-2011 and were renewed in 2012–13, although efforts ceased when most international embassies and aid agencies evacuated their international staff from Yemen. Instead, Ansar Allah started adding their militias to the public payroll in 2015. Between March 2015 and May 2016, Hadi's son Jalal reportedly provided oil importers with the import approval seal of his father.[9] In 2018, Transparency International ranked Yemen 176th of 180 countries in its Corruption Perception Index. In January 2018, the Hadi government announced an official annual budget for the first time since 2014, although no details were made public. Neither the government nor Ansar Allah have published figures showing income generated from taxes, customs revenues and other fees, oil exports and budget support. In October 2018, Hadi dismissed Prime Minister Ahmed bin Daghr over charges of mismanagement and corruption, finally giving in to the STC's demands.

Lack of inclusiveness

Saleh had a long record of excluding potential opponents from access to state resources. Such patterns hardly changed after 2011. When the former ruling GPC and Islah party formed a coalition government in December 2011, other political forces such as Ansar Allah, the Southern Movement and leaders of the 2011 protests were excluded. Unlike Ansar Allah, essential parts of the Southern Movement also boycotted the National Dialogue Conference. Agreed without the consent of important political forces such as Ansar Allah or the Southern Movement, the draft constitution of January 2015 would have deprived Ansar Allah of access to the Red Sea and divided the South into two separate entities not congruent with the borders of the former PDRY. To many, this looked like a return to old autocratic patterns.

Historical grievances

After the unification of the YAR and PDRY, the southern population (which comprises one-fifth of the total population) felt marginalised and neglected in spite of holding most of the country's oil and gas reserves. Like the Maribis in the former YAR's northeast, the southerners derived little benefit from the natural resources in the southern governorates Hadhramaut and Shabwah, with the revenue and plots of land in Aden allocated instead to Saleh's patronage networks. Although not all northern Yemenis are organised in tribes, and tribes can be found in southern Yemen as well, many Adenis in particular equate northern politicians with tribal elites that try to steal southern wealth. An attempt to separate from the more populous north in 1994 resulted in a three-month war between the two former states, culminating in the dismissal of thousands of southern members of the security forces after the defeat of the south.

Abundance of weapons

Weapons of various kinds reach Yemen not only via the west coast and its ports but also through coalition-supported militias selling their weapons on well-established arms markets. Other weapons are said to be smuggled via Mahrah governorate through territory nominally under the control of the Hadi government or the Saudi-led coalition, indicating that economic interests are stronger than political loyalties.[10] The availability of a wide range of firearms, tanks and anti-tank guided missiles not only benefits Ansar Allah but also is essential for AQAP and ISIS–Y, and perhaps even the Somali Islamist group al-Shabaab.

Political and Military Developments

By the end of 2018, Ansar Allah looked weaker than at the beginning of the year. Until late 2017, the rebels' capacities seemed to improve, but the Saudi-led coalition captured major parts of the Tihamah (western coastal plain) in May 2018 and in June advanced towards Hudaydah city, the entry point for most of the goods to northern Yemen. A renewed attack on Hudaydah followed in early November. The UN negotiated short ceasefires in July and November, thus preventing the cut-off of supplies to major parts of the population.

UN-brokered Stockholm meeting

UN Special envoy Martin Griffiths's attempts at arranging direct talks between Ansar Allah and a Hadi delegation in September failed because the Ansar Allah delegation refused to travel unless certain conditions were met (safe travel, evacuation of injured fighters). In November, these demands were fulfilled, and in December, representatives of Ansar Allah and Hadi met for the first time in two and a half years. While the Stockholm consultations resulted in three rather short agreements (ceasefire for the ports of Hudaydah, Salif and Ras Issa, exchange of 15,000 prisoners and a Statement of Understanding on Ta'izz) backed by Security Council Resolution 2451,

no agreement could be found on the reopening of Sana'a airport and the reconstitution of the CBY.

Coming to an agreement on Hudaydah was a major success of the Stockholm consultations, although implementation will be difficult because the agreement is vague and the conflict parties will not readily cede control to UN agencies. Hudaydah is the capital of Yemen's most populous governorate and Yemen's main port city. The port is a major source of revenue for Ansar Allah (which levies customs duties) and of strategic importance. Lacking the necessary resources and industries, Yemen has to import almost all of its staple food, medicine and fuel, even in peacetime. With Sana'a airport closed by the Saudi-led coalition since 2016, paralysing the port or cutting the road from Hudaydah to the northeast means condemning millions of Yemenis to starvation.[11] In 2018, fighting reached the outskirts of the city, the airport and the road to Sana'a but the port and inner parts of the city remained under the control of Ansar Allah. With commercial food imports on the decline and access to humanitarian-aid warehouses blocked by the conflict parties, the situation worsened throughout 2018. In Hudaydah governorate, the majority of districts (17 out of 26) were in an emergency food-security situation in

Figure 2: Timeline of UN-convened peace negotiations

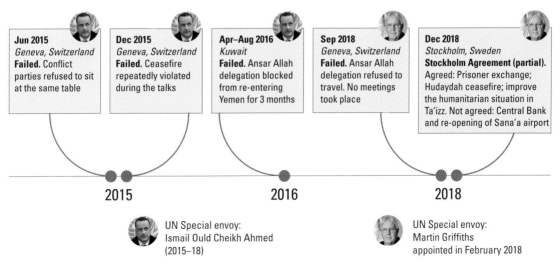

Jun 2015
Geneva, Switzerland
Failed. Conflict parties refused to sit at the same table

Dec 2015
Geneva, Switzerland
Failed. Ceasefire repeatedly violated during the talks

Apr–Aug 2016
Kuwait
Failed. Ansar Allah delegation blocked from re-entering Yemen for 3 months

Sep 2018
Geneva, Switzerland
Failed. Ansar Allah delegation refused to travel. No meetings took place

Dec 2018
Stockholm, Sweden
Stockholm Agreement (partial). Agreed: Prisoner exchange; Hudaydah ceasefire; improve the humanitarian situation in Ta'izz. Not agreed: Central Bank and re-opening of Sana'a airport

2015   2016   2018

UN Special envoy:
Ismail Ould Cheikh Ahmed
(2015–18)

UN Special envoy:
Martin Griffiths
appointed in February 2018

December 2018, while commercial food import reached its lowest level since 2016.

The city of Ta'izz (the capital of Yemen's second-most populous governorate) also received special attention during the Stockholm consultations. In November, a representative of 250 Yemeni women and organisations working on the protection of women and peacebuilding in Yemen reported to the UN Security Council that while taking over the men's tasks to protect them from forced recruitment, abduction, detention and torture, women face all kinds of difficulties including harassment by the various militias. The Stockholm agreement on Ta'izz, however, only acknowledged the need for improving the humanitarian situation. Since 2015, Ansar Allah and the Popular Resistance have been fighting over Ta'izz, thus turning what has been called Yemen's cultural capital into a warzone. In addition, Saudi Arabia- and UAE-supported militias are competing for influence in Ta'izz, with heavy clashes taking place in August.

Interactions among the conflict parties

Though Saudi Arabia and the UAE do not compete over leadership, they do so over the control of territory, by supporting various local forces who sometimes turn against each other. In January 2018, Saudi-supported military units loyal to Hadi clashed with UAE-backed forces in Aden. Though a Saudi Arabia–UAE committee managed to reduce the tension, the matter is far from settled. In Ta'izz, tensions arose between a unit affiliated to the Islah party and the UAE-supported Abu Abbas Brigades, whose leader was designated as a terrorist by the US in 2017. In addition, although the Islah party nominally supports the Hadi government, the UAE has ordered assassinations of their local leaders.

US position

The US is a key factor in future negotiations for a solution of the Yemen conflict. (An intervention by then US defense secretary Mattis reportedly made the Hudaydah agreement possible.[12]) However, the US perspective on Yemen is defined by three strategic interests: fighting international terrorism, ensuring the security of its local allies and US economy. In its war against terror, the US supplied arms worth US$500m to the Saleh regime which it cannot account for any longer, and carried out hundreds of UAV attacks against AQAP (killing civilians as well as suspects) and a limited number of ground operations, such as in Bayda in January 2017.

Sharing the Saudi perspective that Iran is a threat to regional stability, the US government supports the Saudi-led coalition, although Ansar Allah would be a logical partner in its fight against AQAP. The high number of civilians killed by US-supplied arms made headlines in 2018, and after the Saudi government ordered an attack on US-based Saudi journalist Jamal Khashoggi (killed in the Saudi consulate in Istanbul in October 2018), international media turned against Saudi Arabia. In December, the US Senate voted to end US participation in the war in Yemen and blamed the Saudi Crown Prince Muhammad bin Salman for the killing of Khashoggi, although the resolution was largely symbolic, as President Trump has vowed to veto it. In this political atmosphere, the Saudi government might face difficulties in acquiring the US THAAD system, although this would run counter to US arms deals (worth US$110 billion, according to the president) agreed during President Trump's visit to Saudi Arabia in 2017. The US also imports a significant amount of Saudi oil (9% of total US oil imports in 2017) and relies upon Saudi Arabia's capacity as swing producer.[13]

❙ Violent Events

By summer 2018, the number of Saudi-led coalition airstrikes against Ansar Allah had reached 18,000 since 2015.[14] By mid-November, there had been an estimated 125 Saudi-led coalition airstrikes against civilian targets. On 9 August 2018, the Saudi-led coalition bombed a school bus, killing 40 children. However, the number of Saudi-led coalition airstrikes in 2018 decreased to 3,362. More than one-third of them were directed at Sa'ada governo-

rate, where the Ansar Allah movement originated. Saleh al-Sammad (leader of Ansar Allah's Supreme Political Council) was killed in an airstrike on 19 April 2018.

On 2 August, Ansar Allah launched a missile at Jizan in Saudi Arabia, reportedly killing one civilian, while on 5 September Saudi security forces intercepted a missile directed at the Saudi border city of Najran. Missiles targeting Riyadh were intercepted on 26 March, 9 May and 24 June. Though the casualties of the Saudi-led coalition have not been revealed, at least one thousand Saudi civilians and military personnel have reportedly been killed in Yemen–Saudi border raids and missile attacks launched by the Ansar Allah rebel group since the war began.

Assassinations of high-ranking Islah members in southern governorates, which were attributed to the UAE, continued throughout 2018: 16 Islah members were killed, while another 12 escaped assassination attempts.

In January 2018, fighting broke out in Aden ('Battle of Aden') between Hadi supporters, STC demonstrators and militias, reportedly killing 36 people (and wounding 185).

Impact

Humanitarian impact

While military gains have been limited, the humanitarian situation has dramatically deteriorated. Overall, approximately 3m Yemenis have been internally displaced since 2015, with 2m still unable to return home. Approximately 500,000 people were displaced from Hudaydah alone during the second half of 2018. The UN also reported the largest cholera outbreak in modern history: 280,198 suspected cases of cholera were recorded in 2018 alone, with 2,556 deaths registered between April 2017 and October 2018.[15] More than 20m Yemenis require humanitarian or protection assistance, and more than 8m people are at risk of starvation.[16] Even in this disastrous situation, conflict parties are still restricting the movement of humanitarian organisations and delaying the import and distribution of food.[17]

Some 1.2m public servants have had their salaries either not or only partly paid since 2016 when Hadi paralysed the CBY in order to end Ansar Allah's access to its funds. With an average household size of six people, this has directly affected almost 8m people. The situation has been further aggravated by the rapid depreciation of the Yemeni riyal, which accelerated during the second half of 2018 (from YER220 to the US dollar in 2015 to approximately YER600 to the US dollar by late September 2018).[18] Then-prime minister bin Daghr announced in January 2018 that he would restrict the payment of salaries in areas controlled by Ansar Allah to the education and health sectors, thus leaving many public servants in the north unpaid.[19] The breakdown of the economy and the resulting lack of alternatives (some 600,000 jobs have been lost since the war started) is also likely to facilitate the recruitment – including of minors – into the various militias.[20]

Human-rights abuses

On 28 August 2018, the UN Group of Experts on Yemen reported that it had 'reasonable grounds to believe that the parties to the armed conflict in Yemen have committed a substantial number of violations of international humanitarian law'.[21]

Ansar Allah militias impede the delivery of humanitarian aid, and citizens criticising Ansar Allah risk arrest, torture, abduction and death. A committee established by concerned Ansar Allah members to look into cases of alleged abuse was dissolved after it presented a video to its leadership in 2016 showing scenes of overcrowded prison wards.[22] The prisoner exchange agreed upon in Stockholm is also likely to be complicated by a number of factors. As of 2018, Ansar Allah had arrested about 20,000 people. While some have been released (often after their families paid ransom), others may never be found due to lack of proper documentation. According to some reports, more than 100 have died from torture.[23]

In spite of growing international criticism, the Saudi-led coalition maintained its blockade of Sana'a airport, restricted the delivery of humanitarian aid and supplies through the ports of Hudaydah and Salif, and continued attacks on civilian targets.[24] In 2017, reports emerged of secret prisons run by the UAE in south Yemen in which inmates are subjected to torture.[25] The UAE began to release prisoners in 2018 but the facilities do not seem to have been completely handed over to the Hadi government. This could turn out to be a major obstacle, as the prisoner exchange agreed upon in Stockholm presupposes that the government knowns the names and whereabouts of the prisoners nominally under its control.

Militarisation of society and economy

By supplying weapons and recruiting men and boys into the various militias, all parties to the conflict promote the militarisation of Yemeni society and foster a war economy. With around 50 small arms per 100 inhabitants, Yemen has never been short of arms, but the looting of governmental arsenals and the delivery of sophisticated weapons, including anti-tank guided missiles, to militias since 2015 is unprecedented and arms smuggling has flourished. While Saudi Arabia has started arming the tribes of the sparsely populated governorate of Al Mahrah, which so far have not participated in the conflict, Ansar Allah has established a female militia called Zainabiyyat, which targets women critical of Ansar Allah with beatings, arrests and threats to family members.

Impact on Saudi Arabia and UAE

While the Yemeni population bears the brunt of the conflict, the war also has an impact on Saudi Arabia.

The Saudi-led coalition refrains from publishing their fatalities, but they are likely to run into the hundreds.[26] Unlike the UAE, Saudi Arabia avoids deploying Saudi soldiers to Yemen, using mercenaries and allies instead. That the poorer UAE member states contribute more soldiers than Dubai or Abu Dhabi and have thus to cope with more fatalities has been a matter of discussion in the UAE.

Expenses for the war are also massive. Although the Saudi government has not revealed the cost of its military intervention, it has been estimated as being up to US$129bn.[27] In addition, other expenses – such as support of the Hadi government, the relocated Yemeni Central Bank (including a US$2bn deposit in January 2018 and another US$200m in September), humanitarian aid to UN organisations or via the King Salman Foundation, and public-relations campaigns – need to be added. These ancillary expenses may amount to US$10bn for 2018.

Trends

After almost four years of war, none of the actors have achieved their declared objectives. The humanitarian situation is catastrophic, the international community is becoming increasingly critical of the Saudi-led coalition and the influx of more fighters can be expected. In this context, a face-saving exit option for the conflict parties may be more attractive than in the past, especially as Saudi Arabia and the UAE have already reached some undeclared objectives, including access to the Indian Ocean (Saudi Arabia) and control over Yemen's ports and coastal areas (UAE).

Steps taken in 2018 might facilitate future negotiations between Ansar Allah and the Saudi-led coalition: Ansar Allah released two of Saleh's sons in October, the Saudi-led coalition agreed to the evacuation of wounded Ansar Allah fighters in November and consultations took place in Sweden in December. However, the situation is complicated by the weak stance of the internationally recognised government. While the Saudi-led coalition has taken over the paymaster role of the Yemeni government by depositing billions of US dollars in the Yemeni Central Bank and the international community has taken over social-service tasks, Hadi, whose health is fragile,[28] has failed to meet domestic and international expectations of reforming the political and economic system. Even in areas nominally under his control, public services are deficient. Resistance against Hadi and the intervention of the Saudi-led coalition is rising. Parts of the Southern Movement have labelled it an occupation, citizens held demonstrations and sit-ins against the Saudi intervention in Mahrah governorate, and protests even occurred in the remote but strategically important island of Socotra, where the UAE set up a military base. With international attention being short-lived, a comprehensive agreement is not likely to be achieved any time soon.

Notes

[1]   'Islah's Political and Military Ascent in Taiz', Sana'a Center for Strategic Studies, 12 November 2018.

[2]   Douglas Barrie, 'Air power misses the target in Yemen', IISS, 19 September 2018.

3   'Saudi Arabia: Houthi missile strike in Asir province Oct. 18, update 19', *GardaWorld*, 19 October 2018; 'Saudi Arabia intercepts Houthi missile headed for Jizan', *New Arab*, 4 September 2018; 'Situation of human rights in Yemen, including violations and abuses since September 2014', Office of the United Nations High Commissioner for Human Rights (OHCHR), 17 August 2018.

4   Nicholas A. Heras, '"Security Belt": The UAE's Tribal Counterterrorism Strategy in Yemen', *Terrorism Monitor*, vol. 16, no. 12, 14 June 2018; Bel Trew, 'Inside the UAE's war on al-Qaeda in Yemen', *Independent*, 15 August 2018.

5   'Iranians hail Houthi "resistance" for bringing potential end to Yemen war', *Al-Monitor*, 1 November 2018.

6   'Houthis', Missile Defense Advocacy Alliance, June 2018.

7   This estimate refers to 2015–16, when AQAP was at its height. See Elisabeth Kendall, 'Contemporary Jihadi Militancy in Yemen: How Is The Threat Evolving?', Policy Paper 2018–7, The Middle East Institute, July 2018.

8   'Corruption in Yemen's War Economy', Policy Briefing no. 9, Sana'a Center for Strategic Studies, 5 November 2018.

9   Peter Salisbury, 'Yemen's Astonishing Financial Meltdown', *Foreign Policy*, 11 December 2014.

10 Michael Horton, 'Yemen: A Dangerous Regional Arms Bazaar', *Terrorism Monitor*, vol. 15, no. 12, 16 June 2017.

11 Susanne Dahlgren, 'The Southern Transitional Council and the War in Yemen', Middle East Research and Information Project, 3 May 2018.

12 Peter Salisbury, 'Five Steps to Save Yemen's Stockholm Agreement', International Crisis Group, 15 January 2019.

13 'How much petroleum does the United States import and export?', US Energy Administration, 3 October 2018.

14 'Yemen's debilitating war', IISS Strategic Comments, vol. 24, no. 32, November 2018.

15 'Half the population of Yemen at risk of famine: UN emergency relief chief', UN News, 23 October 2018; 'Cholera and malnutrition in Yemen threatens millions', World Health Organization, 27 December 2018.

16 Yemen portal, UN News (https://news.un.org/en/focus/yemen).

17 'Yemen: Humanitarian Access Snapshot (October–November 2018)', UN Office for the Coordination of Humanitarian Affairs (OCHA).

18 'Brief Update on the impact of rapid depreciation of Local Currency (YER) against US dollar on the Prices of Essential Food and Fuel Commodities', Food and Agriculture Organization of the United Nations, 20 September 2018.

19 'Yemen sets first budget since 2014', Reuters, 21 January 2018.

20 'Yemen Humanitarian Update: Covering 13 December 2018 – 15 January 2019', no. 1, OCHA, January 2019.

21 'Situation of human rights in Yemen', (UNHCR), ibid., p. 14.

22 Maggie Michael, 'Ex-inmates: Torture rife in prisons run by Yemen rebels', Associated Press, 7 December 2018.

23 Michael, 'Ex-inmates: Torture rife in prisons run by Yemen rebels'.

24 The Evacuation and Humanitarian Operation Cell (EHOC) of Saudi Arabian Ministry of Defence even prevents delivery of goods cleared by the UN Verification and Inspection Mechanism (UNVIM). See 'Yemen Humanitarian Update: Covering 7–21 November 2018', no. 32, OCHA, November 2018, p. 4.

25 Maggie Michael, 'Detainees Held Without Charges Decry Emiratis' Sexual Abuses', Pulitzer Center, 20 June 2018.

26 'UAE Acknowledges More Army Death in Yemen', *Sayyidali* via *Fars News Agency*; Daniel Byman, 'Saudi Arabia and the United Arab Emirates Have a Disastrous Yemen Strategy', Lawfare, 16 July 2018.

27 Rai al-Yaum, 19 March 2018 (*Mideastwire*, 20 March 2018).

28 Elana DeLozier, 'Yemen's Second-in-Command May Have a Second Coming', The Washington Institute, 9 November 2018.

Middle East and North Africa

5 South Asia

An Indian paramilitary soldier holds a bunch of confiscated poppy buds in Kashmir

Regional Introduction

The armed conflicts active in the South Asia region are diverse but not wholly discrete. In particular, the situations in Afghanistan and Pakistan have numerous connections, and are increasingly relevant to the circumstances in the Indian state of Jammu and Kashmir (India) and Azad Jammu and Kashmir (Pakistan). The CPI–Maoist and northeast India conflicts, meanwhile, are largely discrete and self-contained.

The most prominent conflict-related development in the region in 2018 was the latest set of peace talks on Afghanistan, potentially the most consequential since 2001. Led by the United States Special Representative for Afghanistan Reconciliation Ambassador Zalmay Khalilzad, the talks began in December. Although still at the 'early stages of a protracted process' (as described by Khalilzad), the talks carry great potential for both the country – which has been at war for more than 17 years – and the region as a whole. The process has opened a wider array of potential outcomes for Afghanistan than in the years before 2014, when strategic uncertainty had gripped the country following the decision of the US and NATO combat troops to leave.

By the end of 2018, the US claimed progress towards a draft framework for peace with the Taliban: conditional assurances included the US and its allies withdrawing from the country, in return for the Taliban's commitment to refuse a safe haven to terrorist organisations, such as al-Qaeda. In 2018, direct talks between the Taliban and the Afghan government were yet to start and a ceasefire to be agreed upon. An inclusive national dialogue – which the Afghan government emphasised should be Afghan-led and inclusive of the country's female population – remains essential to advancing peace and seeking comprehensive solutions to the conflict's underlying causes. The warring parties will likely continue to pursue such talks in 2019, but the process will be long and contested, despite the preliminary success of having engaged the Taliban (representing a long-elusive pursuit of US diplomacy).

A new president will be elected in 2019 in Afghanistan, complicating the predictability of the government's position. The Taliban will focus on preserving the early advantage of a direct communication channel with US officials. Though some among their leadership and their ranks are genuinely interested in a non-military solution to the conflict, the Taliban are well aware that their leverage in the negotiations depends on their military successes and their ability to hold and control territory. The situation on the ground will shape the final terms of the agreement, when – or if – it materialises. The process of giving up arms will therefore be slow and gradual, and violence will not cease immediately and homogeneously. Even if peace with the Taliban comes to fruition, however, the agreement will not eliminate all armed violence in Afghanistan, which will continue to be generated by local, tribal and communal disputes or organised criminal activities.

The progress of the talks with the Taliban will have security implications for Pakistan, which is still seeking to close the permissive, mostly northwestern pockets of its territory in which a variety of terrorist and extremist groups have exploited. Throughout 2018, the Pakistani armed forces consistently claimed that the situation had improved amid heightened levels of US pressure to suppress outward-facing terrorism. Attacks by extremist groups on Pakistan's own territory did indeed decrease during the year, indicating that government efforts to target terrorist and militant groups operating on its soil are working. Despite these successes, however, militant

armed violence is unlikely to be fully eradicated in Pakistan in the near future. Local dynamics and the tribe-based organisation of some sectors of Pakistani society, as well as the state's phased approach to militancy (in pursuit of incremental successes in the country's affected areas), will continue to sustain militants' armed violence (including by those seen as 'terrorists' from outside Pakistan). A central challenge in 2019 for Pakistan will be the management of existing internal violence as part of a long-term strategy to degrade its structural causes – a task the Pakistani state has repeatedly demonstrated an ability to undertake decisively. Much of the onus will be on Prime Minister Imran Khan's government, as it transitions into its second year in office. The most challenging costs of Pakistan's management policy (which the state is declaredly seeking to lower) are forced

> Militant armed violence is unlikely to be eradicated

disappearances (of which there are more than 1,800 unresolved cases according to the Commission of Inquiry on Enforced Disappearances) and arbitrary arrests of political activists, students, human-rights defenders, lawyers, journalists, members of religious groups and ethnic minorities (which are prevalent across the country, according to Amnesty International).

Pakistan will remain keen to retain influence in the Afghan peace process and the situation in Afghanistan more generally. In order to avoid instability spilling over to its side of the Durand line – which Afghanistan does not recognise – Pakistan will seek to strike a delicate diplomatic balance assisting the US-led peace efforts, without curtailing its advantage over the Afghan Taliban. Pakistan's new chief of army staff, expected to be appointed in November 2019, will play an important role in the success of this strategy. At the same time, although Pakistan professes to have limited influence over the Afghan Taliban, if uncertainty over the situation in Afghanistan continues, US pressure on Pakistan will likely increase. This would complicate an already fatigued relationship and enhance the scope for miscommunication with and within Afghanistan, in turn increasing uncertainty over the peace process. Pakistan could then face hard national-security dilemmas unprecedented in a generation, across

South Asia

both its western and eastern borders, especially in the case of a deepening downturn of its ties with India.

Much of this would play out in the Indian state of Jammu and Kashmir and in Azad Jammu and Kashmir, which continue to affect and drive the broader relationship between India and Pakistan. Local attacks are often seen as a confrontation, and there are strong indications that these will continue between the two sides. The Indian government will no doubt use the upcoming general elections in April and May 2019 as a platform to continue politicising the conflict and mobilise supporters around a more forceful national-security response to Pakistan's involvement in Kashmir. Though Kashmir did not feature in the Pakistani electoral debate in 2018, Pakistan appeared keen to mobilise public domestic (and international) opinion over the vexed issue. Expectations for the situation to improve will remain low in both countries, although internationally, there are strong beliefs that the situation will not escalate to the point of miscalculation. Much of the outcome will be dependent on mutual restraint along the Line of Control – as demonstrated by Pakistan over the past year – but also on its ability to act against India-focused terrorist and militant groups operating on its soil. Despite tensions between the two countries, the aftermath of the Indian general election could provide an opportunity for both sides to resume their bilateral dialogue for the first time since 2016.

Local violence in the Indian state of Jammu and Kashmir and in Azad Jammu and Kashmir has worsened and will continue to be profoundly affected by India's and Pakistan's domestic political debates and security strategies. The prospects for the local population, living in one of the most militarised zones of the world, seem unlikely to improve and could in fact worsen in 2019 if unrest spikes. The immunity of security forces will remain a matter of controversy as allegations including unlawful killings, involuntary disappearances and disproportionate use of force on peaceful protesters will be slow to dissipate. Armed groups alleged by India to be acting at Pakistan's behest will remain suspected of abuses of their own, including kidnappings, sexual violence and the killing of civilians. In June 2018, the first report published by the Office of the UN High Commissioner for Human Rights (OHCHR) on both the Indian state of Jammu and Kashmir and Azad Jammu and Kashmir called for an international inquiry into systematic human-rights violations on both sides of the Line of Control.

The armed conflicts in northeastern India are the most loosely connected to the rest of the region. In 2019, they will likely continue with low rates of incidents, comparable to 2018. The onset of the general election will see politicians promise more development, not least in relation to New Delhi's attempt to promote the growth of this area through enhanced connectivity with neighbouring regions. The permanency of the gains accrued from New Delhi's quiet, negotiated efforts to lower and manage violence levels will be tested by politicians' rhetoric and attempts to polarise communities for votes. Elsewhere in India, opportunistic Naxalite violence could be stoked by the coming polls. However, the response of security forces and the development promises of electoral patronage politics are likely to overcompensate in many of the parochial, localised environments where Naxalite insurgents have operated.

Afghanistan

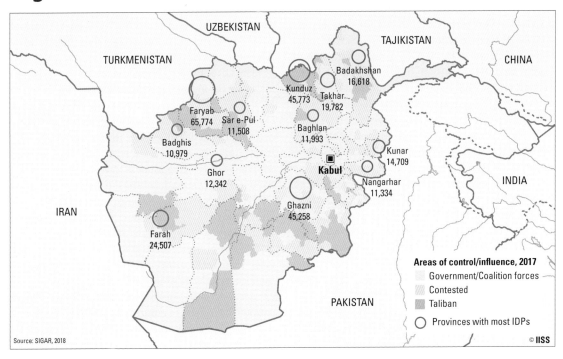

Areas of control/influence, 2017
- Government/Coalition forces
- Contested
- Taliban
- ◯ Provinces with most IDPs

Source: SIGAR, 2018

© IISS

Overview

The conflict in 2018

The conflict in Afghanistan intensified in 2018 according to several indicators. The number of violent events, fatalities and conflict-induced displacements decreased compared to 2017. However, the Afghan government's control of districts also decreased, from 56.8% in 2017 to 55.5% in 2018.[1] The Taliban staged several high-profile attacks that called into question the government's ability to provide security, including an attack on Ghazni city and the offensive against the Hazaras in Ghazni province. The Taliban also claimed credit for an attack that killed or wounded all of Kandahar province's top security leadership and narrowly missed the top US general in Afghanistan.

Peace negotiations made more progress in 2018 than in any other year since the war began. On 21 September, US Secretary of State Mike Pompeo nominated Zalmay Khalilzad as Special Representative for Afghanistan Reconciliation. Khalilzad and US officials met on multiple occasions with Taliban representatives in Doha, Qatar, while the Taliban also engaged in regional diplomacy with representatives

Key statistics	
Type:	Internationalised
IDPs total (2017):	1,300,000
IDPs new (2018):	370,000
Refugees total (2018):	2,600,000
Refugees new (2018):	no data
People in need (2018):	6,300,000

of Iran and Pakistan, as well as several Central Asian countries. However, the talks remained at a preliminary stage and the Afghan government frequently expressed its displeasure at the Taliban's refusal to engage in direct talks with Kabul.

The Afghan government successfully planned and executed parliamentary elections in October 2018, although the process was marred by logistical problems, violence, and claims of fraud and corruption. Economic growth declined in 2018 compared to 2017, and the poverty rate increased.

The conflict to 2018

The conflict in Afghanistan began with the US-led invasion in October 2001 following the 9/11 terrorist attacks. At the beginning of the invasion, the United States' declared objectives were to destroy the al-Qaeda terrorist organisation and to overthrow the Taliban regime that had allowed it safe haven. With a force comprised of special forces and conventional units and a strategic partnership with the Northern Alliance (an anti-Taliban group formed in 1996), the US-led operation removed the Taliban regime from power in November 2001, and the Taliban's structure and leadership quickly dissipated. In December 2001, the Bonn Conference set the groundwork for a new government led by Hamid Karzai.

The period following the invasion was relatively calm and the initial US strategy was to maintain a small footprint. Special forces operated in the country with local partners; conventional units were stationed in Kabul and at Bagram Air Base north of Kabul. This small footprint left space for local strongmen and militia leaders to fill the power void and allowed the Taliban to reconstitute and reorganise in Pakistan. Taliban forces soon began conducting more significant operations in Afghanistan, with violence increasing every year up to 2010. Coalition forces accordingly began increasing troop numbers and expanding their presence throughout the country, with the International Security Assistance Force (ISAF) operating in all regions of Afghanistan by 2006. The number of US security personnel deployed to Afghanistan reached a peak of more than 100,000 in 2010 and 2011. The United States also created provincial reconstruction teams (PRTs) to deploy to the various provinces and establish local provisional governments to expand Kabul's peripheral control. The PRTs, operational between 2006 and 2014, were designed to build the governance capacity of provincial governments, but

little additional direction was given, and each coalition country that operated a PRT incorporated its own preferences and priorities. At its peak – around 2011 – 17 coalition countries operated PRTs in 27 of Afghanistan's 34 provinces.

The US approach changed once US special-operations forces located and killed Osama bin Laden in May 2011. In June 2011, then US president Barack Obama announced the beginning of a troop withdrawal, stating that all combat troops would officially leave Afghanistan by 2014, with only support personnel, advisers and trainers remaining in-country. By the time Obama left office in January 2017, the US had approximately 8,000 troops in Afghanistan. US President Donald Trump frequently criticised US involvement in foreign conflicts, calling for an end to US presence in Afghanistan since 2011, but since taking office has increased troop numbers to their current level of around 14,000. US forces still engage in combat operations, primarily as part of counter-terrorism operations against al-Qaeda and the Islamic State in Khorasan Province (ISIS–KP), and occasionally in counter-offensives against major Taliban operations, such as the assault on Ghazni city in 2018. In December 2018, a US defence official stated that the US would withdraw approximately 7,000 troops from Afghanistan, despite the fact that the Taliban was in control of more territory than at any point since 2001.

Various attempts to bring the parties together for peace talks have failed, although an important breakthrough was made in 2018. Obama attempted to broker a negotiated settlement after the highly publicised release of US Army Sergeant Bowe Bergdahl in 2014, who had been held captive by the Taliban since 2009. The release of Taliban commanders was intended to complement Bergdahl's as a trust-building mechanism to facilitate negotiations, but never took place.

| Forces

Afghan National Defense and Security Forces (ANDSF)

The Afghan National Defense and Security Forces (ANDSF) are comprised of the Afghan Army and Air Force, the National Police, the local police and the National Directorate of Security (Afghanistan's intelligence agency). The ANDSF had approximately 310,000 combined personnel in July 2018. The ANDSF suffer from a number of shortcomings, the most important being the poor quality of recruits and ineffective logistical infrastructure to support them.[2] Desertion rates among conventional units are high.[3] The special-forces commandos, however, do not suffer from the same desertion problems.

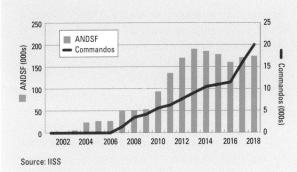

Source: IISS

Figure 1: ANDSF and special-forces-commandos growth

Numbering approximately 20,000, the commandos are effective fighters who are relied upon for most offensive operations, either to prevent districts falling to the Taliban, to rescue besieged outposts or to retake cities and towns. The proven efficacy of the special forces has led to a significant increase in their numbers relative to the regular army, which has decreased or stagnated since 2013 (see **Figure 1**).

Coalition forces

The US-led coalition forces in Afghanistan served under the International Security Assistance Force (ISAF) and *Operation Enduring Freedom* from 2001 until the official end of combat operations in 2014. At that time, the ISAF became *Operation Resolute Support*, while *Operation Enduring Freedom* became *Operation Freedom's Sentinel*. *Operation Resolute Support* remains primarily a training-and-assistance mission while US forces continue a counter-terrorism mission under *Operation Freedom's Sentinel.*

The initial purpose of the coalition forces was the destruction of al-Qaeda and the overthrow of the Taliban regime. After the collapse of the Taliban in 2001, coalition forces began focusing on training, advising and reconstruction, but the return of the Taliban around 2006 and the increase in violence demanded a refocus on a counter-insurgency mission.

The initial coalition presence in Afghanistan was low. The rise in violence led to a surge, with coalition forces reaching a peak of approximately 140,000 in 2011. In 2018, 14,000 US troops were stationed in Afghanistan, with approximately 8,500 assigned to *Operation Resolute Support*. Other NATO countries contributed approximately 7,700, bringing the total troops assigned to *Operation Resolute Support* to 16,200.

The Taliban and the Haqqani network

The Taliban is a fundamentalist Islamist group formed in the Afghan refugee camps in Pakistan during the Soviet occupation from December 1979 to February 1989. Taliban ideology is a mix between Pashtun tribal identity and Deobandi Islam, which is a strict interpretation of Islam (similar to Salafism) common among the madrassas in the refugee camps of Pakistan around the time the Taliban was forming. The Taliban entered the civil war in 1994 in Afghanistan and led the country from 1996 until the US-led invasion in 2001, although the group never completely controlled all of the territory in Afghanistan.

The Taliban was first led by Mullah Mohammad Omar until his death in a Karachi hospital in 2013 (his death was kept secret until mid-2015). His deputy, Mullah Mohammad Akhtar Mansour, took over in July 2015, but was killed in a US airstrike in Balochistan, Pakistan, on 21 May 2016. The group was led in 2018 by Mullah Haibatullah Akhundzada, who took over on 25 May 2016. Together with deputies Sirajuddin Haqqani (leader of the Haqqani network) and Mullah Mohammad Yaqoob (son of Taliban founder Mullah Omar), he heads the Quetta Shura, which directs the military campaign against the Afghan government and coalition forces in Afghanistan. The group has carried out large-scale attacks in major cities, including in Kunduz in September 2015 (and again in September 2016), in Lashkar Gah on 22 June 2017 and on 22 April 2017 near Mazar-e Sharif. The Taliban considers the coalition forces to be illegitimate occupiers of the country and the Afghan government a puppet regime of foreign governments.

Since the US-led invasion, the Taliban has operated 'shadow governments' in districts and provinces throughout Afghanistan, with shadow governors appointed in most districts and shadow provincial governors named in all 34 provinces. As of the end of 2018, the group controlled 59 of Afghanistan's 407 districts (14.5%) and contested the government's control in another 119 (29.2%). Since June 2013, the group has also maintained a political office in Doha, Qatar. Representatives at this office have engaged the US and regional countries in talks and diplomatic meetings. The Taliban also has connections with a variety of other non-state armed groups in South Asia, including al-Qaeda, the Haqqani network, the Islamic Movement of

Uzbekistan (IMU) and Tehrik-e-Taliban Pakistan (TTP).

In 2018, the Taliban was estimated to have between 25,000 and 35,000 personnel and its allied Haqqani network between 3,000 and 5,000 personnel. Although nominally two different organisations, there is little difference between the Haqqani network and the Taliban. The Haqqani network leader, Sirajuddin Haqqani, is the deputy to Taliban leader Mullah Haibatullah. The founder of the group, Jalaluddin Haqqani, has been allied with the Taliban since at least the mid- to late 1990s. In June 2018, the commander of the Kabul Military Training Centre, General Laal Jan Zaheer, said the total number of anti-government militants was more than 77,000, with 5,000 being foreign fighters and 3,000 being ISIS–KP.[4]

Islamic State in Khorasan Province (ISIS–KP)

The Islamic State–Khorasan Province (ISIS–KP) was formed in October 2014 when six senior members of the TTP defected and pledged allegiance to the leader of the Islamic State, also known as ISIS or ISIL, Abu Bakr al-Baghdadi. The group primarily fights against coalition forces, the Afghan government and the Taliban. The organisation has mostly been confined to a few districts in Nangarhar province in eastern Afghanistan.

ISIS–KP has undergone frequent changes in leadership due to a series of targeted killings by US and Afghan forces. Their original leader, Hafiz Saeed Khan, was killed in a US drone strike in Nangarhar province in July 2016. Saeed Khan's successor, Abdul Hasib, was reported killed in a joint Afghan and US special-forces operation on 27 April 2017. Abu Sayed was killed by a US airstrike on 11 July 2018. Another US strike killed Abu Sayeed Orakzai on 25 August 2018. In September 2018, the US Department of Defense estimated the strength of ISIS–KP to be less than 2,000.[5] US special forces and Afghan commandos have been actively engaged in operations to destroy ISIS–KP elements in Afghanistan, with the destruction of ISIS–KP being a high priority for the US in 2018.

Al-Qaeda

Al-Qaeda (meaning 'the base') was formed under the leadership of Osama bin Laden in the aftermath of the Soviet withdrawal from Afghanistan with the strategic vision of providing a base of operations from which to coordinate and enable other jihadist organisations to carry out attacks against the West and against their own local regimes.

Much of the organisation fled to Pakistan following the US-led invasion in 2001. Bin Laden's second in command, Ayman al-Zawahiri, took command of the organisation after the death of bin Laden in May 2011. Al-Qaeda has always preferred targeting the US, as it believes that the US would overextend itself in reacting to attacks and subsequently collapse. As a consequence of such a collapse, local regimes in the Middle East and South Asia that rely on US support would be easier to overthrow. In contrast to ISIS, which attempted to establish a caliphate before the collapse of the US, al-Qaeda believes the caliphate is a longer-term goal. Since the rise of ISIS, the group has been focusing on the cultivation of global alliances.

Al-Qaeda claims to command a network of more than 40,000 fighters throughout the world, with approximately 1,000 in South Asia. However, al-Qaeda's presence in Afghanistan is much more limited than it was during the Taliban regime as a result of a sustained US campaign of drone strikes and an exodus of members from Afghanistan to the conflicts in the Middle East (first Iraq, then Syria and Yemen). The US Department of Defense estimates al-Qaeda membership in the region (including the al-Qaeda in the Indian Subcontinent affiliate) to be approximately 200.[6]

| Drivers

International intervention

Both the presence of coalition troops and other forms of covert and overt interventions in domestic Afghan affairs are key drivers of the conflict. The primary goal of the Taliban is the withdrawal of foreign troops. In 2018, one of the top reasons Afghans believed that the Taliban fights is because of the presence of foreign troops.[7] Foreign troops also give legitimacy to the cause of insurgent groups that frequently inflict collateral damage and injure and kill civilians.

Domestic and socio-economic grievances

It is unlikely that the withdrawal of foreign troops would be sufficient to end the conflict, given the domestic political and socio-economic grievances that also underpin the insurgency. Liberal democratic governance is almost impossible to reconcile with the Islamist form of governance pursued by the Taliban in the late 1990s, which the Taliban is seeking to re-install. A negotiated peace would necessarily have to address this disconnect. Similarly, the issue of women's rights has become of primary concern, with the risk that rights gained since the fall of the Taliban regime will be lost without the presence of coalition forces. Furthermore, economic growth in Afghanistan is slowing, causing a rise in poverty, which could continue to drive violence and conflict even if political grievances were settled through a negotiated peace deal. Taliban attacks in Ghazni province in 2018 against the Hazara minority also showed how ethnic and linguistic differences fuel the conflict.

Regional support for the Taliban

A number of regional powers are involved in the domestic affairs of Afghanistan. According to the former US commander in Afghanistan, General John Nicholson, Russia continues to provide support and assistance to the Taliban, although it is difficult to quantify the nature and extent of this support.

The Taliban also relies on safe havens in Pakistan, with operations coordinated through leadership councils in Quetta and Peshawar. Afghan President Ashraf Ghani has also accused Pakistan of providing logistical support and resources to the Taliban,

particularly following the attack on Ghazni city on 10 August 2018.[8] Pakistan's role regarding the Taliban is complex. During the 2001 US-led invasion of Afghanistan, Pakistan either had no control over the operations of the Taliban in remote regions or only selectively pressured them. There were also reports that Pakistan had taken a more active role in supporting the Taliban, such as in the alleged air evacuation of members of al-Qaeda and the Taliban in November 2001 from locations in Afghanistan as coalition forces closed in.[9]

Democratic deficit

Limited governance and widespread corruption plague Afghanistan. US counter-insurgency doctrine highlights the importance of the legitimacy of the central government in the views of Afghan citizens in the belief that increased government legitimacy reduces the local population's support for the insurgency. The 2018 Asia Foundation survey reported that over 70% of Afghan respondents claimed that corruption was a major problem, although over half (59.6%) believed the government was doing a 'good job' and approximately 41% had confidence in their provincial councils.[10] The overwhelming majority of Afghans were unsympathetic to the Taliban movement, with over 83% of respondents saying they had no sympathy for the Taliban at all, and only 15% saying they had a lot or some sympathy – down three percentage points from 2017. The greater support for the government over the Taliban did not imply overall approval for the government's policies, however: approximately 61% of Afghans said the country was moving in the wrong direction.

Political and Military Developments

Uncertain progress in the peace process

In September 2018, Zalmay Khalilzad was appointed as Special Representative for Afghanistan Reconciliation to lead US efforts towards a negotiated settlement, and unprecedented progress was made towards potential peace negotiations between the US, the Afghan government and the Taliban. There were also significant setbacks, however, and all talks remained exploratory. In June 2018, Ghani called for a ceasefire during the three-day Eid al-Fitr holiday. The Taliban's adherence to the ceasefire

was taken both as a signal of serious intentions to negotiate a settlement, and as a confirmation that the Taliban command had control over their rank-and-file soldiers. In August, Ghani called for a three-month ceasefire, beginning with the Eid al-Adha holiday, but the Taliban rejected it and ambushed a bus with 170 passengers travelling for the holiday, taking the passengers hostage. Afghan security forces rescued 149 of the passengers but 21 remained in Taliban captivity as of December 2018.

South Asia

Challenges in the electoral process

While notable for being entirely planned and executed by Afghans, the parliamentary election in October 2018 was mired in accusations of corruption and poor execution and plagued by confusion, poor logistics and questionable practices. Many districts were unable to vote due to violence, while some polling stations had to open the day after the official election day due to logistical problems. Biometric scanners were used to validate voter identity, but they arrived late and not all districts were able to use them. It was also unclear how votes were to be counted if they were not verified with the biometric devices. Thousands of complaints were filed with the independent Election Complaints Commission and many candidates and parties criticised the legitimacy of the process.[11] The parliamentary elections clearly exposed the logistical and legal inadequacies of the current electoral system in Afghanistan, prompting Ghani to promise reforms to the system and new legislation ahead of the presidential elections scheduled for July 2019.

High ANDSF losses revealed

The ANDSF faced significant levels of pressure and violence in 2018, with several high-profile events leading to large numbers of casualties. In an interview on 14 November 2018, Ghani said that '28,529 of our security forces have lost their lives and become martyrs for our freedom' since 2015.[12] Previous estimates from the government suggested a much lower death rate, with approximately 5,000 security-forces members dying in 2015 and nearly 7,000 in 2016.[13] In October, the Special Inspector General for Afghanistan Reconstruction (SIGAR) reported that ANDSF numbers had decreased by almost 2,000 in only a three-month period in 2018 (April–June).

Cut in US military aid to Pakistan

In 2018, the US cut aid packages intended for Pakistan in an attempt to pressure Pakistan into denying safe haven to insurgent leaders and fighters. In January, the US cut US$500 million in total aid and in September cut an additional US$300m.[14] US leverage over Pakistan is limited, however. The cheapest logistics route to ship material and equipment into Afghanistan is via ocean shipping lanes and then overland through Pakistan. Few viable options exist outside of this route and airlift is unsustainably expensive. Pakistan faces financial difficulties and is seeking relief through both the International Monetary Fund and financial support from countries such as Saudi Arabia, leaving some space for US leverage.

| Violent Events

Insider attacks

At the beginning of 2018, a US report warned that the risk of insider attacks would increase as the 1st Security Force Assistance Brigade (the first US Army unit created exclusively for training and advising foreign militaries) deployed to Afghanistan.[15] The first insider attack occurred on 7 July in Tarinkot district in Uruzgan province, killing one US soldier and wounding two others. Another occurred on 22 October at the military base in Shindand district, Herat province when an Afghan commando opened fire on NATO troops, killing one and wounding two. On 3 November, Brent Taylor, a US Army officer and mayor of North Ogden, Utah, was killed by a member of the Afghan security forces, who was himself killed on the scene by other members of Afghan security.

The most notable insider attack occurred on 18 October in Kandahar province. The top US commander in Afghanistan, General Austin Scott Miller, was meeting with provincial officials when a recently hired member of the governor's security detail opened fire. The highly influential Kandahar police chief General Abdul Raziq was killed and the governor was wounded. Miller was unharmed, but three US personnel were wounded, including Brigadier General Jeffrey Smiley. The Taliban claimed responsibility for the attack.

Siege of Ghazni city

On 10 August, the Taliban launched a large-scale operation against Ghazni, attacking the city of 270,000 residents with approximately 1,000 fighters, occupying government buildings and taking surrounding districts. The Afghan government attempted to downplay the severity of the situation, claiming that government buildings had not been taken. The road to Kabul was cut off, along with electricity and all communications.

Many of the US special-forces and Afghan commando units previously stationed in the city had been pulled from Ghazni to launch offensive operations against ISIS–KP in other provinces. Reinforcements, including US special-forces teams, were sent to retake the city but were delayed or never arrived because of ambushes set along the routes into the city. The Taliban was eventually pushed out after more US and Afghan troops arrived with support from airstrikes and aerial surveillance.

According to US officials, 226 Taliban fighters died in the attack. UN officials reported that approximately 150 civilians also died in the attack. Afghan Brigadier General Dadan Lawang said 112 Afghan security-force members died and 56 were injured. Two days after the initial attack on Ghazni city, Afghan commanders learned that at least 40 commandos stationed west of Ghazni city defending against an attack in Ajristan district had died, while 22 survivors were rescued. Locals carried them out of the area on donkeys after finding them wandering lost in the mountains.

The attacks in Ghazni province came shortly after the US had shifted strategies to pressure the Taliban into peace negotiations through more extensive airstrikes. US military officials often said the strategy was working and that the Taliban was incapable of staging large-scale assaults, but the attack demonstrated that government and coalition claims of a weakened Taliban were exaggerated.

Taliban attacks on Hazaras

In November 2018, the Taliban broke a long-standing truce with the ethnic-minority Hazaras in Ghazni province. According to locals, the Taliban attacked Jaghori district with about 1,000 militants. Jaghori was long considered one of Afghanistan's safest districts and only maintained a small security-force presence. After the attack, 50 of Afghanistan's elite commandos were sent in to guard the district headquarters but were quickly overrun. At least 30 commandos were killed and ten wounded, with a further 50 police officers and militiamen killed.

ISIS–KP and Taliban clash in the north

ISIS–KP operates primarily in the southern area of Nangarhar province in eastern Afghanistan. In 2018, however, a group of ISIS–KP fighters attempted to establish a larger presence in Jowzjan province in the north, specifically in the area of Darzab district. The attempt ended after a major clash with the Taliban on 1 August 2018 that resulted in an overwhelming victory for the Taliban, in which it killed approximately 40 ISIS–KP fighters and took 128 prisoners. Nearly 2,000 Taliban militants gathered in the province for the assault. The surviving ISIS–KP fighters, including the northern commander Mufti Nemat, opted to surrender to government forces rather than continue to face the Taliban offensive. Government officials said more than 200 ISIS–KP fighters surrendered. Major Ahmad Jawid Salim, a spokesman for the Afghan commandos, claimed that 'the Daeshis [ISIS–KP] have been wiped out of the north'.[16]

The clash followed repeated ISIS–KP attacks against the Taliban, including one involving a suicide bombing of a funeral ceremony for a fallen Taliban commander on 17 July in Sar e-Pul province, which killed or wounded at least 20 militants.

Impact

Economic impact

According to the International Monetary Fund, Afghanistan's real GDP grew by 2.3% in 2018 compared to 2.7% in 2017, and was estimated to reach 4% in 2021.[17] The poverty rate continued to increase, however, reaching approximately 55%, from approximately 38% in 2012.[18] With about 400,000 Afghans entering the job market every year and a population-growth rate of 2.7%, Afghanistan will need to significantly increase its economic growth if it is to reduce the poverty rate.

Displacement

The United Nations recorded 364,453 new internally displaced persons (IDPs) as a result of the conflict in 2018. The majority of the IDPs originated from Ghazni, Faryab, Kunduz and Takhar provinces. On 10 August, more than 35,000 people were displaced when the Taliban attacked Ghazni city. The displacement from the Ghazni city assault followed the trend of most displacements in Afghanistan in 2018, with families relocating to other locations within the same district or province.

Drought crisis

Economic performance and human security have also been heavily impacted by the ongoing drought. The UN estimates that the drought has resulted in the displacement of 275,000 people. The UN Office for the Coordination of Humanitarian Affairs (OCHA) estimated that as of September 2018, 2.2m people had been affected by the drought. The UN targeted over 1.3m in need of drought-related assistance and delivered aid to nearly 700,000.[19] Afghanistan will likely see long-term impacts from the drought, with reduced food production, displacements and other economic disruptions.

Trends

A number of systemic issues point to a protracted stalemate in Afghanistan. The negotiating positions of the various parties make an agreement that satisfies all involved difficult. The Taliban increased the number of districts under its control and staged several large-scale operations that physically weakened the security forces and led the international community to doubt that the government can win. Finally, the US announcement on 20 December of a withdrawal of half of its forces boosted Taliban confidence that it still has much to gain by continuing to fight. Importantly, this does not preclude the possibility that the Taliban will negotiate to secure the withdrawal of all US forces and then continue to fight a weakened Afghan government.

Uncertain prospects for peace

Several factors indicate that peace may not be achieved in the short term in Afghanistan. The Taliban has consistently refused to negotiate with Kabul, while the US and Kabul maintain that it must be an Afghan-owned process and the Taliban must negotiate directly with the Afghan government. Of primary concern to the Taliban is the departure of foreign troops, but for the US, maintaining a presence in Afghanistan has great strategic value in countering terrorist organisations. A presence in Afghanistan would also afford the US leverage to counter China's Belt and Road Initiative and Russian activity in the region while maintaining close proximity to one of the largest nuclear stockpiles in the world.

Even if the discrepancies in the parties' positions can be reconciled, there is still uncertainty over what would come next. Some have suggested a renegotiated Bonn Agreement that would reshuffle the Afghan government more to the Taliban's liking. A post-peace-agreement Afghanistan would also have to deal with reconciliation and justice issues, such as whether Taliban militants responsible for civilian deaths would be charged and punished for crimes or be given immunity. Ignoring these issues might make peace more tenuous. Many discrepancies in initial demands, particularly on women's rights, and the wide range of undesirable outcomes makes a negotiated settlement difficult in the short term.

Significantly, violence has increased in recent years, while similar conflicts ended with a negotiated settlement had historically low levels of violence at the time of the agreements. When Colombia successfully negotiated the end of its conflict in 2016, for example, violence had been at an all-time low for more than ten years.

There are some indicators that point towards the peace process being viable and the Taliban's position being weaker than it appears. On several occasions in 2018, rival Taliban factions clashed with each other. Mullah Mohammad Rasul leads a breakaway faction active in Farah, Helmand, Herat and Nimroz provinces that clashed with the mainstream Taliban on 30 November 2018, killing 28 militants and wounding 25 others. The Taliban position would be further weakened if Afghan officials were able to improve their performance in the presidential elections on 20 July 2019, although Khalilzad has said that he hopes for a peace deal before the elections. However, there is no guarantee that the conflict will end even if a peace settlement is reached.

Notes

1 Special Inspector General for Afghanistan Reconstruction (SIGAR), 'Quarterly Report to the United States Congress', 30 October 2018.

2 Daniel Gouré, 'The Key to Success in Afghanistan Is Logistics', *Real Clear Defense*, 23 February 2018.

3 'Afghan security forces "shrink sharply" – US watchdog', BBC, 1 May 2018.

4 J.P. Lawrence, 'Afghan general: There are a lot more Taliban fighters than previously thought', *Stars and Stripes*, 12 June 2018.

5 Lead Inspector General, 'Operation Freedom's Sentinel: Report to the United States Congress, July 1–September 30, 2018', p. 22.

6 Lead Inspector General, 'Operation Freedom's Sentinel: Report to the United States Congress, July 1–September 30, 2018'.

7 The Asia Foundation, 'Afghanistan in 2018: A Survey of the Afghan People', 4 December 2018.

8 Ayaz Gul, 'Ghani Accuses Pakistan of Treating Wounded Taliban Fighters', *VOA News*, 17 August 2018.

9 Seymour M. Hersh, 'The Getaway: Questions Surround a Secret Pakistani Airlift', *New Yorker*, January 2002.

10 The Asia Foundation, 'Afghanistan in 2018: A Survey of the Afghan People', 4 December 2018.

11 'Former warlord Hekmatyar denounces Afghan election "disgrace"', Reuters News UK, 24 October 2018.

12 Ashraf Ghani, comments during video appearance at Johns Hopkins University, Washington DC, 14 November 2018.

13 Rod Nordland and Fahim Abed, 'Afghan Military Deaths Since 2015: More Than 28,000', *New York Times*, 15 November 2018.

14 Clark Mindock, 'Pentagon cancels $300m in aid to Pakistan over failure to tackle militants', *Independent*, 1 September 2018.

15 Lead Inspector General, 'Operation Freedom's Sentinel: Report to the United States Congress, January 1–March 31, 2018'.

16 Najim Rahim and Rod Nordland, 'Taliban Surge Routs ISIS in Northern Afghanistan', *New York Times*, 1 August 2018.

17 International Monetary Fund, 'World Economic Outlook (October 2018)'.

18 World Bank, 'Afghanistan Development Update: August 2018'.

19 OCHA, 'Afghanistan Drought Situation Report', 16 September 2018.

India (CPI–Maoist)

Overview

The conflict in 2018

The decades-long Naxalite insurgency continued in rural areas of central and eastern India, leading to the deaths of at least 303 people during the year. Of several independent insurgent groups, the Communist Party of India–Maoist (CPI–Maoist) posed by far the greatest threat to government forces and civilians. Consistent with previous years, CPI–Maoist's fighters used their mobility and superior knowledge of terrain to evade government forces and relied primarily on improvised explosive devices (IEDs) to inflict losses on security patrols. In addition to fighting government forces, the group also assassinated many civilians suspected of collaborating with police forces, culminating in at least 52 executions.

For its part, the Indian government continued to build up both its security presence and its governance infrastructure in the 'Red Corridor', a term commonly used to refer to territories affected by the insurgency. By providing services and economic development, the government attempted to win the loyalty of civilians who would otherwise provide active or passive support to Maoists. Government forces also continued to encourage surrenders, in addition to carrying out combat operations (several of which were highly effective). Under pressure from combat losses and defections, CPI–Maoist attempted to adapt to the changing balance of power, going so far as to replace its highest-ranking leader (who had led the organisation since 2004) with a younger commander known for orchestrating successful tactical operations. The group's ultimate collapse remains a distinct possibility but is by no means inevitable.

Key statistics	
Type:	Internal
IDPs total (2017):	not applicable
IDPs new (2018):	not applicable
Refugees total (2018):	not applicable
Refugees new (2018):	not applicable
People in need (2018):	not applicable

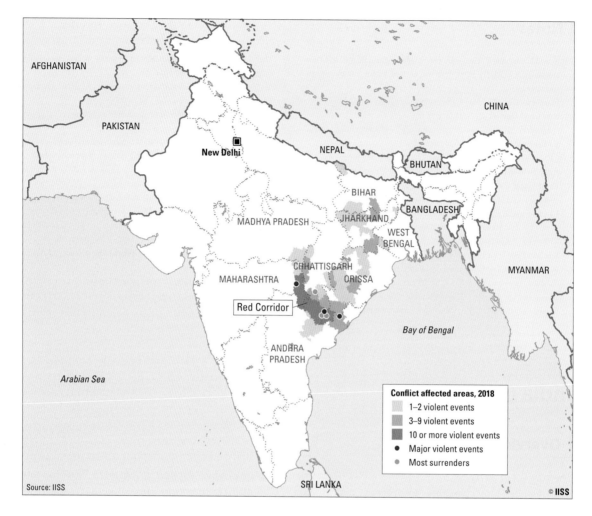

Source: IISS

The conflict to 2018

Communist-inspired movements (known collectively as 'Naxalism') have persisted in the Red Corridor since the 1940s. CPI–Maoist (whose members are commonly referred to simply as 'Maoists') became the most prominent Naxalite organisation in 2004, after forming from the merger of the People's War Group (PWG) and the Maoist Communist Centre (MCC). The group reached the height of its power in the early 2010s, when it controlled and governed vast swaths of 'liberated'

territory, especially in southern Chhattisgarh's Bastar region. The counter-insurgency began gaining ground against CPI–Maoist as early as 2014, a trend that continued into 2018. Since then, fatality ratios have heavily favoured security forces over insurgents, and Maoist fighters and commanders have surrendered in large numbers, usually in exchange for amnesties and financial incentives. However, Naxalism has survived at least two apparent collapses since the 1940s, and may well outlast CPI–Maoist in the event that the group disintegrates.

Forces

Various federal- and state-level law-enforcement agencies are responsible for combatting the Naxalite insurgency, which is almost exclusively driven by CPI–Maoist. Several groups have splintered off

from CPI–Maoist since its formation, but they have posed relatively little threat to the government and civilian communities. The most prominent of these splinter groups, the People's Liberation Front of

India (PLFI), suffered serious damage in 2017 when security forces killed its leader and several commanders in a string of successful combat operations. It appeared that the group had not recovered from these setbacks in 2018; though it suffered several more fatalities in 2018, it inflicted no known damage on security forces or civilians.

Government forces

Manmohan Singh's administration overhauled counter-insurgency efforts in 2012, paving the way for the federal government to play a much larger role in coordinating the separate efforts of each state, as well as significantly expanding the number of federal forces deployed to the Red Corridor. Prime Minister Narendra Modi has continued that approach since coming to power in 2014. By the end of 2018, at least 87 federal law-enforcement battalions were deployed to the Red Corridor – a record high.[1] Most of these battalions belong to the Central Reserve Police Force (CRPF). Like all anti-Naxalite forces, CRPF personnel are police officers, though they are trained and equipped as commando units. They carried out short- and long-range patrols throughout the year, often with local police in combined teams. In addition to these federal forces, each 'Naxal-affected' state has created its own anti-Naxalite police force modelled on the CRPF, which are relatively well armed with light machine guns and mine-detection equipment. The Indian Army does not take part in fighting, but the Air Force often supports police operations with reconnaissance and helicopter transport (especially when evacuating wounded personnel).

Federal and state security forces pursued two main objectives during the year. Firstly, they actively tracked and (upon discovery) attacked insurgents, typically in remote hinterlands. Secondly, they supported the government's hearts-and-minds efforts by providing humanitarian aid to civilian communities (such as free ambulance services) and by physically protecting infrastructure projects (especially road-construction projects).

Aside from killing insurgents, security forces continued to solicit surrenders among CPI–Maoist's high- and low-ranking fighters. The Enforcement Directorate (ED), a federal financial-crimes law-enforcement agency, joined the counter-insurgency effort for the first time in 2018. To encourage surrenders, the ED identified and confiscated or froze financial and real-estate assets belonging to more than 20 commanders, or their families, throughout the Red Corridor.

Communist Party of India–Maoist (CPI–Maoist)

The Communist Party of India–Maoist (CPI–Maoist) is a highly organised group formed from the 2004 merger of the People's War Group (PWG) and the Maoist Communist Centre (MCC). Like all Naxalite groups, it seeks to replace India's parliamentary democracy with a Communist regime by means of guerrilla warfare. CPI–Maoist's highest decision-making body, the Central Committee (CC), delegates authority geographically to lower-ranking committees, which control 'divisions' and 'zones' often corresponding to the borders of Indian states and districts. In turn, divisional and zonal committees delegate power to 'area' committees, which work to tax civilians (or 'collect levies', according to CPI–Maoists), punish suspected police informants and recruit new Maoists. CPI–Maoist's military wing is the People's Liberation Guerrilla Army (PLGA), which is relatively well armed (its cadres are full-time insurgents who often wield light machine guns) and engages government forces in open combat, often supported by local committees' forces.

During the height of its power in the late 2000s and early 2010s, CPI–Maoist conducted large combat operations against government forces, often overrunning fortified police stations and defeating large CRPF patrols in pitched battles. However, government forces significantly increased their combat effectiveness after counter-insurgency reforms in 2012, and CPI–Maoist fighters have increasingly avoided prolonged combat as a result, preferring instead to carry out brief ambushes, often using IEDs.

Drivers

Social and economic inequality
Proponents of 'left-wing extremism' (the government's term for violent Communist-inspired resistance movements) argue that India's caste system creates and sustains social and economic inequalities. To challenge it, non-violent activists

South Asia

and violent insurgents have attempted to mobilise landless farmers in the hinterlands (and occasionally in urban areas) against their landlords, who are separated from their tenants by both class and caste. In recent years, CPI–Maoist has mobilised large numbers of rural tribal (or 'Adivasi') communities, such as the Dongria Kondhs and Gonds, who inhabit some of the least-developed and least-governed regions of India, and who reside outside of the caste system. Mobilised villages provide CPI–Maoist with food, shelter, information, taxes ('levy') and recruits. The Maoists continued efforts to mobilise communities in 2018 (though with fewer signs of success than in previous years) by leveraging these groups' grievances against the state, and particularly against proposed or ongoing mineral-extraction projects.

Despite espousing an anti-mining stance, ties between CPI–Maoist and tribal communities have been eroding for years. After government forces killed CPI–Maoist's last senior-ranking tribal commander during the Balimela Reservoir battle in 2016, there have been no further indications of Maoist recruitment among tribal communities. Instead, many tribal communities in Jharkhand State joined the 'Pathalgadi' movement during 2018, a movement that opposes both Naxalite and government forces and denies the rights of either to enter Adivasi territories. Its members brandish traditional hunting weapons, but have not yet used violence (aside from one unconfirmed report).

Excessive government force

The government's counter-insurgency itself is a secondary driver of the conflict. Counter-insurgency personnel have used force excessively and indiscriminately over the years: at least three legal cases were opened during 2018 into past extrajudicial killings or sexual assaults, and journalists publicised numerous instances of alleged police harassment.[2] In August 2018, a Central Reserve Police Force (CRPF) team killed 15 suspected Maoists camping in Chhattisgarh State's Sukma district. Local activists credibly claimed that all the victims were civilians unaffiliated (or perhaps only nominally so) with CPI–Maoist, though these allegations have yet to be independently verified.[3] In another example, evidence strongly suggests that police secretly executed a medical worker in May in Odisha's Nuapada district on suspicion that he was a Maoist sympathiser.[4] Such incidents, as well as many other less severe encounters between villagers and law-enforcement teams, have almost certainly eroded support for the government. However, aggrieved civilian communities have not necessarily channelled their anger at the government into support for CPI–Maoist, as evidenced by the emergence of the Pathalgadi movement.

Political and Military Developments

Changes in CPI–Maoist territory and hierarchy

The group has attempted to adapt and evolve in response to the government's increased security presence. These efforts continued in 2018 with two important developments. Firstly, CPI–Maoist created the Special Zonal Maharashtra–Madhya Pradesh–Chhattisgarh (MMC) Committee to oversee an attempted expansion into a new swath of territory (the regions of Maharashtra and Madhya Pradesh states where the insurgency has not previously operated and which are therefore not heavily securitised). Secondly, Muppala Lakshman Rao (*nom de guerre* 'Ganapathi'), who has led the organisation since its inception, stepped down from his post in September in favour of his younger second-in-command, Nambala Keshav Rao (*nom de guerre* 'Basavraj'). Ganapathi has retained a position on the Central Committee (CC) and continues to be seen as an intellectual leader, while Basavraj is seen as a seasoned and expert tactician. As a result, CPI–Maoist's tactics and strategies could evolve significantly in 2019.

CPI–Maoist surrenders increase

Overall surrenders increased in 2018, with at least 263 militants, including at least 25 commanders, surrendering to authorities in the course of the year (see **Figure 1**). Surrenders were likely driven in part by the sustained combat effectiveness of the security forces, which made participation in the insurgency more dangerous. Surrenders may also be due to the Enforcement Directorate (ED), which initiated its anti-Naxalite efforts in February by freezing INR860,000 (almost US$13,300) in assets thought to belong to Sandeep Yadav (alias Badka Bhaiya), the commander of CPI–Maoist's Bihar–Jharkhand Special

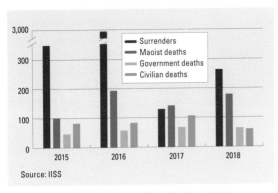

Figure 1: Total surrenders and deaths since 2015

Area Committee. In May, the ED seized assets worth approximately INR14 million (nearly US$200,000) from several Bihar- and Jharkhand-based commanders. These actions have several purposes. Firstly, they make it harder for CPI–Maoist to procure arms, medicines and other equipment needed to sustain the insurgency. Secondly, they are intended to accelerate demoralisation among Maoist fighters. The fact that most of the seized assets were held (and used for personal benefit) by commanders' family members suggests that at least some commanders are placing personal gain above the insurgency's needs. In an effort to discredit targeted commanders in the eyes of their followers, the government publicised this inference after every seizure.

Presumably, the ED's activities should have increased Maoist commanders' incentives to surrender. However, only 25 commanders surrendered in 2018 compared to 45 in 2017, an observation that lends itself to several different interpretations. Possibly, CPI–Maoist's pool of commanders declined considerably, implying that the attrition rate might have remained stable. Alternatively, the government may have already convinced all (or nearly all) of CPI–Maoist's less-committed commanders to 'come above ground', leaving a core of dedicated leaders for government forces to contend with. As an additional alternative, the ED's financial seizures did not credibly threaten most commanders' assets. As there is no clear evidence to support one of these interpretations over the others, it is important to appreciate the uncertainty inherent in assessing the counterinsurgency's impact on CPI–Maoist. Though the group's overall strength almost certainly continued to decline, its remaining forces could conceivably have become either more fragile or more resilient against eventual defeat.

Political assassinations

For the first time since 2013, CPI–Maoist's militants assassinated high-level politicians, killing two elected officials (only one of whom was in office at the time) during a single highly publicised attack in September in Andhra Pradesh's Visakhapatnam district. The group claimed that the attack was in retaliation for the victims' support for bauxite mining, but the assassinations, planned by CPI–Maoist's top leaders, may also have been intended as a show of force to bolster both morale among its fighters and its reputation among civilians. Maoist leaders might also have designed the attack as a strategic ploy intended to induce an indiscriminate security crackdown. Such a crackdown could undermine the government's legitimacy among local populations, to the benefit of CPI–Maoist. Four days after the assassinations, perhaps in line with CPI–Maoist's plan, the federal government coordinated the first of several controversial waves of arrests against 'Urban Naxalites', a group of activists and intellectuals alleged to have been plotting the assassination of Prime Minister Narendra Modi and other officials. International human-rights organisations argued that these arrests violated due process and the civil liberties of the arrestees. Amnesty International's India branch was itself targeted by the federal government in October, and its financial assets frozen by the ED.[5]

Change of government in Chhattisgarh

Chhattisgarh, the state worst hit by the Naxalite conflict, held elections in November 2018, resulting in a landslide victory for the Indian National Congress (usually referred to simply as Congress) and the ousting of the state's incumbent Bharatiya Janata Party (BJP) government. Bhupesh Baghel, Chhattisgarh's new chief minister, announced in December that his approach to the counterinsurgency would be more 'inclusive' than his predecessor's, and that he would attempt to improve governance by creating dialogue with local communities (including surrendered militants). However, Baghel also adopted relatively hardline rhetoric against CPI–Maoist. Whereas Raman Singh, Chhattisgarh's previous chief minister, periodically signalled his willingness to begin peace talks with CPI–Maoist (on condition that the group disarm beforehand), Baghel dismissed the possibility of talks soon after entering office. Possibly, Baghel's decision derives from a personal antipathy towards CPI–Maoist, which killed a total of 27 top Congress party officials and their guards during a well-orchestrated attack on a motorcade in 2013. Regardless, Baghel's rhetoric does not necessarily portend substantial changes on the ground since

both he and his predecessor signalled their support for continued paramilitary operations against CPI–Maoist. Additionally, as Maoist leaders never reciprocated Singh's interests in peace talks, there is no evidence to suggest talks would have taken place had BJP retained its incumbency.

Violent Events

Government and CPI–Maoist forces clash

Both government and CPI–Maoist forces continued to conduct armed operations in 2018. Police patrols attempted to force engagements with Maoists throughout the Red Corridor. Occasionally, police received advance knowledge about the location of Maoist encampments or meeting sites, and carried out well-planned operations against them. Several individual attacks stand out either for their political and strategic implications or for their exceptionally high death counts. In March 2018, CPI–Maoist detonated an IED in Chhattisgarh's Sukma district as a CRPF armoured vehicle drove over it. The blast resulted in the deaths of nine CRPF personnel in the vehicle, and demonstrated the Maoists' ability to punish security forces despite their growing combat-effectiveness. In April, several C-60 Commando teams (Maharashtra State's anti-Naxalite force) attacked a high-level CPI–Maoist meeting on the banks of the Indravati River. The government force, which suffered no casualties, killed at least 40 CPI–Maoist leaders and fighters over the course of the operation. The ambush amounted to CPI–Maoist's single largest loss of life in the group's history, and likely eroded its local command-and-control structures. In September, a CPI–Maoist team assassinated two state-level legislators in Andhra Pradesh State as they travelled via motorcade. The attack triggered outrage among local civilians, who blamed police for failing to provide adequate protection to the motorcade.

Concentration of violence

Consistent with previous years, Naxalite-related violence remained concentrated in Chhattisgarh State, which hosted at least 96 violent events, or nearly half (49%) of all documented executions, exchanges of fire and IED attacks. The majority of the remaining violence occurred in the states of Odisha (17%), Jharkhand (11%) and Maharashtra

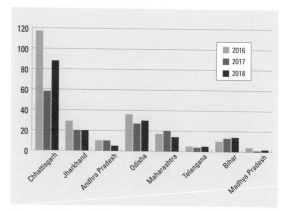

Figure 2: Violent incidents by selected states

(8%), while the states of Andhra Pradesh, Madhya Pradesh and Telangana each also witnessed at least one attack (see **Figure 2**). Though CPI–Maoist publicised its intentions to expand to new territories (to evade government security forces), no strong evidence emerged to suggest the group had achieved this goal – violence was confined to states and districts that have already seen fighting.

Violence in the Red Corridor

Violence in the Red Corridor as a whole, as measured by annual death tolls, remained consistent over the past three years: at least 333, 314 and 303 deaths occurred in 2016, 2017 and 2018, respectively. The fatality ratio of Maoist militants killed per security personnel increased slightly, from 2.1 in 2017 to 2.8 in 2018. Both ratios conform to trends observed since 2014. However, exchanges of fire between militants and security forces have increasingly favoured the latter side. In an effort to adapt to a changing balance of power, Maoists have increasingly relied on hit-and-run-style IED attacks to punish security forces. Accordingly, the proportion of security personnel killed by IEDs rose from approximately 40% in both 2016 and 2017 to just under 60% in 2018.

Civilian casualties decrease

While overall deaths and fatality ratios have not changed drastically, the number of civilian casualties has diminished markedly, from 106 in 2017 to 59 in 2018. The proportion of civilian fatalities (in relation to total Naxalite-related fatalities) also fell, decreasing from 33% in 2017 to 20% in 2018. The 59 confirmed civilian deaths were caused by CPI–Maoist, which targeted people suspected of collaborating with police. Suspected police informants were typically abducted from their homes at night, executed on the outskirts of their villages and left to be discovered by relatives or neighbours the next day. The bodies are commonly found with pamphlets or posters accusing the victim of collaborating with government forces. The falling number of executions suggests either that the insurgency has become less willing to kill civilians or that the government's growing security presence has diminished the group's ability to wield violence with impunity.[6] While CPI–Maoist was responsible for all confirmed civilian fatalities, security forces were likely responsible for a number of unconfirmed civilian deaths. During an August encounter in Chhattisgarh's Sukma district, a CRPF team killed more than a dozen suspected Maoists later identified as non-combatants by local activists (though police disputed this claim). In addition, security forces likely carried out extrajudicial executions. In June, residents from Nuapada district's Bhainsadani village, in Odisha State, carried a human skeleton several kilometres to a non-local police station. The villagers believed the remains belonged to a health professional last seen in April in the custody of local police posted to Nuapada's Boden Station. As Boden police apparently refused to examine the burial site (prompting the villagers' journey to an adjacent police station), the circumstances suggest that the civilian was illegally executed for alleged links with CPI–Maoist.

Impact

CPI–Maoist continues to weaken

Fatality and surrender rates suggest that the government's counter-insurgency efforts have continued to degrade CPI–Maoist's fighting strength since 2013. In January 2018, CPI–Maoist publicised its alarm about the government's increasingly sophisticated efforts to solicit surrenders with a communiqué disseminated throughout the organisation. The communiqué constitutes strong evidence that the (easy-to-observe) yearly count of surrendered militants corresponds with actual (difficult-to-observe) damage to CPI–Maoist's organisational integrity.

Uneven voter turnout in Chhattisgarh elections

Since 2012, the government has sought to address conflict drivers by mitigating civilians' grievances against the state. To that end, government forces have increasingly provided public goods and services, especially transportation and communications infrastructure, to remote communities. Arguably, this strategy showed some positive results in 2018, especially in the context of Chhattisgarh's statewide legislative-assembly elections in November. Voter turnout in the southern half of the state (which hosts the largest concentration of Maoists in the Red Corridor) reached above 70% despite Maoists' efforts (both violent and non-violent) to disrupt polling.[7] This figure was commonly reported by media outlets and interpreted as evidence of widespread support for India's democratic system, and in opposition to CPI–Maoist's Communist vision.[8] The figure is somewhat misleading, however, in that it aggregates turnout for all of southern Chhattisgarh, much of which remains unaffected by the conflict. By comparison, turnout in Bijapur and Konta precincts, the areas hardest hit by the insurgency, reached 49% and 55%, respectively, suggesting Maoists' efforts to disrupt polling met with some success.

The Pathalgadi movement

Outside Chhattisgarh, the spread of the Pathalgadi movement in 2018 may serve as another indicator of the counter-insurgency's impact on civilian communities. More than 200 villages in Jharkhand State populated by 'tribal' communities erected large stone monuments (a local cultural tradition) to signal their support for the movement. Citing violence at the hands of both CPI–Maoist and police, the Pathalgadi supporters have publicly warned all outsiders to stay away from their territories.[9] Similar to the relatively low turnout rates in parts of Chhattisgarh, the Pathalgadi movement suggests that government forces have yet to establish legitimacy and/or civilian protection in many conflict-affected communities.

Trends

End of CPI–Maoist?

Several federal- and state-government officials claimed during the year that CPI–Maoist's demise was imminent and inevitable, or that the movement was in its 'last phase'.[10] On the one hand, there is compelling evidence to support security forces' optimism. As in recent years, relative fatality rates continued to favour security forces. In addition, evidence emerged to suggest that surrender rates among CPI–Maoist's fighters have badly undermined the group's strength. Conceivably, the group could unravel before the end of 2019. On the other hand, CPI–Maoist remained a dangerous force by the end of 2018. It killed at least 128 civilians and security personnel during the year, and demonstrated the ability to evade security forces while travelling long distances across states. For instance, following attacks in June and July that left several of its security personnel dead, Jharkhand State police failed to prevent two separate Maoist teams from travelling back to their respective bases of operation in Bihar and West Bengal states. Additionally, the group has made a concerted effort to adapt its leadership and organisational structure to resist an increasingly robust security presence. If CPI–Maoist successfully builds ties with new communities, or harnesses civilians' grievances against the state, it may rebound and rebuild in coming years.

A diminishing command-level surrender rate may have important implications for CPI–Maoist's future. If commanders have ceased to surrender because the remaining leaders are totally committed to the movement, security forces may be faced with a small but firmly resolved and highly cohesive rebel leadership. Such a leadership corps could steer CPI–Maoist through a great deal more adversity before it finally (if ever) capitulates. Alternatively, the business of rebellion may remain profitable (in spite of the ED's efforts) to commanders and their followers. If so, CPI–Maoist may transition into a wholly criminal syndicate, an organisation dedicated to generating illicit profits rather than achieving a Communist revolution. Maoist insurgents in Bangladesh underwent a similar transition in the 1980s and 1990s before eventually being crushed in the 2000s. If the ED's efforts achieve wide success in coming years, however, this path may be closed to CPI–Maoist.

Possible decrease in support for Modi

The ED's efforts were only made possible by the Modi administration's 2016 'demonetisation' policy, which suddenly voided most of the paper currency in circulation. The policy was designed to pull criminal and militant cash into the licit economy, making it harder for groups like CPI–Maoist (as well as petty criminals) to accrue and use money 'levied' from civilians. It also imposed hardships on many legitimate businesses and individuals, which made the policy extremely controversial and deeply unpopular in many quarters. Had demonetisation proved a clear success in combatting Naxalism (or the Kashmir insurgency), the Modi administration might have been able to use that success to justify its disruptive policy. In lieu of that success, the Indian electorate may become less willing to re-elect Modi in 2019.

Key drivers remain unaddressed

The Naxalite conflict has caused a great deal of human suffering. Unlike most conflicts, however, it has also resulted in rapid state-sponsored economic development. The government has deliberately expanded transportation, electrification and cellular-communication infrastructure throughout the Red Corridor to increase security forces' mobility, and also to persuade civilian communities to reject armed resistance and those who use it. Should CPI–Maoist agree to peacefully negotiate its surrender (an option which the central and state governments have often proposed on condition that the group first disarm), the government's ongoing infrastructure projects may help the Red Corridor to thrive. At the same time, human-rights activists regularly voice anger at the government's counter-insurgency tactics and indigenous movements have periodically challenged the government's policies and legitimacy, such as Jharkhand's Pathalgadi movement.

The counter-insurgency has therefore not succeeded in addressing the drivers of conflict, even though CPI–Maoist has struggled to exploit those same drivers in recent years.

Notes

1 'Maoists plan 3-State Red corridor', *Pioneer*, 27 February 2018.

2 'Sukma "Maoist" arrests divide activists, cops', *New Indian Express*, 26 March 2018, ; 'Prolonged detention of advocate Murugan gross injustice', *Hindu*, 20 January 2018; 'Tribal rights activists questioned', *Hindu*, 4 July 2018; 'Scan on "rape" and "murder" in Maoist drive', *Telegraph*, 2 August 2018.

3 'Encounter victims were innocent: Sori', *Hindu*, 9 August 2018; 'Soni Sori questions Chhattisgarh encounter, police call it above board', *Indian Express*, 12 August 2018.

4 'Villagers walk 15 km to hand over skeleton to police', *Hindu*, 11 June 2018.

5 Amnesty International, 'Government of India Treating Human Rights Organisations Like Criminal Enterprises', 26 October 2018; Amnesty International, 'Bhima Koregaon: Clampdown on Dissent Continues, Three Human Rights Defenders Placed in Police Custody', 28 October 2018.

6 Lisa Hultman, 'Battle Losses and Rebel Violence: Raising the Costs for Fighting', *Terrorism and Political Violence*, vol. 19, no. 2, 2007, pp. 205–22; Jessica A. Stanton, *Violence and Restraint in Civil War* (New York: Cambridge University Press, 2016).

7 Francesca R. Jensenius and Gilles Verniers, 'Studying Indian Politics with Large-scale Data: Indian Election Data 1961–Today', *Studies in Indian Politics*, vol. 5, no. 2, 2017, pp. 269–75.

8 '76.35 per cent voting in Chhattisgarh Assembly polls', *Economic Times*, 21 November 2018.

9 'The Pathalgadi rebellion', *Hindu*, 14 April 2018.

10 'MHA advisor says Maoist insurgency in last stage, but Centre expects more IED attacks', *Hindustan Times*, 24 May 2018.

India (Northeast)

Overview

The conflict in 2018

During 2018, the three major conflicts in India's northeast – in Manipur and Assam states and the Naga-inhabited areas of the region – continued to witness reductions in violence. Violence has been declining in the region since 2010; on 17 January 2018, Union Home Minister Rajnath Singh declared that insurgency-related incidents had dropped from 1,963 incidents in 2000 to 308 in 2017, and that 2017 had the lowest number of insurgency-related incidents in the region since 1997.

The decline was the result of continued, sustained counter-insurgency pressure against armed groups which had not signed up to the 1997 Nagaland State ceasefire, such as the National Democratic Front of Bodoland–Saoraigwra (NDFB–S), and internal fissures in the main non-ceasefire armed group, the National Socialist Council of Nagaland–Khaplang (NSCN–K), which reduced its ability and willingness to conduct major attacks against the security forces.

In Assam State, however, political tensions surrounding the publication of the National Register of Citizens (NRC) and protests against New Delhi's proposed Citizenship (Amendment) Bill to grant automatic citizenship to religious minorities (which would sanction migration from neighbouring countries) threatened to revive the conflict in the state. These tensions gave the main anti-talks faction, the United Liberation Front of Asom–Independent (ULFA–I), the opportunity to increase recruitment and conduct a series of high-profile attacks to declare its public opposition to Delhi's citizenship bill.

Key statistics	
Type:	Internal
IDPs total (2017):	not applicable
IDPs new (2018):	not applicable
Refugees total (2018):	not applicable
Refugees new (2018):	not applicable
People in need (2018):	not applicable

South Asia

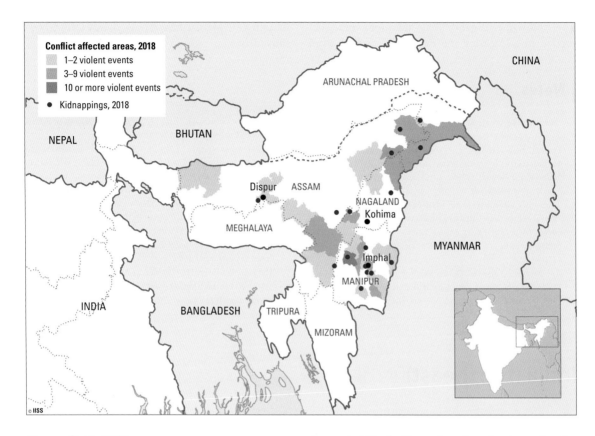

The conflict to 2018

In 1997, the central government ended outright hostilities and initiated peace talks with the major armed group in the northeast region, the National Socialist Council of Nagalim–Isak Muivah (NSCN–IM), resulting in a tense but durable ceasefire. In August 2015, the two parties signed a secretive document that was heralded as a framework for a final peace accord to take place in the coming years. While the terms of the 'Framework Agreement' became clearer during 2018, tensions over the status of 'Greater Nagalim' (a belt of territory encompassing all of Nagaland, the hills of Manipur, part of central Assam and northeastern

Arunachal Pradesh) continued to dominate the discussion of any lasting resolution to the conflict. The issue has dominated the politics of the Naga conflict since the creation of Nagaland State in 1962.[1] It came to a head in 2001 when the government was forced to backtrack from extending the ceasefire with the NSCN–IM (which covered only Nagaland State) following a violent backlash in Manipur.[2] Indeed, growing clarity surrounding the terms of the agreement, which reportedly grants non-territorial constitutional concessions to Nagas within Greater Nagalim, arguably revived anxieties in Manipur, Assam and Arunachal Pradesh.

Forces

Government and state forces

The Indian central government continued to deploy the armed forces and five central police/paramilitary agencies, in addition to each state government's law-enforcement agencies, to conduct counter-insurgency operations in the states of Assam, Manipur and Nagaland (see **Table 1**).

The composition of force deployments in the region largely remained unchanged in 2018. The Indian Army and the Assam Rifles (a central paramilitary force officered by the army) retained leading operational roles in the conduct of counter-insurgency operations, particularly in Arunachal Pradesh, upper eastern Assam, Nagaland and the

Force	Organisation Type	Role and Deployment
Indian armed forces	Military force	Army: Counter-insurgency (Assam, Manipur, Arunachal Pradesh, Nagaland), border defence Air Force: Supply, logistics
Assam Rifles	Paramilitary force	Counter-insurgency (Assam, Arunachal Pradesh, Manipur, Nagaland), border defence
State police	Local law enforcement	Counter-insurgency (Assam, Manipur), anti-extortion policing (Nagaland)
Central Reserve Police Force	Central police force	Policing support (Assam, Manipur)
Border Security Force	Central armed police force	Border defence, limited internal security
Indo-Tibetan Border Police	Central armed police force	Border police, limited internal security
Central Industrial Security Force	Central armed police force	Installation defence

Table 1: Indian government forces

hill areas of Manipur. Deployments of the army and Assam Rifles are geared towards 'area domination', an approach which involves a series of interconnected outposts along a 'counter-insurgency grid', conducting regular patrols to disrupt insurgent activity.[3]

While police forces are ill equipped compared to their military and paramilitary counterparts, they nonetheless played crucial counter-insurgency roles in localities such as the Imphal municipal area in Manipur State, where the 1958 Armed Forces (Special Powers) Act (AFSPA) – providing legal cover for the armed forces to operate in areas of 'disturbance' – was lifted in 2015. Similarly, in urban centres of Nagaland such as Dimapur, specialist anti-extortion police units checked the taxation practices of several Naga outfits collecting revenue from businesses, though the peace process compels these security forces to exercise a degree of restraint when pursuing these extortion networks.

The ongoing Supreme Court investigation into the army's role in extrajudicial killings and the implications of the AFSPA is challenging the Indian Army's role as the main counter-insurgency force in the region. On 28 January 2018, Chief of Army Staff General Bipin Rawat declared that it was not an appropriate time to amend the provisions of the legislation. During August, it emerged that more than 700 army officers have challenged cases filed against security personnel in operational theatres, including the northeast. On 10 September, the army's top leadership seemed to be seriously reconsidering a recalibration of its operational role in the northeast, while criticising the Supreme Court investigation for leading local commanders to be 'overcautious',

arguing that this stance had caused an increase in army casualties in states such as Manipur.

Non-state armed groups

Non-state armed groups in the region can be broadly divided into groups engaged in some form of peace talks with the government and groups opposed to negotiations (see **Table 2**).

In Manipur, the Kuki National Organisation (KNO) and United People's Front (UPF) – the two main umbrella organisations representing Kuki armed groups – signed a Suspension of Operations agreement in 2008 but did not substantively begin peace talks until June 2016. The People's Liberation Army (PLA) and the conglomerate of six Manipuri armed groups under the Coordination Committee (CorCom) are opposed to holding any talks with the Indian government. These groups have conducted joint operations with other anti-talks armed groups such as ULFA–Independent (ULFA–I) and the National Socialist Council of Nagaland–Khaplang (NSCN–K).

The two main insurgent groups in Assam – the United Liberation Front of Asom (ULFA) and National Democratic Front of Bodoland (NDFB) – have undergone a number of splits into pro-talks and anti-talks factions. In 2009, ULFA split into ULFA–Pro-Talks Faction (ULFA–PTF) and ULFA–I; the NDFB has split on two occasions, firstly into the NDFB–Ranjan Daimary (NDFB–RD) and NDFB–Progressive (NDFB–P) factions in 2008, while the NDFB–RD faction suffered a further split with the formation of NDFB–Songbijit (NDFB–S) in 2012. The anti-talks factions linked up with other anti-talks factions in the region as part of their involvement

Table 2a: Key armed groups known to be in talks with the Government of India[4]				
Armed Group	**Formed**	**Area of Operation (by State)**	**Operations**	**Main Rivals**
Kangleipak Communist Party–Lamphel (KCP–Lamphel)[a]	1980 (KCP); date of breakaway unknown	Plains of Manipur	Formally surrendered group	Non-ceasefire signatory groups (i.e., UNLF)
Kuki National Organisation (KNO)	1988	Kuki-populated areas of Manipur	(Umbrella organisation: no operations of its own)	NSCN–IM
Kuki Revolutionary Army (KRA)	2000	Kuki-populated areas of Manipur	Illicit economic activity including extortion	Rival Kuki armed groups
National Democratic Front of Bodoland–Progressive (NDFB–P)	2009	Western Assam	Ceasefire	NDFB–S
National Socialist Council of Nagaland–Khaplang/Khango Konyak (NSCN–K/KK)	2018	Eastern Nagaland	Peace talks	NSCN–IM, NSCN–K/YA
National Socialist Council of Nagaland–Kitovi-Neokpao/Unification (NSCN–KN/U)	2007 (NSCN–KN and NSCN–U formed); 2011 (NSCN–KN/U formed)	Nagaland, Arunachal Pradesh	Factional clashes, ceasefire, limited clashes with security forces	State forces (limited clashes), NSCN–IM
National Socialist Council of Nagalim–Isak Muivah (NSCN–IM)	1988	Nagaland, Naga-populated areas of Assam, Manipur, Arunachal Pradesh	Clashes with rival groups, limited clashes with state forces, illicit economic activity including extortion and kidnapping	State forces (limited clashes), NSCN–K, ZUF, Kuki armed groups
ULFA–Pro-Talks Faction (ULFA–PTF)	2009	Assam	Peace talks, participates in peaceful protests	n/a
United People's Front (UPF)	1977	Kuki-populated areas of Manipur	(Umbrella organisation: no operations of its own)	NSCN–IM
United Socialist Revolutionary Army (USRA)	Date of breakaway from ZRA unknown	Hill areas of Manipur	Illicit economic activity including extortion	Rival tribal factions
Working Committee (WC)	2016	Nagaland	Limited intra-factional clashes, extortion	NSCN–IM

in the umbrella organisation, the United National Liberation Front of Western South East Asia (UNLFWSEA). Among the Naga groups, the NSCN–K, having engaged in dialogue with the government since 2001, left the process in 2015 and immediately returned to armed operations. The NSCN–K remains the only major armed group opposed to talks in the state and chairs the UNLFWSEA.

Drivers

Politics of identity, whether through secessionist sentiments or the desire to create local ethnic 'homelands', have long featured as major drivers behind the conflicts in northeast India. While violence decreased steadily in 2018, many of the underlying social, political and economic drivers of the armed conflict remain present, with some appearing to re-emerge as catalysts for renewed social and political unrest.

Identity politics
In Assam State, the ULFA insurgency and Bodo insurgencies have historically opposed the settlement of non-local migrants among indigenous communities.

Table 2b: Key armed groups known to be not in talks with the Government of India[a]

Armed Group	Formed	Area of Operation (by State)	Operations	Main Rivals
Coordination Committee (CorCom)	2011	Manipur, Arunachal Pradesh	Umbrella organisation: coordinated strikes, individual armed-group extortion programmes	State forces
Dimasa National Army (DNA)	Early 2000s	Dima Hasao district in Assam	Extortion, limited clashes with security forces	State forces
National Democratic Front of Bodoland–Saoraigwra (NDFB–S)	2012	Western Assam	Ethnic violence	State forces
National Socialist Council of Nagaland–Khaplang (NSCN–K)[b]	1988	Eastern Nagaland, Myanmar, Arunachal Pradesh, Manipur	Cross-border strikes	State forces NSCN–IM
National Socialist Council of Nagaland–Khaplang/Yung Aung (NSCN–K/YA)[c]	2018	Eastern Nagaland, Myanmar, Arunachal Pradesh, Manipur	Cross-border strikes, joint operations with allies	NSCN–K/KK
People's Liberation Army (PLA)	1978	Manipur, Arunachal Pradesh	Strikes in coordination with allies	State forces
People's Revolutionary Party of Kangleipak (PREPAK)	1977	Plains of Manipur	Coordination with allies via CorCom	State forces
Thadou People's Liberation Army (TPLA)	2015	Thadou-populated areas of Manipur	Clashes with security forces	State forces
United Liberation Front of Asom–Independent (ULFA–I)	2009	Northeastern Assam, Arunachal Pradesh	Extortion and extortion-related violence, strikes on security forces, public bombings	State forces
United National Liberation Front (UNLF)	1964	Manipur	Limited strikes against security forces, moral policing killings	State forces, rival Meitei armed groups (i.e., KCP–Lamphel)
United Tribal Liberation Army–Poukhai (UTLA–P)	2002 (UTLA)	Kuki-populated areas of Manipur	Clashes with rival armed groups	Rival UTLA factions
Zeliangrong United Front (ZUF)	2011	Zeliangrong-populated areas of Manipur, Nagaland, Assam	Clashes with NSCN–IM	NSCN–IM

[a] Armed operations suspended; [b] as of 2018, the original NSCN–K has split into NSCN–K/YA and NSCN–K/KK; [c] in talks with the government of Myanmar

Local politicians have exploited popular fears of the social, economic and cultural impacts of immigration in the years following India's independence in 1947, and particularly during the 1979–85 Assam Agitation. Even though the intensity of the ULFA insurgency has declined since 2010, the question of native identity and legitimate citizenship still causes political tensions.

Insurgent political economy

Years of conflict have fundamentally altered the political economy of the region, which is now plagued by criminal practices such as extortion and kidnapping. Extortion payments from civilians, businesses and construction projects form a significant portion of insurgent groups' revenues and therefore shape their interactions with civilians.

For many analysts, this indicates that insurgencies in the region have simply descended into criminality and lost their ideological underpinnings.[5] Yet armed groups adopt these tactics as part of their wider efforts at establishing local or regional rebel governance structures, often issuing press releases regarding 'tax collection' in order to project an image of regularised governance.[6] On 24 May, for example, the NSCN–IM's regional secretary in

Dima Hasao district issued a request that village and ward chairmen submit their tax forms to the group's regional office in the district by 25 June. Similarly, the Working Committee (WC) – an umbrella organisation of six Naga armed groups – announced on 15 June that it would no longer exempt businesses run by non-locals from its 'tax' collections, indicating a political angle in its efforts to reshape power relations in favour of 'local' Nagas.

These parallel governance networks have historically extended into and penetrated state structures. Developing taxation relationships by appealing to 'natural allies' within the state has allowed groups such as the NSCN–IM to consolidate financial and political support, providing a steady stream of funds and ensuring that the state government does not act against its interests. A number of Naga armed groups have penetrated Nagaland state-government structures over the years, with state politicians typically linked with either the NSCN–IM or the NSCN–K. During 2018, the fall of the Zeliang government (linked to the NSCN–K) created the space for investigation, and the National Investigation Agency (NIA) duly summoned Zeliang on 28 March. On 31 May, the NIA revealed that ten state-government officials had siphoned funds to the NSCN–K. In Manipur, an NIA investigation into the disappearance of 56 pistols from the Manipur State Rifles during 2016–17 revealed on 30 July 2018 that the pistols had been delivered to Kuki armed groups – including the Kuki Revolutionary Army (KRA) and United Kuki Liberation Front (UKLF) – by a Congress party lawmaker and ethnic Kuki.

Political and Military Developments

State Assembly elections

Little tangible progress had been made in peace talks between the central government and the NSCN–IM since the signature of the 'Framework Agreement' in August 2015, despite government assurances to the contrary. The February State Assembly elections in Nagaland shifted the focus away from the peace talks in the early months of 2018, despite calls from civil-society organisations for 'no election without solution'. The key contestants in the election were the Congress party, the ruling Naga People's Front (NPF), the Bharatiya Janata Party (BJP) and the Nationalist Democratic Progressive Party (NDPP). The NPF on 23 January outlined its plans to retain its alliance with the BJP, but on 3 February the BJP declared its intention to form an electoral alliance with the NDPP. The BJP's investment of political clout and resources into the campaign culminated in Prime Minister Narendra Modi's visit to the state on 22 February, when he told crowds that the peace process would be solved in the coming months. The BJP–NDPP alliance secured 32 seats, enabling the NDPP's Neiphiu Rio to be sworn in as chief minister on 8 March. As a result, Nagaland joined Manipur (2017) and Assam (2016) as a further key victory for the BJP in a region that had previously held out as a Congress stronghold (see **Figure 1**).

The question of Greater Nagalim

Modi's grand promise for a solution within months was more a product of careful political rhetoric in advance of the upcoming election than a realistic assessment of the trajectory of the peace process. Indeed, the issues dominating the agenda of the peace talks remained seemingly deadlocked on the question of the integration of the Naga-inhabited areas of neighbouring Assam, Manipur and Arunachal Pradesh into what the NSCN–IM considers to be the entity of Greater Nagalim.

Rumours surrounding the broad contours of the settlement nonetheless suggested that the parties were nearing a compromise of sorts on the question of Greater Nagalim, possibly granting 'special rights' to Nagas on 'land and resources' in the three states.

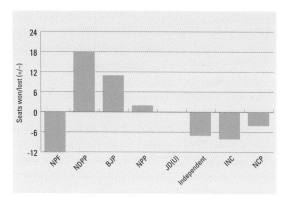

Figure 1: Nagaland electoral results by seats won/lost

While the central government would not formally parcel off parts of Manipur, Assam and Arunachal Pradesh, the contents of the Framework Agreement afforded special status and 'special arrangements' to Nagas living in these states, in the form of autonomous territorial councils, as confirmed by the government's mediator, R.N. Ravi, in July.

The two parties appeared to be approaching a resolution when on 22 August Ravi announced to a parliamentary committee that the NSCN–IM had dropped its demand for Greater Nagalim. The group issued a carefully worded rebuttal on 26 August, saying that it had never softened its position on the unique history and rights of the Nagas while failing to directly challenge Ravi's remarks. The remarks indicated the group's broader dilemma, in which it must retain a 'strong' negotiating position vis-à-vis the Indian government in order to prevent defections to opposing Naga factions while at the same time conveying to its constituents that it is the only group capable of delivering tangible results in the peace process.

The divulgence of these details of the negotiations to the public failed, however, to reassure other communities in neighbouring states that fervently oppose any formal recognition of Naga political and insurgent influence in the state. People demonstrated in Manipur against any redistribution of political power, whether on a territorial or non-territorial basis.

Other peace processes

The Indian government made minimal progress with other armed groups in the region in 2018. On 2 June, a police raid on the residence of the leader of the WC in Jotsoma, Kohima district in Nagaland State, led to the group announcing its withdrawal from talks. Protests from local civil-society organisations led the group to resume talks by 12 June.

In Manipur State, the appointment of a new government interlocutor for talks with the Kuki armed groups in January 2018 led to talks in New Delhi between the central government and the two major Kuki umbrella organisations, the Kuki National Organisation (KNO) and United People's Front (UPF). Beyond the submission of initial demands in January, however, the talks slowed down and the group issued warnings of a possible return to armed hostilities. The group submitted a demand for the creation of an autonomous council in the

Kuki-inhabited areas of Manipur, but progress stalled throughout the year. On 15 September, the KNO threatened to abandon the peace process, although the group renewed its Suspension of Operations agreement along with the UPF on 25 September.

A third split in the NSCN–K

The NSCN–K plays an instrumental role in coordinating the operations of anti-peace-talks factions in the northeast, but suffered its third split in seven years during the summer of 2018. The split fractured the group into an Indian faction (led by Khango Konyak) and a Burmese Naga faction (led by Yung Aung). The split fragmented the group's hardline position on peace talks with the Indian government, a position adopted in April 2015 after the group renounced the ceasefire with New Delhi.

In 2011 and 2015, Indian Naga groups defected, denouncing an increasing dominance of Burmese Nagas led by then-leader and founder S.S. Khaplang. After Khaplang's death in June 2017, fissures emerged again over whether to open negotiations with the Indian or the Myanmar government. The NSCN–K also changed military tactics. It was responsible for at least 79 fatalities between 27 March 2015 and 10 June 2017, but only 15 under Konyak's leadership (from 10 June 2017 to 27 August 2018). Konyak's comparatively restrained approach has reportedly drawn accusations of incompetency from factions within the group.[7]

The Myanmar government's attempts to push the NSCN–K into more active involvement with its Union Peace Conference provided the immediate catalyst for the Burmese faction to oust Konyak. On 25 July, the Myanmar armed forces launched an operation against NSCN–K camps in Taga, Sagaing region within Myanmar and did not allow the group's leader to leave the Kukwang Valley. On 17 August, Konyak was 'impeached' and allowed to flee to India with at least 100 militants had followed Konyak. Other NSCN–K camps along the India–Myanmar border were reportedly contemplating joining his faction.

Upon the group's split, both the Indian and Burmese factions began back-channel negotiations with their respective choices of negotiating partner.[8] The Indian faction attempted to open a dialogue with the Indian government, seeking the support of eastern Naga civil-society organisations such as the Eastern Naga People's Organisation (ENPO) as intermediaries in the process. On 15 October, Isak Sumi, the new 'general secretary' of the NSCN–K's Khango Konyak faction, said that the group and the Indian central government were already seeking to resume peace talks. The faction's demands reportedly included releasing top functionaries from jail and affording the remaining incarcerated militants the status of political prisoners, indicating that the group was softening its sovereignty-only preconditions. The Indian government's interlocutor said on 1 November that New Delhi had never abrogated the ceasefire and was open to talks but only with the original NSCN–K rather than a separate entity.

Tensions surrounding the Citizenship Bill

The central government's attempts to pass the Citizenship (Amendment) Bill (proposed in 2016), which would grant citizenship to Hindus, Sikhs, Jains and Christians from Afghanistan, Bangladesh and Pakistan, generated considerable political opposition and growing unrest. On 9 May, a senior ULFA–Pro-Talks Faction (ULFA–PTF) leader, Jiten Dutta, warned that the Kakopathar-based faction of the group would withdraw from the peace talks and take up arms if the bill passed. On 13 November, ULFA–PTF leader Anup Chetia suggested that the crisis over the citizenship bill had fuelled Assamese nationalist sentiments and increased recruitment. The intelligence arm of the Assam police shared these concerns; on 11 November, Director General (Special Branch) Pallab Bhattacharyya said that the Citizenship Amendment Act had given a 'fresh lease of life' to ULFA–I, noting that at least eight youths had joined the organisation from 1 September to 11 November and a further eight had been arrested attempting to do so.

Violent Events

The armed conflicts in the states of Assam, Naga and Manipur witnessed 78 fatalities in 110 violent events throughout the year, compared with 95 fatalities in 2017, 165 in 2016 and 260 in 2015.

Geographic concentration

According to the Indian government's Ministry of Home Affairs, insurgency-related incidents concentrated in Arunachal Pradesh State and the areas in immediate proximity. Violent events there increased by 22% in 2017 compared to 2016, in contrast to the declines in violent incidents of 56% in Assam, 67% in Nagaland and 28% in Manipur. Three of the state's easternmost districts – Changlang, Longding and Tirap – provide an access route into Myanmar, where most of the anti-peace-talks groups are camped. As the incoming Director General of Police in Assam, Kuladhar Saikia, acknowledged on 5 May, counter-insurgency operations in Assam have tended to push insurgents into Arunachal Pradesh, highlighting the importance of coordinating with security forces in the three districts of Arunachal Pradesh.

The dispersion of violent events in and around Arunachal Pradesh State in 2018 saw just 12 of the region's violent events taking place within the state itself, though these resulted in ten fatalities (including two army personnel) compared to nine in 2017 (when no army personnel were killed). Violent events remained most heavily concentrated in Manipur (42.7%) due to the continued presence of multiple armed groups in contested areas such as Noney (19.5%), where these armed groups clash with one another and the security forces. The presence of a significant business community in the Imphal Municipal area, particularly Imphal West district, provides armed groups with opportunities for extortion revenues, and accounted for 28% of the violent incidents in the state.

Violent events by armed group
NDFB–S

Sustained counter-insurgency operations succeeded in reducing violence in the region in 2018 and significantly reduced the ability of non-ceasefire-signatory armed groups to inflict casualties on other actors (see **Table 3**). This was particularly apparent in the case of the NDFB–S. Since conducting large-scale ethnic killings in Western Assam in December 2014, *Operation All Clear* has significantly weakened the organisation.[9] On 23 April, the Ministry of Home Affairs released data indicating that 60 NDFB–S militants had been killed since the start of *All Clear* up to the end of 2017, while 1,015 were arrested. As a

Table 3: Fatalities by armed group, 2018

Armed Group	State	Number of Fatalities				
		Security forces	Civilians	Other militants	Own losses	Total
ULFA–I	Assam	5	9	0	4	18
NSCN–K	Naga	3	1	0	9	13
NSCN–IM	Naga	1	1	4	7	13
ZUF	Assam, Naga, Manipur	0	0	2	6	8
PLA	Manipur	1	0	0	5	6
NSCN–U	Naga	0	0	0	5	5
NDFB–S	Assam	0	0	0	5	5
UNLF	Manipur	0	2	1	0	3
PREPAK	Manipur	2	0	0	0	2
USRA	Manipur	0	0	0	2	2
KCP–Lamphel	Manipur	0	0	1	1	2
UTLA–P	Manipur	1	0	0	0	1
TPLA	Manipur	1	0	0	0	1
KRA	Manipur	0	0	0	1	1
DNA	Assam	0	0	0	1	1

result, the group was unable to inflict any casualties on security forces or civilians in 2018 and suffered five fatalities, four of which were the result of security-forces operations.

NSCN–K
Similarly, although the NSCN–K caused the second-highest number of fatalities in 2018, this constituted a drop compared to the period between 27 March 2015 and 10 June 2017 (from the group's abrogation of the ceasefire agreement to S.S. Khaplang's death).[10] The internal differences in approach that led to the group's split had an impact on operational decision-making.

ULFA–I
In November, one of its deadliest months in Assam in recent years, the ULFA–I killed five civilians in one incident at Sadiya Saikhowaghat, Tinsukia district, on 1 November. Three weeks later, the group detonated a bomb at Demow, Sivasagar district, killing two civilians. On 13 October 2018, the group detonated a bomb in Fancy Bazaar, Guwahati city, in one of its biggest attacks on the capital in recent years, injuring four in what it called an 'explosive statement' levelled at the Citizenship (Amendment) Bill.

NSCN–IM
Despite the NSCN–IM's long-standing participation in a ceasefire agreement with New Delhi, the group remained active and was implicated in several armed clashes with rival groups, such as the Zeliangrong United Front (ZUF), which caused 13 fatalities in 2018. On 7 August, ZUF militants killed one NSCN–IM militant in Khumji, Noney district of Manipur, and on 1 September one ZUF militant during a clash in Nungnang, Tamenglong district in Manipur. The NSCN–IM and security forces also launched direct operations against one another in contested areas such as Arunachal Pradesh and Manipur. On 25 May, one NSCN–IM militant was killed after Assam Rifles personnel launched an operation against a hideout in Longding district of Arunachal Pradesh, while on 5 March, an army soldier was killed during a clash with NSCN–IM militants in Noney district of Manipur. On 30 June, 25 NSCN–IM militants ambushed an Assam Rifles convoy in Motongsa, Changlang district of Arunachal Pradesh, while four days later security forces attacked an NSCN–IM camp in the area. The clashes are indicative of the ambiguous rules governing interactions between the state and NSCN–IM in the states not governed by the ceasefire (restricted to Nagaland).

South Asia

Kidnappings

There were 26 kidnapping incidents across the three conflicts throughout the year, which were predominantly concentrated in and around Manipur (50%). On 10 March, armed individuals kidnapped two railway-construction workers in Makru, Tamenglong district in Manipur. On 17 May, Assam Rifles personnel revealed that at least 12 labourers working on the construction of the Northeast Frontier Railway had been abducted along National Highway 37, the primary road linking Imphal to Jiribam in Manipur. Armed groups typically employed kidnappings and threats of violence when extortion payments (usually charged to contractors, construction workers and businesses within armed groups' areas of influence) were late or outstanding. For example, on 10 February, NSCN–IM militants kidnapped a contractor in Changlang district of Arunachal Pradesh after the contractor reportedly paid only half of the ransom of INR10 million (US$142,215) demanded by the group (the hostage was released three days later without any indication as to whether the outstanding ransom was paid).

Impact

Economic impact

New Delhi's 'Act East' programme, initiated in 2014 as an extension to India's post-1991 'Look East' policy, seeks to improve connectivity between India and Southeast Asian countries through the development of secure and reliable access corridors into neighbouring states such as Myanmar. The armed groups' continued efforts to impose taxes on road and rail infrastructure development continued to threaten this strategy. Reports of harassment and violence against road-construction workers in Nagaland during 2018 illustrated the challenges the state government faced in implementing the Nagaland Road Maintenance Policy 2017, a government venture to ensure effective road maintenance. Crucial arteries connecting Moreh, a town on the international border with Myanmar, to Imphal and Nagaland remained under the control of the NSCN–IM, which imposes levies at multiple toll gates on the highway. On 22 April, reports emerged that trucks transporting goods from Manipur to the rest of India were increasingly being threatened by Naga armed groups along the highways, with the effect of driving up commodity prices in the state.

Diplomatic agreements between India and Myanmar nonetheless promised to increase cross-border trade and enhance prospects for human development in the areas immediately adjacent to the international border. On 11 May, the two countries consolidated their existing agreements for visa-free travel along a 16 kilometre zone at the border, which passes through the states of Arunachal Pradesh, Nagaland, Manipur and Mizoram. The agreement, which is designed to encourage cross-border trade and to preserve communities living along the border, was extended to allow citizens of both countries to access health and education services.

Declining violence raises political concerns

Despite the fact that violence declined in the region during 2018, different branches of the government viewed the security situation differently. The possibility of reducing the coverage of the AFSPA provoked opposition from the state government of Assam, which feared that the withdrawal of armed forces could render the state vulnerable to heightened militant activity. In July, the Ministry of Home Affairs suggested reducing the areas covered by the Armed Forces Special Powers Act, but was met with opposition from the Defence Ministry and the army. The state government ultimately rejected the proposal, extending the act across the state for a further six months on 29 August. The members of a parliamentary standing committee commented that the committee was 'unable to comprehend the divergent perceptions of the situation in Assam'. The reluctance to withdraw the act was indicative of the longer-term entrenchment of the army in the northeast, but it also reflected an anxiety that the army's withdrawal would undermine a central pillar of this apparatus, placing the bulk of responsibility for facing the insurgency on the state governments and local security forces.

The state government's anxieties are perhaps not misplaced. The failure of the state and central governments to reconcile the tensions between the National Register of Citizens and the Citizenship (Amendment) Bill created a polarised political climate in Assam in 2018, leading to many *bandhs* (strikes) and rallies. Assamese-speaking communities have campaigned against the citizenship bill whereas Bengali Hindu migrant communities in the Barak Valley have supported it (as the bill would consolidate their bid for citizenship). Combined with the small but not insignificant resurgence of ULFA–I, these tensions indicate that the two programmes have contributed to the re-emergence of the political grievances that caused the Assam Agitation and the original ULFA insurgency in the 1980s and 1990s.

Trends

Prospects for conflict resolution

Despite continued reductions in violence in the region, the fundamental drivers of conflict and instability in the region remained unresolved and retained the potential to re-escalate into serious civil unrest and insurgency. In Assam, tensions between the National Register of Citizens process and the Citizenship (Amendment) Bill threatened to reopen the political space that ULFA–I had previously been able to exploit successfully. In the contiguous Naga-inhabited areas of Manipur, Assam and Arunachal Pradesh, even guarantees of territorial integrity failed to reassure communities that Nagas could be granted benefits at their expense in the event of a government peace deal with the NSCN–IM. Thus, the underlying tension of the Greater Nagalim vision is likely to produce civil unrest if a peace accord is reached in 2019.

NSCN–K: a return to peace talks?

The split within the NSCN–K increased the likelihood that at least part of the group will return to substantive peace talks during 2019. On 7 December 2018, the Konyak faction of the group unilaterally revoked the NSCN–K's abrogation of the ceasefire in 2015. In December 2018, the two parties initiated informal talks in New Delhi to discuss the group's possible inclusion in the peace process. The government's insistence on 1 November that it would not negotiate with a new faction nonetheless indicated that New Delhi was approaching the Khango Konyak faction with a degree of caution. During 2019, the faction will need to demonstrate its ability to win enough support within the NSCN–K in order to establish itself as a credible partner in the negotiations.

It remained unclear whether and how the split in the NSCN–K would impact the operational viability of the UNLFWSEA, since the NSCN–K has played a central role in hosting, training and coordinating with allied Assam- and Manipur-based armed groups such as the ULFA–I and the CorCom, facilitating access to India via corridors from Myanmar into eastern Nagaland and Arunachal Pradesh. On 3 December, a joint raiding party of NSCN–K and ULFA–I militants were killed in Mon district of Nagaland, suggesting that the split had failed to drastically impact the group's operational viability in the immediate term. However, if the Indian faction is able to consolidate in Mon district of eastern Nagaland during 2019, then it would likely enhance the Myanmar faction's reliance on access corridors into India via Arunachal Pradesh. Such dynamics could impact the operational viability of the UNLFWSEA, meaning the activities of the NSCN–K's Yung Aung faction and the status of counter-insurgency operations in Arunachal Pradesh will be particularly noteworthy during 2019.

Unsolved conflict drivers

Across each conflict theatre, armed groups remain active and involved in violence against civilians, rival armed groups and (to a lesser extent) security forces. As well as political drivers, armed groups continue to be driven by the requirement to secure funds through extortion and kidnapping, with implications for human security and economic development in the region. These underlying drivers, which are fundamentally linked to the political drivers, remain entrenched components of the conflict ecosystem and are unlikely to be dislodged by any major political progress during 2019.

General election in 2019

Upcoming elections 2019 risk distracting policymakers. The Indian government might let the general election pass before re-engaging with peace processes in earnest, as it did in the case of the Nagaland State Assembly elections of 2018. The

South Asia

citizenship bill is the issue most at risk of politicisation in Assam. Given the salience of this political issue, the extent to which the 2019 general election will intersect with the peace processes and political drivers of conflict in the region will also determine whether violence will continue to decline.

Notes

1   Government of India and Naga People's Convention, 'The 16 Point Agreement between the Government of India and the Naga People's Convention', 1960.

2   'Firing Toll to 14, Further Curfew Relaxation', *Sangai Express*, 22 June 2001; 'Truce to Be Restricted to Nagaland State', *Sangai Express*, 27 July 2001.

3   Angel Rabasa et al., *Money in the Bank: Lessons Learned from Past Counterinsurgency (COIN) Operations*, RAND Counterinsurgency Study, Paper 4 (Santa Monica, CA: Rand Corporation, 2007), p. 55.

4   This is a non-exhaustive list indicating the most significant armed groups in the region.

5   Gautam Das, *Insurgencies in North-East India: Moving towards Resolution* (New Delhi, India: Centre for Land Warfare Studies,

2013), p. 3; Arvind Sharma, 'The Psychological Effects on Defence Forces', in *Internal Conflicts: Military Perspectives*, ed. V.R. Raghavan (New Delhi, India: Vij, 2012), pp. 205–22 (pp. 206–7).

6   Alex Waterman, 'Compressing Politics in Counterinsurgency (COIN): Implications for COIN Theory from India's Northeast', *Strategic Analysis*, vol. 41, no. 5, 2017, pp. 447–63 (pp. 451–52).

7   Giriraj Bhattacharjee, 'NSCN–K: Coup!', *South Asia Intelligence Review*, vol. 17, no. 9, 2018.

8   Prabin Kalita, 'India, Myanmar Pull off NSCN(K) Split', *Times of India*, 3 October 2018.

9   Sushil Kumar Sharma, 'Operation All Out against Bodo Militants: What Next?', *Institute for Defence Studies and Analyses*, 2016.

10 Bhattacharjee, 'NSCN–K: Coup!'.

India–Pakistan (Kashmir)

Overview

The conflict in 2018

The conflict in the Indian state of Jammu and Kashmir escalated in 2018, with frequent gunfights between armed groups and the state. Approximately 490 people died in conflict-related incidents in 2018, making it the deadliest year for Kashmir in a decade. The rebel groups suffered approximately 252 fatalities, and the Indian security forces 80, including 30 army personnel. At least 160 civilians were killed, including 31 children and 18 women. The government announced a month-long ceasefire in mid-May, but armed skirmishes continued, while more than 1,400 ceasefire violations were recorded along the Line of Control (LoC) between India and Pakistan, displacing tens of thousands of civilians. The Indian security forces achieved some of the objectives of *Operation All-Out* (launched in 2017) by killing ten of the 12 most-wanted rebel commanders and forcing the armed groups into retreat.

The conflict to 2018

Since the independence of India and Pakistan in 1947, the unresolved status of Kashmir has been a source of conflict. The first war between India and Pakistan in 1947 left the territory partitioned, and the second in 1965 failed to shift the dividing LoC. Although guerrilla warfare in Kashmir was initiated by the Jammu and Kashmir Liberation Front (JKLF) in the late 1980s with an agenda of an independent

Key statistics	
Type:	International
IDPs total (2017):	805,000
IDPs new (2018):	165,000
Refugees total (2018):	no data
Refugees new (2018):	no data
People in need (2018):	not applicable

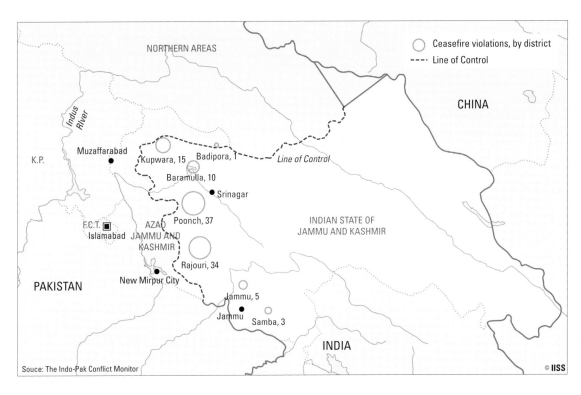

Souce: The Indo-Pak Conflict Monitor

state, it was pro-Pakistan groups, such as Hizbul Mujahideen (HM) and Lashkar-e-Taiba (LeT), who would later dominate and sustain the insurgency. Both HM and LeT seek to merge the whole territory of Kashmir into Pakistan. After giving up arms in 1994, the JKLF has been marginalised, but overwhelming support among Kashmiris remains for an independent state.

On the political front, the All Parties Hurriyat Conference (APHC), an alliance of more than 20 groups, is at the forefront of the self-determination movement in Kashmir. The APHC's two main demands are that India should accept Kashmir as a dispute, and that negotiations should involve Indian, Pakistani and Kashmiri representatives. While Pakistan supports the APHC, successive federal governments in India have so far refused to entertain its demands. India's official position is that Kashmir is an 'integral part' of the country, though New Delhi has offered separate talks with the APHC within the framework of the Indian constitution. Pakistan, on the other hand, maintains that the Kashmir issue must be resolved within the framework of the United Nations Security Council, which has passed resolutions

stating that the question of Kashmir should be decided through a plebiscite with two options for Kashmiris: remaining within India or accession to Pakistan.

From 2003 onwards, partly owing to the post-9/11 environment, the number of insurgency-related incidents gradually decreased in Kashmir from 3,401 in 2003 to 708 in 2008, together with the number of fatalities (from 3,073 to 505 in the same period). The current phase of the armed conflict is partially a consequence of the 2010 street protests, which were brutally quelled by the Indian security forces, with more than 100 protesters killed and hundreds more jailed. Following the killing of the charismatic HM commander Burhan Muzaffar Wani on 8 July 2016, violence has intensified, shrinking the political space of the unionist parties in the region. To stem the momentum of the growing militancy, the ruling Bharatiya Janata Party (BJP) gave free rein to the Indian security forces to kill militants and repress their civilian support structure through *Operation All-Out*. Since 2016, more than 600 rebels have died in the conflict, the majority killed in army raids inside their hideouts, but civilian deaths and injuries have also surged.

South Asia

Forces

State forces

There are an estimated 600,000 to 700,000 Indian security personnel (including army, police, paramilitary and other auxiliary forces) deployed in the state of Jammu and Kashmir. With a troop-to-civilian ratio of 1:12, Kashmir is one of the most militarised regions in the world. The Indian counter-insurgency apparatus in Kashmir is comprised of the Indian Army's elite Rashtriya Rifles (RR), the paramilitary Central Reserve Police Force (CRPF) and Border Security Force (BSF), and the Jammu and Kashmir Police (JKP) and its counter-insurgency wing Special Operations Group (SOG). Military operations against armed groups are jointly conducted by these forces, with the JKP primarily involved in intelligence gathering and surveillance.

The primary objective of the Indian government is to contain the spread of militant recruitments and kill the rebels. On 12 November, Indian Army chief Bipin Rawat stated that 'if the [Kashmiri youth] still do not behave and continue with violence, then the alternative left is to neutralise them'. On 28 November, Rawat said that limited hybrid warfare against Pakistan was advisable, and that inside Kashmir he would prefer 'a new integrated response strategy which is focussed on governmental outreach, political dialogue, good governance, situational awareness, domination and intelligence-based operations'.

United Nations Observer mission

In March 1951, the UN Security Council, under Resolution 91 (1951), established the UN Military Observer Group in India and Pakistan (UNMOGIP), with a mandate to monitor the ceasefire in Kashmir. From May to October, UNMOGIP's headquarters are located in Srinagar in the Indian state of Jammu and Kashmir, and from November to April in Islamabad, Pakistan. UNMOGIP's main headquarters supervises field stations on both sides of the LoC.

Hizbul Mujahideen (HM)

Hizbul Mujahideen (HM) has been active since the late 1980s and is the largest indigenous guerrilla organisation in Kashmir, with approximately 128 militants in 2018. Comprised mainly of local Kashmiris, HM is headed by Syed Salahuddin, who is based in Muzaffarabad (Azad Jammu and Kashmir). HM's operational commander in the Indian state of Jammu and Kashmir is Riyaz Naikoo, who succeeded Sabzar Bhat in May 2017 after the latter was killed in a gunfight in Kashmir's Pulwama district. A former teacher, Naikoo is widely seen as a sharp-minded militant leader with effective organisational and communication skills.

Lashkar-e-Taiba (LeT)

With approximately 141 militants, Lashkar-e-Taiba (LeT) has the most combatants operating in Kashmir and seeks to merge the whole state with Pakistan through a war of attrition against India. Founded by Pakistan-based cleric Hafiz Muhammad Saeed in the late 1980s, LeT is a proscribed organisation that India accuses of carrying out the 2008 Mumbai attacks. LeT has considerable assets within both Pakistan and Afghanistan: in the wake of the 2016 uprising in Kashmir, LeT was able to organise large rallies inside Pakistan and collect millions in donations for its 'Kashmir cause'. Better trained than the local HM forces, LeT militants have carried out some of the deadliest attacks on Indian security forces in the conflict. For example, on 25 June 2016, two LeT militants ambushed Indian paramilitary vehicles on a secured highway in Pampore town, killing eight officers and injuring 20 more. Through its commanders such as Abu Qasim and Abu Dujana, LeT has attracted dozens of Kashmiri recruits in the past few years.

Jaysh-e-Mohammad (JeM)

Created in 2000 by Pakistani national Maulana Masood Azhar, Jaysh-e-Mohammad (JeM) seeks to merge Kashmir with Pakistan. After the 9/11 attacks, JeM was banned by Pakistan's government, though it continues to operate under different names. The outfit was routed in Kashmir a few years ago, but signalled its comeback in August 2017 by carrying out a deadly pre-dawn attack at the police headquarters in Pulwama district, killing eight Indian security personnel. JeM's exact strength in Kashmir is unknown, but more than 60 local youth had reportedly joined the outfit between January and October 2018. The re-entry of JeM into Kashmir presents a challenge to Indian security forces, as JeM is known for its audacious attacks, highly trained fighters and use of sophisticated weapons. A greater number of improvised explosive device (IED) and grenade attacks may occur in the future, as the well-trained members of the group might be instructing the local recruits in manufacturing and using the bombs.

The 'new age militancy'

The 'new age militancy' in Kashmir owes its name to the highly motivated and tech-savvy local rebels, whose considerable social-media presence has made them widely popular in Kashmir, especially among the youth. These local recruits, however, have not been able to initiate any major offensive against the Indian security forces, and large numbers have been killed in army raids inside residential houses or hideouts. Unlike the Kashmiri militants of the early 1990s, they are poorly trained and lack resources.

The dense presence of the Indian security forces and intelligence networks prevent them from properly training or practising in the open.

The militancy is believed to receive a large proportion of arms and ammunition from across the LoC through local conduits, although some of the new recruits have also acquired weapons by snatching service rifles from soft targets, such as security guards of banks and other public establishments. Since March 2015, Kashmiri rebels and police defectors have seized around 34 rifles and a pistol over nine separate incidents. In September 2018, a personal security officer of Aijaz Mir, legislator in the ruling People's Democratic Party (PDP), fled with seven AK47s and a pistol (the officer subsequently joined HM).

Drivers

Stalled peace process

Expectations of a political breakthrough rose when peace talks between India and Pakistan began in the mid-2000s and local recruitment into armed groups declined. The peace process was suspended by India after the 2008 Mumbai attack, however, and an uprising in 2008 and street protests in 2010 changed the situation in Kashmir. The Indian government did not enact the recommendations of state-appointed officials who had investigated the 2010 street protests, and in the absence of any political initiative, another uprising occurred in 2016.

Major world powers such as the United States maintain that Kashmir is a bilateral issue and must be addressed by India and Pakistan alone. In the absence of international interest or mediation, the status quo continues, making some of the young people in Kashmir vulnerable to the propaganda of transnational Islamist networks such as al-Qaeda and the Islamic State, also known as ISIS or ISIL.

Demographic youth bulge

By 2011, Kashmir's youth constituted more than 30% of the population. A proportion of this demographic grew increasingly disillusioned with political processes and less averse to the armed movement as the administration of Kashmir became more militarised, human-rights abuses by Indian security forces continued, and the state cracked down on political protests. Facing torture and constant harassment,

some of the jailed young protesters later joined armed groups. The 'new age militancy' emerged, led by youth rebels such as Burhan Wani, whom the young generation of Kashmir related to and started hero-worshipping.

Rise of Hindutva politics

In general, the rise of Hindutva (or Hindu nationalist) politics in mainland India has created the conditions for the armed conflict in Kashmir to thrive and escalate. The shrill rhetoric of Hindutva nationalists directed against India's Muslim minority and the mainstreaming of the Hindutva ideology means there is wider support for the heightened repression and of muscular policy against Kashmiri Muslims. The Hindutva nationalists openly call for demographic change in Muslim-majority Kashmir, raising fears and anxieties among Kashmiris and further exacerbating the political tensions in the region.

Cross-border armed groups

State repression within Kashmir allows Pakistan-based armed groups to infiltrate the LoC and fight Indian security forces. Although Pakistan's armed forces have proscribed some of these organisations and shut down their camps in Pakistan, they have also facilitated the infiltration of armed groups into Kashmir by shelling Indian border posts to distract the Indian security forces. Having bases inside

South Asia

Pakistan allows the armed groups to easily arrange logistics and weapons, and find recruitments away from the control of the Indian security forces. This support structure and safe environment is essential for these groups to recover and sustain their strength despite incurring heavy losses.

Political and Military Developments

Bilateral peace process remains frozen

Despite peace overtures from the Pakistani government headed by Imran Khan, including a September 2018 letter by Khan to Indian Prime Minister Narendra Modi requesting the resumption of dialogue, the bilateral peace process remained frozen in 2018. The scheduled meeting on 26 September between the foreign ministers of the two countries at the sidelines of the UN General Assembly in New York was called off by India within 24 hours of confirmation. The two reasons cited by the Indian foreign ministry – the killing of Indian security personnel by militants in Kashmir and the issuing of postal stamps by the Pakistani government that featured deceased Kashmiri rebel leader Wani – occurred before the talks were confirmed.

Some analysts believe that for the BJP government the timing of the talks was not appropriate. Three days after the scheduled meeting, the Indian government was planning to celebrate 'Surgical Strike Day', the anniversary of the 29 September 2016 cross-LoC military raid which allegedly targeted suspected militants inside Azad Jammu and Kashmir. The purported surgical strike had come after four heavily armed gunmen carried out a pre-dawn attack on an Indian Army camp in Uri (near the LoC), killing 19 soldiers and wounding nearly 80 others.

Collapse of state government

In February 2015, the People's Democratic Party (PDP) and the right-wing BJP formed an unexpected coalition government. In the 2014 elections for the 87-member state assembly, the PDP had won 28 seats in the Muslim-majority Kashmir Valley and the BJP had swept the Hindu-dominated areas of the Jammu region with 25 seats. This alliance, however, ultimately proved a political disaster. It created deep resentment in Kashmir against the PDP, and the pro-Indian parties in general, because the PDP's election campaign had focused on stopping the 'anti-Muslim' BJP from acquiring power in the state.

In June 2018, the PDP–BJP government collapsed after the BJP withdrew from the coalition, citing security concerns in the Valley and failings of the state government. As a result, the incumbent governor, N.N. Vohra, assumed control of Kashmir. His image as a moderate bureaucrat made his administration acceptable to most, but he was soon replaced. On 21 August, the BJP government in New Delhi appointed its former national vice-president Satya Pal Malik as the new governor of Jammu and Kashmir, which was perceived as a strategic move by the BJP to forge, with the help of the local party People's Conference (PC), a new alliance government by causing defections in the PDP, the National Conference (NC) party and the Congress party. By increasing its control over Kashmir, the BJP further stoked resentment among the Muslim residents.

On 21 November, reports emerged that the PDP, NC and Congress had come together in an unprecedented coalition to form a new government and checkmate the BJP's plan. In response, Malik dissolved the state legislative assembly, which had been temporarily suspended after the collapse of the civilian government in June. Through secret parleys and horse-trading, the BJP appeared to be forging a 'third front' in Kashmir – comprised of PC, defectors from NC, Congress and PDP, plus some independents – to form a new government. The PDP and NC believed that New Delhi was again trying to divide and weaken Kashmir-based political parties to gain more control over the politics of the state, and vehemently opposed the BJP's move.

Constitutional challenges

The BJP government has stated that it aims to abrogate Article 35A of the Indian constitution, which debars non-state subjects (i.e., people not ordinarily residents of the Indian state of Jammu and Kashmir) from acquiring immovable property in the region. Since 2014, some non-governmental organisations and private citizens – believed to be aligned with the Indian far right – have submitted petitions in the Indian Supreme Court demanding the abrogation of articles 370 and 35A. If the court decides in favour of these petitions, the BJP, which has an absolute majority in the Indian parliament, could potentially remove Article 35A. (The BJP would, however, need the concurrence of the state legislative assembly.)

The potential removal of Article 35A from the constitution raised anxiety among Kashmiris in 2018, who feared that the BJP plans to engineer demographic change in Kashmir by settling Indian Hindus in the region along the lines of Israeli settlements in the occupied Palestinian territories. In August, the call by the Joint Resistance Leadership (JRL) for general strikes received an unprecedented response, with many organisations, trade unions and civil-society members giving their full support. In a statement on 5 August, JRL said: 'the people of this state have a unique identity, a rare distinctiveness and heritage ... No Kashmiri can think of allowing any tinkering with this uniqueness, which is also known as state subject law.' On 5 and 31 August 2018, Kashmiris observed a complete strike against the Supreme Court petitions. At least 12 protesters were injured during clashes with Indian security forces.

Order was restored on 31 August as the Supreme Court deferred its hearing of the petitions until January 2019. Nevertheless, the challenge to Article 35A had brought people together across the ideological divide. In a significant move, both of the unionist parties, the NC and the PDP, decided to boycott the local urban-bodies elections in October as a mark of protest.

Local elections

In mid-September, the State Administrative Council under Governor Malik decided to hold elections for urban local bodies (ULB) and rural bodies (Panchayat). The government announced that elections would be held on a non-party basis (i.e., the candidates would stand without party affiliations). The JRL, comprised of the top Kashmiri separatist leaders Syed Ali Geelani, Mirwaiz Umar Farooq and Yasin Malik, asked people to boycott the polls, while the militant groups threatened the candidates.

The ULB elections were held in four phases on 8, 10, 13 and 16 October. Turnout was very low, with only 8% of the electorate casting ballots in Kashmir Valley. There were no candidates in 181 wards out of the 598, and 231 candidates were elected unopposed. The boycott by the NC and PDP played to the advantage of independents and the Congress party, which took the most wards.

The Panchayat elections were held in nine phases on 17, 20, 24, 27 and 29 November and 1, 4, 8 and 11 December. In comparison to the ULB elections, there was an increase in voter turnout, though in the Kashmir Valley it was only 41%, compared to 83% in the Jammu division. Only 1,656 out of the 17,059 wards in Kashmir were contested; in 4,537 wards the candidates were elected unopposed. In southern Kashmir, which has seen much unrest and violence in the past two years, people largely stayed away from the polls, with only 95 out of the total 5,847 wards seeing any polling.

For India, conducting elections in Kashmir has diplomatic significance as it allows the government to ward off international pressure by showing that political processes are in place and Kashmiris do participate. The APHC and rebel groups see participation in elections as counter-productive, because India uses the vote to argue against the Kashmiri self-determination movement at international forums.

Crackdown on social media

Dozens of social-media accounts and posts were removed during 2018 as the Indian government sought to regulate the behaviour of the local media and counter the anti-India narrative in Kashmir. In July, the Jammu and Kashmir Police (JKP) registered a case against a local news agency, Current News Service, for 'providing space' for a letter written by scholar-turned-militant Manan Wani. In late August, JKP also arrested journalist Asif Sultan, allegedly targeted for writing a cover story on the late HM commander Burhan Wani for the magazine *Kashmir Narrator*, though JKP formally accused him of harbouring militants. On 2 December 2018, the English daily newspaper *Kashmir Reader* reported that JKP had arrested an assistant professor, a journalist and a lawyer for their posts on social media.

Rise in local recruitment

In 2018, the number of active militants in Kashmir rose above 300 for the first time in a decade, with 164 youths joining armed groups by the end of October. The figure marked a significant increase in recruitment compared to previous years, with 124 local youths becoming militants in 2017 and 88 in 2016.

On 1 April 2018, 13 militants were killed in separate gunfights in southern Kashmir. The huge impact of their funerals drove an increase in recruitment, with approximately 35 local young men joining armed groups within a few weeks, including 25-year-old Shamsul Haq Mengnoo, the brother of an Indian police officer. (Mengnoo's cousin was among the slain rebels.) In total, 64 youths joined armed groups in three months between June and August.

Armed groups using more diverse weaponry

In an effort to reverse their losses against the security forces, armed groups in Kashmir attempted to diversify their use of weaponry in 2018. In addition to armour-piercing 'steel core' bullets, which were first used in August and December 2017 and caused substantial losses to Indian security forces, the armed groups also revived the use of improvised explosive devices (IEDs) to target Indian security forces in 2018. On 6 January, Jaysh-e-Mohammad (JeM) militants remotely triggered an IED in the main market of Sopore town in north Kashmir, killing four police personnel and injuring several others. The previous instance of an IED attack had occurred in 2016, when HM successfully detonated an IED in the town of Tral, south Kashmir, killing three police personnel. In 2018, HM carried out IED attacks on 28 May and 18 October.

Armed groups also used sniper rifles in 2018. On 18 September, a Central Reserve Police Force (CRPF) trooper in Pulwama district was injured in the first sniper attack. A month later, in three separate sniper attacks, three Indian security personnel were killed inside their camps. It is believed that the militants may be in possession of US-made M4

carbines mounted with night-vision devices. In November 2017, Indian security forces found an M4 rifle in Aglar village of Pulwama district, where three JeM militants were killed in an overnight gunfight. The same gun was seen for the first time on the shoulders of popular HM commander Sameer Tiger in one of his social-media photos, generating much public interest about the presence of a US-made weapon inside Kashmir. It is possible that the gun travelled from Afghanistan to Kashmir through the LoC.

Arrests

The Over Ground Workers (OGWs) network provide vital logistical support to the militant groups. The JKP consider them the backbone of the armed opposition, as without OGWs rebels cannot easily move around or get information and food. Some OGWs are also militants-in-waiting. Zeenat-ul-Islam was first arrested in 2008 for being an OGW and later joined HM in 2015, becoming a top rebel commander.

In 2018, approximately 750 OGWs were arrested by the Indian security agencies. On 13 November, the JKP detained a female OGW on the outskirts of Srinagar city, claiming that she was carrying 20 grenades and a cache of ammunition. In some cases, arrested OGWs have been instrumental in security agencies locating militants. For example, it was the arrest of two OGWs in the late evening on 23 November that led Indian security forces to a hideout in dense orchards in Anantnag district, where six armed rebels – including LeT and HM commanders – were killed in a pre-dawn gunfight.

Violent Events

April gunfights in southern Kashmir

In one of the biggest operations of 2018, Indian security forces killed 13 HM militants in three separate gunfights in southern Kashmir's Shopian and Anantnag districts on 1 April. Four civilians and three army soldiers were also killed. During protests on 1 April, around 100 civilians were injured by the security forces. In response to these killings, JRL issued a call to strike on 2 April. Educational institutions closed, and exams were postponed by the government authorities.

Attacks rise in winter

Between 15 September and 5 December, Indian security forces killed 85 militants, dealing a huge blow to the armed opposition. In November alone, 39 militants were killed, most of them (22) in the last ten days of the month. November was the deadliest month of the conflict in 2018 with 61 deaths, including 13 civilians and nine members of the security forces. While the mounting rebel deaths showed that the Indian security forces had created a strong intelligence network, the weather conditions also played a part. Snow and cold mean that armed groups cannot survive in jungles in the winter, so they take shelter among the civilian population, where paid informers tip off the police or army about the presence of militants.

Killings of informers

As armed groups suffered mounting casualties in army raids, they began targeting police personnel and their relatives and suspected civilian informers. There were at least 45 police fatalities in 2018 and several significant cases of abduction. On 30 August, militants kidnapped 11 relatives of JKP personnel from the four districts of south Kashmir after Indian security forces arrested the father of HM commander Riyaz Naikoo and two brothers of Lateef Tiger, another HM commander, as well as setting fire to the houses of several militants. Although the abducted relatives of the police personnel were later released by militants, the event was demoralising for JKP personnel. A week after the dramatic abductions, the director general of JKP, Shesh Paul Vaid, was removed from his post.

On 15 November, Nadeem Manzoor was killed in Safanagri, Shopian district. Two days later, suspected militants abducted Huzaif Ashraf of Kulgam district, cut his throat and dumped his body in an apple orchard in nearby Hermain village. The militants recorded these killings and posted them online.

In 2018, militants killed at least eight Special Police Officers (SPOs) and threatened others with the same fate if they did not resign. The militants suspected that the SPOs – an auxiliary force of JKP with a strength of 30,000 personnel – were discreetly staying in civilian areas to track them. The fact that the armed groups could locate 'informers' and abduct them suggests that they had cultivated their own intelligence network, a network that had penetrated the security agencies. In late September, at least 30 SPOs handed in their resignations on social media following the killing of their three colleagues by HM earlier that month. To stem this resignation spree, which was demoralising the police force, the state government immediately suspended the internet for a week. Furthermore, the wages of SPOs were doubled from a paltry INR3,000 (US$43) to INR6,000 (US$86) per month.

Despite beating and killing many suspected informers, militants continued to be tracked down and killed in targeted army raids, indicating that the deterrence tactic of the armed groups had failed to erode the human-intelligence network of the security agencies. The reason for this is the conflict economy: each militant killing brings from around US$9,000 to US$14,000 for the security-force team involved, and a part of that reward goes to the informer, who is subsequently appointed as an SPO on an ad hoc basis.[1]

Impact

Civilians attacked by security forces

In 2018, Indian security forces killed at least 40 civilians during pro-militant protests near gunfight sites; injured the eyes of 360 people after firing metallic pellets with pump-action shotguns; and blasted around 120 private properties where militants were cornered (and to discourage civilians from sheltering rebels). New army camps were set up deep in civilian areas, often leading to coercion and harassment, especially of local youth. After 15 years, in mid-2017, the Indian Army reintroduced Cordon and Search Operations (CASOs), which involve intrusive house-to-house searches and the frisking of civilians. In 2018, Indian security forces launched an estimated 275 CASOs, creating resentment among the civilian population. In southern Kashmir villages, there were reports of women suffering sexual assaults and the vandalism of private properties during CASOs.

Civilians displaced along the LoC

Armed skirmishes along the LoC increased significantly in 2018, with more than 1,400 violations of the ceasefire (signed in November 2003) that killed dozens of soldiers and civilians on both sides of the LoC. In May 2018, more than 100,000 residents living along the border were displaced due to heavy shelling by the armed forces of the two countries. Facing shelling from the Indian side, the Pakistani armed forces had targeted Hindu-dominated areas in Jammu region, triggering anti-government protests, which pressured the BJP government to de-escalate the situation.[2] On 30 May, the two armed forces declared a truce, giving respite to the displaced citizens.

Human-rights abuses

In June 2018, the Office of the United Nations High Commissioner for Human Rights (OHCHR) published a report highlighting the human-rights abuses inflicted by the Indian security forces in Kashmir. The report focused on the human-rights situation in the Indian state of Jammu and Kashmir since the outbreak of the mass civilian uprising in July 2016, and urged India to establish impartial and independent investigations into all civilian killings and human-rights abuses committed by Indian security forces and non-state armed groups. The report also acknowledged the issue of sexual violence (such as the 1991 Kunan Poshpora mass rape), enforced disappearances since 1989 (approximately 8,000 cases) and mass graves in Kashmir.

Calling on India to repeal the controversial Public Safety Act and Armed Forces (Special Powers) Act, which give total impunity to its forces in Kashmir, the report said that these laws have 'created structures that obstruct the normal course of law, impede accountability and jeopardize the right to remedy for victims of human rights violations'. The report also highlighted the human-rights situation in Azad Jammu and Kashmir, especially with regard to the misuse of anti-terrorism laws for arbitrary arrests, restrictions on freedom of expression and religious discrimination. In a major development for the Kashmiri pro-independence movement, the report recommended to both India and Pakistan to 'fully respect the right of self-determination of the people of Kashmir as protected under international law'.

Trends

Operation All-Out *to continue*

While killing more than 250 rebels in Kashmir in 2018, India could not eliminate the armed opposition. The Indian government is therefore likely to continue *Operation All-Out* against the armed opposition in Kashmir. This will at least allow the unionist parties in Kashmir to regain the political space that has shrunk in recent years due to growing militancy, especially in southern Kashmir, which unionist politicians avoid visiting. As the killing of rebels has not stopped new recruitments, however, a review of this policy is likely. Some Indian security experts have suggested a more political approach to Kashmir, stressing that normalcy can be brought to Kashmir through good governance and development. Others believe that nothing will change unless the political aspirations of Kashmiris are addressed. This would involve restoring autonomy to Kashmir, which has been gradually eroded by successive governments in New Delhi through the extension of several federal laws to the state (through at least 47 Presidential Orders between 1954 and 1994), in violation of the original constitutional agreements between Kashmir and New Delhi.

Back-channel diplomacy

Although Dineshwar Sharma, the interlocutor appointed by New Delhi, made several trips to Kashmir in 2017 and 2018 to convince the APHC to engage in dialogue, he has not yet succeeded in bringing the APHC to the table. The APHC will not enter into talks unless the Indian government accepts Kashmir as a dispute and releases political prisoners.

The surprise visit of the former prime minister of Norway, Kjell Magne Bondevik, to Kashmir on 23 November was seen as an indication of New Delhi's willingness to facilitate back-channel diplomacy on Kashmir. Bondevik, who heads the Oslo Center for Peace and Human Rights, met the two senior leaders of the JRL, Syed Ali Geelani and Mirwaiz Umar Farooq, in Srinagar and visited the LoC and Azad Jammu and Kashmir, where he met AJ&K President Sardar Masood Khan.

Some observers believed that Bondevik's visit to Kashmir, which severely restricts the entry of foreign journalists and dignitaries, was mere optics to distract the international community after the OHCHR report of June 2018 indicted the Indian government for gross human-rights violations in Kashmir and acknowledged the right to self-determination of the people of Jammu and Kashmir. However, the fact that the JRL willingly met Bondevik indicates a different story. If a new government comes to power in India after the spring 2019 elections, Bondevik may again mediate talks between the federal government and the APHC, because the latter would be willing to accept Bondevik as a third-party interlocutor. Such an arrangement would also maintain Kashmir's status as an international dispute rather than dilute it as an internal issue of India.

Pakistan may be willing to resume talks

Pakistan must also be involved for any talks between India and the APHC to succeed. If the past is any indication, talks between the two countries may resume after the Indian general election in spring 2019. Currently, Pakistan is grappling with an economic crisis, so improved relations with India can help its trade. The influential Pakistan Army are likely to support Imran Khan, as the resumption of the peace process would allow it to concentrate on the western border with Afghanistan. The negotiations on Kashmir between India and Pakistan will likely be under the framework of the 'Four Point Formula' suggested by the former Pakistan president General Pervez Musharraf and former Indian prime minister Manmohan Singh. This involves the phased withdrawal of troops; free movement of people across the LoC with no alteration of existing boundaries; self-governance short of independence; and a joint supervision mechanism in Jammu and Kashmir, involving India, Pakistan and Kashmir. Though the APHC would be unwilling to accept this arrangement, the Khan government and the Pakistan establishment in general have shown indications of proposing such a plan.

Tensions surrounding Article 35A hearing

The first few months of 2019 will be crucial because of the scheduled hearing on Article 35A – a judgment abrogating the article would trigger violent protests in Kashmir. Violence is also likely due to political considerations, at least until the first half of 2019, as in the run-up to the general elections in spring 2019, the BJP will prefer an aggressive military campaign in Kashmir in order to win nationalist voters. However, the formation of a new government in India after the May 2019 election may still open the possibility of resumption of talks and de-escalation of the conflict. If the alliance of the opposition parties in India succeeds in defeating the BJP, the new Congress-led government could restart the peace process with Pakistan, which would help to de-escalate the situation both within Kashmir and along the LoC, as was seen during the previous phase of the India–Pakistan peace process between 2004 and 2008.

Notes

1   Haseeb Drabu, 'Militancy, not militants', *Indian Express*, 19 December 2018.

2   Christophe Jefferlot, 'Ceasefire Violations in Kashmir: A War by Other Means?', Carnegie Endowment for International Peace, 24 October 2018.

Pakistan

Overview

The conflict in 2018

Terrorist attacks in Pakistan continued to decline in 2018 due to counter-terrorism operations (primarily *Operation Radd-ul-Fasaad)* led by the security forces and police. Terrorism-related violence surged ahead of the July general elections that saw the centrist Pakistan Tehreek-e-Insaaf (PTI) come to power and Imran Khan sworn in as prime minister. An estimated 262 terrorist attacks took place in 2018, against 370 in 2017, leaving more than 200 security personnel and 381 civilians dead.[1]

Key statistics	
Type:	Internal
IDPs total (2017):	250,000
IDPs new (2018):	75,000
Refugees total (2018):	135,000
Refugees new (2018):	no data
People in need (2018):	1,200,000

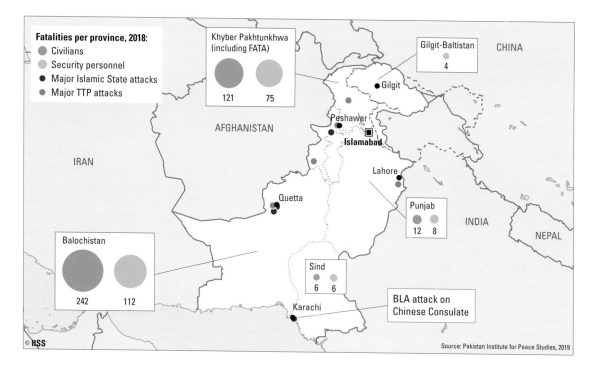

The two groups responsible for the majority of attacks were the Tehrik-e-Taliban Pakistan (TTP) and the chapter of the Islamic State, also known as ISIS or ISIL, in Afghanistan and Pakistan, known as the Islamic State–Khorasan Province (ISIS–KP). Offshoot groups such as Jamaat-ul-Ahrar (JuA) and Lashkar-e-Jhangvi al-Alami (LEJ–A) were less active this year as compared to 2017.

Balochistan was the province worst affected by armed violence and suffered the highest number of casualties as Baloch insurgent groups, most notably the Balochistan Liberation Army (BLA), continued to launch attacks. Baloch insurgents were responsible for several attacks against Chinese civilians and assets (consulate premises), in particular (though not exclusively) those connected with the China–Pakistan Economic Corridor (CPEC). Baloch insurgents were also responsible for several attacks against security forces and election staff, particularly in the Kech district of Balochistan. The Federally Administered Tribal Areas (FATA) in the northern areas of Pakistan were the second-worst-affected region by terrorism-related violence, where the armed forces cracked down on suspected terrorists that mostly directed their violence at state institutions. Nonetheless, the government continued to make progress to merge FATA with the province of Khyber Pakhtunkhwa (KPK).

Barelvi extremism continued from 2017, particularly through the establishment of Tehrik-e-Labaik Pakistan (TLP), a group that supports blasphemy laws and participated in the 2018 general elections.

The conflict to 2018

Pakistani security forces have been engaged in a counter-insurgency struggle with the TTP in FATA and KPK (northwest Pakistan) since 2009, but with limited success due to the absence of a coherent counter-terrorism strategy. Following the attack on the Army Public School in Peshawar by the TTP in December 2014, Pakistan drafted its first counter-terrorism policy, the National Action Plan (NAP). Additionally, operations led by security forces – including *Operation Zarb-e-Azb* (2014) and *Operation Radd-ul-Fasaad* (2017) – were launched to counter the TTP, various sectarian terrorist groups (such as the anti-Shia organisation Lashkar-e-Jhangvi), as well as al-Qaeda. These operations led to a gradual reduction in terrorism and religiously motivated violence across Pakistan between 2014 and 2018. However, sectarian and religiously motivated violence has continued to affect all regions of Pakistan, especially FATA and Balochistan (both bordering Afghanistan), as well as selected areas of Sindh province, including Karachi.

Balochistan in particular has a long history of insurgency. The first four 'phases' of insurgency in Balochistan were periods of armed conflicts between Baloch insurgents and state forces in 1948, 1958, 1962 and 1973, with the fifth phase beginning in 2003. Demands of the insurgents have ranged from greater political autonomy for the province to complete independence from Pakistan.

Forces

State forces

Counter-terrorism operations in Khyber Pakhtun-khwa (KPK), the Federally Administered Tribal Areas (FATA) and Balochistan are primarily led by the Pakistani Army and paramilitary forces, including the Frontier Corps (Balochistan), the Sindh Rangers (Karachi), and the Frontier Constabulary (KPK), as well as civilian law-enforcement agencies, including provincial police forces and their Counter-Terrorism Departments (CTDs).

To further the gains made by military and paramilitary forces, the Pakistani government relies upon military courts to prosecute suspected terrorists and armed combatants. Military courts were established after the Army Public School attack in the city of Peshawar in December 2014 and are empowered to try civilians under the Twenty-First Constitutional Amendment, passed in 2015. The power to sentence a terrorist to death rests with the Chief of Army Staff (Pakistan Army). According to Major General Asif Ghafoor, the director general of Inter Services Public Relations (ISPR), the media wing of the Pakistan Army, at least 345 terrorists were sentenced to death between 2014 and 2018. In November and December 2018 alone, army chief General Qamar Javed Bajwa confirmed the death sentences of 26 'hardcore terrorists'. In total, 617 people have been convicted for terrorism-related offences between January 2015 and December 2018.[2]

Tehrik-e-Taliban Pakistan (TTP)

The Tehrik-e-Taliban Pakistan (TTP, or the Pakistani Taliban) is an umbrella organisation of various militant groups formed in 2007 by the mujahideen who fought with the Afghan Taliban in Afghanistan. The TTP opposes the Pakistani state and seeks to enforce sharia law. The group originally operated in Pakistan's FATA area, but since the start of the military crackdown in 2014 (*Operation Zarb-e-Azb*), has fractured and is operating largely from Afghanistan, carrying out sporadic attacks in Pakistan in 2018.

The TTP's exact strength remains disputed, ranging from 5,000 to 30,000 fighters. Targeted operations by the armed forces and infighting led a number of factions to break away, including Jamaat-ul-Ahrar. Disputes over succession following the death of Mullah Fazlullah in a US-led drone strike in Afghanistan in June 2018 also created a number of internal rifts. As of December 2018, the group was commanded by Mufti Noor Wali Mehsud, while Muhammad Khurasani remained its primary spokesperson. In October, the TTP released a manual for its members, advised them to resolve their internal differences and gave new instructions on how to carry out suicide attacks more strategically and selectively. The manual was an attempt by the TTP to re-establish itself and curtail suicide attacks against civilians, a tactic which has created disputes among its militants. In 2018, the TTP continued to target state security forces in Pakistan, primarily the police. The TTP was held to be responsible for 79 terrorist attacks across Pakistan in 2018, primarily in KPK and FATA.[3]

Islamic State of Khorasan Province (ISIS–KP)

ISIS's Khorasan chapter (ISIS–KP) made its appearance in Pakistan in 2015, although its presence was long denied and later underplayed by state officials. Following claims of attacks in 2017 on shrines in Sindh and Balochistan provinces, ISIS–KP was recognised as a prominent threat. In 2018, ISIS–KP claimed five terrorist attacks in Pakistan, including four in Balochistan. Beyond its demands for strict adherence to sharia law and a rejection of democratic governance in Pakistan – policies in line with the Salafi ideology of the Islamic State of Syria and Iraq – ISIS–KP has directed its violence against Pakistani Shias in a bid to exacerbate sectarian tensions.

In early 2017, ISIS–KP's estimated strength in Pakistan was around 1,800.[4] ISIS–KP continued to perpetrate attacks in Pakistan in 2018 while retaining its base in Afghanistan, including suicide bombings, targeted killings and abductions. Besides Shi'ites, ISIS–KP also targeted Christians, police officials and politicians. The group's main areas of operations in Pakistan are in Balochistan province, which shares a border with Afghanistan and has been a gateway for ISIS-affiliated militants since 2015. The group has been aided by Pakistan-based groups who share strategic, logistical or ideological objectives, including Lashkar-e-Jhangvi al-Alami.

Balochistan Liberation Army (BLA)

The Balochistan Liberation Army (BLA) counts on between 2,000 and 3,000 militants, though many Baloch militants from different separatist groups surrendered to Pakistani security forces in 2018. It is one of the six separatist groups opposing Chinese investment and assets in Pakistan (such as China–Pakistan Economic Corridor, or CPEC), considered as a form of colonial oppression. Baloch insurgents have carried out ambushes, gun and improvised explosive device (IED) attacks against security personnel and workers, but in 2018 also adopted suicide attacks as a new tactic. BLA claimed 23 terrorist attacks in Balochistan and two in Karachi in 2018.

Militant splinter groups and factions

Since 2016, Lashkar-e-Jhangvi al-Alami (LEJ–A) have provided logistical, tactical and strategic assistance to ISIS–KP. ISIS–KP and LEJ–A have an ideological affiliation and both target the Shia minority as well as state security forces.

Jamaat-ul-Ahrar (JuA), a TTP offshoot, has also been less active in 2018, with its spokesman Assad Mansoor having surrendered to the security forces in January.

Hizb-ul-Ahrar (HuA) was more active than other offshoots in 2018. A splinter group of JuA, HuA was created by Umar Khurasani and Aziz Yousufzai in November 2017 with militants based across the border in Afghanistan. The split likely occurred over divergences on the policy of attacking civilians. HuA attacked police and army officials in 2018, including a suicide attack on Pakistani troops in Mastung, Balochistan in August and a targeted killing of a police official in Karachi in October. HuA further claimed a rocket attack in Mohmand agency, allegedly carried out against a Pakistani checkpoint from across the border in Afghanistan. In April, HuA claimed two suicide attacks in Quetta in which six police personnel were killed.

| Drivers

Ethnic grievances

Ethnic Pashtun, Baloch and Sindhi grievances drive part of the armed conflict in Pakistan. These grievances result from political and economic discrimination by a state in which the army and the system of governance have been largely dominated by Punjabis (the ethnic majority). The Pakistani state forces (including the army and police) are accused by these ethnic minorities of violently repressing and marginalising minority populations. Dissidents are often targets of extrajudicial killings and enforced disappearances.

A peaceful Pashtun Tahafuz (Protection) Movement (PTM) emerged in January 2018 to protest the extrajudicial killing of Naqeebullah Mehsud by the Karachi police, who suspected Mehsud of being a terrorist. Mehsud was in police custody for days prior to his death. The PTM called for equal rights for the Pashtuns in Pakistan, investigations into enforced disappearances and missing persons, and the removal of mines from FATA.[5] The PTM further denounced the TTP for an armed attack on a PTM gathering in northern Pakistan.

Baloch groups also lobbied for missing persons. The Baloch insurgency in Balochistan and Karachi against Chinese assets and workers drew attention to the economic grievances of the Baloch, especially regarding the question of whether CPEC was intended to benefit the local Baloch in Pakistan.[6] CPEC is a Chinese-driven infrastructural project prospectively worth around US$62 billion as of 2017, part of China's larger development framework, the Belt and Road Initiative (BRI). CPEC allows China to construct multiple infrastructural facilities (such as transportation networks and a port in Gwadar) in Balochistan, Sindh, Punjab and KPK.

Pakistan blames India for fuelling the grievances of Baloch groups in Balochistan, especially those demanding independence from Pakistan, such as the BLA. Ethnic Sindhis, victims of enforced disappearances by state officials since 2017, continued to be abducted in 2018, leading to demonstrations across Sindh province as protesters demanded information on the victims' whereabouts.[7]

Religious divides

The Pakistani society has a Sunni majority (approximately 80% of the population) and a Shia minority (approximately 14%). The rise of Barelvi extremism in 2017 has made it vulnerable to sub-sectarian extremism within its Sunni population. Barelvi Sunnis are the majority within the Sunni population in Pakistan but were traditionally known to be moderate and non-violent, with state security forces engaging in armed conflict primarily with Deobandi Sunni groups (such as the TTP). However, the issue of blasphemy – a chief cause advocated by Barelvi militants and hardliners – has become a driver of violence across the country and has radicalised pockets among Pakistan's Barelvi Sunnis.

Confrontations between violent Barelvis and the state began in 2017 with the advent of a new religio-political group, the TLP, a staunch advocate of blasphemy laws, formed to represent Barelvi Sunnis. In 2017, the TLP violently protested against an electoral reform it deemed blasphemous, shutting down one of the primary roads leading to the capital in a three-day-long sit-in that resulted in clashes with the police and the eventual resignation of the then-law minister.

Political and Military Developments

Elections

In July 2018, Pakistan held its third consecutive democratic elections that saw Imran Khan elected as prime minister during the deadliest month of the year – in particular, election-related violence struck Balochistan and KPK. It is widely believed that Khan has the backing of the armed forces, indicating that civil–military relations could be the most stable during his tenure than they have ever been in the decade since the end of military rule. Khan's election means that the civilian and military leadership are likely to be closely aligned on security issues and internal and regional conflicts. Khan's PTI benefited from a surge in popularity after the former government of Pakistan Muslim League–Nawaz (PML–Nawaz) was weakened by the Panama Case judgments that led to the disqualification, trial and imprisonment of former prime minister Nawaz Sharif and his daughter Maryam Nawaz in the months leading up to the elections.

The elections also saw the rise of the TLP as a strong electoral contender and political force, pulling voters from existing parties such as the Pakistan Muslim League–Nawaz (PML–Nawaz), PTI, Muttahida Qaumi Movement (MQM) and the Pakistan People's Party (PPP), and securing two provincial assembly seats from Karachi. In August, the TLP rallied against a Dutch caricature contest, demanding that the new government of Imran Khan cut political and diplomatic ties with the Netherlands on grounds of blasphemy. In late October, the TLP organised countrywide protests and sit-ins to voice their disapproval of the Supreme Court verdict that acquitted Asia Bibi, a Christian woman who was wrongfully accused of blasphemy and sentenced to death in 2010. In late November, the state authorised a police-led crackdown against TLP workers who participated in the protests in 2018, leaving several people wounded, while hundreds of TLP members were arrested, including its chief Khadim Hussain Rizvi, who was taken into 'protective custody'. Senior leaders of the TLP, including Rizvi, were charged with sedition and terrorism. The state crackdown against the TLP saw other Barelvi groups withdrawing their support for the TLP, but exposed the possibility of militancy from the Sunni Barelvi population.

KPK–FATA merger

With the support of all major political parties (including PTI, PML–Nawaz, PPP and MQM), the National Assembly voted in favour of a constitutional amendment that officially recognised the KP–FATA merger. The merger will grant FATA an improved constitutional status that will guarantee better socio-economic conditions for the residents of tribal areas, an outcome that is likely to have a direct impact on militancy in FATA. Furthermore, the merger is likely to do away with a colonial-era legal framework, the Frontier Crimes Regulation, and extend the jurisdiction of the higher courts of Pakistan to the residents of FATA. This could reduce the appeal of Islamic clerics (and their associated militants), whose sharia-inspired administration of justice has traditionally competed with the court system. The government of PTI and Pakistan's armed forces reiterated their support for the merger (or 'mainstreaming') of FATA and promised to complete the process.

Pakistan placed on FATF grey list

The Financial Action Task Force (FATF), an international intergovernmental grouping watching over terrorism financing, placed Pakistan on its 'grey list' in June again. Being placed on the grey list weakens Pakistan's international standing and could compromise its position in negotiations with the International Monetary Fund, but will not necessarily affect Pakistan's economy.[8]

Although Pakistan and China maintained their strong business relationship over CPEC, China chose not to support Pakistan unconditionally at the FATF. This position revealed Beijing's growing frustration with Islamabad's lack of a coherent anti-terrorist policy and inadequate response to the insurgency in Balochistan, where militant groups have attacked Chinese nationals and assets. China will preside over the FATF in 2019–20.

Rising tensions with US

Pakistan's relationship with the United States took a bitter turn in 2018. In January, US President Donald Trump took to social media to accuse Pakistan of providing a safe haven for terrorists. Pakistan's then-foreign minister Khawaja Asif responded that Trump was 'blaming Pakistan' for the United States' 'failure' in Afghanistan. In November 2018, Trump reiterated that Pakistan 'don't do anything for us'. In December, Pakistan facilitated the first talks between the US and the Taliban, opening the possibility of a change in tone in the relationship.

Security operations

Operation Radd-ul-Fasaad was launched in 2017 against the Pakistani Taliban to further the gains made in *Operation Zarb-e-Azb* (2014). Primarily, the army carried out attacks against militants and insurgents in Balochistan (15 attacks) and KPK (13 attacks), supported by paramilitary forces (such as the Frontier Corps in Balochistan) as well as the Counter-Terrorism Departments (CTDs) of provincial police forces.

The *Karachi Operation*, which targets criminal and militant groups in the city, entered its fifth year in 2018, led by the paramilitary force Sindh Rangers and the Karachi police. Due to this operation, Karachi experienced a 62% decrease in the number of terrorist attacks between 2017 and 2018, although there were a number of significant terrorist attacks in the second half of 2018, such as the attack on 23 November on the Chinese consulate by a Baloch separatist group, the BLA. In these security operations, law-enforcement and security personnel arrested militants, most of whom were affiliated with the TTP, Lashkar-e-Jhangvi and ISIS–KP. However, apex committees – formed in December 2014 to oversee the implementation of the National Action Plan and military operations – did not meet as frequently as in preceding years.[9]

Violent Events

At least 105 militants were killed in counter-terrorism operations in 2018, compared to 524 in 2017. This decrease indicated a cooling down in security operations, likely the result of decreasing terrorist activities in the country (see **Figure 1**). Security and law-enforcement personnel continued to be targeted by militants, however, primarily in KPK, FATA and Balochistan. In total, 217 security personnel were killed in terrorist attacks in 2018, including 73 army officials and at least 67 police officials (see **Figure 2**). US-led uninhabited aerial vehicle (UAV) strikes supported the counter-terrorism operations, killing five people in the tribal regions of FATA, including militants associated with the Haqqani network.

Political attacks

The deadliest attack in 2018 took place in Mastung, Balochistan province. At least 149 people were killed in a suicide bombing that targeted an election-campaign rally. The attack was claimed by ISIS–KP, who was also responsible for an attack against four Christian civilians in Balochistan in April. In November, ISIS–KP claimed the bombing in Orakzai, KPK, that targeted Shia Muslims at a marketplace and claimed 33 lives.

In July, terrorists associated with the Pakistani Taliban targeted and killed Haroon Bilour, a senior politician of the Awami National Party (ANP), along with 12 other civilians. The TTP claimed that

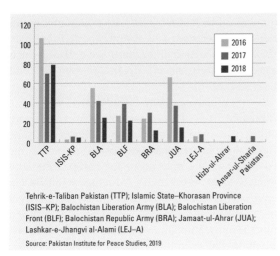

Tehrik-e-Taliban Pakistan (TTP); Islamic State–Khorasan Province
(ISIS–KP); Balochistan Liberation Army (BLA); Balochistan Liberation
Front (BLF); Balochistan Republic Army (BRA); Jamaat-ul-Ahrar (JUA);
Lashkar-e-Jhangvi al-Alami (LEJ–A)

Source: Pakistan Institute for Peace Studies, 2019

**Figure 1: Incidents attributed to or claimed by militant
groups, 2016–18**

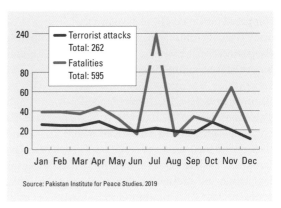

Source: Pakistan Institute for Peace Studies, 2019

Figure 2: Terrorist attacks and fatalities per month, 2018

the suicide attack was in retaliation for the military operations against the group, as well as revenge for the previous ANP government in KPK.

Baloch separatist attacks

Baloch separatists were also responsible for a number of violent attacks in 2018, including against Chinese targets. In August, the BLA carried out a suicide attack on a vehicle transporting Chinese engineers in Balochistan, leaving six injured. In November, the BLA claimed the armed attack on the Chinese consulate in Karachi that killed two civilians, two police officials and three militants.

In January, LEJ–A claimed an IED attack on the security forces in Balochistan. In May, JuA claimed a suicide attack in Nowshera; in March, an attack on a polio-vaccination team in Mohmand agency, KPK; and in January, an attack on paramilitary forces (also in Mohmand agency).

Impact

Pakistan's role in regional geopolitics

Pakistan's conflict dynamics remained diverse and continued to have an impact on its relations with the US, China and Afghanistan. The Trump administration continued to criticise the Pakistani state for insufficiently combatting terrorism and for patronising militants associated with the Afghan Taliban and the Haqqani network. Nevertheless, in the latter half of 2018, Washington reached out to Islamabad for help in talks with the Afghan Taliban. In December, two days of peace talks between the US and the Taliban took place in the United Arab Emirates, part-facilitated by Pakistan.

Successful peace talks with the Afghan Taliban and stability in Afghanistan could significantly benefit both Pakistan's internal security as well as the process of repatriation of Afghan refugees. Depending on the specific outcome of those nascent Afghan peace talks, militants engaging in conflict in Pakistan (such as the TTP and ISIS–KP) may be cut from safe haven in Afghanistan. This would cement the gains made by military operations in Pakistan. Border management looked set to remain a challenge, owing to Afghanistan's historic reluctance to recognise (as Pakistan does) the Durand Line as the international border separating the countries.

Chinese investment

Chinese stakes in Pakistan continued to increase through CPEC, but attacks against Chinese targets in 2018 revealed the vulnerability of those investments and negatively affected Islamabad's business relations with Beijing. Pakistan continued to dedicate a substantial number of security officials (drawn from the provincial police departments, the army and the navy, in addition to private-security companies) to protect CPEC projects in 2018. Despite these efforts, China rejected Khan's petitions for financial relief in November.[10]

South Asia

Humanitarian impact

The ongoing military operations in northwest Pakistan, coupled with violence in KPK/FATA and Balochistan, continued to challenge the safety and security of internally displaced persons (IDPs). According to the Office of the United Nations High Commissioner for Refugees (UNHCR), 96,384 IDPs were registered in KPK in 2018, of whom 83,454 had returned to their places of residence (a total of 13,909 families). Pakistan does not have a clear policy or legislation for addressing the repatriation of IDPs, however, and IDPs continued to lack access to education, healthcare and other basic services, besides facing challenges in integrating in host communities.

Of the almost 1.4 million registered Afghan refugees in Pakistan in 2018, 14,017 were repatriated to Afghanistan in 2018, bringing the total number of Afghan refugees who voluntarily repatriated between 2002 and 2018 to 4.37m. More than 30,000 undocumented Afghans were also repatriated. Most Afghans were repatriated from KPK and Balochistan.

In September, Khan – himself a Pashtun – expressed support for the repatriation process, which is overseen by UNHCR, although human-rights organisations have expressed concern at the coercive tactics employed by the Pakistani security forces.[11] Many of the registered refugees in Pakistan have been in the country since the 1980s, following the Afghan war against Soviet forces (1979–89), and have formed familial and marital ties in Pakistan. Khan offered to grant citizenship to Afghans born in Pakistan, but backtracked on this promise a day later.

Trends

The Pakistani state forces are likely to continue *Operation Radd-ul-Fasaad* and the *Karachi Operation* in 2019, although gains made from these operations would be bolstered by a more coherent and detailed counter-terrorism policy. The government has yet to implement the National Internal Security Policy (NISP 2018), which was drafted and submitted by the then outgoing government of PML–N. PTI continues to rely upon the National Action Plan (2014), which is a far more limited policy. Without the implementation of the NISP, Pakistan is much less likely to defeat religious and sectarian extremism, and recruitment and financial support for the Pakistani Taliban, ISIS–KP and Baloch insurgents will continue in 2019.

Militant groups retain the ability to travel across the Afghanistan–Pakistan border, allowing them to carry out attacks in Pakistan and sustain a low-intensity conflict. Pakistan is likely to continue accusing India of fuelling the insurgency in Balochistan and enabling separatist groups to carry out anti-state activities, but its own discriminatory rhetoric against the ethnic Balochis will continue to fuel many ethnic grievances in the province. Efforts to delegitimise the PTM and harass its workers could similarly exacerbate Pashtun grievances and widen the gap between Pashtuns and the Pakistani state, potentially providing militant groups (especially the Pakistani Taliban) with recruitment opportunities within Pakistan. Should military operations slow down, and socio-economic development within formerly conflict-ridden areas fail to materialise, militants are likely to regroup and hurt Chinese and other inward investments to the country.

The state has yet to re-establish full control over FATA and Balochistan. Although PTI and the armed forces have expressed their support for the KPL–FATA merger, its implementation has yet to be completed. A lack of progress on this merger could further stoke Pashtun grievances and see confrontations between the PTM and state security forces.

In 2019, the groups most likely to perpetrate violence in Pakistan are ISIS–KP, the TTP and Baloch separatists. TTP offshoots and defectors have been seen to liaise with ISIS–KP, as the latter's profile grows in Afghanistan. ISIS–KP is therefore likely to continue striking targets in Pakistan, particularly in Balochistan and Sindh. Pakistan will need to cultivate closer relations with the Afghan government and security forces to improve intelligence sharing and collection and curtail the movement of ISIS–KP militants. This is a tall order given the difficulty Afghanistan and Pakistan have historically had to effect counter-terrorism cooperation and insulate it from the see-saw quality of their relations. Pakistan will also need to address Baloch grievances to address key underlying causes of the insurgency while enforcing the writ of the state in the province to prevent its exploitation by other armed militant groups.

Notes

1. Pakistan Institute for Peace Studies (PIPS), 'Pakistan Security Report 2018', Islamabad, 2019; PIPS, 'Pakistan Security Report 2017', Islamabad, 2018.

2. Reema Omer, 'Yet another extension?', *Dawn*, 5 January 2019.

3. 'PIPS Security Report 2019', p. 74.

4. For a breakdown of this estimate, see Antonio Giustozzi, *The Islamic State in Khorasan* (London: Hurst, 2018), pp. 60–1.

5. Abubakar Siddique, 'New Nationalist Movement Emerges from Pakistan's Pashtun Protests', *Gandhara*, 11 April 2018.

6. 'China Consulate Attack: Why Pakistan's Baloch separatists are against Beijing', *Deutsche Welle*, 23 November 2018.

7. 'Protest against "enforced disappearances" in Sindh intensifies', *Dawn*, 25 May 2018.

8. Shahid Karim and Usman Hayat, 'Pakistan on FATF's grey list: what, why, and why now?', *Dawn*, 6 July 2018.

9. Apex committees were formed after the APS attack in December 2014 and were intended to meet on a quarterly basis. These committees were formed on both provincial and federal levels and comprised of civilians and military leaders.

10. Adnan Rasool, 'Was Imran's visit to China a failure? Yes. Here's why', *Dawn*, 6 November 2018.

11. Human Rights Watch, 'Pakistan: Mass Forced Returns of Afghan Refugees', 13 February 2017.

6 Sub-Saharan Africa

Electoral banners are displayed in the Ndjili district of Kinshasa, DRC

Regional Introduction

In sub-Saharan Africa, crime, jihadism, insurgency and communal violence are all facets of the current active conflicts. Transnational trends converge and overlap with grassroots dynamics – linking local violence across different areas; protracting, exacerbating and entrenching pre-existing disputes and causing spillovers across borders and regions. Political exclusion, institutional and governance weakness, poverty, and a lack of access to resources, job opportunities and land all combine to fuel resentment and sustain armed violence locally. Porous borders and limited state capacity facilitate the movement of armed groups and weapons across large swaths of territory; allow international terrorist and criminal networks – such as the Islamic State, also known as ISIS or ISIL, and al-Qaeda – to exploit sub-national grievances and communal disputes; and shield roving bandits from the reach of national and international security forces.

Country-specific factors drive armed violence in Cameroon, Central African Republic (CAR), the Democratic Republic of the Congo (DRC), Lake Chad Basin, Mali, Nigeria, Somalia, South Sudan and Sudan, while at the same time initiating, prolonging or exacerbating conflicts in neighbouring countries.

For example, in Mali, jihadist groups have exploited a long history of neglect and exclusion to further their trafficking networks and challenge the state's overstretched security apparatus; and in turn, the Malian civil war affects the Sahel region as a whole. It fuels, for example, Burkina Faso's home-grown violence by bringing international radical ideologies into contact with long-standing colonial-era grievances in the country's marginalised and impoverished north. Similarly, al-Shabaab's ability to operate in Somalia depends in part on the support it receives from its Kenyan cells, which facilitate logistics and prepare attacks against Kenyan targets. Boko Haram exemplifies the ability of the region's armed groups to move across borders, exploiting local geography and state weakness in their pursuit to connect transnational networks, while preserving their communal roots.

Forced displacement and climate change are the main non-violent influences on the region's conflict dynamics. Conflict-induced displacement makes sub-Saharan Africa the region with the most refugees and internally displaced people (IDPs) in the world, according to the United Nations High Commissioner for Refugees (UNHCR) and the Internal Displacement Monitoring Centre (IDMC). The movement of people occurs in both directions and in most countries in the region. Although the Anglophone separatist conflict in Cameroon has so far remained contained in the country's north-western and southwestern regions – after Nigeria quickly dismantled the insurgents' safe havens along its eastern border – more than 30,000 people have fled to Nigeria since the end of 2017, straining the resources of the remote communities in Cross River State. More than 400,000 people have, in turn, sought refuge in Cameroon's northern provinces, fleeing Boko Haram's violence in Nigeria and cattle-rustling and rebel bands in CAR. Climate change has also had a devastating impact on the politico-economic fabric of agricultural societies in sub-Saharan Africa, and has fuelled violence in the region. Its indirect impact on armed conflict is evident in the Lake Chad Basin and central Nigeria, where land mismanagement and reduced access to ever-shrinking water resources exacerbate long-standing disputes between farmers and pastoralists. The state's inability to provide political and institutional mechanisms for peaceful resolution, together with the increased availability of automatic weapons from transnational smuggling networks, connect otherwise contained local conflicts and greatly intensify their lethality.

The internal dynamics of non-state armed groups is the other key driver of conflict and politics in sub-Saharan Africa. Against the backdrop of weak states in East and Central Africa, armed groups are becoming stronger political actors despite their highly unstable configurations. Constantly fragmenting conflict parties form volatile re-alignments and create fluid alliances and fresh opportunities for temporary pay-offs. In CAR, the initial confrontation between two rebel and self-defence groups, Séléka and anti-Balaka, fractured into a constellation of armed groups and criminal bands pursuing narrower interests. With varying degrees of territorial control, these new groups fight each other and the state to exploit natural resources and the cattle trade. In these conditions, with the government controlling only about a quarter of the country's territory, conflict parties will likely continue to use their military capabilities to get a larger share of political power, rather than seeking a genuine resolution to the conflict. The DRC also experienced a dramatic increase in local, and particularly self-defence, militias in 2018. Contrary to this trend, in South Sudan, the number of armed groups, which increased steadily from 2015–16, decreased in 2018, as groups focused instead on consolidating power in their areas of operation.

> Jihadist groups exploit a long history of neglect and exclusion

Political developments and electoral processes may lead armed violence in sub-Saharan Africa to continue or even increase in 2019. In 2018, many presidents in Central and East Africa sought to extend their time in office. Many of these attempts led to protests and corresponding violent crackdowns against popular mobilisation in the DRC, Sudan and Zimbabwe, and eventually resulted in a fully fledged armed conflict in Cameroon. In Burundi, Tanzania and Uganda, for example, long-serving presidents have regularly employed military operations against political opposition. These deeply entrenched and unsolved weaknesses of governance, including corruption and a lack of commitment to democratic and inclusive processes, fuel and protract conflict once violence emerges.

Many of the 15 national elections to be held in sub-Saharan Africa in 2019 (and particularly those in Burkina Faso, Cameroon, Chad, Mali, Madagascar and Mozambique) may exacerbate these dynamics and serve as opportunities for further violence.

Peace prospects remain slim for all active conflicts in sub-Saharan Africa, even for South Sudan, where a peace agreement was signed in September 2018. The African Union Mission in Somalia (AMISOM) is preparing to withdraw from the country, but al-Shabaab is not defeated. Similar to the situation in Afghanistan, it is likely that the international community will eventually seek to agree on a ceasefire with the group, after acknowledging that it cannot fully eradicate it. The mixed success of AMISOM in the Somalian conflict may also be part of a larger trend that suggests the African Union (AU) is losing relevance as a peacemaking body on the continent. Sub-regional organisations, such as the Economic Community of West African States (ECOWAS), have fared better than the UN and the AU in peacemaking initiatives. With governments becoming increasingly recalcitrant or even actively resistant (as in the case of the DRC) towards multilateral interference, sub-regional partners seem better able to make inroads and have their voices heard. The Southern African Development Community (SADC), for example, has been more vocal and effective than the AU at urging politicians in Angola, the DRC and Mozambique to respect their elected term times.

Bilateral mediators have had even more success than sub-regional peacemaking bodies this year. Saudi Arabia and the United Arab Emirates brokered the historic summit formally ending the Eritrean–Ethiopian conflict and re-establishing diplomatic ties and a border crossing. Bilateral actors have also been active in curbing violence and negotiating agreements over changes in leadership, such as in Darfur. This engagement reveals the increasing geostrategic interest of the Gulf countries in the region, and particularly in the Horn of Africa – an interest mainly rooted in great-power politics, as well as the exploitation of resources and commercial and security infrastructure, such as the need to control ports in the Red Sea and the Gulf of Aden. The UAE, for example, uses Eritrea as a tactical base to launch attacks on Yemen; Saudi Arabia plans to build a military base in Djibouti; Qatar and Turkey are funding the upgrade of a port in Sudan; and Russia and the United Kingdom are exploring opportunities in Somaliland. The United States is not far behind, branching out from its traditional counter-terrorism focus. This competition, pitting Qatar and Turkey against Saudi Arabia and the UAE, manipulates domestic interests, particularly in Somalia and Sudan. Similar dynamics are unfolding in Central Africa, where Russia is establishing its presence through private security deals with the governments of CAR and Sudan.

Cameroon

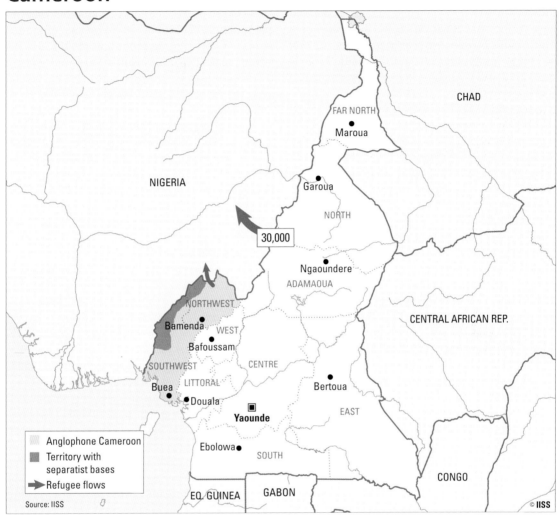

Source: IISS

© IISS

Overview

The conflict in 2018

The conflict in Cameroon escalated significantly in 2018 and spread throughout the regions of Northeast and Southeast Cameroon. In January, 47 members of the self-proclaimed interim government of the 'Republic of Ambazonia', including its leader Julius Ayuk Tabe, were extradited to Cameroon from Nigeria. In February, the government created a new military region headquartered in Bamenda, Northwest Region, to help coordinate a counter-insurgency campaign. Since then, the number of engagements between separatist groups and government forces have increased from scattered skirmishes to regular clashes. Separatist groups have

expanded their tactics to include road blockades and attacks on the educational system, including the kidnapping of teachers and students, and arson. The

Key statistics

Type:	Internal
IDPs total (2018):	440,000
IDPs new (2018):	no data
Refugees total (2018):	35,000
Refugees new (2018):	no data
People in need (2018):	no data

government has used 'scorched-earth' tactics that include attacks on villages and indiscriminate killings. At the same time, the conflict has taken on a much more fragmented character as the number of groups has proliferated and the political movement behind the Anglophone cause has remained fractured. In October, President Paul Biya won re-election and began his 36th year in power. While international attention on the conflict has grown, there have not been any concerted efforts at conflict resolution. As of November 2018 there were at least 437,000 internally displaced persons (IDPs) in Cameroon and 30,000 refugees in Nigeria.

The conflict to 2018

The conflict in Anglophone Cameroon (the Northwest and Southwest regions of Cameroon) began in late 2016 when a series of protests and general strikes led by lawyers, teachers and other civil-society organisations sought to foreground issues affecting Cameroon's English-speaking citizens. Anglophones, who constitute approximately 20% of the population, called for the roll back of policies of perceived cultural, economic and political discrimination dating back to the abolishment of federalism in 1972. The positions of the various groups of demonstrators ranged widely. A large segment of the protesters were associated with the Cameroon Anglophone Civil Society Consortium (CACSC), which supports political decentralisation or a return to federalism. Others, such as the Southern Cameroons National Council (SCNC), demanded succession and self-determination as an independent nation named 'Ambazonia'. There were no sustained or credible efforts at political reconciliation in 2017, which created a dynamic of mutual escalation between the protesting groups and the government. The government at times used violence to dissolve demonstrations and arrested several members of the protest movement under charges of domestic terrorism.

By late 2017, the protests had evolved into a secessionist movement (see **Table 1**) centralised in the Anglophone regions and led by the Southern Cameroon Ambazonia Consortium Front (SCACUF) and the rival Ambazonia Governing Council (AGC). Both organisations operate from abroad and draw senior leadership from expatriate Cameroonians, but also coordinate local membership in Anglophone areas. In October 2017, SCACUF proclaimed an interim government and elected Julius Ayuk Tabe as president. The AGC elected Lucas Cho Ayaba as commander-in-chief, and formed the Ambazonia Defence Forces (ADF), which has been at the forefront of an armed insurgency against the Cameroonian government. The ADF uses guerrilla tactics and makeshift weapons to attack government forces, and uses violence to compel citizens to participate in economic and political boycotts of public places (known as 'ghost towns'). In addition, several smaller militias and self-defence groups, many of which operate independently, have emerged. The Cameroonian government deployed one of its elite forces, the Rapid Response Brigade (BIR), which has been criticised for human-rights violations.

Forces

State forces

The government has relied heavily on Cameroon's military police (the gendarmerie) and elements of its elite military force, the Rapid Response Brigade (BIR), to suppress the insurgency. The BIR was created in 2008 to combat banditry along Cameroon's frontiers, but has since been used as an intervention force to combat Boko Haram in the north and Anglophone separatists in the south. To fight separatists, in February 2018 the Cameroonian government created a newly designated military region that covers Northwest and Southwest Cameroon called RMIA 5. The region is headquartered in Bamenda and led by General Agha Robinson Ndong. The counter-insurgency operation, which began in earnest in June 2018 with an increase in raids on suspected separatist camps and sympathetic villages, is referred to as *Operation Jackal*.

The gendarmerie and particularly the BIR have access to modern weaponry and armoured vehicles, and receive training from the United States and France. More recently, the BIR received a number of *Panthera* T6 armoured personnel carriers from Minerva Special Purpose Vehicles (MSPV) to be used specifically in urban settings in Northwest and Southwest Cameroon. The size of the military deployment is unclear, but the government can draw on 12,500 army servicemen and 9,000 paramilitaries. Both the BIR and the gendarmerie have been accused of human-rights abuses such as arson, rape, torture and indiscriminate violence.

Anglophone insurgency: Ambazonia Defence Forces (ADF) and the Southern Cameroons Defence Forces (SOCADEF)

The Ambazonia Defence Forces (ADF) was formed in late 2017 as the military arm of the Ambazonia Governing Council. The ADF is the largest armed group, and in 2018 was led from abroad by Lucas Cho Ayaba. Its goal is to establish an independent state of Ambazonia in the territories of Cameroon that were formerly under British colonial rule. Estimates place the group's strength between 1,500 and 3,000 fighters, spread out across approximately 20–50 camps in rural areas of Northwest and Southwest regions. The ADF uses mainly makeshift and old weapons together with improvised explosive devices (IEDs) to launch ambushes and quick attacks on government forces deployed in Anglophone Cameroon, and to deploy temporary roadblocks.[1] The ADF has also been linked to kidnappings and some violence against civilians, although it explicitly condemns such activities.

The Southern Cameroons Defence Forces (SOCADEF) is a smaller armed separatist group of approximately 100 members that operates mainly in Meme Division, Southwest Region, and is led from abroad by Ebenezer Derek Mbongo Akwanga. SOCADEF has claimed responsibility for several attacks on government forces and shares similar aims and tactics as the ADF. It is unclear how much coordination occurs between SOCADEF and the ADF.

Self-defence groups

Approximately 12 self-defence groups operate throughout Southwest and Northwest Cameroon, formed following a call from the self-proclaimed interim government in February 2018 to begin an 'era of self defence'. Information on most self-defence groups is limited, but among the more well-known groups are the Seven Karta Militia, the Ambazonia Restoration Army, the Manyu Tigers/Tigers of Ambazonia, the Manyu Ghost Warriors and the Southern Cameroon Defence Force (SCDF). Some groups coordinate with SCACUF through the Ambazonia Self Defence Council (ASDC), while others operate independently. These groups are minimally armed, and their explicit goal is the protection of Anglophone citizens from government forces. While ostensibly committed to defence rather than active insurgency, some groups such as the Manyu Ghost Warriors have been implicated in attacks on security forces.

Smaller armed militias

There are numerous smaller armed militias operating in the Southwest and Northwest regions of Cameroon. The main known groups are the Vipers, the Lebialem Red Dragons and the Amba Boys/Ambaland Forces. These groups use guerrilla tactics and improvised weaponry to attack government forces. However, they have also attacked on schools and businesses to compel them to participate in political and economic boycotts, and have carried out a number of prominent kidnappings of schoolchildren for ransom. In total, there are approximately 500 to 1,000 fighters in these groups, but information is limited.

Drivers

Historical perceptions of discrimination
The conflict's root causes date back to the colonial history of Cameroon. At independence in 1960, the country was bifurcated between a larger French-speaking territory and a smaller English-speaking region. Between 1962 and 1972, Cameroon operated as a federation, but first president Ahmadou Ahidjo used state institutions and his control of the budgets to eliminate rival political parties and consolidate power in a single-party regime under his

Cameroonian National Union (CNU). In 1972, a referendum to abolish federalism and create a unitary state easily passed, but with significant opposition from Anglophone areas.

Since then, Anglophone perceptions of cultural, economic and political discrimination have grown. Under Ahidjo, the perception was that resources were tilted towards his political allies and members of his Fulani ethnic group in Northern Cameroon. In 1982, power contentiously transitioned to Paul

Biya, and the ruling coalition shifted towards privileging the South and the Beti ethnic group. Residents of the Anglophone regions perceive themselves as the major losers from these arrangements. Common criticisms include the lack of major infrastructural investments in their regions; disregard for bilingualism in the public sector and higher education; the absence of a bench for common law on the Supreme Court; and lack of access to major government portfolios. In the 1990s, these issues were at the heart of opposition activity during the transition to democracy. The opposition Social Democratic Front (SDF) is considered an Anglophone party, and its members have supported decentralisation and a return to federalism for decades, while groups such as the SCNC have advocated for independence.

Patronage, corruption and weak democratic accountability

Rampant corruption and weak democratic accountability have also exacerbated the Anglophone sense of alienation. The office of the presidency, which oversees a vast state apparatus used to distribute patronage to supporters, dominates the political system in Cameroon. The president can single-handedly appoint most government positions, including influential regional governors and district officers. The president can also dissolve parliament and commands all the armed forces. According to Transparency International's 2018 Corruption Index, Cameroon ranks 152nd out of 180 countries in terms of perceptions of corruption. In 1992, the office of the prime minister was reinstated and has subsequently always been allocated to an Anglophone, although given the power of the presidency, many Anglophones view this concession as merely symbolic.

In 1992, Cameroon transitioned to multiparty elections, but the ruling Cameroon People's Democratic Movement (CPDM) has continued to dictate politics, in part through electoral manipulation and violence.[2] A process of gerrymandering and a disproportionate electoral system have also increasingly disadvantaged opposition parties, who occupy only 18% of parliamentary seats. In 2008, Biya changed the constitution to abolish term limits and then won re-election in 2011. In 2018, he won a seventh consecutive term in power. The perception of an entrenched status quo and an exclusive and

powerful elite has pushed many Anglophones to consider full autonomy as the only solution.

Imposition of French-speaking magistrates

The initial protests in Southwest Cameroon were driven by an increase in the appointment of French-speaking magistrates in Anglophone regions in late 2015. While common law is recognised in English-speaking regions, the country's legal system is based primarily on French civil law. At the time there was no common-law bench on the Supreme Court, and no common-law Bar association. Anglophone lawyers further complained that many essential laws are never translated into English, and that French-speaking magistrates who are unfamiliar with common law push cases into the French legal system. On 11 October 2016, Anglophone lawyers began a 72-hour strike in Buea and Bamenda. Shortly thereafter, the Common Law Bar Association was created to advocate for their interests. These strikes extended throughout 2016, and expanded into a protest movement that included the major teacher associations and student groups from the University of Buea and the University of Bamenda (in Southwest and Northwest Cameroon respectively).

Dynamics of mutual escalation

The protest movement began largely peacefully, but the government's aggressive response created a dynamic of mutual escalation. An ad hoc negotiations committee led by the prime minister was met by distrust in Anglophone areas (the majority of its members were French-speaking), and it failed to make headway after government forces violently dispersed protesters. During a protest march in Bamenda on 22 November 2016, more than 100 individuals were arrested, while in December 2016, government forces used live ammunition and killed four people. After negotiations collapsed, the CACSC began to coordinate wider-scale strikes known as 'ghost town' campaigns. In response, on 17 January 2017 the government used its authority under a 2014 anti-terrorism law to ban the SCNC and the CACSC and arrest the CACSC leadership on charges of terrorism. Internet services were suspended for long periods of time in early 2017, which had a significant economic effect on the region's nascent tech industry.[3]

Consequently, many Anglophone advocates began to shift their position from narrower

Table 1: The Anglophone movement

Political Organisation	Description	Related to
Southern Cameroon Ambazonia Consortium Front (SCACUF)	An umbrella organisation of several Ambazonian independence groups, which later evolved into the Interim Government of Ambazonia. SCACUF is responsible for international advocacy and fundraising.	Interim Government, AGC
Self-proclaimed interim Government of Ambazonia	Self-proclaimed independent interim government was founded in October 2017 and operates outside of Cameroon. The acting president is Samuel Ikome Sako, after the elected president Julius Sisiku Ayuk Tabe was extradited from Nigeria. The ultimate objective is independence, pursued through 'ghost-town' campaigns and the coordination of 'self-defence' groups (through ASDC).	SCACUF, ASDC
Ambazonia Governance Council (AGC)	An umbrella organisation of local Ambazonian independence groups founded in 2013, it operates mainly outside of Cameroon. The current leader is Ayaba Cho Lucas. The AGC is responsible for international advocacy and fundraising, but also supports violence against government forces and oversees the ADF. The AGC was a constituent member of SCACUF, but now operates a parallel and at times rival political structure.	SCACUF, ADF
Ambazonia Self Defence Council (ASDC)	A coordination mechanism created by the interim government in March 2018 to unite four local self-defence groups (the ARA, TTA, SCDF and Manyu Ghost Warriors).	Interim Government, Self-Defence Groups
Southern Cameroon National Council (SCNC)	A now-banned organisation that has advocated for Anglophone independence since its foundation in 1995.	
Social Democratic Front (SDF)	The major Anglophone political party, which currently holds 18 of 180 seats in the National Assembly. The SDF advocates for a return to federalism through government negotiation.	
Cameroon Anglophone Civil Society Consortium (CACSC)	A now-banned umbrella organisation of civil-society groups that helped coordinate the protest movement in 2016 and 2017, during which it was the main negotiating partner of the government.	
Major Armed Groups		
Ambazonia Defence Forces (ADF)	The largest and most active armed separatist group, with approximately 1,500 members operating in most areas of Northwest and Southwest Cameroon and led by Lucas Cho Ayaba. The ADF considers itself the official military of independent Ambazonia, under the guidance of the AGC.	AGC
Southern Cameroons Defence Forces (SOCADEF)	A smaller separatist group of approximately 100 members that operates mainly in Meme Division and is led by Ebenezer Derek Mbongo Akwanga. SOCADEF was founded as the military wing of the Southern Cameroon Youth League, one of the constituent members of the AGC. The degree of cooperation with the ADF is unclear.	AGC
Self-defence Groups		
Seven Karta Militia	Founded by taxi drivers in Manyu Division.	
Ambazonia Restoration Army (ARA)	Likely the largest armed self-defence group, encompassing several smaller local groups.	ASDC
Manyu Tigers/Tigers of Ambazonia (TTA)	Operates mainly in Manyu and Meme divisions.	ASDC
Manyu Ghost Warriors	Operates mainly in Manyu Division.	ASDC
Southern Cameroon Defence Force (SCDF)	Operates primarily in Meme Division.	ASDC
Small Militias		
The Vipers	Approximately 50 members.	
Lebialem Red Dragons	Operates mainly in Lebialem Division.	
Amba Boys/Ambaland Forces	General term for over a dozen small militias that operate throughout Northwest and Southwest regions. Likely responsible for most kidnappings and targeting of civilians.	

grievances within the legal and educational realms to demands for a return to federalism or even secession. In response, the government began to frame the Anglophone issue as a direct threat to the stability of the country, although it made some conciliatory concessions. The government announced a recruitment drive of bilingual teachers and created a National Commission for Bilingualism and Multiculturalism. During the legislative session of March 2017, bills were passed that created a new common-law bench on the Supreme Court and common-law departments at Francophone universities. However, Anglophones saw these measures as insincere and coming too late. Throughout 2017, the ghost-town campaigns expanded, and the security forces continued to use violence against demonstrators. Between September and October 2017, they opened fire on protesters across Anglophone Cameroon, killing 17 people. By late 2017, SCACUF and several small militias were already active, and the Anglophone movement had become factionalised over goals and tactics.

Permissive international environment

Cameroon enjoys a unique status in international circles given its historical ties to France and its role in regional national-security operations. Cameroon's relationship with France dates back to the post-colonial period, when important military and economic partnerships were developed.

French bilateral aid has been a significant source of government revenue, especially during periods when other lenders rescinded aid over Cameroon's poor democratic record and weak implementation of economic reforms. In return, Cameroon has offered France preferred access to primary commodities and remains a French ally in international arenas. Since 2001, Cameroon has also occupied an important position as the gateway to Central Africa and an ally in the war on terror. Cameroon contributes troops to the Multinational Joint Task Force (MNJTF), which fights the terrorist group Boko Haram. In 2018, there were 300 US military personnel and a drone base in Northern Cameroon. Cameroon is also a member of the G5 Sahel Force (FC-G5S), which was formed in 2014 as a regional military-coordination mechanism.

The international response to the government's crackdown on the initial protest movement was muted, and since the beginning of the conflict there has been no sustained international (or regional) effort to curtail violence and bring an end to the conflict. During the protests, many countries and international organisations – including Canada, the European Union, France, Germany and the United Kingdom – made no public statements on the evolving violence. Others such as the US and the African Union expressed concern and encouraged dialogue, but took no concrete diplomatic steps to resolve the conflict.

Political and Military Developments

Extradition of Ambazonia interim government

The conflict took on a new international dimension on 30 January 2018 when 47 members of SCACUF, the Ambazonian self-proclaimed interim government, were arrested and extradited from Nigeria to Cameroon. These figures included the president of the self-proclaimed interim government, Julius Sisiku Ayuk Tabe. Most of these individuals had filed asylum requests with the United Nations High Commissioner for Refugees (UNHCR), which led international human-rights organisations to criticise Nigeria for violating the principle of non-refoulement (not forcing asylum seekers to return to the country of their persecution). The Nigerian government seemed to initially cooperate with UNHCR, but then likely agreed to the extra-

dition to strengthen its strategic partnership with Cameroon. In November, ten members of SCACUF, including Ayuk, were charged with inciting terrorism and 'hostility against the motherland' and as of December 2018 were still awaiting trial.

Increased separatist activity

Following the extraditions, the number of engagements between security forces and various separatist forces increased sharply. In 2017, groups mainly operated in the Southwest Region (five divisions in particular), but in 2018, groups were active in 12 divisions across both Southwest and Northwest regions. While there were approximately 15–20 violent events in January 2018 throughout Northwest and Southwest Cameroon, by December

2018 there were 75–80. The ADF has remained the largest and most organised armed group, but throughout 2018 dozens of smaller militias and self-defence groups formed and were responsible for some of the violence.

The tactics used by these groups also expanded in 2018. In 2017 and early 2018, separatist tactics mostly included hit-and-run attacks and ambushes on police outposts, military patrols and border crossings. However, throughout the rest of 2018 they began to include the use of roadblocks, kidnappings and violence against civilians. In particular, the educational sector in rural areas has come under duress as part of a strategy to enforce a boycott of state services. In November, 79 schoolchildren were abducted near Bamenda. Most were released shortly thereafter, with no major separatist group claiming responsibility for the incident. Similar tactics were used to intimidate potential informers and reduce turnout during the March senatorial and October presidential elections.

Presidential elections

Following senatorial elections in March, Biya announced that he would run again as the CPDM's presidential candidate. The president has been in power since 1982, and the question of his succession has been the source of intense factionalism and speculation within the ruling party amid the absence of institutionalised mechanisms for selecting a successor. By 2018 no consensus replacement candidate had emerged, and the Anglophone crisis led to a prioritising of political stability and continuity. Biya's candidacy ended internal debate within the ruling party, but also signalled an endorsement of the status quo in place essentially since 1982 (when Biya became president).

Armed groups deliberately intimidated citizens in Anglophone areas to boycott the October election, resulting in election turnouts of 5% and 10% in Northwest and Southwest regions respectively. Biya won with 71% of the vote. Subsequent petitions by opposition candidates to the newly formed Constitutional Court claiming that the elections had been marred by fraud were rejected. The president appointed most of the Constitutional Court's members, which limited its independence.

Increased international attention

In 2018, the conflict received more international attention compared to the previous two years. In January 2018, the Commonwealth Secretary-General Patricia Scotland travelled to Anglophone Cameroon and encouraged the government to open dialogue with the Ambazonian self-proclaimed interim government. In May 2018, the UN declared a humanitarian crisis and began to organise international aid across the border in Nigeria. At the same time, however, the US Ambassador to Cameroon Peter Barlerin came under heavy criticism for telling Biya that he 'should consider his legacy' as the election approached – his words were received as undue pressure on Biya to end the crisis quickly or to resign. In June, the US Congress was briefed on the situation and 50 members of the German parliament called for a review of aid to Cameroon. Following pressure from the UK and Germany, in November Cameroon's major patron France sent a delegation that reportedly threatened in private to withdraw military aid unless dialogue channels with separatists were established.[4] In addition, Human Rights Watch and Amnesty International issued major reports showing extensive evidence of human-rights violations committed by both government forces and separatist groups. Still, no real policy developments ensued from the international community.

Violent Events

Sporadic attacks in Southwest Region

In early 2018, the conflict was concentrated in rural areas, primarily along the Nigerian border in Southwest Region (Ndian and Manyu divisions in particular). Armed groups associated with the ADF and other militias launched numerous hit-and-run attacks on police stations, border crossings and military convoys, and carried out a more limited number of kidnappings of police officers, civil servants and mayors, as well as attacks on teachers and traditional chiefs. Government forces launched raids on villages suspected of harbouring separatists, which led to the internal displacement of approximately 80,000 people towards major cities, and to approximately 20,000 refugees crossing into Nigeria.

Battle of Batibo and ADF advances in Mezam and Boyo divisions

On 3 March, separatist forces attacked a military convoy on the Bamenda–Batibo highway, following an ADF announcement in late February that it controlled significant territory along the highway in Mezam and Boyo divisions (Northwest Region). In what was reported as the conflict's deadliest attack to date, approximately 70 members of the Cameroonian armed forces and more than 100 separatist fighters died. In response, government forces carried out mass arrests and destroyed several villages in the Batibo sub-division, causing the displacement of approximately 4,000 people. In April, the ADF forced government forces to withdraw from the town of Belo (Boyo Division), which the government did not retake until later in May.

Fighting in Fako Division

While separatists and the Cameroonian armed forces continued to clash throughout the Southwest Region, in June a significant proportion of the conflict became concentrated along the Buea–Kumba road and Fako Division. Separatist forces imposed roadblocks to disrupt local commerce, and launched frequent incursions against military outposts into the towns of Buea, Ekona, Kumba and Tiko. Separatist attacks increased in September and October to commemorate the first anniversary of the beginning of the conflict, and to disrupt Unification Day and the upcoming presidential election. Starting in September, in view of the elections, the Cameroonian government committed additional forces to end road blockades and to retake territories throughout Fako Division, causing a sharp increase in clashes in these areas, with reports of entire neighbourhoods and villages being destroyed. In November, separatist groups increased their use of kidnappings in these areas, in particular targeting schools. By December, many sections of the Kumba–Buea road were still obstructed by separatist roadblocks.

Fighting in Mezam and Menchum divisions

In early 2018 there were numerous clashes throughout Northwest Region as well, but by June they became heavily concentrated along the Wum–Bamenda road in Mezam and Menchum divisions. Separatist forces attempted to impose an economic blockade in Bamenda, and took territory near the towns of Chomba, Njikwa, Oku and Zhoa. Government forces later dismantled several separatist camps and destroyed the village of Zhoa. A four-day battle with separatists began on 23 September in the town of Bafut, during which two separatists and 12 government soldiers were killed. Services in Bafut were heavily disrupted until late November.

On 4 November, a militia affiliated with the Amba Boys kidnapped 79 schoolchildren and three teachers from a boarding facility near Bamenda, and transported them to Bafut, marking the first attack against such a large civilian population. The kidnapping was likely used to intimidate civilians into a school boycott. The victims were released days later unharmed, although the teachers remained in the group's custody. The ADF condemned the kidnappings and it remains unclear whether the action had the desired effect.[5]

Major clashes in Lebialem Division

There was a concentration of fighting in Lebialem Division (Southwest Region), in particular between government forces and smaller militias such as the Red Dragons. On 25 July, a major battle occurred in which both sides claimed victory. More than 100 militia members and 100 soldiers were reportedly killed in the fighting.[6] On 5 August, the government raided separatist camps in Tabil.

Conflict expands to new geographical areas

By the end of 2018, clashes were reported between separatist and government forces in all the divisions of Southwest and Northwest regions, and in some areas of Littoral and West regions. On 27 September, separatists forced the government to withdraw from Balikumbat in Ngo-Ketunjia Division (Northwest Region). There were also several battles around the town of Ndop in this division, including a successful prison break. By November there were also reports of attacks and kidnappings in Noun Division (West Region) and Moungo Division (Littoral Region), marking the first time the conflict spread from the Anglophone region.

Impact

The situation in Anglophone Cameroon deteriorated significantly in 2018, with serious humanitarian and economic consequences. The geographic reach of the conflict expanded and the government began a violent counter-insurgency campaign that had a devastating impact. In addition, the conflict disrupted an already-tenuous democratic environment. Biya's re-election was both symptomatic of broader factors that have sustained the conflict, and a response to the threat of instability posed by the conflict. Cameroon plays a strategic role in regional stability, which is also potentially under threat if the crisis continues.

Humanitarian impact

The expansion of the conflict and the government's use of harsh counter-insurgency tactics have taken a significant humanitarian toll. According to the Cameroonian government, approximately 200 security personnel and 800 separatists have been killed. Reporting on civilian casualties is uneven, but some sources indicate that since late 2017 between 400 and 1,000 people may have been killed. Human-rights organisations reported that government forces destroyed approximately 100 villages, and the UN Office for the Coordination of Humanitarian Affairs (OCHA) reported in November that at least 437,000 people had been internally displaced, with 246,000 in the Southwest Region alone. The UNHCR assessed that there were 30,000 refugees in Nigeria, of whom 52% were under 18 years old. There are also reports of human-rights violations on both sides of the conflict, and – outside of some minor civil-society initiatives – there is no current effort at reconciliation. The separatist focus on disrupting the educational system and limiting commerce with French companies has also had a profound impact. Many schools have remained closed for the academic year, and the universities in Buea and Bamenda have been targeted in kidnapping attacks.

Economic impact

The Anglophone economy is based primarily on the export of palm oil, coffee and cocoa. Trade with Nigeria is a primary source of goods and there is a nascent IT sector concentrated around the University of Buea (referred to as 'Silicone Mountain'). The conflict has led the state-run palm-oil company Pamol to shut down mills in Ndian and Meme divisions. Likewise, many coffee and cocoa plantations have been abandoned by private enterprises, and the Cameroonian Development Corporation (CDC) has been unable to pay nearly 20,000 workers employed in various local firms. Consequently, exports have declined by nearly 80% and approximately 60,000 agricultural workers have become unemployed. Along the Cameroon–Nigeria border there has been a slowdown in trade of basic goods such as fabrics, electronics and foodstuffs. Frequent internet shutdowns in 2016 and 2017 have brought investments into the IT sector to a halt, and many enterprises have moved to Douala or Yaoundé, in Littoral Region and Centre Region respectively.

Political impact

The conflict has impacted democratic processes in Cameroon and strained the ruling party. Previous elections in Cameroon have persistently been criticised over issues of electoral integrity. Likewise, the many violations of freedom of assembly and expression have not instilled confidence in the political system. Nonetheless, opposition parties have participated in elections and wielded some political power in the legislature. The conflict and separatist campaign to boycott elections in 2018 led however to the lowest electoral turnout in Cameroon's history (approximately 10% in Anglophone areas and 50% in total). The opposition soundly rejected the election results, and their participation in the 2019 parliamentary elections is uncertain. Moreover, the conflict has exposed rifts within the ruling CPDM over the government's tactics. The re-election of Biya stifled much of the internal debate within the party over the Anglophone crisis, but factionalism remains a factor.

Regional stability

Cameroon plays an important role in regional security cooperation, which the Anglophone conflict places at some threat. Cameroon is a member of the MNJTF and contributes troops to the UN's stabilisation mission in Central African Republic. Moreover, Cameroon patrols a lengthy border with Chad and Central African Republic that is porous to smuggling and other illicit activities. In late September 2017, Cameroon was forced to close the border with

Central African Republic in response to armed-group activity. While the Cameroonian armed forces has made significant advances against Boko Haram in the Far North Region, continued conflict in Anglophone regions could divert much-needed military resources and raise the risk of the group's resurgence and increased criminal activity along Cameroon's rural borders.

Trends

By the end of 2018 the conflict remained in a condition of uncertainty. Since August, the government has increased its counter-insurgency efforts and gained more control over major urban areas in Anglophone Cameroon. However, separatist groups still operate with ease in rural areas where infrastructure is poor, and have been able to impose long-term blockades on major thoroughfares in Northwest and Southwest regions. Likewise, insurgent groups have adjusted and increasingly adopted new tactics such as kidnappings, while maintaining strong ties with the diaspora community in Nigeria, France and the US, an important source of funding. While international attention to the conflict has increased, there is no sustained effort to end the conflict.

The fragmentation of the Anglophone movement has also been a key impediment to conflict resolution. Throughout 2018, the self-proclaimed interim government of Ambazonia and the ADF eclipsed the civil-society-based protest movement that was still paramount in 2017. There are now numerous armed groups with different political aims, and deep divisions between the political and armed opposition. By the end of 2018, the Catholic Church began efforts to coordinate an All-Anglophone Conference that would resolve this internal factionalism and lead to negotiations with the government.[7] However, these efforts have not yet borne fruit and it is not clear whether they can satisfy the more radical demands of armed groups. Unless some consensus can be forged over what a negotiated outcome might look like, the fragmentation of the movement is likely to perpetuate the conflict in 2019.

The re-election of Biya helped ensure near-term political stability, but did little to resolve the fundamental causes of the conflict. Within the ruling coalition there are disagreements over the government's strategies, and some advocate for a harsher crackdown on the insurgency as a prerequisite for any negotiations. Biya's re-election also signalled to the various separatist groups that the status quo will continue and that their demands for autonomy would not be achieved through legal means. In late 2018, the Biya regime announced plans for a disarmament, demobilisation and reintegration commission, which seemed to indicate some openness to reconciliation. However, Biya offered no tangible concessions to Anglophone demands for political restructuring. The government still appears willing to address most of the cultural grievances that it negotiated on in 2016, and might cede some ground on issues of decentralisation, but it is unlikely to agree to a return to federalism, let alone secession of Anglophone regions.

Notes

[1]   Emmanuel Freudenthal, 'Cameroon's Anglophone War, Part I: A Rifle as the Only Way Out', *IRIN News*, 12 June 2018.

[2]   Erika Albaugh, 'An Autocrat's Toolkit: Adaptation and Manipulation in "Democratic Cameroon"', *Democratization*, vol. 18, no. 2, 2011.

[3]   Abdi Latif Dahir, 'How Do You Build Africa's Newest Tech Ecosystem When the Government Shuts the Internet Down', *Quartz*, 3 February 2017.

[4]   'Two Macron Envoys in Yaounde to Discuss Anglophone Crisis', *West Africa Newsletter*, no. 788, 20 November 2018.

[5]   'Schoolchildren in Cameroon Released Days After Abduction by Separatists', *VOA News*, 7 November 2018.

[6]   'Separatists and Government Forces Sent Out Conflicting Reports in the Battle for Lebialem', *National Times*, 25 July 2018,

[7]   International Crisis Group, 'Cameroon's Anglophone Crisis: How the Catholic Church can Promote Dialogue', ICG Briefing no. 138, 25 April 2018.

Central African Republic

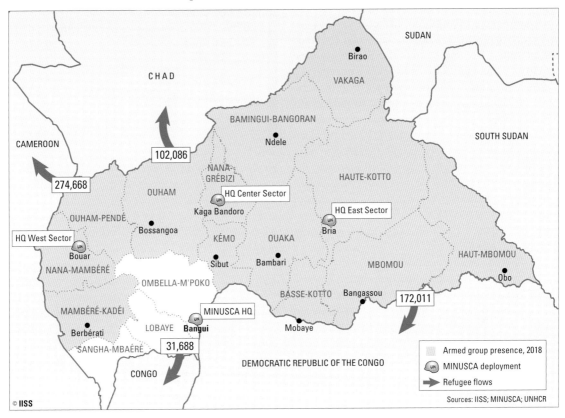

Sources: IISS; MINUSCA; UNHCR

Overview

The conflict in 2018

The fundamental dynamics of the conflict in the Central African Republic (CAR) remained the same, with localised fighting between armed groups and sporadic attacks against civilians and peacekeepers. The United Nations Multidimensional Integrated Stabilization Mission in the Central African Republic (MINUSCA) continued to face critical capacity gaps that impeded its ability to uphold its civilian-protection mandate consistently. In April 2018, UN peacekeepers conducted an operation against armed groups in the predominantly Muslim PK5 – the main trade district of the capital Bangui, triggering new tension between Muslim and non-Muslim communities in the capital, as well as between MINUSCA and the ex-Séléka armed groups (that purport to protect the Muslims). In May, violence broke out between Muslim and non-Muslim communities in another major city, Bambari, Ouaka prefecture. This key road connection and trade centre in central CAR

was declared a gun-free zone by MINUSCA in early 2017 in an attempt to end intercommunal fighting.

The African Union mediation process remained stalled in 2018. Negotiations were due to begin in June but were delayed indefinitely. AU mediation was also challenged by an unexpected Russian initiative. With the support of the Sudanese government, on 10 July and 28 August Moscow invited warlords and government officials to Khartoum to discuss a parallel peace deal.

The conflict to 2018

Following a failed early 2013 peace deal mediated by the Economic Community of the Central African States (ECCAS) with then-president François Bozizé, the Séléka marched into Bangui. After overthrowing Bozizé on 24 March 2013, however, the Séléka coalition proved unable to establish a functional government. The state collapsed, lacking any effective ministries or security services.

In a situation of near anarchy, a self-defence group called the anti-Balaka emerged in western CAR and entered Bangui on 5 December 2013. To protect Bangui's citizens, France launched *Operation Sangaris* on 5 December 2013. The Séléka coalition fled from Bangui but stationed some fighters in PK5.

As anti-Muslim violence spiralled in Bangui, most Muslims in western CAR fled to neighbouring countries (Cameroon and Chad) or remained trapped in enclaves surrounded by anti-Balaka forces. *Operation Sangaris* ended in October 2016 and UN peacekeepers deployed throughout the country. A transitional government was established and elections organised in 2016 under international supervision. Former prime minister Faustin-Archange Touadéra was elected president and formed a government.

Since 2015, the initial conflict between the anti-Balaka and the Séléka coalition has turned into a chaotic confrontation between many armed groups (the number of armed groups increased from ten in 2015 to 17 in 2018). After leaving the capital city, the Séléka coalition splintered into several armed groups that took over north, east and central CAR. While the conflict initially sharpened divisions

Key statistics	
Type:	Internationalised
IDPs total (2018):	650,000
IDPs new (2018):	no data
Refugees total (2018):	580,000
Refugees new (2018):	25,000
People in need (2018):	2,900,000

between the Muslim and Christian communities, it has now an intercommunal dimension indicated in the shifting alliances between various predatory armed groups, including factions of the ex-Séléka rebel alliance and anti-Balaka militias. Despite the presence of 11,000 peacekeepers, the training of CAR armed forces (FACA) by the European Union and Russia, and vital financial support from donors, 70% of CAR territory is under the control of armed groups and most of the country remains lawless. The elected government only controls the western part of the country, but even in government-controlled areas, basic services for the population have not been restored.

Forces

State forces

The Central African army, which consists of approximately 7,000 soldiers, is being retrained by the European Union and Russia in order to fulfil its mandate and improve the security situation. Operational capacity is improving: 243 soldiers have been deployed in Am Dafok, Boali, Bouar and Moungounba without MINUSCA or partner support, while 612 EU-trained personnel have been deployed in Bangassou, Bouar, Dekoa, Obo, Paoua and Sibut.[1] The Central African armed forces received contributions from bilateral partners (China, France, Russia and the United States), including armaments, vehicles, communications and other equipment.

United Nations Multidimensional Integrated Stabilisation Mission in the Central African Republic (MINUSCA)

The UN Security Council on 10 April 2014 (Resolution 2149) established the United Nations Multidimensional Integrated Stabilization Mission in the Central African Republic (MINUSCA), mandated to protect civilians; support the peace process; deliver humanitarian assistance; support the extension of state authority, the deployment of security forces and the preservation of territorial integrity; disarm, demobilise and reintegrate former combatants; promote and protect human rights; and address the illicit exploitation and trafficking of natural resources.

MINUSCA's total force strength as of December 2018 was 13,595, including 1,768 troops, 153 military observers, 292 staff officers and 2,050 police units. Bangladesh, Burundi, Cameroon, Egypt, Gabon, Mauritania, Morocco, Pakistan, Rwanda and Zambia are the main troop contributors, while Senegal and Jordan contribute police units.

Popular Front for the Renaissance of Central African Republic (FPRC)

Led by Abdoulaye Hissène and Noureddine Adam, the Popular Front for the Renaissance of the Central

African Republic (FPRC) is one of the most powerful and structured armed groups in CAR. The FPRC comprised Rounga, Goula, Chadian and Sudanese fighters, but most of the Goula left the movement in 2017–18 after internal fighting and joined the RPRC.

The FPRC has developed a political agenda based on the protection of Muslims and the partition of the country. In 2015, Adam briefly proclaimed the creation of an independent state in northeastern CAR, the Logone Republic and has since then unsuccessfully tried to reunite the ex-Séléka groups. According to the UN Panel of Experts, the FPRC has set up parallel administrative structures and taxation mechanisms and its leadership is well connected in Chad and Sudan.

Union for Peace in Central Africa (UPC)

The Union for Peace in Central Africa (UPC) is a Fulani armed group headed by Ali Darassa. It was the first group to split from the Séléka coalition in 2014 and is one of the most powerful armed groups in CAR. Thanks to its regional connections and its involvement in the cross-country cattle business, the group can also draw on extensive financial resources.

The expansion of the UPC-controlled territory in 2015 and 2016 caused the creation of an anti-UPC coalition (FPRC, MPC and some anti-Balaka groups), which in 2017 and 2018 fought the UPC in eastern and southern CAR. In May 2018, the UPC made a peace deal with the RPRC that was still holding at the end of the year. Unlike the FPRC, the UPC does not have political aspirations. Its agenda is restricted to Fulani interests, including ending violence against the Fulani in CAR and the regulation of cattle migration.

Patriotic Movement for Central Africa (MPC)

The Patriotic Movement for Central Africa (MPC) was formed in mid-2015 when Mahamat al-Khatim left the FPRC and created his own group. The MPC is mostly comprised of Chadian fighters and dominates a large swathe of territory from the Chadian border to Kaga-Bandoro in central CAR. The group is well connected in Chad and heavily involved in the cattle migration from Chad to CAR.

Popular Rally for the Reconstruction of Central Africa (RPRC)

The Popular Rally for the Reconstruction of Central Africa (RPRC) is an armed group formed by Goula fighters and led by Zakaria Damane. It is located in the northeast of CAR and its main opponents are the FPRC and the UPC, although in May 2018 the RPRC signed a peace deal with the UPC.

National Movement for the Liberation of the Central African Republic (MNLC)

The National Movement for the Liberation of the Central African Republic (MNLC) is an MPC splinter group created in 2017 by Ahmat Bahar and located in northwest CAR, close to the Chadian border. In 2018, despite the initial split, it re-established a working relationship with the MPC.

Movement of the Central African Liberators for Justice (MLCJ)

The Movement of the Central African Liberators for Justice (MLCJ) is a small armed group based in Birao and Bria in northeast CAR. This Kara militia preceded the Séléka rebellion, having originally splintered from the Union of Democratic Forces for Unity (UFDR). Previously run by Abakar Sabone, it is now led by Gilbert Toumoudeya, although the group is no longer very active.

Return, Reclamation and Rehabilitation (3R)

Return, Reclamation and Rehabilitation (3R) is a Fulani armed group that emerged in late 2015 at the northwest border between CAR and Cameroon. Its leader, Sidiki Abass, has been protecting the pastoralist communities at the border against anti-Balaka cattle thieves (the Ndalé gang). Sidiki Abass advocates the return of the Fulani refugees from Cameroon and the protection of their cattle.

The 3R fought against the Ndalé gang until the two parties signed a peace deal (brokered by MINUSCA) in December 2017. Since then, the 3R has not been involved in new fighting. However, it maintains its military capacity and in October 2018 expressed its intention to create a political platform.

Siriri Coalition

The Siriri Coalition is a Fulani armed group that emerged in late 2017 at the border between CAR and Cameroon, in the Amada-Gaza sub-prefecture. It initially protected the cattle sent to CAR's grazing fields against anti-Balaka groups, but then turned to banditry. It is the smallest Fulani armed group, with no known leadership or political agenda.

Democratic Front of the Central African People (FDPC)

The Democratic Front of the Central African People (FDPC) was created by Martin Koumtamadji (also known as 'Abdoulaye Miskine'), who ran a militia for then-president Ange-Félix Patassé in the early 2000s. After the successful Bozizé putsch against Patassé in 2003, Miskine fled and formed FDPC. Its area of operation is the Baboua sub-prefecture close to the Cameroonian border. Miskine was arrested on 16 September 2013 in Bertoua in eastern Cameroon. In response, his militiamen kidnapped Cameroonians and Central Africans, as well as a Polish priest, and asked for an exchange. Miskine was released on 27 November 2014, along with 27 hostages. He currently lives in Congo-Brazzaville but still leads the small group, the strategy of which is essentially local banditry.

Anti-Balaka

The anti-Balaka groups – the term means 'anti-bullets of AK-47', suggesting the group's invulnerability – are a loose network of mostly Christian and animist militias with mainly local agendas. They were initially an anti-Muslim self-defence movement that emerged in response to the Séléka violence in western CAR in late 2013, and were then mainly comprised of members of the Gbaya ethnic group (including orphans and former soldiers).

The term 'anti-Balaka' has come to encompass a broad range of armed actors, including criminal gangs. These militias are poorly armed and usually affiliated with one of the two principal Bangui-based anti-Balaka coordinating branches (the branch run by Maxime Mokom and the branch run by Sebastien Wenezoui and Patrice-Edouard Ngaïssona), which are increasingly thought to represent personal interests rather than any clear agenda. The group's original political demand – the return of former president François Bozizé from exile in Uganda – has become less relevant, given that Bozizé has been absent from the political scene since 2013.

In 2017, the anti-Balaka movement extended its territorial reach thanks to the emergence in southeastern CAR of the so-called 'self-defence' groups made up of local tribes such as the Banda and Nzakara. Despite their initial anti-Séléka motive, some of the anti-Balaka groups have now formed alliances with Muslim armed groups.

Revolution and Justice (RJ)

Revolution and Justice (RJ) is a small armed group created by Armel Sayo in 2013 and located in Ouham-Pendé prefecture. RJ did not align to the anti-Balaka nor the Séléka in 2013–14 but fought against any armed group trying to settle in its territory.

Armel Sayo supported the transitional government in 2014 and became minister of sports until 2016. Since then, his leadership was repeatedly challenged. Raymond Belanga created a splintered group (RJ–Belanga) but was assassinated in 2017 by elements of the MNLC. In January 2018, RJ agreed to participate into the disarmament, demobilisation and reintegration (DDR) programme.

Lord's Resistance Army (LRA)

The Lord's Resistance Army (LRA) is a rebel group run by Joseph Kony that emerged in northern Uganda in the late 1980s. Its fighters moved to CAR and South Sudan after the failure of peace negotiations in 2008. Their survival strategy is based on poaching, theft and village attacks. Small groups of LRA combatants terrorise the rural villages in southeastern CAR (Mbomou, Haut-Mbomou and Haute-Kotto prefectures). They live in the bush, are poorly armed and have been accused of many human-rights violations, including child abductions.

Drivers

Economic predation

The UN estimates that 70% of CAR is controlled by armed groups. These armed groups are self-funded and have economic ties with political and economic actors. They rely on revenues generated through predation of trade routes and exploitation of natural resources such as diamonds, gold, wildlife and cattle. The sophistication of the armed groups' predatory strategies varies but most of the clashes between and within them are due to disputes over the control of resource-rich territories and the management of predation operations. The anti-Balaka groups are notorious for their infighting when it comes to sharing their gains, while the most powerful Muslim groups (the FPRC, MPC and UPC) have set up their own taxation mechanisms and have diversified their sources of revenue. Ex-Séléka and anti-Balaka roadblocks are widespread and are at the core of the political economy of CAR's conflict: without the revenues generated from the roadblocks, armed groups would struggle to retain their rank and file. It is estimated that the FPRC, MPC and UPC collectively collect at least €3.6 million (US$4.2m) a year from taxing the cattle circuit, and another €2.5m (US$2.9m) from Sudanese trade routes.[2]

Socio-economic rivalries under religious disguise

In the course of the conflict, hate speech and incitement to ethnic and religious violence emerged often, with some anti-Balaka groups carrying out targeted attacks against the Muslim population. These attacks have a social and economic dimension as well: traders are mostly Muslim, and Muslim entrepreneurs tend to dominate business sectors, such as clothing, transportation and the artisanal trade in diamonds and gold. Despite the many mixed marriages, relations between Muslims and the rest of the population are often tainted by social jealousy.

Revival of an historic divide

The Séléka power grab in March 2013 marked a fundamental reversal of CAR's traditional political landscape. Since independence, the struggle for power was the prerogative of military officers drawn from savannah and riverside communities (in central and southern CAR). Previous coups were carried out by senior army officers, sometimes supported by Chadian mercenaries, as in 2003. These mercenaries of the 2003 coup became the leaders of the coup in 2013, which led a rebel force composed of Muslims from the north and the east to take power for the first time. The emergence of the Séléka was perceived by the rest of the country as a literal 'invasion', awakening the collective memory of slaving raids led by Muslim traders between the

sixteenth and nineteenth centuries that depopulated entire regions of CAR. Exploiting this anxiety, politicians used the fear of the Muslim 'invaders' to mobilise support and create youth militias for their own protection.

Regional security interests

Chad and Sudan have taken advantage of the conflict in CAR to solve issues of domestic security. The two neighbouring countries have generated many militiamen in the course of their long histories of conflict, but with the appeasement in Darfur and the end of the civil war in Chad, these fighters became jobless. Some of them were hired by the Séléka and provided a substantial force in 2012–13. Many returned home after the Séléka coalition disbanded, or deployed in other battlefields (notably Libya), but some ex-Séléka armed groups still have Chadian and Sudanese fighters in their ranks.

Militas take control of cattle migration

The involvement of militias in cattle migration is a key driver of violence in the rural areas of north and central CAR. Each year during the dry season, thousands of cows are moved from Sudan and Chad to the grazing fields in CAR. This migration is a major source of revenue for the Sudanese and Chadian cattle owners but it drives local conflicts between the pastoralists and the farming communities in CAR. Lack of state services, erosion of traditional dispute-resolution mechanisms, cattle theft, widespread use of AK-47s by herders and frequent interventions of the Chadian army against cattle thieves have gradually turned the annual cattle migration into a major and seasonal security risk. As a result, the Chadian and Sudanese cattle owners now rely on armed groups to secure the cattle movement, while the farming communities organise local self-defence groups against the armed herders, thereby exacerbating the resentment against the Muslim pastoralists in general and the Chadian and Sudanese in particular.

Political and Military Developments

France–Russia tensions

Just after opposing the delivery of weapons by France in the UN Security Council, in late 2017, Russia began sending military equipment and

instructors for the Central African Army. In 2018, Moscow stepped up the involvement in CAR by providing a security adviser to the president, supporting the deployment of some CAR army units,

Sub-Saharan Africa

signing a military-cooperation agreement with CAR and funding a new radio station (Lengo Songo). More significantly, it sponsored a new peace initiative that competes with the AU-led mediation supported by France, leading to rising tensions between Moscow and Paris.

In order to counter Russian influence, French diplomats used the UN General Assembly in September 2018 to arrange a show of support for the AU-led mediation initiative in CAR. UN Secretary-General António Guterres recommended that the initiative become a joint UN–AU task implemented by a high-level figure appointed by both the UN and the AU. In response, Russian diplomats insisted that the UN should recognise the positive role played by Russia in CAR. French diplomats opposed the Russian motion, which led to a delay in the renewal of MINUSCA's mandate. The mandate was eventually renewed on 13 December by the UN Security Council, but Russia and China abstained from voting on the resolution.

In late 2018, the French ministers for foreign affairs and defence visited Bangui, where they announced an increase in financial and military support to the CAR government comprising €24m (US$27.7m) in development aid and 1,400 assault rifles.

No start to AU negotiations and local ceasefires
The effort by the AU to mediate a political solution to the conflict has been progressing slowly since mid-2017. The AU panel organised several meetings in 2017 and 2018 with 14 armed groups. The result of these lengthy discussions was the formulation of 104 demands, combined in a single document on 30 August 2018 which was submitted to the government, but no subsequent negotiations.

Several local peace initiatives have progressed in parallel, and some have been successful. Peace accords were signed in 2018 between armed groups, local administrators and civil-society representatives in Bangassou, Briam, Batangafo and Markounda. Tthese agreements are only ceasefires and do not address the causes of the conflict – widespread poverty and long-term bad governance – but they may help to prevent violence, albeit only in the short term.

Justice in a time of war
In May 2014, the CAR transitional government referred the situation in CAR to the International Criminal Court (ICC), which opened investigations into alleged war crimes and crimes against humanity by both Séléka and anti-Balaka forces in the period since 2012. On 17 November 2018, Alfred Yekatom (also known as 'Colonel Rambo') became the first CAR warlord to be delivered to the ICC. Yekatom was a well-known anti-Balaka commander during the transition (2014–16) and was elected as a member of parliament in 2016. He was arrested in October 2018 after he drew his gun and fired into the air in the CAR parliament during an altercation – taking advantage of this arrest, the ICC prosecutor indicted him. Yekatom is suspected of having committed war crimes and crimes against humanity, including murder and recruitment of child soldiers in late 2013 and early 2014.

On 12 December Patrice-Edouard Ngaïssona, national coordinator of one of the factions of the anti-Balaka movement, was arrested in a Paris airport. He was indicted by the ICC for war crimes and crimes against humanity committed between September 2013 and December 2014. On 31 December, French authorities confirmed that he would soon be extradited to The Hague.

The Special Criminal Court for CAR (SCC) – a hybrid judicial mechanism created in 2015 – is also responsible for prosecuting crimes committed during the CAR conflict. Mainly funded by international aid, the SCC is comprised of foreign and national magistrates and is designed to deal with serious human-rights violations committed from 1 January 2003. On 2 July 2018, the SCC rules of procedure and evidence were promulgated and the court was officially inaugurated on 22 October 2018.

Early preparations for next elections
President Touadéra created his own party, Mouvement Coeurs Unis (United Hearts), in order to run again in the 2021 elections. On 8 November, the first congress of this new political formation was organised in Bangui.

The dismissal of Karim Meckassoua, the chairperson of the National Assembly, on 26 October after Touadéra organised a vote of no confidence also signalled that the president is thinking about re-election. Meckassoua, who has opposed the government since 2016 and become Touadéra's main opponent, was replaced by Laurent Ngon-Baba, a low-profile Muslim former minister.

Violent Events

The CAR conflict has high impact on vulnerable populations. In late 2018, violence took a new turn with several attacks against camps for internally displaced persons (IDPs).

Operation Sukula

On 7 and 8 April 2018, MINUSCA and FACA launched *Operation Sukula*, a joint intervention designed to remove self-defence groups from the PK5 district of Bangui. The operation unintendedly triggered an increase in intercommunal tensions and a series of violent clashes from early April to early May. According to a report by the UN Panel of Experts, the violence led to 'the highest number of casualties in the capital during a 30-day period since 2014, with at least 70 people killed and 330 injured, most of them civilians'. MINUSCA was accused of using excessive force during this operation, faced a hostile media campaign and proved to be unable to neutralise armed groups in the PK5 neighbourhood despite its superiority in troops and equipment.

Violence returns to Bambari

Bambari is a strategic town located in the centre of the country that was declared free of armed groups by MINUSCA after its intervention in early 2017. During a year of relative quiet, reconstruction began and many non-governmental organisations started using the city as a hub for their operations in the centre of CAR. In May 2018, however, the murder of a taxi driver triggered a new surge in violence in Bambari between the UPC (which had maintained a strong influence in the city despite MINUSCA troops) and anti-Balaka groups. From May to the end of the year, the UPC attacked NGO offices, MINUSCA peacekeepers and FACA. One priest was murdered during the fighting.

New fighting in Mambéré-Kadeï

While Mambéré-Kadeï prefecture used to be a quiet area, fighting erupted throughout the year due to the presence of the Siriri Coalition. In 2018, this newly formed armed group extended its reach in the north to the Gamboula border area with Cameroon. It raided Amada-Gaza town and clashed with MINUSCA troops (one peacekeeper was killed on 17 November) and another unidentified armed group (reportedly 3R) on 11 November).

Violence against IDPs

Displaced people represent a significant proportion of the total population in prefectures such as Haute-Kotto (85%), Haut-Mbomou (45%), Nana-Grébizi (32%) and Ouaka (30%).[3] In 2018, IDP camps were attacked at Bria in the east, at Batangafo in the north-west and Alindao in the south. Camps at Alindao and Batangafo were set ablaze, obliterating years of work and leaving tens of thousands of people destitute. The UPC attack on the IDP camp in Alindao in November was motivated by suspicions that it was a safe haven for anti-Balaka fighters. Two priests were among the victims. As a result, the Catholic Church boycotted the national-day celebrations on 1 December.

Murder of Russian journalists

On 30 July 2018, three Russian journalists were killed on the Dekoa–Sibut road in Kémo prefecture (their bodies were recovered by MINUSCA personnel the next day). The murders were attributed to Muslim bandits, but their presence is unlikely in this area. The journalists, who were affiliated with the Russian news-media organisation the Investigation Control Center, came to CAR in order to investigate the activities of Russian private military contractors.

Impact

The humanitarian situation in the Central African Republic remains catastrophic. In December 2018, the UN Office for the Coordination of Humanitarian Affairs (OCHA) reported that 2.9m of the 4.6m population in CAR needed aid, and 1.9m were food insecure.[4] OCHA also estimated that there were 648,516 IDPs in CAR and 574,638 refugees in neighbouring countries, mostly in Cameroon, Chad and the Democratic Republic of the Congo.

Risk of famine

Over 75% of the population in CAR relies on subsistence agriculture. Except for the southwest, many rural communities have lost access to their livelihood, resulting in large food gaps only marginally mitigated by humanitarian food assistance. According to the IPC Acute Food Insecurity analysis update conducted in August 2018, approximately 550,000 people were facing emergency food insecurity conditions and approximately 1.35m people were in crisis. Populations with acute food insecurity were mainly found in the Batangafo, Kaga-Bandoro, Rafai zones and prefectures of Ouham-Pendé, Nana-Grébizi, Ouaka and Haut-Mbomou.

Insecurity and humanitarian access

CAR remained one of the most dangerous countries for humanitarian actors in 2018, with armed groups actively targeting aid workers (see **Figure 1**). From January to October 2018, OCHA recorded 338 security incidents against aid workers.[5] Robberies, burglaries and looting of humanitarian organisations and assets are on the rise. In 2018, 46 vehicles of humanitarian organisations (trucks and cars) were hijacked. Several aid workers have been killed: the most notorious incident took place close to Markounda on 25 February when six aid workers were murdered by unidentified armed men. The most dangerous areas for humanitarian workers are the prefectures of Ouham, Ouaka and Nana-Grébizi.

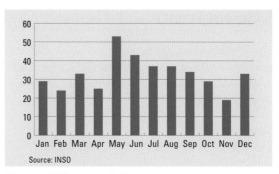

Source: INSO

Figure 1: NGO security incidents

The causes of these attacks are the fragmentation of the armed groups and the lack of command and control in most of the militias; their consequences, the disruption of logistics activities and the restriction of humanitarian access. From April to May, 15 NGOs suspended their activities in a dozen localities in the sub-prefectures of Bambari, Batangafo, Bria, Ippy, Kaga-Bandoro and Kabo. In the war-torn city of Bangassou, Mbomou prefecture, humanitarian assistance was temporarily suspended in March and April 2018 after the looting of humanitarian organisations' offices and threats to their personnel. In September, a further seven humanitarian organisations suspended their operations.

Trends

The conflict in CAR is gridlocked owing to the lack of effective governance, disputes between international actors and the lack of efforts to counter the armed groups' predation strategy. In 2018, the solution to the CAR crisis became a contentious issue between Paris and Moscow, and this new rivalry will likely hamper the role of the UN in CAR in 2019. Consensus on peace enforcement is needed, but the UN Security Council is divided and the UN and the AU engage in a counterproductive institutional rivalry. As a result, the two institutions have

not yet jointly appointed a new special envoy as recommended by the UN secretary-general and have not solved their differences on the issue of amnesty for armed groups' leaders. Touadéra's electoral manoeuvring has also begun. Despite the start of an AU-led peace negotiations in late January 2019 in Khartoum, the fighting between armed groups looks likely to continue and the humanitarian situation to further deteriorate as MINUSCA remains unable to enforce a peace deal.

Notes

1   UN Security Council, 'Report of the Secretary-General on the Central African Republic, 15 June–15 October 2018', S/2018/922, 15 October 2018.

2   International Peace Information Service, 'Central African Republic: A Conflict Mapping', August 2018, p. 46.

4   IPC, 'Central African Republic (CAR): Acute Food Insecurity

Situation in August 2018: Update of the projected IPC Acute Food Insecurity analysis conducted in March 2018', September 2018.

5   UN Office for the Coordination of Humanitarian Affairs (OCHA), 'Bulletin humanitaire', no. 40, December 2018.

6   OCHA CAR, 'Civilians Need Urgent Protection and Assistance in the Central African Republic', 21 November 2018.

The Democratic Republic of the Congo

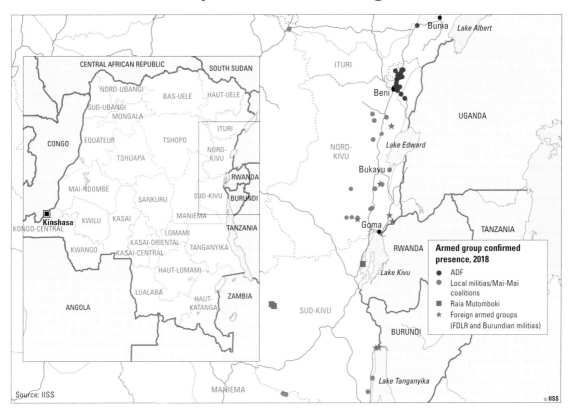

Source: IISS

Overview

The conflict in 2018

The political situation in the Democratic Republic of the Congo (DRC) continued to be crucial to the country's dynamics of armed violence in 2018. For most of the year, doubts about whether elections would take place as scheduled and whether President Joseph Kabila would run for a third term in office (or how he might otherwise attempt to retain power) raised tensions within the political system and had a direct impact on the security situation. In August, however, Kabila nominated a successor and the election went ahead on 30 December 2018.

In an increasingly polarised climate, the government continued to crack down on political freedoms and exacerbated local conflict dynamics. Violence continued to be widespread across eastern DRC, with armed groups attacking the civilian population, the army and each other. The political turmoil offered new opportunities for armed groups, which

attempt to improve their bargaining position.[1] In response to the government's military operations in 2018, numerous armed groups attacked security forces and United Nations peacekeepers, leading to an intensification of the humanitarian crisis. The Allied Democratic Forces (ADF) was again the deadliest group, killing more than 230 civilians, dozens of soldiers and eight peacekeepers, despite the heavy presence of the Congolese Army and UN peacekeepers in the Beni area.

While most domestic and international observers agreed that the widely unpopular Kabila should step down, the opposition did not manage to overcome its internal fragmentation, whereas international actors, including the UN Organization Stabilization Mission in the Democratic Republic of the Congo (MONUSCO), failed to show the necessary resolve to change the regime's behaviour. A number of unforeseen developments, such as two Ebola outbreaks, the release of former vice-president

Sub-Saharan Africa

Jean-Pierre Bemba by the International Criminal Court (ICC) and the choice of Emmanuel Ramazani Shadary as Kabila's successor, made for an eventful year. At the end of 2018, it looked as though Kabila's skilful manoeuvres would allow him to maintain his patrimonial system and retain control of the country after the elections, though possibly indirectly. The formal post-electoral arrangements and the shape of the next Congolese government may prove to be mostly a façade.

The conflict to 2018

There are numerous, simultaneous and decentralised armed conflicts in the DRC, which occur at the local level but are shaped by regional and national dynamics. Since 2015, existing conflicts have been exacerbated by a severe political crisis, caused by Kabila's unwillingness to respect the Congolese constitution and step down after two consecutive terms in office. Instead of organising elections foreseen for November 2016, the ruling majority delayed the voting process under the pretext of technical and logistical problems, a strategy that became known as *glissement* ('slippage'). Meanwhile, Kabila organised several 'political dialogues', mainly for political window-dressing and to further fragment the

Key statistics	
Type:	Internationalised
IDPs total (2018):	4,500,000
IDPs new (2018):	no data
Refugees total (2018):	no data
Refugees new (2018):	75,000
People in need (2018):	12,800,000

opposition. Kabila's clinging on to power increasingly provoked political and armed resistance, which the government countered with repression and widespread human-rights abuses. After security forces had killed dozens of civilians during several protests, the government banned all demonstrations in September 2016 and increased its efforts to curtail assemblies, thereby reducing the capacity of the opposition to exert pressure through mass mobilisation. As the political crisis further delegitimised the regime, the already volatile situation in the east deteriorated while new armed conflicts emerged in the central and western parts of the country, leading to a major humanitarian emergency, particularly in the Kasai provinces.

Forces

More than 120 armed groups are active in the DRC, predominantly in the eastern provinces of North and South Kivu, Ituri, Bas- and Haut-Uele, Tanganyika, Maniema and Haut-Katanga. Since 2016, insurgencies have emerged in formerly peaceful areas in the Kasai (centre) and Bandundu (west) provinces. Armed groups prey on local populations, fight each other over land and resources, and increasingly attack state security forces. While their sheer number, increasing fragmentation and shifts in leadership and alliances make a comprehensive description of each armed group difficult, they can be divided into two broad categories.

Local armed groups

Most armed groups in the DRC are outgrowths of community-based self-defence militias. Many initially mobilised against the (perceived) threat of a Rwandan invasion, but over time became more concerned with sustaining and projecting their

power. More recently, as the Kabila administration is seen as illegally hanging on to power, the narrative of local mobilisation has shifted and many armed groups have started attacking state institutions. Despite their generic labels, such as Mai-Mai (referring to magic protection) and Raia Mutomboki (literally 'angry citizens'), these groups are distinct and frequently fight each other for control over land and resources. Their size can range from a dozen to several hundred members. Prominent examples are the Nande-based Mai-Mai Mazembe in North Kivu province and Mai-Mai Yakutumba from the Bembe community in South Kivu province. In parallel and partly in response to the community mobilisation by self-proclaimed indigenous groups, Congolese Hutu and Tutsi – reinforced by several migratory waves from Rwanda and Burundi – have also formed militias, such as the Nyatura (Hutu) groups in North Kivu and Banyamulenge (Tutsi) militias in the highlands of Uvira and Fizi, South Kivu province.

Foreign armed groups

Foreign armed groups in the DRC started as rebellions against neighbouring countries but changed their orientation as they became entangled in Congolese dynamics. They rank among the best-equipped and most capable forces. While some Burundian groups, such as the RED–Tabara (Resistance for the Rule of Law in Burundi), have only recently become more active in the DRC, most foreign armed groups have been present for decades, integrating into local communities and building patronage relationships with provincial and national politicians.

A prime example is the Democratic Forces for the Liberation of Rwanda (FDLR), which emerged from the Hutu population and security forces that fled Rwanda after the 1994 genocide. The FDLR was formerly among the most formidable armed groups in the DRC, with sophisticated equipment and up to 7,000 disciplined and highly trained fighters. In recent years, it has been reduced to fewer than 1,000 elements as a result of military operations and infighting.

Currently, the deadliest group is the Allied Democratic Forces (ADF). Established in western Uganda at the end of the 1980s, the group has been involved in mass killings of civilians in Beni territory since October 2014, seemingly in collaboration with local groups and parts of the army.[2] The UN Group of Experts estimated the ADF to have between 400 and 450 armed elements in mid-2018. Following military operations, the ADF have retaliated by attacking the FARDC, UN peacekeepers and local civilians. Some of these attacks have been surprisingly sophisticated for an organisation which is known to operate with light weapons in loosely organised groups. Although an international Islamist connection remains possible, it is more likely that the group has received arms, fighters and logistical support from other local armed groups and parts of the Congolese army, with whom the ADF has collaborated in the past.

State forces

Congo's national-security forces operate in shifting alliances with armed groups and regularly commit more than half of all human-rights violations. The perception that local populations are affiliated with armed groups, together with poor troop discipline, leads security forces to target civilians. In response to rising protests, since 2015 President Kabila has also deployed the security forces against opposition members and peaceful demonstrators.

The Armed Forces of the Democratic Republic of Congo (FARDC) is estimated to have at least 140,000 soldiers, but many are of retirement age or disabled.[3] Insufficient training, irregular pay and dysfunctional equipment further limit the army's operational capacity. Besides border skirmishes, including incidents with Rwanda and Uganda in 2018, the FARDC is operating against more than 120 armed groups active mainly in the country's east. In 2018, the many (re)deployments made the army susceptible to attacks and often led to a subsequent re-emergence of armed groups.

The Congolese National Police (PNC) is estimated to have at least 100,000 personnel. As with the FARDC, the majority of police officers receive insufficient training and remuneration, and face multiple challenges related to lack of equipment.

The Republican Guard has between 10,000 and 15,000 personnel who are directly under the control of the president. The Republican Guard wears distinct red berets, has better equipment and is paid more regularly than the FARDC. They often conduct critical military missions and have been deployed against peaceful protesters in recent years.

Headed by Kalev Mutond, a Kabila loyalist under UN sanctions, the DRC national intelligence agency (ANR) is estimated to number approximately 10,000 personnel, but counts on numerous informers and collaborators across the country. Previously known for opportunistic extortion, the ANR has become notorious for illegally detaining and abusing journalists, activists and opposition members.

MONUSCO

The United Nations Organization Stabilization Mission in the Democratic Republic of the Congo (MONUSCO) started as a small observation mission in 1999 (then named MONUC) and gradually became the biggest and most expensive peacekeeping mission in the world. In 2007, MONUSCO was the first to receive a mandate to prioritise the protection of civilians. Since then, the mission has been at the forefront of protection where innovative instruments and practices are developed and subsequently mainstreamed into other peacekeeping contexts. Following a gradual downscaling process since 2017, MONUSCO is currently authorised to deploy 16,215 military personnel, 660 military observers and staff officers, 391 police personnel, 1,050 personnel of formed police units and 4,415 civilian staff, but has deployed considerably fewer, following the General Assembly's financial decisions. The majority of its peacekeepers are from India (2,906), Pakistan (2,731) and Bangladesh (1,884). Since March 2013, MONUSCO has possessed unique offensive capacities with the Force Intervention Brigade (FIB), consisting of South African, Tanzanian and Malawian soldiers. Although the FIB has the mandate to operate independently, MONUSCO mainly conducts operations in support of the Congolese army.

Drivers

Past wars

Many complex and interwoven issues, largely rooted in the DRC's troubled past, drive today's armed conflicts. The extraordinarily brutal colonial era still has a detrimental impact on politics and governance. When the Congolese gained independence from Belgium in 1960, the former colonial power initiated a split of the resource-rich Katanga region, leading to the deployment of the first UN peacekeeping mission. Together with the Central Intelligence Agency (CIA), the Belgian government instigated the killing of Congo's first prime minister Patrice Lumumba in 1961, inaugurating a precedent for violent regime change. Eventually, the Western-backed Joseph-Désiré Mobutu came to power in 1965 and stayed for the following 32 years by constructing client networks and employing divide-and-rule tactics. Mobutu was eventually ousted by a rebellion in 1997 led by President Kabila's father Laurent, in what became known as the First Congo War. Shortly thereafter, a second rebellion erupted – this time against Laurent Kabila – dubbed 'Africa's World War' because of the involvement of nine neighbouring states.[4] Extensive fighting during both wars and the connected decades of low-intensity conflicts in the east of the country have made the opportunity cost of violence low, driven the proliferation of armed groups and exacted a heavy toll on physical and social infrastructure. Many of the former fighters demobilised after those wars have not been successfully reintegrated into either a functioning army or civilian life. Hasty disarmament, demobilisation and reintegration (DDR) efforts rendered Congolese security forces undisciplined and inefficient. Entrenched grievances, the wide availability of arms and a lack of alternatives provide a steady flow of young men to armed organisations.

Fractionalisation

The DRC's numerous armed conflicts emerge from power struggles along national, regional and ethnic divides. Although the population exhibits strong national pride, kinship politics are usually at the heart of alliance formation and decision-making in Kinshasa as well as in the regional or provincial capitals. Since colonisation, central rulers have applied divide-and-rule strategies, pitting the more than 200 ethnic groups against each other and using troops from some areas to put down resistance in others. Long-term dictator Mobutu notoriously continued to reinforce inter-group conflicts in order to weaken and fragment possible opposition. His ambivalence regarding the recognition of citizenship for Congolese Tutsi (Banyamulenge and Banyarwanda) made this group dependent on his patronage and set it against indigenous populations. The Congo wars, as well as continued fighting in the country's east, further exacerbated these ethnic divisions and entrenched grievances. Similarly, Kabila exploited ethnic divides to create diversions and reduce the likelihood of a viable opposition, for instance, fuelling recent violence between Hema and Lendu militias in Ituri province, and recruiting members of the former eastern rebel group M23 to crack down on demonstrators in central and western DRC.[5] As a result, local disputes over land and power quickly take on an ethnic dimension, while the *ethnicisation* of the state and security institutions continue to drive tensions.

Poor governance and mismanagement

Mismanagement hampers the country's economy and has ruined its means of production. With only a handful of university graduates at independence, the country was unprepared to manage its vast infrastructure and mineral wealth. The hasty nationalisation of land and property under Mobutu's 'Zaïrianisation' reinforced rent-seeking tendencies, ruining infrastructure and leading to a massive decline in production, particularly in the mining sector.

Since coming to power after the assassination of his father in 2001, Joseph Kabila has favoured the shadow economy over implementing required reforms and good-governance standards, and has thus been unable to deliver on his 2006 election promise to improve infrastructure, sanitation, health services, schooling and employment. The limited reform of the security sector, for example, has failed to fundamentally improve the pay of soldiers, resulting in diminished operational capacity and widespread abuses against civilians.

Patronage and corruption
Desolate living conditions and frustration over the lack of change also drive the country's armed conflicts. The Human Development Index ranks the DRC 176th out of 189 nations. Instead of addressing the malaise, Congolese elites engage in illicit businesses and massive embezzlement of state resources. Kabila's family has come to own more than 80 companies across all sectors of the economy, including banking, mining and telecommunication, with hundreds of millions of dollars in revenue.[6] Estimated at three times the national budget, corruption dwarfs DRC's development investments – and the problem extends beyond individual self-enrichment. Mobutu established a patrimonial system in which the patron needs to distribute resources and support in order to ensure allegiance. As a way to gain illicit funds, Congolese officials sell state property, such as mining licences, below market value in exchange for kickbacks.[7] Meanwhile,

subordinates are required to prove their worth to the patrons. Chronically underpaid civil servants – from teachers to traffic police to army generals – are expected to 'gain' additional income to survive and deliver a required amount of funds upwards. This distributive style of governance counters organised planning and auditing efforts, reinforces the illicit flow of resources and puts personal relations ahead of qualifications and accountability. As a result, the predatory state institutions remain weak but omnipresent.

Kabila clinging onto power
Kabila's reluctance to relinquish power has caused an acute political crisis that has had a direct impact on the security and humanitarian situation. Depending on the office for privilege and protection, Kabila, elected in 2006 and confirmed in 2011, sought to change the constitution, which limits presidents to two terms in office. When that failed and opposition to a third term became apparent across the political spectrum, the government cited technical and logistical issues to delay the elections initially due in November 2016. Invoking a caretaker clause in the constitution, Kabila stayed in power for two more years, during which his government repressed political opposition and used the security apparatus to crack down on mounting protests, further polarising national politics. Armed resistance against Kabila grew, exacerbating existing conflicts in the east and provoking new violence in the central Kasai and western Bandundu provinces, which in turn allowed the government to position itself as the guarantor of stability and national security.

Political and Military Developments

Presidential elections
After a tumultuous campaigning period, the long-awaited presidential elections took place on 30 December in a relatively peaceful environment. The National Episcopal Conference of the Congo (CENCO), however, reported 1,543 irregularities (from observing 12,300 of the 21,000 polling stations), including failing voting machines, denied access to registered voters and election observers, and illegal campaigning outside voting stations.[8] As many as 846 polling stations were established in prohibited areas and armed groups intimidated voters

in Rutshuru and Masisi territories (North Kivu). In Walungu, South Kivu province, three people died when violence broke out over alleged fraud. Seven civilians were seriously injured in clashes between supporters in Ditunda, Kasai province.

In the run-up to the elections, the Congolese parliament passed laws excluding Congolese living abroad – many of whom are government critics – and granting former presidents a number of privileges, including immunity. The government also insisted on the use of 106,000 electronic voting machines, despite unreliable electricity in rural areas, while the registration of more than 6.7 million individuals (16.6% of the electorate) without complete data raised concerns of fictitious voters. Finally, the Independent National Electoral Commission (CENI) disqualified a large number of likely opposition voters – 1.2m of the total 40m – by postponing the elections in Beni, Butembo (North Kivu province) and in Yumbi (Mai-Ndombe province) until March 2019, under the pretext of security and/or Ebola-related risks.[9] The government also repressed civil-society and political opposition, with 1,054 restrictions of democratic rights documented by the UN alone. The campaigning period (22 November to 21 December) was marked by heavy institutional support for Kabila's presidential candidate, Emmanuel Ramazani Shadary and restrictions against the major opposition candidates (Martin Fayulu and Félix Antoine Tshisekedi) that led to clashes between protesters and security forces in which one police officer and at least nine civilians died and many more were injured and arrested.

Divided opposition

Congo's opposition groups were unable to overcome their divisions and agree on a unified candidate. In addition to the personal ambitions of their leaders, the division was the result of the parties' different constituencies, often representing a region or a specific ethnic group. President Kabila is known exploit to these differences to keep the opposition weak and fragmented.

Former vice-president Jean-Pierre Bemba, who represents the western Equateur province, joined the list of opposition heavyweights in the presidential race after his surprise acquittal by the ICC in June. While Bemba was ultimately disqualified for witness tampering at the ICC, the exiled Moise Katumbi was unable to register his candidacy because he was barred from re-entering the DRC. With Katumbi and Bemba excluded from the race, there was some hope that the opposition could agree on a unified candidate, Félix Tshisekedi being the most likely aspirant. The Kofi Annan Foundation convened a meeting on 9–11 November, during which seven key opposition figures, including Katumbi and Bemba, formed the Lamuka (wake up) coalition and chose Martin Fayulu as their candidate. However, Tshisekedi retracted from the deal less than 24 hours later, claiming that his 'base' did not accept the results of the vote and had requested that he run for president instead. While Vital Kamerhe followed suit and decided to run with Tshisekedi under the electoral platform CAP pour le changement (Cach), Katumbi and Bemba stayed in the Lamuka coalition and continued to support Fayulu.

Relations with the international community

The Congolese government has continued to push back against international interference under the pretext of national sovereignty. Kabila announced at the UN General Assembly that the DRC would not tolerate any outside interference in the elections and it would cover their full cost. He also reiterated his request for MONUSCO's withdrawal. Shortly before the elections, Kabila expelled the European Union ambassador. Over the year, he cancelled visits by UN Secretary-General António Guterres and African Union Commission Chairman Moussa Faki Mahamat, claimed to be too busy to see US Ambassador to the UN Nikki Haley and rejected the nomination of Thabo Mbeki as South Africa's new special envoy to the DRC.[10]

In January, the Belgian government redirected aid (US$31m) allocated for the Congolese government to humanitarian organisations and non-governmental organisations, citing concerns over human-rights abuses and delays in the electoral schedule. In response, the Congolese foreign ministry closed the Belgian development agency (ENABEL) and the Belgian-led European consulate (Maison Schengen) in Kinshasa. Brussels recalled its ambassador in April.

Military operations

The Congolese army conducted different operations against armed groups in North and South Kivu, Ituri, Maniema, Haut-Katanga and Kasai provinces in 2018. In some instances these operations were successful, but often resulted in counter-attacks. Overall, military operations failed to fundamentally improve civilian security, while in some cases they even deteriorated it.

As in previous years, the ADF remained the focus of military operations. Major operations were launched in January – including tanks, heavy artillery and counter-insurgency tactics – and succeeded in shelling ADF strongholds and taking control of two major camps, but the ADF responded, killing hundreds of troops. In September, MONUSCO and the FARDC launched joint offensives in and around the Mayangose forest area. While the FARDC continued to do the core of the fighting, MONUSCO contributed with patrols, aerial support and medical support, but at times also responded to ADF incursions directly. These operations did not stop insurgent attacks, which instead increased, with the ADF attacking UN peacekeepers, premises and assets, and severely restricting humanitarian access in the midst of the Ebola outbreak.

In South Kivu, the FARDC conducted operations against the Mai-Mai Yakutumba-led National People's Council for the Sovereignty of Congo (CNPSC) and ethnic-Bafuliro Mai-Mai militia in the Ruzizi plain. While these operations were successful in initially displacing these groups, for instance from the Ubwari Peninsula, and leading to the surrender of approximately 600 fighters, Yakutumba elements eventually regrouped in the Itombwe forest and launched a series of retaliatory attacks against the FARDC.

In Ituri, the deployment of an additional 1,300 army and police personnel in April and the launch of *Operation Hero* in May against the Front for Patriotic Resistance in Ituri (FRPI) temporarily succeeded in curtailing the group's activities. The FARDC also launched an offensive against Lendu militia in Djugu territory. Similar patterns of military operations, temporary displacement and retaliatory attacks occurred in Tanganyika in response to Mai-Mai activities, addressing Kamuina Nsapu threats in Kasai Central province and a number of other Mai-Mai groups in North and South Kivu.

Protests against the UN

North Kivu's population and particularly the people of Beni protested regularly against the inability of the FARDC and the UN to protect them from the abuses and massacres committed by the ADF. On several occasions protesters threw stones at MONUSCO patrols, injuring peacekeepers.

Inter-ethnic violence

Inter-community conflicts continued to fuel local violence across the DRC. In Ituri province, the violence between Lendu and Hema communities that had begun in December 2017 intensified in 2018. At least 110 people died and more than 300 houses were destroyed during clashes between the two groups in February and March alone. As a result,

at least 40,000 people sought refuge in Uganda and more than 32,000 fled to the provincial capital Bunia, including 20,000 seeking shelter at the Bunia General Hospital. In April the security situation stabilised, and some displaced people returned. In September, clashes erupted between Lendu militias and the FARDC. On 15 September, nine soldiers and six civilians died following an attack by the Lendu militia on a FARDC position in Muvaramu (80 kilometres northeast of Bunia). Additional attacks occurred throughout September, resulting in the deaths of at least five soldiers and eight militiamen. During a particularly deadly attack on 3 November, assailants killed 16 soldiers and 20 civilians in Muganga. A few days later, on 9 November, Lendu militias allegedly killed nine soldiers and wounded 14 more in Landjo (25 km northeast of Djugu town).

Similar inter-community violence also continued between Nande and Nyanga militias in Lubero, and Nande and Hutu militias in Rutshuru territory of North Kivu province; between Banyamulenge and self-proclaimed indigenous Bafuliro, Banyindu and Babembe groups in Bijombo, South Kivu province; between the Luba and Twa in Haut-Katanga; and between ethnic Chokwe Bana Mura militia and Lubaphone populations in the Kasais.

In mid-December, a new community conflict emerged between Batende and Banunu ethnic groups over a burial ground in Yumbi, Mai-Ndombe province. Given the remote and previously stable location at the northwestern border of the DRC and the eventful election preparations, the massive violence was at first under-reported. The killing of at least 535 people appeared to be the result of a very well-organised attack against the Banunu, possibly involving local authorities and security forces. A conflict over a local burial quickly escalated, possibly due to pre-independence tensions and local power struggles stemming from the recent division of the Bandundu province into several smaller provinces. In addition, the two communities were on opposing sides of the electoral spectrum, with the Batende mainly supporting the presidential majority, while the Banunu were largely supporters of Martin Fayulu's Lamuka coalition.[11]

Attacks against wildlife parks

The presence of militias in different wildlife parks across eastern DRC, as well as tensions between affiliated local communities and the park management about the use of the land, led to frequent violent episodes. On 17 February, armed men killed seven people during an attack on a vehicle by the Okapi Wildlife Resort between Ituri and North Kivu province, while on 9 April, Mai-Mai militants killed six people in Virunga National Park, North Kivu.

On 11 May, Nyatura elements attacked a vehicle belonging to the Congolese Institute for Nature Conservation (ICCN), 27 km north of Goma, killing one park ranger and kidnapping two British tourists. Although the tourists were subsequently released, the ICCN announced that the Virunga Park would remain closed until at least 2019.

Violent Events

Attacks by the FRPI

In 2018, the FRPI again committed the largest number of documented human-rights violations out of all armed groups. Between mid-July and mid-August, FRPI members conducted 14 raids on villages in southern Irumu territory and raided another 16 villages in the areas of Gety and Aveba in the first week of October.

Attacks by the CNPSC

On 24 May, the CNPSC coalition launched a major attack on Banro's Salamabila mining site and a connected FARDC camp in Maniema province, which resulted in the deaths of 37 Mai-Mai, 21 soldiers, two police and two civilians. On 11 August, Mai-Mai Malaika attacked a Banro truck from Namoya gold mine in Maniema and killed two civilian passengers, while kidnapping two drivers and two soldiers.

Attacks by the ADF

The ADF intensified its attacks on civilians, FARDC and MONUSCO in Beni, North Kivu province in 2018, causing at least 245 deaths and committing numerous abductions. On 19 January, the ADF killed 24 FARDC soldiers and wounded 13 more in Parkingi. On 24 May, ADF elements attacked an army position north of Mbau, resulting in the deaths of 12 FARDC soldiers and 16 militants. After Ebola was declared in Beni, ADF attacks intensified. Notably on 24 August, suspected ADF militants attacked an army position in the Ngadi neighbourhood of Beni town, leading to the deaths of 17 FARDC and seven militants. On 22 September, suspected ADF killed at least 14 civilians and four soldiers during a six-hour attack on Beni town. The attack also led to a suspension of activities to tackle Ebola prevention in the area. During an offensive on 15 November against a major ADF stronghold in Kididiwe (20 km from Beni), eight UN peacekeepers

and at least 12 Congolese soldiers were killed. On 6 December, ADF militants killed at least 12 civilians in Mayangose and in two separate attacks on 22 and 26 December, the Kipriani area of Beni town was attacked, resulting in at least 13 civilian deaths.

Attacks by the LRA

Joint MONUSCO–FARDC operations succeeded in curtailing activities of the Lord's Resistance Army (LRA) in 2018. Small groups of suspected LRA elements committed isolated ambushes throughout the year, looting and abducting for self-sustenance rather than with strategic objectives. Throughout all of 2018, Invisible Children's crisis tracker reported a total of 45 incidents but only two fatalities, figures similar to 2017 but different from the group's bloody killings of the past.

Attacks by Burundian armed groups

The year saw a marked increase in the activity of Burundian groups in the Ruzizi plain as well as the middle and high plateaus of Uvira territory. RED–Tabara reportedly reinforced its presence in the highlands around Lemera and Bijombo, siding with Mai-Mai groups against the Banyamulenge. Similarly, the movement of the Burundian National Liberation Front (FNL) into Fizi and Uvira increased and the group collaborated with local Mai-Mai militias, amid rumours of Rwandan support. In response to the threat at the border, the Burundian army repeatedly entered Congolese territory in pursuit of these groups. On 14 November, clashes between Burundian armed forces (supported by the FARDC) and FNL in Uvira and Fizi led to 16 deaths. At the beginning of December, the FARDC repeatedly clashed with FNL, Mai-Mai Yakutumba and She Hassan groups in Majaga forest in Fizi territory, reportedly killing 12 militants over two days.

Attacks by the FDLR

Previously weakened through military operations and infighting, the FDLR became more active in Rutshuru and Masisi territories of North Kivu province towards the end of the year. On 5 September, the FDLR killed four people during an attack on the Goma–Rutshuru route. On 5 November, the FARDC clashed with a coalition of FDLR and Nyatura Domi fighters in Masisi, resulting in the deaths of six militiamen and one soldier. On 10 December, the FDLR made an incursion into neighbouring Rwanda, where it clashed with Rwanda Defence Force (RDF), leading to the deaths of at least five FDLR fighters and three RDF soldiers.

It is probably in response to this incursion that the Congolese army decided to arrest the FDLR's spokesperson and number three in the organisation, Ignace Nkaka (also known as 'The Forger'), and head of intelligence, Jean Pierre Nsekanabo, on 15 December. Over following two days, the FDLR reportedly attacked the FARDC in Kasizi village and Mount Mikeno area, killing seven and injuring nine soldiers. A FARDC spokesman denied rumours that the clashes were in fact with the Rwandan army – as had happened before in that area. On 18 December, the FDLR allegedly staged a larger attack on Sake, a town close to Goma, killing seven civilians and kidnapping three.

Impact

Human-rights abuses

The Congolese population bore the brunt of the violence in 2018, with armed groups and security forces purposefully targeting civilians and causing displacement. The UN Joint Human Rights Office (JHRO) reported 6,831 human-rights violations were committed in 2018, representing a 5% increase from 2017 (6,497) and a 32% increase from 2016 (5,190). As in previous years, state agents, notably the army and the police, committed 61% of these violations. At least 1,169 extrajudicial and summary executions were verified in 2018. Given the exigent standards for these verifications, the vastness of the country and the organisational challenges to human-rights reporting, the real number of killings is likely much higher. The killings in Yumbi alone would raise these numbers significantly. Armed actors also continued to commit sexual violence, with about a thousand new victims in 2018. Many armed groups continued to recruit children, which remained the main violation among the 2,573 documented violations of children's rights.

Epidemics

Violence in 2018 facilitated the spread of epidemics, while epidemics exacerbated the vulnerability of people affected by violence. On 1 August, only eight days after a previous Ebola outbreak in northwestern Equateur province was declared over, a second outbreak was declared approximately 2,000 km away in Mangina (30 km southwest of Beni), North Kivu province. The World Health Organization (WHO) quickly started rVSV-ZEBOV vaccinations and the US-developed an experimental treatment called mAb114. These measures reduced the rate of new infections but the virus spread to the regional trading hub of Butembo, neighbouring Ituri province and the Ugandan border, provoking fears of a larger epidemic, while on 27 September, the WHO raised the risk estimation from 'high' to 'very high'.

As of 31 December, there were 608 Ebola cases in the second outbreak, including 560 confirmed and 48 probable, leading to 368 deaths. While the Ebola outbreaks attracted international attention and support, other, less-reported epidemics had broader repercussions for the local population. Cholera spread to 13 of the 26 Congolese provinces over the course of the year, with more than 30,000 cases and at least 1,000 deaths, while there were at least 842 cases of measles, leading to a minimum of 566 deaths.

Humanitarian need and access

The humanitarian situation in the DRC remained dire and has worsened in some regards. By 31 December, the UN Office for the Coordination of Humanitarian Affairs (OCHA) estimated the number of people in need to be 12.8m. Of these, an estimated 44% (5.6m) are children. Although almost 1m people returned to their areas of origin in 2018, at least 2.1m were newly displaced by violence in Ituri, the Kivus, Tanganyika and Yumbi.[12] According to the UN High Commissioner for Refugees (UNHCR), the number of Congolese refugees in neighbouring countries further increased from 622,000 as of end of

2017 to 814,975 by the end of 2018.[13] While the cumulative figure for internally displaced persons (IDPs) has been controversial in light of the Congolese government's pushback on discussing its 'internal affairs', it is estimated at approximately 5.6m as of December 2018. Most of these IDPs are accommodated by host families, putting additional strain on already impoverished communities.

Insecurity in conflict-affected provinces severely hindered the delivery of humanitarian aid. Armed groups repeatedly targeted relief workers, prompting aid organisations to suspend their operations in parts of North and South Kivu provinces. Given its comparatively strong field presence, Médecins Sans Frontières (MSF) was particularly affected. Insecurity also hindered the Ebola response in Beni territory, making the treatment of victims and the monitoring of possible infections difficult. For instance, on 16 November, a clash between FARDC and ADF fighters in the Boikene area of Beni led to the suspension of emergency centres and the evacuation of 16 WHO staff to Goma. The climate of violence also negatively influenced the attitude of the population towards health workers, leading to several disruptive protests and violent incidents, particularly in response to safe burial procedures.

Trends

The political situation will continue to have major implications for the armed conflicts in 2019. Brazen attempts to falsify the electoral results or further delays in the transition of power could lead to a major escalation that might pull in some of the neighbouring states and require a greater international engagement. A change of guard is, on the other hand, likely to calm the political climate and positively impact the security situation. Most Western diplomats agree that MONUSCO should quickly be wrapped up after the milestones of successful elections and a peaceful transition of power. However, even a peaceful transition is unlikely to result in major change for the DRC in the foreseeable future. The political class, government institutions and civil society all operate in established ways that require long-term engagement, possibly over decades. Therefore, corruption, bad governance, roaming armed groups and ill-equipped security forces will in all likelihood continue to be part of the DRC's immediate to mid-term future.

Kabila likely to remain in control
Kabila is determined to remain in power and has repeatedly shown in the past his creativity in developing ways to attain this goal. When it became clear that running himself for re-election was not viable, he handpicked a successor. However, given that Ramazani has proven a highly unpopular choice, Kabila will have already developed several moves that he can choose from based on the positions of the other stakeholders and the development of events. Kabila has control over the security forces and state institution, which allowed him to cut off protests and makes a coup or successful rebellion unlikely during his tenure. MONUSCO appears unable to play a role, and a larger intervention by regional powers or the EU is highly improbable.

New government may bring improvements
A new regime might be able to engage in more benevolent forms of governance after dealing with the fallout from the election. One of Kabila's major shortcomings was his failure to deliver on his 2006 promises of improved employment, infrastructure and services, which made him deeply unpopular and hindered his 2018 attempts to extend his presidency. The new government might address some of the issues more effectively, starting by streamlining the administration and leveraging its unique position in the global commodity market.

Key factors
Three factors will be key in 2019. The first is the capacity of the new president to wrest actual power from Kabila, although his chances will be low, given the outgoing president's success in manipulating the political system and setting up a parallel power network. The second factor will be the direction of the economy and its (perceived) effects on the living conditions of the population. Thirdly, the degree of (dis)integration within the ruling majority will also be a key area, as many of its members may grow increasingly frustrated by the personal costs inflicted on them by Kabila's self-centred deal-making.

Notes

1   Christoph Vogel and Jason Stearns, 'Kivu's intractable security conundrum, revisited', *African Affairs*, vol. 117, no. 469, 1 October 2018, pp. 695–707.

2   Congo Research Group (CRG), 'Inside the ADF Rebellion', November 2018.

3   Congolese Analyst Jean-Jacques Wondo estimates the FARDC to contain up to 164,000 soldiers.

4   Gérard Prunier, *Africa's World War: Congo, the Rwandan Genocide, and the Making of a Continental Catastrophe* (Oxford: Oxford University Press, 2009).

5   Human Rights Watch, '"Special Mission": Recruitment of M23 Rebels to Suppress Protests in the Democratic Republic of Congo', 4 December 2017.

6   CRG, 'All The President's Wealth: The Kabila Family Business', 19 July 2017.

7   Franz Wild, Vernon Silver and William Clowes, 'Trouble in the Congo: The Misadventures of Glencore', *Bloomberg Businessweek*, 16 November 2018.

8   Jason Stearns, 'The Congo Elections: Where Things Stand', CRG, 3 January 2019.

9   Giulia Paravicini, 'Three Congo opposition areas excluded from presidential election', Reuters, 23 December 2018.

10 Janosch Kullenberg, 'Confronting Kabila', IISS blog, 28 July 2018.

11 Liselotte Mas and Chloé Lauvergnier, 'Hundreds killed in Yumbi, DR Congo: "People were finished off with machetes"', *France24*, 21 January 2019; 'Revealed: DRC's "invisible" massacre', *Times Live*, 9 February 2019; '"Along the Main Road You See the Graves": U.N. Says Hundreds Killed in Congo', *New York Times*, 29 January 2019; 'Sud-Kivu : l'armée burundaise est intervenue à Uvira pour combattre ses opposants soutenus par le Rwanda', mediacongo.net, 16 November 2018.

12 OCHA, 'Calcul du nombre de personnes déplacées en RDC', Q4 report, 2018.

13 UN High Commissioner for Refugees (UNHCR), 'DR Congo', 31 December 2018.

Lake Chad Basin (Boko Haram)

Overview

The conflict in 2018

The crisis in the Lake Chad Basin worsened in 2018. While Boko Haram and Islamic State West Africa Province (ISWAP) insurgents intensified their attacks on military bases and civilian populations in the region, they also faced increased military pressure. In order to survive, the insurgency became more adaptable and more sophisticated. The year ended with no clear attempt at conflict resolution, but rather an intensification of insurgent attacks. The government made concerted attempts to win hearts and minds among local populations, which were also targeted by armed groups' recruitment drives.

The conflict to 2018

Between 1999 and 2001, 12 of Nigeria's northern states adopted sharia law and a growing number of northerners began calling for the adoption of sharia law across the country. This sentiment, together with growing socio-economic inequality, gave rise in 2002 to a group that became known as the Nigerian Taliban, led by the charismatic preacher Mohammed Yusuf. The group's ultimate goal was to establish sharia law in Nigeria and destroy the country's Western-influenced institutions, including education and democracy.

The group first attracted international media attention in 2009 when it launched a number of attacks against police officers. In response to the violence, the Nigerian government deployed the armed forces. The conflict killed more than 1,000 people and led to the arrests of hundreds of members of the group. By July 2009, the security forces had killed Yusuf and the group's strength appeared to be declining.

However, the desire to revenge Yusuf's extra-judicial killing became a key rallying point for Boko Haram, and in 2010 the group re-emerged and confirmed its transition from religious movement to insurgent organisation under the leadership of former second-in-command Abubakar Shekau. In response, on 15 June 2011 the government launched *Operation Restore Order*. The conflict subsequently extended into neighbouring Cameroon, Chad and Niger, which previously had only been used as safe havens by the group.

Sub-Saharan Africa

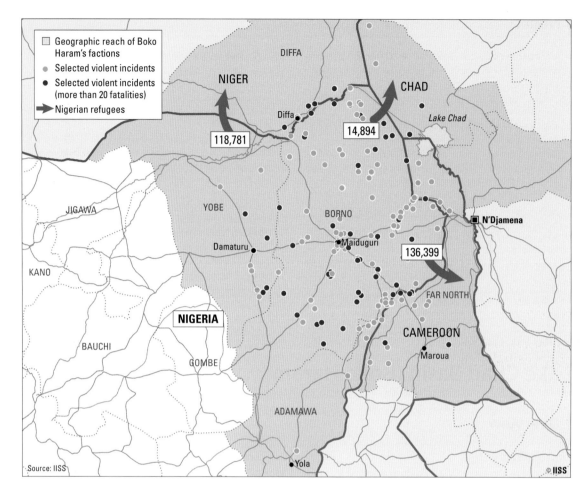

By spring 2013, reports indicated that Boko Haram was controlling territory around its camps in Borno State. This threat to national sovereignty and widespread violence prompted the government to declare a state of emergency in the states of Adamawa, Borno and Yobe and to launch the largest military deployment in the country since the civil war (Biafra War) of 1967–70. Despite some progress, violence did not diminish.

In 2015, Boko Haram pledged its allegiance to the emir of the Islamic State, also known as ISIS or ISIL, and adopted the new name the Islamic State West Africa Province. This development added to the complexity of the picture and produced frictions within the group and the emergence of different methods and targeting.

The military offensive that followed Nigerian President Muhammadu Buhari's appointment in May 2015, together with more concerted regional efforts under the Multinational Joint Task Force

(MNJTF), weakened Boko Haram and ISWAP. The insurgency was no longer able to carry out attacks across the country or hold territory. Activities became primarily concentrated in the northern part of Borno State and borderlands of Niger, Cameroon and, to a lesser degree, Chad, while violent and coordinated attacks, abductions and widespread use of suicide bombers, including women and children, continued.

Key statistics

Type:	Internationalised
IDPs total (2018):	2,500,000
IDPs new (2018):	no data
Refugees total (2018):	no data
Refugees new (2018):	no data
People in need (2018):	10,700,000

Forces

Multinational Joint Task Force (MNJTF)

The Lake Chad Basin Commission (LCBC, comprising Cameroon, Chad, Niger and Nigeria) established the Multinational Joint Task Force (MNJTF) in 2015 with the support of the African Union. Headquartered in N'Djamena, Chad, the MNJTF is primarily tasked with neutralising the threat of Boko Haram. In addition, the remit of the force includes the facilitation of stabilisation programmes and the return of internally displaced persons (IDPs) and refugees. The MNJTF has four major sectors, corresponding to each of the countries around Lake Chad, and comprises military contingents from Cameroon, Chad, Nigeria and Niger. (Benin joined the MNJTF in 2017.) Though the exact size of the MNJTF is unknown, it is estimated to comprise approximately 8,700 troops. In 2015, the United States sent 300 personnel to support the fight against ISWAP. Both the US and France consider the Lake Chad Basin crucial to defeating ISIS, which is believed to be preparing to make significant inroads in the region following the losses it suffered in Syria and Iraq in 2017 and 2018.

The European Union is the MNJTF's main donor, but funding has been subject to delays and shortfalls since the group's creation. Nigeria and France pledged US$250 million to the force's first budget in 2015, but this amounted to only a third of the total required, impacting the provision of equipment: as of June 2016, the force reportedly had only 11 vehicles and some radio equipment. However, 61 vehicles were handed over to the MNJTF by the AU on 15 March 2018, and 129 night-vision goggles in April 2018.[1] Despite pressure to deliver on its mandate, the lack of adequate funds has hampered the MNJTF's ability to match the sophistication of the insurgency. To prioritise the protection of their territorial integrity, some nation-states have pursued national-security strategies over commitment to regional security cooperation.

Nigerian Army

Ensuring the territorial integrity of the state is the primary focus of the Nigerian government and armed forces. The Nigerian Army comprises approximately 100,000 active personnel, with 80,000 paramilitary members. Defence spending increased significantly with the launch of *Operation*

Restore Order in 2011 (from US$1.54 billion in 2010 to US$2.62bn in 2011). Although defence spending subsequently decreased, 2018 witnessed a rise as the government faced pressure to produce results. However, despite heavy spending, reports of disaffected soldiers were still numerous in 2018, with faulty and outdated equipment a concern. The armed forces suffered significant numbers of casualties over the year, which the Nigerian Army refused to disclose for most of 2018.[2]

Tactics recently developed by the Nigerian Army include the use of motorcycles to improve mobility, culminating in the creation of a special motorcycle squad as part of *Operation Lafiya Dole*.

Civilian Joint Task Force

Since 2013, a civilian-led response to the insurgents has emerged in the Lake Chad Basin. This force, known as the Civilian Joint Task Force (CJTF) and best understood as a vigilante group, has provided support to the MNJTF through discreet surveillance, local knowledge and intelligence gathering. The overall strength of the CJTF is unknown, but it claims to have approximately 26,000 fighters in Borno State alone.[3] Throughout the year, hundreds of CJTF vigilantes were released (many were children, including some as young as 11) and are in the process of being absorbed by the Nigerian Army.

Islamic State in the West African Province (ISWAP) and Boko Haram

Boko Haram pledged allegiance (*bay'ah*) to the Islamic State, also known as ISIS or ISIL, in March 2015 and later rebranded itself as the Islamic State West African Province (ISWAP).

In the summer of 2016, a rift within ISWAP emerged. Abu Musab al-Barnawi, son of Boko Haram's late founder Mohammed Yusuf, was designated leader of ISWAP, sidelining Boko Haram's chief Abubakar Shekau. The ensuing dispute led to two separate organisations: Shekau's 'traditional' Boko Haram, which continued to carry out indiscriminate and opportunistic attacks against military, government and civilian targets; and ISWAP under Barnawi, which claimed to prefer the strategic targeting of military personnel and infrastructure, as well as foreigners. In August 2017, Barnawi released a video in which he accused Shekau of betraying the teachings of the group's founder Yusuf, and predicted that the Nigerian Army would soon defeat his faction. The primary objective of both factions – the establishment an Islamic caliphate in the Lake Chad Basin – remains the same. Competition between the two factions stems more from the need to attain political clout than any fundamental divergence of purpose.

ISWAP is estimated to have between 1,500 and 3,500 fighters. As well as targeted attacks, ISWAP conducts kidnappings to gain leverage with the government over freeing captured ISWAP fighters. Alongside a conventional small-arms capability, the group also deployed drones in 2018.

Boko Haram is estimated to have approximately 7,000 fighters. The group mostly uses suicide bombings and kidnappings in addition to guerrilla warfare to pursue its goal. The group's use of suicide bombings and the execution of kidnapped hostages increased in 2018 to instil fear in the population and refute claims by the Nigerian government that the group's strength has been degraded. The group also continued to attack military formations and bases in Nigeria's North East zone, as well as ambushing military convoys. The insurgents were also reported to be using anti-aircraft guns and rocket-propelled grenades (RPGs).

Drivers

Socio-economic grievances
The North East zone of Nigeria has one of the highest rates of poverty in the country, together with high levels of illiteracy and a significant number of out-of-school children. Boko Haram and ISWAP have been able to take advantage of the situation by recruiting many youth into their cause, offering spiritual glorification and financial rewards. Addressing the challenge posed by the group thus requires not only a military campaign but also a multifaceted approach addressing the socio-economic challenges that continue to fuel the conflict.

Radical ideology
Radical ideologies still serve an important function in providing motivation for the insurgency. Indeed,

Boko Haram (and ISWAP) can be characterised as a Salafi-jihadi group. The immediate driver of the ongoing conflict is the quest to create an Islamic caliphate based on sharia law to erase 'Western' influence in the region. From its early days, Boko Haram has strived to present its radical version of Salafism as the antidote to societal 'evils' represented by Westernised corrupted elites, inequality and poverty and Islamic religious leaders who, in the eyes of Mohammed Yusuf, had gone astray by adopting moderate positions.

ISWAP appears to be more open and flexible to negotiations with the governments of the region compared with Boko Haram, which has from its inception attacked government institutions and the United Nations.

Political and Military Developments

Pressure on Buhari ahead of elections
International and domestic political pressure to bring the insurgency to an end increased on the Buhari administration throughout the year. With general elections slated to take place on 16 February 2019, the federal government intensified its military campaign against the insurgency in 2018 to ensure that no part of Nigerian territory fell to Boko Haram, as had been the case in previous years. Buhari and his party, the All Progressives Congress (APC), campaigned in 2015 on the promise of defeating Boko Haram, but that promise is far from being fulfilled

as the conflict rages on, which cast doubt on Buhari's prospects of re-election.

UK–Nigeria security partnership
As part of international efforts to counter Boko Haram and ISWAP, on 29 August 2018 British Prime Minister Theresa May announced the first-ever defence and security partnership between the UK and Nigeria. Under the terms of the partnership, the UK would supply training and equipment to allow the Nigerian armed forces to combat the threat of improvised explosive devices (IEDs). The UK also

offered to train full Nigerian Army units and help deliver a £13 million (US$16.9m) programme to educate 100,000 children, as well as challenging insurgent narratives that are used in recruitment drives. These initiatives are just the latest in a well-cemented relationship between the UK and Nigeria which, notwithstanding ups and downs, has long featured military training, counter-terrorism cooperation, and extensive diplomatic efforts and development programmes.

Boko Haram and ISWAT remain operational

The Shekau-led Boko Haram faction remained operational in the central and southern parts of Borno State, while ISWAP continued to maintain its hold on the northern part of the state. Mamman Nur, the leader of an ISWAP faction, was killed by his own lieutenants in August 2018, allegedly in a dispute over his handling of ransom monies, but more likely as a consequence of strategic divergences with Shekau. ISWAP subsequently established bases and focused operations in the Lake Chad region along northern Borno State in areas previously controlled by Nur's faction.

Violent Events

The most significant attacks in 2018 took place in northeastern Nigeria, although insurgency groups continued to launch attacks in Cameroon, Chad and Niger which were repelled by the MNJTF. Between July and December 2018 – the most intense period of fighting – more than 700 troops, particularly Nigerian troops, were reported to have been killed and their equipment seized by ISWAP.[4] Violence was concentrated in the North East zone, including the towns of Baga, Doron-Baga, Kross Kawwa, Bunduran, Kekeno and Kukawa, all of which were reported to have come under the control of ISWAP after the Nigerian armed forces were driven away.

Increase in suicide bombings and attacks on mosques

Since their inception in 2011, the use of suicide attacks has been one of Boko Haram's preferred methods of attack. Suicide bombers accounted for an increased number of deaths in 2018. In the first half of 2018, there were 30 suicide bombings that led to the deaths of 297 people. Attacks on mosques also increased in 2018, which some analysts interpreted as a display of grievances against supporters of Buhari, who is Muslim, as well as targeting moderate Muslims in general. Female suicide missions are now a consolidated trademark of the Lake Chad Basin insurgency, with children often being among the (forced) perpetrators. Following an apparent three-month pause, November saw the return of this tactic.

Insurgency attacks against the Nigerian Army

In 2018, Boko Haram and ISWAP attempted to regain control of some of the territories they had lost. ISWAP made persistent attempts to overrun the town of Monguno, Borno State, which were repelled by the Nigeran Army's special forces, with 200 insurgents reported dead.

In some cases the groups were successful in seizing control. On 14 July, ISWAP fighters dressed in military uniforms overran a military base in Jilli village in Yobe State, killing approximately 12 troops. In November 2018, Boko Haram killed approximately 23 soldiers and wounded 31 when it overran the military base in Metele, Borno State.

Insurgents launched a series of attacks on Doron Naira and Dogon Chukun, two islands along Lake Chad, in December 2018. These attacks were targeted at civilians, particularly those in the fishing community. From 28 to 30 December, violence erupted between ISWAP and Nigerian soldiers in the town of Baga, near the border with Chad, leading to the withdrawal of Nigerian troops attached to the MNJTF base and the dismissal of 167 officers of the Nigerian Police Force after they refused to participate in a counter-terrorism offensive. ISWAP reportedly seized weapons belonging to the MNJTF in Naga.[5] The insurgents were also reported to have overrun a naval fighting base and a marine police base in the area.

Other towns that were affected by the violence include the local towns of Doron-Baga, Kross Kawwa, Bunduran, Kekeno and Kukawa. ISWAP fighters killed locals only when they displayed some form of resistance, marking a change in the group's tactics in 2018.

Impact

Socio-economic challenges

The conflict has had a devastating effect on economic activities in the local communities within the Lake Chad Basin. In ISWAP-controlled towns and villages on the Nigerian shores of Lake Chad, farmers are made to pay tax before being granted access to their farmlands, while fishermen are taxed before they are allowed to leave with their catch. These measures have resulted in a significant decline in socio-economic activities.

Humanitarian impact

The ongoing conflict has produced more IDPs and created the conditions for a famine in Nigeria's North East zone. As a result of the violence, many fishermen and farmers have fled to Maiduguri, the capital of Borno State, others to Damasak, Borno State, and Gaidam, Yobe State. As of 30 November 2018, there were some 232,000 Nigerian refugees displaced in Cameroon, Chad and Niger due to the insurgency, while an estimated 6,000 refugees were reported to have fled Borno State after the clashes around Baga town on 26 December, with many fleeing to Chad.[6]

Human-rights abuses

Amnesty International was expelled from Nigeria in December 2018 after consistently accusing the Nigerian Army of committing human-rights abuses in its campaign against terrorist groups. The government accused the international organisation of damaging the morale of its soldiers fighting terrorism. In mid-December, the Nigerian Army suspended the activities of the UN International Children's Emergency Fund (UNICEF) in northeastern Nigeria, accusing the organisation of spying for insurgents and undermining the counter-terrorism operation by reporting on alleged human-rights abuses committed by the Nigerian armed forces. The suspension was lifted a few hours later after an emergency meeting with UNICEF.

Increasing civic division

The failure of the government to end the insurgency in 2018 emboldened the opposition party, the People's Democratic Party (PDP), to criticise Buhari's administration for its failures, while the continuing threat from the insurgent factions led to growing distrust towards the government among the civilian population. Many citizens criticised the government's counter-terrorism operations in 2018 for letting the insurgency cause too many deaths. Others feared the government due to the human-rights record of the Nigerian Army. These political dynamics fuelled divisions among citizens. Some alleged that the government has been less proactive in the fight against the insurgents due to the religious connotations of the conflict, with some Christian critics accusing Buhari (a Muslim) of being sympathetic to the insurgents.

Trends

Prospect of peace remains dim

The conflict will continue in 2019 and the political leadership of the affected states will struggle to address the root causes of the conflict. The prospects for a resolution of the conflict seem unlikely in 2019 and a peace deal would probably only materialise at heavy cost to Nigeria. While the government has indicated its willingness to negotiate with Boko Haram in the past, the internal divisions between the Shekau-led Boko Haram and ISWAP make the coalescing of a credible partner for the peace dialogue unlikely.

The federal government and the government of Borno State are pursuing plans to repatriate those affected by the conflict, including financial compensation for families of police officers and soldiers who have lost their lives fighting the terrorist groups.

The risk of the conflict spilling over into neighbouring states beyond the Lake Chad Basin is slim, as the insurgency does not currently have the necessary structure or sufficient capacity. To achieve such an objective, the terrorist groups would have to set up training facilities, supply channels and recruitment plans, which they are currently unable to do in places outside of their spheres of influence due to tighter security measures.

The Nigerian armed forces are expected to ramp up their counter-terrorism operations against the insurgents in 2019. The US is likely to continue providing support in the form of intelligence sharing through its African Command (AFRICOM), while France will pay close attention to the conflict due to its strategic relationship with the Francophone countries in the region; should its interests be threatened, it may intervene directly.

Notes

1   'The AU Commission hands over of Night Vision Goggles (NVGs) to the Multinational Joint Task Force against Boko Haram', African Union website (www.peaceau.org), 5 April 2018.

2   Timileyin Omilana, 'Army finally release casualty figures of Metele attack', *Guardian Nigeria*, 29 November 2018.

3   Crisis Group, 'Watchmen of Lake Chad: Vigilante Groups Fighting Boko Haram', Report no. 244, 23 February 2017.

4   'Eighth Report of The Secretary-General on the threat posed by ISIL (Da'esh) to international peace and security and the range of United Nations efforts in support of Member States in countering the threat', United Nations Office of Counter-Terrorism, 29 January 2016.

5   'Boko Haram mounts major offensive on Monguno, Damasak, other Borno towns', International Centre for Investigative Reporting, 30 December 2018.

6   Charley Yaxley, 'Thousands of Nigerian refugees seek safety in Chad', United Nations High Commissioner for Refugees (UNHCR) press briefing, 22 January 2019.

Mali (The Sahel)

Overview

The conflict in 2018

In 2018, jihadism continued to spread throughout Mali, exploiting the overstretched state and long-standing historical grievances of Mali's more remote regions. Armed groups attacked military, international and civilian targets, with central Mali at the epicentre of violence. The climate of fear created by the growing jihadist presence since the coup of 2012 has prompted many communities, both geographical and ethnic, to rely on 'self-defence' militias to provide security. In reality, the proliferation of armed actors throughout the country has coincided with a marked increase in civilian casualties.

Some small successes were achieved in stopping the spread of jihadism throughout the country. Counter-terrorism efforts by the national government and the international forces, particularly in the tri-border area between Mali, Niger and Burkina Faso, achieved some progress in dismantling jihadist camps and neutralising some high-level leaders. However, these limited results came alongside reports of widespread abuses by the security forces, including mass extrajudicial killings.

What the events of 2018 have perhaps most clearly demonstrated is that the current conflict in Mali is not the same conflict that erupted in 2012, and not the same conflict that the 2015 Algiers Accords attempted to pacify. As stated in a July 2018 report by Peace Direct, a non-governmental organisation working in the country, 'Mali is not experiencing a civil war in the conventional sense but a complex, multidimensional security crisis of interlinked micro-conflicts'. Given that many of the drivers of the 2012 conflict still exist today, the 2015 Algiers Accords may still have a role to play in promoting a more equitable and stable Mali. However, the evolution of the conflict has rendered the agreement increasingly ill-equipped to deal with the new challenges facing the country.

Key statistics	
Type:	Internationalised
IDPs total (2017):	40,000
IDPs new (2018):	no data
Refugees total (2018):	160,000
Refugees new (2018):	no data
People in need (2018):	3,200,000

Sub-Saharan Africa

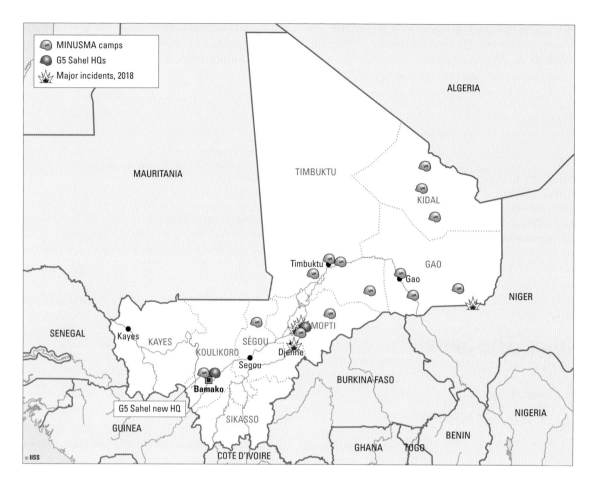

The conflict to 2018

The path to disorder began in January 2012, when northern populations (most notably the Tuareg ethnic group) staged the fourth rebellion since Mali achieved independence from France in 1960. Due to a long-standing concentration of resources and attention in southern Mali, where the majority of the population resides, northern Malians had long felt disconnected from the state and sought their own state, called the 'Azawad'. The rebellion, led by groups such as the National Movement for the Liberation of Azawad, won territory and influence, and quickly partnered with nascent extremist groups led, in part, by Algerian fighters travelling south. In March 2012, a group of Malian soldiers staged a coup and ousted then-president Amadou Toumani Touré. Their seizure of power crippled Bamako's capacity, and the joint forces of the rebel and extremist groups were able to win significant territory, including the three largest cities in northern Mali – Gao, Kidal and Timbuktu – by April 2012.

Eventually, the difference in ideology caused a split between the extremist groups and the rebels of the north, and the territory claimed for the Azawad fell solely into the hands of the extremists by July. Following calls by the Malian government for international assistance, France sent troops to retake the extremist-controlled areas of northern Mali for the Malian government. By July 2014, French forces had achieved that goal, and the Algiers Accords process began to reconcile the needs of the original northern rebel forces and the Malian state.

The Algiers Accords in 2015 officially ended the rebellion of 2012–15 and attempted to provide a way forward for Mali. It was signed by the relevant armed actors at the time: non-jihadist rebel groups active in the northern regions. Yet the jihadist presence once again expanded rapidly after the French shifted strategies to support Bamako in consolidating power, and the Algiers Accords have no provisions or considerations in place in reference to the extremist threat, which appeared to be neutralised in 2015 but was the primary cause of violence in 2018. As a result, any movement to implement the Algiers Accords, including expanding the state's presence and continuing negotiations on provisions like impunity for signatory fighters, appears ineffectual and slow to curb current violence. Stalled progress on both humanitarian and political issues has contributed to further disenfranchisement of the Malian people and exacerbated existing grievances.

Forces

The Malian conflict is characterised by numerous highly fluid and interconnected armed groups, some consisting of only a dozen people, whose allegiances regularly shift. Attribution of security incidents to a particular group is therefore complicated by the large number of armed groups, their varying sizes and the often remote location of the incident.

Malian Armed Forces (FAMa)

The Malian Armed Forces (FAMa) plays the primary role in responding to security incidents around the country, including jihadist activity. The Malian Army consists of 10,000 active army personnel. In addition, the government records 7,800 paramilitary officers, 1,800 gendarmerie, 2,000 members of the National Guard, 1,000 national police officers and approximately 3,000 militiamen. A recruitment campaign has also been running since 2017 for an additional 10,000 soldiers. The Malian Ministry of Defence changed leadership in 2018 following the presidential election in July, and was headed by Tiémoko Sangaré at the close of the year. In 2018, the Malian Army worked closely with the United Nations Mission in Mali, French forces and the G5 Sahel Joint Task Force.

United Nations Multidimensional Integrated Stabilization Mission in Mali (MINUSMA)

The United Nations Multidimensional Integrated Stabilization Mission in Mali (MINUSMA) is a comprehensive mission with the specific purpose of supporting the implementation of the 2015 Algiers Accords. Strategic priorities for the mission include reconciliation; supporting defence and security; supporting the rule of law throughout the country; the protection of civilians; and providing humanitarian assistance.

MINUSMA does not have a counter-terrorism mandate, and so does not engage with military campaigns against jihadist bases, unlike French soldiers and the FC-G5S. However, MINUSMA is responsible for providing evacuations to Malian Army personnel, French soldiers and FC-G5S soldiers undertaking those tasks. Since operations began in 2013, MINUSMA's mandate has focused on the northern regions that were active in the rebellion of 2012–15. In June 2018, its mandate shifted slightly to place more emphasis on supporting the restoration of the state in central Mali. Reports indicate that MINUSMA plans to deploy additional personnel to the Mopti region and the town of Sévaré in early 2019. As of December 2018, peacekeepers were deployed in the cities of Bamako, Mopti, Dyabali, Douentza, Goundam, Timbuktu, Ber, Gossi, Gao, Ansongo, Menaka, Kidal, Tessalit and Aguelhok.

UN peacekeepers are high-profile targets for extremist groups, and are often targeted through the use of roadside explosives. MINUSMA has one of the highest mortality rates among the world's peacekeeping missions: since its inception in 2013, 177 MINUSMA personnel have been killed. MINUSMA employs 1,421 civilians, 11,632 troops, 38 experts, 1,767 police, 446 staff officers and 146 UN volunteers in the country, while MINUSMA's budget for July 2017 to June 2018 was US$1.05 billion.[1]

French forces

French forces first entered the conflict in 2013 with *Operation Serval*, responding to an official request by the Malian government for French assistance following the jihadist occupation of multiple Malian cities, including Timbuktu. The insurgency was quickly driven out of the most populous areas, and *Operation Serval* was replaced by the stabilisation-focused *Operation Barkhane* in 2014. *Operation Barkhane*'s mandate is to continue supporting counter-terrorism efforts across the Sahel, both by conducting missions and by building capacity in the Malian security forces, with a focus on fighting the terrorist threat directly and supporting partner forces, including the FC-G5S and the Malian Army.

Sub-Saharan Africa

In 2018, they saw particular success in launching offensive attacks against insurgent groups and their hideouts across the country. *Operation Barkhane* also works closely with MINUSMA, though MINUSMA does not conduct offensive counter-terrorism campaigns. *Operation Barkhane* consists of a 4,000-strong force active across Burkina Faso, Chad, Mali, Mauritania and Niger.

The Joint Force of the G5 Sahel (FC-G5S)

The Joint Force of the G5 Sahel (FC-G5S), originally created in March 2017, is comprised of approximately 5,000 troops drawn from the G5 Sahel states (Burkina Faso, Chad, Mali, Mauritania and Niger) and is designed to create a coordinated, transnational response to terrorism threats in the region. Its mandate includes combatting terrorism, transnational organised crime and human trafficking. The first phase of the FC-G5S is to improve security along the shared borders of the G5 Sahel through cooperation between the security forces and the deployment of joint patrols. The force is intended to act as a complement to both MINUSMA and *Operation Barkhane*, while filling in gaps such as addressing organised crime.

The FC-G5S consists of seven battalions. An additional counter-terrorism brigade based in northern Mali is expected to be formed sometime in 2019. The organisation is directed by the defence ministers of the G5 Sahel countries and commanded by a general from one of the participating nations.

The FC-G5S enjoys significant international support, particularly from France under President Emmanuel Macron. Nevertheless, the organisation has struggled to deliver in 2018. The G5 Sahel states faced budget shortages and lack of predictable financing, which led to unnecessary delays in 2018. Troop deployment has also proved slow, reportedly due to the absence of secure and fortified operating bases, capacity and equipment. The headquarters of the force in Sévaré, central Mali, was the target of a terrorist attack in June 2018. Subsequently, Mauritanian General Hanena Ould Sidi replaced the Malian commander of the force, and the headquarters were moved to the more stable city of Bamako.

Self-defence groups (ethnic and village militias)

Small armed groups representing a community, sometimes geographical but often ethnic, have become increasingly widespread in Mali, particularly throughout the central regions of Mopti and Ségou. Ethnic militias – one category of self-defence group – are usually formed to protect fellow ethnic members from an enemy (often a neighbouring ethnic group). Similarly, village militias are typically assembled for the sake of protecting a specific community or area from an enemy, but that enemy is far more variable. Depending on the community, that enemy could be roving bandits, jihadist groups, signatory rebel groups, other village militias, other ethnic communities or even the state. To complicate matters further, ethnic militias and village militias are not mutually exclusive, though some village militias are not specific to one ethnicity and some ethnic militias comprise the citizens of multiple villages. There is no reliable estimate of how many self-defence groups are currently operating in Mali (most analysts employ words such as 'myriad' or 'countless' to refer to the scale of the phenomenon).

The two types of self-defence groups also pose related, but distinct, challenges. The village militias often operate in highly isolated and disenfranchised locations (such as the far north) and change alliances rapidly. They have also been linked to banditry. Their small size and geographical isolation means that they are often difficult to track, but the sheer number of village militias collectively constitutes a highly destabilising force.

Ethnic militias, comparatively, operate largely in central Mali and gained significant notoriety in 2018 for a number of offensive attacks against the Fulani people in particular, in the belief that the Fulani are supportive of the jihadist cause. The most notorious ethnic militia in 2018 was Da Na Amassagou ('the Hunters Who Confide in God'), formed in May from the Dogon ethnic group, which was responsible for the numerous violent incidents against Fulani communities near the Koro area and officially opposed the signing of a peace agreement with Fulani leaders. Their attacks had high casualty counts, indicating that Da Na Amassagou had access to advanced weaponry.

In many cases, young men are encouraged to join these armed groups to protect their homes and families. Jihadist organisations and larger armed groups tend to prey upon village and ethnic militias as sources of new recruits. Their tactics include both violence and intimidation of the militiamen, as well as non-violent proselytising.

Group to Support Islam and Muslims (JNIM)

Jamaat Nusrat al-Islam wal-Muslimeen (JNIM) was formed in 2017 from three jihadist groups – Ansar Dine, al-Mourabitoun and al-Qaeda in the Islamic Maghreb (AQIM). JNIM acts as the official branch of al-Qaeda in Mali, and in September 2018 was estimated to have between 1,000 and 2,000 fighters. The group is led by former Ansar Dine leader Iyad Ag Ghaly, and has the stated goal of bringing sharia law to areas under its control.

JNIM conducted frequent and high-profile attacks throughout 2018 against military and international targets, as well as against tourist infrastructure. The targets chosen and the methods employed also indicated an increasing lack of concern with avoiding civilian casualties. The group regularly utilises suicide bombers, improvised explosive devices (IEDs) and armed men on motorcycles to conduct attacks, and also perpetrates complex attacks with advanced weaponry (including missiles) against fortified positions such as UN bases.

Islamic State in the Greater Sahara (ISIS–GS)

Islamic State in the Greater Sahara (ISIS–GS) is a nascent extremist group operating in the tri-border area between Mali, Burkina Faso and Niger. In 2018, its frequent and ambitious attacks gained it significant influence. ISIS–GS claimed responsibility for a number of high-profile attacks against military positions and kidnappings of foreign personnel, besides targeting civilians and towns. As of June 2018, ISIS–GS had claimed 15 attacks, but they were presumed to be responsible for many more. Information regarding the structure and composition of ISIS–GS is limited. The Combating Terrorism Center at Westpoint estimated it had approximately 425 recruits in July 2018.[2]

Drivers

A myriad of violent actors

The presence, strength and ambition of jihadist organisations is the most immediate driver of violence and insecurity in Mali. Escalating ethnic violence is also contributing to instability in central Mali. While tensions between ethnic groups have existed for decades, resulting in regular skirmishes, this dynamic has deteriorated in recent years due to an influx of small arms and the presence of jihadist actors. Weapons are known to have travelled south from Algeria and Libya into Mali, or from Burkina Faso in the east. Trafficking networks through the Sahara in northern Mali have also provided significant revenue to armed actors in the region, funding the rebellion first and jihadist activity more recently. More generally, the increasing radicalisation of a previously unifying religion – Islam – has also created or exacerbated divisions between communities. Attempts to defend communities often create new cycles of violence, with some anti-jihadist communities launching pre-emptive attacks against neighbouring communities to neutralise a perceived jihadist threat (see **Figure 1**).

Failed promises, failed institutions

Extremism has flourished in part because of the lack of state capacity and presence in central and

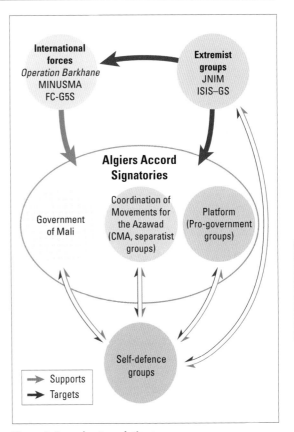

Figure 1: Armed-actor relations

northern Mali. As of December 2018, only 34% of civil administrators were at their posts in the northern and Mopti regions.[3] Military presence is concentrated in major cities, leaving isolated villages vulnerable to jihadist attacks or influence. The borders of Mali, especially in the north and east, are notoriously porous and allow for many illicit trade routes that provide both funding and fighters from regions around West and North Africa.

The state presence that does exist is unable to provide needed government services consistently. At the end of 2018, 716 schools were closed due to violent conflict and crime, 60% of which were in the Mopti region of central Mali. The closures affected approximately 213,800 children. Field research undertaken in 2018 indicated that communities appreciated the jihadists' efforts to crack down on corruption, manage natural-resource conflicts and administer justice – which respondents contrasted directly with the failings of the Malian state.[4] The deteriorating humanitarian situation has also exacerbated insecurity. The state faces a plethora of challenges in food security, education and responding to natural events such as floods, but lacks the capacity to respond, and has been unable to secure sufficient outside support to do so. The perceived lack of action by the Malian state contributes to distrust and discontent among the population.

Historical divisions
Mali is an ethnically diverse but deeply divided nation. The divisions are numerous, with some deriving from disputes over land and natural resources, and others from differing lifestyles (such as pastoral, hunter/gatherer, nomadic). There is also a geographic divide between southern Malians and northern Malians. These tensions were exploited and compounded by French colonists, with leaders in Bamako providing privileged positions and resources to people living in what was referred to as 'Mali utile' – the south. Attempts by previous governments to address community tensions only worsened the problem. Historically, brutal repressions to stop inter-ethnic conflict left deep grievances in communities and a lasting resentment of the state. More recently, the government has relied on negotiation to quell tensions, but the negotiated promises often went unfulfilled.

Lack of structural reform
Most foreign support comes in the form of counter-terrorism operations. While an important component of promoting stability in Mali, the focus on radicalisation diverts attention and funding away from the systemic drivers of the conflict. The responsibility of much of the peacebuilding activity falls to MINUSMA, which does not have a counter-terrorism mandate but is tasked with responding to decades' worth of inequality, resentment and corruption. The sheer scale and ambition of its mandate – bringing peace in the face of jihadism, while ushering in structural and societal changes that will alter the country significantly – necessitates multiple actors and a re-prioritisation of funds and political commitment towards long-term structural changes. Without greater financial and political support for agencies working to encourage the necessary structural changes to Malian society, the neutralisation of the current jihadist threat will not be enough to ensure peace and stability over the longer term.

Political and Military Developments

Presidential election
The presidential election on 29 July 2018 resulted in the re-election of President Ibrahim Boubacar Keïta after a run-off vote against opposition candidate Soumaïla Cissé. The election process won praise from international observers, despite accusations of voter fraud from the opposition. Smaller security incidents, such as suspected jihadists destroying election material or forcing closures of polling stations, occurred outside of major cities and in remote regions of Mali, but remained concentrated in the Mopti region. Notably, fewer security incidents occurred in the far north, parts of which are jihadist strongholds. The Malian Ministry of Territorial Administration estimated that the voting process was cancelled or disrupted due to insecurity in nearly one in five polling stations in the north and centre of the country, although MINUSMA said that the number of voting stations nationwide that did not open accounted for only 3.8% of the total. Its

records also indicated that at least 50 polling stations were ransacked in Mopti, Ségou and Timbuktu over the course of the day.

With a decisive 67% of the vote in the August run-off election, Keïta has been given a strong mandate to continue addressing the violence, although his governing style is often criticised for its unilateralism. After legislative elections were postponed in September 2018 due to security concerns, opposition parties urged more cooperation in parliament. In the last quarter of 2018, Prime Minister Soumeylou Boubèye Maïga began far-reaching consultations with political and societal actors, including signatory armed parties and unions, to promote inclusive political and institutional reforms.

Strikes continue

Strikes have been commonplace in Mali since the 2015 Algiers Accords. In the face of widespread insecurity and little movement on social issues, Malian people continued to participate in mass protests and strikes around the nation in 2018. Magistrates began a three-month strike in late August, calling for a change to poor working conditions and a salary raise, and causing a backlog and stalled the judicial process for hundreds of Malians. Election organisers also went on strike prior to the 29 July vote over poor working conditions, threatening to disrupt the vote. If such issues remain unaddressed, discontent with the government may push Malians to accept alternative governance – including by jihadist movements.

Achievements in the peace process

The peace process advanced throughout 2018, fulfilling some of the promises set forth in 2015. The Truth, Justice and Reconciliation Commission began accepting testimonies in January 2017 and as of 28 December 2018 had received 10,247 depositions.[5] By September, the government had nominated interim authorities for 21 of the 24 districts in northern regions of Mali, previously without government representation. This act served the dual purpose of expanding state presence while promoting a sense of democracy and accountability for historically disenfranchised

regions such as Gao, Kidal, Menaka and Timbuktu. Parliament also began consultations on the creation of additional municipalities, as well as increasing the number of regions from 11 to 21. Parliament also adopted a national Security Sector Reform strategy. An ad hoc disarmament, demobilisation and reintegration (DDR) process for combatants from signatory groups working in cooperative joint patrols was operational in Gao, Timbuktu and Kidal in November. The fighters were integrated into the national army. Negotiations continued throughout the year on the limits of impunity for signatory rebel fighters (mandated by the Algiers Accords) and how to best support the national reconciliation process. Finally, a 'Pact for Peace' was signed in October, reiterating the signatory parties' commitment to the peace process and to reinvigorate implementation efforts. Critically, 2018 saw promising cooperation between signatory armed groups. The ceasefire between rebel groups, routinely violated over the previous two years, held fast for most of the year Mixed patrols, comprising members of the Malian Army and signatory rebel fighters, took place throughout 2018.

More spending to improve security

According to the Malian government, 11.7% of the state budget was dedicated to defence in 2018. (A further 4.3% of the total budget was dedicated to 'social protection' and 5.6% earmarked for 'order and public security', although it was unclear exactly what services fell under each of these categories.[6]) The International Conference for the Economic Recovery and Development of Mali, held in 2015, promised approximately US$4.24 billion in development assistance over a four-year period. An estimated 90% of the funds had been distributed by the end of 2018, with 40% of the funds earmarked for the north.

The 2019 budget, passed in September 2018, saw an increase in expenditures of 3.42% as compared to the 2018 budget. The increase is directly attributable to the implementation of the Algiers Accords, the operationalisation of the new administrative regions and reforms of the security forces.

| Violent Events

Extremist organisations, community self-defence militias or Malian security personnel were primar-

ily responsible for the violent events of 2018. While the majority of attacks were perpetrated by JNIM or

ISIS–GS, some incidents could not be conclusively linked to one group or another, particularly incidents linked to ethnic or village militias, which are often reported as jihadist groups, by either government forces or the media.

The UN recorded 229 attacks throughout the year, 34% of which occurred in the Mopti region, where 40% of all jihadist attacks took place.[7] Notably, the frequency of attacks in the restive Kidal region, largely considered the centre of the original 2012 rebellion, consistently decreased from 16 attacks in the first quarter of 2018 to seven in the final quarter. Gao, on the other hand, saw an increase in attacks during the year (15 in the first half compared to 27 in the second half of the year). In the last quarter of 2018, 57% of the total reported human-rights violations occurred in either the Mopti or Ségou region.

In past years, security personnel were the most likely targets, but civilian casualties rose sharply in 2018. Between June and September, the UN recorded 287 civilians casualties, the highest number since MINUSMA began in 2013. (A further 5,000 people were displaced during that same period.) This spike is partly due to the specific targeting of civilians by self-defence militias and jihadist organisations such as ISIS–GS, but also reflective of the overall increase in violent events, which resulted in more collateral casualties, and the frequent use of IEDs by extremist groups (particularly JNIM). The total number of IED incidents in 2018 was 192, compared to 124 in 2017.[8] Civilians were heavily impacted by these roadside bombs – between January and October 2018, 192 civilians died by buried explosive, more than double the number of IED-related civilian deaths in all 2017 (91). In total, 43% of IED attacks took place in either the Mopti or Ségou region, up from 22% of incidents in 2017.

JNIM

In 2018, JNIM organised attacks of varying complexity against a wide array of targets. In a notable attack in April, members of JNIM dressed as MINUSMA personnel and attacked the UN camp in Timbuktu using a UN vehicle, causing the deaths of a peacekeeper, seven French soldiers and two Malian civilians. The UN camp in Menaka was attacked for the first time in 2018, in early September. An additional two peacekeepers were killed during an attack on the Ber (Timbuktu) camp on 27 October. In total, ten peacekeepers were killed in 2018. In late

June, JNIM operatives conducted a highly successful suicide attack against the G5 Sahel headquarters in Sévaré, in Mopti, inflicting a considerable blow to the fledgling counter-terrorism force and killing two Malian soldiers and injuring 11. Despite these successes, JNIM took heavy casualties in the last half of the year during French and G5 Sahel joint counter-terrorism missions. In particular, two leaders of the movement Almansour Ag Alkassim and Amadou Kouffa, were killed within the same month by French raids.

ISIS–GS

ISIS–GS has been contending with a large-scale, coordinated assault on its territory in the tri-border area by signatory groups, the French army and the FC-G5S since early February 2018. Though casualty reports vary greatly by organisation, clashes typically result in double-digit casualties for the jihadist group.

ISIS–GS launched a number of attacks against members of the signatory armed groups in 2018, resulting in the deaths of at least 40 rebel fighters between June and September 2018 in the Menaka region (eastern Mali). ISIS–GS was also thought to be responsible for significant attacks against towns and population centres throughout the summer, usually using armed individuals on motorcycles. In a particularly deadly week at the end of April, 42 Tuareg were killed in multiple attacks throughout the Menaka region; on 27 April, 31 on 27 April and 11 more on 1 May.

Self-defence groups

A surge of inter-ethnic violence in 2018 resulted in the deaths of hundreds of civilians, with Human Rights Watch documenting abuses in 42 villages and hamlets in the Mopti region in 2018. Attacks on villages were often accompanied by widespread pillaging, destruction of buildings, arson and theft. Reporting of incidents suffered, however, as conflicting information was often released about both the perpetrators and the targets (for example, a Fulani community may have been referred to as jihadists in official reports).

In 2018, the Da Na Amassagou, a Dogon self-defence group, rose to prominence after having rarely had any significant influence over political processes and engaged in many targeted attacks against nearby Fulani. The group rejected a peace agreement brokered on 28 August to stop violence in the restive Koro region, in Mopti, which it saw as insufficiently inclusive and unable protect their community from the Fulani.[9]

Security forces

The Malian Army's forward role in conducting counter-terrorism operations resulted in the deaths of 111 Malian soldiers over the course of 2018. The security forces were also accused of significant abuses of power, including mass arrests and extra-judicial mass killings. FAMa allegedly killed 14 civilians on 6 April, 11 children on 13 May, ten Fulani citizens on 15 May and 12 prisoners on 19 May – all in the Mopti region.[10] The Malian Army maintained the victims of the 19 May incident were 'terrorists', but the community denied the claim.[11] On 20 June, then-defence minister Tiéna Coulibaly admitted that Malian soldiers were responsible for the summary execution of 25 individuals, who had been buried in three mass graves in central Mali. All the victims were from the Fulani ethnic group.

Impact

Deepening humanitarian crisis

The spread of violence and the ineffective response of the government was extremely detrimental to the humanitarian situation in Mali. A 2018 update to the UN Human Development Index ranked Mali 182nd out of 189 countries, roughly the same place as in previous reports. Some 5.2 million Malians were in need of humanitarian assistance in 2018, compared to 3.8m in 2017. More than 700 schools did not open at the beginning of the school year in October due to insecurity – in December alone, school closures affected more than 213,000 children across Mali. The provision of life-saving goods and services was complicated by the increasing danger for humanitarian workers and limited access to remote regions. The widespread use of IEDs in particular increasingly prevented aid workers from travelling. As of December 2018, humanitarian actors were the target of 194 security incidents, compared to 133 in 2017 and 63 in 2016.

Mass violence in central Mali resulted in a sharp increase in internally displaced persons (IDPs), with serious ramifications on the stability of both the central region of Mopti and the rest of the country, as increasing displacement strains existing state resources and capacities, and fuels societal grievances. The number of IDPs across Mali almost doubled from 2017 to mid-2018 – as of September 2018, there were 77,046 IDPs, with 139,978 Malian refugees currently residing in neighbouring countries.[12] The number of IDPs from Mopti alone increased from 2,000 in April to 12,000 by the end of August.

Rates of acute malnutrition remained high in 2018, though a good rainy season resulted in improvements from 2017. As of November 2018, 2.5m people were considered food insecure, with approximately 185,000 requiring immediate food assistance.[13] Despite the good growing season, more than 70,700 people were affected by floods in 2018, which caused the destruction of homes, livestock and food supplies.[14] The Malian state struggled to secure the requisite funding for emergency assistance: as of 3 December 2018, only 52.4% of the required US$329.6m (requested under the 2018 UN Humanitarian Response Plan) had been provided, though still represents an increase in total funding, breaking a steady decline in international financial support since 2014. Only 43% of the requested funds in 2017 (US$304.7m) was fulfilled.[15]

Backfiring counter-terrorism strategies

In some cases, misguided counter-terrorism and/or stabilisation policies led to more violence and grievance. The International Crisis Group reported that, over the long term, government and international actors have worsened ethnic tensions in central and northern Mali, as they tried to capitalise on self-defence groups to act as government proxies against the jihadists. Self-defence groups were provided with significant financial and materiel support, which are in some cases now being directed at other citizens. The fact that jihadists enjoy support because they are perceived as providing better governance than the state is both alarming and an indication that the Malian state must improve its capacity if counter-terrorism strategies are to bear fruit.

Resilient economy

The widespread violence has yet to have serious ramifications on the overall economic output of the

West African nation. According to the World Bank, Mali's GDP growth rate declined from 5.4% in 2017 to 4.9% in 2018, but that is expected to rise to 5% in 2019. The growth is largely the result of agricultural activities (cotton) and trade. While household consumption is the primary source of demand in Malian society, the violence in the centre and north has not yet led to widespread changes in spending.

Challenges to the Algiers Accords

Despite the progress made on implementing the Algiers Accords in 2018, and sustained support from international and domestic parties, insecurity in Mali still threatens the agreement. With continuing delays in the peace process, and increasing attention and funds diverted to countering terrorism, there is a risk that signatory armed groups may abandon negotiations. This strategy may not guarantee them more power or influence, as by the end of 2018, the signatory groups were largely fragmented and held little territory. Members of armed groups still stand to gain from DDR programmes if they continue with the process. Barring a major military collapse, the peace agreement is likely to hold fin 2019.

Increasing human-rights violations by the Malian security forces greatly undermined any progress achieved on implementing the peace agreement. By alienating the population and eroding trust in institutions, Malian security personnel are making citizens more vulnerable to extremists and self-defence militias, and creating grievances that may persist for decades.

Trends

Lack of counter-terrorism resources

It is unlikely that the Malian Army, French forces, MINUSMA and the FC-G5S will reduce their operations in the coming year. Extremist organisations have proven to be dynamic and fluid adversaries, appearing undeterred by counter-terrorism campaigns. By exploiting existing grievances and capitalising on holes in the security structure, jihadist organisations such as JNIM and ISIS–GS are likely to gain more ground and influence over the next year.

The FC-G5S and the UN must contend with inconsistent funding and resources that directly hinder their efforts. In October, UN Secretary-General António Guterres identified these materiel shortfalls as greatly limiting the reach of MINUSMA in properly fulfilling its mandate, noting the lack of medium-utility helicopters in Mopti and Timbuktu, as well as the desperate need for armoured personnel carriers. The FC-G5S, once considered a potential 'home-grown solution' to the region's transnational terrorism problems, will likely continue to enjoy international support but lack sufficient funding in 2019.

Rising regional instability

Due to the porous nature of borders in the Sahel, instability in Mali is likely to have consequences for neighbouring countries, as signalled by the increased frequency of attacks near the border with Niger and Burkina Faso in 2018. ISIS–GS may seek to coordinate or share resources and fighters with internal insurgencies in these countries. Extremist activity and illicit trade routes in Algeria, Libya, Mauritania, Niger and Nigeria are also likely to exacerbate the Malian conflict. The destabilisation of Mali will be both a cause and a symptom of its neighbours' instability.

Humanitarian situation remains severe

The humanitarian situation in Mali is unlikely to improve in 2019, despite pleas for increased aid and support. Humanitarian actors are increasingly under threat, and the constant state of insecurity hinders their ability to provide aid or reach isolated communities. According to the UN, the monthly average for security incidents affecting humanitarian workers between 1 January and 31 August 2018 was 18.3; in 2017, it was 11.5 per month and only 3.5 in 2016.[16] As violence grows increasingly widespread, it is unlikely that this trend will reverse. In turn, the humanitarian situation will continue to exacerbate the main drivers of the conflict.

The human-rights situation in Mali is also deteriorating rapidly. From June to September, the UN recorded 518 victims of human-rights abuses and violations (compared with 475 victims during the April to June period). Between June and September, nine cases of conflict-related sexual violence were recorded, compared to 16 cases recorded during

2017.[17] The Malian security forces were involved in 18 human-rights violations over the June to September period, JNIM was responsible for 47 abuses and community self-defence groups for 49 cases.[18] It will prove extremely difficult to contain these well-armed, motivated and numerous community militias – even if the Malian government were not already contending with a sophisticated and well-resourced jihadist threat.

Peace requires a new vision

The 2015 Algiers Accords are not yet dead, and the necessary work of implementing their provisions will continue in 2019. However, the provisions of the agreement are not sufficient to meet the challenges currently facing Mali, including many structural and social issues that continue to fuel insecurity in the country.

Notes

1   UN Peacekeeping, 'MINUSMA Fact Sheet: Deployed number of personnel as of January 2019'.

2   Jason Warner and Charlotte Hulme, 'The Islamic State in Africa: Estimating Fighter Numbers in Cells Across the Continent', *Combating Terrorism Centre Sentinel*, vol. 11, 2018, pp. 21–30.

3   UN, 'Situation in Mali', December 2018.

4   Ibrahim and Zapata, *Regions at Risk,* 2018.

5   UN, 'Situation in Mali', December 2018.

6   Government of Mali, 'Budget Citoyens Du Mali Loi de Finances 2018', 2018.

7   International Federation for Human Rights, 'Central Mali: Populations caught between terrorism and anti-terrorism', 20 November 2018.

8   UN, 'Situation in Mali', December 2018.

9   Philip Kleinfeld, '"I have lost everything": In central Mali, rising extremism stirs inter-communal conflict', IRIN, 2018.

10 UN, 'Situation in Mali', December 2018.

11 'UN says Malian army killed 12 civilians', eNews channel Africa, 27 June 2018; Economist Intelligence Unit, 'Military faces accusations of extra-judicial killings', *The Economist*, 17 April 2018.

12 OCHA, 'Humanitarian Bulletin – Mali: July–August 2018', 2018.

13 OCHA, 'Mali: Overview of 2019 Humanitarian Needs (November 2018)', 18 January 2019.

14 OCHA, 'Bulletin Humanitaire – Mali: Septembre–mi-Novembre 2018', November 2018.

15 OCHA, 'Mali: Humanitarian Response Plan – Fact Sheet (January to December 2017)', 21 January 2018.

16 OCHA, 'Humanitarian Bulletin – Mali: July–August 2018'.

17 UN, 'Situation in Mali', September 2018; UN, 'Report of the Secretary-General on conflict-related sexual violence', S/2018/250, 23 March 2018.

18 UN, 'Situation in Mali', September 2018.

Nigeria (Farmer–Pastoralist)

Overview

The conflict in 2018

Violence between pastoralists and farmers in Nigeria increased in 2018, causing more fatalities than in 2017, with clashes becoming more frequent.[1] Farmer–pastoralist violence was most severe in central Nigeria and in parts of the northwest and northeast. Violence also increased in the south, but to a lesser extent. The worst-affected states in 2018 were Adamawa, Taraba, Plateau, Benue, Kaduna and Zamfara. The conflict between the Bachama and Fulani communities in Adamawa State continued from the previous year, while on 23–24 June at least 218 people were killed in Plateau State in Fulani attacks, leading to a wave of recriminatory violence against Muslims. In Zamfara State and Birnin Gwari, Kaduna State, continuing rural banditry compounded conflicts between Hausa and Fulani communities.[2]

The conflict to 2018

Recent divisive national and local politics, together with increasing demographic and ecological pressures in rural areas, have exacerbated the intermittent historical tensions between pastoralists and farmers and broadened the conflict geographically. Though much of the violence is localised and involves specific pastoralist and farming communities, it has steadily become more widespread and

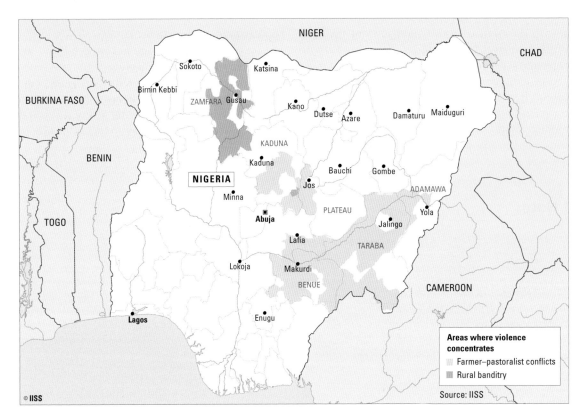

Areas where violence concentrates

Farmer–pastoralist conflicts

Rural banditry

Source: IISS

© IISS

connected across different areas. There is some circulation of fighters between conflict zones, and often rural violence is triggered by violence and instability in urban areas.

In 2001, Muslim–Christian violence between Fulani herders and local farmers in Plateau State began during the 7–12 September riots in Jos, as violence spread from urban to rural areas of the Jos Plateau. As the pastoralists were particularly badly hit in this period, the conflict spiralled into reprisals on Berom and Irigwe villages over subsequent years, a situation which successive governments not only failed to resolve but also at times inflamed. There was a resurgence of mass violence in January 2010 that has continued intermittently ever since. The violence also affected stability in neighbouring states due to the displacement of pastoralists from Plateau.

In neighbouring Kaduna State, riots against the results of the 2011 presidential election also spread from urban to rural areas, leading to violence between pastoralists and farmers in the south of the state. Fulani agro-pastoralists were not involved in the post-election riots but were targeted due to their religious and ethnic identities. The rioting spread

across towns and cities in northern Nigeria, where both Christians and supporters of the then-ruling People's Democratic Party (PDP) were targeted. This violence rekindled long-standing ethno-religious tensions in Kaduna city and Kafanchan town and precipitated retaliatory attacks on Muslims in majority Christian areas of southern Kaduna. As a result, cooperative relations between farmers and herders deteriorated in many southern Kaduna districts, some of which subsequently experienced revenge attacks by the pastoral Fulani.

Benue State has also seen high levels of violence (especially since 2016), in which herders have attacked many villages and destroyed crops, while in

Key statistics

Type:	Internal
IDPs total (2018):	no data
IDPs new (2018):	no data
Refugees total (2018):	245,000
Refugees new (2018):	43,000
People in need (2018):	7,100,000

some areas farmers and militias have killed herders and stolen cattle. A badly performing state governor, Samuel Ortom, seized the opportunity and adopted populist measures – introducing an anti-open-grazing law that effectively banned pastoralism in Benue State – partly to divert public attention from his non-payment of civil-servant salaries for months. The Livestock Guards militia, established in 2017 by the Benue State government to enforce the ban on open grazing, clashed with Fulani pastoralists and expelled them from large areas of Benue, seizing and shooting cattle in the process and triggering large-scale attacks by herders on farmers in Benue at the end of 2017 and the beginning of 2018.

While clashes between pastoralists and farmers have become widespread in Nigeria over the past decade, there are still areas of coexistence and relative amity. Even within states and local government areas (LGAs) that have experienced armed clashes, the distribution of violence varies significantly, suggesting that this is not a generalised conflict between pastoralists and farmers or Muslims and Christians, but violence that follows specific local and regional logics.

Forces

The main actors are transhumant pastoralists – rearing cattle and sheep – and sedentary farmers who grow grains (millet, maize and sorghum), vegetables and fruit. The pastoralists are mainly ethnic Fulani (Fulbe/Mbororo), while the ethnicity of the farmers varies depending on location. The Fulani are predominantly Muslim and the farmers in most of the conflict areas are Christian. Local vigilante groups and the Nigerian security forces are also involved, as are armed bandit gangs and cattle rustlers.

Nigerian security forces

Nigerian security forces intervened in pastoralist–farmer conflicts in 2018 with varying effectiveness. The armed forces and police are overstretched due to their deployment in many conflict areas across Nigeria. The Nigerian armed forces number less than 140,000 personnel across all services, with some rank-and-file soldiers complaining of low pay and poor welfare. The police are especially under-resourced, with 377,000 personnel for a country of more than 190 million people, with a large proportion of those officers tied up in protection duties for VIPs (politicians and others).[3] The ability or willingness of the security forces to protect civilians, who bear the brunt of communal violence, is often lacking. The deployment of the armed forces and police likely prevented farmer–pastoralist conflicts from escalating and spreading, but the conflicts persisted and the armed forces have harmed non-combatants in their operations, including by aerial bombing. Most community self-defence groups and militias have emerged to counter the lack of state protection for the civilian population, though some vigilantes work with the army, air force and police to provide information on the location of belligerents.

Fulani herders

The Fulani are the largest pastoralist group in Nigeria and own most of the country's livestock.[4] They generally live in dispersed settlements and camps and can mobilise across a wide area when tensions with farmers escalate into violence. Fulani groups are highly decentralised, being divided into clans (*leyyi*) and sub-clans. Individuals have significant autonomy on whether to fight or retaliate for a perceived wrong, a decision which may be made without community leaders knowing. For some conflicts, mobilisation happens more officially. If Fulani camps or settlements are attacked on a large scale and there is no government response, the leaders (*ardo'en*) of a clan or a community may sanction a call to arms. When violence intensifies, support may be solicited from both extended family members and neighbouring Fulani groups (the sharing of kola nuts usually seals such agreements). Youth leaders and vigilantes may also mobilise fighters.

Where violence becomes large-scale, Fulani pastoralists mobilise along religious (mostly Muslim) and ethnic lines. Alliances often form between different Fulani groups or clans, but rarely across ethnic lines: non-Fulani Muslims (such as Hausas) are not normally invited to join in the farmer–pastoralist fighting. The increased availability of small and light weapons among pastoralists has increased the deadliness of their attacks on villages and agricultural

Table 1: Main groups fighting against the Fulani in central and northern Nigeria

State / LGA	Groups	Other Information
• Adamawa • Numan, Demsa and Lamurde LGAs (Numan Federation), Mayo Belwa LGA	• Bachama/Bwatiye, Bata, Bali, Bille, Yendam and others	• Conflict between the Bachama and Fulani communities in Numan and Demsa LGAs in November 2017 spread as mobilisation widened to include other ethnic groups and LGAs – as listed here – forming one zone of conflict.
• Taraba • Lau, Yorro, Zing LGAs	• Bakula (seven ethnic groups including Kunini), Yandang, Karimjo, Mumuye, Bachama. Jukun fighters recruited from Wukari	• Part of the same zone of conflict as that in Adamawa in 2018, allied with the Bachama and other groups in Numan, Demsa and Mayo Belwa LGAs to fight the Fulani.
• Wukari, Ibi, Gassol, Bali, Takum, Ussa, Kurmi LGAs	• Jukun, Kuteb, Tiv, Ndola	• Tiv–Jukun conflict in Taraba, 1990s–2000s; Tiv–Fulani conflict in Benue in 1990s; Fulani–Jukun alliance in 2001 against Tiv in Taraba; now all three sides in separate conflicts against each other. Ndola-Fulani conflict occurred in 2018 (Kurmi LGA).
• Sardauna LGA	• Mambilla militias; alliance with Kaka and Kambu	• Mambilla political leaders allegedly instigated villagers to attack settled Fulani agro-pastoralists to seize land in June 2017.
• Benue	• Tiv, Idoma, Igede and Agatu ethnic groups; Benue State Livestock Guards	• The Tiv are one of the largest ethnic minorities in Nigeria, numbering in the millions. Tiv farmers are mobile and expanded their land by practising shifting cultivation.
• Nasarawa	• Eggon, Alago and Tiv ethnic groups; Ombatse militia (Eggon ethnic group)	• Ombatse is an Eggon militia and socio-cultural movement that fought conflicts with the Alago and on a smaller scale with Fulani herders. They also ambushed the Nigerian police/State Security Service in 2013. Ombatse's leader, Baba Alakyo, reportedly killed in 2014.
• Plateau • Barkin Ladi, Riyom, Jos South, Bassa	• Berom and Irigwe ethnic groups	• Berom–Fulani and Irigwe–Fulani conflicts on the Jos Plateau began in September 2001, then resurfaced in January 2010 until present, triggered by urban violence in Jos city.
• Zamfara	• Militant Vigilante Group (yan sakai) (Hausa, Muslim)	• Militant Vigilante Group engaged in combat with bandits across state and accused of stirring wider inter-ethnic conflict between Fulani and Hausa in Zamfara State.

communities, and vice versa. The main guns available include AK-47s, G3s, Mark 4 rifles, locally made single-barrel shotguns (Dane guns), 'Lebanons' (double-barrel shotguns) and a variety of other locally made guns.[5] Automatic weapons are illegal in Nigeria but readily available from gun smugglers. Pastoralists have better financial means to buy them thanks to their wealth in cattle – an AK-47 or comparable gun costs approximately two bulls. These are deployed in communal conflicts and by bandits, while Fulani vigilantes – usually armed with locally made weapons such as Dane guns – combat banditry and cattle rustling with some success in parts of Taraba and in southern Plateau State (Wase LGA) and uphold public morality through a code of conduct (pulaaku), playing a key role in local security provision.

Farmers and ethnic militias

Farming communities also mobilise on an ethnic basis, but unlike Fulani combatants, in some cases also form alliances across ethnic lines, using a Christian religious identity to mobilise members (for main groups fighting the Fulani, see **Table 1**).

Armed bandits and cattle rustlers

Armed bandits are most prevalent in northwest Nigeria, particularly in and around Zamfara State where they attack Hausa villages and coerce Fulani pastoralists by stealing their cattle, demanding money and cooperation in exchange for stolen herds. They are armed with small and light weapons and usually attack villages on motorcycles. According to eyewitnesses, the bandits deployed up to 50 motorcycles in some attacks, each bike carrying three men, all armed and shooting while on the move (this tactic was first used in Nigeria by Boko Haram in July 2009). Some would then dismount and continue the attack on foot while the motorcycle riders waited on the edge of the village to make a swift exit at the end of the operation. Roving bandits have killed several thousand people in the northwest since 2012. From their forest bases in Zamfara the bandits also attack Birnin Gwari LGA, Kaduna State, and parts of Sokoto and Katsina States. Banditry has existed for decades in some areas of north-central and northeast Nigeria, becoming more acute with increased conflict.

The ringleader of the bandits in Zamfara was Buharin Tsoho, popularly known as 'Buharin Daji' ('Buhari of the forest'). An ethnic Fulani, whose gangs pillaged their own ethnic group as well as Hausa farmers, he nonetheless gained hundreds of followers through coercion and by exploiting existing tensions between farmers and pastoralists over land. Buhari was killed in March 2018 by one of his associates, but his surviving men and other gangs continued to terrorise Zamfara and contiguous states. In 2018, criminals involved in banditry and cattle rustling in Zamfara began spreading out to other parts of northern Nigeria as far as Adamawa State in the northeast.

Some of the large sums made from cattle rustling and kidnapping-for-ransom are used to buy guns and for personal enrichment, but the gangs live in the forests at low cost, leaving ample margins for channelling money for other purposes. The complicity of state officials is widely thought to have perpetuated banditry; the bandits appear to be politically connected at the highest levels of government in Zamfara State.

Boko Haram

Boko Haram became a predatory force in rural areas of Borno State and contiguous areas of Yobe and Adamawa from mid-2013, when they were forced out of metropolitan Maiduguri by the Civilian Joint Task Force and the military. As the insurgency spread through rural Borno, Boko Haram raided farmers' grain stores and pastoralists' livestock. They killed thousands of civilians and displaced much of the rural population, who having lost their livelihoods and wealth fled in destitution as internally displaced persons (IDPs) and refugees, mainly to urban areas. There are still 2m people displaced in northeast Nigeria and more than 232,000 Nigerian refugees in Cameroon, Niger and Chad. Many of these people are farmers or pastoralists. There were still raids in 2017–18, but fewer in number compared to 2015–16 because herders and farmers had fled so much of rural Borno by then. When the Islamic State West Africa Province (ISWAP) faction formed in 2015, it sought to improve relations with local civilians and focused its fight on the Nigerian armed forces, allowing a resumption of farming and pastoralism in some areas. However, people commuting from Maiduguri to farm, rear livestock or collect firewood are still being attacked and killed.

| Drivers

Breakdown of farmer–pastoralist arrangements
Pastoralism has a long history in Nigeria, with most of the cattle and sheep in the country still owned and reared by pastoralists. Pastoralism generally requires transhumance – the movement of herders and their animals, often on a seasonal basis between dry and rainy seasons, as well as the daily journeys between pastures and water points. Historically, mutually beneficial rules and regulations guided the interaction between farmers and pastoralists, enabling them to coexist in the same rural space. Reciprocity, however, has weakened in recent years. Farmers are increasingly not respecting the user rights of pastoralists to grazing land and water. Farmers are also seizing land owned by pastoralists, which, together with land seizures by urban-based political elites, has resulted in the loss of grazing land and the blockage of livestock routes. Many grazing reserves, which are protected by law in northern Nigeria, have been cultivated or repurposed. On the other side, increasing competition over resources has brought pastoralists into farming land, where pastoralists' livestock frequently destroy crops.

Unlike other West African countries, Nigeria does not have a pastoral code or clear rules setting out the rights and responsibilities of pastoralists and farmers. There is no official framework stipulating how farming and livestock activities should be managed. Existing laws and customs, such as those governing grazing reserves and livestock routes, have not been enforced due to a combination of weak state institutional capacity in rural areas and vested interests whereby local elites appropriate land that had been set aside for pastoralists. At the same time, there is no formal oversight of herders to regulate their mobility, vaccinate cattle and ensure they do not encroach onto farms and destroy crops.

Increasing competition over land and water

Competition over land and water in Nigeria has increased due to several factors. The most important is population growth. Nigeria's population has more than quadrupled since independence in 1960, from 45 million to an estimated 190m in 2018. In northern Nigeria, which has the highest population growth rate in the country, increased population density has led to severe pressure on land and the loss of rural livelihoods. Farmers have expanded the land area under cultivation, including to riverine areas for dry-season farming that were used by pastoralists in the dry season, raising tensions with pastoralists seeking grazing land and access to rivers and streams for drinking water for their livestock.

Deforestation has also severely degraded the savannahs of central and northern Nigeria, increasing soil erosion, reducing biodiversity and reducing the productivity of agriculture and pastoralism.[6] This has contributed to more extensive agricultural practices and increased competition for good-quality land. In addition, the decimation of tropical forests by cultivators and loggers in southern Nigeria has paradoxically opened more of the south to pastoralists, creating tensions with farmers in environments that were previously unsuitable for cattle.

Weak state

The state is not proactive in addressing environmental and social problems, and often compounds them. Weak rural governance means there is no support for farmers and herders to increase productivity, better integrate livestock and crop farming, and manage land and water resources. Land grabs by political elites further marginalise rural people, while state-level anti-open-grazing laws (as implemented in Benue State) actively prejudice pastoralists. The situation is compounded by a weak public educational system, especially in central and northern Nigeria, which reduces the ability of affected rural communities to diversify their livelihoods. Nomadic schools

have largely collapsed through state neglect and the diversion of funds by officials.

Another feature of state weakness is impunity and injustice. Nigeria's court system is dysfunctional and corrupt, and police capacity is limited. When disputes arise, such as over land ownership, crop damage or theft of livestock, it is difficult and expensive to resolve them via legal means, and people take justice increasingly into their own hands. The perpetrators of violent attacks are then almost never prosecuted. In June 2017, Mambilla militias allegedly killed 728 Fulani people in Taraba State, but known suspects were released in September on the request of the Taraba State Attorney General without ever going to trial. The ready availability of illegal weapons further exacerbates the consequences of this turn to violence, increasing the number of fatalities in the attacks.

Erosion of pastoralist oversight mechanisms

In many cases young men and boys are no longer properly supervised by their parents or elders when herding cattle. Leaving young herders unaccompanied for months at a time exposes them to risks – including drug abuse and recruitment into criminal gangs – and it makes it harder to maintain good relationships with farmers and village leaders. Young Fulani men responsible for herding livestock for their families or as hired herders have become increasingly susceptible to drug abuse. This scourge has spread from urban to rural areas in northern Nigeria. Drug addicts cannot control livestock and this is a cause of conflict with farmers.

Ethnic and religious prejudice

Nigeria is the most populous state in Africa and the most ethnically and linguistically diverse. It is also about half Muslim and half Christian. There is much coexistence and amity across ethnic and religious lines, but there is also prejudice and animosity between some communities. This is partly historic and contextual and partly ideological. In central and southern Nigeria, a widespread Christian viewpoint is that Fulani pastoralists are vanguards of a northern Islamisation agenda, with conflicts perceived as being religious rather than resource-based. The Fulani still often refer to non-Fulanis as *haabe* (plural) or *kaado* (sing.), pejorative terms denoting non-Muslim 'blacks' (and often used for non-Fulani Muslims such as Hausas too). In contrast, a view among the pastoral Fulani is that they are attacked and denied access to land by some ethnic groups due to their Muslim religious identity and their status as Fulani nomads. Their self-perception is of a socio-cultural crisis and vulnerability, which is also a problem in far northern states, with grazing land and pastoral livelihoods not well protected.

Land disputes are often articulated in ethnic terms between farmers and pastoralists, with assertions that the Fulani have neither tenure nor user rights on land as they are 'outsiders' or 'latecomers' to areas they have migrated to, even in cases where they did in fact buy land or had been settled or grazing on it for generations.

Political and Military Developments

Politically instigated violence

The increase in violent clashes between pastoralist and farming communities in 2018 was due to an escalation in specific states – Adamawa, Taraba, Benue, Nasarawa and Plateau – and a surge in attacks by gangs of bandits in Zamfara and north-west Kaduna.

Some of the violence was politically instigated in the lead-up to Nigeria's 2019 elections. This includes the anti-open-grazing laws introduced in four states, and particularly its enforcement in Benue State, but also the violence on the Mambilla Plateau which was orchestrated by elites in Jalingo, the Taraba State capital. The banditry in Zamfara, spreading to neighbouring states, also appears to be perpetuated by officials in the Zamfara State government. More generally, there was a failure of federal and state governments to prevent violence, even when there were warning signs or clear risks of escalation.

Military response

The main security response of the federal government was through military-led operations (including air-force bombing, which hit many civilians). However, even where the army and air force recorded successes against armed combatants, the impact was often fleeting, as armed groups would often return after the soldiers left. Overall, the presence of soldiers in the conflict zones probably did reduce the number of attacks on civilians by armed groups, but the record was uneven and there were cases of large attacks occurring even with soldiers stationed nearby (as on the Jos Plateau in June 2018).

Notable military operations in 2018 included *Operation Safe Haven* in Plateau State, a peacekeeping operation launched in 2010 in response to conflicts in Jos city and the rural hinterland of Jos (ethno-religious and farmer–herder conflicts). *Operation Whirl Stroke* in Benue, Nasarawa and Taraba states commenced on 18 May 2018, with the aim of restoring law and order to communities affected by clashes between farmers and pastoralists and rural banditry, while *Operation Whirl Stroke 2* – a military operation to fight banditry in Zamfara and Kaduna states – was launched on 29 June 2018.

Operation Sharan Daji – launched in May 2016 to fight armed banditry and cattle rustling in northwest Nigeria, with a main focus on Zamfara State – continued in 2018, while the air-force operation *Diran Mikiya* commenced on 31 July 2018 to 'locate and neutralise' armed bandits in northwest Nigeria. While some of the bandit hideouts were reportedly destroyed by the air force, there were also multiple reports of non-combatants being bombed in rural areas – particularly pastoralist families.

Violent Events

Attacks were committed by farmers and pastoralists throughout 2018 on each other's villages and settlements, and in markets and other public places, and are too numerous to list in full.

Clashes in Adamawa and Taraba states

Bachama and allied farming groups clashed with Fulani herders in the areas around Numan, Demsa, Lamurde and Mayo Belwa Local Government Areas (LGAs) in Adamawa State, and in Lau, Yorro and Zing LGAs in Taraba State. Many groups mobilised to form a Christian alliance against the Muslim Fulani, while Jukun fighters were hired from Wukari (Taraba State) to assist the Bachama and their allies.

In Adamawa State, 30 villagers were reportedly killed and 23 injured in a Fulani attack on

Bachama/Bata communities in Demsa on 27 February. On 14 July, attacks on Fulani villages and camps in Bidda and other parts of Mayo Belwa resulted in the deaths of 27 Fulani residents.

In Taraba State, attacks between January and February in Lau resulted in 55 reported deaths among farming communities. Many pastoralists were also killed in Lau between January and September 2018, but the exact number was unclear. Between 5 and 8 July, in the rainy season, 70 people were reportedly killed in violence between pastoralists and farmers in Lau and Yorro LGAs.

In the central and southern zones of Taraba State (Wukari, Ibi, Gassol, Bali, Takum, Ussa, Kurmi LGAs), violence peaked during the dry season (January to April), exacerbated by an influx of herders from Benue State due to the anti-open-grazing law there. On 11 April, 25 people were killed in an attack allegedly by a Fulani militia on the village of Jandeikyula, Wukari LGA.

From 1 March, there was another round of serious violence on the Mambilla Plateau, Sardauna LGA, Taraba State. This followed the Mambilla militia attacks of June 2017. The violence in 2018 was less extensive than that of 2017, but it still may have resulted in more than a hundred deaths. A difference was that the Fulani in most of the affected areas, especially near Nguroje, Maisamari and Yelwa, had allegedly armed themselves, leading to more fatalities among the Mambilla than in the previous year.

Benue State

In Benue State, shootouts between livestock guards and Fulani herders continued in the first quarter of 2018, leading to fatalities among the pastoralists, livestock guards and villagers that were either involved in the clashes or targeted by pastoralists. Most of the pastoralists were forced out of Benue State, with loss of life and cattle, leading to retaliatory attacks.

At least 80 farmers (mainly Tiv) were reported killed in attacks in January, mainly in Guma and Logo LGAs. On 5 March, 26 people were reported killed in an attack on Owusu village, Okpokwu LGA.[7] On 24 April, two priests were among 16 villagers killed in Mbalom village, Gwer East LGA. Fulani gunmen were suspected but the identities of the attackers were not confirmed. Attacks continued intermittently for most of the year, but they were highest in the first half.

The Fulani reported that at least 37 pastoralists were killed in clashes with the Livestock Guards from November 2017 to February 2018, and that more than 1,700 cows were seized and 95 cows shot and killed in Logo, Guma, Oturkpo and Oju LGAs.

Plateau State

In Plateau State, tit-for-tat killings in the first half of 2018 precipitated a wave of major violence in June in the latest iteration of the conflict between the Fulani and Berom communities that began in September 2001 and saw a resurgence from January 2010. Armed gangs, mainly Berom, in Fan district of Barkin Ladi LGA had been rustling Fulani cattle and frequently killing herders. On 21 June, four Beroms were killed, leading to a reprisal the same evening in which five Fulani men were killed when their vehicle was stopped on the road at Heipang.

On 23–24 June, at least 218 Christians were killed in Fulani attacks on more than 15 villages, with Gashish and Ropp districts in Barkin Ladi LGA accounting for 203 of the recorded fatalities, including children and elderly people. The victims were from different ethnic groups because some of the settlements were ethnically mixed, but the majority were Berom. Muslims were not targeted. In the aftermath of the attacks, irate youths blocked the main roads in the area, dragging Muslim passengers out of vehicles and killing them.

Violence between the Fulani and Irigwe farmers in Bassa LGA, on the northwest side of the Jos Plateau, also continued. The Irigwe recorded 54 Fulani attacks between September 2017 and October 2018, in which 238 Irigwe people were killed. On 5 October alone 19 Irigwe were killed in Ariri village, Miango district, in a night attack. There were also Fulani fatalities in the conflict, but fewer than the Irigwe suffered as most pastoralists had left the villages beforehand.

Banditry in Zamfara State and Birnin Gwari, Kaduna State

Communities in Zamfara State and Birnin Gwari, Kaduna State, suffered many attacks and several hundred fatalities in 2018. The attacks were perpetrated by roving bandits, who were predominantly Fulani, while most of the victims were Hausa farmers and some pastoralists. Violence flared regularly throughout the year, resulting in high numbers of fatalities. In Zamfara State, on 15 February, 41 people were killed in Birane village, while on 24 May, 27 farmers were killed in a bandit attack on Malikawa village, Gidan Goga district. On 4 June, an attack on Jarkuka village, Anka LGA, killed 26 people. In Birnin Gwari, 40 miners were killed in Janruwa village on 28 April.

Impact

Deepening ethnic and religious divisions

The conflict between pastoralists and farmers was one of the top national-security issues in Nigeria in 2018 for federal and state governments and security forces, as well as in media reporting. Military interventions increased in 2018. In media accounts of farmer–pastoralist conflicts, the pastoralists' side of the story was rarely told and the Fulani as an ethnic group were often negatively stereotyped, with reporting and analysis repeatedly citing 'Fulani militias' and 'suspected herdsmen' as the sole violent actors, portraying the other conflict groups as victims and not also as actors. As farmer–pastoralist conflicts were widespread and politicised, there was a tendency towards ethnic and religious interpretations of the violence, exacerbating social divisions.

Socio-economic impact

The violence had a negative impact on crop and livestock production in the conflict-affected areas. About 25% of Nigerians are severely food insecure and the farmer–pastoralist conflicts have contributed to this. Half of Nigerians live in rural areas, mostly working in agriculture, which constituted 25% of GDP in 2018.[8] Overall, the agricultural sector (crops, livestock, forestry, fisheries, with crops making up some 90% of recorded agricultural GDP) reportedly grew by only 2.12% in 2018, below the population growth rate of 2.6% and down from 3.45% in 2017 and 4.11% in 2016. Attacks on villages were accompanied by the destruction of crops, with persistent insecurity in the aftermath of violence preventing farming from taking place. Pastoralists, on the other side, have had large numbers of cattle stolen or killed and have lost access to grazing land.

In some cases, the conflicts have resulted in pastoralists taking over land from farmers (as on parts of the Jos Plateau) or farmers preventing pastoralists from entering communal land (Benue State) or seizing pastoral land (much of the Mambilla Plateau). The conflicts have also affected socio-economic relations between farmers and pastoralists, leading to a breakdown in what were previously mutually beneficial exchange relations. Pastoralists boost rural markets, buying grains and other farm produce, while manure from their cattle is used to fertilise farms.

Humanitarian impact

The farmer–pastoralist conflicts in Nigeria have been marked by communal violence that has cost thousands of lives and displaced several hundred thousand people. In the affected areas, entire villages and pastoralist camps were burned down, crops destroyed, farms abandoned, and livestock killed or stolen. The IDPs in Taraba State increased from 67,111 in June to 112,197 in October, and in Adamawa State from 178,977 in June to 197,713 in October, largely due to farmer–pastoralist conflicts (most of the existing IDPs in Adamawa were from the Boko Haram insurgency; some displacement was also caused by flooding).[9] The Plateau State Emergency Management Agency recorded 35,000 people displaced, in 20 IDP camps, as a direct result of the June attacks in Barkin Ladi LGA; while in Bassa LGA, the Irigwe community recorded 11,587 IDPs by October.[10] In November, a Plateau State government commission of inquiry estimated there were more than 50,000 IDPs from farmer–pastoralist violence in Barkin Ladi, Riyom, Jos South, Bokkos and Bassa LGAs, most of them recent IDPs but some displaced since 2010.[11] In February, the governor of Benue State estimated there were 200,000 IDPs in his state (official number of farmers displaced excluding herders displaced into Nasarawa and Taraba states).[12] In all these cases, many IDPs were not counted because they were residing with family members or in host communities rather than IDP camps. The overall assistance provided to the IDPs fell far short of their needs, but some support was provided by churches, non-governmental organisations and communities.

Trends

The conflict had limited bearing on election preparations ahead of the 2019 presidential vote. In October 2018, Atiku Abubakar (popularly known as Atiku) won the primary elections for the opposition People's Democratic Party, to stand against the incumbent Muhammadu Buhari in February 2019. Atiku, a businessman and establishment politician, is also Fulani, but he is seen as more neutral than Buhari, who many Christians perceive through a religious lens. The marked differences between the two Fulani presidential candidates reduced the political significance of the farmer–pastoralist conflicts during the electoral campaign, as anti-Fulani stereotyping was no longer useful in the national political discourse, even if the issue remained locally prominent.

Emerging government livestock policy

Intensification of production and more integration and cooperation between the livestock and farming sectors are much-needed responses to demographic and environmental pressures in Nigeria. The federal government's 'National Livestock Transformation Plan 2018' is an emerging policy response to the farmer–pastoralist conflict. The plan attempts to address the issues holistically and includes investment in the livestock sector, but there are debates over whether the proposed ranching system could work in Nigeria, given the infrastructural constraints and capital investment needed. It is not clear if ranches would benefit or disenfranchise the pastoralists, and where the land would be made available. In the proposed model, the livestock sector also appears to be treated independently from crop farming.

In general, federal policy has been moving towards trying to curtail pastoral mobility and transhumance, rather than permitting it in a regulated system of stock routes and grazing reserves. By viewing mobility as inherently problematic rather than trying to facilitate a more ordered system of mobility, the state may not make the interventions that are needed to improve pastoral livelihoods

and resolve the conflict with farmers. In any case, a change in the livestock-production system, if it happens, will be gradual. Also, agricultural intensification will take time to achieve, especially with the current low levels of investment (only 1.8% of the national budget). The expansion of farmland, and competition for land, is likely to continue, further raising tensions between farmers and pastoralists. Whether state governments in central and northern Nigeria will reserve land for livestock grazing is a political issue that is likely to play out differently in different states.

Risk of increased violence in Taraba

A significant risk in 2019 would be if the present governor of Taraba State, Darius Ishaku, wins a second term and decides to actively enforce Taraba State's anti-open-grazing law along the lines of that in place in Benue State. In 2018, the governor started training marshals to enforce the law, but this scheme was disbanded by the federal authorities. Taraba is an important agricultural state, but it is also vital for livestock. Pastoralists have a historic presence in Taraba, unlike in much of Benue, and there are more livestock in Taraba than Benue. Taraba is already riven with ethno-religious conflicts and farmer–pastoralist clashes, and there is little doubt that the enforcement of the anti-open-grazing law there would lead to large-scale violence.

State and civil-society reconciliation initiatives between communities have not resolved the conflicts or reduced the violence. The recommendations of government commissions of inquiry are never implemented and state- or NGO-sponsored attempts at dialogue are not followed up with action to address the concerns of different sides in the conflict. Conflict-resolution initiatives are only likely to succeed if the structural causes of the conflict are addressed, which requires federal government involvement to keep the excesses of state governments in check.

Notes

[1] According to Nigerian newspaper reports monitored by Nigeria Watch, there were 1,867 deaths in farmer–pastoralist conflicts in 2018, compared to 390 in 2017. However, many of the violent

deaths in these conflicts are not reported, or they are underreported, particularly those occurring in remote rural areas (http://www.nigeriawatch.org). It should be noted that the 2017 figure of 390 is inaccurate, being much too low according to the author's fieldwork; more people were killed on the Mambilla Plateau alone in June 2017.

2   Murtala Ahmed Rufa'I, *Cattle Rustling and Rural Banditry in Zamfara State*, Centre for Peace Studies, Usmanu Danfodio University, Sokoto. Unpublished book, 2017.

3   Olly Owen, 'Government Properties: The Nigeria Police Force as Total Institution?', *AFRICA: Journal of the International African Institute*, vol. 86, no. 1, 2016, pp. 37–58.

4   Pastoral Fulani likely number several million people in Nigeria (projection from 1950s data), where the largest Fulani population live. The 2006 Nigerian census and preceding ones were inaccurate and did not record ethnicity or religion.

5   Amnesty International, 'Harvest of Death: Three Years of Bloody Clashes between Farmers and Herders in Nigeria', 2018, pp. 35–7.

6   On the impacts of reduced biodiversity on agricultural productivity, see UN Food and Agricultural Organisation (FAO), 'The State of the World's Biodiversity for Food and Agriculture', ed. J. Bélanger and D. Pilling, FAO Commission on

Genetic Resources for Food and Agriculture Assessments, 2019.

7   '26 killed as herdsmen sack Benue village in fresh attack', *Vanguard,* 7 March 2018.

8   National Bureau of Statistics, 'Nigerian Gross Domestic Product Report (Q4 & Full Year 2018)', February 2019.

9   International Organization for Migration (IOM), 'Nigeria: Displacement Tracking Matrix', DTM Round 23 Report, June 2018; DTM Round 24 Report, August 2018; DTM Round 25 Report, October 2018; DTM Round 25 List of Wards Assessed, October 2018.

10 'Summary of overall impact assessment of attacks carried out on Irigwe people by Fulani herdsmen between September 2017 and October 2018'. Information provided by the Rural Youth Integral Support Initiative (RUYISI) – Miango, Bassa LGA, Plateau State.

11 'With Thousands Dead, Many More Homeless, Plateau's Economy Plummets', *Nigerian Tribune*, 16 November 2018.

12 UN Office for West Africa and the Sahel (UNOWAS), 'Pastoralism and Security in West Africa and the Sahel: Towards Peaceful Coexistence', UNOWAS Issue Paper, August 2018.

Somalia

Overview

The conflict in 2018

The violent stalemate between al-Shabaab and the Somali state largely continued in 2018. While al-Shabaab found itself under increasing military pressure, there was little evidence to suggest that its defeat was imminent, with the group retaining considerable territorial control in southern Somalia and pervasive influence elsewhere. Al-Shabaab continued to launch attacks close to seats of government power in Mogadishu and elsewhere in 2018. In the last quarter of 2018 alone, checkpoints at the Presidential Palace and a hotel popular with government ministers were subject to separate bombing attacks, with each killing tens of people. Government ministers continued to be targeted for assassinations. In southern Somalia – al-Shabaab's territorial stronghold – military victories against the group were numerous but short-lived, with militants returning as soon as troops withdrew.

Somalia's political troubles instead worsened in 2018 as the agreements meant to chart the country's future fell apart. In September, the relations between the federal and member-state governments broke down, with five member-state administrations

announcing that they were ceasing cooperation with the federal government due to its failure to provide security and respect member-state authority. In December, the fears of the member states that the federal government was prepared to intervene in their elections were confirmed when the federal government arrested Mukhtar Mansur Robow. Robow, the former al-Shabaab deputy leader who defected and then later became a candidate in the South West State election, was struck off the ballot and taken to a Mogadishu prison, while 300 of his supporters were arrested and 15 people were killed in ensuing clashes.

Key statistics	
Type:	Internationalised
IDPs total (2018):	2,600,000
IDPs new (2018):	no data
Refugees total (2018):	955,000
Refugees new (2018):	no data
People in need (2018):	4,200,000

Sub-Saharan Africa

Source: IISS

The conflict to 2018

At its core, the conflict between the federal government of Somalia and the al-Shabaab insurgency is a fight to impose governance. After the collapse of the authoritarian regime of Siad Barre in 1991, a decade-long civil war erupted. The Union of Islamic Courts (UIC), a grassroots Islamist movement, restored a degree of order through the early to mid-2000s, but the US-backed Ethiopian invasion of Somalia in 2006 destroyed the UIC's control. An internationally backed Transitional Federal Government (TFG), which had previously been based in Kenya, then set up an interim capital in the city of Baidoa. The al-Shabaab insurgency emerged from the UIC's former enforcement wing with the aim of overthrowing the TFG and establishing an Islamic state in Somalia. In 2007, African Union forces spearheaded by Uganda began supporting the TFG militarily in its fight against al-Shabaab, an operation that has since

expanded to become the African Union Mission in Somalia (AMISOM).

The TFG was inaugurated in Mogadishu in 2012 as the federal government of Somalia. Despite its international backing, the federal government lacks legitimacy in Somali society and remains largely unable to exercise control over areas outside of Mogadishu. Insecurity is not the only inhibitor to government control. Somalia is made up of federal member states, each of which has its own administration. Somalia claims to have six federal member states – Puntland, Galmudug, Hirshabelle, South West, Jubaland and Somaliland, as well as the Banadir Regional Administration containing the capital Mogadishu. However, Somaliland considers itself to be a sovereign state and has not recognised Mogadishu's authority over it since it declared independence in 1991. Puntland also declares itself to be an autonomous region, although it does not seek independence.

Relations between the federal government and the member states are extremely tense and marked by stiff competition for authority. Hopes for a fresh start were raised in 2017 with the election of President Mohamed Abdullahi Mohamed (popularly known as 'Farmajo'). Farmajo managed to forge a series of cooperative agreements with the administrations of the member states, including the 2017 Security Pact – an agreement that was to be the road map for Somalia to take control of its own security as AMISOM prepared to leave. He also said he would defeat al-Shabaab within two years. The events of 2018, however, have shown that the group's enduring defeat remains a distant prospect.

Forces

Somali National Army (SNA)

The federal government's Somali National Army (SNA) is being built from an amalgamation of former clan and warlord militias. According to the 2017 Security Pact, the SNA should comprise a minimum of 18,000 soldiers, as well as 4,000 *Danab* ('Lightning') special forces. The Ministry of Defence has between 22,000 and 32,000 SNA personnel on its payroll. However, the actual number of soldiers is significantly smaller, with the payroll being inflated by 'ghost soldiers' and troops' dependants.[1] A recent estimate put the real number of soldiers at 19,800. Factionalism remains rife, both along clan lines and because some integrated militias still operate with a degree of independence from the force.

Several international efforts to train the SNA are under way, with the European Union, Turkey, Qatar and the United States currently being the most involved. While having multiple training partners speeds up the pace of training, it also risks failing to overcome pre-existing divisions within the SNA and institutionalising new ones. The multitude of trainers means that different units have adopted different practices and military cultures. The lack of unity and morale within the force also exacerbates the problem of corruption, a factor that harms the SNA's acquisition – and retention – of resources.

An Operational Readiness Assessment (ORA) conducted in September 2017 found that 30% of SNA soldiers did not have weapons and that the army lacked the artillery, shoulder-launched missiles and heavy machine guns needed to repel al-Shabaab attacks from a distance. SNA commanders and the federal government insist that the United Nations arms embargo on Somalia (imposed in 1992) prevents them from obtaining the necessary weapons. By contrast, the UN Group of Experts reported in 2018 that the SNA has received approximately 20,000 weapons from foreign partners since the partial lifting of the arms embargo in 2013, enough for one per soldier. Shortages are likely down to a prolific trade in weapons by SNA soldiers, who are known to have sold weapons to al-Shabaab.

The SNA has four command divisions (12th, 21st, 43rd and 60th) and is spread around Somalia's territory across eight operational sectors (12th, 21st, 43rd, 49th, 48th, 54th, 26th and 60th). The SNA's future operations are looking increasingly uncertain, however, since the breakdown of relations between the federal and state administrations may affect where the army can operate, how it will operate within member-state territories and whether the member states will contribute to its growth.

African Union Mission in Somalia (AMISOM)

The African Union Mission in Somalia (AMISOM) is one of the largest, longest-running and most complex peacekeeping missions in the world. It is also arguably the most militarised, often closer to a conventional military operation than a peacekeeping one. The mission is currently composed of approximately 21,564 troops, provided by five Troop Contributing Countries (TCCs) – Uganda, Burundi, Djibouti, Kenya and Ethiopia.

AMISOM still lacks a unified command-and-control system, hindering the viability of joint-sector operations with troops from different TCCs and inadvertently giving al-Shabaab safe haven between sector border areas. AMISOM's efficacy is also inhibited by its bureaucratic complexities – the result of numerous international donor and management bodies struggling to assert their authority. This not only blights the mission's ability to secure funding quickly and reliably, but also inhibits its capacity to strategise, since it cannot be sure of what resources it will receive when. AMISOM's resource shortages are significant, including a lack of air assets and ground equipment in some sectors. AMISOM did acquire its first uninhabited aerial intelligence, surveillance and reconnaissance (ISR) system in 2018, which includes three uninhabited aerial vehicles (UAVs), donated by the US in order to improve security along AMISOM's logistical supply routes.

AMISOM's mandate is meant to end after the general election due to be held in 2020, and AU leadership intends for the mission to have fully withdrawn from Somalia by 2021. TCC military leaders have vehemently disputed this goal, openly saying that a premature withdrawal will reverse the gains made against al-Shabaab.

On 30 July 2018, the UN Security Council adopted Resolution 2431, reauthorising AMISOM's mandate until 31 May 2019 but pledging to reduce the number of troops to 20,626 by 28 February 2019. In December, AMISOM asked Burundi to prepare to withdraw 1,000 troops in anticipation of meeting this target, but Bujumbura protested and said that all TCCs should be reducing their forces proportionately instead. It is unclear how effectively AMISOM will be able to dictate withdrawal terms to the TCCs, especially if TCC governments threaten to withdraw their cooperation in the immediate term.

Al-Shabaab

Harakat al-Shabaab al-Mujahedeen (commonly referred to as al-Shabaab) has been the official affiliate of al-Qaeda in the Horn of Africa since 2012. Al-Shabaab officially shares al-Qaeda's global jihadist objective – building a global Islamist caliphate – and more immediately aims to create an Islamist state in Somalia. Ideological motives vary within the group, however, with the leadership generally being most concerned with 'global jihad' while fighters on the ground are more motivated by opportunism, desire for political influence or by grievances against the federal government. Since the government is dependent on external (and particularly Western) support, many Somalis see it as illegitimate and corrupt – a factor that al-Shabaab exploits.

Al-Shabaab has a tenacious grip of control over much of southern Somalia and in the Galgala Mountain region of Puntland. However, its territorial hold is inconsistent. Al-Shabaab's case shows that a permanent monopoly of force over a given territory is not essential for maintaining authority. A near-monopoly for most of the time is good enough. While it is often forced out of an area for the duration of a military offensive, al-Shabaab quickly restores its influence – if not outright control – once AMISOM/SNA forces withdraw to their forward operating bases. Al-Shabaab continues to exert its influence over the local populations, since residents know that they are bound to return.

In accordance with its Islamist aims for Somalia, al-Shabaab attempts to govern populations through sharia law in areas it controls. The group is often the most consistent provider of services in these contested areas of southern Somalia, since the government's reach does not extend to many rural places. Al-Shabaab's services are limited – primarily to the provision of justice, education and security – but they are often considered less corrupt than those of the government. The group maintains functional – if sometimes contentious – relationships with local clan leaders. Moreover, civilians can benefit from integrating into al-Shabaab structures. For instance, when a woman marries an al-Shabaab fighter, the group's protection is automatically extended to her whole family.

Al-Shabaab's conventional force comprises approximately 5,700 fighters, who are divided into smaller armies (*jaysh*, pl. *juyush*).[2] Each *jaysh* is assigned to a particular region. There are also smaller special-forces units assigned to complex operations. Al-Shabaab also has an intelligence wing, known as Amniyat. The Amniyat is thought to have a formidable reach in Mogadishu, as well as over the border in Kenya, where it receives help from al-Shabaab's Kenyan support wing al-Hijra. Al-Hijra facilitates cross-border logistics, as well as attacks against Kenyan targets.

The coordination between these multiple units and the fact that fighters can call on other *juyush* for reinforcements during battle suggests that the group remains relatively cohesive and centralised. Al-Shabaab is led by Ahmed Umar Diriye, better known as Abu Ubaidah. Analysts have raised the possibility of a leadership crisis, since Abu Ubaidah is rumoured to be suffering from kidney disease. Al-Shabaab has, however, been historically resistant to fracture. After the death of the previous leader, Ahmed Abdi Godane, there were similar speculations of a leadership crisis, yet splits did not materialise.

Islamic State in Somalia (ISIS Somalia)

The branch of Islamic State, also known as ISIS or ISIL, in Somalia is a far less pressing threat to Somalia than al-Shabaab. Al-Shabaab nevertheless sees it as a rival that must be defeated, and in December vowed to eliminate it altogether. ISIS Somalia is comprised of approximately 70 fighters who are concentrated in the Bari region of Puntland and led by the elderly al-Shabaab defector Abd al-Qadir Mumin. Mumin is reportedly ill, and his deputy Mahad Moalim was found dead on a Mogadishu beach in October 2018. ISIS Somalia is struggling to pay its existing fighters, and so is unlikely to expand significantly. Its limited capacity is reflected by the low number of small-scale attacks it has committed this year – four shootings, resulting in three fatalities in total.

Drivers

Governance challenges

The federal government continues to lack widespread legitimacy and the capacity to govern the majority of Somalia. As long as the government cannot establish effective service provision, or is perceived as the weaker provider of security, Somalis will continue to seek alternative providers, including al-Shabaab. Indeed, al-Shabaab has established itself as the federal government's key competitor in governance as well as in military terms. Within its areas of control, al-Shabaab's governance is widely perceived as more effective than that provided by Mogadishu. Al-Shabaab courts are often visited by civilians living outside the group's territory, since they are seen to operate swiftly and without the corruption of the official justice system. Even al-Shabaab fighters who are disillusioned with the group remain in it because they do not believe there is a better alternative. The Mogadishu-based Hiraal Institute interviewed al-Shabaab fighters and found that despite low morale in the group, fighters felt they had a better life than they would outside of the group. The informants also indicated that they did not trust in the government's ability to protect defectors, given that the government could not protect its own politicians from assassination.[3]

Clan challenge to political unity

The breakdown of the Barre regime in 1991 led to the militarisation of clan tensions and the formation of clan militias which subsequently fought in the civil war and continue to be a source of violence. Unlike the Barre regime, the federal government is trying to accommodate clan structures within national politics rather than trying to suppress them. Clans have nevertheless continued to present a challenge to political unity on the scale of a nation-state.

There are four 'major' clans in Somalia – the Darod, Dir, Hawiye and Rahanweyn. These four clans were used as the basis of the '4.5' power-sharing system in the 2017 election, which was meant to accord equal representation to Somalia's four major clans and due representation to minor clans.

Major clans are clan families, stemming from a common patrilineal ancestor. Within each of these are myriad sub-clans. At a local level, the most significant clan unit is the Diya group – that in which members share a common customary-law system (*xheer*) and are socially contracted to pay *mag* (compensation) in the event of crimes against each other.

The clan is both a stabilising influence and a source of volatility in Somalia. At the micro level, individuals can seek security by invoking shared clan identity. Mutual assistance between members of a Diya group is socially mandated – if a member of a Diya is killed, their fellow members are obliged to seek revenge or compensation for their death. Clan association thus offers a degree of protection through deterrence of violence. Clan leaders are also a consistent authority in Somali life, and so can be effective brokers in dispute resolution, even around matters that are not necessarily clan-based. In late November, al-Shabaab abducted two Kenyan herders on the Somali–Kenyan border for failing to pay their *zakat* tax – a religious tax al-Shabaab demands from those under its control. The herders' release was eventually arranged through negotiations between the herders' and the militants' local clan authorities.

However, at a more macro level, clan loyalties can fracture political arrangements, or make unstable forms of exclusion. Mogadishu landlords often refuse to rent to tenants of different clans, and likewise prospective tenants prefer to have a landlord of the same clan, since they will be bound by customary obligations to act fairly. This preference has compounded Mogadishu's housing crisis, caused by vast numbers of displaced persons from southern Somalia seeking refuge. Since the lucrative housing sector in the city is run informally along clan lines, competition for control of housing has intensified inter-clan fighting and urban conflict. In more rural areas, competition for resources emerges along clan lines. In November, ten people were killed in Galgaduud region after two rival clan militias fought over grazing land and boreholes.

Lack of central-government authority

The legacy of the Barre regime has left Somalis distrustful of state centralisation. The present federal state system aimed to decentralise the state, and also to compensate for the federal government's limited capacity. However, the system is troubled by a lack of consensus over what federal authority means, what its limits are and on what basis a federal state should claim authority. The net result is a state in which the federal and member-state governments persistently compete for authority.

This contestation is exacerbated by a series of internal and external factors. Externally, donors, investors and international interests find direct dealings with the member-state governments more expedient than dealing with the federal government, although this undermines the federal government's authority. This situation also increases competition within and between member states, who are aware that there is little Mogadishu can do to restrain them. This makes building political consensus extremely challenging. Political elites and clan interests also impact the politics of member-state governments, often leading to the exclusion of minorities from the political process.

Territorial disputes

The relationship between clan and territory is rarely clear in Somalia, a situation that can lead to violence. A key problem is that the justificatory bases for territorial claims are themselves contested. Historical clan territories ('clan-states') and former colonial borders have both been used in advancing member-state claims to authority.

The territorial dispute between Puntland and Somaliland is a case in point. The self-declared sovereign state of Somaliland (which remains unrecognised by the international community) bases its borders on the former British protectorate of Somaliland. Puntland is an autonomous regional state within Somalia but, like the rest of Somalia, does not recognise Somaliland's independence or its borders. Puntland justifies its territorial claim to the area genealogically: the state is the power centre of the Harti clan family, and the Dhulbahante and Warsangeli clans that inhabit the disputed Sool and Sanaag regions along the Puntland–Somaliland border are part of the Harti clan family.

This struggle played out violently in 2018. The town of Tukaraq was taken by Somaliland forces in a battle with Puntland forces on 8 January, leading to the displacement of 2,500 people and numerous casualties on both sides. A Puntland-backed militia attacked Tukaraq again in May, leaving over a hundred people dead. Further clashes between regional clan militias have added to the violence over 2018.

Climate change

Adverse weather patterns are exacerbating the precarious agricultural livelihoods of rural Somalis. While 2018 has seen a moderate improvement in rainfall and food security, longer-term projections suggest that the climate in the Horn of Africa will become increasingly inhospitable. Even as the situation eased slightly in 2018, the effects of climate instability on social tensions were apparent. In the first half of 2018, 100,000 internally displaced persons (IDPs) surveyed in Mogadishu reported being displaced by military offensives in southern Somalia. In the same period, 167,000 were displaced by 'slow-onset disasters' such as drought and lack of livelihood.[4] This is but one wave of urbanisation that is putting untenable pressure on housing in Mogadishu and exacerbating inter-clan urban conflict. Shortages of food and water also exacerbate social divisions in rural areas, and in extreme circumstances lead to violence.

Political and Military Developments

Federal disputes and foreign policy

On 8 September 2018, after a four-day conference of the inter-state Council for Inter-State Cooperation (CIC), five member-state governments (Jubaland, Puntland, South West, Galmudug and Hirshabelle) said they were ceasing cooperation with the Farmajo administration because of its failure to ensure the country's security and to respect federal authority.

In October, the CIC declared that it would form an Inter-State Security Force to combat al-Shabaab. Each member-state government on the CIC declared it would contribute 1,000 troops towards the force.

These plans do not appear to have progressed since. However, the stand-off between the federal and member-state governments means that the 2017 Security Pact – which is guiding AMISOM's exit strategy and was based on federal and member-state cooperation – is no longer viable.

There were several factors behind the September severance of relations. Foreign policy was a principal driver, particularly in regard to the Gulf states. The United Arab Emirates has long had a tense relationship with Mogadishu. When the Gulf crisis erupted in June 2017 over Qatar's alleged support to Islamist groups, the UAE believed the federal government was too close to Qatar, while Mogadishu suspected the UAE of manipulating Somali federal politics for its own ends. This suspicion was due to the Emirati port-development company DP World striking deals with Somaliland and Puntland states.

In 2017, DP World secured a contract to develop Bosaso Port in the autonomous federal state of Puntland, and in early March 2018, DP World secured another contract to develop Berbera Port in Somaliland. Somaliland declared independence from Somalia in 1991 but is not recognised by Mogadishu or the international community. However, its internal stability and strategic location on the Gulf of Aden attracted the UAE and Ethiopia, both of whom want to establish commercial and military bases there. Ethiopia secured a 19% stake in the Berbera Port, with the view of ensuring maritime access for its economy. The federal government was enraged at being bypassed, declaring the entire deal void a week later and banning DP World from operating in Somalia. This has had no effect on the deal, with the development of Puntland and Somaliland's ports continuing throughout 2018.

Somali–Emirati relations soured further in April 2018 after Somali authorities seized an Emirati plane containing US$10 million in cash. The federal government claimed that the cash was intended to help the UEA buy influence with federal member states and circumvent Mogadishu's authority. The UAE ended several arrangements with Somalia in response, including its contributions to the military training of the SNA. Several member-state governments – chiefly those with existing or potential Emirati investments – voiced their objections to Mogadishu's stance and reiterated support for the UAE.

These foreign-policy differences were not expressly cited as a reason for the September severance of relations by the member-state governments. However, Farmajo angrily exclaimed in November that the state administrations were overstepping their bounds by getting involved in foreign policy – the exclusive purview of the federal government. Yet the fact that Mogadishu has been unable to stop DP World's port development may encourage the member states to pursue foreign interests unilaterally, further undermining the existing legal framework for a decentralised Somali state.

Regional political change

In June 2018, the new Ethiopian Prime Minister Abiy Ahmed implemented the UN peace agreement with neighbouring Eritrea, which had originally been signed in 2000. The two countries rapidly resumed relations after two decades of hostility. In the following month, Somalia also reconciled with Eritrea after 15 years of diplomatic severance over accusations that Eritrea was funding al-Shabaab. That same month, Eritrea, Somalia and Ethiopia signed a tripartite agreement in which they agreed to cooperate and bolster economic and security ties and regional peace. They pledged to establish a Joint High-Level Committee to further these goals.

While this is certainly positive news for regional stability, Somalia's internal disputes over foreign policy continued throughout these diplomatic developments. Farmajo narrowly escaped a motion to impeach him in November, after several lawmakers declared that the cooperative agreements with Ethiopia and Eritrea were unconstitutional because parliament had not been consulted. The necessary number of signatures for the motion was not met, but it still led to a further political rift between the president and the Lower House. Multilateral regional agreements may ultimately decrease the chances of internal crises over foreign policy in Somalia, since international players will be less able to sidestep national interests.

Al-Shabaab adopts flexible tactics, retains capability

Analysis of al-Shabaab's methods of attack in 2018 indicated some loose, if not fixed, trends in tactical change in relation to the number of offensives that the group faced in the period. For the purpose of this analysis, two categories of al-Shabaab attack tactic are considered: low-exposure and high-exposure attacks. Low-exposure attacks make use of tactics that expose a small number of al-Shabaab fighters to potentially lethal violence, for example, targeted assassinations, suicide attacks or attacks making use of remotely detonated explosives. High-exposure attacks make use of tactics that expose high numbers of al-Shabaab fighters to potentially lethal violence, for example, ambush attacks on security forces or raids, particularly on military bases, convoys of armed vehicles or other well-guarded targets.

Al-Shabaab tends to use the periods when there are fewer military offensives against the group to increase the number of high-exposure attacks (i.e., ambushes/raids), particularly on security-force targets such as military bases.

In months where al-Shabaab conducts fewer high-exposure attacks (see **Figure 1**), there are some observed increases in low-exposure or remote attacks (e.g., remote improvised explosive devices, targeted assassinations). Suicide attacks are a relative rarity and are usually directed against high-value, high-security targets, particularly Mogadishu hotels.

These shifts in tactics are, however, temporary. For instance, while numbers of ambushes and raids were low in October and December, the number in November was unusually high. While November's rise in ambushes did coincide with a low number of operations against the group, these were not vastly lower than average.

Insofar as their tactics of violence can be revealing, there is little evidence to suggest that the group is being progressively incapacitated by the military operations against it.

Violent Events

Combat in southern Somalia

The main fronts in the battle between security forces and al-Shabaab remained overwhelmingly concentrated in southern Somalia, with the regions of Lower Shabelle in Hirshabelle State and Lower Juba in Jubaland State experiencing the bulk of the fighting in 2018. This concentration is partly because each area contains a strategically important coastal city (Mogadishu and the Banadir administrative region, and Kismayo respectively). The more northern regions of South West and Jubaland states also experienced high levels of violence. Gedo region in the north of Jubaland state also continued to be highly affected because of the Kenyan border on its western edge, across which al-Shabaab fighters frequently move.

The key challenge for security forces and, more broadly, for the federal government, in southern Somalia is ensuring that military victories translate into lasting government control. A number of areas of southern Somalia were retaken from al-Shabaab control in 2018, but the group easily recaptured lost areas after troops withdrew. In February, AMISOM and SNA forces recaptured the town of Sablale in Lower Shabelle. Yet in May, multiple reports emerged of a woman being stoned to death for adultery by al-Shabaab in a public square in Sablale, and the town was described as being entirely under al-Shabaab control. This pattern will persist until a permanent government and security presence is maintained in these areas.

Attacks in Mogadishu

Mogadishu continues to be the highest-value target for al-Shabaab, as attacks there damage the federal government's infrastructure and hurt its personnel. On 22 December, a double car-bombing occurred near the Presidential Palace in Mogadishu, killing 20 people in the blasts, including members of the security forces. One blast targeted a checkpoint at the palace's rear entrance, while the second bomb exploded near the entrance to the nearby national theatre and resulted in predominantly civilian casualties. Politicians were regular targets for assassination attempts in Mogadishu. In March 2018, a female MP from South West State Parliament, Ruqiya Abshir, was shot outside her Mogadishu residence by suspected al-Shabaab attackers. In August 2018, Somali Deputy Defence Minister Abdullahi Olad Rooble escaped an al-Shabaab assassination attempt in the form of a planted IED. The IED killed a civilian when it detonated.

To what extent al-Shabaab intends to target civilians is a matter of debate. After the devastating truck bombing near the Safari Hotel in October 2017, which killed more than 500 people, there were demonstrations against al-Shabaab in the streets of Mogadishu and the group received widespread condemnation from Somalis. The fact that al-Shabaab did not claim responsibility for the attack suggests that the bombing had not gone as planned. Somali intelligence investigators say that the true target of the attack was a Turkish military base.

It seems that al-Shabaab attacks are primarily designed to strike political targets. However, there is evidence to suggest the group also intends to kill a limited number of civilians in these attacks to highlight the federal government's inability to provide security for its citizens. The group's history of launching attacks on Mogadishu hotels can also be interpreted in this light. While Mogadishu's expensive hotels are not technically government buildings, they are mostly owned by political elites or people with powerful connections to the government. The hotels also frequently serve as bases for international visitors and representatives. This makes them symbolic and high-value targets, albeit risky ones since they are usually well defended.

The Sahafi hotel attack in November 2018, which killed 52 people, is one such example. The

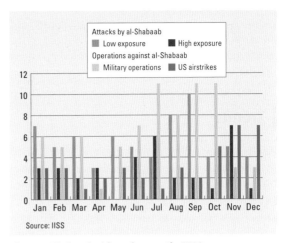

Figure 1: Violent incidents by month, 2018

hotel is opposite Somalia's Criminal Investigations Department, and al-Shabaab claimed to be attacking the government officials that frequented the hotel. However, the use of four car bombs followed by gunmen attempting to storm the hotel suggests that a number of civilian casualties were also likely intended.

Impact

Displacement

One of the most significant consequences of violence in Somalia is displacement, particularly in central-southern areas. Somalia was believed to have as many as 2.6m IDPs in 2018. Between August and November, 34,000 people were displaced as a direct result of extended clashes between security forces and al-Shabaab. This displacement drives a deeply unstable urbanisation process, since the majority of IDPs flee to urban and peri-urban areas, particularly Baidoa, Galkayo, Kismayo and Mogadishu. An informally run, usually clan-based housing market in each of these cities (especially Mogadishu) has resulted in high levels of eviction and secondary displacement. Since many of these urban IDPs previously depended on agriculture for a living, they lack employment and money with which to buy necessities. They thus face shortages of food and water, as well as poor sanitation and other protection issues, such as restrictions on movement and arbitrary arrest.

Food insecurity

Approximately 5.7m Somalis are food insecure according to the World Food Programme, with 2.7m unable to meet their daily food requirements. There is a debate as to whether food insecurity is a cause or a result of conflict in Somalia. In reality, conflict and food insecurity are concurrent and often mutually exacerbating factors. Conflict is one cause of food insecurity, but it is not the only one. Climate change also exacerbates insecurity too. A 2018 survey of farmers in Afgoye district in Lower Shabelle asked respondents about the key challenges to crop production. Some 55% of respondents said that climate change was a key obstruction and 60% cited water shortages, while 60% agreed that violence was a key challenge.[5]

Conflict does compound other drivers of food insecurity. Violence causes displacement, which prevents farmers from harvesting their crops. Likewise, the urbanisation that results from displacement reduces the amount of food being produced domestically. This in turn impacts livelihoods in the longer term and economic development. Agricultural products represent 93% of Somalia's exports and are responsible for 75% of its GDP.[6] Declines in the yields of these products have a negative impact on the national economy. As Somalia's conflict increases the dependence of the population on food aid, the availability of which reduces the market value of farmers' crops, which in turn impacts agricultural production.

Trends

AMISOM's mandate is meant to end after a 2020 general election – intended to be Somalia's first election with universal suffrage since the start of military rule in 1969. At present, insecurity makes a one-person one-vote election impossible. Nevertheless, AMISOM has so far indicated that it is committed to this timeline, which would see the mission fully withdrawn by 2021. If the political deadlock between the federal and member-state governments continues, and if AMISOM maintains its departure date, Somalia faces a security vacuum, given the unpreparedness of the SNA to assume security responsibilities.

AMISOM is to begin drawing down its forces in 2019, a factor that will likely reduce its capacity to take territory from al-Shabaab, and to retain it. Drawdowns will require changes to the structure and distribution within the forward operating bases, which risks creating larger pockets of territory for al-Shabaab to gain a stronger foothold. Al-Shabaab has undoubtedly been depleted as a force since its peak in the late 2000s, and is thus unlikely to make major strategic gains while AMISOM remains in Somalia. Nevertheless, 2019 may see incremental gains for al-Shabaab as armed opposition to it thins. The key determinants of how the conflict will play out will be political ones. If the federal government and federal member states reconcile and recommit to building an effective SNA, reducing corruption and improving service provision, al-Shabaab will face a much stronger challenge in the medium term. Without these steps, however, Somalia's security will be deeply vulnerable.

Notes

[1] Vanda Felbab-Brown, 'Developments in Somalia', Brookings Institution, 14 November 2018.
[2] The Hiraal Institute, 'Al-Shabaab's Military Machine', 2019.
[3] The Hiraal Institute, 'Al-Shabaab's Military Machine', 2019.
[4] Internal Displacement Monitoring Centre, 'City of Flight: New and Secondary Displacements in Mogadishu', November 2018.
[5] Mohamed Ibrahim Abdi-Soojeede, 'Crop Production Challenges Faced by Farmers in Somalia: A Case Study of Afgoye District Farmers', *Agricultural Sciences*, vol. 9, no. 8, 30 August 2018.
[6] World Bank, 'Agriculture Remains Key to Somalia's Economic Growth and Poverty Reduction', 28 March 2018.

South Sudan

Overview

The conflict in 2018
The conflict between the government of South Sudan and rebel forces continued throughout 2018, although the number of armed clashes dropped during the latter part of the year. Fighting was concentrated in the Equatoria, Bahr el-Ghazal, Unity and Upper Nile regions.

In September 2018, President Salva Kiir, Riek Machar and several other opposition groups signed the Revitalised Agreement on the Resolution of the Conflict in the Republic of South Sudan (R-ARCSS) in Addis Ababa, Ethiopia. The National Salvation Front (NAS) and six other groups did not sign. As per its name, the agreement was intended to

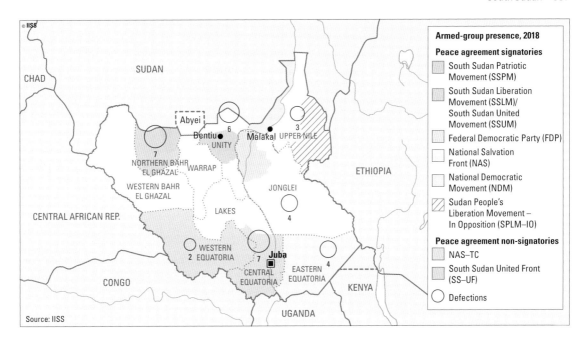

Armed-group presence, 2018

Peace agreement signatories

South Sudan Patriotic Movement (SSPM)

South Sudan Liberation Movement (SSLM)/ South Sudan United Movement (SSUM)

Federal Democratic Party (FDP)

National Salvation Front (NAS)

National Democratic Movement (NDM)

Sudan People's Liberation Movement – In Opposition (SPLM–IO)

Peace agreement non-signatories

NAS–TC

South Sudan United Front (SS–UF)

Defections

Source: IISS

revitalise the 2015 peace deal and end the conflict through a power-sharing arrangement. It had an immediate impact in reducing the number of armed clashes in the remainder of the year, although significant fighting continued in Eastern Equatoria State between the Sudan People's Liberation Movement/ Army (SPLM/A) and the non-signatory NAS–TC.

In July 2018, the United Nations Security Council passed Resolution 2428, extending sanctions to 31 May 2019 as laid out in Resolution 2206 (2015). The prohibition included a travel ban and assets freeze on two high-ranking individuals – an act South Sudan's representative described as a 'slap in the face' of those engaged in the ongoing peace-negotiation process. The US also placed sanctions on retired Israeli military official Israel Ziv, South Sudanese businessman Obac William Olawo and Gregory Vasili, Kiir's brother-in-law, as 'leading entities whose actions have extended the conflict'.[1] Ziv reportedly used an agricultural company as a front to supply arms and ammunition to both sides in the civil war. Approximately US$150 million worth of weapons were sold to the government, including rifles, grenade launchers and shoulder-fired rockets.

South Sudan's humanitarian situation remained dire in 2018. As of early 2018, there were approximately 2.2m South Sudanese refugees in neighbouring countries and 1.9m internally displaced persons (IPDs). Approximately 80% of recorded refugees and IDPs are women and

children. In February 2018, the UN Office for the Coordination of Humanitarian Affairs (OCHA) warned that, without humanitarian assistance, approximately 7m people (60% of the pre-crisis population) faced famine, while some 5.3m people — or 48% of the population — were estimated to be facing severe food insecurity in the post-harvest season.[2]

The conflict to 2018

South Sudan, the world's youngest nation, plunged into conflict in 2013 after Kiir accused then-vice-president Machar of attempting a *coup d'état*. The SPLM/A divided in two, with soldiers affiliated with Machar forming the SPLM–In Opposition (SPLM–IO). Soldiers loyal to Kiir then searched the streets, hunting for ethnic Nuer thought to be loyal to Machar. Fighters from both sides went on a killing rampage, raping and pillaging their way through towns and villages. As reports of massacres began to

Key statistics	
Type:	Internationalised
IDPs total (2018):	1,900,000
IDPs new (2018):	no data
Refugees total (2018):	2,215,000
Refugees new (2018):	110,000
People in need (2018):	7,100,000

Sub-Saharan Africa

spread, so did revolts across the country. The conflict that had predominantly been between two old rivals and over disagreements within the SPLM/A quickly turned into a conflict where ethnicity was used as a recruitment mechanism and split the country down ethnic lines, contributing to rifts between tribes and subsections of society.

The two main groups signed the Agreement on the Resolution of the Conflict in the Republic of South Sudan (ARCSS) on 17 August 2015. However, the security situation worsened and the agreement subsequently fell apart. Kiir would later go on to form a Transitional Government of National Unity (TGoNU) in April 2016 with SPLM–IO general Taban Deng Gai as vice-president but without opposition leader Machar. Machar returned to Juba in 2016, but fighting broke out between the forces of Kiir and Machar only a few weeks later, leaving 300 people dead and starting a new wave of displacement and violence.

Forces

Since the outbreak of conflict and the formation of the SPLM–IO in December 2013, 19 major new armed groups have emerged. This number does not include many of the smaller local self-defence militia groups that emerged as community-protection forces against the SPLM/A.

The number of shifts in allegiance decreased in 2018, but there were still between 31 and 33 defections of commanders and generals to and from the SPLM/A or to other existing rebel groups or to form new groups. Some splinter groups defected back to the SPLM/A, while other forces joined the NAS or SPLM–IO.

Sudan People's Liberation Movement/Army (SPLM/A) (now South Sudan People's Defence Forces)

President Salva Kiir heads the Sudan People's Liberation Movement/Army (SPLM/A). Prior to the outbreak of fighting in 2013, the SPLM/A had 745 generals – 41 more than the four branches of the United States armed forces combined.[3] In 2018, Kiir continued to use promotion to shore up his support in the army, promoting an additional 120 army officers to the rank of major general in August. There were still some defections from the SPLM/A in 2018, while a few opposition groups decided to return to the SPLM/A since the signing of the R-ARCSS. In October, Kiir renamed the SPLA the South Sudan People's Defence Forces (SSPDF).

Sudan People's Liberation Movement–In Opposition (SPLM–IO)[4]

The Sudan People's Liberation Movement–In Opposition (SPLM–IO) consists of a heterogeneous group of political and military rebels led by former South Sudanese vice-president Riek Machar. Machar, a Nuer and the third-in-command (after John Garang and Salva Kiir) in the early days of the SPLM/A, broke with the SPLM/A in 1991 and commanded troops that led the massacres in Bor district, killing almost 2,000 civilians. Machar rejoined the SPLM/A in 2002 but left again in 2013 to form the SPLM–IO. The SPLM–IO includes prominent leaders such as General Johnson Olony, who defected from the SPLM/A in 2014 and once included Taban Deng Gai, the current First Vice-President of South Sudan, who was widely believed to be the mastermind behind the July 2016 fighting in Juba designed to remove Machar as head of the SPLM–IO.

National Salvation Front (NAS), now NAS and NAS–TC

Prior to August 2018, the National Salvation Front (NAS) was led by Thomas Cirillo Swaka, who is from the country's Equatoria region and was previously associated with SPLM–IO. Cirillo was Kiir's former deputy head of logistics who resigned in February 2017 and accused the president of turning South Sudan into a 'tribal army'. The group also refused to sign the R-ARCSS in 2018 and aims to establish a genuine federal system focused on managing and administering land. In 2018, Butrus George, a commander heading a group of 400 soldiers, defected from the SPLM–IO to the NAS. In August 2018, the NAS spilt into two – NAS and NAS–TC – the latter being led by Cirillo.

South Sudan–United Front (SS–UF)

Formed in April 2018, the South Sudan–United Front (SS–UF) is led by Paul Malong, South Sudan's former military chief who attempted to stamp out the SPLM–IO in July 2016. The SS–UF was founded to 'arrest the carnage' of South Sudan's ongoing civil war. Malong was formerly the governor of Northern Bahr el-Ghazal State and South Sudan's military chief, and widely perceived as the true power behind Kiir's presidency.

Malong is perceived as a threat to South Sudan,

Table 1: List of armed groups operating in South Sudan, December 2018				
Armed Group Name	**Leadership**	**Association**	**Established**	**Zones of Control**
Federal Democratic Party (FDP)	Gabriel Changson	Opposition (South Sudan Opposition Alliance; SSOA)	August 2015	Fangak
National Democratic Movement (NDM)–Tiger Faction New Forces (TFNF)	Lam Akol	Opposition (SSOA)	September 2016	Fashoda
National Salvation Front (NAS)	Khalid Butrous	Opposition (SSOA)	March 2017	Kapoeta, Imatong, Yei River, Murle
South Sudan Liberation Movement (SSLM)	Bapiny Montuil	Opposition (SSOA)	October 2016	Northern Liech
South Sudan National Movement for Change (SSNMC)	Joseph Bakosoro	Opposition (SSOA)	January 2017	Amadi, Gbudwe, Maridi, Tambura, Yei River
South Sudan Patriotic Movement (SSPM)	Costello Garang, Abdel Bagi Ayii	Opposition (SSOA)	April 2017	Aweil East
South Sudan United Movement (SSUM)	Peter Gadet	Opposition (SSOA)	July 2017	Northern Liech
South Sudan People Defence Force (SSPDF), formerly Sudan People's Liberation Movement/Army (SPLM/A)/Transitional Government of National Unity (TGoNU)–South Sudan Armed Forces	Salva Kiir	Government		Presence throughout the country, excluding opposition areas
Sudan People's Liberation Movement–In Opposition (SPLM–IO)	Riek Machar	Opposition	December 2013	Greater Upper Nile, Greater Equatoria (Yei River, Gbudwe, Maridi, Amadi, Kapoeta and Imatong) and Greater Bahr-el Ghazal (Wau and Lol)
United Democratic Republic Alliance (UDRA)	Gatwech Koang Thich	Opposition (SSNDA)	February 2017	changing zone
National Agenda (NA)	Joseph Ukel Abango	Opposition (SSOA)	Not known	changing zone
South Sudan National Democratic Alliance (SSNDA), groups include NAS–TC	Thomas Cirillo Swaka and Kornelio Kon Ngu	Opposition (SSNDA)	Early November 2018	changing zone
People's Democratic Movement (PDM)	Hakim Dario	Opposition (SSOA)	Not known	changing zone
SPLM Leaders Former Detainees (SPLM/A–FDs), a group of 10 former detainees (G-10)	Pagan Amum	Opposition (SSOA)	Not known (est. 2014)	changing zone
People's Liberal Party (PLP), umbrella parties in the High-Level Revitalization Forum in Addis Ababa, Ethiopia	Peter Mayen Majongdit	Opposition (SSOA)	Not known	changing zone
South Sudan United Front (SS–UF)	Paul Malong/ William Ezekiel Kujo Deng	Opposition	April 2018	changing zone
Shilluk Agwelek militia	Loyal to Johnson Olony	n/a	Not known	Shilluk land in South Sudan's Upper Nile
South Sudan People's Patriotic Front (SSPPF)		n/a	October 2015	

and the SS–UF was not invited to the June 2018 peace talks in Khartoum. However, Malong's position weakened when he was relieved of his duties as chair of the SS–UF and reappointed interim chair. Brigadier General Chan Garang told reporters in August that he and more than 300 officers and soldiers were leaving the SS–UF and coming back to the government side.

National Democratic Movement (NDM)

The National Democratic Movement (NDM) is a Shilluk rebel group led by the former agriculture minister Lam Akol. The group is made up of members from the Tiger Faction New Forces who fought during the second Sudanese conflict with the aim of reversing the creation of 28 states in August 2015.

People's Democratic Movement (PDM)

The People's Democratic Movement (PDM) is led by Hakim Dario. The PDM rejected[5] the R-ARCSS and split from the South Sudan Opposition Alliance (SSOA) to join a new coalition called the South Sudan National Democratic Alliance (SSNDA). Within this group was Josephine Lagu Yanga, a former member of the PDM negotiating team who was sacked and later announced she would be leading members to support the R-ARCSS. Yanga is the daughter of the former leader of the Anya Nya who was defeated by the SPLM/A under John Garang.

South Sudan National Movement for Change (SSNMC)

The South Sudan National Movement for Change (SSNMC) is led by Joseph Bangasi Bakosoro, the former governor of Western Equatoria State, although in September 2018 a faction of the group announced that he had been removed as chairman due to his endorsement of R-ARCSS. However, several SSNMC military commanders rejected the faction's announcement and asserted that Bakosoro remained the leader of the group.

Shilluk Agwelek militia

The Agwelek forces have fought alongside both the SPLM/A and the SPLM–IO. Primarily focused on defending Shilluk land in Upper Nile State, the group is predominantly loyal to General Johnson Olony, who sides with the SPLM–IO. In 2018, sources on the ground said Olony was moving troops along the border in preparation for an attack.

| Drivers

Structural tensions within SPLM/A

Since its foundation in 1982, the SPLM/A has suffered from structural divisions related to leadership style, the overall aim of the group and power sharing. Fundamental differences emerged with regard to the desirability of maintaining a united Sudan or campaigning for secession of the south, while the planned transfer of power from President Kiir to vice-president Machar failed to take place, precipitating the group's split in 2013. The political and structural divisions within the SPLM led to the mobilisation of fighters along ethnic lines (Kiir belongs to the Dinka community while Machar is a Nuer). In 2013, this led to significant violence along ethnic lines, which has resulted in ethnicity becoming a dimension of the conflict. However, the relationship between ethnicity and the conflict in South Sudan is more complex than a Nuer–Dinka dichotomy, given that the two main tribes in the country are internally heterogeneous and politically separated.[6] This has allowed subnational leaders to resourcefully shift associations, aggravating South Sudanese politics.

Creation of states

Fuelling the conflict has been Kiir's practice of signing peace agreements and then decreeing by presidential order the creation of new states that benefit Dinka communities. It is widely believed the Jieng Council of Elders, a group of Dinka leaders who advise Kiir, has put pressure on Kiir to create more states. In December 2015, Kiir increased the number of states from ten to 28, with a further four being created in January 2017, taking the total number to 32. (This was done without consultation with the parties to the August 2015 peace agreement, opposing groups or local communities.) The creation of the additional states further eroded the capacity of local chiefs, weak (or non-existent) state institutions and local government systems, causing considerable tensions at the national level and fuelling local conflicts across the country. The division

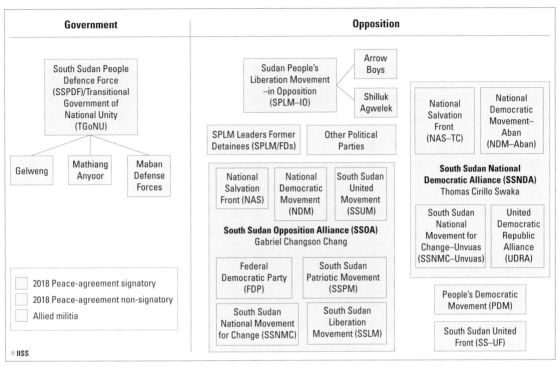

Figure 1: Conflict parties

of states has created significant problems in the former states of Upper Nile, Equatoria and Western Bahr el-Ghazal, particularly for communities from the Shilluk Kingdom in the Upper Nile. This system has in turn fuelled the rise of local rebel groups and splinter groups who are determined to claim back land that they see as rightfully theirs, and thus chose not to sign the R-ARCSS. The creation of states along ethnic lines also not only creates further division among the ethnic communities but also allows tribal areas to be consolidated to preserve indigenous majority rule in the area.

Abuse of power

The SPLM/A and its political leaders have been engrossed in short-term political management that serves the needs of the individual leaders and not the people of South Sudan. The SPLM/A's power extends to its absolute control over the executive and legislative arms of government: all policies that the government implements come from the SPLM/A political programme. Within this framework, the SPLM/A has ignored the value of political experience and competency as required criteria for appointments. Governors appointed to the 32 states are active generals or returning political defectors

and many became ministers or legislators overnight, without any formal experience. Capacity in the local councils and districts suffered as a result of this political manoeuvring. The SPLA/M position has instead strengthened, thanks to the centrally appointed governors supporting the government agenda.

Weak leadership

Since 2005, South Sudan has experienced a combination of disintegration of local institutions and communal networks and ethnic segmentation. Weak institutions and poor economic management characterised South Sudan under the SPLM/A and the National Congress Party (NCP) when the country was still part of Sudan. During 2018, weak leadership at both the national and local levels continued to erode the few governance systems that existed within the country.

Since the signing of the Comprehensive Peace Agreement in 2005, the sole focus of South Sudan and the UN Mission in Sudan (UNMIS), later renamed UN Mission in South Sudan (UNMISS) has lacked a strategy for resolving many of the local tensions or inter-communal pastoral infighting and instead focused on building the new state from the centre.[7]

Political and Military Developments

The Khartoum Declaration for power sharing

In June 2018, Sudanese President Omar al-Bashir facilitated a meeting between Kiir and Machar in Addis Ababa, Ethiopia, in an attempt to broker an agreement between the parties. Many saw Bashir's intervention as an effort to salvage the Sudanese economy, given that Sudan is dependent on oil, the production of which relies on South Sudan's oil infrastructure, which was damaged when war broke out in 2013, drastically cutting oil supplies. At a subsequent meeting in Khartoum on 5 August 2018, Kiir and Machar signed a preliminary power-sharing agreement that laid the groundwork for Machar to be returned as first vice-president, as well as creating the provision for an additional four vice-presidents. The deal puts in place a framework for creating a new transitional government by May 2019, which includes a process for choosing ministers and sets requirements for the participation of women and rebel groups. The Khartoum Declaration also promised a permanent ceasefire, reforms in the security sector, rehabilitation of oil wells and the improvement of the South Sudan infrastructure, although as of December 2018 no tangible steps had been made to achieve these milestones.

R-ARCSS peace agreement

Kiir, Machar and several other opposition groups under the South Sudan Opposition Alliance (SSOA) umbrella signed the R-ARCSS in September 2018. As part of the agreement, parliament will expand from 440 to 550 members to accommodate opposition groups and the various armed groups operating in the country. Machar will be also reinstated as first vice-president, along with four other vice-presidents. The R-ARCSS also mandates power sharing at state and local government levels, including the allocation of official positions (including governors, speakers of state legislatures and councils of ministers) as TGoNU 55%, SPLM–IO 27%, SSOA 10% and OPP 8%.

However, there were signs in late 2018 that the implementation of the agreement was falling behind the mandated schedule. Under R-ARCSS, the country will retain the 32-state system. As part of the deal, an Independent Boundaries Commission (IBC) – designed to consider the number and boundaries of the states – was to be established within two weeks of the agreement being signed, but was still not in place as of December 2018. Notably, there are no monitoring and enforcement mechanisms in the R-ARCSS to hold the TGoNU accountable (R-ARCSS

Figure 2: Selected key events

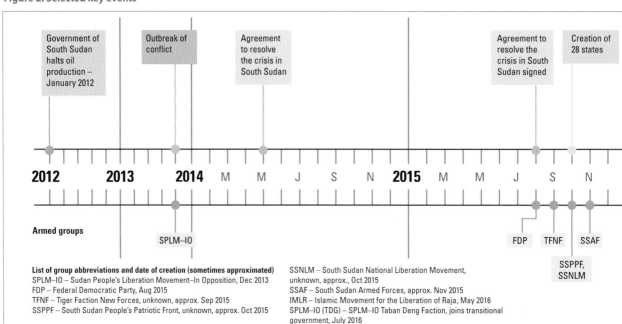

states: 'the parties shall agree on self-monitoring mechanisms'). This makes it harder for the African Union's Ad hoc Peace and Security Committee for South Sudan (the C5, comprising Algeria, Chad, Nigeria, Rwanda and South Africa), the UN and the Intergovernmental Authority on Development (IGAD) to hold the parties accountable. In 2018, the UN Security Council, the AU and IGAD made little effort to punish ceasefire violations.

Questions also remain over how opposition forces will be integrated into a unified army. The R-ARCSS stipulates that the armed groups are to

be integrated into a single unified force within eight months of signing the agreement; they are to be screened and classified according to known military criteria; and clear criteria are to be followed for recruitment in the army, police, national security and other services. Ineligible individuals shall be referred to disarmament, demobilisation and re-integration (DDR). Uncertainty remains over how this programme will be implemented and funded, given that Troika members (the US, United Kingdom and Norway) did not agree to the agreement and have resisted funding the implementation process.

Violent Events

In June 2018, government forces launched counter-insurgency operations in south and west Wau, northwestern South Sudan, forcing thousands to flee to the UN protection of the civilian camp in Wau. In May, there was a surge of violence in Unity State between government forces loyal to Vice-President Taban Deng and opposition forces. The two sides clashed over territory, which was likely linked to the government's attempt to consolidate power before signing a peace agreement. Heavy fighting was also reported in September between the South

Sudanese army and SPLM/A–IO in Equatoria and Unity regions when the government army attacked opposition forces in Mirmir and Kuok payams in Southern Liech State and in Mundu area, Lainya county in Yei River State.

Overall levels of violence and armed clashes dropped after the R-ARCSS was signed in September 2018. The number of recorded incidents in 2018 was around 250, mainly comprising the armed clashes between SPLM/A and NAS–TC in the Equatorial region. During the latter parts of the year, after the

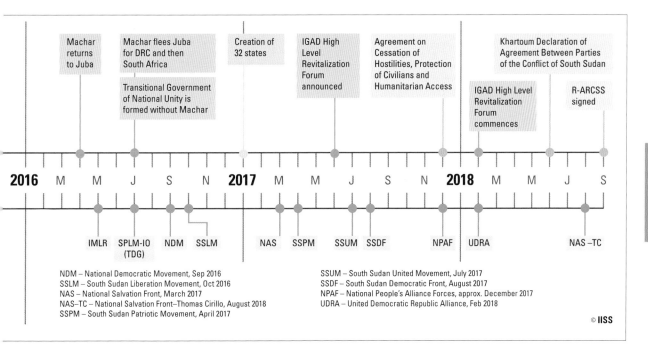

NDM – National Democratic Movement, Sep 2016
SSLM – South Sudan Liberation Movement, Oct 2016
NAS – National Salvation Front, March 2017
NAS–TC – National Salvation Front–Thomas Cirillo, August 2018
SSPM – South Sudan Patriotic Movement, April 2017

SSUM – South Sudan United Movement, July 2017
SSDF – South Sudan Democratic Front, August 2017
NPAF – National People's Alliance Forces, approx. December 2017
UDRA – United Democratic Republic Alliance, Feb 2018

© IISS

Sub-Saharan Africa

signing of the peace agreements, fighting occurred in Mukaya Payam, north of Yei town, and in Rokon area west of the capital Juba on the Juba–Maridi road. The main towns – Yei and Rokon – of the Greater Equatoria region were largely quiet after the agreement was signed, but armed clashes continued to displace populations in rural areas of southern Central Equatoria State (Morobo, Yei, Lainya and Kajo-Keji counties), in Mundri East county (Western Equatoria State) and in Kapoeta South county (Eastern Equatoria State).

Impact

Attacks on aid workers

In 2018, South Sudan was ranked the most dangerous place for humanitarian-aid workers for the third consecutive year according to research by Humanitarian Outcomes, with approximately one-third of the total attacks on aid workers across 22 countries taking place in South Sudan. In September, ten soldiers were sentenced for an attack on the Terrain hotel in 2016, just after the outbreak of fighting in Juba, in which 50 to 100 soldiers stormed the building, killing a South Sudanese journalist and raping foreign aid workers.

Humanitarian impact

A study published by the London School of Hygiene and Tropical Medicine in September 2018 estimated that 382,000 people had died between December 2013 and April 2018 as a result of the conflict.[8] By the end of December 2018, the UN High Commissioner for Refugees (UNHCR) reported that there were more than 2.2m refugees, while OCHA reported 1.87m IDPs. As of 31 December 2018, there were more than 789,098 South Sudanese refugees in Uganda, 852,080 in Sudan and 422,240 in Ethiopia.

The delivery of aid in South Sudan is seven times more expensive than Somalia, largely because of the logistical difficulty in moving aid around a country with almost non-existent infrastructure. According to a World Bank report, less than 2% of the country's primary road network was paved as of 2011.[9] Humanitarian funding remained below what was needed, with OCHA reporting that only 61% of the US$1.7 billion target had been received in 2018.[10]

Civilian victimisation

On 30 November 2018, Médecins Sans Frontières (MSF) reported that it had treated 125 women and girls who were raped, beaten and brutalised in Rubkona county, northern South Sudan, in the ten days between 19 and 29 November 2018. MSF found that some of the girls were as young as ten years old, while other women were older than 65. Many of the survivors had been whipped, beaten or clubbed with sticks and rifle butts.

Economy

When conflict broke out in 2013, the government of South Sudan halted oil production, hampering its own economy as well as that of Sudan. The country's GDP per capita dropped from US$1,111 in 2014 to under US$200 in 2017. South Sudan's economic collapse continued in 2018, although inflation slowed to 49% in September 2018 from 161% in March 2018 (inflation peaked at 835% in October 2016). The slowing inflation was due to the resumption of oil production after Sudan and South Sudan signed an agreement on 27 June in Khartoum that paved the way for the joint repair of oil infrastructure damaged by conflict. South Sudan is the most oil-dependent country in the world, with oil accounting for almost all exports and approximately 60% of the country's GDP. Outside the oil sector, livelihoods are concentrated in agriculture and pastoralism, which have been severely disrupted by the fighting.

International community

The international community remains divided over South Sudan. The US demonstrated little interest in the situation in 2018 and continued to threaten to cut aid. The lack of funds affected the ability of the Ceasefire and Transitional Security Arrangements Monitoring Mechanism in South Sudan (CTSAMM) to properly monitor the peace agreement. (CTSAMM monitors the warring parties through its Monitoring and Verification Teams (MVTs) located in 12 of the most conflict-affected areas in South Sudan.) US President Donald Trump's new policy for Africa focused on cutting loans and other resources to the South Sudanese government.

Trends

Uncertain prospects for peace agreement

So far, Kiir has failed to promote dialogue with existing armed groups and an environment favourable to peace. The president instead focused on consolidating power and strengthening his position in the capital and the region.

For peace to succeed, the transitional government (to be established in May 2019) will need to negotiate fairly with individual armed groups and engage with disaffected communities at the grassroots level. However, the parties involved in this agreement have yet to show a genuine commitment to and ownership of peace internally. South Sudan could revert to a stateless entity if the current peace agreement fails again, which could lead to a wave of widespread famine and conflict. Such a vast ungoverned space would create a severe regional security vacuum.

The peace deal requires focus on the national level, but also local mechanisms to help support local peace processes. The implementation of the peace accord must also strike the right balance between peace and justice, in which it may be hampered by a lack of institutional capacity. It is unclear that the judicial system in South Sudan will be able to handle many of the cases that have emerged from the fighting at the local levels. Many of the SPLM/A troops and leaders could be prosecuted, and it is clear that South Sudan's leaders would not accept such a scenario.

The methods of enforcement and implementation of the peace agreement must be sufficiently resilient to deal with spoiler groups who may seek to undermine or overturn the agreement. As this new and highly fragmented nation continues to battle with itself, the prospects of peace in South Sudan will likely remain dim for the next year.

Sudan's influence may decrease levels of violence

The involvement of Sudanese President Omar al-Bashir in support of the R-ARCSS peace talks between the SSOA and the government of South Sudan indicates that violence may decrease in 2019. The agreement appears to have led to a reduction in fighting in 2018, but it remains to be seen if this reduction will continue once the rainy season (approximately the end of April to the end of November) has passed in 2019. (There tends to be less fighting during the rainy season due to undeveloped roads and non-existent transport links.) However, if the protest in Sudan continues, this could undermine Bashir's ability to control Machar's rebels, who may try to renege on the agreement.

Notes

1   US sanctions were also placed on Information Minister Michael Makuei, high-ranking military official Malek Reuben and former army chief General Paul Malong.

2   World Food Programme, 'Nearly two-thirds of the population in South Sudan at risk of rising hunger', UN Children's Fund, Food and Agriculture Organization of the United Nations, 26 February 2018; Integrated Food Security Phase Classification (IPC), 'South Sudan Key IPC Findings: January–July 2018', 26 February 2018.

3   World Bank, 'South Sudan–Country Engagement Note', 7 November 2017; Alex DeWaal, 'Visualizing South Sudan: The Culprit: The Army', World Peace Foundation, 13 March 2014.

4   Small Arms Survey, 'The SPLM-in-Opposition', Human Security Baseline Assessment for Sudan and South Sudan, September 2015.

5   'South Sudan president says Awan has to return to prove his innocence', *Sudan Tribune*, 8 January 2018.

6   Cherry Leonardi, Leben Nelson Moro, Martina Santschi and Deborah H. Isser, 'Local Justice in Southern Sudan', United States Institute of Peace, 24 September 2010; Øystein H. Rolandsen, 'Land, Security and Peace Building in Southern Sudan', Peace Research Institute Oslo, December 2009.

7   Robert Gerenge, 'South Sudan's December 2013 conflict: Bolting state-building fault lines with social capital', *African Journal on Conflict Resolution*, vol. 15, no. 3, January 2015, pp. 85–109.

8   Francesco Checchi, Adrienne Testa, Abdihamid Warsame, Le Quach and Rachel Burns, 'Estimates of crisis-attributable mortality in South Sudan, December 2013–April 2018', London School of Hygiene and Tropical Medicine, September 2018.

9   Rupa Ranganathan and Cecilia M. Briceño-Garmendia, 'South Sudan's Infrastructure: A Continental Perspective', World Bank, Policy Research Working Paper, September 2011.

10 UN Office for the Coordination of Humanitarian Affairs (OCHA), 'Humanitarian Bulletin: South Sudan', no. 12, 30 December 2018.

Sub-Saharan Africa

Sudan

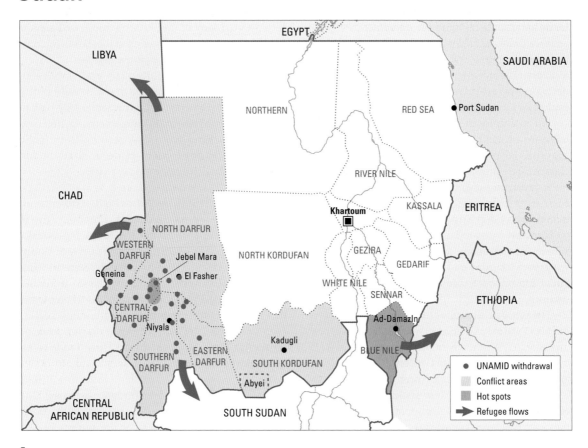

| Overview

The conflict in 2018

Despite slow progress in the peace process, violence continued to decrease in 2018, as insurgencies in Darfur and the Two Areas (the states of Blue Nile and South Kordofan) faltered while the government continued to consolidate its territorial control. In the Two Areas, the year was notable for the continued absence of air attacks by government forces and the declaration of a ceasefire between the two rival Sudan People's Liberation Movement/Army–North (SPLM/A–N) factions in mid-February. In Darfur, fighting remained restricted to the Jebel Marra front, where the Sudanese armed forces sought to eliminate the last positions controlled by the Sudan Liberation Movement faction led by Abdel Wahid al-Nur (SLM/A–AW). The other main Darfur rebels – the Justice and Equality Movement (JEM) and the SLM/A branch led by Minni Minnawi (SLM/A–MM) – remained inactive in the region and agreed

to resume peace talks in the framework established by the Doha Document for Peace in Darfur (DDPD).

Although clashes involving rebels and government forces decreased, violence against civilians continued throughout the year, including raids by the Rapid Support Forces (RSF); attacks on internally displaced persons (IDPs) and returnees; and abductions, sexual violence and intercommunal clashes. Despite continued insecurity, the United Nations–African Union Hybrid Operation in Darfur (UNAMID), which deployed in 2006, continued to reduce its peacekeeping activities in line with its intention to exit Sudan by 2020.

As of the end of December 2017, there were approximately two million IDPs in the country.[1] As of late 2018, there were approximately 337,200 Sudanese refugees in Chad, 273,100 in South Sudan, 44,600 in Ethiopia, 10,800 in Libya and 3,000 in Uganda. The humanitarian situation remained precarious for displaced people, whom the government is increasingly encouraging to return home despite ongoing attacks on returnees. While humanitarian agencies benefited from decreased restrictions on their activities following the lifting of US sanctions on Sudan in October 2017, logistical issues and government bureaucracy continued to pose obstacles to aid delivery. Disagreements between the SPLM–N and the government over aid also prevented humanitarian access in the Two Areas, but the government's acceptance of a UN proposal to provide aid in South Kordofan in September may improve the humanitarian situation in the region. Finally, starting in mid-December, a massive wave of protests calling for regime change spread across the country, threatening President Omar al-Bashir's 30-year rule.

The conflict to 2018

Sudan has been affected by multiple civil wars since independence in 1956. The current conflict consists of protracted rebellions in Darfur and the Two Areas. In Darfur, rebels took up arms against the government in 2003 to fight against the marginalisation of 'non-Arab' tribes in the region.[2] The government responded with the mass killing of civilians by the armed forces and the paramilitary Janjaweed (a militia composed of nomadic, mostly Arab tribesmen), leading to an International Criminal Court (ICC) indictment against Bashir for war crimes and crimes against humanity in 2009, and for genocide in 2010. At least 300,000 people have been killed in the conflict to date.[3]

In Blue Nile and South Kordofan states, the conflict originates in the war between Khartoum and the rebels of the Sudan People's Liberation Movement/Army (SPLM/A) from 1983 to 2005 that ended with the signing of the Comprehensive Peace Agreement (CPA) in 2005. The referendum that led

Key statistics	
Type:	Internationalised
IDPs total (2017):	2,000,000
IDPs new (2018):	no data
Refugees total (2018):	715,000
Refugees new (2018):	15,000
People in need (2018):	5,500,000

to the independence of South Sudan in 2011 was not held in the Two Areas, despite the identification of the people from the Nuba Mountains and Blue Nile with the South. In a context of unresolved issues, including the failure to integrate SPLM/A fighters into the army, fighting broke out following the disputed election of a governor from the ruling National Congress Party (NCP) in South Kordofan in May 2011. When the SPLM/A faction that remained in the Two Areas (SPLM/A–N) rebelled against the government, demanding greater autonomy and reforms, Khartoum responded with counter-insurgency tactics similar to those employed in Darfur, including aerial bombings followed by ground attacks in civilian areas.

In 2011, the creation of the Sudan Revolutionary Front (SRF), an alliance between Sudan's main rebel groups, brought the two conflicts together by uniting the Darfur rebels with SPLA–N fighters. The violence intensified in 2013–14 when the government launched a series of dry-season offensives, relying on locally mobilised militias and shelling civilian villages to suppress rebellions in Darfur and the Two Areas. Fighting then started to scale down after the Sudanese government announced a unilateral ceasefire in both conflict zones in July 2016, ahead of the removal of US sanctions against the government.

Forces

The Sudanese armed forces currently fight alongside the RSF against two rival factions of the Sudan People's Liberation Movement–North (SPLM–N) in the Two Areas, and against the insurgents of the Sudan Liberation Movement faction led by Abdel Wahid al-Nur (SLM–AW) in the Jebel Marra front in Darfur. The other Darfur groups, the Justice and Equality Movement (JEM), the SLM branch led by

Minni Minnawi (SLM–MM) and the Transitional Council (SLM–TC), are now reportedly operating in the south of Libya and South Sudan, outside their initial strongholds in Darfur.

Sudanese armed forces

The Sudanese armed forces are composed of a regular army (estimated to number 100,000 personnel), a navy (1,300 personnel) and an air force (3,000 personnel). The army possesses weapons imported mostly from Russia, China and Bulgaria (as well as Iran until 2014), including battle tanks, armoured vehicles and reconnaissance vehicles. Sudan's Military Industry Corporation (MIC) also produces rockets, heavy artillery, machine guns and light weapons. The Sudanese armed forces' main objective is to suppress regional insurgencies and to maintain the regime of Bashir's National Congress Party (NCP), which has been in office since 1989.

While regularly renewing its unilateral ceasefires since 2016, the government continues to seek a military victory instead of a negotiated settlement with rebels, using force to prevent rebels from gaining control over new territory. The Sudanese armed forces have extensively used modified Antonov aircraft and attack helicopters against rebels and civilians suspected of supporting them in the past, but aerial bombardments have diminished since the government's ceasefire declaration in 2016. The regular armed forces fought less frequently against rebels in 2018, as counter-insurgency attacks are now mostly carried out by government militias.

Rapid Support Forces (RSF)

The Rapid Support Forces (RSF) is a militia set up by the government in 2013 to fight against rebel groups in the country, and is now the main counter-insurgency force in Darfur and the Two Areas. With an estimated size of 10,000 to 40,000 troops, the RSF is mainly composed of former Arab pastoralist militias, including the Janjaweed, which have been progressively integrated into the Sudanese armed forces and the National Intelligence and Security Service (NISS) since the mid-2000s.[4]

Formally merged into the Sudanese armed forces in January 2017, the RSF, led by Mohammed Hamdan Dagolo (also known as 'Hemmeti'), are now also in charge of patrolling the borders and countering various forms of dissent, including peaceful protests. Known for their scorched-earth strategies, the RSF operate jointly with the armed forces in counter-insurgency offensives. Often supported by aerial bombardments, militiamen storm villages to kill civilians before burning crops, destroying houses and looting property.[5] RSF fighters also engage in isolated attacks including cattle raids, rapes, looting and abductions.

Sudan Liberation Movement/Army (SLM/A) factions

Established in 2001 in Darfur with the objective to overthrow the Khartoum government, the Sudan Liberation Movement/Army (SLM/A) split in 2005 due to leadership rivalries and ethnic tensions within its ranks.

Abdel Wahid al-Nur faction (SLM/A–AW)

Operating in Jebel Marra, the Sudan Liberation Movement/Army–Abdel Wahid (SLM/A–AW) comprises around 1,000 fighters (mainly Fur, one of the largest 'non-Arab' ethnic groups in Darfur) who are skilled at guerrilla tactics in mountainous areas. The group is weaker than before, mainly due to Abdel Wahid's continuing self-imposed exile in Paris, where he has lived since 2006. The SLM/A–AW continues to fight against the armed forces and rejects the peace process, requesting that the government demobilise Arab militias, provide security for IDPs and reform land-ownership rights before the group enters into peace talks.

Minni Minnawi faction (SLM/A–MM)

Originally based in South and East Darfur states, the Sudan Liberation Movement/Army–Minni Minnawi (SLM/A–MM) is also present in South Kordofan State through its involvement in the SRF. Weakened in Sudan after it joined the government from 2006 to 2010 following a peace agreement, the faction is now strengthening its capacities in Libya alongside the Libyan National Army led by General Khalifa Haftar, allegedly in preparation for a return to insurgent fighting in Sudan. Minni Minnawi's exile outside Sudan has affected command and control and led to multiple internal divisions within the SLM/A–MM.

Transitional Council (SLM/A–TC)

Established in 2015 out of a group of SLM fighters defecting from the Abdel Wahid faction, this group is mainly composed of Fur fighters, and allegedly cooperates with the SLM/A–MM in Libya and South Sudan. The Sudan Liberation Movement/Army–Transitional Council (SLM/A–TC) leader, Mohammed Abdelsalam (also known as 'Tarada'), was reportedly executed by government forces in May 2017. In 2018, the SLM/A–TC reported the deaths of five of its detained members due to alleged torture and ill-treatment by the security services.

Justice and Equality Movement (JEM)

The Justice and Equality Movement (JEM) was created in 2003 in Darfur with the objective of toppling Bashir and addressing the regional marginalisation of non-Arab communities. The movement has an Islamist ideology and was led by Khalil Ibrahim, from the Zaghawa tribe, until his death in December 2011. The group is now led by Khalil's brother, Gibril. Although subject to splits and shifting alliances (the main breakaway faction being the JEM–Dabajo), the JEM is more disciplined and better equipped than the other groups. Once the most powerful group in Darfur after its 2008 attack on Omdurman, the rebel group appears to have left the region in 2013 to establish bases in Kordofan State, as well as in South Sudan and Libya.

Sudan People's Liberation Movement/Army–North (SPLM/A–N)

Emerging as the northern branch of the Sudan People's Liberation Movement/Army, which fought against the Sudanese government during the Second Sudanese Civil War from 1983 until the secession of South Sudan from Sudan in 2011, the SPLM/A–North (SPLM/A–N) now continues to fight against Khartoum in Blue Nile and South Kordofan states.

Coming from various tribes of the Nuba Mountains, SPLM/A–N fighters adhere to SPLM/A founder John Garang's 'New Sudan' ideology, aiming to address the marginalisation of peripheral regions. A large part of the SPLM/A–N's equipment comes from the capture of arms and vehicles from the Sudanese armed forces. Contrary to the Darfur rebels, the SPLM/A–N employs more conventional military equipment and tactics, preferring to seize and hold territory.

In March 2017, the SPLM/A–N split into two factions after disagreements over leadership and strategy. The faction based in South Kordofan State is led by Abdelaziz al-Hilu (SPLM/A–N al-Hilu), who prioritises demands for self-determination, and the faction based in the Blue Nile is led by Malik Agar, who advocates national reforms. In early 2018, the two forces repeatedly clashed in Blue Nile State.

Sudan Revolutionary Front (SRF) coalition

Established in 2011 with the aim of overthrowing Bashir, the Sudan Revolutionary Front (SRF) is a coalition of the main rebel groups in Sudan: the SLM/A–AW, SLM/A–MM, the JEM and the SPLM/A–N, and, since July 2018, the SLM/A–TC. The joint force is composed of troops and vehicles from the main rebel groups, which are mobilised on an ad hoc basis for military operations. The Front benefits from the combination of the Darfur groups' guerrilla tactics and use of 'technicals' (non-standard tactical vehicles) together with the SPLM/A–N's focus on territorial gains.

However, the coalition has not launched any major offensive since its raid on Abu Kershola in April 2013 and has been affected by internal divisions over the peace process. In October 2015, following disagreements over leadership, the rebel umbrella group split into two factions, which agreed to reunify in July 2018. While remaining committed to armed rebellion, the SRF is also part of the 'Sudan Call', an opposition coalition mainly composed of the SRF, the National Umma Party (NUP), the National Congress Party (NCP) and civil-society groups that seeks democratic change through comprehensive negotiations involving all rebel groups, instead of separate peace discussions for Darfur and the Two Areas. In 2018, the Sudan Call has repeatedly met with the AU High-Level Implementation Panel (AUHIP) to discuss the peace process.

Sudanese Revolutionary Awakening Council (SRAC)

Established in January 2014 and controlling positions around Kabkabiya in North Darfur State, the Sudanese Revolutionary Awakening Council (SRAC) is composed of local tribal chiefs and approximately 3,000 militiamen. The SRAC is led by former Janjaweed chief Musa Hilal, who has been alternating between supporting and opposing the government since 2003. Hilal was arrested in November 2017, along with members of the Borders Guards Force militia who refused to either hand over their weapons or join the RSF. Khartoum accuses the militia of seeking cooperation with the Darfuri rebel groups training alongside Haftar's forces in Libya, a claim rejected by Hilal. While initially wary of directly confronting Khartoum militarily, the SRAC officially announced the start of its armed struggle against the Sudanese armed forces in November 2018.

Drivers

Regional and ethnic cleavages

In the peripheral areas of the states of Darfur, Blue Nile and South Kordofan, rebellions emerged out of the grievances of marginalised non-Arab tribes over the political, cultural and socio-economic domination of Arab elites from Khartoum. Seeking to establish a homogeneous Muslim Arab culture as a national model, the NCP based its rule on identity politics to the detriment of minorities, notably through the appointment of Arab officials from the centre to leading local-government positions. Peripheral tribes' feeling of alienation favoured the emergence of insurgent political agendas directed at overthrowing the regime and establishing a multi-ethnic state. In Darfur, the *Black Book*, published anonymously in the early 2000s, expressed the frustrations of the Fur, Masalit and Zaghawa communities and motivated them to wage war against Khartoum.[6] Likewise, in the Two Areas, adherence to the revolutionary 'New Sudan' ideology, advocated by SPLM founder John Garang since the 1980s, encouraged members of the historically marginalised Nuba tribes to resume the SPLM/A's armed struggle in 2011.

Competition for resources

Sudan has a long history of intercommunal disputes over land, water, gold and other resources, often pitting nomadic herders against sedentary farmers. While these issues were resolved through communal mediation in the past, the regimes in place since independence have removed local governance mechanisms in order to reinforce their central authority. Furthering the colonial era's disruption of traditional land-allocation patterns, Khartoum's undermining of the ability of local chiefs to settle disputes encouraged ethnic rivalry as a basis for resource competition.[7] From the 1980s onwards, tensions over land and water were aggravated by environmental degradation and resource depletion, in a context of severe drought.[8] In addition to increased inter-clan resource competition, land dispossession and the unequal allocation of resources nurtured armed rebellions against the central government. In Blue Nile and South Kordofan states, rebels are resisting Khartoum's taxation of locals, citing the government's failure to remit any of the revenues generated by oil extraction in these areas back to the local people.[9]

Authoritarian rule

Bashir firmly controls Sudan's political system, having been in office since a military coup in 1989. While multi-party elections took place in 2010 and 2015, in practice the electoral process is marked by irregularities and fraud and political opponents are violently repressed. The public sector's inability to compensate for the redistributive functions of weakened traditional governance mechanisms, the absence of representative central institutions, along with harsh restrictions on freedom of expression, encourage marginalised communities to turn to armed struggle as a way to address their grievances. The sharia-based judiciary controlled by the security services enables arbitrary arrests and human-rights violations, and weak rule of law in conflict areas allows armed groups and governmental militias to perpetrate crimes against civilians with impunity. Because recognising the role of national politics in the conflict would highlight the need for reform, which could undermine his authority, Bashir prefers to adopt a piecemeal approach to the conflict by portraying the rebellions in Darfur and the Two Areas as distinct instances of local unrest.

Regional relations

Unresolved border issues and regional instability have also fuelled the conflicts. After South Sudan's independence in 2011, tensions remained between Khartoum and Juba over Abyei, an oil-rich area home to the northern Misseriya nomads and the southern sedentary Ngok Dinka. As the parties still disagree on the population eligible for a referendum, Khartoum exerts de facto administrative control, while the UN Interim Security Force in Abyei (UNISFA) peacekeeping force provides security in the region.

Khartoum and Juba have repeatedly accused each other of backing rebellions against their respective governments.[10] Similar accusations have been levelled at other neighbours, especially Libya and Chad, as the shared ethnicity of Darfur tribes with Chadian groups and former Libyan leader Muammar Gadhafi's support of Arab militias in the region have favoured the spread of insurrections across borders.[11] After the improvement of Sudan's relations with Chad in 2010 and the fall of Gadhafi in 2011, sources of support for Darfur armed groups subsided. However, in 2015 Darfur rebels began cooperating with various Libyan militias, thereby accessing new positions, equipment and personnel.

Political and Military Developments

Roadmap Agreement

Despite efforts to revive the African Union-mediated Roadmap Agreement – a two-track mechanism aiming to prepare rebels from both Darfur and the Two Areas to sign a ceasefire and resume peace negotiations with the government – negotiations between the main parties had reached a deadlock by the end of 2018.

In 2016, the government and some opposition groups had signed a first version of the Roadmap Agreement but subsequently failed to agree on a ceasefire (see **Figure 1**). In October 2016, the government concluded the national dialogue mandated by the Roadmap Agreement without the input of the Sudan Call group, which had boycotted the process. As the 2016 roadmap was rendered obsolete in the face of these political developments, the AU High-Level Implementation Panel (AUHIP) proposed to amend it in September 2018. Under the newly proposed Roadmap Agreement, the parties would take part in constitutional reforms and participate in the next presidential elections directly after signing a peace deal, without trust-building mechanisms and preparatory meetings. However, the Sudan Call rejected this proposal, viewing it as favouring the government. In December, the AUHIP suspended consultations with the coalition for an undetermined period after refusing to meet with Sudan Call members that did not take part in the 2016 process, including the SPLM/A–N faction led by Malik Agar.

Darfur peace talks

While the SLM/A–AW continued to reject the peace process, the JEM and the SLM/A–MM agreed to negotiate with Khartoum using the 2011 DDPD as a basis, on condition that a New Independent Implementation Mechanism (NIIM) for a future peace agreement was established. Following unsuccessful talks throughout the year, the government's eventual acceptance of this condition led to the signing of a pre-negotiation agreement in December, paving the way for future talks on a ceasefire agreement (planned for January 2019), followed by peace negotiations in Doha. The Sudan Call urged the mediation to extend these discussions to all of its members to make the process inclusive.

Two Areas talks

In February, the Sudanese government and SPLM/A–N al-Hilu faction held talks for the first time since August 2016, and repeatedly met during the remainder of the year, but failed to overcome their disagreement on humanitarian access. Fearing that the armed forces could use the flow of aid to send troops to rebel-controlled areas, the rebel group requested that part of the humanitarian aid be delivered through the border with Ethiopia, which the government viewed as a tactic to infiltrate weapons to isolated rebel positions. In November, the government accepted South Sudanese President Salva Kiir's offer to mediate peace negotiations with rebels in the Two Areas and to reunify the rival SPLM/A–N factions. The scope of this mediation remains unclear,

Figure 1: Previous peacemaking initiatives for Darfur (2006–16)

May 2006	May 2011 and April 2013	March 2016
Abuja Agreement (Darfur Peace Agreement)	**Doha Document for Peace in Darfur (DDPD)**	**Roadmap Agreement**
Signatories: GoS, SLM–MM Mediator: African Union	Signatories: GoS, Liberation and Justice Movement (LJM), JEM–Bashar Mediator: Qatar	Signatories: GoS, JEM, SLM–MM, SPLM–N, National Umma Party Mediator: African Union High Implementation Panel

as the government's chief negotiator later declared that talks under Kiir's facilitation would not supersede existing negotiation frameworks.

Disarmament

In July 2017, the Sudanese government initiated a disarmament campaign in Darfur and South Kordofan states. In October 2018, assessing that enough time had passed for civilians to hand over their weapons voluntarily, the authorities started a forcible phase of the operation. Officially aiming to fight against insecurity, the campaign has also been used as a counter-insurgency strategy, notably by targeting remaining border guards and tribal militias who refused to join the RSF. This approach generated new tensions, with the Hilal's Revolutionary Awakening Council (SRAC) beginning an armed insurgency against Khartoum in November, after members of Musa Hilal's Border Guard Forces were tried for refusing to hand in their weapons.

UNAMID withdrawal

In July, UNAMID reduced its troops from 8,735 to 4,050 and withdrew from ten sites in Darfur, in line with the mission's objective to exit Sudan by 2020. Due to ongoing fighting in Jebel Marra, the mission opened a new site in the area in 2018, but peacekeepers were repeatedly denied access by both rebels and government forces. While the UN Security Council used the reduction in violence to justify the mission's drawdown, the decision to exit Darfur amid ongoing insecurity appeared to be due to lack of resources, which could worsen if US President Donald Trump delivers on his intention to cut the United States' contributions to the UN peacekeeping budget. Improved relations between the US and EU and Sudan, following increased cooperation on counter-terrorism and migration issues, likely also played a role in ending UNAMID's mandate, which Khartoum has advocated for years. The withdrawal strategy sparked criticisms among the Darfur rebels, who continued to question the mission's neutrality after UNAMID head Jeremiah Mamabolo suggested that the UN take action against SLM/A–AW leader Abdel Wahid al-Nur for his continuation of armed rebellion in Darfur.

UNISFA

In September, the UN Security Council proposed to send additional troops for the UN Interim Security Force for Abyei (UNISFA), which has been deployed in the disputed region since 2011, in order to adapt the mission to continued tensions and the absence of local police authorities. Khartoum opposed the proposal, fearing that increased UNISFA presence would threaten its control over local administration. The UN Security Council eventually extended the mission's protection mandate until May 2019, decreasing troops from 4,500 to 4,140 while augmenting the police contingent from 50 to 345. While renewing the mandate to support the Joint Border Verification and Monitoring Mechanism (which tasks Sudan and South Sudan with monitoring a temporary buffer zone) until April 2019, the Security Council stressed that this extension would be the last one, unless the parties show progress in key issues, including border demarcation.

Regional relations

Sudan improved its relationships with several neighbouring countries in 2018. In 2017, relations with Egypt were tense after Khartoum accused Cairo of supporting Darfur rebels seeking to return from Libya, adding to unresolved territorial tensions over the disputed 'Hala'ib Triangle' and disagreements over Ethiopia's construction of a giant dam on the Nile. Seeking to ease their bilateral relations, Egyptian President Abdel Fattah al-Sisi and Bashir met in July 2018, agreeing later to establish a joint border-protection force, and to strategic partnerships and investments.

In addition to Egypt, Sudan also planned to set up joint patrolling forces with Libya and Ethiopia, citing the protection force already set up with Chad in 2010 as a model. The Sudanese government also decided to reopen its border with South Sudan, previously closed amid accusations that Juba was harbouring South Kordofan rebels.

South Sudanese peace agreement

In September 2018, the parties to the conflict in South Sudan, Kiir and former vice-president and current rebel leader Riek Machar signed a peace agreement (brokered by Khartoum) in Ethiopia. Khartoum and Juba agreed to the joint repair of oil installations that had been damaged by conflict, which could accelerate the resumption of oil production in South Sudan and benefit the Sudanese economy, which was severely hit by the loss of oil revenues following secession.

Protests

The last days of 2018 were marked by the rise of a mass popular protest against the Sudanese government. Following International Monetary Fund recommendations, Khartoum adopted austerity measures in early 2018, including restrictions on cash withdrawals and subsidy cuts for basic commodities. The subsequent surge in bread and fuel prices in January provoked a first wave of protests in Khartoum, which the authorities repressed by detaining dozens of people. Demonstrations and strikes then continued to take place sporadically throughout the year, leading to multiple detentions of protesters, activists and journalists. In mid-December, as the price of bread tripled, and in the midst of severe fuel and cash shortages, thousands of people demonstrated in Port Sudan (Red Sea State), Wad Madani (El Gezira State), Atbara and Berber (River Nile State) and Khartoum.

Starting as spontaneous anti-inflation demonstrations, the protests quickly intensified and spread across the country in late December, with people setting fire to governmental offices and calling for regime change. The movement was spearheaded by professional associations, civil-society actors and opposition parties, as well as parties defecting from the ruling coalition. As with previous protests, the authorities used tear gas, sticks and live ammunition to disperse the protesters. At least 37 people were killed in the first five days of protests alone and hundreds were detained. Despite the state of emergency in several states, and the reported social-media shutdown, thousands of people continued to take part in rallies demanding Bashir's resignation.

| Violent Events

Fighting in Jebel Marra

Fighting between the government and rebels continued in Jebel Marra, Darfur State, where the government sought to eliminate the last SLM/A–AW positions. During their offensives, the armed forces assaulted villages using heavy artillery against both rebel soldiers and unarmed civilians, displacing thousands of people. In early July, the government gained control of the last rebel stronghold in northern Jebel Marra, and the SLM/A–AW unsuccessfully attempted to recapture its base in Golol from the government. On 18 September, the SLM/A–AW announced a three-month unilateral ceasefire to allow the delivery of aid to civilians affected by the rainy season, while accusing the government of taking advantage of this ceasefire to pursue attacks in southern Jebel Marra using aircraft and artillery. In November, the RSF government militia announced its objective to eliminate all SLM/A–AW positions by February 2019. The other Darfur groups, the JEM–Gibril, the SLM/A–MM and the SLM/A–TC, repeatedly renewed their unilateral ceasefires and remained inactive.

Fighting in the Two Areas

Fighting in the Two Areas continued to scale down, although government forces and rebels clashed twice in the Blue Nile in 2018. The Sudanese armed forces continued to refrain from aerial bombings, having ceased such operations at the end of 2016. Along with the government's unilateral cessation of hostilities, the SPLM/A–N al-Hilu faction renewed its ceasefire, which has been in place since July 2017. However, in April 2018, the army and the RSF assaulted positions held by the SPLM/A–N Agar. According to the rebel group, which had declared a six-month unilateral ceasefire in December 2017, the RSF bombarded the group's forces in the Blue Nile's Taka and Kalkoa mountains and used aircraft to pinpoint rebel positions prior to the attack. The government militia announced the capture of multiple rebel positions in the region following the clashes. Another clash erupted on 7 December, during which the government reportedly attacked positions in the El Angessana Hills, where SPLM/A–N forces are stationed.

In February 2018, heavy fighting took place between the two SPLM/A–N factions in Blue Nile State, killing and injuring dozens of people and displacing at least 500 families. The Agar faction claimed that al-Hilu's forces moved into Blue Nile from the Nuba Mountains with tank crews and ammunition, but without sufficient skills and equipment to carry out extensive attacks. No fighting was reported after these clashes, and the SPLM/A–N Agar declared a unilateral cessation of hostilities on 3 March, which still held at the end of the year.

Sub-Saharan Africa

Impact

Displacement

Continued fighting and attacks on civilians in Darfur's Jebel Marra was the main cause of new displacement in 2018. Clashes between the Sudanese armed forces and the SLM/A–AW, along with intercommunal fighting, displaced thousands in nearby towns and mountainous caves. Around 11,500 people found refuge in Rokero town and Jemeza village alone.

In the Two Areas, communal fighting and internal conflict between the SPLM/A–N factions at the beginning of the year caused the internal displacement of approximately 12,000 people in Blue Nile State. This added to the 47,392 IDPs reported to be in need of aid in February 2018 in the area, at which time there were also 179,665 IDPs in need of humanitarian assistance in South Kordofan State.

Whereas the unilateral ceasefires renewed by the government and rebel groups alike were not fully implemented, the reduction of aerial bombings encouraged thousands of refugees and IDPs to spontaneously return to their hometowns. In January, the last group of Sudanese refugees in the Central African Republic returned to South Darfur after ten years of asylum. The lack of basic infrastructure, along with frequent attacks by militias and armed settlers occupying returnees' lands, pushed many IDPs in Darfur to refuse to leave their camps, leading to criticisms of the government's efforts to encourage returns without guaranteeing IDP protection. While Sudan, Chad and the UN High Commissioner for Refugees (UNHCR) planned to repatriate 20,000 Darfuri refugees from Chad in 2018 and facilitated the return of three convoys of refugees since April, the project was suspended due to insecurity and lack of resources. Resuming in November, these repatriation efforts allowed the return of 1,760 Sudanese refugees from Chad in 2018.

Food insecurity

Food insecurity in Sudan remained severe, affecting 4.7m people in 2018.[12] Inflation increased to 72.9% in December 2018 from 25.2% in December 2017,[13] undermining the purchasing power of vulnerable households and preventing them from buying food as the price of basic commodities surged. Civilians were particularly affected in rebel-controlled areas. Aid agencies recorded dire malnutrition in parts of Jebel Marra, Blue Nile and South Kordofan states as ongoing clashes amid floods and drought continued to impede food production. Impeded access to farmland due to the presence of settlers also prevented IDPs from cultivating their lands, threatening food supply for displaced people. In the Two Areas, ceasefire violations targeting agricultural lands forced civilians to move from rebel-held areas to government-controlled areas, where access to food is easier, which could be part of a deliberate government strategy to weaken rebel positions.

Humanitarian access

Approximately 5.5m people were in need of aid in Sudan as of February 2018, including 3.1m in Darfur.[14] Since the lifting of US sanctions in October 2017, humanitarian organisations, including the International Committee of the Red Cross (ICRC), reported reduced governmental restrictions for travelling and for launching new projects, but a new law requiring humanitarian organisations to obtain approval from a national partner to operate in Sudan posed new challenges to aid agencies. Complex bureaucratic procedures, poor infrastructure and low electricity supply, in addition to the fuel shortage that started earlier in the year, continued to prevent timely and efficient aid delivery.

These obstacles were even greater in rebel-controlled areas, where flows of people and goods remain limited. The continuing fighting in Jebel Marra temporarily slowed the delivery of basic services in the region, including the provision of water. The deadlock between Khartoum and the SPLM/A–N over the supply route for aid delivery has continued to prevent humanitarian access to the Two Areas. In South Kordofan State, the government accepted a UN initiative to deliver aid in rebel positions in late September, but the SPLM/A–N rejected it. Sudan remained on the United States' list of sponsors of terrorism, which restricts the country's eligibility for debt relief, investments and international aid. In November, the US expressed its readiness to remove Sudan conditional on progress in key areas, including humanitarian access.

Attacks on civilians

Fighting in Jebel Marra involved the destruction, burning and looting of civilian villages by government and RSF troops. There were also multiple reports of RSF members assaulting, killing, abducting and torturing civilians suspected of supporting the SLM/A–AW in Jebel Marra. In the Two Areas, attacks on unarmed civilians by government forces and allied militias continued, although information on such attacks remained scarce due to limited access. While the SPLM/A–N took action against perpetrators of human-rights violations within its own personnel, there was no evidence of the Sudanese government investigating or prosecuting soldiers responsible for crimes against civilians.

Efforts by local chiefs and security forces to disarm civilians and prevent the escalation of tensions encouraged an overall decrease in inter-communal violence, but clashes over land and large-scale cattle raids continued to take place in Darfur and the Two Areas. In Darfur, displaced farmers were repeatedly attacked by new settlers seeking to dissuade IDPs from returning to their villages. Women and girls working on their farms or picking firewood were the frequent targets of attacks by armed pastoralists, which included sexual violence, looting and murders.

Trends

Bashir's rule

Although Bashir previously declared his intention to resign from power in 2020, when the next elections are due to be held, the NCP appointed him as its candidate for the next elections by removing the two-term limit from its charter in August 2018. Condemning this decision, opposition movements started campaigning against the proposed constitutional amendments (required to allow Bashir to run again). The mass protests of December 2018, if sustained into 2019, could weaken the government and may lead Bashir's allies to force him to step down.

The protests may also have a bearing on the direction of peace talks. The exclusion from African Union-mediated peace negotiations of the SPLM–Agar faction, which supports the Sudan Call's objective to address national-governance issues through comprehensive talks, helped Khartoum's strategy of dividing the conflict into local issues and avoid discussing national reforms. The popular protests against Bashir at the end of 2018 may give weight to rebel groups' demands for a comprehensive peace framework that addresses national issues. Having officially supported the protesters' calls for regime change, rebel movements could be less willing to compromise if anti-government protests continue to intensify. This could further undermine the prospect of a negotiated settlement with the government.

Future sources of insecurity

The conflict could resume in Darfur outside Jebel Marra if the JEM, the SLM/A–MM and the SLM/A–TC use the resources and weapons received in exchange for their alleged mercenary activities in Libya to prepare for a potential return to fighting in Darfur.[15] In Blue Nile State, a future Sudanese armed forces offensive similar to the current operation in Jebel Marra could take place, as the government has reportedly been using the rise in resources induced by the removal of US sanctions in October 2017 to build up its military capabilities north of Blue Nile. Finally, the forceful phase of the disarmament campaign will likely allow the RSF to justify intensified attacks against targeted groups and communities.[16]

Displacement

In November, the government, with the help of the RSF, started to implement its plan to dismantle IDP camps and turn them into permanent residential areas in Darfur. In North Darfur State, the first step of the plan aims to resettle 45,000 people from the Abu Shouk, Al-Salam and Zam Zam camps. The authorities declared that IDPs would be given the option of either acquiring a parcel of land in the new settlements, resettling to existing towns or returning to their hometowns. Camp residents complained about being pressured to adopt the latter option amid ongoing violence against returnees.[17] The government's camp-dismantling policy, unresolved land-ownership issues for returnees, the presence of uncollected weapons among new settlers and a context of impunity that facilitates attacks by armed groups (including the RSF) on IDPs and returnees, will likely continue to create a climate of insecurity for displaced people in Darfur.

Sub-Saharan Africa

UNAMID withdrawal

In this context, UNAMID's withdrawal strategy could undermine the progress made in civilian protection and create a security vacuum in Darfur by leaving the area in the hands of the RSF, which is one of the main perpetrators of human-rights violations in Sudan.[18] The UN Security Council has claimed that the withdrawal has not had any negative impact so far, but precise information on the consequences of the UNAMID exit remains scarce.

Notes

[1]   Reliable figures on fatalities and displacement in Sudan remain scarce due to restricted access to affected areas, together with a lack of information on interrupted returns and renewed displacements. Using government information, the United Nations currently estimates the number of IDPs to have decreased from 2.3 million to 2m in 2017, but this number is still under verification. See OCHA, 'Sudan: Darfur Humanitarian Overview', 1 February 2018, p. 5.

[2]   The division between 'Arabs' and 'non-Arabs' in Sudan is the outcome of an ideological and political construct that simplifies a complex history of flexible ethnic identities. See Alex De Waal, *Famine That Kills: Darfur, Sudan,* 2nd edn, (Oxford: Oxford University Press, 2005), p. iv.

[3]   This official UN estimate has not been updated since 2008.

[4]   IISS, *The Military Balance 2018* (Abingdon: Routledge for the IISS, 2018), p. 439; UN Security Council, 'Final report of the Panel of Experts on the Sudan established pursuant to resolution 1591 (2005)', S/2017/1125, 28 December 2017, p. 10, paragraph 26.

[5]   Akshaya Kumar and Omer Ismail, 'Janjaweed Reincarnate Sudan's New Army of War Criminals', *Enough Project*, June 2014.

[6]   Alex Cobham, 'Causes of Conflict in Sudan: Testing The Black Book', *European Journal of Development Research*, vol. 17, no. 3, 2005, pp. 462–80.

[7]   Ahmad Sikainga, 'The World's Worst Humanitarian Crisis: Understanding the Darfur Conflict', *Origins: Current Events in Historical Perspective,* vol. 2, no. 5, February 2009.

[8]   Jeffrey Mazo, 'Chapter Three: Darfur: The First Modern Climate-Change Conflict', in *The Adelphi Papers*, IISS, vol. 49, no. 409, 2009: pp. 73–86.

[9]   International Crisis Group, 'Sudan's Spreading Conflict (I): War in South Kordofan', Africa Report No. 198, February 2013, p. i.

[10]   Security Council Report, 'Sudan and South Sudan, June 2015 Monthly Forecast', 1 June 2015.

[11]   Sikainga, 'The World's Worst Humanitarian Crisis'.

[12]   OCHA, 'Sudan: Humanitarian Dashboard', June 2018.

[13]   'Sudan's inflation rise to 72,94% in December', *Sudan Tribune,* 19 January 2019.

[14]   The 0.7 million increase compared to the prior year is partially due to improved access to needs assessments in previously unreachable areas. OCHA, 'Humanitarian Needs Overview, Sudan', February 2018.

[15]   Ann Strimov Durbin, 'The Darfur genocide 15 years on: What has changed?', *Jewish World Watch, 8* October 2018.

[16]   Small Arms Survey, 'Lifting US sanctions on Sudan, Rationale and Reality', HSBA Report, p. 37.

[17]   'North Darfur displaced reject Abu Shouk camp re-planning', Radio Dabanga, 29 March 2018.

[18]   Amnesty International, 'Sudan: Downsized UN Mission Not an Option Amid Ongoing Attacks in Darfur', 29 June 2018.

Index